BURPEE
THE COMPLETE
VEGETABLE & HERB
GARDENER

BURPEE
THE COMPLETE
VEGETABLE & HERB
GARDENER

A Guide to Growing
Your Garden Organically

By Karan Davis Cutler

PHOTOGRAPHY BY DAVID CAVAGNARO

MACMILLAN • USA

MACMILLAN
A Simon & Schuster Macmillan Company
1633 Broadway
New York, NY 10019-6785

Library of Congress Cataloging-in-Publication Data
Cutler, Karan Davis.

Burpee—The complete vegetable & herb gardener: a guide to growing your garden organically / Karan Davis Cutler; edited by Barbara W. Ellis
      p. cm.
      Includes index.
      ISBN 0-02-862005-4 (hardcover)
      1. Vegetable gardening. 2. Herb gardening. 3. Organic gardening.
      4. Vegetables. 5. Herbs. I. Ellis, Barbara W. II. Title.
SB324.3.C88 1997
635'.0484—dc21   97-14564
                                                        CIP

Manufactured in the United States of America
10 9 8 7 6 5 4 3 2 1

EDITOR,
BARBARA W. ELLIS

INTERIOR & JACKET DESIGN,
STAN GREEN / GREEN GRAPHICS

ILLUSTRATIONS,
ELAYNE SEARS

ACKNOWLEDGMENTS

Special thanks go to Barbara Ellis, the world's most thoughtful and patient editor, and to Charlotte DuChene, Jennifer Bennett, Paul Dunphy, and Stan Green. And to the extraordinarily generous and helpful Dr. James R. McFerson, Plant Geneticist, USDA-ARS, Cornell University in Geneva, New York, who was willing to answer every question, no matter how foolish or obscure. These individuals have done their best to keep me from looking stupid; whatever errors remain, and I hope they are few, are my responsibility alone.

Many other individuals have also made contributions to this book, including Steve Bellavia and Kathy Warren, Johnny's Selected Seeds; Richard Burrell, D.V. Burrell Seed Growers Co.; Jake Chapline; Robert Crabtree, Yale University; Rosalind Creasy; George Dickerson, Extension Horticulture Specialist, New Mexico State University; Erv Evans, North Carolina State University; Sarah M. Gallant, Pinetree Garden Seeds; Gerry Hood, Canadian Sphagnum Peat Moss Association; Doreen Howard, *Gardener's Companion Newsletter*; Dianne Johnson, USDA National Agricultural Statistics Service; Amy Fay Kasica, Cornell Cooperative Extension; Alice Krinsky, Shepherd's Garden Seeds; Rosie Lerner, Consumer Horticulture Extension Specialist, Purdue University; Bill McDorman, Seeds Trust-High Altitude Gardens; Dale E. Marshall, USDA, Michigan State University; Marianne C. Ophardt, Washington State University Cooperative Extension; Marlene Merrill; David Robsond, University of Illinois Extension Specialist; Judy Sheldon; Bill Sidnam, Orange County (CA) Register; Philipp W. Simon, University of Wisconsin; Ronald C. Smith, North Dakota State University; Marc Tosiano, USDA New England Agricultural Statistics Service; and William W. Weaver, Seed Savers Exchange (Pennsylvania).

Finally, I'd like to thank my husband Steve, who had the good sense to spend most of the past year on sabbatical in Switzerland and North Carolina, leaving me free to work and fret without interruption.

PHOTOGRAPHY CREDITS

Unless otherwise noted below, all photographs are by David Cavagnaro.

Karan Davis Cutler: pages 8 (right), 21, 38, 74, 79 (top), 81 (all), 103 (top left & right), 151, 285 (top left, center, & right, bottom left), 321, 358, 360

Stan Green: pages 9 (right), 24, 37, 40, 48, 50, 53, 79 (bottom), 132, 134, 146, 147

W. Atlee Burpee Co.: pages 3, 13, 25, 41, 67, 97, 123, 143, 185 (top right), 210 (left), 234 (left), 235, 245 (left & right), 290, 297 (right), 298, 313 (left), 325, 326, 330 (left), 333 (left), 352, 401 (right), 404 (top center)

Seminis Vegetable Seeds, Inc.: pages 185 (bottom right), 213, 403 (center row, right)

Alf Christianson Seed Co.: 363

Pan American Seed Co.: 404 (top right)

C O N T

E N T S

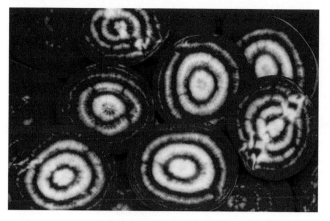

INTRODUCTION

W. Atlee Burpee & Company began as a poultry and small animal breeder in the 1870s, but by the late 1890s had become the world's largest garden seed company. The company has both witnessed and created many of the changes that have transformed gardening during the last 100 years. Nowhere else in horticulture have there been as many exciting new trends and products as in vegetables and herbs. Perhaps this is because humankind has always searched for new food items in a persistent, dogged manner. When geneticists and plant breeders like Atlee Burpee adapted European vegetables to the North American climate, the flood of new varieties they created helped encourage farmers to expand their landholdings and experiment with new crops. Thousands of gardeners followed suit. The result was what many have called the Golden Age of American Gardening, which lasted from about 1880 to 1930.

We are now in the Platinum Age: There are more choices today than ever before, ranging from the charming "old is new again" antique varieties to the latest hybrids with their spectacular yields. In addition, herbs have never been more popular than now. Not only do they provide a satisfying substitute for sodium, but also look and smell wonderful in the garden. Finally, the seeds of most vegetables and herbs are so well grown today that the risk of poor germination is almost non-existent.

Atlee Burpee would have some difficulty recognizing the contemporary home vegetable and herb garden. The love of birds and butterflies, the preponderant use of mulch and compost, as well as the distinctive styles of many gardeners—mixing flowers, herbs, and ornamental vegetables in the same beds, for example—are just some of the marvelous new features that would pique his interest. As the creator of such breakthrough varieties as 'Golden Bantam', the first yellow sweet corn, 'Iceberg' lettuce, and the first bush lima bean, Mr. Burpee would feel much more at home among the futuristic tomatoes, peppers, basils, and sorrels in our many research and test gardens across the United States.

We are extremely happy to offer our many long-standing customers, as well as newcomers to the gardening scene, this excellent compendium of information, knowledge, and wisdom on the art—and science—of vegetable and herb gardening. Author Karan Davis Cutler, along with Barbara Ellis and her team, have done a first-rate job of making a worthy addition to the general gardening literature—both Burpee and non-Burpee—on this very useful subject.

Happy Gardening!

GEORGE BALL, JR.
President, W. Atlee Burpee & Company

PART I

VEGETABLE & HERB GARDENING FROM THE GROUND UP

WHEN HE SAID, "GARDENS ARE NOT MADE BY SINGING 'OH, HOW BEAUTIFUL,' AND SITTING IN THE SHADE," Rudyard Kipling hit the nail on the head. Gardens do take work—they're built and tended "from the ground up." Good site selection, an assortment of well-chosen tools, and a soil-improvement program are the basic building blocks for a successful garden—one that will allow time for sitting in the shade and enjoying the sight of ripening vegetables and herbs. Planning is another part of the recipe for success. In the pages that follow, you'll also find techniques for fitting everything from early season peas and lettuce to summer crops of tomatoes and peppers into a manageable space and spreading out the harvest to avoid an avalanche of produce one week followed by nothing the next. The basics of good garden care—the satisfying work that goes into a good garden—are also covered, from getting plants off to a good start with proper sowing and transplanting techniques, to weeding, mulching, watering, and preventing pest and disease problems.

FRESH TASTE GUARANTEED. Homegrown vegetables and herbs provide garden-fresh taste that is simply not available from grocery-store produce. A backyard garden also makes it possible to grow unusual vegetables, such as these heirloom tomatoes and peppers, which are unavailable from most commercial sources.

CHAPTER ONE

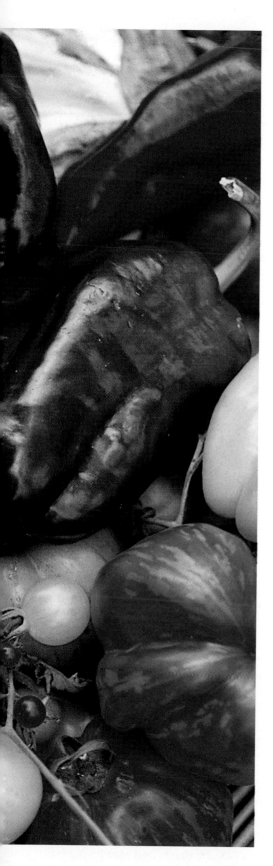

GROWING YOUR OWN

Who would look dangerously up at planets
that might safely look down at plants?
JOHN GERARD, *The Herball*, 1597

WITH FAMILIAR AND EXOTIC PRODUCE CROWDING THE SUPERMARKET SHELVES FROM JANUARY TO December and farmers' markets making a comeback throughout the country, it may seem senseless to plant vegetables and herbs. But it's not, as anyone who does it will tell you. There's a wheelbarrowful of reasons to grow your own.

To start, there's pleasure in knowing that the pesto was made from your basil and garlic. You're allowed to gloat quietly as you carve the 79-pound 'Big Max' pumpkin that you grew from a seed the size of a thumbnail. A backyard garden may be self-reliance on a small scale, but the satisfactions are the same. Freeze or can part of your harvest—or save seeds from your crops—and the sense of independence swells. Plus gardening is good exercise: Thirty min-

LETTUCE 'SPECKLES'. *This pretty heirloom leaf lettuce has sweet, apple green leaves flecked with red-brown to maroon spots.*

utes of digging, weeding, or harvesting burns 150 calories. It takes you outdoors into the sun and air as well. Even the landless can reap gardening's benefits by farming in pots, window boxes, and even Mason jars. And anyone can grow vegetables and herbs—city or country dweller, woman or man, old or young. Best of all, growing things is fun.

If you factor in your time, it's clear you won't save huge amounts of money by growing vegetables and herbs, but it's still entertaining to run the numbers. The next time you buy sweet corn at a farm stand—25¢ an ear—remember that a packet of 100 seeds, which should produce 200 ears, costs $2. That's 2¢ an ear. One $3 artichoke plant yields about 20 buds, which comes to 15¢ a heart. Compare that with $2 to $3 per heart at the supermarket, and start separating eggs for the hollandaise sauce with a happy spirit.

Furthermore, growing your own is the best way—in fact, the only way—to sample more of the world's amazing storehouse of cultivated vegetable and herb varieties. You won't find 'White Rabbit', 'Yellow Tommy Toe', or 'Nebraska Wedding' tomatoes at the supermarket. 'Nootka Rose' garlic, a red silverskin type from the San Juan islands of Washington, or 'Big John' pole bean, a white-seeded bean that's been grown in Kentucky since the Revolutionary War, won't be in the produce section either. Even the best-stocked farm stand is unlikely to sell white-kerneled 'Luther Hill' sweet corn or 'All Cream' lettuce, a ruffled-leaf cultivar, green with pink edges.

You won't find many of these seeds for sale either. Over the years, thousands of heirlooms have been dropped from the catalogs of large seed houses. Most are older, home-garden cultivars (cultivated varieties) of vegetables and herbs that put a premium on outstanding flavor. They have been dropped in favor of hybrids bred for commercial growers—types that ripen in a concentrated period of time and are tough enough to stand up to mechanical harvesting. Continued consolidation within the seed industry further endangers access to heirloom and even many modern cultivars developed for home gardens.

'Stovewood' beans, 'Early Frame' cucumber, 'Mr. Topp' tomato, and hundreds of other names appear to be gone forever. Smaller and specialized seed companies, such as Ronniger's Seed Potatoes and Alfrey Seeds (a kitchen-table operation that specializes in chili peppers), have been instrumental in keeping many home-garden cultivars available to gardeners. A modest sample of heirlooms is sold by seed firms with a particular interest in open-pollinated (OP) cultivars, such as Southern Exposure Seed Exchange and Seeds Blüm. The premium collections of old-time and home-garden cultivars, however, are available only from the U.S. Department of Agriculture (USDA) and nonprofit organizations. The USDA normally makes its seeds available only to researchers and scientists, but nonprofit seed-preservation groups, such as Seed Savers Exchange and CORNS, supply seeds to any interested gardener. (See the Appendix on page 419 for addresses of these organizations.)

The work of these volunteer organizations is vital, important enough for Seed Savers Exchange founder Kent Whealy to be given a John D. and Catherine T. MacArthur Foundation Fellowship—widely known as a "genus" award—in 1990. When plants, wild or cultivated, become extinct, everyone loses not just a part of what was and is but a part of what might be. Gone are 'Stovewood' pole beans, reported to bear enormous pods with seeds 2 inches across. Gone, too, are all possibilities of crossing 'Stovewood' with other beans to produce new cultivars that are better than either parent. Unlike china, furniture, and other family heirlooms, antique vegetables and herbs are living things. Seeds can't be collected and stored indefinitely in a glass jar. They need a gardener, because they have to be grown to be preserved. When you

A GROWING HERITAGE. *Unlike most antiques, heirloom vegetables can't be stored on a shelf indefinately— since they are living things, they must be grown to be preserved. This garden of heirloom vegetables at Seed Savers Exchange's Heritage Farm features heritage kale, Swiss chard, and summer squash.*

FAMILY TRADITIONS. *Heirloom vegetables can often be traced to a particular family or ethnic group who developed them and passed them down from generation to generation. Plants could have been selected because of a specifically desired color or shape or because they were especially well adapted to the region.*

choose to plant (and save seeds of) 'Queen Anne's Pocket Melon', 'Fortin's Family' rutabaga, 'Grandpa's Leaf' lettuce, or any of the thousands of cultivars of vegetables and herbs meant for back-yard gardens, you are protecting the past *and* enriching the future.

OUR GARDENING HERITAGE

Gardening, if we're to believe the story of Adam and Eve and the apple, is the oldest profession. One way or another, gardens have been around almost forever, putting food on our tables as well as joy and beauty in our lives. Gardening is also America's favorite avocation. Today, nearly 75 per-cent of all U.S. households dig and plant, every-thing from 3-foot window boxes in Manhattan to 3-acre vegetable patches in Kansas. What and

how much we grow have changed dramatically over time, however.

Colonial Americans, wonderfully practical souls, transplanted not only themselves but their favorite plants to the New World. John Winthrop, Jr.'s seed order, which traveled from England to the Massachusetts Bay Colony aboard the Lion in 1631 and cost him 160£, was light on ornamentals and heavy on vegetables and herbs—a typical 17th-century New England garden designed "For Meate or Medicine." Onions, parsley, carrots, parsnips, radishes, pumpkins, and cabbages were ordered in greatest quantity; cauliflower seeds were the most costly of the 59 items. Winthrop also included angelica, basil, cress, fennel, lovage, marjoram, pars-ley, rosemary, savory, and thyme, suggesting that he liked his "meate" well flavored.

By the middle of the 19th century, scores of new

HEIRLOOM HARVEST. *For anyone who has never looked beyond white bakers, the array of shapes, sizes, and colors that potatoes come in is quite a surprise. This collection of heirloom potatoes, labeled for overwintering, is from the Seed Savers Exchange.*

vegetables and herbs were being grown. Fearing Burr's *The Field and Garden Vegetables of America*, first published in 1863 with a second edition in 1865, is a 667-page compilation of "Nearly Eleven Hundred Species and Varieties; With Directions For Propagation, Culture and Use." It provides an A-to-Z record of the era's taste and includes everything from *Agaricus campestris* (mushrooms) to *Zea mays* (corn). His list abounds with peas (172 cultivars) and turnips (82 cultivars, plus "turnip cabbage," "turnip-rooted celery," and "turnip-rooted chervil"), neither of which show up on contemporary lists of most popular vegetables. Tomatoes, Burr notes, were still not agreeable "to a majority of tastes," but that didn't keep him from describing 35 cultivars. Interestingly, he includes specialty crops like orach,

pak choi, purslane, cress, and endive, crops that have become *de rigueur* in gourmet seed catalogs today.

How much we grow also has changed over time. Home gardens have become smaller, so the declaration in an 1867 garden book that between 200 and 500 celery plants "are usually required for use by an ordinary family" is eye-opening. Similarly, a book on cooking and gardening (*The Secrets of Many Gardens*) written in 1924 takes growers to task for producing *more* than they need. Learning from a gardener that the household would consume 2 tons of potatoes in a year, the author, Mrs. Philip Martineau, consults with the cook and does a little math. Only 1 ton a year is necessary. "Just an error in calculation, needing five minutes to put right," she concludes.

Another great change in the past 150 years is the increased popularity of eating uncooked vegetables. Salads are more fashionable than ever, although they aren't new. The poet Virgil (70–19 B.C.) wrote an ode to the salad (the word comes from the Latin for "salt," *sal*, a derivation originating with the Roman practice of eating greens that had been dipped in salt). The earliest English salad recipe, which dates from about 1390, was for a mixture of herbs, greens, onions, and leeks. Elizabethans were more adventuresome: They started their salads with herbs and greens, such as lettuce, purslane, sorrel, dandelion, mustard, cress, spinach, chicory, chives, as well as turnip and radish greens, then topped them with flowers, including petals of violets, borage, primroses, gillyflowers, and especially nasturtiums, a new import from the West Indies.

Despite the salad's ancient roots, eating raw vegetables and herbs remained out of favor for centuries. Suspicion was rampant. The kitchen notebooks of Leonardo da Vinci (1452–1519) are crammed with meat recipes (shoulder of serpent, pierced pigs' ears, leg of loon, and more) but give short shrift to uncooked vegetables. Da Vinci acknowledged that his cook, Battista, was fond of "serving me with unwashed lettuce, and this I normally give to my dog ...."

Tomatoes were still believed to be toxic as late as 1820, when Robert Johnson gobbled up a basketful on the steps of the Salem, New Jersey, courthouse to prove their safety. The event has been widely reported over the years and may have helped change public attitudes about tomato safety. In truth, Johnson's act of vegetable valor probably

ORNAMENTAL EDIBLES. *Although many gardeners grow their vegetables in a separate plot, there's no reason many edibles can't be incorporated in flower beds and borders. This garden at Seeds Blüm in Boise, Idaho, features cabbages and other brassicas combined with Gem series marigolds, which have edible flowers.*

MAKING THE MOST OF SPACE AND TIME. *Raised beds and intensive planting are just two ways to garden more efficiently. Raised beds are the answer to a wide variety of soil problems. Intensive planting allows today's time-pressed gardeners to harvest a bounty of produce from a minimum of space.*

never occurred, but that hasn't stopped it from being believed. (In fact, it was even dramatized in 1949 in the "You Are There" CBS television series, thereby creating the peculiar situation of viewers being there while Johnson wasn't.) Little by little, then, vegetables and herbs were rescued from suspicion and from being boiled or stewed beyond recognition. By the end of World War II, most Americans were confirmed fresh-vegetable eaters, a serendipitous conjunction of a heightened interest in health and nutrition and better methods of transportation and storage.

VEGETABLES AND HERBS TODAY

Today, the value of eating fresh vegetables and herbs is unquestioned. There are hundreds of cultivars of lettuce, beans, and tomatoes, scores of cucumbers, peppers, peas, radishes, and spinach, and dozens of cabbages, eggplants, and scallions. Still, breeders work around the clock to produce more cultivars. Tomatoes consistently head the most ordered list at U.S. seed companies. The tally kept by the National Garden Bureau, which counts both seed and bedding-plant sales, is similar: tomatoes first, followed by peppers, cabbages, cucumbers, squash, and beans. Basil is the most planted herb, followed by parsley, chives, and dill. The National Gardening Association, using information from its annual sur-

vey of American gardeners, leads off with tomatoes, followed by peppers, onions, cucumbers, beans, lettuce, carrots, corn, radishes, and cabbages. Tomatoes or cabbages, basils or dills, hybrids or heirlooms, this wealth is only as far away as the catalogs of a few good seed companies and seed exchanges.

What's next for vegetables and herbs? The sky's not the limit, since all sorts of plants and seeds have been blasted into outer space. In one project, more than 12.5 million 'Rutgers California Supreme' tomato seeds circled Earth aboard a satellite, then were retrieved by the crew of the *Columbia*. Back on Earth, the seeds were distributed to more than 3 million schoolchildren and 64,000 teachers in all 50 states, the District of Columbia, and 34 foreign countries.

There are no rampageous killer tomatoes to report, although the informal responses suggest that space-exposed seeds germinated and initially grew faster than did Earth-bound seeds. Plants from space-exposed seeds also had higher levels of chlorophyll and carotenes than the homebodies had. Over time, however, the terrestrial tomatoes equaled their more adventuresome counterparts, and no significant differences were found between the Earthlings and the space travelers.

The experiments continue: Seed Savers Exchange members are making third-, fourth-, and fifth-generation NASA seeds available to other amateur growers. And the seeds-in-space study,

SUMMER BOUNTY. *Although gardeners grow vegetables and herbs for all sorts of reasons—for fresh taste, food that is free of dangerous chemicals, or a bountiful harvest—an undeniable benefit is the pleasure of watching a garden grow and caring for the plants from sowing seed to gathering the harvest.*

while it revealed no death-dealing mutations, was not without its casualties. "Dear NASA," wrote one young gardener. "My name is Matt. I am in grade 2. I really enjoy growing my plants. Here are my results. My Earth seed did not grow. My space seed grew, but it fell off my desk. It died."

Exchanging seeds and horticultural knowledge isn't a space-age event. Gardeners have always been a friendly and generous lot. "Wee Brothers of the Spade find it very necessary to share," an English plantsman wrote to the prominent Virginian John Custis in 1735. Today, more than 1,000 Seed Savers Exchange members offer seeds from their home gardens—nearly 12,000 cultivars of vegetables and herbs—to other members each year, clear evidence of the hospitality that infects people who grow plants. "I had a very bad year due to health problems," one California member wrote. "All requests not filled yet will be filled eventually. I apologize for the delay." And from an North Carolina gardener: "Will be happy to exchange seeds and correspond all year. I grow many plants not listed and will save seeds for anyone interested."

Gardening is a companionable activity, but it is also an opportunity for solitude, a time to reflect, an occasion to use your imagination. Gardeners live in the future, forever required to think weeks, months, even years ahead. Use the experience of others, copy whatever appeals to you—it would be foolish

HEALTHY EXERCISE. *Whether you are stringing a bean trellis, digging in the soil, or just pulling weeds, gardening is good exercise.*

not to take advantage of those who have gone before—but remember that your garden is your creation. It is personal. It should contain the vegetables and herbs that you like. Whether rigidly geometric or wildly casual, it should be a place where you feel at home.

GARDENS AND NATURE

Like mountain climbers, gardeners both conquer and cooperate with the natural world. By coercing tomatoes and beans from soil that if left alone would be producing sugar maples, big bluestem grass, goldenrods, or cactuses, we have our way with the land. But sensible gardeners, like mountaineers older than 55, know there are limits. Wise garden makers are mindful of the natural world they inhabit. They use "sustainable" methods in order to maintain a healthy environment. They rotate crops, conserve soil and water, use biological controls. It's what organic gardening is all about—working with nature. Good gardeners are stewards of the Earth's richness, aware of its balance and diversity, and willing to help protect them. This means rejecting easy solutions—renouncing toxic prescriptions that kill pest insects along with the insect allies that help control them naturally, for example. It means thinking in the long rather than the short term, adding compost and animal manures to the garden rather than a 25-pound bag of 10–10–10. It means seeing the broad rather than the narrow picture.

Growing your own in harmony with nature also ensures that your vegetables and herbs are safe to eat—that they haven't been treated with toxic chemicals. While "Wash it first" remains sensible advice, you know that it's dirt you'll be scrubbing off, not insecticides or fungicides. Turning your back on chemical controls may mean that some of your harvest will be slightly less perfect-looking than the produce at the supermarket, but any blemish is offset by knowing that your vegetables and herbs are free of poisons.

THEY'RE GOOD FOR YOU

New studies keep reinforcing what your mother knew: Vegetables are good for you. Not only do they contain vitamins and fiber, they help prevent disease. Interestingly, the value of phytochemicals, or plant chemicals, is enhanced by eating the whole food. A salad is mightier than a pill.

The lists below indicate good sources of various vitamins and minerals, with "good" meaning an average serving contains at least 10 percent of the Recommended Dietary Allowance (RDA). An asterisk (*) indicates a high source of the vitamin or mineral in question—25 percent or more of the RDA per average serving.

Vitamin A
Good sources of beta carotene and other carotenoids (vitamin A):
Broccoli
Carrot*
Chicory
Endive
Escarole
Kale*
Melon
Mustard
Pepper, sweet red*
Pumpkin
Romaine and cos lettuce
Spinach*
Sweet potato*
Swiss chard*
Tomato
Turnip green*
Watermelon
Winter squash*

Vitamin B
Good sources of one or more of the B vitamins:
Bean, lima
Broccoli
Collard*
Pea
Potato
Turnip green

Vitamin C
Good sources of vitamin C:
Artichoke, globe
Asparagus
Bean, green & yellow
Bean, lima
Broccoli*
Brussels sprout*
Cabbage*
Cauliflower*
Chicory
Collard*
Endive
Escarole
Kale*
Kohlrabi*
Melon*
Mustard*
Okra
Parsnip
Pea
Pea, edible-podded*
Pepper, sweet*
Potato*
Pumpkin
Radish
Romaine lettuce
Rutabaga*
Scallion
Spinach
Squash, summer & winter
Swiss chard
Tomato*
Turnip
Turnip green
Watercress
Watermelon*

Having a garden gives the adage "Don't pick corn before the water is boiling" full meaning. However fast the jets that move vegetables and herbs from California or Mexico to your supermarket, nothing matches the minute it takes to walk between a backyard garden and the kitchen. Nothing equals the quality of produce harvested and eaten at the moment it reaches peak flavor and nutrition: snow peas gathered while they are still young and tender, spinach and lettuce leaves cut the moment they are large enough to eat, tomatoes picked when they are fully colored and ripe, or parsnips pulled from the ground after being sweetened by autumn's first frost.

That's what growing and harvesting your own vegetables and herbs is all about: having a degree of independence; having a safe supply of fresh, good-tasting produce; and knowing, while you're sliding a fat slice of 'Earliana' tomato and two leaves of 'Tango' lettuce into the season's first BLT, that producing the crop was just as pleasurable as consuming it will be.

Folic Acid
Good sources of folate (folacin, folic acid):
- Artichoke, globe
- Asparagus
- Bean, dried
- Beet
- Black-eyed pea*
- Broccoli
- Brussels sprout
- Cauliflower
- Chickpea
- Chicory
- Chinese cabbage
- Corn
- Endive
- Escarole
- Lentil*
- Mustard
- Okra
- Parsnip
- Pea
- Romaine lettuce
- Spinach*
- Turnip

Calcium & Iron
Good sources of calcium or iron:
- Bean, lima
- Broccoli
- Collard*
- Kale
- Turnip greens

Magnesium
Good sources of magnesium:
- Artichoke, globe
- Bean, lima
- Broccoli
- Okra
- Spinach
- Sunflower seed
- Swiss chard

Potassium
Good sources of potassium:
- Artichoke, globe
- Asparagus
- Bean
- Bean, dried*
- Bean, lima*
- Bean, soy*
- Cauliflower
- Chickpea
- Corn
- Jerusalem artichoke
- Lentil*
- Melon
- Parsnip
- Pea
- Potato*
- Pumpkin*
- Rutabaga
- Spinach*
- Squash, winter*
- Sweet potato*
- Swiss chard
- Tomato*
- Watermelon

Fiber
Good sources of dietary fiber, at least 2 grams per average serving:
- Artichoke, globe
- Bean, green & dried
- Bean, lima
- Beet
- Black-eyed pea
- Broccoli
- Brussels sprout
- Cabbage
- Carrot
- Chickpea
- Lentil
- Okra
- Parsnip
- Pea
- Pea, edible-podded
- Potato
- Spinach
- Squash, winter
- Sunflower seed
- Sweet potato
- Tomato

PLANNING PAYS OFF. *A well-planned garden provides good growing conditions—sun, fresh air, and good soil—for a wide range of vegetables, including popular crops such as tomatoes and pole beans.*

CHAPTER TWO

GETTING STARTED

What we call the beginning is often the end
And to make an end is to make a beginning.
The end is where we start from.

T.S. ELIOT, *Four Quartets*, 1942

FORTUNATELY, GREEN THUMBS AND GARDENERS ARE MADE, NOT BORN, a fact that anyone starting a first garden should keep in mind. According to Henry Mitchell, "There are no green thumbs or black thumbs. There are only gardeners and non-gardeners" (*The Essential Earthman*, 1981). Successful gardens are much the same—they don't come instantly into existence. Establishing a garden that is a manageable size and selecting a good site are important first steps in any successful garden. After that, learning plays an essential role. Careful observation, reading about new techniques and crops, talking about gardening with fellow gardeners, along with good old trial and error are the secrets to figuring out just what will work best for you.

DETERMINING GARDEN SIZE

The size of a vegetable garden begins with how much space you have available. Lack of space is limiting, but it isn't fatal. A garden can be as small as one 6-inch clay pot of chives or extend farther than the eye can see. A well-planned 600 square feet (20 by 30 feet) should keep a family of four flooded with vegetables and herbs, but a pint-size plot of 9 square feet can still provide a summer full of salads. Even a 2-foot-long window box will hold a half-dozen different herbs, and one 'Sweet 100' tomato plant will yield hundreds of fruits.

Moreover, there are plenty of space-saving techniques, such as intercropping and trellising, that can increase the harvest without requiring a larger garden. (For more on these techniques, see Chapter 5.) Some vegetables are more space-

CROP YIELDS

Yields vary according to the garden conditions and the cultivar planted, but these estimates for some of the most popular vegetables will give you a sense of the size of the harvest when crops are spaced according to usual seed-packet directions. To get an idea of how many fruits you would harvest, divide the total yield by the approximate weight per fruit. For 'Big Boy' tomatoes, which weigh 1 pound or more, the calculation is easy. 'Viva Italia' hybrid paste tomatoes average 3 ounces each, for an average yield of 533 fruits per 100-foot row. The next question to ask yourself is whether you really need 100 'Big Boy' or 533 'Viva Italia' tomatoes—probably not, so plant accordingly.

In addition, most gardeners won't want an entire 100-foot row maturing all at once—or a 25- or 10-foot one for that matter—unless they plan on canning or freezing the produce. See "Succession Planting Basics" on page 83 for planting techniques that stretch out the harvest over weeks or months.

Vegetable	Average yield per 100-foot row	Vegetable	Average yield per 100-foot row
Asparagus	30 pounds	Okra	100 pounds
Bean, bush	120 pounds	Onion	80 pounds
Bean, pole	150 pounds	Parsley	40 pounds
Beet	125 pounds	Parsnip	100 pounds
Broccoli	80 pounds	Pea	20 pounds
Brussels sprout	75 pounds	Potato	100 pounds
Cabbage	150 pounds	Radish	100 bunches
Carrot	100 pounds	Rhubarb	75 pounds
Cauliflower	100 pounds	Spinach	40 pounds
Corn	10 dozen ears	Squash, summer	150 pounds
Cucumber	120 pounds	Squash, winter	100 pounds
Eggplant	100 pounds	Sweet pepper	50 pounds
Leek	125 pounds	Sweet potato	100 pounds
Lettuce, leaf	50 pounds	Tomato	100 pounds
Melon	50 fruits	Turnip	75 pounds
		Watermelon	40 fruits

SIZE ISN'T EVERYTHING. *A large garden isn't the only way to produce bumper crops of vegetables. Before digging up all your available space, consider how much time you have to care for a garden. Plan on using space-saving techniques, such as intercropping and trellising, to produce the most in the space you can manage.*

efficient than others too. Based on yields per square foot, value per pound, and seed-to-harvest time, the National Garden Bureau rates tomatoes as the most space-efficient vegetable, followed by scallions, leaf lettuce, summer squash, snow peas, onions, beans, and beets. Sweet corn, melons, and pumpkins fall at the bottom of the list.

Keep in mind, though, that even if you have room to spare, it's easier and faster to sow a 100-foot row of peas than to weed it—or harvest it. Gardens take time, and the no-care garden doesn't exist. If you know your time is limited, as you thumb through the seed catalogs don't be seduced into buying far more seeds than you can plant—or care for. Also bear in mind that some vegetables take more time than others. Peas, which require trellising, and leeks, which must be hilled up with soil as they grow, are two examples. (See "Easy Vegetables & Herbs," below, for a list of the easiest-to-grow crops.) Some herbs are more versatile in the kitchen than others, and these are the best bets for time-pressed herb gardeners. Start with basil, thyme, and oregano, then add chives, parsley, dill, tarragon, and rosemary if you have room and time. If you have only a couple of hours a week to spend with a hoe in your hand, restrain your enthusiasm and start small. Three 5-foot-long rows (lettuce, peas, and beans, perhaps), one 3-foot double row of scallions, four plants each of tomato, cucumber, cabbage, and broccoli, one hill of summer squash, plus a small herb collection (basil, dill, parsley, and chives) will be plenty to keep you busy.

If you find you have more time, greater interest and experience, and an expanding appetite for vegetables and herbs, you can always enlarge your garden. You can add another 50 or 100 square feet to the garden proper, but another option is to set an extra tomato in the back of the perennial border, tuck a few 'Red Robin' basil plants next to the lamb's ears for contrast, or start a 'Lumina' pumpkin in a patio pot and allow it to wander across the lawn, producing its startling white-skinned fruits as it goes.

SELECTING A GARDEN SITE

Knowing where to place a vegetable garden requires only knowing what vegetables like, and there's no mystery to that. Thomas Hill set forth the basics 400 years ago in *The Gardener's Labyrinth*, the first garden book written in English. Still, few of us have the perfect site: a sunny, sheltered, well-drained, southwest-sloping, generous-size plot of organically rich loam located near an infinite source of water. Faced with heavy clay soil, 100-foot maples blocking the sun until noon, or children demanding space to play soccer, most gardeners must compromise. Fortunately, it is possible to compromise *and* produce vegetables and herbs. Not planting cucumbers where their vines will trail across the shortcut to the garage is obvious, but some dos and don'ts of garden placement may surprise you. Above all, consider the eternal basics—sun, air, water, soil—before you start digging.

SUNSHINE

"Let there be light" was the first exhortation from above, and surely one with the gardener in mind. When you are selecting a spot to grow vegetables and herbs, sunshine is the most critical and least negotiable ingredient. Sun-poor gardens are slow to warm in spring, susceptible to diseases, and notorious for producing spindly plants and harvests. All the aluminum foil, white mulch, mirrors, and other tricks used by those saddled with really shady gardens won't produce even a small basket of beefsteak tomatoes.

In cool northern gardens, sun is doubly important, but in relentlessly hot regions, afternoon shade can be an asset. Wherever the location, nearly all plants require a minimum of 6 hours of sun daily; in most parts of the country, 8 hours is better, and all day is best. If your only spot for a garden is partially shaded, you will have the best luck with vegetables and herbs that tolerate semi-darkish settings.

EASY VEGETABLES & HERBS

If this is your first garden, try these simple-to-grow crops. All are sown from seed and are rarely troubled by diseases or pests.

Basil	Pea
Bean	Radish
Beet	Spinach
Cucumber	Summer squash
Dill	Swiss chard
Leaf lettuce	

FRESH AIR

Plants need fresh air as well as sun—Thomas Hill warned that "evil aire … doth not only annoy and corrupt the plants … but choke and dul the spirits of men." Women too, no doubt, so avoid placing a garden in a low area where air stagnates and remains colder. Cool air pools in valleys and hollows, even in modest dips in the landscape; these locations are notorious for holding the local record for late frosts in spring and early frosts in autumn. In contrast, a garden on a gentle slope with a southern exposure and good air circulation is likely to escape most early-fall and late-spring frosts. Tightly enclosed spots should be avoided too. A garden that is boxed in by a garage wall and a solid fence won't receive the sun and breezes that keep plants thriving. Poor air circulation encourages diseases, such as powdery mildew and early blight, especially in the Southeast and other regions with high humidity. If your loca-tion requires a tall barrier to protect your garden from neighborhood pets and wildlife, make sure it doesn't prevent plants from getting all the fresh air and sun they need.

WIND PROTECTION

Some protection from the wind is desirable, though. At worst, a cold wind can wipe out new transplants; at best, it slows their growth. Hot winds also can be destructive by desiccating, or dehydrating, plants and causing catfacing and other blemishes on fruits. If your garden regularly receives winds in the 15-mph range, it needs per-manent protection. A windward barrier—trees, hedge, fence, wall, or building—not only safeguards plants from wind damage but also reduces soil ero-sion as well as moisture and heat loss. Experiments show that a burlap windbreak only 2 feet tall can increase air temperature by 2 to 3 degrees. On a smaller scale, individual plants like tomatoes or peppers can be protected from unpredictable cold or unceasing winds by growing them in cages or frames that have been wrapped in either burlap or a floating-row-cover fabric, such as Reemay.

Like children, living windbreaks have a way of getting bigger. Set them at a distance of four or five times their ultimate height, and keep them in bounds by regular pruning. If positioned too close—less than 6 feet away—their roots will filch moisture and nutrients needed by your corn and cabbages. The roots of any tree will compete with vegetables and herbs, so situate your garden well beyond the drip line, or root zone, of trees, especially shallow-rooted species like willows and maples. Some gar-deners also dig a 2-foot-deep trench around their garden, severing any tree roots they encounter; before they refill the trench, they line one wall with a fabric weed mat to discourage new root growth. Above all, stay far, far away—at least 100 feet—from black walnut trees, which exude juglone, a chemical that is allelopathic, or toxic, to peas, tomatoes, and many other vegetables.

GOOD DRAINAGE

Wet ground—where "the watriness shall exceed," as Hill put it—is an inhospitable place for a garden. It is a signal that the spaces between the particles of soil, through which water and air travel, are extremely small. Waterlogged soil is air-poor soil. Plant roots, which need air as well as moisture, actu-

---

VEGETABLES & HERBS FOR PARTIAL SUN

Except in extremely hot regions, veg-etables and herbs do best in full sun, 10 hours or more. The following species will tolerate partial sun—6 hours per day—but yields and fruit size may be smaller than normal.

Angelica	Lemon balm
Arugula	Lovage
Beet	Mint
Broccoli	Mustard
Cabbage	New Zealand
Carrot	spinach
Chervil	Parsley
Chinese cabbage	Pea
Chives	Radish
Corn salad	Scallion, or
Endive &	green onion
escarole	Sorrel
Garden cress	Spinach
Horseradish	Swiss chard
Kale	Turnip
Leaf lettuce	Watercress

PLAN FOR CONVENIENCE. *For crops harvested fresh and frequently, the best site is often the most convenient one. This garden makes it easy to pop out the kitchen door to harvest leaf lettuce, basil, and other herbs, plus edible flowers such as nasturtiums.*

ally grow in these minute spaces rather than in the soil particles themselves.

Take a look at your potential garden site after a rain. Is there standing water? Does the turf remain soft and soppy for 2 or 3 days after a storm? Is there a temporary stream? If the answers are yes, it may be a location to reject. While solving a minor drainage problem is only a matter of loosening compacted subsoil or improving porosity by adding organic matter, seriously waterlogged locations probably have to be drained. That can be a whopping undertaking, one involving drain tiles, dry wells, and other expensive options. Better to put the garden elsewhere, although it may be possible to circumvent a moderately wet site by creating raised beds.

Conversely, gardeners in arid regions sometimes create sunken beds to collect much-needed mois-

ture or install permanent irrigation systems. If your garden is unlikely to receive the weekly inch of rain that is the rule-of-thumb measure for most plants, position it near a reliable source of water—or devise a plan to get water to your vegetables and herbs and to conserve what moisture is available. If water is as scarce as rain, you may want to pass on crops, such as eggplant, that require more-than-average amounts of moisture, and give more room to herbs, most of which need less-than-average moisture.

GOOD SOIL QUALITY

Soil, while it receives the most attention from the experts, is the least important consideration when siting a garden. That's because soil is less fixed than the other basics. Structure can be altered, pH adjusted, fertility improved. One simple indication of healthy, fertile soil is the presence of earthworms. These "intestines of the soil," as Charles Darwin called them, feed on organic matter and then deposit their waste, or castings, at the entrance to their burrows. Scientists have calculated that the 750,000 to 1 million earthworms contained in an average 1-acre plot digest between 15 and 20 tons of soil each year.

SIMPLE SOIL DRAINAGE TESTS

Use one of the two tests below to assess your soil's porosity, that is, how fast or slowly it drains.

To determine whether your soil drains too slowly, dig a 1-foot-deep 1-foot-wide hole and fill it with water. Refill the hole the next day, and keep track of how quickly it drains: If it takes longer than 12 hours, drainage is poor and you should plant elsewhere.

To determine whether your soil drains too quickly, water your garden thoroughly. If, after 48 hours, the soil is dry to a depth of 6 inches, it drains too rapidly to support a vegetable garden and should be heavily amended with organic matter.

LOCATION, LOCATION, LOCATION. *When it comes to vegetable gardens, out of sight is often out of mind. This garden's location next to a walkway makes it hard to forget when plants need weeding, watering, or other attention. Chinese mustards and cabbages share space with flowers to create a showy display.*

Earthworms, despite their lowly status, are particular creatures. They won't thrive just anywhere. They require moist, organically rich soil. If the ground becomes too dry, they become dormant; if it is saturated with water, the worms are driven to the surface to breathe, where they are in danger of drying out or being eaten. Earthworms are also highly sensitive to chemicals. Examine a shovelful of moist soil. If it contains three or four earthworms, you probably have fine ground for growing vegetables and herbs.

Over time, goodly applications of compost and animal manures can transform almost any plot into "fat earth," the country term for fertile soil. Adding organic matter, such as straw, leaves, grass clippings, and green manures, is the best way to cure the ills of both sand and clay. (See Chapter 4 for details on improving soil.) Still, it makes sense to begin with the best soil possible. That usually means not plant-ing alongside buildings, where the ground is typically backfill. Because of leaching from concrete foundations, this soil also may be highly alkaline, or even contaminated from lead paint if the building is an old one. Old dump sites, septic tanks, and leach fields are other potential contamination sources, so site your garden *at least* 20 feet from them. Finally, if there is evidence that soilborne diseases, such as fusarium and verticillium wilt, lurk in the location you've chosen, solarize your soil. (See "Solarizing the Soil" on page 151.)

EASY ACCESS

If it's possible, do place your garden where you can easily see and admire it. Gardens that are located out of sight quickly become gardens that are out of mind. If you don't see the weeds, it's easy not to pull them. If you don't see that your cucumbers have begun to bloom, you'll be days late removing the floating row covers you laid down to discourage cucumber beetles. A garden set close by demands to be watched; it screams "Now." You'll want to tend and harvest it. Many vegetables— beans and summer squash are two—mature in the blink of an eye. Wait to harvest and you'll be gathering a basketful of inedible produce.

Convenience and timeliness may mean turning the front lawn into a vegetable patch or creating an "edible landscape." While edible landscaping is not a new idea—people have been tucking vegetables and herbs among their dooryard flowers for centuries—it is an increasingly popular one, driven by smaller and smaller yards. Its culmination is container gardening, raising vegetables in pots and boxes, which allows even an apartment dweller to be a farmer. Ever alert to social trends, seed companies now offer bite-size tomatoes for hanging baskets and cucumbers that don't spread to compete with fuchsias and petunias for a place on your deck.

PLANT WHAT YOU EAT. *When deciding what to grow, start with what your family likes to eat. If they'll eat yellow crookneck summer squash, grow that, and consider branching out to round, delicate-tasting 'Ronde de Nice' zucchini. This planting also features handsome 'Lacinato' Italian kale.*

DECIDING WHAT TO GROW

Vegetables come in all forms: as leaves (lettuce), as stalks (celery), as flowers (broccoli), as fruits (tomato), as seeds (corn), and as modified roots (beet). And they come in all sizes, from carrots, which can be spaced 2 inches apart, to melons, which require a 6-foot separation from their nearest neighbor. Remember, too, that most vegetables and herbs are annuals. They do their business in one season: Between planting and the first snow, they sprout, flower, fruit, and die. They have, as the American garden writer Richardson Wright put it, "a short life and a merry one."

A handful of biennial vegetables and herbs, species such as cabbage, carrot, and parsley, take 2 years to set seed, but even these crops are grown as annuals, harvested in their first season. A smaller number of vegetables, including asparagus, horseradish, and rhubarb, are perennials; these live 3 years and more. Finally, depending on where you live, there is a good-size collection of perennial herbs, such as chives, thyme, and oregano.

Flower or stalk, annual or perennial, always plant what you and your family like and will eat. If you hate cabbage and cilantro, don't grow them. If you want to freeze tomato sauce, put in another dozen paste tomatoes. Remember that some vegetables—zucchini is a prime example—produce extravagant quantities of fruit. One plant is enough. In contrast, sweet corn requires plenty of colleagues to pollinate, and one stalk rarely yields more than two ears. If you have room for only four plants, erase corn from your garden plan, use the space for something else, and patronize the local farm stand. You may want to choose crops or cultivars that are otherwise unavailable, things such as chicory, lemon basil, an heirloom watermelon like 'Moon & Stars', or 'Corno di Toro Giallo' pepper, an 8-inch yellow sweet pepper shaped like a bull's horn. And if this is your first garden, start with easy crops, with leaf rather than head lettuce, broccoli rather than cauliflower. (See "Easy Vegetables & Herbs" on page 16 for more suggestions.)

CONSIDER CONTAINERS. *Containers filled with vegetables and herbs can be as attractive as they are useful. Not only do they create gardening space for the landless, they also make it easy to grow often-used crops right outside the kitchen door.*

THE IMPORTANCE OF PLACE & TIME

It's important not to set yourself up for failure by planting vegetables and herbs that have little chance of succeeding in your region. Ornamental gardeners depend on hardiness zones to help determine what they can grow. These zones are distinct regions established by the United States Department of Agriculture (USDA) based on average annual low temperatures. But while knowing your zone is essential to growing ornamentals, it is less important to food gardeners, since most vegetables and herbs are handled as annual crops. What is important is the length of your growing season, the average number of days from the last frost in spring to the first frost in autumn. (See "Determining When to Plant" on page 98 for more on frost dates.)

Growing-season length, which you can obtain from the local Cooperative Extension Service or from an experienced neighborhood gardener, tells you whether or not a crop has time to ripen in your location. (You'll also find first and last frost dates as well as growing-season lengths for cities across the country in the Appendix beginning on page 419.) Many leaf lettuces, for instance, are ready to pick 50 days after you sow their seeds, but head lettuces, such as icebergs, can take 75 days or more. Summer squash matures in as few as 45 days after transplanting, but a seedless watermelon like the hybrid 'Triplesweet' takes twice that time. Eggplant, a native of the tropics, needs between 4 and 5 months of warm days to stroll from seed to harvest. Knowing that your growing season is only 112 days long, as it is in Flagstaff, Arizona, will help you determine whether and when to start seeds indoors and what cultivars to choose. If your growing season is a truncated one, fill your garden with crops that mature quickly—see "Quick-Maturing Vegetables & Herbs," below, for a list—and keep your eye out for short-season cultivars, such as 'Earligold' melon, 'Dusky' eggplant, and 'Quickie', a bicolor corn that matures in 65 days. And be grateful that you're not living in Barrow, Alaska, where there are only 8 frost-free days a year.

The last- and first-frost dates, which are averages based on temperature data collected over many years, are garden guideposts. If your frost-free date is April 15, for instance, you know that hardy plants, those like spinach that can tolerate exposure to freezing temperatures, probably can be planted as early as March 15. Highly tender crops—plants like basil that hate cold and won't survive even a hint of frost—shouldn't go into the garden until 2 or 3 weeks *after* the frost-free date. Similarly, if you know that October 18 is the first-frost date, you can

QUICK-MATURING VEGETABLES & HERBS

The following crops mature in fewer than 65 days in all but extreme conditions when sown from seed or planted as bulbs.

Bean, bush	Okra
Beet	Pea
Chives	Radish
(from bulbs)	Scallion, or
Corn salad	green onion
Garden cress	Spinach
Kale	Summer squash
Kohlrabi	Swiss chard
Leaf lettuce	Turnip
Mustard	Watercress
New Zealand spinach	

GARDEN RECORDS BOOST YIELDS. *Over the years, a journal with notes on planting dates, pest and disease problems, fertilizer applications, crop rotations, and other details can be invaluable. Records allow you to build on past successes and avoid past mistakes, thus improving garden performance.*

quickly count back to determine that a fall crop of spinach, which takes about 45 days to mature, needs to be planted by the first week in September.

While last- and first-frost dates are invaluable to gardeners, remember that they are *averages*. Just because your first-frost date is November 10 does not mean that the mercury won't drop to 24°F on Halloween. While you're collecting weather information—a good source is the National Weather Service—find out the average temperatures for your region. If you live in an area with cool summers and are addicted to ratatouille, you'll need to give eggplant special help to grow and ripen. Discover, too, your location's average rainfall for each month of the growing season. Knowing that your garden probably will receive less than an inch of rain in July should affect how closely you plant in April and how heavily you mulch in May—as well as make clear that you'll have to hire someone to water your garden when you go to the beach in July. All this weather information, combined with knowledge about the vegetables and herbs you want to grow, increases your chances of success.

While you're collecting information, talk to other local gardeners about what vegetables and herbs do well for them. Ask for specific recommendations. Many "locally adapted" cultivars exist that are suited to a particular region. They may have especially good performance in the environmental conditions where they were developed or have multi-resistance to common diseases of their locale. For example, 'Tappy's Finest', a pink-red tomato, does well in moderate to cool conditions like those in the West Virginia mountains where it originated. Similarly, 'Homestead 24', a tomato introduced in 1966, was developed for hot coastal areas and is a favorite with gardeners in Florida. Such locally adapted plants will do best in your garden.

KEEPING RECORDS

Once you begin gardening, become an information source yourself. National and state records are helpful, but your records are the most accurate and useful index to your garden. Every location has its own characteristics—features that make it different from other spots, even nearby ones. It may be protected from wind and located on a southern slope, which means you can plant a week earlier than others in your area; or one corner of your garden may be wet and can't be tilled as early as the rest of the plot can. These local variations are called microclimates, and they can be as large as your town or county or as small as the 10-foot strip between your garage and the next-door neighbor's fence.

Keeping a journal is a good way to record the peculiarities of your garden and of the vegetables and herbs you grow. It doesn't have to be a daily account—although daily weather records are invaluable—but try to make frequent entries. Jot down important information and activities, such as how many plants of each crop were enough for your needs; what you planted where; when you sowed or transplanted crops; when you side-dressed with compost; what pests gave you trouble. Don't forget to record successes as well as failures. Every gardener has plenty of both.

Another form of keeping records is to be sure to label plants—beginning when the seed or transplant goes into the garden. Names are easy to forget. Conscientious labeling—and recording observations in a journal—is the only way most gardeners can remember that the pale yellow sunflowers they liked last year were the cultivar 'Moonwalker'; or that 'Valeria' lettuce, a small, frizzy endivelike cultivar, had a bitter aftertaste; or that 'Mountain Pride' tomato had better resistance to early blight than any tomato they ever grew.

Records allow gardeners to avoid past mistakes and repeat past successes. Just keep in mind that as one robin doesn't make a spring, one year's results don't make hard-and-fast rules. One year's results are one year's results. But if 'Imperator Long' carrot has performed poorly 4 years in a row in your rocky soil, it's time to try a short-rooted variety. If you like 'Celebrity' tomato as much in the fifth season as you did in the first, it belongs at the top of next year's seed list. And if, in honor of your English ancestors, you've planted peas on St. David's Day for 3 years and they never once germinated, it's time to ignore that British tradition and wait until the soil reaches at least 45°F.

TOOLS OF THE TRADE. *A well-chosen collection of basic garden tools makes gardening easy and efficient. Essential for every toolshed are soil-moving tools such as a shovel, fork, and a wheelbarrow, along with one or more types of hoes.*

CHAPTER THREE

GARDEN TOOLS & EQUIPMENT

*Man is a tool-using animal. Without tools
he is nothing, with tools he is all.*

THOMAS CARLYLE, *Sartor Resartus*, 1834

MOST EXPERIENCED GARDENERS CAN DIVIDE
THEIR TOOLS AND EQUIPMENT into four categories. There
are the "Can't Do Without" items, old friends that go to the garden almost every time the gardener does. There are "Very Useful"
tools and equipment, which get frequent use. Third are the
"Awfully Handy" devices that aren't used regularly but seem
indispensable when the need comes up. Last, collecting dust in a
dark, out-of-the-way corner of the garage, is a sizable assortment
of garden contraptions, each of which belongs under the heading
"It Seemed Like a Good Idea at the Time."

Buying tools and equipment is like reading a seed catalog: It's
easy to get carried away, to believe you need one of everything.
Begin outfitting modestly so that 5 years from now, your "It
Seemed Like a Good Idea at the Time" gadgets don't outnumber

BUY THE BEST. *To avoid wasting money on gardening equipment that you may rarely use, start with a few basic tools—a rake, a hoe, a trowel, and a spade or garden fork are a good beginning. It makes sense to always buy top-quality tools; not only will they make your work easier, with good care, they'll last a lifetime.*

everything else you own. Focus first on the essentials, such as spade, shovel, rake, and hoe. These tools, especially the traditional models, make the first cut because of their versatility.

A common garden hoe, for example, is designed to cultivate the soil and remove weeds, but it can do much more. It can make rows and furrows, cover and tamp seeds, create mounds and beds, hill up plants, break clods, dig holes, open drainage ditches in summer, and create swales in winter to redirect snowmelt. Notch its handle, and a hoe is a yardstick. Swing it wildly, and it's an instrument for encouraging snakes to move out from under the cabbages and into the woods, or the neighbor's yard.

What you'll need in addition to the most basic tools and equipment depends on where you garden, the size and style of your garden, and what crops you grow. And the size of your pocketbook.

Regional differences can be marked. Gardeners in the far north, for instance, wouldn't be without polyethylene mulches, floating row covers, and cold frames. In hot, arid parts of the country, shade cloth, hoses, sprinklers, and even irrigation systems are crucial to growing vegetables and herbs. Country gardeners plagued by deer and other wildlife put electric fencing near the top of their "Can't Do Without" list; while city gardeners with neighbors an arm's length away swear by barrel composters. If your vegetables and herbs are tucked between ornamental plants throughout your landscape, you won't have any use for an old-fashioned wheel cultivator. But if your garden is a traditional one, a straight-edged plot with rectilinear rows separated by evenly spaced lanes, a wheel cultivator is just the ticket.

Tools and equipment are the biggest investment, other than land, that a home gardener makes. If you choose wisely, they are a long-lasting investment too. Buy the best tools you can afford, even if it means spreading your purchases over several years. Consider renting power equipment, such as a tiller, or sharing the purchase with a friend. Unless a local business is having an end-of-the-season sale—and you're certain that the price has been reduced—there aren't many "deals" on tools. Cheaper means cheaper.

At the same time, don't be seduced by glossy catalogs that tuck a few eyebrow-raisingly expensive imported forks and spades made of titanium and teak between French café umbrellas and rattan love seats. European garden tools are among the best—Bulldog is one name famous for quality—but first-rate equipment is also manufactured in this country and sold at local nurseries and farm stores, even at a few national chains (look for brands that come with a lifetime guarantee). A handful of down-to-earth mail-order companies also specialize in garden tools and equipment. These firms offer the widest selection of domestic and imported garden tools and equipment. Prices can differ rather shockingly, so it's worth writing for several catalogs and comparing costs.

SIGNS OF QUALITY

Equipment for growing vegetables and herbs begins with basic tools—spade, shovel, hoe, rake. Choosing a spade or hoe might appear to be an easy decision, but the offerings are so great that even experienced gardeners can feel overwhelmed. Launch your tool shopping with a consideration of materials and construction.

HANDLES

Spade, shovel, hoe, or rake, look for handles made of hardwood—either white ash or hickory. Handles should be free of knots, the wood grain should be even and tight and run the length of the handle. Douglas fir and other softwoods, which won't survive hard use, are commonly used in less expensive tools. Avoid them, and beware of handles that have been painted, a practice used to disguise softwoods.

Some tools come with steel handles, either solid steel, which is heavier than wood, or tubular steel, which is lighter than wood. Designed for professionals, steel handles are stronger than wood but also more costly, and their extra strength is rarely necessary when working in a backyard vegetable or herb garden. Fiberglass, solid-core fiberglass, and wood/fiberglass composite handles are another option. Lighter and usually stronger than wood, they're also more expensive, boosting the cost of a tool by one-third or more.

Whether you choose a long, straight handle or a short handle with a T- or D-grip handle on your digging tools is a matter of personal preference. A wooden T grip, designed for two-handed trenching and edging, is suited for use more in the ornamental than in the food garden. If you prefer a short rather than a long handle, look for one with a D grip made of wood or metal, not plastic. If it's an all-metal D grip that is slipped over the end of the handle, examine it to see that it's securely attached. The best construction is a wooden D grip that is part of the handle itself. Also known as a Y-D grip, in this arrangement, the wooden handle is actually split to form the Y. In top-of-the-line brands, the base of the Y is reinforced with a metal collar.

METALS

Years ago, most garden tools were made of cast iron, which is both brittle and heavy; today, the best tools are made of heat-treated high-carbon steel. Look for words like "forged," "drop-forged," or "tempered." What you don't want are "stamped steel" tools,

---

CARING FOR TOOLS

If you've gone to the trouble and expense of buying good tools and equipment, it makes sense to give them a careful cleaning at the end of the garden season. It makes even more sense to clean each time you use them.

- Scrape off all dirt with a coarse brush, wooden paint stirrer, or dry corncob.

- Wipe metal parts with an oily rag to prevent rusting.

- Clean and dry wooden handles. At the end of the season, sand and apply tung oil to protect the wood.

- Keep tools well sharpened.

CONNECTIONS

The Achilles' heel of most tools lies in the connection between wood and metal. Most tool heads or blades are attached to their handles in one of five ways. Look for tools with solid-socket or solid-strap construction. Never buy tools with open-socket construction.

SOLID SOCKET & SOLID STRAP. *These constructions are hallmarks of well-made tools. In solid socket, the bottom 10 to 12 inches of the handle is encased in a forged socket, or collar, which is secured with a pin or rivet. Strong and light. Solid strap is similar to solid socket construction except that metal straps are part of the socket and extend up the handle. Very strong but heavy.*

EYE SOCKET. *The handle is threaded through an eye in the blade like an ax's and secured with a pin. Primarily used on mattocks and grubbing hoes. Strong but heavy.*

TANG-AND-FERRULE. *The tool head has a projecting tang, or prong, that is inserted vertically into the handle. The handle is then fitted with a 6-inch metal ferrule, or collar, which is secured with a rivet. Light but less strong than solid socket, solid strap, or eye socket.*

OPEN SOCKET. *The bottom 10 to 12 inches of the handle is wrapped partway by the socket, or collar, leaving the handle exposed in the back. Light but very weak.*

which are stamped out of metal sheets. Forged tools, which are made from a single piece of rolled steel, are heavier and far stronger. Nor do you want spades, shovels, or forks—tools for heavy jobs like turning the soil—that are made from cast aluminum, although aluminum is a suitable material for hand tools such as trowels.

Stainless-steel tools, usually imported from a venerable British firm with an appointment to Her Majesty the Queen, are available in a few upscale stores and catalogs. Stainless steel is strong and it doesn't rust, but it's prohibitively expensive and not significantly better than high-carbon steel. Given good care, a high-carbon-steel tool won't rust. And while stainless-steel tools hold an edge better than high-carbon-steel tools, they are extremely difficult to sharpen.

TOOLS FOR DIGGING

The flat-bladed spade is the traditional garden tool, good for digging, lifting sod, cutting roots, edging, and trenching. Most come fitted with a short handle. Shovels, widely available with long or short handles, have rounded blades and an angled bottom edge. They're good for digging and turning soil, as well as for moving around soil and other materials—that is, for "shoveling." Short-handled spading forks, the easiest digging tool to insert into the ground, are made for turning in cover crops as well as turning, loosening, and aerating soil and compost.

Most digging tools are obtainable in more than one style and size. Long handles give you more leverage; short handles give you more control. Try to select a model that you can manage easily—don't be put off with terms like "lady's spade," which are frequently used for sized-down tools. Unless cheaply made, these smaller tools are just as strong and useful as their bigger cousins are, and they may be a far better match for your body.

Any digging tool should be made from forged steel and fitted with an ash handle. Be wary of spades and shovels that have a frog, or fold, on the back of the blade (below where the handle attaches). Called hollow-back construction, the frog is designed to increase the tool's strength and signals that the blade was made from stamped metal. In closed-back tools, a steel triangle is welded over the frog to increase the blade's strength.

SPADES

The historical digging tool for gardeners, the spade can have a flat or near-flat rectangular blade (about 7 by 11 inches) with a straight or slightly angled bottom edge and a short handle with either a T or D grip. The standard spade is about 4 feet long and weighs between 5 and 6 pounds (all-steel models can weigh as much as 8 pounds). For comfort and good leverage, the spade should be long enough to reach your waist when the blade is inserted in the ground. Look, too, for a footrest, or tread, on the top of the blade to cushion your foot while you're digging. There are dozens of variations of the spade, including models with long blades for trenching and nursery work and lighter models with small heads. Price range: $50 to $70.

SHOVELS

If you regularly scoop or move soil, compost, or other materials from place to place—and what gardener doesn't?—you'll need a shovel. Shovel heads

---

MAINTAINING AN EDGE

Garden tools work best when they're clean and sharp. Use a flat or half-round coarse, or bastard, file with a double-cut tooth pattern. Digging tools, such as shovels, should be sharpened at a sharp angle on the inside edge; hoes and other weeding tools should be filed at a shallower angle, which creates a sharper edge for cutting, typically on the outside edge. Always sharpen the beveled edge of a tool blade, never the flat edge. Use the flat side of the file for flat edges, the half-round side for curved edges.

To sharpen, clamp the tool in a vise and grasp the file with two hands. File on the forward stroke, pushing away from the tool blade. Continue until you create a burr, or small lip, on the opposite side of the blade. Remove the burr by running the file along the blade's opposite side.

GARDEN FORKS. *An ideal all-around digging tool, a garden fork can be used for turning under cover crops, loosening soil, and unearthing root crops.*

(about 8 by 12 inches), which are rounded and typically have a pointed bottom edge, are attached to the handle at an angle (the greater the angle, the less the gardener has to bend). Check for a footrest, or tread, on the top of the blade to cushion your foot while you're digging. Long-handled shovels are more common on construction jobs, but many gardeners prefer a short-handled model with a D grip.

Both types weigh an average of 5½ pounds. Lighter, short-handled models with smaller heads (6 by 8 inches) are known as floral shovels and are fashioned for small transplanting jobs and for work in cramped spaces. Price range: $35 to $60.

GARDEN FORKS

Garden forks are nothing more than spades with 12-inch tines rather than a rectangular blade. Unsurpassed for loosening and turning soil, forks are also suited for digging root vegetables such as potatoes. Heavier models, known as English pattern forks, have four square or rectangular tines; spading forks have four flat tines. Most forks are fitted with a 30-inch-long D-grip handle and weigh about 5 pounds. Choose a model with a head that measures between 6 and 8 inches wide—wider forks tend to be awkward and heavy. The handle should come to your waist when inserted in the ground. Price range: $35 to $55.

TROWELS

Trowels are for transplanting in the garden as well as for working in pots, window boxes, and other containers. Many trowels are sold in a set that also includes a hand fork for digging and a claw for weeding and stirring the soil surface. For general use, choose a wide- rather than a narrow-bladed trowel, although the narrow type is helpful if you're growing vegetables and herbs in pots. Most designs—those made from a single piece of high-carbon steel or those with a steel blade and a wooden, molded plastic, or cushioned grip—are acceptable. Pick a trowel that feels good in your hand. Price range: $10 to $20.

DIGGING ERGONOMICALLY

To reduce back strain, make sure the handle of your spade, shovel, or fork is straight up and down. Keep your back straight, place your foot on the tread, and allow your weight to push the blade into the ground. Bend at the waist, and use your knees to angle the spade forward, then straighten your waist and knees to lift the load.

TUNING UP TINES

The tines of garden forks, especially flat-tined types, can become bent when working in heavy or rocky soil. To straighten a tine, drive a 4-foot piece of 1-inch galvanized pipe into the ground, leaving 1 foot above ground, or clamp the pipe securely in a vise. Insert the bent tine in the pipe, and bend it until it's properly aligned.

TROWELS. *Ideal for slipping seedlings into tight spots, trowels are best held with the thumb on top, so that they can be stabbed into the soil like a dagger.*

TOOLS FOR RAKING AND CULTIVATING

Digging is a big job, but only the first job. After the ground is opened, it has to be broken down, mixed, smoothed, and kept friable. There are clods to whack, beds to build, furrows to set, seeds to cover, and weeds to chop. These chores are not for spade or shovel but for two other essential tools—a rake and one of the many variations on the hoe.

COMMON GARDEN RAKE

Beginners are often surprised that a long-handled rake is one of gardening's "basic three," along with a spade or shovel and a hoe. It's indispensable for grading soil, forming and smoothing seedbeds, breaking up clods, covering seeds that have been broadcast, as well as for tasks like clearing stones, weeds, and other debris and spreading lime, manure, compost, and other organic matter. There are only a few variations on the garden rake, slightly different styles and sizes, so purchasing this tool is one of the gardener's easier assignments.

The standard garden rake has between 14 and 16 slightly curved or straight steel teeth and weighs about 4 pounds. Most rake heads measure from 12 to 16 inches wide. Pass on any rake with a head broader than 16 inches, which is too heavy and large to control easily.

Garden rakes are available in two styles: levelhead (or flathead) and bowhead. A levelhead rake head attaches flush to the handle by a center tang, forming a T. Bowhead rakes have curved tangs that run from each end of the rake head to the handle. They're stronger and better balanced than levelhead rakes, and their bow construction gives them a bit of springlike action. Both can be flipped over to give soil a final smoothing. If your garden is small and its soil is in top condition, you may be able to get by with a light aluminum rake; otherwise, choose a rake with a forged head and fitted with a sturdy ash handle that comes up to your chin. Price range: $20 to $45.

After the ground is dug, vegetable and herb gardeners probably spend more time with a hoe than with any other tool. According to horticultural funny men Henry Beard and Roy McKie, the hoe's name "derives from the fact that when its blade is stepped on, its handle delivers a sharp rap to the gardener's brow, at which point he cries 'Hoe!' or 'Oh _____!' or 'Holy _____!'"

HOES

There is a barnful of hoes to choose from already, yet new ones are introduced every year. Selection is further complicated by every type of hoe having several variations; and every type and variation has more than one name and comes in more than one size. After a few seasons in the garden, it's easy to

---

VARIATIONS ON A THEME

Gardeners swear by several variations of the common garden hoe. Try hefting one or more of the following at your local garden supplier to see whether you prefer them to the standard model.

Floral Hoe. This version, designed for Lilliputian gardens and gardeners, is a smaller, lighter version of the garden hoe. Its handle length is about 50 inches, its weight 1 pound.

Swan-Neck Hoe. Also known as the gooseneck hoe and Stalham hoe, this differs from the garden hoe only in its extremely long, curved metal shank, or neck, which allows the gardener to stand straighter while pulling the blade along the soil surface.

Onion Hoe. This hoe masquerades under several names but is easy to identify by its wide (7 to 12 inches), shallow (2 to 3 inches) blade that is sharpened on both bottom and side edges. Onion hoes are made for in-tight cultivation and weeding rather than digging and chopping; extra-wide models are helpful for making raised beds.

Collinear Hoe. Wide but even more shallow-bladed than an onion hoe, the collinear hoe is a lightweight tool for slicing off small weeds.

---

find yourself owning a half-dozen hoes, everything from a 6-pound mattock to a featherweight bio-cultivator, a single narrow claw designed for deep cultivation. Despite their differences, all hoes and hoelike tools are designed to cultivate the soil or remove weeds or both.

Which to buy first? It depends. Does your garden have wide rows or tightly interplanted beds? Would you rather draw a hoe toward you, push it away from yourself, or both? How strong are you? Whatever style—or styles—you settle on, make sure the blade and neck are made from a single piece of forged steel. If you can own only one hoe, the common garden, or draw, hoe is still the best all-purpose tool. If you have room and a budget for two or three hoes, add an oscillating hoe for weeding and a tined hoe for breaking up the soil.

Common Garden Hoe. Also known as the American pattern hoe and the draw hoe, the common garden hoe is a workhorse, made for chopping, digging, weeding, and cultivating. It has a broad, straight blade, measuring about 6 by 4 inches, that is sharpened on the outside bottom edge, and a rounded or scalloped top. The blade is attached at approximately a 70-degree angle to the handle by a curved neck. Handle lengths vary from 50 to 70 inches, weights from 2 to 3 pounds. (See "Variations on a Theme," left, for several alternative options.) Price range: $20 to $35.

Warren Hoe. An American native invented in 1870, the Warren, or cultivating, hoe is shaped like an arrowhead. Its sharp point is perfect for making rows and furrows. It can then be turned over so that the "ears" on the top of the blade can be used to cover the seeds. A warren hoe is also useful for grubbing out stubborn clumps of weeds and for hilling up crops, such as potatoes. Price range: $20 to $35.

Grub Hoe. A grub hoe is a tough-job tool, meant for breaking up hardpan and digging out rocks and roots. Its long, thick handle, which attaches through an eye socket, and heavy near-square blade reveal its prehistoric origin. Still popular in Europe and Asia, grub hoes are weighty— as much as 8 pounds—and are only occasionally needed in an established garden. Price range: $20 to $40.

Oscillating Hoe. Some hoes are made primarily for weeding. Best among them is the oscillating hoe, which is designed for slicing off weeds just below the soil surface. Its blade looks like a stirrup and is hinged so that it moves back and forth slightly when pushed and pulled (in contrast to a common garden hoe, which is pulled toward the gardener). Also known as the hula hoe, action hoe, and stirrup hoe, the oscillating hoe has been around for less than 50 years but is considered an essential tool by gardeners who have tried it. Look for a model with a long ash handle and a 5-inch-wide carbon-steel stirrup. If you plant closely, you may want to seek out a model with a 3-inch-wide stirrup. Avoid more expensive oscillating hoes with stainless-steel blades: They are difficult to sharpen, and a keen blade is crucial to this tool's performance. Price range: $20 to $35.

Scuffle Hoe. Similar to an oscillating hoe, a scuffle hoe is also built for weeding, not cultivating, but its blade is not hinged. There are many versions, all of which have solid blades set parallel to the ground that cut on the push stroke. A few scuffle hoes are sharpened on more than the front edge and can be both pushed and pulled. Blade shapes vary, everything from crescent and triangular to rectangular and round. Names vary too—cavex hoe, Dutch hoe, and push hoe are three of the most common. The swoe, the most unusual version, is sharpened on three sides and looks like a golf club. Price range: $25 to $40.

Tined Hoe. The tined, or fork, hoe is an under-appreciated garden tool that is good for uprooting weeds, aerating the soil, and digging in compost and other organic matter. A 5-inch-wide forged-steel head with four tines is standard, though three-tine versions are also available. Light—about 2

pounds—and easy to use, it is unsurpassed for breaking up a crusted soil surface. Be sure to choose a forged rather than a welded model. (Also built for cultivating the soil is a single-tined hoe known as a biocultivator, or finger hoe. Its merit lies in opening the soil more deeply than three- or four-tined hoes. Some models have a copper rivet on their tip that releases trace amounts of copper into the soil to help control fungal diseases.) Price range: $30 to $45.

Wheel Cultivator. As old-fashioned as a butter churn, wheel, or high-wheel, cultivators are rugged and simple, valuable in large gardens with long, straight rows. Able to maneuver in tight, narrow spaces, many cultivators come with several options—tines, weeding knives, plow blades—but the tines are the most useful attachment. Traditional models have a large wheel (at least 22 inches in diameter) and widely spread handles; 20th-century designs have a much smaller wheel, making them easier to push and balance. Price range: $65 to $80.

EQUIPMENT FOR CARRYING

All gardeners must haul things to and from the garden. Everyone needs a heavy plastic 5-gallon bucket (you can probably pick up a free one at a construction site) and a basket for carrying the harvest. If your vegetable and herb plot is tiny, a bucket and basket may be all you need. For gardeners willing to spend a little extra, there are shallow wood-strip baskets called trugs, which are created for gathering vegetables, herbs, and flowers and for carrying hand tools. A wire harvest basket made of galvanized steel is another practical investment. Its open construction lets you hose off your produce without removing it from the basket and then permits quick drying.

Those who tend more than a few herbs and one tomato plant need something on wheels for carrying—something that is larger than a 5-gallon bucket and stronger than the little red wagon the neighbor's kids outgrew a decade ago. Bypass yard buggies and other oddball contraptions, and go straight to the two best alternatives: a wheelbarrow and a two-wheel garden cart.

Wheelbarrows are more maneuverable than garden carts, able to turn on a dime, and fit in a 12-inch row. They're also more manageable on hills and easy to dump. Furthermore, they can be

HOEING ERGONOMICALLY

To reduce back strain, choose a light hoe that has a handle at least 54 inches long. There are two ways to hold a hoe: thumbs down or thumbs up. Thumbs down is the way most gardeners were taught—it feels more natural but forces you to bend over when you work. If your back is bothering you, try hoeing with both thumbs pointed up. This position requires (and builds) strong arms but allows you to stand up straight while working.

HANDY HAULING. *Whether it's mulch, compost, or soil, every gardener needs to move heavy loads from one place to another. A conventional wheelbarrow is a good choice for maneuvering in tight spaces. For adults, buy a contractor's wheelbarrow, which carries more and is sturdier than lighter-weight models.*

pushed up and down planks and serve as containers for mixing soil and compost, even concrete. Garden carts are easier to push and to keep upright—no balancing required—and can handle heavier, larger, and bulkier loads. Both are useful, if you can afford both; whichever you choose, buy the largest model your bank account and muscles can manage.

Wheelbarrow. A tray with handles set over a wheel pretty much describes a wheelbarrow; a model with a large, extra-deep tray is known as a contractor's wheelbarrow. It's more expensive, but its sturdy construction and greater carrying capacity (6 cubic feet) make it worth the extra dollars. Look for a model with ash handles, an inflatable tire, and a seamless 18-gauge steel or a heavy polyethylene tray. Wheelbarrows with polyethylene trays typically weigh about 10 or 15 pounds less than similar steel-tray models, and they won't rust,

an important advantage. Lightweight "lawn" wheelbarrows, which cost half as much as contractor's models do, are rarely a good investment. Price range: $100 to $175.

Two-Wheel Garden Cart. A deep wooden box on two wheels sums up the garden cart. Large enough to hold several bales of hay and other heavy, unwieldy loads—the big models can bear as much as 400 pounds—the garden cart can handle just about anything a backyard gardener might need to haul. The classic model has a hinged front panel, which can be swung open or removed for dumping, and is open on the back end. Look for a cart with a box made of ½-inch treated plywood rather than metal, a steel frame and axle, 26-inch spoked wheels with inflatable tires, and a hinged, detachable front for easy unloading. Buy a large cart (about 42 inches wide) if you can fit it into your budget. Price range: $175 to $275.

ERGONOMIC TOOLS

Clever designers have created all sorts of tools and equipment—trigger-grip hand tools, knee pads and kneeling benches, long-handled seed sowers, and more—so that gardeners don't have to give up growing vegetables and herbs after the first arthritic twinge or after any physical limitation. For more information, write the American Horticultural Therapy Association, Wightman Road, Suite 300, Gaithersburg, MD 20879, or the National Gardening Association, 180 Flynn Avenue, Burlington, VT 05401.

OTHER USEFUL TOOLS & EQUIPMENT

A shovel, rake, hoe, bucket, and garden cart are enough to get your garden under way, but they aren't enough to keep you going season after season. Many items that make gardening easier and more productive—floating row covers, compost bins, and other equipment designed for specific tasks—are detailed in upcoming chapters. That still leaves a handful of items that won't be your first purchases but shouldn't be too far down your shopping list.

Pocketknife. Things always need to be cut in the garden, including ripe melons and tomatoes, so make sure you have a sharp knife in your pocket. It need not be one designed specifically for garden work, such as a grafting or pruning knife, but it should be sturdy and well made. A knife with a single 2¼-inch carbon-steel blade is a good choice. Price range: $10 and $20.

Pruning Shears. Hand pruners are useful for slicing through stubborn pumpkin stems and other cutting tasks. For work in the vegetable and herb garden, choose a pair with high-carbon-steel blades that are strong and can maneuver in small spaces. A pair of high-quality needle-nose, or straight bypass, pruners is a good choice; a pair of bypass shears, which has a curved cutting blade sharpened on the outside edge offset from a counter blade, is also satisfactory. Avoid anvil shears, which are not meant for cutting twine and other thin materials and are difficult to snuggle into tight spots. Good pruners are designed so that they can be taken apart to sharpen or replace the blades. To keep track of your pruning shears, purchase a leather scabbard ($10). Price range: $20 to $35.

Watering Can. Both polyethylene and galvanized-steel (steel that has been treated with zinc to make it weatherproof) watering cans get the job done. Polyethylene models are lighter and don't corrode. Avoid copper and brass cans for outdoor use. Select the largest size you can carry comfortably and will fit under your faucet. (Oval-shaped cans are often easier to carry than round ones are, because they don't bump into your leg as easily when carried.) Check the sprinkling head, or rose, to make sure it applies water evenly and gently and is detachable for cleaning. Price range: $12 to $25.

Hose. While it's true that rubber hoses don't kink and are strong and durable, they're also expensive and surprisingly heavy. If you have the muscles to pull a heavy hose, rubber is the best choice; otherwise, look for a high-quality vinyl hose that is reinforced with a layer of synthetic mesh. Any hose you buy should have at least a ⅝-inch diameter, heavy brass couplings, and a pounds-per-inch (psi) rating of 500. Brass nozzles are more expensive, but they last forever (choose a twist type, which can be set and left at different spray patterns without being held). Price range: $25 to $35 for 50 feet.

File. Paying good money for a top-notch shovel or hoe is a wasted deed unless you have a file to keep it sharp. A bastard file—the term refers to the file's coarse teeth—with a double-cut tooth pattern is the standard choice for touching up the edges of garden tools. For ease of use, pick a file that is at least 10 inches long, either a flat mill file or a half-round model, which is flat on one side and half-round on the other. Price range: $10 to $15.

Outdoor Thermometer. Although plants are a remarkably agreeable lot, willing to grow in less than optimum conditions, they are sensitive to the temperature of the air. An outdoor thermometer can help tell you when it's time to move transplants to the garden or when to open the vent on a cold frame, and it's essential for keeping records for your garden. Especially helpful are maximum/minimum models, which indicate highest and lowest temperatures reached since the thermometer was last set, as well as the current temperature. Price range: $10 to $20.

Soil Thermometer. Seeds and the roots of transplants are as sensitive to the temperature of the soil as young stems and leaves are to the temperature of the air. You can risk ruining an outdoor thermometer by burying it in the soil for 45 minutes, but it's a better idea to buy a soil thermometer, which consists of a long metal spike topped with a small dial. Top-of-the-line models measure temperatures from 0° to 220°F, which is a greater range than most gardeners need. Models with a more narrow range, such as 20° to 180°F, are also less expensive. Price range: $15 to $30.

POWER EQUIPMENT

Having help from a gasoline engine or electric motor has undeniable advantages, but unless your plot is very large—more than 3,000 square feet, say—and you have very limited time to spend working in it, buying expensive power equipment may be overkill. Add engine noise and pollution, infrequent use, and a small garden, and it's clear that renting or borrowing are more sensible options. Purchasing used equipment is another money-saving alternative. If you decide on the secondhand route, make sure *before* you write the check that the engine starts easily and that there are no signs of oil or other leaks and no excessive vibrations or grinding noises.

Tillers. If used sensibly, tillers are unbeatable machines for preparing soil quickly in spring and fall and for turning green manures, compost, and other organics into the soil. They save countless hours of backbreaking work but should not be used for routine weeding and cultivation. Whether buying, borrowing, or renting, look for a tiller that has rear-mounted tines. In front-mounted-tine models, the tines propel the machine, while in rear-mounted-tine machines, the wheels push the tiller. Models with rear-mounted tines are easier to operate and don't have wheels in the back to compact the soil you've just cultivated. A model with a 5-horsepower gasoline engine has plenty of power to handle a 600- to 1,200-square-foot garden. Models with 5-horsepower-and-up engines have more features than smaller tillers, including a reverse gear, deeper tilling, and the ability to freewheel, or move the machine without the tines engaged. Price range for rear-tine models: $700 for a 3-horsepower model with only a forward gear to $2,800 for a large, full-featured machine.

Chipper/Shredders. They're loud, dangerous, and relatively new to the home gardener, but if you have leaves to burn or mounds of organic refuse to dispose of, a chipper/shredder is a godsend. The

---

POWER-TOOL MAINTENANCE

Always store power tools under cover, and clean them after every use. In the fall, after you've put the garden to bed, prepare your tiller or chipper/shredder for storage. Manufacturers recommend a professional tune-up for most gasoline-powered equipment after 100 hours of use.

In the fall:

- Clean and dry power equipment thoroughly.

- Either run the engine dry of gasoline and completely drain the carburetor, or add a fuel stabilizer to a full tank of gasoline.

- Disconnect the spark plug; clean and check the gap (replace plug every 2 years).

- Put a teaspoon of oil in the spark-plug hole, and slowly turn the engine over four or five times.

- Change the oil.

- Clean or, if necessary, replace the air filter.

- Sharpen, straighten, and balance blades.

- Lubricate all of the controls and bearings.

In the spring, fill the tank with fresh fuel, and turn the engine over three or four times to clean the excess oil out of the cylinder—*then* reconnect the spark plug. The engine should start on the first pull.

CONVENIENT STORAGE. *Having a small storage shed for tools and other equipment right next to the garden can be a great time saver, eliminating the need to haul an unwieldy assortment of tools from the garage. It also makes it easy and more convenient to put tools away.*

larger your property or garden, the larger the machine you'll need, but a model with a 5-horsepower gasoline engine is enough for most home gardeners. Anything smaller probably isn't worth buying. Look for models that include a plastic tamper and a reusable cloth bag, as well as wheels for easy moving. Price range: $800 to $2,000.

GARDEN WEAR

You don't need special clothing to work in the garden. No one is checking at the gate to see that you're wearing an organic cotton, garment-dyed farmer's shirt and trousers with a button-on tool pouch. Loose-fitting canvas pants with double knees and large pockets—billed as "gardener's pants" in mail-order catalogs—are durable and comfortable, but you can plant garlic or pick corn wearing an old bathrobe if you like.

FOOTWEAR

You do need sensible footwear, however. Anyone running power equipment should invest in a pair of heavy leather work books with steel toes.

Otherwise, wear what keeps your feet happy while remembering that some shoes and boots designed with the gardener in mind are worth a second look.

Garden Clogs. Available in open- and closed-heel models, lightweight, durable polyurethane garden clogs, which look like wooden shoes from Holland, are more comfortable than they appear. Good brands provide excellent arch support (less good ankle support), and they can be hosed off after you work in wet soil. Not meant to wear for spading or tilling, a pair of clogs is a good "second" purchase. Price range: $30 to $50.

Rubber Boots. Affectionately known as "Wellies" in England, over-the-sock boots in mid-calf and knee-high versions are waterproof and easy to clean. Available in PVC and other compounds as well as rubber, garden boots don't give much in the way of arch support and are hot in summer; liners are available for gardeners with cold feet. Price range: $30 to $65.

Gumboots. Created by L.L. Bean for hunters, gumboots and shoes are a compromise—leather uppers and rubber shoes—that many gardeners have embraced. Moderately good foot support and excellent protection from the wet. Gumboots are available in mid-calf styles, but gardeners will be interested in the ankle-high, shoe, and moccasin models. Price range: $30 to $70.

OTHER GARDEN WEAR

In addition to comfortable clothing and footwear, make sure you have:

Gloves. While some jobs in the garden—sowing tiny carrot seeds is one—are better done bare-handed, be sure you have a pair of gloves to protect your hands from blisters and cuts. Look for a design and size that fits well. For many tasks, inexpensive cotton work gloves may be all you need, but gloves made from goatskin, sheepskin, or cowhide will last longer and give your hands better protection. Price range: $3 to $18.

Hat. All the warnings about the dangers of the sun's ultraviolet rays aren't meant only for swimmers and surfers. Wide-brimmed or billed, cloth or straw, wear a hat that gives your face and neck protection from the sun and is ventilated for coolness on hot days. And it never hurts to pick a hat that makes you look good. Get into the habit of augmenting the protection your hat provides with an ample dose of sunblock. Price range: $10 to $20.

INCLUDE FUN FEATURES. *Whirligigs, scarecrows, sundials, and other garden ornaments may or may not contribute to your harvest, but all add a personal touch to your garden and make it more fun to work in.*

Safety Equipment. In addition to heavy leather shoes, gloves, and a hat, gardeners should wear earmuffs ($15 to $22) and goggles ($10 to $20) that meet American National Standards Institute safety standards when running power equipment. In addition to long pants and sleeves, be certain to wear goggles and a respirator ($35 to $50) when applying horticultural sprays.

GARDEN ORNAMENTS

After you've outfitted yourself, it seems only fair to perk up your garden's appearance. Growing vegetables and herbs may be a practical enterprise, but a garden is also a place to express yourself and to have a little fun. Don't hesitate to add an ornament or two to your vegetable patch or herb bed. English garden writer Beverley Nichols (an avowed ornament hater who once described a stone Cupid as looking like "a very horrible baby that has been petrified just as it was having an acute attack of wind") confessed he was inexplicably carried away while on a shopping trip for a sundial. Instead of coming home with a traditional brass timepiece, he returned with a stone balustrade, 180 feet long, to which he couldn't resist adding 9-foot Doric pillars.

Doric pillars probably aren't your style, but a statue of Saint Fiacre, the patron of gardeners, makes a graceful addition to the food garden; so does a sundial, either a simple model or something more unusual, such as a multi-ringed armillary sphere. Informal folk-garden ornaments include whirligigs and scarecrows. Neither is a permanent solution to marauding birds, which quickly habituate, but whirligigs add color and interest to the garden. And a scarecrow, even if it doesn't keep avian visitors from pulling up sweet-corn seedlings to reach the sprouting kernel, is preferable to a propane cannon booming every 15 minutes. Think of it as an opportunity to get rid of the garish Hawaiian shirt that hangs in your closet.

TOOL FOR THE MIND

For the enthusiast, the next best thing to gardening is reading about gardening. (See "Reading About Gardening" in the Appendix.) Begin building a library with general reference books, then consider adding specialized titles on topics that interest you. You may want to subscribe to a national garden magazine, such as *Kitchen Garden*, *National Gardening*, or *The Herb Quarterly*; also available are many state and regional horticultural publications and specialized magazines and newsletters, such as *Off the Vine*, which focuses on heirloom tomatoes.

Most gardeners would agree with the sentiments of the late Katharine White, an avid gardener who was also an editor for *The New Yorker*: "Whatever may be said about the seedsmen's and nurserymen's methods, their catalog writers are my favorite authors and produce my favorite reading material." Seed companies range from large established houses, such as W. Atlee Burpee & Co., which offers a broad inventory of vegetables, herbs, and flowers, to specialized firms, such as Kitazawa Seed Co., which sells seeds for Asian vegetables, and Richters, whose stock-in-trade is herbs. There is also a good supply of regional companies—Seeds of Change, located in New Mexico, is one—and even a organization of regional seed-saving groups called CRESS (Conservation and Regional Exchange by Seed Savers). All together, there are well over 200 U.S. and Canadian seed companies to choose from, and most of their catalogs are free or cost only a dollar or two. Get your name on at least a dozen mailing lists, and consider becoming a member of Seed Savers Exchange or some other nonprofit seed-preservation group.

RICH SOIL PAYS OFF. *Organic gardeners know that rich, healthy soil is the key to a bountiful garden. The secret is to feed the soil and let the soil feed the plants.*

CHAPTER FOUR

IMPROVING THE SOIL

I find that a real gardener ... is a man who cultivates the soil .... If he came into the Garden of Eden, he would sniff excitedly and say, "Good Lord, what humus!"

KAREL ČAPEK, *The Gardener's Year*, 1931

OLD-TIMERS SWEAR BY THEIR NOSE, TONGUE, AND EYES TO JUDGE SOIL QUALITY, claiming that the good stuff has a sweet fragrance and flavor along with a characteristic color. Tints of blue and blue-gray betray wet clay soil; red and yellow indicate dry sandy soil; dark brown and black announce fertile soil, rich in organic matter. Weeds are another clue to soil quality. A stand of horsetail or broom sedge signals sandy ground; bindweed, mustard, and quack grass thrive on hardpan. (For more on these green clues to soil quality, see "Reading the Weeds" on page 42.)

The bad news is that all garden soils are not created equal. It

41

may seem that yours was lifted straight from a sand dune or a clay pit, a hopeless prospect for growing vegetables and herbs, while your neighbor's has the look and texture of chocolate cake. What makes good soil? Good aeration, good drainage, good water retention, balanced pH, balanced nutrients, and a good supply of organic matter. How do you know if you have good soil—soil that will produce prizewinning patty-pan squash and 'Big Rainbow' tomatoes the size of softballs? Sniffing, tasting, consulting a color wheel, and keying weeds aren't the only ways to discover what kind of soil you have. And you don't have to be an old-timer to know that any soil can be improved—or to improve it.

UNDERSTANDING SOIL TEXTURE

Half of what we call soil actually is air and water. Of the other half, 5 percent is organic matter—or should be; the rest, about 45 percent, consists of bits of rocks and minerals. That last 45 percent is the place to begin. Determining your soil's texture, by calculating the proportions of the different sizes of solid particles it contains, tells you not only what you have but also how to improve it. Knowing what you're digging in before you dig also tips you off to what assistance your crops may need as the garden season progresses. For example, grow 'Red Sails' leaf lettuce in sandy rather than clay soil, and it will require more frequent watering and mulching and extra fertilizer. 'Red Sails' planted in clay will have to be cultivated more frequently to keep the soil aerated. Forewarned is forearmed.

Scientists classify soils by the size of the particles they contain. The largest particle sizes top out with boulders, then move down through cobbles, pebbles, and gravel. Although the stone walls that serpentine through New England are a reminder that some soils have larger particles than others, most gardeners aren't plagued with boulders or even

READING THE WEEDS

Healthy populations of weeds—not single plants—provide a fairly reliable guide to soil quality, prompting one wit to observe, "Read it and weep, then weed it and reap." Mosses, coltsfoot, docks, joe-pye weed, oxeye daisies, and plantains are some of the plants that signal heavy, wet soil. Acid soils often support telltale growths of Eastern bracken fern, cinquefoil, coltsfoot, dandelions, docks, hawkweeds, knotweed, mosses, mulleins, nettles, sheep sorrel, stargrass, and swamp horsetail. Bladder campion, goldenrods, henbane, mustards, saltbush, and sow thistle flourish in alkaline soil. If all weeds look alike to you, invest in a field guide to plants in your region and start "reading."

Dandelion, Taraxacum vulgare

Common Plantain,
Plantago major

Sow Thistle, Sonchus *sp.*

cobbles and must cope with only a sprinkling of pebbles and gravel. Nearly all backyard soils are composed of a mix of the three smallest types of particles: sand, silt, and clay. The particle-size differences between sand, silt, and clay may seem insignificant unless you consider an equal weight of each. One pound of sand contains 2½ *million* particles; a pound of silt contains 2½ *billion* particles; and a pound of clay, 40 *trillion* particles.

Sand particles are the most irregular as well as the largest of the three. That makes sandy soil easy to cultivate when wet or dry. At the same time, it warms quickly and drains in a flash, losing both moisture and nutrients in the process. Clay soil has the smallest particles, 0.002 millimeters or less in diameter, too small to be seen without the help of an electron microscope. Clay retains moisture and nutrients better than sand or silt do, but it stays wet

and cool in spring, which delays getting started outdoors. It also is brick-hard when dry. Silt falls between sand and clay. Its particles are often coated with clay, which gives it a characteristic slippery feel. Gardeners (and soil scientists) call soil that has moderate amounts of all three types of particles "loam." It's what most of them don't have.

Henry Beard and Roy McKie, authors of the hilarious book *Gardening: A Gardener's Dictionary*, recommend inviting a child to play in your garden to determine your soil's texture: "Inspect the results. Is it a castle, a tasteful little ashtray, or a messy mud pie? That's really all there is to it." Truth be told,

COLLECTING SOIL SAMPLES. *To collect a sample for determining soil texture or to test its pH, first remove the surface layer of organic matter. Then collect a slice of soil to a depth of about 6 inches. For a complete "picture" of your soil, collect several samples from different spots in the garden.*

OVERCOMING SOIL PROBLEMS

Problem soil doesn't mean you have to give up on gardening. Here are strategies for coping with some problems you may encounter.

Waterlogged Soil. Change garden location; provide drainage; break up hardpan; create raised beds; lighten soil by adding organic matter.

Arid Soil. Water more frequently or irrigate; create sunken beds; improve moisture retention by adding organic matter.

Saline Soil. Provide good drainage; add gypsum and wash away excessive salts by drenching the soil with fresh water; irrigate often with fresh water; mulch heavily to reduce evaporation; avoid fertilizers that contain salts.

Contaminated Soil. Test soil to identify contaminant; maintain a near-neutral pH level in soil; fallow contaminated soil; contact your Cooperative Extension Service for specific remedies.

Diseased Soil. Keep plants healthy; grow disease-resistant cultivars; mulch; rotate crops; adjust soil pH to appropriate levels; solarize garden. (See "Solarizing the Soil" on page 151 for directions.)

DETERMINING SOIL TEXTURE

The best method of appraising soil texture is to fill a large, straight-sided, clear-glass jar two-thirds full with water. Add a cup or so of dry pulverized soil from your garden—soil dug vertically like a core sample—and a teaspoon of dishwasher detergent. Screw on the jar's lid and shake. Then let the jar sit overnight. When everything has settled, the soil will be layered. The sand will rest on the bottom of the jar, the silt above it, and the clay—looking more like muddy water than a solid layer—atop the silt.

Now measure each layer and determine its percentage. If your sample were to contain 1 inch of sand, 2 inches of silt, and 3 inches of clay, that's a total of 6 inches. To calculate the percentage of each, divide the total (6) into each measurement: 6 into 1, 6 into 2, and 6 into 3, which gives you 17 percent sand, 33 percent silt, and 50 percent clay.

With only 17 percent sand, it's a good guess that your soil is heavy, not light. Use the "USDA Textural Triangle," below, to determine exactly what kind of dirt you'll be getting under your fingernails.

Not surprisingly, the example above scores a solid "clay" on the triangle. It's going to retain moisture and nutrients but will be slow to dry and warm in spring and is probably underaerated. It is soil that needs improving before it will produce a generous harvest of vegetables and herbs.

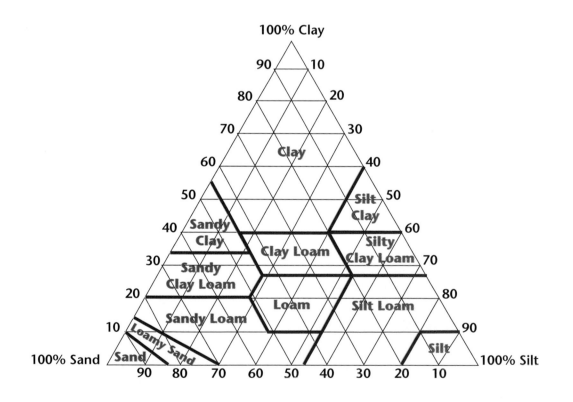

USDA TEXTURAL TRIANGLE. *To determine your soil's texture, locate the percentages of sand, silt, and clay. From each of the points, draw a straight line inward that is parallel to the side adjacent in a counterclockwise direction. The area where the three lines intersect is the classification of your soil.*

their tongue-in-cheek advice is right on target. If you don't have a child to muck around for you, one way to get a rough idea of your soil's texture is use another old-timers' trick. Scoop up a handful of damp soil and squeeze it. If it doesn't form a ball, it is primarily sand, what gardeners call a "light" soil. If it remains in a ball when you open your fist and feels sticky and smooth, it's mostly clay, or a "heavy" soil. Loam, in contrast, forms a ball but crumbles easily when touched.

UNDERSTANDING SOIL STRUCTURE

Trying to change your soil's texture isn't realistic, even if you're willing to haul truckloads of sand or clay. But you *can* improve a soil's structure. Structure is the degree to which soil particles cling together to form what scientists call "aggregates." Sand hardly binds at all; clay binds so strongly that it's close to impenetrable when dry. In contrast, soil with good structure, also called good tilth, holds together but still leaves plenty of "pore space." It is this space—half of soil's volume—that permits essential water, air, roots, and other underground life to travel with ease. Soil with good structure is well aggregated and hangs on to moisture and nutrients, yet it lets excess water drain through it, preventing waterlogged conditions and allowing adequate space for soil air. It is friable: It doesn't pack into hardpan when wet, and it doesn't blow away when dry. You can squeeze a handful into a ball, but when you open your hand, the ball crumbles without difficulty.

Physical events, such as freezing and thawing, help soil particles aggregate. Cultivating is another way to affect structure, although gardeners can do more harm than good if they till when the ground is too wet or too dry—or if they overtill. (See "R$_x$ for Tilling," right, for more on proper tilling.) Farmers have discovered that cutting back on traditional plowing not only reduces erosion but improves soil structure and increases yields. "Conservation tillage" is now used on 99 million acres of cropland, slightly more than one-third of all planted acreage in the U.S. While that's an increase of 27 million acres in only 2 years, it's unlikely that all large farms will go as far as Ruth Stout, the originator of the "no-work garden." Rather than turning the soil each year, Stout maintained a permanent 8-inch mulch of straw and other organic matter on her vegetable bed. In spring, she pulled back the mulch to sow seeds or set transplants, then gradually replaced the mulch around the small plants as they grew. With her method, tilling, fertilizing, and weeding are unnecessary.

Anything that compacts the soil—repeatedly walking or driving heavy equipment on it, for example—destroys the open soil structure that plants need. It's a good argument for creating raised beds that are bordered by paths and for heavy mulching, which helps reduce pressure on the soil when you walk across it. Another tactic to reduce compaction is to place boards between crop rows to spread your weight as you work in the garden.

R$_x$ FOR TILLING

Mechanical tillers are great helpers—they save hours of digging and produce smooth seedbeds—but they can do too good a job. Run a tiller back and forth a half-dozen times, and its blades can turn healthy garden soil that is dry into powder or compact wet soil into a sticky mass. Tilling can also create a hardpan layer below the soil you have tilled. To avoid damaging soil with a tiller, use the following guidelines:

- Use a tiller sparingly, for preparing soil in the fall or spring or for turning in a cover crop of compost or green manure.
- Don't till when the soil is wet: If you squeeze a handful of soil and it doesn't crumble when you open your fist, it's too wet to work.
- Don't till when the soil is extremely dry.
- Don't overtill—one pass should be enough.
- Don't use a tiller for everyday weeding and cultivation.

KEEP OFF THE SOIL. *To protect the soil you've worked so hard to improve, avoid walking or sitting on it, both activities that cause compaction, destroying soil structure. Boards placed across a bed make a convenient path, and if you need to sit on the soil to transplant or weed, sit on a large sheet of plywood to distribute your weight.*

LIFE DOWN BELOW

Unless you specialize in growing carrots or potatoes, it's easy to overlook what's happening under the soil's surface. There's plenty going on down there! Ninety-five percent of the soil may be rock particles, air, and water, but plants depend on that other 5 percent, the portion that is—or once was—alive.

In addition to miles of plant roots and tons of dead plant and animal matter, soil is home to billions of bacteria, actinomycetes, algae, fungi, viruses, and other microflora, as well as an enormous miscellany of macrofauna—creatures that are visible without magnification. Ants, beetles, centipedes, grubs, nematodes, slugs, snails, spiders, springtails, worms, and moles are but a few of the animals that spend all or part of their lives underground. Scientists estimate than an acre-foot (a volume 1 acre large and 1 foot deep) contains as much as 3 tons of living organisms. Most of them reside near the soil's surface, in the top

6 or 8 inches where you are gardening. There, in an energetic yet delicate balance of small and large, plant and animal, the living underworld feeds on organic matter—and on each other.

Soil organisms are essential to healthy soil and crops, but not all underground dwellers have the gardener's interests in mind. For example, cutworms are fond of chewing through the stems of young plants; the soilborne fungal disease fusarium wilt attacks cabbage, celery, melons, peas, potatoes, spinach, tomatoes, turnips, and more. Rotating crops, regular cultivating, fallowing, and composting are four safe ways to help curb troublemakers. More drastic treatments include toxic fumigants like methyl bromide, but they are indiscriminate, killing allies as competently as they kill foes. In the long run, keeping the menagerie in the soil healthy and diverse is your most important weapon for controlling subterranean problems.

Keeping soil dwellers vigorous is also the key to

good soil structure and tilth. As these plants and animals churn and tunnel their way through the netherworld, they open and aerate it. As they turn organic matter into humus, the stable dark organic matter that is left after complete decomposition, they simultaneously emit substances that dissolve rocks into smaller particles and help bind those particles together into aggregates. The gardener's job is to give the underground flora and fauna what they need: air, water, and plenty of food. Add organic matter, and your soil will develop a structure that allows air and water to get to its living constituents. Add more organic matter, and the residents will have plenty to eat.

IMPROVING SOIL STRUCTURE

Because organic matter is constantly broken down into humus by the soil's underground mix of living organisms, it must be resupplied regularly. Adding organic matter is the single most important thing you can do to improve your garden soil and ensure the success of the vegetables and herbs you plant. Organic matter helps soil preserve moisture and nutrients, improves its structure, moderates its pH, and increases its fertility. You may not have that ideal balance of sand, silt, and clay that equals pure loam, but you can have soil that acts like loam—soil that is easy to work and fertile.

It's not possible to transform a sandy or clayey plot into dark rich soil in 6 months, but you can do it in three or four seasons. So while organic matter isn't an overnight cure, it is an all-purpose one. It is the horticultural equivalent of Lydia E. Pinkham's Vegetable Compound, the popular 19th-century remedy for *every* woman's *every* ill. Sandy soil? Add organic matter. Silty soil? Add organic matter. Clay soil? Add organic matter.

While adding any kind of organic material will help your garden, the structure of sandy soils are improved most by adding fine materials like compost. Clay soil, which tends to hold too much water, is best enhanced by more bulky matter, such as half-composted plants and green manures, which are crops of grasses, legumes, and other plants that are sown to be turned into the soil. Remember, too, that organic materials decompose more rapidly in warm regions, more slowly in cold ones, more rapidly in sandy soils, more slowly in clayey ones. Gardeners in the South will need to add organic matter to the soil and mulch more often than do those living north of the Mason-Dixon line.

It's hard to imagine a garden with too much organic matter, but before you haul in tons of leaf mold and horse manure and build a 10-bin composting system, take a look at a handful of your topsoil. If you can see bits of organic matter, small pieces of stalks, leaves, or roots, your soil may need only maintenance, not a major overhaul. If you don't see any signs of organic matter—if the soil looks like "pure dirt"—you need to put your garden on a high-organic diet.

ADDING ORGANIC MATTER

You can add organic matter by digging or tilling it into the soil, by applying a mulch, or by planting a green-manure or cover crop. For the best results, do all three. To start a year-round soil-improvement campaign, follow the cycle below.

First Spring. Begin the first spring by digging or tilling 3 or 4 inches of well-rotted manure, compost, leaf mold, or other organic matter into the soil.

Early Summer. The first season, and seasons thereafter, once the soil has warmed and crops are up, mulch the garden with compost, straw, grass clippings, or some other organic mulch. Keep the garden mulched throughout the garden season.

Fall. In the fall, as soon as any portion of the garden is free, turn the mulch into the soil and plant a green manure. Annual crops like hairy vetch, red clover, and winter rye will help stop erosion and keep down weeds, as well as enrich the soil.

Second and Subsequent Springs. In the spring, spread 2 or 3 inches of organic matter on top of the cover crop, and turn them into the soil. (If you grew buckwheat or some other tall cover crop, cut or mow it before you spread organic matter.)

From there on, it's only a matter of repeating the *cycle*. Remember that it is a cycle. You can get started any time of year. If it's fall, don't wait until spring. Apply mulch, dig or till it in, and plant a cover crop. If it's midsummer and your garden is already producing vegetables and herbs, mulch between the plants. Once the soil has achieved good tilth, adding 1 or 2 inches of fine organic material, such as compost, or 4 to 5 inches of straw, chopped leaves, or other more bulky matter to your garden each year should keep your soil healthy. Do a little exploratory digging. If the earthworms are plentiful, you've done a good job.

SMALL-SCALE COMPOSTING

Commercial barrel and drum composters—priced anywhere from $75 to $400—are useful in urban and suburban areas, where appearance and space are important. They also make compost more quickly than a traditional open pile. Look for a model that is easy to move and turn, and remember that you must stop adding raw materials at some point so that the decomposition process can be completed.

You can make your own outdoor composter out of a plastic trash can by removing its bottom (to attract earthworms) and drilling aeration holes in its sides and lid, as shown below.

Another option for do-it-yourselfers is to make a simple enclosure with wood framing and hardware cloth. The model shown below keeps composted materials contained, and a hinged side provides easy access, both for turning and for collecting finished compost.

MAKING COMPOST

What kind of organic material you add to your soil may depend on where you live. If your garden is surrounded by large deciduous trees, shredded leaves are an obvious choice. Choose pine needles if you live where pines are endemic, or animal bedding and manure if you live near a stable or farm. Each has its merits, but the top choice in every gardener's book? Compost.

Consider compost's advantages. It contains not only organic matter and nutrients but a generous measure of the underground organisms that keep soil healthy and productive. Its dark color absorbs heat from the sun, warming the soil. You can make it yourself from many different—and free—materials, such as grass clippings, leaves, weeds, kitchen scraps, and more. Composting is nonpolluting and means not overloading landfills. No wonder compost is referred to as "brown gold." Better still, the alchemy of brown gold is no guarded secret: Combine a mix of organic matter in a pile, and keep the pile moist and aerated. Microorganisms do the rest. As the bumper sticker says, "Compost Happens."

Composting has become a horticultural icon in America—there are systems so complicated that it takes a book to detail them. In *Country Colic* (1944), American humorist Robert Lawson contended that "a compost heap requires scarcely more attention than an ailing panda and in the short space of two or three years will reward you with enough rich, black gook to fill one entire window box." But don't let such contentions discourage you. Left alone, any pile of organic material will break down over several years. This laissez-faire approach, known as cold composting, requires no effort beyond the piling. No layering, no wetting, no turning or aerating, no covering or uncovering. Cold, or anaerobic, composting is slow, though, and the temperature within the pile probably won't climb above 100°F, making it unlikely that weed seeds or disease organisms will be destroyed.

STEPS TO FASTER COMPOST

Speeding up the process—and heating up the pile to kill weed seeds and disease organisms—is a fairly simple matter, and you don't need to buy an aerator that attaches to your electric drill or add commercial activators to your pile. Compost really does happen. If you want to speed up the happening, use the guidelines that follow.

Balance high-nitrogen and high-carbon matter. The right combination of organic materials—the food for the millions of microorganisms that will do the composting—guarantees that decomposition takes place more quickly. The right combination also ensures that the pile will heat up to temperatures as high as 160°F, which will kill many weed seeds and pathogens. A good rule of thumb is 3 parts dry brown or yellow materials that are high in carbon, such as straw, leaves, and sawdust, to 1 part green succulent or wet matter that is high in nitrogen, such as kitchen waste, grass clippings, and animal manures. (See "Compost Ingredients," right, for a list of other suitable materials.) Too much of the first, and decomposition moves at a snail's pace; too much of the second, and the pile's odor will have the neighbors complaining. Layering the pile is the classic approach, but it isn't necessary—mixing materials together works just as well. Just make sure your blend of carbonaceous and nitrogenous materials is approximately 3 to 1.

Shred or chop before you add. Shredding or chopping organic matter is another way to expedite decomposition. If you add woody or leathery materials, such as tree twigs or oak leaves, shredding them first is essential for timely decomposition. If

NO-TURN AERATION. *For the benefits of aeration without the work of turning a compost pile, drill holes along the length of plastic PVC pipe. Incorporate the pipes either horizontally or vertically as you add materials to your pile.*

COMPOST INGREDIENTS

Efficient composting depends on the correct balance of organic matter. Matter high in carbon is typically brown and dry, while matter high in nitrogen is generally green and succulent. The proper balance for optimum composting is about 25:1 carbon to nitrogen (C:N). Don't worry about exact proportions—start with 3 parts brown and dry (carbon) for every 1 part green and succulent (nitrogen). Here are the approximate C:N ratios for common compost-pile ingredients. Ratios of 30:1 and lower are considered high-nitrogen; ratios above 30:1 are high-carbon.

Nitrogen Rich

Poultry manure (fresh)	12:1
Vegetable wastes	12:1
Alfalfa hay	12:1
Pig manure (fresh)	14:1
Grass clippings	17:1
Seaweed	17:1
Weeds (green)	20:1
Coffee grounds	20:1
Cow manure (fresh)	20:1
Horse manure (fresh)	25:1
Sweet clover	24:1

Carbon Rich

Horse manure with bedding	45:1
Leaves (dry)	60:1
Cornstalks	60:1
Pine needles	70:1
Straw	80:1
Timothy hay	80:1
Sawdust	300:1
Hardwood chips	560:1
Newsprint	600:1

TWO-BIN COMPOSTER. *For large-scale composting, consider making a two-bin composter—this one is made of leftover wooden pallets wired together. Use one bin to gather materials for composting and the other for the finished pile. Serious hot-composters will want to add a third bin and turn the finished pile from one bin to the other every two weeks to speed decomposition.*

COMPOST CAUTIONS

Some organic materials, such as tree limbs, large pieces of wood, and leathery leaves like those of large-leaved or evergreen magnolias break down slowly and should not be added to a compost pile unless they are first chopped or shredded. Avoid, too, anything that may carry pathogens, such as pet or human feces. Here are some other materials to keep out of the compost pile:

- Diseased plants
- Grass clippings or any organic matter that has been sprayed with an herbicide or pesticide
- Noxious weeds that have gone to seed or that spread by creeping stems and roots
- Allelopathic matter, such as black-walnut and eucalyptus leaves, which will stunt the growth of many plants
- Poisonous plants, such as castor bean and oleander

- Large amounts of highly acidic matter, such as pine needles
- Items, such as bones, meat scraps, or grease, which will attract wildlife to your compost pile

KEEP COMPOST HANDY. *The best place for any composting operation is near the garden, where adding organic material to the pile is an easy matter and the finished compost is right where you need it.*

you're in a hurry, shredding or chopping everything you add to the compost pile—every grapefruit rind and flower stem—will speed their decomposition.

Keep the pile aerated. Composting quickly also depends on supplying enough air to the pile and to the microorganisms that are doing the decomposing. Good aeration begins with keeping the pile under 5 feet tall and not tamping it down. It ends with time spent on the working end of a pitchfork. Rather than turning the pile and trying to keep it in one place, some gardeners build side-by-side compost bins or piles. Once a pile cools down, they fork it into the next bin or create a second pile, which quickly heats up. Another aeration technique is to bury lengths of perforated PVC or drainpipe horizontally and vertically in the pile (see the illustration on Page 49.)

Consider pile size. Studies show that a pile measuring between 3 and 5 cubic feet—either freestanding or contained—is the most efficient and workable for making compost, but the pile can be any size you want. It takes about 9 cubic feet of finished compost to cover 100 square feet 1 inch deep.

Keep the pile moist but not wet. Choose a well-drained location, or elevate the pile so that it doesn't become waterlogged and drown the aerobic organisms it contains. In rainy regions, a loose cover keeps a pile from becoming saturated; if your climate is hot and arid, sprinkle the pile with water if it becomes too dry and cover it to retain moisture.

Although hot composting is fast—determined gardeners can make usable compost in a couple of months—it has some disadvantages. It requires stockpiling materials and creating an entire pile at one time, being fairly precise about its contents, making adjustments constantly, and turning the pile every 2 or 3 days. It's great to have compost in 60 days, but remember that the much higher temperatures created during hot composting can kill off beneficial as well as pathogenic organisms. If you're determined to turn your vegetable peelings and leaves into finished compost at breakneck speed, or if you want to build a compost bin, or want to compost indoors, there are plenty of books to help you. (See "Reading About Gardening" in the Appendix for suggestions.)

FAST BUT EASY COMPOST

For most time-pressed backyard gardeners, the best composting method is somewhere between the extremes of no maintenance cold composting and labor intensive hot composting, a middle way that involves modest attention to the carbon-nitrogen balance, an occasional fluffing of the pile, and watering when the pile dries out. To make compost

---

COMPOSTING PROBLEMS & SOLUTIONS

If your compost pile isn't working as you expected—or would like—there may be an easy remedy.

Problem: Undecomposed materials in pile.
Solution: Remove them and add them to the next pile. In the future, don't add large solids, such as pieces of wood, that are slow to break down; or shred them before adding.

Problem: Pile doesn't heat up.
Solution: Add more high-nitrogen matter, such as fresh animal manure or grass clippings.

Problem: Pile is wet and smells.
Solution: Turn pile more frequently; add high-carbon matter, such as dry leaves.

Problem: Center of pile is dry and hasn't decomposed.
Solution: Turn pile, wetting it thoroughly; cover with plastic to retain moisture.

Problem: Pile is warm and damp only in center.
Solution: Pile is too small. Rebuild and enlarge it to at least 3 feet wide, long and high.

Problem: Seedlings are sprouting on top of pile.
Solution: Don't add plants that have set seed. Increase temperature of pile by adding high-nitrogen materials. Keep pile moist and turn frequently.

that will be ready to use in about 4 months, follow the steps below.

1. Spread a 6-inch layer of dry material over the area to be covered.

2. Spread a 2-inch layer of succulent material.

3. Spread a 1-inch layer of soil.

4. Sprinkle lightly with lime or wood ashes.

5. Water thoroughly, but do not soak the pile.

6. Repeat the process until the pile is approximately 5 feet tall.

7. Cover the pile with a plastic tarp.

8. After 2 weeks, remove the tarp, and turn the pile with a fork; turn again at 5 and at 7 weeks.

Fast or slow, you will want to maintain more than one pile so there will always be a place to put this week's potato peelings or the quack grass you just pulled out of the flower border. Don't be put off by complicated schemes. If cold composting fits your schedule, that's the method to use. However it's made, compost will do wonders for your soil's structure and fertility.

Using Green Manures

Green manures—also known as cover crops because they blanket and protect soil—are another first-rate way to add organic matter to the garden. Backyard growers, if they sow them at all, typically sow green manures in late summer or fall, then turn them into the soil the following spring with a tiller or by hand. Some gardeners underplant their gardens with green manures like white clover—creating a living mulch that keeps down weeds and improves and protects the soil. As one expert put it, undersowing a green manure is like planting a desirable weed. For example, sweet clover can be undersown with pumpkins or melons. Recently, USDA scientists established that tomato plants set in a cover of hairy vetch not only had fewer insect problems but were twice as productive as plants grown without a cover of vetch. (See "Green Manures" on page 60 for a rundown of the best cover crops.)

Even if you don't underplant your tomatoes with vetch or sow clover between your rows or beneath your melons, you can plant a green manure once the harvest is over. Don't bother to wait until the entire garden is fallow—sow green manures spot by spot. If you don't have another crop to follow the peas and radishes, plant annual ryegrass or clover. If your garden stays wet in spring, go ahead and turn in the green manure in late fall; otherwise, incorporate it when you prepare your soil in the spring, about 3 weeks before you plant. If your garden is larger than you need, consider keeping a portion of it covered with a green manure for the entire year. Seed it in the spring, then turn the manure crop under before it sets seed, and replant. Buckwheat, which grows so densely that it crowds out weeds, is a good choice. Annual rye is another possibility, or alternate the two. Never leave the soil bare.

The roughly two dozen common green manures are often divided into two groups: nonlegumes and legumes. Nonlegumes, which are typically grasses like winter rye, grow quickly and are valued for adding organic matter to the soil. Leguminous crops, such as alfalfa, clovers, and vetches (and vegetables like peas and beans), have the extra advantage of returning nitrogen to the soil through a cooperative arrangement with a group of underground bacteria called *Rhizobium*. If you want to see whether your legumes are fixing nitrogen, pull up a plant or two and check their roots for small pinkish nodules. If there are none, purchase an inoculant—a powder that contains *Rhizobium* bacteria—and add it to your soil. One warning: Many strains of *Rhizobium* exist, so read the label on the inoculant powder to be sure that it is appropriate for the legume you plan to sow.

There are other differences between green manures. Be sure to choose a crop that matches your garden's needs and conditions and fits into your growing schedule. In most parts of the country, nonlegumes like barley, winter rye, and other grasses are good choices for winter cover crops. Planted in the fall, they should be turned into the soil in spring. Legumes, such as clovers, beans, peas, and hairy vetch, are good spring and summer crops—ideal plants for improving the soil of any ungardened portion of your vegetable patch. Buckwheat, millet, and Sudan grass are also good summer crops. All should be tilled under in the autumn. One caution: Low-growing crops, such as clovers, are far easier to incorporate into the soil by hand than are tall plants like buckwheat.

The benefits of green manures change as the

GREEN-MANURE BENEFITS. *Underplanting a crop with a green manure such as clover keeps down weeds and protects the soil during the growing season. Cut back green-manure plants that threaten to overtake the crop. At season's end, dig the remains into the soil to add organic matter.*

crop matures. Turn under young plants, and they decompose quickly. They add less organic matter to the soil, but their nutrients are available almost immediately. Manure crops that are in the flowering stage decompose more slowly when turned under. They add more organic matter to the soil and improve its structure, but their nutrients are released more slowly. Don't wait for a cover crop to set seed. Seeds sprout, and an unwanted green manure is a weed.

SOIL FERTILITY & FERTILIZERS

Soil fertility is related to soil structure, but it's something more. Fertility requires the presence of essential elements, or nutrients, that vegetables and herbs need to grow and fruit. Water is the element plants need most—and need in largest amounts. Three other vital elements—carbon, hydrogen, and oxygen—come from the air. But the rest, the mineral nutrients, are mostly supplied to plants by the soil. Since nutrients are lost through overcropping, erosion, and leaching, they must be regularly replenished. A good mix of organic matter contains all the nutrients plants need, so regularly adding compost, leaves, green manures, or other humus-producing materials to your garden usually guarantees your soil will have everything that your crops will need. Usually, but not always.

Some vegetables and herbs demand larger amounts of a particular nutrient. Corn demands high levels of nitrogen and phosphorus; cucumbers, squash, and pumpkins do best when there is an abundance of phosphorus in the soil; carrots and cabbages need a plentiful supply of potassium. Beans and peas, which have the ability to fix, or take, nitrogen from the atmosphere, can flourish in soil that is nitrogen-poor. Parsley's demands are relatively small; it uses more nitrogen and potassium than phosphorus. So do tomatoes, but tomatoes are "heavy feeders" and require far higher levels of nutrients than parsley does. The plants themselves are the best index to whether or not nutrients are missing from the soil. Foliage that is pale, purplish on the underside, mottled or curled, as well as fruits that are undersized are warnings that the soil isn't providing everything your plants need. (See "Signs of Nutrient Deficiencies" on page 124 for more symptoms to look for.)

The subject of fertilizers stirs up the old organic-

WORKING IN ORGANIC FERTILIZERS. *A garden fork is the instrument of choice when it's time to incorporate compost, well-rotted manure, or other organic materials into the soil.*

versus-nonorganic debate. It's true that plants can't tell the difference between nitrogen that comes from synthetic sources and nitrogen that comes from natural sources. But your soil and the underground life that dwells there *can* tell the difference. Organic fertilizers and amendments are more than food for plants. They are food for the microorganisms that live underground. They break down slowly, which helps plants resist disease and other stresses throughout the growing season. Most synthetic fertilizers dissolve immediately, sometimes leaching out before they are of any benefit whatsoever.

UNDERSTANDING ORGANIC FERTILIZERS

Organic fertilizers also have the advantage of containing many nutrients, not just nitrogen (N), phosphorus (P), and potassium (K). These are horticulture's Trinity, the three essential elements packaged in a bag of synthetic 5–10–10 or 10–10–10. (A "simple" fertilizer contains one of the three elements; a "compound" fertilizer, two of the three; a "complete" fertilizer, all three.) But vegetables and herbs need more than nitrogen, phosphorus, and potassium. They want ample doses of sulfur, magnesium, and calcium, as well as small amounts of seven minor nutrients, or micronutrients: boron, chloride, copper, iron, manganese, molybdenum, and zinc. All of these elements are available from natural sources.

The nitrogen-phosphorus-potassium, or N-P-K, numbers, which designate the percentage content of those elements, appear on bags of organic as well as synthetic fertilizer. (The percentage numbers on similar organic products, such as blood meal, can differ depending on how they were produced.) Steamed bonemeal, a compound organic fertilizer, is marked 1–11–0, making it 1 percent nitrogen, 11 percent phosphorus, and 0 percent potassium. Another compound organic substance, unleached wood ash, is designated 0–1.5–8. It contains no nitrogen but has a modest amount of phosphorus and is high in potassium. Unlike a bag of synthetic fertilizer, which contains only the three major nutrients, both bonemeal and wood ash contain calcium and micronutrients. (See "Applying Organic Fertilizers" on page 62 for analyses of the most common organic fertilizers.)

Don't be mislead by the lower nutrient-analysis numbers that some organic fertilizers and additives carry. By law, the numbers refer to the percentage of nitrogen, phosphorus, and potassium that is *immediately* available to plants. Since many organic fertilizers break down slowly, their nutrients are released over time rather than all at once. Rock phosphate, for instance, is about 30 percent phosphorus, but only 3 percent is available immediately, so its N-P-K label reads 0–3–0, not 1–30–0.

All the elements have a consequential role in creating healthy, productive plants. Nitrogen is essential to plant growth and the development of dark green leaves. Phosphorus is basic to growth, too, and to the production of healthy seedlings and strong roots, and to flowering and fruiting. Potassium is crucial to photosynthesis, plant vigor, and flowering, as well as to hardiness and resistance to disease, cold, and drought. Too little calcium

PLANT pH PREFERENCES

Most vegetables and herbs prefer a pH range between 6.5 and 7.0 but will grow well in soil that ranges from 6.0 to 7.0. The vegetables below require or tolerate soil that is either more acid (below 6.0) or more alkaline (above 7.0). If your soil is chronically acid or alkaline, adjust the pH or choose plants that have better tolerance to your conditions.

Asparagus 6.5–7.5	Garlic 5.5–7.5	Rhubarb 5.0–6.8
Beet 6.5–7.5	Leek 6.0–7.5	Shallot 6.5–7.5
Brussels sprout 6.0–7.5	Melon 6.0–7.5	Spinach, New Zealand
Carrot 5.5–6.8	Mustard 5.8–6.5	6.5–7.5
Cauliflower 6.0–7.5	Okra 6.8–7.5	Sunflower 6.0–7.5
Celery 5.5–7.5	Onion 6.0–7.5	Sweet potato 5.5–6.5
Cucumber 6.0–7.5	Peanut 5.8–6.2	Thyme 5.5–7.0
Eggplant 5.5–6.8	Potato 5.8–6.5	Watermelon 5.5–7.0
Endive 5.5–7.0	Radish 5.5–6.5	

A NATURAL pH INDICATOR

Bigleaf hydrangea (*Hydrangea macrophylla*), which blooms in midsummer, is a reliable indicator of soil pH. If all the hydrangea flowers in your neighborhood are pink, the soil pH in your location is above 7.0; if they are blue, the pH is probably 6.5 or lower. If there are both pink and blue flowers, or if the blooms are a muddy purple, the soil pH is neutral (7.0).

causes leaf drop and dieback; dieback is also the result of too little boron. Not enough sulfur, and plants are spindly and pale; an iron shortage translates into yellow leaves, or chlorosis; stubby roots and wilting indicate a chlorine deficiency. Plants tell us when the soil's fertility is imperfect, but sorting out which nutrients are missing isn't always easy. Blotchy leaves can mean a manganese deficiency, but they can also signal a lack of potassium or zinc.

In one way or another, organic matter is the passkey to the elements that vegetables and herbs need. Not only does it supply nutrients to the soil, but it also, like a browser on the World Wide Web, helps plants access, or make use of, those nutrients. If you're constantly enriching your soil with compost, green manures, or other organics, and your vegetables and herbs are thriving, don't worry about soil fertility. But if your plants are spindly and harvests are meager—or if you've created a brand-new garden—have your soil tested. Autumn is the recommended season for having a soil test done, but you can do one any time of year. Basic tests measure levels of phosphorus, potassium, calcium, and magnesium (most labs don't test for nitrogen). You can also have more extensive analyses done, including tests for micronutrients and organic matter. Basic soil analyses cost around $10 and are available in most states through state universities and/or the Cooperative Extension Service, which is listed in telephone books under the name of your county or state university. For extensive soil tests, which are considerably more expensive, you may have to go to a private soil-testing laboratory. (See "Soil-Testing Sources" in the Appendix for a list.)

THE ROLE OF pH

A soil analysis discloses more than what nutrients are or are not present in your soil: It reports your

---

NUTRIENT SOURCES

Incorporating a diverse mixture of organic materials in your soil is the best way to increase its fertility. Not all organic substances are created equal, however. If a soil test identifies particular deficiencies, you can correct the imbalance by applying an appropriate organic additive. (See "Applying Organic Fertilizers" on page 62 for estimated analyses of these materials.)

Nitrogen Sources
Alfalfa meal
Blood meal
Coffee grounds
Cottonseed meal
Fish emulsion
Fish meal
Guano
Legumes
Manures
Soybean meal

Phosphorus Sources
Bonemeal
Colloidal phosphate
Rock phosphate
Fish emulsion
Liquid seaweed
Poultry manure

Potassium Sources
Dairy manure
Granite meal
Greensand
Kelp meal
Sul-po-mag
Wood ashes

Calcium Sources
Aragonite
Bonemeal
Colloidal & rock phosphates
Eggshells
Gypsum
Limestone

Magnesium Sources
Dolomitic limestone
Epsom salts
Sul-po-mag

Sulfur Sources
Epsom salts
Gypsum
Manures
Organic matter
Sul-po-mag

Micronutrient Sources
Alfalfa hay
Animal manures
Compost
Eggshells
Granite meal
Grass clippings
Kelp meal
Leaves & weeds
Rock phosphate
Soybean meal
Wood ashes
Worm castings

soil's pH, its level of acidity or alkalinity. (If you prefer, you can purchase an inexpensive kit from a garden center or mail-order company and test your soil's pH yourself.) The pH scale runs from 1 to 14. A score of 7.0 is neutral. Anything below 7.0 is acid, or sour; anything above 7.0 is alkaline, or sweet. Keep in mind that the pH scale is logarithmic, not arithmetic. That means that each numerical increase represents a tenfold change: pH of 5.0 is 10 times—not 2 times—more acid than a soil that registers 6.0, and 100 times more acid than neutral (7.0) soil. A small change in the pH number means a large change in the soil.

Knowing your soil's pH is important for two reasons. First, a few crops—celery is one—can tolerate a huge pH range, from very acid to very alkaline. But most vegetables and herbs do best in soil with a pH that ranges between 6.5 and 7.0. Some exceptions, such as potatoes, prefer quite acid soil; fewer insist on an alkaline pH. To grow these pH-sensitive crops successfully, you may have to make adjustments to your soil. (See "Plant pH Preferences" on page 55 for a list of crops that grow outside the normal 6.5 to 7.0 range.) Second, soil that is either very acidic (below 5.0) or very alkaline (above 7.8) locks up nutrients that plants need—or releases them in amounts that can be toxic. Extreme alkalinity or acidity also can harm earthworms and other indispensable organisms that live underground.

Acid soils need lime; alkaline soils, sulfur. Altering soil pH isn't rocket science (see "Changing pH," below, for guidelines), but be cautious of one-size-fits-all formulas. The soil's texture and current pH reading affect how much lime or sulfur should be added. Clay soils, as well as humus-rich ones, are slower and more difficult to adjust than are sandy soils. Acid soils are easier to fix than are alkaline ones. Small changes are more manageable than great ones are. Remember, too, that modifying soil

CHANGING pH

General guidelines for raising or lowering pH are a place to begin. If you have any doubts, add less than the amounts recommended below.

Raising pH
To raise soil pH one unit (for example, from 5.0 to 6.0), add to

Sandy soil: 30 pounds of ground limestone per 1,000 square feet.

Loam soil: 70 pounds of ground limestone per 1,000 square feet.

Clay soil: 80 pounds of ground limestone per 1,000 square feet.

Lowering pH
To lower soil pH one unit (for example, from 7.5 to 6.5), add to

Sandy loam: 10 pounds of sulfur per 1,000 square feet.

Loam soil: 13 pounds of sulfur per 1,000 square feet.

Clay soil: 20 pounds of sulfur per 1,000 square feet.

Beyond Lime & Sulfur
Lime and sulfur aren't the only ways to change your soil's pH. Wood ashes can be used to raise soil pH and are also a source of phosphate and potassium. More soluble than ground limestone, they act quickly. Apply them in spring and use them cautiously—no more than 2 pounds per 100 square feet annually. They are slightly caustic, so avoid getting them on plant foliage. Other additives for a too-acid soil are bonemeal and ground egg, clam and oyster shells.

Sphagnum peat is frequently recommended as an alternative to sulfur for lowering soil pH. While it has the advantage of adding organic matter to the soil, peat is expensive and is, for all practical purposes, a nonrenewable natural resource. Better additives for a too-alkaline soil are oak-leaf mold, pine needles, sawdust, wood chips, cottonseed meal, and fresh manure.

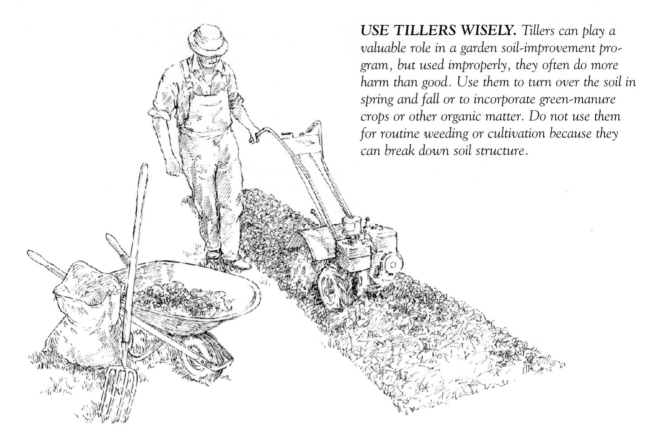

USE TILLERS WISELY. *Tillers can play a valuable role in a garden soil-improvement program, but used improperly, they often do more harm than good. Use them to turn over the soil in spring and fall or to incorporate green-manure crops or other organic matter. Do not use them for routine weeding or cultivation because they can break down soil structure.*

pH takes more than one season. Don't be in a hurry. Twice the recommended dosage won't work twice as fast or twice as well: Too much lime or sulfur creates problems rather than solves them. If the soil in your region is chronically acid (as it is in most of the eastern U.S.) or alkaline (as it is in many parts of the West), controlling pH will be a lifelong chore. Finally, compost and other decomposed organic matter help stabilize pH. You may never have to purchase lime or sulfur if your garden soil is rich in humus.

IMPROVING SOIL FERTILITY

Improving a soil's fertility is relatively simple once its pH is within a healthy range and you've identified what nutrients are lacking. Gardeners have been known to go to extremes to feed their plants. An English vicar, the story goes, grew such wonderful roses that members of his parish bullied him into giving up his secret: "I bury a cat under each bush," he confessed. You may prefer to add a balanced organic fertilizer—many are available on the market, and they are easy to apply—or you can select the appropriate organic additive to correct your soil's deficiency.

Organic fertilizers and additives can be grouped in five loose classes: animal manures, green manures, dried animal parts, compost, and rock powders.

Animal Manures. Fresh manures are high in nitrogen and can burn plants; they should be composted before using or applied in the fall. (Nutrients from fresh manures are rapidly available to plants; dry or composted manures release their nutrients more slowly.) In addition to nitrogen, phosphorus, and potassium, most animal manures contain sulfur, calcium, and micronutrients. Manures are also a good source of organic matter.

Green Manures. As well as providing organic matter to the soil, green manures, or cover crops, slowly release a balanced variety of nutrients. Alfalfa, for example, contains nitrogen, phosphorus, potassium, sulfur, calcium, magnesium, and micronutrients. (Nutrients contained in most plant "meals," such as alfalfa, cottonseed, or soybean meal, are immediately available to plants.)

Compost. The nutrient value of compost, a complete fertilizer, depends on what it was made from and how it was made (most compost is rated about 1–0.5–1; to increase the value of your compost, keep the pile covered to prevent leaching). In addition to nitrogen, phosphorus, and

ADD ORGANIC MATTER WITH MULCH. *Organic mulches, such as chopped leaves, straw, hay, or even dried grass clippings, help not only to control weeds and keep moisture in the soil but also to improve soil fertility. As they break down, they add organic matter to the soil. Turn them under at the end of the season.*

potassium, compost contains sulfur, calcium, magnesium, and micronutrients—everything your plants need.

Dried Animal Parts. Most fertilizers made from dried animal parts, such as blood and ground bones, are rapidly available to plants. Nutrient contents vary widely: Fish and blood meal are high in nitrogen; steamed bonemeal is high in phosphorus and calcium.

Rock Powders. The minerals in rock powders, such as rock phosphate, limestone, granite meal, and gypsum, are released slowly. Although they are often rich in calcium and micronutrients, most rock powders are not complete fertilizers.

USING FERTILIZERS

Using organic fertilizers and additives isn't an exact science. This year's compost isn't exactly the same as last year's; the manure from your barn isn't exactly the same as the manure from the local stable; your grass clippings aren't exactly the same as your neighbor's. Don't be disturbed by these uncertainties. Vegetables and herbs are fairly forgiving. Too much nitrogen can create serious problems, but if you overdo the phosphorus or potassium, you'll still have a good harvest. If you're going to err, though, too little is better than too much.

Adding organic fertilizers is more than a question of what and how much. It's a matter of timing. While some organic additives are highly soluble—wood ash and dried blood are two—most organics need time to release their nutrients. Granite dust and rock phosphate, two slow-release sources of phosphorus, must be applied in autumn to be of use to plants in the spring. It's valuable to be able to read your plants—to connect leaves with purple undersides to a phosphorus deficiency in the soil—but the overall goal is to anticipate what your soil may need. That's the key—concentrate first on what your *soil* needs. The shopworn phrase is worth repeating: Feed the soil, not the plant. Smart Gardening 101.

It's also worth repeating that soils routinely enriched with compost, green manures, and other organic matter usually have everything that plants need: a slightly acid pH, a full complement of essential nutrients, and good tilth. Healthy soil produces good vegetables and herbs. It's that simple.

GREEN MANURES

Green-manure crops add both organic matter and nutrients to the soil. To sow, broadcast seeds—spreading handfuls of seeds as evenly as you can—then rake. Water the area and keep it evenly moist until seedlings appear.

TYPE	WHEN TO SOW	SEEDING RATE (lbs. per 1,000 sq. ft.)
LEGUMES		
Alfalfa	Spring	1
Beans, fava	Spring or fall	6
Beans, soy	Spring	5
Clover, alsike	Spring to late summer	0.5
Clover, crimson	Fall	1
Clover, ladino	Spring to late summer	0.5
Clover, red	Spring to late summer	0.5
Clover, sweet (yellow or white)	Spring to summer	0.5
Clover, white Dutch	Spring to summer	0.5
Cowpeas	Spring	5
Hairy indigo	Spring	0.5
Lespedeza	Spring	1
Lupine, white or blue	Spring	1
Pea, field or Austrian	Spring or fall	5
Trefoil, birdsfoot	Spring	0.5
Vetch, hairy	Spring to fall	1.5
NONLEGUMES		
Barley	Spring or fall	2.5
Brassicas (kale, radish, etc.)	Spring to fall	0.5
Bromegrass, smooth	Fall	1
Buckwheat	Spring to summer	2–3
Millet, pearl	Spring to summer	1
Oats	Spring or fall	2.5
Rye, winter	Fall	2.5
Ryegrass, annual	Spring or fall	1–2
Sudan grass; sorghum	Spring to summer	1
Wheat, winter	Late summer	2–3

Reprinted from *Start with the Soil*, © Grace Gershuny.
Permission granted by Rodale Press, Inc., Emmaus, Pennsylvania.

WHERE ADAPTED IN UNITED STATES	COMMENTS
All	Perennial; deep-rooted; needs good drainage; neutral pH
All	Annual; edible bean
All	Annual
North	Tolerates wet, acidic soil
South to Central	Winter annual
All	Tolerates traffic; wet or droughty soil
North to Central	Perennial; good phosphorus accumulator
All	Needs good drainage & neutral pH; yellow clover tolerates dry conditions
All	Perennial; tolerates traffic
South to Central	Annual; drought-resistant
Deep South	Needs warm, well-drained soil; resists root knot nematode
South	Good for restoring eroded, acidic soil
All	Tender annual; good biomass producer
All	Annual; best combined with grain crop
All	Comparable to alfalfa but tolerates poor soil
All	Best combined with rye; good biomass producer; winter-hardy
All	Needs pH 7–8; use spring varieties in North
All	Fast-growing, cool season; do not allow to set seed
North	Cold-hardy winter cover crop
All	Tender; good smother crop; phosphorus accumulator
All	Fast-growing warm-season smother crop; tolerates low pH
All	Tolerates wide pH range; avoid heavy clay; good "nurse crop" for legumes
All	Suppresses weed growth when turned under
All	Widely adapted; rapid grower
All	Tolerates poor drainage; rapid biomass producer in hot weather
All	Needs pH 7–8 and good fertility

APPLYING ORGANIC FERTILIZERS

The table below provides information on various types of organic fertilizers, including benefits, average analysis (nitrogen–phosphorus–potassium, or N–P–K ratio), and application rates. Application rates are given in ranges per 1,000 square feet, designed to be used in conjunction with a soil test.

ORGANIC AMENDMENT	PRIMARY BENEFIT	AVERAGE ANALYSIS
Alfalfa Meal	Organic Matter	5–1–2
Apple Pomace	Organic Matter	0.2–0–0.2
Aragonite	Raises pH	96% Calcium Carbonate
Bat Guano (ancient)	Nitrogen	2–8–0 plus Calcium
Bat Guano (fresh)	Nitrogen	10–3–1
Blood Meal	Nitrogen	10–0–0
Bluegrass Hay	Organic Matter	1.8–0.6–1.8
Bonemeal (steamed)	Phosphate	1–11–0
Borate Rock (borax)	Trace Minerals	10% Boron
Calcitic Limestone	Raises pH	65%–80% Calcium Carbonate
Cattle Manure (dry)	Organic Matter	2–2.3–2.4
Coffee Grounds	Nitrogen	2–0.3–0.2
Colloidal Phosphate	Phosphate	0–2–0, 18% Total P2O5
Compost (dry/bagged)	Organic Matter	1–1–1
Compost (homemade)	Organic Matter	Up to 4–4–4
Compost (mushroom)	Organic Matter	0–0–1
Corn Stover (dry)	Organic Matter	1.2–0.4–1.6
Corn Stover (green)	Organic Matter	0.3–0.1–0.3
Cottonseed Meal	Nitrogen	6–2–1
Cowpeas (dry)	Organic Matter	3.1–0.6–2.3
Cowpeas (green)	Organic Matter	0.4–0.1–0.4
Crab Meal	Nitrogen	4–3–0.5
Dolomitic Limestone	Raises pH	51% Calcium Carbonate, 40% Magnesium Carbonate
Eggshells	Calcium	1.2–0.4–0.1
Epsom Salts	Balancer	10% Magnesium, 13% Sulfur
Feather Meal	Nitrogen	11–0–0
Fescue Hay	Organic Matter	2.1–0.7–2.4
Fish Emulsion	Nitrogen	4–1–1; 5% Sulfur
Fish Meal	Nitrogen	6–3–3
Flowers of Sulfur	Balancer	99% Sulfur

If your soil is of good fertility, apply the material at the lower end of the range; for poor soils, use the higher end. To feed your soil with a balanced supply of nitrogen, phosphorus, potassium, and micronutrients, combine materials high in each element at the recommended rate and apply.

RATE PER 1,000 SQ. FT.	COMMENTS
25–50 lbs.	Natural plant growth stimulant
100–250 lbs.	Contains trace minerals
25–100 lbs.	Can replace limestone
10–25 lbs.	High analysis fertilizer
10–30 lbs.	High analysis fertilizer
10–30 lbs.	Fertilizer and animal repellent
100–250 lbs.	Apply as mulch
10–30 lbs.	Feeds plants directly
3–5 ozs.	Use only if boron tested deficient
25–100 lbs.	Releases slowly; apply in fall
100–200 lbs.	Compost before applying
Mix in compost	Acidic; use with limestone
20–80 lbs.	Raises pH
50–200 lbs.	Avoid sludge-based compost
400–2,000 lbs.	25% Organic Matter
50–350 lbs.	Check for pesticide residues
100–250 lbs.	(Dry cornstalks)
400–1,000 lbs.	(Green cornstalks)
10–35 lbs.	Request "feed grade"
100–200 lbs.	
400–800 lbs.	
50–150 lbs.	Helps control harmful nematodes
25–100 lbs.	Use only if magnesium tested deficient
25–100 lbs.	Also contains trace minerals
1–5 lbs.	Use sparingly; can be sprayed
10–30 lbs.	
100–200 lbs.	
4 oz.–2 qts.	Usually also contains sulfur
10–30 lbs.	
2–20 lbs.	Lowers pH

Continued on page 64

APPLYING ORGANIC FERTILIZERS—CONTINUED

ORGANIC AMENDMENT	PRIMARY BENEFIT	AVERAGE ANALYSIS
Granite Meal	Potash	3%–5% Total Potash
Grass Clippings	Organic Matter	0.5–0.2–0.5
Greensand	Potash	7% Total Potash
Gypsum	Balancer, Calcium	22% Calcium, 17% Sulfur
Hairy Vetch	Organic Matter	2.8–0.8–2.3
Hoof and Horn Meal	Nitrogen	12–2–0
Horse Manure	Organic Matter	1.7–0.7–1.8
Humates	Organic Matter	
Kelp Meal	Complete Fertilizer	1.4–0.5–2.5
Lespedeza Hay	Organic Matter	2.4–0.8–2.3
Oak Leaves	Organic Matter	0.8–9.4–0.1
Orchard Grass Hay	Organic Matter	2.3–0.7–2.8
Oyster Shells	Calcium	33% Calcium
Peat Moss	Organic Matter	pH range 3.0–4.5
Pig Manure	Organic Matter	2–1.8–1.8
Potassium Sulfate	Potash	0–0–50
Poultry Manure (dry)	Organic Matter	4–4–2
Red Clover Hay	Organic Matter	2.8–0.6–2.3
Rock Phosphate	Phosphate	0–3–0, 30% Total Phosphate
Sawdust	Organic Matter	0.2–0–0.2
Sheep Manure (dry)	Organic Matter	4–1.4–3.5
Soybean Meal	Nitrogen	7–0.5–2.3
Sul-Po-Mag	Potash, Magnesium	0–0–22, 11% Magnesium, 22% Sulfur
Sweet Clover Hay	Organic Matter	2.2–0.6–2.2
Timothy Hay	Organic Matter	1.8–0.7–2.8
Wheat Bran	Organic Matter	2.6–2.9–1.6
Wheat Straw	Organic Matter	0.7–0.2–1.2
White Clover (green)	Organic Matter	0.5–0.2–0.3
Wood Ash (leached)	Potash	0–1.2–2
Wood Ash (unleached)	Potash	0–1.5–8
Worm Castings	Organic Matter	0.5–0.5–0.3

RATE PER 1,000 SQ. FT.	COMMENTS
25–100 lbs.	67% Silicas plus 19 trace minerals
200–500 lbs.	
25–100 lbs.	32 trace minerals
5–40 lbs.	Do not apply if pH is below 5.8
100–200 lbs.	Grown as winter cover crop
10–30 lbs.	
100–200 lbs.	Let rot before applying
15–50 lbs.	Variety of humic acids
10–40 lbs.	60 trace minerals
100–200 lbs.	
100–250 lbs.	
100–200 lbs.	
25–100 lbs.	Works very slowly to raise pH
As needed	Use around acid-loving plants
100–200 lbs.	Compost before applying
3–8 lbs.	Very soluble, use with caution
25–100 lbs.	Compost before applying
100–200 lbs.	
10–60 lbs.	32% Calcium, 11 trace minerals
100–250 lbs.	Must be well rotted
25–100 lbs.	Compost before applying
10–50 lbs.	
5–10 lbs.	Does not change pH
100–200 lbs.	
100–200 lbs.	
100–200 lbs.	
100–250 lbs.	
400–800 lbs.	Grown as summer cover crop
5–20 lbs.	Raises pH
3–10 lbs.	Very soluble; use with caution
50–250 lbs.	Includes 11 trace minerals

ROWS OR BEDS—OR BOTH. *Planting in a mix of beds and conventional rows, as well as intercropping and succession planting are all layout techniques that help make the most of available space in any garden. Use them to make room for all your favorite crops from leaf lettuce to tomatoes.*

CHAPTER FIVE

LAYING OUT THE GARDEN

It is one of the most bewitching sights in the world to observe a hill of beans thrusting aside the soil, or a row of early peas just peeping forth sufficiently to trace a line of delicate green.

NATHANIEL HAWTHORNE,
Mosses From an Old Manse (1845)

TO TRADITIONALISTS, VEGETABLES AND HERBS OUGHT TO GROW IN ROWS AS PRECISE AS A PLUMB line. But tradition is optional. Your garden doesn't have to be as uncompromising as a Marine Corps haircut. It can be as gloriously haphazard as a patchwork quilt. It can be one large plot filled with 20-foot rows or divided into five rectangular beds. It can be several small round gardens, each filled with like-minded plants or with a mix of flowers, vegetables, and herbs. A garden

CONSIDER WIDE-ROW PLANTING. *Planting crops in closely spaced rows or bands saves space and maximizes yields compared with conventional single-row plantings. Wide paths between rows provide access to the plants from either side making weeding, harvesting, and other tasks easy.*

can consist entirely of hanging baskets and pots on a deck or patio too. Your choice—or choices, for your garden can be some of each—depends on your space, your crops, and your fancy.

Once the garden site is set (see Chapter 2, "Getting Started"), you must decide how to use the space. Experienced gardeners always advise making a plan before stringing lines and sowing seeds, although a good many of these experts plant without making one. (They are the same people who can't name the carrot they've grown but were *absolutely positive* when they planted it in March that they wouldn't need a label to remember it was 'Early Scarlet Horn'.) So do what they say, not what they do: However you lay out your garden, first compose it on paper.

ROWS OR BEDS

A plan does more than confirm that you planted 'Earliwax', not 'Golden Wax', bean. A plan helps you avoid mistakes and use space efficiently. It helps you maintain healthy soil and extend the length of the harvest season. Before deciding between 'Red Rubin' and 'Purple Ruffles' basil, or how many 'Butternut' squash plants you'll need, or anything else, settle on the basic layout of your garden. Rows or beds? Or both?

TRADITIONAL ROWS

Laying out a garden in rows is uncomplicated. It simplifies calculating how much seed you'll need—most seed packets tell how many single-row feet their contents will sow—and organization is straightforward. String a line and plant—a row of lettuce, a row of carrots and beets, a row of parsley and basil, a row of cucumbers, three rows of beans, two rows of tomatoes, four rows of corn. Moreover, crops that must be hilled up as they develop—potatoes and leeks are two—are far easier to grow when planted in rows. Overall, though, growing all your vegetables and herbs in long single rows makes sense only if the garden is so large that you must cultivate it by machine.

GROW A FREE-FORM GARDEN. *There's no rule that vegetables have to be planted in arrow-straight rows. This kitchen garden, filled with herbs, salad greens, and flowers, produces a bumper harvest for the table and looks colorful and attractive while doing it.*

For most home gardeners, planting in conventional rows has fewer advantages than disadvantages. Because the garden is level with the surrounding land, it may drain poorly and be slow to dry and warm in spring. Intercropping is difficult in narrow rows. Single-row schemes also use space inefficiently, for the distance between plants must be greater than in beds—as much or more space is allotted to paths than to plants, which means you must cultivate a larger area. Paths, which compact and damage soil structure, must be kept free of weeds or covered with a mulch, making more work. The bottom line is, if your layout consists of single rows, you'll have to spend extra time and energy maintaining your garden.

If you're not ready to turn your traditional single-row garden into one filled with beds, at least consider planting in broad bands, with two or more rows seeded closely together to form a wide row. Wide rows are real space savers. A 12-inch-wide 10-foot-long row of colorful French butterhead lettuce 'Merveille des Quatre Saisons' plants spaced 1 foot apart (10 plants) and bordered by 18-inch paths would occupy 40 square feet (4 by 10 feet). Set those 10 lettuces side by side in a 2-foot-wide 5-foot-long strip bounded by 18-inch paths, and the garden shrinks to 25 square feet (5 by 5 feet).

BED BENEFITS

But why stop halfway when cultivating vegetables and herbs in beds has so many advantages for the

BENEFIT BY MAKING BEDS. *Created by mounding up soil, long, free-standing beds are easy to make, use space efficiently, and concentrate soil-improvement efforts where they really count. This garden features a handsome planting of salad greens for cutting, with repeating triangles of minzuna next to purple mustard.*

GARDEN WALKWAY OPTIONS

Rather than being left bare, paths between permanent raised beds should be covered with materials that are dense enough to stifle weeds, easy to maintain, and attractive. Among the possible choices are:

- Gravel, flagstone, or sand.

- Black plastic, roofing shingles, tar paper, heavy cardboard, newsprint, or carpet covered with a 3-inch layer of organic material, such as wood chips.

- A 4- to 6-inch layer of organic matter, such as shredded bark, wood chips, sawdust, shredded corncobs and cornstalks, chopped leaves, pine needles, straw, hay, or grass clippings.

- A green manure, such as alfalfa, rye, white clover, or vetch. When used this way, green manures must be mowed, but the trimmings can be dried and spread over the beds as mulch, then worked into the soil at season's end.

- Grass, which also must be mowed.

home grower? If you live in a hot, dry region and have sandy soil, you're probably better off with flat beds—or sunken beds—which will retain more moisture and dry out more slowly. In frigid regions, hilling, which helps raise the temperature of the soil, is a preferable option to single rows. In most parts of the country, raised beds, which are like large bottomless containers, give gardeners the most benefits. The advantages of growing vegetables in beds include:

Efficient Use of Space. Beds increase gardening space by reducing the number of paths. Crops now occupy two-thirds of the garden rather than one-third. Beds also lend themselves to intercropping, as well as intensive and succession planting, and make crop rotations simpler. They increase yields simply through better use of space.

Soil Improvement. Beds not only reduce soil compaction and improve soil structure, they allow soil to drain and warm more quickly in spring. In addition, they make containing and correcting soil problems easier.

Season Extension. Because soil warms up more quickly in spring—raised beds help extend the growing season.

Time- and Money-Saving Design. Beds reduce costs because only productive areas of the garden are cultivated, enriched, and watered. They require less maintenance and are more convenient to tend.

Add attractiveness to that list, and it's hard to say no to raised beds. The technique is as old as the Bronze Age but was largely abandoned in industrial nations until the onset of the ecology movement in the 1970s. Then, a concern for the environment, an interest in growing healthful and safe food, a desire to create beautiful food gardens, and increasingly smaller backyards combined to renew interest in this ancient practice.

RAISED-BED OPTIONS

You can build permanent raised beds or create new beds each year. Each alternative has its strengths and drawbacks. If you're not sure what's best for your location, begin with freestanding beds. You can always make them permanent next year.

Freestanding Beds. Inexpensive and simple to create, freestanding beds are made by hilling up soil with a hoe. They can be resized or shifted easily, reducing the risk of soilborne diseases. They warm and drain more quickly than enclosed beds do and are more accessible to power equipment. They also require regular maintenance to keep the soil mounded up, however. Because of their uncontained, sloping sides, they are less space-efficient and are more susceptible to soil erosion and to water and nutrient runoff.

Permanent Enclosed Beds. Handsome and permanent, raised beds enclosed by wood, stone, or some other material are less subject to soil erosion than are freestanding beds. They retain moisture better and provide an effective barrier against invasive weeds. In addition, they make full use of the

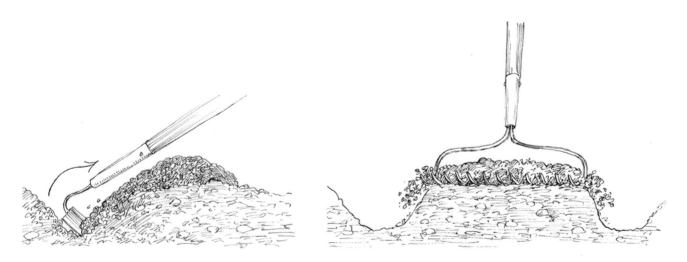

SIMPLE RAISED BEDS. *If you aren't sure what the permanent layout of your garden will be, freestanding raised beds, created by mounding up soil with a hoe, raking the top smooth, and leveling it off, are the best option.*

cultivated space because there are no sloping sides. On the downside, they are also more costly and time-consuming to build, can make digging or rototilling difficult, and can shelter unwanted wildlife, such as slugs.

You can frame enclosed beds with a variety of materials—everything from wood beams, timbers, and railroad ties to flagstones, bricks, and cement blocks. Wood frames should be treated with a non-toxic preservative for longer life. Sink the frame a couple of inches into the soil for additional support, and don't overfill. To avoid excessive erosion, the frame should rise 2 or 3 inches above the surface of the bed. If you're only half-decided on raised beds, you can create a semi-permanent frame with bales of straw or hay.

LAYOUT BASICS

A rough outline of your garden plot is all you need at first. Graph paper is helpful but not essential— just make certain that the scale is reasonably accurate and that you've marked how the sun hits your garden. Knowing the sun's path will tell you where to place tall or trellised plants, such as sunflowers and pole beans, so that they won't shade diminutive neighbors. Running rows and beds east to west gives plants the greatest exposure to light and is the orientation most gardeners use. If your climate is sultry, you may want to plant on a north-south axis and set tall plants where they will screen lettuce, summer greens, and other crops that tend to wilt in the hot afternoon sun. Finally, rather than take their direction from the movement of the sun, hillside gardeners always should plant across the slope to discourage erosion.

Next, work out how many rows or beds your garden can hold and what size they'll be. Rows can be any length. Be sure to factor in paths: Eighteen inches is a commonly recommended width, but if you plan to use a heavy-duty tiller or want to take an oversize cart into the garden, make sure that the paths will easily accommodate your equipment.

Beds should be sized between 3 and 5 feet wide. The goal is to make beds no broader than your reach from either side so that you never need to walk on them. Squat down and stretch out your arm. That distance doubled minus an inch or two should be the maximum width. If you know that you'll be using plastic mulches or floating row covers for pro-

tection against the cold or insects, keep in mind that most garden fabrics come in 6-foot widths. Plastic covers used with standard hoops to create a cloche will span about 3 feet. The length of a bed is unimportant, but don't make it so long that you're tempted to walk across rather than around it—an important benefit of raised beds is that their soil is never compacted.

All the beds in your garden don't have to be the same dimension, but if they are, you can move covers, cloches, cold frames, and other equipment from one to another without having to resize them. Same-size beds also make crop rotations and amending the soil easier. Consistency, in this case, is neither foolish nor a hobgoblin, and even those contrary "great souls" Henry David Thoreau referred to would want to embrace it.

PREPARING THE BEDS

"The operation of digging [is] a fine healthy occupation, not only from its calling the muscles into vigorous action, but from the smell of the new earth … ," Jane Loudon wrote in 1845 (*The Lady's Country Companion*). Louden lived in London, where she and her husband maintained a modest-size garden, so it's unlikely that her knowledge of digging was firsthand. If not intimate, her view was accurate. Digging, as experienced gardeners know, is an exhausting pleasure.

DOUBLE DIGGING

Hand digging, more specifically double digging, is the classic technique for creating raised beds. Used for 5,000 years, it was late-19th-century French gardeners who made the method famous. Double digging— so named because you dig two spade-lengths, or spits, deep—is a formidable job (the British call it "bastard trenching"), but it doesn't have to be done every year. Fall is the best time, but whenever you dig, make sure the soil is neither too wet nor dry to be worked. To test it, turn over a little soil and squeeze a handful. If it doesn't form a ball, it's too dry. Water the area thoroughly and wait a day before digging. If it forms a solid, sticky ball, it's too wet. Let it dry out for a day or more. If the handful holds together but doesn't pack densely, it's ready for the spade. Follow the steps under "Double Digging Basics," right, to prepare the soil in a new bed.

By aerating the soil, double digging will "raise"

DOUBLE DIGGING BASICS

To double dig, first mark the dimensions of the bed with string or a sprinkling of flour, lime, or white sand. Next, use a spade to skim the sod off the bed and set it aside. Then follow the steps below.

1. Dig a trench one spit deep and two spade-widths broad, placing the soil in a wheelbarrow or cart.

2. Using a spading fork, loosen the subsoil at the bottom of the trench until you reach a total depth of about 2 feet. Place a single layer of sod, vegetative side down, over the loosened subsoil. Using the spade, cut the sod into smaller pieces. If your soil has poor structure or is depleted of nutrients, add a layer of organic matter, such as rotted manure or compost.

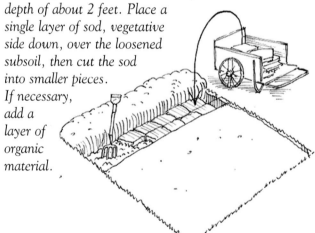

3. Dig a second trench alongside the first, placing the topsoil from the second trench in the first trench.

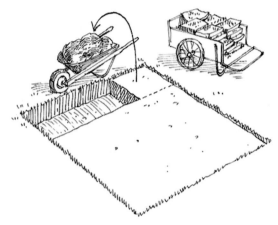

4. Using a spading fork, loosen the subsoil at the bottom of the second trench until you reach a total depth of about 2 feet. Place a single layer of sod, vegetative side down, over the loosened subsoil, then cut the sod into smaller pieces. If necessary, add a layer of organic material.

5. Dig a third trench alongside the second, continuing the established process until the entire bed has been dug.

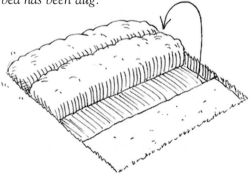

6. Fill the last trench with the reserved topsoil from the first trench. Add any needed soil amendments, and work them in with a spading fork or rake. Break up any large clods, and rake the beds smooth.

AN EFFICIENT LAYOUT. *The large raised beds in this garden accommodate a wide range of crops. Mulched paths wide enough for a garden cart make it easy to haul in compost or other supplies.*

a bed several inches, but you can add more soil, compost, or other organic matter to elevate it even farther. Be careful not to overdo it in hot, dry regions, where the exposed sides of freestanding raised beds are quickly baked by the sun. If you prepare beds in autumn, leave the soil rough so that it erodes less easily during the winter. Better still, sow a green manure to hold the soil. (See "Using Green Manures" on page 52 for directions.)

OTHER PREPARATION OPTIONS

If double digging isn't your cup of tea, or if your soil has been cultivated before and already is in good tilth, there are other ways to prepare the ground for raised beds. Whether you depend on muscles or gasoline engines, begin by removing sod. Weeds and grasses, even tiny bits of stems and roots, have a wondrous ability to survive and sprout. A non-back-breaking way to get rid of vegetation is to smother it

by laying down a heavy black plastic cover 6 months before you prepare ground for planting.

Single digging—using a spade, shovel, or fork to turn the topsoil one spit deep—is a respectable alternative if you want to work by hand. Remove any sod and add it to your compost pile (place it upside down). After the entire garden is dug, spread a layer of compost, well-rotted manure, or grass clippings and turn it in. Create beds by digging out paths and adding that topsoil to the beds. Or use a tiller, a rear-tine model if possible, so that you won't compact the soil you've just worked. Again, remove sod first. Then till the entire plot (See "R_x for Tilling" on page 45), spread a layer of organic matter, and till or rake it in. Finally, dig out paths, adding the soil from the paths to the new beds.

Building beds properly the first time means not having to start from scratch the following year. Instead of having to double- or single-dig your soil again, a minimal tilling may be all it needs to ready it for planting. Some home gardeners have become no-till growers by mulching their raised beds heavily throughout the year; then, in spring, they pull the mulch aside just long enough to warm and plant in the fertile soil lying beneath. No-till gardening may be less successful in cold regions with heavy clay soil, where the aerating and warming that come from turning the soil are indispensable.

Laying Out the Garden

Now comes the real challenge. Laying out a garden is like juggling a dozen balls. You have to allow simultaneously for the limits and demands of the location, the soil, the crops, and the gardener. What do you want to grow? Is it a good match for your location? When should you plant? How much should you plant? How much space will it take? What does the crop require? How will the crop affect the soil? How does one crop affect another?

It's hard to know where to begin. Unless you have acres to spare, you'll want to use space as efficiently as possible. Everyone wants to maximize yields. Some decisions, such as selecting what you want to grow, should be made early on so that there's plenty of time to order seeds. But before you make any final decisions, you need to run through all the variables—the what, where, and when of layouts.

A logical first step is to determine what you want to grow. Compile your list of vegetables and herbs, and calculate how many plants are needed to produce the size harvest you want. (See "Crop Yields" on page 14 for harvest estimates per 100-foot row.) The temptation is always to plant more than you can consume or care for, so once the planting list is complete, take a second look. Will you really eat a dozen cabbages? One healthy 'Royal Marvel' plant can produce 100 Brussels sprouts. Do you really need 15 plants? Make a rough comparison of what you want to produce with the room you have to produce it, remembering that it's easier to thin your garden before you plant it. Cut back now, especially if you're new to gardening.

CROPS ON THE MOVE

Healthy soil means healthy plants. Except for asparagus, chives, and other perennial vegetables and herbs that should be located where they can grow undisturbed, rotating crops is essential to both soil and plants. By alternating what you grow in a specific location, you can better maintain soil fertility—different plants rob the soil of different nutrients—and reduce pest and disease problems. Multi-year crop-rotation plans can become complicated, so begin with three easy rules.

Rule One. Don't plant a crop in the same place it grew the year before.

Rule Two. Don't plant crops with similar nutrient needs in the same place each year.

Rule Three. Don't plant crops that have similar pest and insect problems—typically plants that are members of the same family—in the same place year after year.

PLANT APPETITES

Another common approach to rotating crops is to divide them into "heavy feeders," "light feeders," and "soil feeders" as follows:

Heavy Feeders. This group includes most vining plants—cucumber, melon, and squash—along with cabbage and its kin—broccoli, Brussels sprout, and cauliflower. Most leaf vegetables, including celery, kale, lettuce, spinach, and Swiss chard as well as asparagus, beet, corn, eggplant, rhubarb, and tomato are also heavy feeders.

Light Feeders. Among the light—or at least less heavy—feeders are carrot, chive, garlic, leek, onion, parsnip, pepper, potato, radish, rutabaga, shallot, sweet potato, Swiss chard, and turnip. Most of the best-known culinary herbs are light feeders, with parsley being the one exception.

Soil Feeders. Legumes like beans and peas, along with all cover crops, actually improve the soil. Now the crop-rotation cycle is heavy feeder → light feeder or legume → heavy feeder → light feeder or legume.

Rule One is simple enough to follow. If yours isn't a brand-new garden, think back to last season. If you grew cucumbers in the southeast corner of your plot, don't plant them there this year. Where should you put them? Now it becomes clear why it's smart to start on paper. Move to Rule Two: Plant them where they follow crops that don't have identical nutrient requirements.

It's possible to make an exact analysis for each crop—a nutrient-by-nutrient breakdown—but most gardeners settle for dividing vegetables and herbs into four general groups:

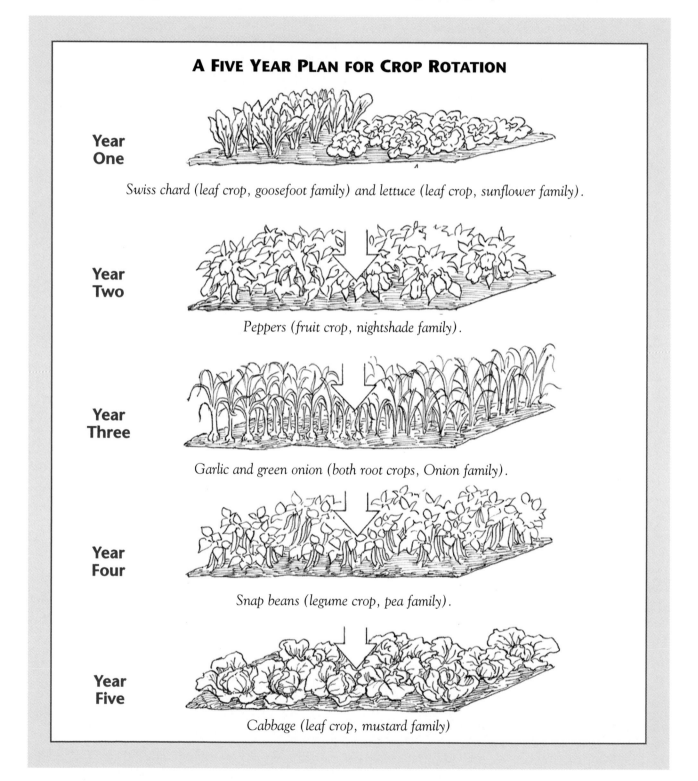

A FIVE YEAR PLAN FOR CROP ROTATION

Year One

Swiss chard (leaf crop, goosefoot family) and lettuce (leaf crop, sunflower family).

Year Two

Peppers (fruit crop, nightshade family).

Year Three

Garlic and green onion (both root crops, Onion family).

Year Four

Snap beans (legume crop, pea family).

Year Five

Cabbage (leaf crop, mustard family)

Fruit Crops. These include corn, cucumber, eggplant, squash, and tomato, which are heavy phosphorus users.

Leaf Crops. These include basil, broccoli, cabbage, kale, lettuce, and spinach, which are heavy nitrogen users.

Root Crops. These crops, including beet, carrot, onion, and potato, are heavy potassium users.

Legume Crops. Legumes such as bean and pea, as well as cover crops like clover, alfalfa, and vetch, return nitrogen to the soil.

Keep in mind that generalizations are generalizations. Corn siphons not only phosphorus but nitrogen from the soil; tomatoes need a generous supply of potassium and nitrogen as well as phosphorus. And legume crops, which are soil "improvers," can precede or follow any crop.

A sensible 5-year rotation cycle for a garden bed is leaf crop → fruit crop → root crop → legume crop → leaf crop. Translated into real plants, it could be salad greens followed by peppers, then carrots and beets, then beans, then broccoli. Another 5-year rotation plan is fruit crop → leaf crop → root crop → legume crop → fruit crop. That could translate to summer squash then cabbage followed by potatoes then peas and then tomatoes.

Next, add in Rule Three, the warning to move around members of the same family. Cucumbers belong to the gourd family, Cucurbitaceae, a group of mostly viners that includes melons, pumpkins, squash, and watermelons. So don't plant 'Sweet Slice' where 'Big Max' pumpkin grew last year. Nearly all of the most popular vegetables and herbs are members of only 11 plant families:

Carrot family, *Apiaceae*: anise, carrot, celery, chervil, cilantro, dill, fennel, lovage, parsley, parsnip

Goosefoot family, *Chenopodiaceae*: amaranth, beet, chard, spinach

Gourd family, *Cucurbitaceae*: cucumber, melon, pumpkin, squash, watermelon

Grass family, *Poaceae*: corn and other grains

Lily family, *Liliaceae*: asparagus

Mint family, *Lamiaceae*: basil, lemon balm, marjoram, mint, oregano, rosemary, sage, thyme

Mustard family, *Brassicaceae*: broccoli, Brussels sprout, cabbage, cauliflower, collard, horseradish, kale, kohlrabi, radish, rutabaga, turnip, watercress

Onion family, *Alliaceae*: garlic, leek, onion, shallot

Nightshade family, *Solanaceae*: eggplant, pepper, potato, tomato

Pea family, Fabaceae: bean, peanut, pea

Sunflower family, *Asteraceae*: endive, globe artichoke, Jerusalem artichoke, lettuce, sunflower, tarragon

It's almost as easy as Pick One From Column A, One From Column B, One From Column C, but

ROTATION WISDOM

In addition to general guidelines, there are specific bits of rotation wisdom that may run against some of those general guidelines that experienced growers have learned to follow. Some of the recommendations are the worse kind of folklore—widely accepted but specious notions—but others, like the ones below, are worth trying.

- Squash and other vine crops, which shade out weeds, can be good preceding crops for root vegetables.
- Potatoes do well after corn.
- Corn does well after legumes.
- Cabbages do well after onions.
- Legumes and green manures are good preceding or following all crops.

Keep careful records, and after several years of growing vegetables and herbs, you will be able to add wisdom of your own.

ROTATION PLANNING. *Wide-row plantings make it easy to keep track of rotations because plants move in blocks. Here, Chinese cabbage, a leaf crop, is growing next to onions, a root crop, and beans, a legume crop.*

not quite. In a few cases, a good rotation for the soil doesn't jibe with a good plant-family rotation. A helpful way to chart crop rotations is to write the name (and its "type" and family) of each vegetable and herb that you want to grow on an index card. Then spread the cards out on the kitchen table, and move them around until you have created a layout that benefits both your soil and your crops.

A 5-year plan for one bed might be: Swiss chard (leaf crop, goosefoot family, Chenopodiaceae) and lettuce (leaf crop, sunflower family, Asteraceae) → peppers (fruit crop, nightshade family, Solanaceae) → garlic and green onion (both root crops, onion family, Alliaceae) → snap beans (legume crop, pea family, Fabaceae) → cabbage (leaf crop, mustard family, Brassicaceae)

Don't panic if it seems there are too many things to think about at once. Just do the best you can. No one follows all the rules all the time. If the potatoes must go where the peppers were last year, put them there. If you can't move your tomatoes to

a new location, you can't. It doesn't mean you have to give up growing tomatoes. But when you are unable to follow a good rotation plan, make doubly sure you return to the soil all the nutrients that your plants have taken from it by adding organic matter and sowing green manures, and be excessively watchful for signs of soilborne plagues.

Corn, for instance, eats up nitrogen and phosphorus nearly as fast as Golden Staters use water. To replace those elements, you may need to add—in addition to the annual application of compost, animal manures, or other organic matter—alfalfa meal, blood meal, or fish meal for nitrogen, as well as bonemeal or rock phosphate for phosphorus. Tomatoes are susceptible to anthracnose, leaf spot, fusarium wilt, blights, and other diseases that lurk in the soil. Be vigilant: Watch your plants for signs of stress and infection. If your rotation scheme has shortcomings, make a special effort to choose disease-resistant cultivars. Rotating crops is easier and more effective in a large garden than in a small one, but any crop rotation is better than no crop rotation at all.

Filling In the Layout

Once you've set up general crop rotations—what plants go where—start filling in your garden plan. Since you already know that tall plants like corn have to be located where they won't stop the sun from reaching groundhuggers like untrellised cucumbers, saving space will likely be your overriding concern. For most backyard gardeners, space is finite, while desire and ambition are infinite. Lodging everything you want to grow in the room you have available may seem impossible at first. Fortunately, a number of techniques can help you fit more in your garden, giving greater yields and spreading them over a longer period of time.

SPACE-SAVING PLANTING TECHNIQUES

If you've decided to farm in beds rather than in single rows, you've already taken advantage of an important space-saving method. Now each row doesn't have to be bordered by paths, so rows can be set far closer together. While you're at it, capitalize on a hexagonal planting pattern—an odd-numbered row of plants across the bed followed by an even-numbered row—to maximize space. This staggered, equidistant arrangement creates diagonal rows in the bed (rather than rows that are parallel or perpendicular to the bed's sides) and lets you fit the most plants into the area you have. The bed's width and the plant's size determine the planting pattern. The same bed might hold a 2–1–2 staggered planting for cabbages, but a 6–5–6 planting for upright-growing romaine lettuces. In a hexagonal pattern, each plant has all the room it needs but sits close enough to its neighbors to shade the vacant soil. You'll still want to mulch your garden, but this intensive planting scheme will help reduce moisture loss and retard the growth of weeds.

Another route to maximizing space is to grow plants vertically instead of horizontally. For many vegetables, staking or trellising also improves plant health by providing better air circulation and exposure to the sun and yields superior produce by keeping fruits off the ground. Pole beans and peas climb successfully on their own, but cucumbers, squash, melons, and tomatoes will need some help

ascending. Whatever support you provide (see "Plant Support Systems" on page 80 for options), make sure it is well anchored, strong, and plenty tall, and put it in place early—immediately after

continued on page 82

HEX PLANTING SAVES SPACE. *Lettuce seedlings in this raised bed are arranged in a hexagonal planting. When mature, they'll fill the entire bed, leaving little room for weeds.*

SMALL-GARDEN SOLUTIONS. *In a small plot, finding room for all the crops you want to grow can be a challenge. Fortunately, space-saving techniques, such as hexagonal planting, along with planting crops in succession and trellising, will help make the most of limited space.*

PLANT SUPPORT SYSTEMS

You can build plant supports from any material: wood, bamboo, metal, plastic, wire, string, and more. If you live in the Southwest or another torrid region, beware of metal and wire components; when heated by the sun, they can burn young plants. Wood supports should be treated with a nontoxic preservative (avoid pressure-treated wood, which contains toxic compounds). If you want to do it yourself, the USDA Forest Products Laboratory recommends a mixture of paraffin wax (1 ounce, melted in a double boiler), turpentine (1 gallon less 2 cups), and boiled linseed oil (1½ cups).

Many gardeners now extol PVC (polyvinyl chloride) piping for building supports. Strong, durable, and easy to work with, lightweight PVC frames and trellises can be disassembled quickly and stored when not being used. Whatever materials you use, make sure your support is tall and strong enough to hold the plants it is intended to support.

Stakes

Wooden stakes set 1 foot deep into the ground are an inexpensive and simple way to brace plants like tomatoes. Use 6-foot-long 2-by-2s, and install guy wires if additional support is necessary. Use cloth strips to tie stems loosely to the stake.

Cages

The support of choice for tomatoes, wire cages are the epitome of easy, but pass on the lightweight models carried by most garden centers. Instead, make your own cages. Use 5- or 6-inch-square mesh wire for large-fruit crops like tomatoes, and form cylinders 24 inches in diameter. Anchor each cage with one or two wooden stakes; otherwise, they are liable to topple under heavy fruit loads. Make sure the cage is tall enough to handle the plant you're growing—cages for vigorous indeterminate tomatoes like 'Sweet 100' should be at least 5 feet tall. You can also cage a single plant with four 6-foot wooden stakes encircled at 1-foot intervals with twine—or cage an entire row or bed by surrounding it with stakes set at 2-foot intervals ringed with twine. An advantage of cages, round or square, is that they can be converted easily to minigreenhouses by draping or circling them with clear plastic.

A-Frames

Angled supports, such as A-frames, are ideal for cucumbers, melons, sweet potatoes, and other crops that lack sturdy stems and are better at sprawling than climbing. Build a hinged wooden frame at least 5 feet tall, cover it with 5-inch mesh wire or wood laths spaced 5 inches apart for large-fruit crops (poultry wire or plastic netting work well with peas and beans), and allow plants to ramble over it.

Trellises

Vertical trellises best suit beans and peas, plants that climb without much assistance and whose fruits are light. Tomatoes, cucumbers, and squash can be trained to grow straight up, but they will need regular tending—tying and weaving—and their heavy fruits may require individual support. To build a simple trellis, run a section of heavy mesh wire between two sturdy, well-anchored end posts, with supporting stakes set every 3 or 4 feet between the two end posts. For light crops, such as peas, substitute plastic netting for the mesh wire—or make a string trellis. You can also train plants to ascend wood or bamboo trellises. If any support is a permanent structure, such as a fence, be sure to rotate the crops you grow on it to avoid insect and disease problems.

Weaving

Weaving is a variation of vertical trellising; it requires well-anchored end posts and supporting stakes set every 3 or 4 feet between the two end posts. Weaving consists of running a line of heavy-duty natural-fiber twine 8 to 12 inches from the ground and along the plants, securing it to each stake as you travel up the row. When you reach the other anchor post, fasten the line and head back up the row, enclosing the plants between the two lines. Add new strands at 6- or 8-inch intervals, as the plants grow. To make the job go faster, place the ball of twine on a stick

STRING TRELLIS. *These beans are climbing "mesh" made by strings run first vertically and then horizontally. The horizontal strings are looped around the vertical ones where they intersect.*

TEPEE END SUPPORTS. *For extra support from a lightweight trellis, erect tepees at either end of the row. Run a support across the top to hold string for the crop to climb.*

TOMATO CAGES. *Store-bought cages are generally too small for most tomatoes, although they may suffice for shorter determinate tomatoes.*

SIDEWAYS STRINGING. *This system for peas uses A-frame end supports for sturdiness, and strings that run horizontally.*

for quick unraveling. When the garden season is over, cut down the plants, twine and all, and add them to the compost pile. Good candidates for weaving include peas and tomatoes.

Stringing

Another variation of vertical trellising that is ideal for twining plants, stringing involves well-anchored end posts and a heavy wire stretched between the two. Tie one or two lengths of heavy-duty natural-fiber twine to stakes set at the base of each plant; leaving some slack in the line, knot the other end of the twine around the overhead support. As the plant grows, guide its stems around the twine.

Tepees

An easy way to trellis twining crops like beans is to run them up a pole tepee. Use five or more saplings (leave the bark on), bamboo poles, or 1-by-2s that are at least 8 feet long; set them 4 to 6 inches into the soil, and lash them together at the top with heavy twine. To tepee crops like peas and cucumbers, which clasp with small tendrils, wrap the structure with chicken wire.

A CAGE VARIATION. *A half-hoop of wire mesh gives plants enough support to keep the fruit off the ground. This system is suitable for determinate tomatoes only.*

sowing seeds or setting out transplants. Above all, don't procrastinate if your plants need help climbing. Tying, weaving, or threading long, large stems and vines is difficult at best, impossible at worst.

DECIDING WHEN TO PLANT

With considerations of *what* and *how* you plant out of the way, move to *when* you plant. Just as some vegetables and herbs need more nitrogen or water than others do, some can withstand cold or heat better than can others. Eggplants, cucumbers, and summer squash are tender vegetables, unable to tolerate frost. Peas, broccoli, and spinach love cool temperatures and can put up with some frost. Sandwiched between the two are semi-hardy plants like carrots and lettuce, which tolerate cool conditions but not below-freezing temperatures.

Consider, too, the when of the harvest. One hundred 'Derby' bean plants may produce the total yield you have in mind, but if you want to eat fresh beans all summer long, you'll need a planting strategy. One option is to sow fewer seeds at 1- or 2-week intervals rather than the entire 2-ounce packet all at once. The result is small crops of beans that mature every 1 or 2 weeks over a longer period of time. An alternative tactic is to plant several cultivars of the same crop simultaneously—a cultivar that matures quickly, one midseason type, and a

SOME LIKE IT HOT

Knowing what conditions—cool or warm—a vegetable or herb prefers is important in determining when to plant it and in growing it successfully. As a general rule, plants whose leaves, immature flowers, and/or roots are edible can tolerate cool conditions. (Three exceptions are New Zealand spinach, sweet potatoes, and peanuts.) Crops that flower and then produce edible fruits tend to need warm conditions. (Two exceptions are peas and fava beans.)

Heat-Tolerant Crops
In the list below, an asterisk (*) indicates crops that are very tender and will not survive even light frost.

Basil*	Cucumber*	Pepper*	Squash*
Bean	Eggplant*	Pumpkin*	Sweet potato*
Bean, lima*	Melon*	Soybean	Tomato
Cowpea	Okra	Spinach, malabar	Watermelon*
Corn	Peanut*	Spinach, New Zealand	

Cold-Tolerant Crops
In the list below, an asterisk (*) indicates crops that will tolerate some frost without damage.

Artichoke, globe	Celery*	Kohlrabi*	Radish
Asparagus*	Chicory	Leek*	Rhubarb*
Beet	Chive*	Lettuce	Salsify*
Broccoli*	Collard*	Mustard	Scallion*, or
Brussels sprout*	Cress	Onion*	green onion
Cabbage*	Endive	Parsley	Spinach*
Cabbage, Chinese	Garlic*	Parsnip	Swiss chard
Carrot	Horseradish*	Pea*	Turnip*
Cauliflower	Kale*	Potato	

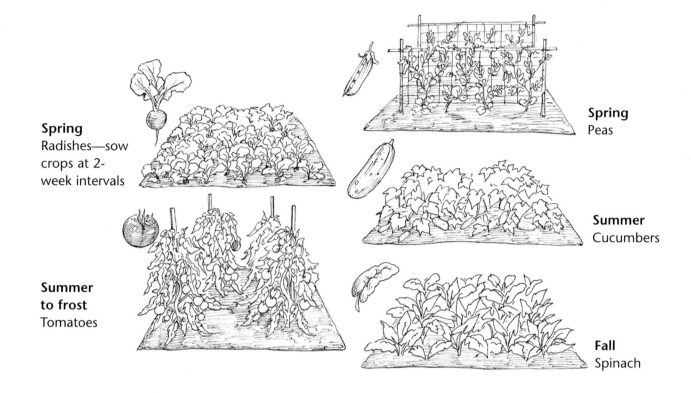

Spring
Radishes—sow crops at 2-week intervals

Summer to frost
Tomatoes

Spring
Peas

Summer
Cucumbers

Fall
Spinach

EFFICIENT SUCCESSION PLANTING. To keep garden space producing, follow spring plantings of cold-tolerant crops with summer plantings of heat-tolerant ones. If your season is long enough, follow summer crops with a fall planting of cold-tolerant ones.

late-yielding one. For example, you could grow 'Kotlas' for early tomatoes, 'Pilgrim' for midseason fruits, and 'Rutgers' for a late harvest.

The bottom line is that everything isn't planted at the same time. While that does complicate planning—it would be easier to sow every seed and set out every transplant early one sunny morning in May—it allows you to reduce waste by stretching out the harvest over weeks or months instead of days. It also allows you to increase yields by making double, even triple or quadruple, use of garden space during the course of the season. Making several sowings of the same crop or following one crop by another in the same space in a single season is called succession planting.

SUCCESSION PLANTING BASICS

Making several sowings of crops like beans, lettuce, or peas is a simple form of succession planting. Sow four crops of lettuce at 2-week intervals, and the

first crop will be ready for harvest before seedlings of the fourth one are up out of the soil. By the time the fourth crop is ready for harvesting, any leftover first-crop plants will be ready for the compost pile. That brings us to the second type of succession planting, which requires that you plant a second crop *after you've harvested* the first.

To identify what vegetables or herbs can be planted in succession, begin with the length of your growing season. Then choose two or three crops whose combined days-to-maturity numbers don't exceed the length of your season, making sure that you have selected both cool- and warm-weather plants. For example, if your average growing season is 120 days long, you could sow the hybrid savoy spinach 'Melody' 2 weeks before the last frost. When it's harvested—in about 50 days—you can fill the space with tomato or pepper transplants. Or set out 'Dark Red Norland' tubers in early spring, and dig "new" potatoes 10 weeks later; then replant

SPREAD OUT THE HARVEST. *Use succession planting to avoid producing heaps of produce that go to waste. Here, a crop of head lettuce (left) is ready for harvest as leaf lettuce (right) is just getting started.*

MATCHING HARES & TORTOISES. *Intercropping allows you to grow fast and slow crops together to maximize harvests. Here, rows of fast-growing, green and red leaf lettuces that are nearly mature have been interplanted with still-small leeks.*

the bed with a yellow wax bean, such as 'Goldkist' or 'Rocdor', or a French filet bean like 'Triumphe de Farcy'.

Succession planting has a seasonal logic: Quick-maturing, cold-tolerant plants are planted for a spring crop and are followed by vegetables and herbs that prefer warm weather for summer. If there's still time, the summer crop is followed by cold-tolerant plants for a fall harvest or overwintering. In the truncated growing season of USDA Zone 3, succession planting might be no more than peas followed by a fall crop of radishes, or lettuce supervened by onions. In Zone 5, it could be spinach followed by corn succeeded by kale, or spinach followed by bush beans supplanted by radishes. In Zone 8, the succession might be cabbages planted in February, followed by tomatoes set out in late spring and, to close the growing season, a fall crop of mustard.

Keep in mind that you can combine both types of succession planting: Two or three spring sowings of cold-tolerant lettuce could be followed by a summer crop of heat-loving beans.

What you plant and when you plant it depends on where you live. Gardeners with mild winters and hot summers grow cool-weather crops in fall and winter; warm-weather crops are begun in late winter and early spring. Gardeners with mild winters and summers grow cool-weather crops throughout the year; they sow warm-weather crops in late spring. In regions with cold winters and hot summers, cool-weather crops are planted in early spring and/or early fall, warm-weather crops in spring. For expert advice, talk to other gardeners in your neighborhood, or contact your local Cooperative Extension Service. (See "Regional Planting Progressions" on page 98 for guidelines on what to plant when.)

INTERCROPPING FOR HIGH YIELDS

A first cousin of succession planting is intercropping, or interplanting. This technique makes double use of bed space by growing two or more crops together that mature at different times. Intercropping not only increases yields, but reduces insect and disease problems as well. After all, diversity in the garden, as in nature, is the foremost defense. By mingling different plants, you deny diseases and pests a clean shot at a single large target.

To plan your own intercropping schemes, keep the length of your growing season in mind and pick vegetables and herbs that grow and mature at different speeds, some quickly, some more slowly. (See "Horticultural Hares & Tortoises" on page 86 for suggestions.) For a spring planting, you could intercrop 'Ruby', a red leaf lettuce that's ready to pick in 48 days, and a savoy cabbage, such as 'Julius', a blue-green hybrid that takes 75 days to form a mature head. By the time 'Julius' spreads out, 'Ruby' has made her way to the salad bowl.

There are dozens of intercropping possibilities: spinach and peas, celery, or Brussels sprouts; radishes and celery or peppers; peas and cabbage or tomatoes; lettuce and tomatoes, peppers, or beets; mesclun and pole beans; scallions and carrots or broccoli; early corn and pumpkins; onions and tomatoes; pole beans and summer greens; and many more. When making intercrop pairings, try to choose plants that have similar or complementary cultural needs but are from different families (to discourage insect and disease problems). Take care, too, that the crop that matures first can be harvested without disturbing its slowpoke partner. Some root vegetables, whose harvesting disturbs the soil, may be poor choices for intercropping. Similarly, the historic American garden duo of pole beans and corn is a pairing that works well only if you plan to leave both crops in the garden until they dry.

Again, don't be overwhelmed by all this horticultural juggling. You don't *have* to intercrop or plant successively; you can use one bed to grow tomatoes and nothing else. You don't *have* to trellis sweet potatoes or cucumbers; you can let them ramble. Your garden layout can be as simple or as complicated as you want. If you're new to growing vegetables and herbs, look again at your seed list—you're likely to have more success if you plant 5 rather than 10 crops. After a few seasons' experience, you'll be designing complex layouts with the best of them.

SCHEDULING 101

By now, it's apparent that keeping track of *what* you are planting and *when* you want to plant it can be complicated, but it doesn't have to be. A schedule written out in winter—long before the spring planting rush—makes it easy to keep track of sowing and

COMPANION PLANTING

Companion planting is another form of intercropping, one based on the supposed capacity of one plant to enhance another. There is evidence that tansy and rue repel some insect pests and that marigolds deter nematodes. There's verification that underplanting tomatoes with hairy vetch increases yields and decreases insect and disease problems. Researchers also have established that golden Marguerites (*Anthemis tinctoria*), coriander, dill, fennel, and fern-leaf yarrow (*Achillea filipendulina*) are five of the best plants for attracting beneficial insects, such as ladybugs, parasitic miniwasps, hover flies, and lacewings. However, in spite of the many articles and books devoted to the subject— *Good Neighbors: Companion Planting for Gardeners* by Anna Carr is one bestseller—most of the evidence about companion planting is anecdotal. As one horticultural curmudgeon put it, "Much has been written, little has been proved." With that caveat in mind, refer to the list below for some of the most recommended garden "companions."

Asparagus and tomatoes	Eggplants and beans
Beans and potatoes	Peppers and carrots
Beets and onions	Potatoes and horseradish
Cabbages and celery	Pumpkins and corn
Carrots and peas	Squash and corn
Cucumbers and radishes	Tomatoes and basil

transplant dates. A calendar with ample writing space for each date works well for this, but a list of dates and crops to sow or transplant is fine too. Whatever method you choose, post your schedule somewhere that it is easy to see and refer to—many gardeners use the refrigerator.

You'll find recommendations on scheduling specific crops in the individual Plant Portraits in Part Two of this book. Spring plantings are figured from the average last-spring-frost date. To schedule indoor sowings, simply count backward from that date for the recommended number of weeks. Jot down the sowing date on your calendar. Outdoors, sowing and transplanting can be done before or after the last-frost date, depending on the crop, but they're scheduled the same way. Fall crops, which

HORTICULTURAL HARES & TORTOISES

Use the lists below to create intercropping combinations by matching short-season hares with long-season tortoises. Keep in mind that days-to-maturity numbers aren't written in concrete. Vegetables that mature in 65 days in southern Missouri may take 80 days to ripen in North Dakota.

Also remember that for crops that are typically grown from seedlings started indoors, such as eggplants and tomatoes, the days-to-maturity numbers listed in seed catalogs are counted from the transplant day, not from the day the seed was sown. Finally, don't overlook the short-season cultivars breeders have produced for gardeners living in regions with abbreviated growing seasons. 'Earlivee', 'Seneca Daybreak', and 'Quickie', for example, mature nearly a month sooner than most cultivars of sweet corn.

Short-Season Crops

On average, the following crops take 55 or fewer days from seed to harvest.

Arugula	Kale	Radish
Bean, bush	Kohlrabi	Scallion, or green onion
Beet	Lettuce, leaf	Spinach
Bok Choy	Mustard	Squash, summer
Cilantro, or coriander	New Zealand spinach	Swiss chard
Corn salad, or mâche	Okra	Turnip
Garden cress		Watercress

Long-Season Crops

The crops listed below require, on average, 70 or more days from seed to maturity.

Anise	Collard	Parsnip
Basil	Corn	Peanut
Bean, lima	Eggplant	Pepper, sweet & chili
Borage	Endive & escarole	Potato
Broccoli	Fennel	Pumpkin
Brussels sprout	Garlic	Rutabaga
Cabbage	Leek	Sage
Caraway	Lettuce, romaine	Squash, winter
Cauliflower	& head	Sweet marjoram
Celeriac	Melon	Sweet potato
Celery	Mesclun mix	Tomato
Chervil	Onion	Watermelon
Chicory	Parsley	

are figured from the average first fall frost, aren't quite as straightforward—see "Planning for Mid-season Planting" on page 134 for directions on scheduling them.

List each sowing of each crop to keep track of succession plantings and intercropping. Biweekly reminders to sow more leaf lettuce or peas, or an entry to plant a row of cabbage and lettuce, take away the worry of staying on schedule and break down ambitious planting schemes into doable steps.

Keep in mind that you'll have to stay flexible when it comes to real planting dates, though, because weather, soil temperature, and other factors affect the best times to plant. (See Chapter 6, "Planting the Garden," for information on deciding when to plant as well as for techniques to get a jump on the season.)

CREATING EDIBLE LANDSCAPES

You might want to lay out an edible garden that is also "for show," one that capitalizes on the ornamental qualities of its resident plants. For instance, why not create a formal design like an Oriental carpet's that takes advantage of the rich colors of many vegetables and herbs?

Gardeners have been creating artful food gardens for centuries, patches as beautiful as they are

EDIBLES & ORNAMENTALS. *This ornamental bed combines Swiss chard and variegated-leaved 'Alaska' nasturtiums, which have spicy-tasting edible leaves and flowers, with brightly colored coleus.*

EDIBLE ORNAMENTALS

This short list includes some of the most striking and colorful edible plants that can be used effectively in a perennial border; don't forget that any vegetable or herb, from 8-foot corn plants to creeping thyme, can be incorporated into a landscape. Set food plants where they will enhance the overall design, and remember not to place them alongside tea roses or other ornamentals that are regularly sprayed for diseases or pests.

Artichoke	Cauliflower	Endive & escarole	Red mustard
Asparagus	Celery	Fennel	Red orach
Basil	Chamomile	Kale	Rhubarb
Bean (bush & vining cultivars)	Chives, garden & garlic	Lettuce	Sage
Bok Choy	Cilantro	Marjoram	Summer squash (bush cultivars)
Borage	Cucumber (bush cultivars)	Okra	Swiss chard
Burnet		Oregano	Thyme
Cabbage	Dill	Parsley	Tomato
Carrot	Eggplant	Pepper, sweet & chili	

FORMAL HERB GARDEN. *Culinary and medicinal herbs have long been planted in separate gardens, a system that is especially sensible because many herbs are perennial. These formal rectangular beds are edged with santolina on the outside, garlic chives along the inner paths.*

productive, as well as incorporating vegetables and herbs in their flower beds and borders. But modern gardening trends and forceful champions like Rosalind Creasy and Robert Kourick (see "Reading About Gardening" in the Appendix for books on the subject) have created an explosion of "edible land-scapes." Simply put, an edible landscape is one that includes food plants as a part of the overall landscape rather than exiling them to a plot of their own.

If you're an edible landscaper, you'll need to find spots that not only meet the cultural demands of your vegetables and herbs but take advantage of their ornamental qualities—of their flowers, foliage and/or fruits, and even their fragrance. Borage, for example, has clusters of cobalt-blue flowers and handsome, fuzzy gray-green leaves; chili peppers, such as 'Hungarian Wax', 'Sizzler', and 'Charleston Hot', produce waxy green fruits that turn yellow, red, and orange. You may want to grow creeping thyme

in a sunny location between paving stones, where its fragrance will be released when you step on it. Or set three eggplants where their foliage and fruits will augment the purple launched earlier in the season by the bearded and Siberian iris. A tall tomato like 'Sweet 100' needs a place in the back of your peren-nial border to show off its bright red fruits, but save a spot up front for 'Lollo Rosso', a compact lettuce with crinkled crimson leaves. Culinary herbs are tra-ditional companions for flowers—what about edging a flower border with a string of 'Green Globe' basils, tidy bushes the size of soccer balls? Pole and runner beans can do double duty as flowering vines. Globe artichokes and their arching, gray-green, fernlike leaves and lavender thistlelike flowers are an edible substitute for look-alike globe thistles (*Echinops* spp.). The message of edible landscaping is that not having a discrete plot shouldn't stop anyone from growing vegetables and herbs.

GROWING GARDENERS

Children are like their elders when it comes to gardening: Enthusiasm is unbounded in spring; it wanes when weeds and pests grow thick; and it is restored when the harvest begins. But children are not adults. Their initial excitement is greater, their boredom is quicker to develop and longer to last, and their ability to see ahead is more limited. Only rarely are children steadfast gardeners, yet they love to participate. To help them do so successfully, make sure their involvement matches their abilities and limitations. For them, gardening should require less strength and endurance, less knowledge and constancy, and, when possible, less delay.

Above all, children require gentle forbearance in the garden—your willingness to sacrifice a few bean plants to novice efforts with a hoe, your tolerance of meandering rows of scallions and unevenly spaced tomatoes. Forget about the lost carrots while a youngster learns how to thin seedlings. Ignore the water sprayed through the screen door, and assume the lettuce got its share. Refuse to notice the three immature peppers picked with every full-size one. Pretend that keeping a tomato worm in a jar is fun. At the same time, gently remind young gardeners to be prudent, to walk carefully, to pull cautiously, to touch gingerly, and to stay 200 yards away from the picture-perfect eggplants that your neighbor plans to enter in the county fair.

Here are some helpful tips for gardening with children:

Allow children to plan their own gardens. Children should grow their favorite vegetables, herbs, and flowers, not yours. At the same time, failure isn't a fun teacher. Try to steer them toward plants that are easy and quick-maturing—radishes and peas rather than artichokes and celery. Also help them lay out their plots so that crops will flourish.

Allow children to have their own space. A child's garden need not be large—4 by 4 feet is plenty for a small child—but locate it centrally. Don't exile children to the back of the yard where nothing will grow, including their interest.

Share your own garden. Children delight in working side by side, but they are not fools. They will want to do the same jobs you enjoy—planting, watering, harvesting—and will be as impatient with pulling weeds as you are. Be generous.

Don't grade on tidiness. Harping about weeds in the garden will kill children's interest long before the bindweed smothers the beans.

Don't be afraid of a little dirt. Grazing is one of the great advantages of growing your own.

Be inventive. Create a garden hideaway for children by setting up a pole tepee, covering it with poultry wire, and planting runner beans. Plant a pizza garden, a pickle garden, or recreate Mr. McGregor's garden. Carve initials in an immature squash, and watch them grow. Sow a vegetable maze or a checkerboard garden. Grow a giant pumpkin. Design and make fancy plant labels. Put up a scarecrow.

Take the garden indoors. Cooking with children can be as much fun as gardening with them.

In a nutshell, don't preach, do teach; don't show, do share. Above all, remember that gardening is not like learning to cross the street safely. Gardening is not mandatory, no matter how much you love it.

A CHILD'S HIDE-OUT. A tepee planted with pole beans creates a child-size garden hideaway.

EDIBLE ORNAMENTALS. *This garden features a series of beds shaped like pieces of pie with grass paths between them. Each piece of pie is planted with a slightly different mix of edibles and ornamentals.*

Special Garden Layouts

Today's smaller yards and busier schedules have meant that fewer people are putting in large gardens filled with a plant list that runs from anise to zucchini. Rather than a giant melange of vegetables and herbs, many gardeners are planting only one or two crops or several different cultivars of one crop. Or they're mixing flowers, vegetables, and herbs together in the same plot or creating theme and seasonal gardens. Food gardens have become more personal and limited. Specialization may be the best option for your location or your busy life. Perhaps a tiny plot filled with nothing but spring salad plants or a garden just for children is right for you. What about a dooryard herb garden—or an herb garden in a barrel—or a pumpkin patch crammed with a half-dozen different cultivars? Or a 19th-century garden to harmonize with your Victorian house, a garden filled with heirloom, or older, cultivars, such as 'Thomas Laxton' pea, 'Country Gentleman' corn, and 'Jenny Lind' melon? Or a garden of Lilliputian vegetables, everything from 'Presto' turnip and 'Little Finger' carrot to 'Golden Midget' corn and 'Baby Pam' pumpkin? Or, for those who like food hot enough to make a gringo cry, a Tex-Mex garden, overfilled with black and pinto beans, chilies, cilantro, epazote, jicamas, tomatillos, tomatoes, and tortilla corn?

It's great fun to compile lists of plants for specialized gardens. You can pursue any interest, from an extra-narrow one, such as growing only the plants Thomas Jefferson cultivated at Monticello, to something broader, like vegetables and herbs for Asian cuisine. Here are lists for four specialized gardens, but don't be shy about creating your own, choosing plants that fit your interests, taste, and location. (For two other specialty garden ideas, see the entries on *Edible Flowers* on page 248 and *Mesclun* on page 301 in the Plant Portraits section of this book.)

HEIRLOOM THEME GARDEN. *You may decide to dedicate an entire garden to heirloom or old-time cultivars. This planting features heirloom kales and squashes combined with parsley, basil, and marigolds.*

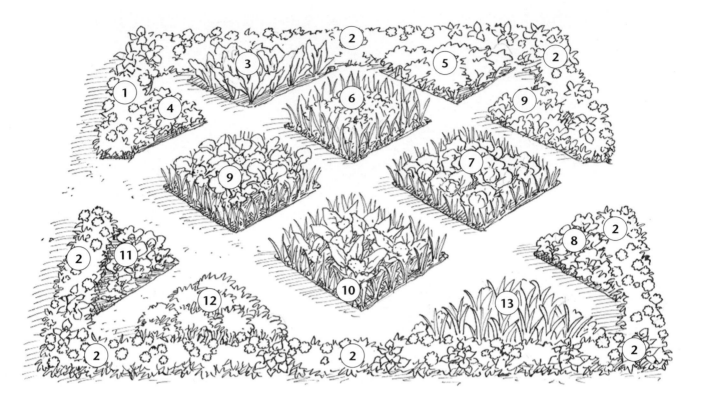

AN ORNAMENTAL VEGETABLE GARDEN. *To plant a garden that is both pretty and productive, consider intensively planted raised beds filled with ornamental vegetables. Succession plant to maximize yields—follow spring crops, such as lettuce, with summer crops, such as bush beans, for example, or consider intercropping schemes. Above, listed by number is an example: 1. Basil and parsley 2. Marigolds 3. Ruby chard, edged with radishes 4. Sierra Lettuce 5. Carrots 6. Mesclun, edged with garlic 7. Ruby ball lettuce, edged with scallions 8. Tango lettuce 9. Snow Crown cauliflower, edged with shallots 10. Green Comet broccoli, edged with scallions 11. Rosy lettuce 12. Carrots 13. Leeks, edged with radishes*

AN ITALIAN GARDEN

Growing the ingredients of minestrone, spaghetti sauce, pesto, and other Italian dishes is almost as good as a visit to Naples or Florence. Many of the cultivars listed below are heirlooms, revered for their rich flavor.

Arugula: 'Italian Wild Rustica'

Basil: 'Fino Verde Compatto'/'Picollo', 'Mammoth', 'Napoletano', 'Genovese'

Bean: 'Borlotto', 'Cannellini', 'Green Anellino', 'Marvel of Venice', 'Stregonta', 'Trionfo Violetto', 'Viola Cornetti', 'Yellow Anellino'

Beet: 'Chioggia'

Black salsify: *Scorzonera hispanica*

Broccoli raab: 'De Brocoletto', 'Rappone', 'Romanesco'

Cardoon: *Cynara cardunculus*

Eggplant: 'Agora', 'Rosa Bianca', 'Violetta Lunga', 'Violette di Firenze'

Florence fennel: 'Zefa Fino', 'Romy'

Garlic: 'Early Red Italian', 'Sicilian'

Globe artichoke: 'Purple Sicilian', 'Violetto'

Lettuce: 'Lollo Rosso', 'Rossa di Trento', 'Valeriana'

Marjoram: *Origanum majorana*

Onion: 'Borettana Cipollini', 'Giallo di Milaon', 'Italian Torpedo', 'Red Florence', 'Rossa di Milano'

Parsley: 'Catalogno', 'Gigante D'Italia'

Peppers: 'Corno di Toro', 'Figaro', 'Marconi'

Radicchio: 'Red Treviso', 'Red Verona'

Summer squash: 'Fiorentino', 'Zucchette Rampicante'

Swiss Chard: 'Argentata', 'Monstruoso'

Tomato: 'Costoluto Genovese', 'Milano', 'Principe Borghese', 'San Marzano', 'San Remo'

A TEA GARDEN

This sampler of tea plants is only a place to begin— any edible herb also can be used to make tea time a more interesting experience.

Alfalfa, *Medicago sativa*

Angelica, *Angelica archangelica*

Anise hyssop, *Agastache foeniculum*

Bee balm, *Monarda* spp.

Catnip, *Nepeta cataria*

Chamomile, *Anthemis nobilis*

Comfrey, *Symphytum officinale*

Dill, *Anethum graveolens*

Lemon balm, *Melissa officinalis*

Lemon thyme, *Thymus* x *citriodorus*

Mint, *Mentha* spp.

Sage, *Salvia officinalis*

Sweet cicely, *Myrrhis odorata*

A HIGH-NUTRITION GARDEN

Breeders have been successful at enhancing the nutritional content of many vegetables, including increasing carotene levels in carrots, cauliflower, cabbage, and squash. They have also increased vitamin C in peppers and potatoes and vitamins A and C in tomatoes. Here's a garden that's better for you.

Carrot: 'Beta Champ', 'Healthmaster', 'Ingot',

Cauliflower: 'Orange Bouquet'

Chinese cabbage: 'Orange Queen'

Potato: 'Butte'

Pepper: 'Hungarian Hot Wax', 'Sweet Banana'

Squash: 'Jade-A'

Tomato: 'Caro Rich', 'Double Rich', 'Peacevine'

A LILLIPUTIAN GARDEN

A garden of miniature vegetables and herbs— which don't necessarily grow on miniature plants—can delight both children and adults. The list includes true miniature cultivars and standard ones, such as 'Jersey Golden Acorn' squash, that were bred to be picked when the fruits are extremely small.

Bean, filet: 'Vernandon', 'Etalon', 'Aiguillon', 'Astrelle'

Beet: 'Dwergina', 'Crimson Beauty', 'Little Ball'

Carrot: 'Parisienne', 'Baby Finger', 'Tiny Sweet', 'Partima'

Cauliflower: 'Snow Crown'

Corn: 'Golden Midget', 'Early Arctic', 'Early Sunglow'

Cucumber: 'Vert de Petit Paris'

Eggplant: 'Easter Egg', 'Little Fingers'

Leek: 'Albinstar', 'King Richard'

Lettuce: 'Tom Thumb' bibb, 'Little Gem' romaine, 'Pom Pom' oakleaf

Melon: 'Minnesota Midget'

Onion: 'Early Aviv'

Pepper, sweet: 'Jingle Bells'

Pumpkin: 'Baby Bear'

Squash: 'Sunburst' scallop, 'Jersey Golden' acorn, 'Arlesa' zucchini

Tomato: 'Red Robin', 'Golden Pygmy', 'Micro-Tom'

Turnip: 'Presto', 'Red-Topped Milan'

Watermelon: 'Sugar Baby'

CONTAINER GARDENS

You don't have to be short on space to grow edibles in containers—they can be a part of an edible landscape or simply positioned to put frequently used salad ingredients or herbs within easy reach. If you are short on space, though, containers are the only way to grow vegetables and herbs. Whatever your reasons, container gardens on decks, patios, rooftops, and balconies can be as ornamental as they are productive. Plant a large pot with ruby chard, red nasturtiums, and carrots, or a half barrel with eggplants, borage, garlic chives, and purple alyssum, and visitors will be astonished to learn that your colorful containers can be harvested as well as admired.

Containers are the place to begin. Anything with good drainage will serve: wood, plastic, fiberglass, clay, concrete, or metal. Except to house a single herb plant, a 3-gallon container is as small as you should go; a 5-gallon container is better. Don't overpot, but give crops plenty of room, both above and below ground. Salad crops can thrive in soil only 6 inches deep, but crops like carrots need soil at least a foot deep for their delving roots. Finally, use containers that are heavy enough not to topple in wind. Anchor them, if necessary, and don't set a freestanding trellis in a container. If you grow climbing

CONTAINING SPREADING HERBS. *These terra-cotta chimney liners, which are set with 8 to 10 inches underground to make them sturdy, are a handsome containment solution for herbs that spread.*

vegetables, such as peas, set the container alongside a fence, wall, or other sturdy, independent support.

Container-grown vegetables and herbs need everything crops planted in the garden need—sun, water, good soil—but they also present special challenges. First, garden soil is best left in the garden. Instead, use a commercial mix—augmented with compost—or create your own potting soil by mixing together equal parts of soil, compost, sand, and per-

---

CROPS FOR CONTAINERS

Just about any food plant can be grown in a container, but breeders have made the life of landless gardeners easier by developing a compact, ideally suited for pots and boxes. Among the best are:

Basil: 'Dwarf Italian', 'Greek Miniature'

Beet: 'Baby Canning', 'Little Ball'

Broccoli: 'Dandy Early', 'Green Comet'

Cabbage: 'Minicole', 'Fast Ball', 'Flash'

Carrot: 'Little Finger', 'Baby Spike'

Cauliflower: 'Early Snowball'

Cucumber: 'Bush Champion', 'Spacemaster'

Dill: 'Fernleaf'

Eggplant: 'Morden Midget', 'Bambino' clutch of cultivars that are smaller and more

Kale: 'Dwarf Green Curled'

Melon: 'Minnesota Midget'

Parsley: 'Extra Curled Dwarf'

Pea: 'Early Patio'

Pepper: 'Gypsy', 'Jingle Bells'

Radish: 'Comet', 'Sparkler'

Summer squash: 'Burpee Hybrid', 'Peter Pan', 'Gold Rush'

Swiss Chard: 'Compacta Slow Bolting'

Tomato: 'Yellow Canary', 'Patio', 'Tumbler', 'Small Fry', 'Whippersnapper'

ORNAMENTAL AND EDIBLE. *Many vegetables and herbs are as attractive as they are edible. They can easily be accommodated in the vegetable garden but are just as at home in flower beds and borders, raised beds, or in window-box or container gardens. While flowering cabbage and kale, used here as edging plants, are strictly ornamental, they can be used as garnishes.*

lite or vermiculite. For a soilless mix, combine 2 parts compost, 2 parts sphagnum peat, 2 parts vermiculite, 2 parts perlite, and 1 part sand. Another common formula for filling containers is 1 part commercial potting soil, 1 part compost, and 1 part coarse sand. (Always use coarse builder's sand, not the sandbox variety, for potting mixes.) When the growing season ends, add the "soil" from the containers to the compost pile and begin fresh the following year.

Second, vegetables and herbs planted in containers need more watering and feeding than they would if grown in the garden. Soil in containers dries out quickly (soil in clay and wood containers dries out even faster than it does in containers made of plastic or fiberglass; soil in dark-colored containers dries out faster than in light-colored ones). Container-grown plants also deplete soil nutrients rapidly. You'll need to give plants a bimonthly feeding of a balanced water-soluble organic fertilizer (heavy feeders also may require a monthly foliar spray of diluted manure tea or fish emulsion) and to water frequently. The need to cultivate and weed, happily, is almost nonexistent.

PRETTY AND PRACTICAL. *Space-efficient, high-yield planting schemes can be ornamental too, as this wide bed of mixed leaf lettuces planted in a hexagonal pattern prove. The lettuce is interplanted with seedling leeks.*

CHAPTER SIX

PLANTING THE GARDEN

To every thing there is a season,
and a time to every purpose under the heaven:
A time to be born, and a time to die;
a time to plant, and a time to pluck up
that which is planted ...

ECCLESIASTES

IF "START SMALL" IS THE FIRST PIECE OF ADVICE TO
GIVE NOVICE GARDENERS, "DON'T RUSH" should be the
second. The proverb says that God helps those who get up early.
Alas, no one can help those who plant too early. Vegetable and
herb seeds begun too soon indoors grow into weak, leggy,
root-bound seedlings long before it's warm enough to put them
in the garden. Seeds sown too soon outdoors rot in the cold
wet soil or germinate at glacial speed. Seedlings transplanted
prematurely are vulnerable to disease and often are permanently

stunted if not killed outright by frosty ground and air. You can start thinking about and planning your garden whenever you wish, but don't start planting until the time is right.

The right time, of course, differs from region to region. Gardeners in Houston, Texas, begin transplanting tomato seedlings the second week in March; in Raleigh, North Carolina, tomatoes go outdoors the last week of April. In central Indiana, the date is May 10; 2 weeks later in Prosser, Washington, and Fargo, North Dakota; the first week in June in northern Minnesota. You don't have to travel great distances to find great disparities in planting dates. The differences are considerable even in a tiny state like Vermont. In St. Albans, a northwestern town located on the shore of Lake Champlain, tomato transplants are set out around May 9. Drive 75 miles due east to Lemington, a northeastern Vermont town set on the banks of the Connecticut River, and June 7 is the date tomatoes go into the garden.

Determining When to Plant

Knowing exactly when the danger of frost has past—or when it returns—has always been an uncertain business, even for experienced gardeners. In 1684, John Evelyn, one of the founders of England's Royal Horticultural Society, wrote in his diary, "I went to see how the frost and rigorous weather had dealt with my garden, where I found many of the greens utterly destroyed." The complaint of naturalist Gilbert White, recorded 100 years later, has a familiar ring: "Ice thick as a crown piece. Potatoes much injured, and whole rows of kidney-beans killed: nasturtiums killed."

The average last-spring-frost and first-fall-frost dates of your location determine when to sow seeds, indoors or out, and when to transplant. *Average* is a crucial word here. Some springs, the last frost occurs weeks after the average frost-free date; other years, it occurs weeks before. October 14 may be your average first-frost date, as it is in Boise, Idaho, Des

REGIONAL PLANTING PROGRESSIONS

Although frost dates differ from area to area, seasonal planting progressions are fairly consistent within the larger regions of the country. Certainly, there are always exceptions to general rules—enormous variations exist in regions as large as the Southwest or South, for example—but the following progressions generally apply. Check with an experienced gardener if you have any doubts about when to sow or transplant a crop.

Mid-Atlantic, Northeast, Midwest, and Rocky Mountains. In most parts of the country, cool-season crops that will tolerate near-freezing temperatures can be planted in early spring and, depending on how much time they require to mature, again in midsummer for an autumn harvest. Warm-season plants are sown in late spring, after the danger of frost has passed, for summer harvesting.

South. In this region, most cool-season vegetables and herbs are planted in late winter and/or in late summer; warm-season crops are seeded in early spring.

The Coastal Northwest. Cool-season crops are planted from late winter to mid-spring and again in late summer; warm-season plants are sown from mid- to late spring.

The Southwest. Cool-season crops are seeded from early spring (February, in some areas) to May; cabbage and related crops are sown in early summer for a fall harvest; fast-maturing cool-season crops, such as lettuce, are planted in early fall; warm-season vegetables and herbs are planted in early spring.

Southern California. Southern California is a world unto itself. Here, cool-weather vegetables are planted from September through February; warm-season crops are sown in March and April; and fast-maturing cool-season crops, such as lettuce, from September through May. Many crops can be grown throughout the year.

Moines, Iowa, and Kingston, Rhode Island, but your neighbors—or gardeners in any of those towns—can tell horror stories about the year the mercury slid below 32°F in September. Weather is more settled in some parts of the country than others, but scientists warn that most Americans can expect temperatures significantly different from the "averages" one year out of every six.

Despite the inevitable and devastating exceptions, it's important to be familiar with the average last- and first-frost dates. They—and the condition of your soil—are the most dependable planting timepieces you have. Local gardeners, the local Cooperative Extension Office, and the National Weather Service can provide the average frost dates for your location. You'll also find first- and last-frost dates, along with growing-season lengths, for cities across the country beginning on page 422 of the Appendix. You'll find recommendations on scheduling specific crops in the individual Plant Portraits in Part Two of this book. See "Scheduling 101" on page 85 for suggestions on determining and keeping track of planting and transplant dates.

WEATHER & DAY-LENGTH CONSIDERATIONS

While gathering data on frost dates, get some information on average temperatures for your location. Don't overlook the obvious: Standard outdoor and soil thermometers are indispensable garden equipment. Both day- and nighttime temperatures affect the growth of plants, and soil temperature is every bit as crucial as the temperature of the air. Knowing average air and soil temperatures—and keeping records for your own garden—will help you to determine whether spring is coming faster or slower than usual in a given year and to fine-tune planting dates from year to year.

A few vegetables and herbs are affected by day length, and this can affect *when* you plant as well as *what* you plant. Give day-length-sensitive crops the wrong conditions, and they flower too quickly or fail

SPRING PLANTING. *For an early-spring crop, start leaf lettuce indoors and move hardened-off plants to the garden about 3 weeks before the last spring frost. In this garden, mounded beds, sloped to catch the early-spring sunshine, help warm the soil.*

DON'T RUSH TO PLANT. *Warm-weather crops like peppers and tomatoes may survive a too early planting, but waiting to plant until the soil has warmed up gets plants off to a better, more vigorous start.*

to flower altogether. The influence of light and dark on plants, called photoperiodism, is one of the major botanical findings of this century. It actually is the length of darkness, not light, that is crucial to the development of flowers, but plants are nonetheless characterized as short-day (short days are required for flowering), long-day (long days are required for flowering) and day-neutral (day length doesn't affect flowering). Spinach, for instance, is a long-day plant, but gardeners grow it for its leaves, not its flowers. One reason to plant it in the spring or fall, when the days are shorter, is to *discourage* it from flowering. You'll find specific information on dealing with day-length-sensitive crops in the individual Plant Portraits in Part Two of this book.

Understanding photoperiodism has been a particular boon to commercial flower growers who now fool hundreds of ornamentals—poinsettias and chrysanthemums are two—into blooming out of season. It's also spurred plant breeders to develop light-sensitive edible cultivars that do well in different regions. The ability of onions to form bulbs is influenced by day length, so gardeners in the North, where the days are longer, plant long-day cultivars, such as 'Early Yellow Globe' and 'Redman'; Southerners grow 'Granex', 'Red Bermuda', and other short-day cultivars. If your leaf and root crops are bolting prematurely, scan the seed catalogs for cultivars bred for your climate and latitude. Otherwise, you can leave counting the sunny hours to sundials.

USING SIGNS OF THE SEASON

Before climatologists began compiling records, gardeners relied on natural signs for timing planting. Reasonable people disagree about astrological gardening, but some garden folklore has a reliable and scientific basis. Especially valuable is advice based on plant phenology, the study of recurring natural events and their relationship with climate. Many of the scores of old phenological sayings are as reliable as the National Weather Service's average frost dates. For example:

> *When the dogwood flowers appear,*
> *Frost will not again be here.*

> *When elmen [elm] leaves are as big as a penny,*
> *Plant kidney-beans,*
> *if you mean to have any.*

In 1956, botanists organized a phenological network in the United States and Canada using the Persian lilac *Syringa persica* 'Red Rothomagensis' as the indicator plant. By matching the dates of the lilac's four stages of growth, or phenophases, with meteorological data, they've been able to forecast crop yields and insect infestations and to recommend when to plant different vegetables and herbs. In northern New England, for example, cool-weather crops can be planted safely when 'Red Rothomagensis' begins to leaf, the first phenophase; tender crops, such as cucumbers, shouldn't be planted until it is in full bloom, the third phenophase.

Keeping phenological records for your garden is an engaging and useful garden project—and another reason to keep a garden journal. You don't have to grow 'Red Rothomagensis'; instead, correlate weather with plants, especially native species, that grow in your yard. Several seasons of observation may lead you to discover that the time to seed chili peppers indoors—8 weeks before they can go into the garden always coincides with bloodroot (*Sanguinaria canadensis*) flowering; or that perfect weather for transplanting cucumber seedlings concurs with the first blooms on the crabapple; or that a fall crop of 'Alderman' peas sown after the rudbeckia 'Goldsturm' begins to blossom never has time to form pods. Don't draw conclusions precipitately, but if the first blooms of the fringed bleeding heart (*Dicentra eximia*) have appeared within 1 or 2 days of the frost-free date for 5 years in a row, it's a natural gardening indicator worth planting by.

ALTERING SOIL & AIR TEMPERATURES

It's impossible to create August in March, but you can boost the temperature of both soil and air to get a small jump on spring. There is an arsenal of techniques and equipment that permit gardeners to pre-warm the soil before moving transplants to the garden or to protect tender transplants from inclimate weather. These same techniques and equipment can be used to lengthen the growing season in autumn. (See "Extending & Ending the Season" on page 139 for more on these techniques.)

While you're fooling Mother Nature, though, remember that planting in sodden soil is nothing more than a head start on failure. Cold is the usual problem for most gardeners, but don't forget to monitor the soil and air temperatures around your plants as spring moves into summer. Many edibles—tomatoes are a prime example—drop their blossoms if the air becomes too hot. Similarly, most vegetable and herb plants stop growing when the soil reaches a temperature of 85°F.

SOIL-WARMING TECHNIQUES

Start with traditional methods to help warm soil. Well before you plant, remove any sod or organic mulches, rough the soil surface, and construct hills, mounds, or freestanding raised rows and beds, which expose more soil to the sun. This may be all you need to do in southern regions; in colder parts of the country, you can create your own greenhouse effect by laying down a plastic mulch several weeks before you sow seed or set out transplants.

HORTICULTURAL PLASTICS

The complicated chemical world of plastics is based on large molecules called polymers (Greek for "many units"), which are made up of smaller units, or monomers, such as ethylene or propylene. Combine several monomers, and you get polyethylene or polypropylene, two of the most important horticultural plastics. Most plastics are available in several weights.

Polyethylene. The stuff of clear and colored mulches, as well as slitted and knitted row covers like VisPore, polyethylene is the most widely used horticultural plastic. Sold under names like Agplast, it's tough and waterproof.

Polyester. This is the plastic used to make Reemay, the original spun-bonded floating row cover. Spun polyester is permeable to water and air.

Polypropylene. Also used to make row covers (sold under names such as Agronet and YardTek), polypropylene is more opaque and durable than spun polyester; it is permeable to water and air.

Polyvinyl alcohol. Used to make plant covers, such as Tufbell, polyvinyl alcohol is permeable to air and actually absorbs water. It is stronger and longer-lasting than are other horticultural plastics—it is also more expensive.

TUFBELL ROW COVERS. These row covers, suspended on hoops, are made of strong, long-lasting polyvinyl alcohol.

Black plastic mulch helps retain moisture and smother weeds but, compared with clear plastic, is second-rate at raising soil temperature. Clear plastic, which permits light to be transmitted directly to the ground, raised soil temperatures 20 degrees in experiments in northern gardens. In a southern location, the effect is even greater—as much as 40°F—which may be more heat than is good. If you live in USDA Zone 6 or higher, black plastic probably is a better choice for your garden. Be prepared, too, that clear plastic also encourages weed seeds to sprout. Halfway between black and clear plastics are the relatively new infrared transmitting (IRT) mulches. Colored dark green, they're better than clear plastic at controlling weeds while allowing more heat to reach the soil than black plastic does.

Seal the edges of any plastic mulch with soil or U-shaped pins fashioned from coat hangers; at planting time, slit the plastic wherever you want to seed or set transplants. You may also want to punch small holes in polyethylene mulches, which are impervious to water, to allow moisture to reach the soil. Once the weather warms, clear plastic mulches must be either removed or covered with straw or another organic matter; otherwise, the soil will become overheated. Black and IRT mulches can be left in place throughout the growing season in most parts of the country.

PLANT COVERS FOR WARMING AIR

Temporary covers are the answer to warming the air around plants, although few covers provide much protection when the thermometer falls below 20°F. Gardeners have been using plant covers for centuries, employing everything from the shirts off their backs to the elegant 17th-century French market growers' straw, and glass bells, which have become collectors' items. Today, glass, straw and, except in emergencies, shirts (and sheets, bedspreads, towels, and blankets) have pretty much been abandoned for plastic.

Called cloches (*cloche* is French for "bell"), these covers are usually set in place in the evening and removed in the morning; well-ventilated models can be left in place until the danger of frost and cold is past. Mail-order catalogs and garden centers sell many sizes and shapes of polyethylene and polypropylene caps and domes. The most popular and effective commercial model is the Wall O'Water, a ring of connected vertical plastic tubes set over a plant and then filled with water; the water

WARM SOIL WITH PLASTIC. *Black plastic, shown here mulching sweet potatoes, controls weeds and retains soil moisture, but it doesn't warm the soil as effectively as clear plastic does.*

stores heat during the day and radiates it during the night.

It's not difficult to make plant covers, but keep in mind that most will provide only a few degrees of protection. A pot, paper bag, or newspaper (folded into a hat) can serve as a nighttime cover; remove it during the day. You can turn a 1-gallon plastic milk jug into a mini-greenhouse by removing its bottom. If the weather warms during the day, be sure to remove its screw cap for ventilation. Or surround stakes or wire cages with plastic sheeting for protection against the cold. To create your own walls-of-water, ring a plant with 2-liter plastic soda bottles filled with water, then encircle them with plastic sheeting.

Continuous cloches are easier and quicker to install than individual covers are. You can size them to protect three or four plants, a row, or an entire

CONTINUOUS CLOCHES. *Metal or PVC half-hoops and sheets of polyethylene make it easy to protect a row or an entire bed of plants from chilly spring temperatures. Be sure to ventilate plants on sunny days.*

HOMEMADE FROST PROTECTORS. *Milk jugs with the bottoms removed make mini-greenhouses for pepper plants. Caps on the jugs hold in heat at night, but remove them during the day for ventilation.*

LIGHTWEIGHT ROW COVERS. *Floating row covers are so lightweight they can be laid loosely over a seedbed or newly transplanted seedlings. Weight down the corners to keep them from blowing away. To use them to keep out pest insects, bury the edges with soil.*

bed. Tunnels made from sheets of 4- to 6-mil polyethylene suspended on PVC (polyvinyl chloride) piping or metal half-hoops become temporary greenhouses. They give a few degrees of protection at night but can raise the mercury 10 degrees or more during the day. Roll back the plastic on sunny days, or you may cook your plants. To improve nighttime performance, set 1-gallon plastic jugs filled with water under the tunnel; the water heats up during the day, then radiates its warmth when darkness falls. Another option is to create a tunnel out of semi-rigid fiberglass, either smooth sheets or translucent corrugated roofing.

Far easier to use are floating row covers, drapes of spun-plastic fabric that are lightweight, air- and water-permeable, and durable enough to last from two to four garden seasons. Row covers rest on the plants themselves—they weigh about ½ ounce per square yard—so no hoops are necessary. Light transference runs between 85 and 95 percent; frost protection also varies, from 2 to many as 10 degrees. (Savvy gardeners have discovered that double, even triple, layers significantly improve on those numbers.) The covers also provide protection from wind, which can desiccate young plants

Spread covers over a seedbed or newly transplanted seedlings, leaving plenty of slack for plant growth, and secure the edges so that the wind does not blow them away. Because they allow light, air, and water to reach plants, floating row covers can be left on the garden far longer than most continuous cloches. This is especially true of those made from polyethylene, which turns them into a blue-ribbon barrier against flea beetles, radish maggots, and other pests. But don't forget that their ability to exclude pests also means that honeybees can't reach your plants; remove row covers when insect-pollinated vegetables and herbs, such as cucumbers and melons, begin to bloom.

COLD FRAMES

Cold frames are bottomless boxes with clear plastic or glass lids. While movable models are available from mail-order catalogs, most gardeners build their own cold frames and set them in a permanent location outside the garden plot. Good for germinating cold-hardy plants, such as cabbage and broccoli, and for hardening off, or acclimating, seedlings that have been sprouted indoors, cold frames also can be used to grow winter crops. Many gardeners recycle storm windows to make the lid, or sash, for a cold frame; the box can be built of wood, brick, stone, or even bales of straw. (A *hot bed* is similar to a cold frame except that it uses heat generated from either electric cables or a pit of fresh manure buried under the seedbed.)

Cold frames can heat up quickly on sunny days, and the heat can damage or kill plants. The temperature inside the frame is controlled by opening the lid. This can be done manually by simply watching the temperature and propping up the lid with a notched stick when it gets too high. Gardeners who are away from home during the day probably will want to equip their frame with a solar-powered vent opener, which will monitor the temperature and open the top automatically.

LOWERING TEMPERATURES

For gardeners in some locations, the goal is lowering, not raising, temperatures. Soil can be cooled—and moisture retained—by mulching heavily with compost, straw, or another organic material and by planting in recessed rather than raised beds. To bring down the air temperature, provide shade. Laying out your garden so that tall crops shade sun-sensitive ones is the least expensive option. You can erect screens of lath, snow fencing, burlap, cheese-cloth, or some other material that permits good ventilation. Or use a woven polypropylene shade fabric. Floating row covers also make good shade cloths. They can be laid directly on plants but are more

MULTIPURPOSE COLD FRAME. *Spring is the busiest time in a cold frame, when they are filled with newly sown flats of seeds and plants that are being hardened off. They can also be used to grow winter crops of cool-weather greens and other plants.*

effective if they are suspended on hoops above the plants, which permits air to circulate better. New on the market is a polyvinyl alcohol (PVA) row-cover shade cloth that has been impregnated with silver-finish aluminum for high light and heat reflection. Sold under the name Silver Turfbell, it is more effective and longer-lasting than most row covers, as well as more expensive. Finally, portable cold frames—their sashes replaced by shade cloth—can be used to protect crops from sun.

SELECTING SEEDS

Inside the protective skin of a seed is not the promise of life but life itself. "In this tiny casket," New Englander Celia Thaxter wrote in 1894, "lie folded roots, stalks, leaves, buds, flowers, seed-vessels . . . all that goes to make up a plant which is gigantic in proportion to the bounds that confine it as the oak is to the acorn."

Seeds vary in appearance and size, from the familiar near-square corn kernel (100 to 200 seeds per ounce) to the brownish ridged ovals that turn into carrot plants (23,000 seeds per ounce). They differ in the soil temperature they prefer for germination (95°F for corn, 80° for carrots) and the length of time they can be stored (1 or 2 years for corn, 3 or 4 for carrots). But all seeds, small and large, are plants-in-waiting. Give them the right conditions, and they reveal the treasure within. "I have great faith in a seed," Henry David Thoreau wrote. "Convince me that you have a seed there, and I am prepared to expect wonders."

Plant breeders and seed sellers have added to the wonders that come from seeds by creating thousands of new cultivars of vegetables and herbs. Plant breeding is a mixed bag of successes and failures, a two-faced creature like Janus, the Roman patron of January, which is the very time of year when the breeders release their newborn. Buying seeds, too, requires looking back and ahead, considering old wrinkles as well as the latest ones. As always, a bit of skepticism marks an intelligent shopper and also qualifies gardeners as spiritual descendants of Katharine White. Her wonderful grumbles about the seed industry's fixation with the novel were collected as *Onward and Upward in the Garden* by her husband, E.B. White, in 1979. Her complaints weren't the first, however. Gertrude Jekyll, the *doyenne* of British garden writing, beat White by eight decades. "There is no merit whatever in novelty or variety unless the thing new or different is distinctly more beautiful, or in some such way better than an older thing of the same class," she wrote in 1899.

UNDERSTANDING SEED SHORTHAND

Truth be told, seed breeders are responsible for an embarrassment of sins: for tomatoes without zip, watery and limp lettuce, chilies masquerading as sweet peppers, and corn so sweet that it should be served for dessert. At the same time, gardeners have breeders to thank for cucumbers that flourish in plots the size of hand towels, for beans more resistant to viruses than their growers are, for compact dill plants that don't blow down in the wind, and for spinach that refuses to bolt. To take advantage of

the benefits that breeders have wrought, make sure you know the basics of seed shorthand. Be prepared for a seed packet that reads:

'KING ARTHUR' SWEET PEPPER
F_1 Hyb • BLS,PVY,TEV,TMV
Thick Long Blocky • Green/Red
Germ 75 degrees/10 days • In 6-8 wks
Sun • Space 18 inches • 72 Days
100 seeds (Net Wt. 500 mg)
Pack for 1997 • USA • Germ 75%
Very Good Seeds Co. • First Eden, MO

Here's a translation:

'King Arthur' sweet pepper. The top line is the name of the plant whose seeds are contained in the packet. Vegetable and herb cultivars, or varieties, are usually designated in print by single quotation marks—'King Arthur'. (Botanists recognize a technical difference between a cultivar and a variety, but gardeners generally use the terms interchangeably.) Sweet Pepper is the common name of the plant, but all plants also have a botanical name consisting of a genus and species name (the pepper's is *Capsicum annuum*). The botanical name is indicated by italics or underlining.

F_1 Hyb. This phrase means 'King Arthur' is a first-generation hybrid, a cross between two stable but dissimilar parent strains. Plants grown from the seeds in the packet will have better-than-average vigor and uniformity, but seeds saved from those plants won't produce 'King Arthur' peppers. If you save seeds from 'King Arthur' peppers—or any other hybrid—for next year's garden, you'll undoubtedly be disappointed in what comes up. The plants are unlikely to resemble the hybrid you planted.

In contrast to seeds saved from a hybrid plant, seeds from an open-pollinated (OP), or nonhybrid, pepper like 'Yankee Bell' *will* produce plants and fruits that are identical to their parent. Open-pollinated cultivars are the result of someone, usually a home gardener, finding an unusual or clearly superior plant, saving its seeds, and planting them the next year—then saving the seeds of the best fruits of the best offspring and planting again and again and again. In time—five generations or more—the characteristics valued, such as larger size, better flavor, or greater hardiness, are stabilized.

BLS,PVY,TEV,TMV. These initials tell you that 'King Arthur' plants are resistant *but not* *immune* to bacterial leaf spot, potato virus Y, tobacco etch virus, and tobacco mosaic virus. Good seed catalogs provide keys to the disease resistance of specific vegetables and herbs. If your garden is packed with viruses, fungi, and other plagues, the more letters the better. Remember, though, that the most disease-resistant cultivars are not always the most flavorful ones. (See Chapter 8 for more information on plant diseases.)

Thick Long Blocky. 'King Arthur' is a long, block-shaped sweet pepper with thick flesh, ideal for stuffing, roasting, grilling, or slicing into a stir-fry or salad.

Green/Red. 'King Arthur' is green if picked while still immature, which is when gardeners typically harvest sweet peppers. Fruits left on the plant until maturity turn bright red.

Germ 75 degrees/10 days. This shorthand explains the germination requirements of 'King Arthur'. In other words, seeds sown in soil kept at 75°F should sprout in 10 days. Each vegetable and herb has an optimum range of temperatures at which its seeds germinate. For peppers, the range is 65° to 95°F.

ALL-AMERICA SELECTIONS

Watch for the designation "AAS" (All-America Selections) when you buy vegetable and herb seeds. The letters indicate that the cultivar has been grown in more than 60 trial gardens located throughout the United States and, when compared with similar cultivars, has been judged outstanding by independent horticultural experts. AAS, the only national program that focuses on cultivars for home gardeners, began handing out prizes in 1932. Many older winners, such as 'Clemson Spineless' okra and 'Stringless Black Valentine' bean, are still favorites; among the most popular recent winners are 'Sugar Snap' pea, 'Red Sails' and 'Salad Bowl' lettuces, 'Fanfare' bush cucumber, and 'Celebrity' tomato.

In 6-8 wks. Plants should be started indoors 6 to 8 weeks before the average frost-free date for your region.

Sun. 'King Arthur', like all sweet and chili peppers, should be grown in a site with full sun for best performance.

Space 18 inches. Transplants should be spaced 18 inches apart when set in the garden.

72 Days. This is the days-to-maturity number: There should be green peppers ready to pick 72 days *after you set transplants in the garden.* For direct-seeded crops, such as beans and peas, the days to maturity are counted from the time the seeds go into the ground rather than when seedlings are transplanted outdoors. The total number of days required to grow 'King Arthur'—from seeds to fruits—is approximately 135.

100 seeds. The packet contains approximately 100 seeds.

500 mg. The seeds in the packet weigh 500 milligrams, or 15/1000 of an ounce. If that doesn't sound like much, remember that 1 ounce of pepper seeds will produce between 4,000 and 6,000 plants.

Pack for 1997. The seeds were packaged for the 1997 garden season. Most seeds packed for 1997 were grown in 1995, although they may have been grown even earlier.

USA. The seeds were grown in the United States.

Germ 75%. You can expect 75 of the 100 seeds in the packet to germinate, which is about 70 more plants than two people need.

Very Good Seeds Co., First Eden, MO. The name and location of the retail company that *packaged* the seeds. Most seed companies do not grow all—or even any—of the seeds they hawk.

By federal law, vegetable—and herb—seed packets need carry only the species and cultivar or variety names, and net weight, although compliance is uneven. The envelopes to be avoided are the ones marked with oversimplified statements such as "PEANUTS Easy to Grow Anywhere." Heat-loving peanuts, which take 130 days to mature, are not easy to grow anywhere. Just ask a northern gardener. So buy from seed companies that provide useful and complete information—either on the seed packets or on planting guides enclosed with your order.

Plant breeders have focused most on the needs of commercial agriculture. Qualities important to home gardeners, such as flavor, have taken a back-

FROM SEEDS TO SEEDLINGS. *Fresh, properly stored seeds will germinate into vigorous seedlings like these young sunflowers. The best time to plant, and whether seeds should be sown indoors or out, will vary depending on the crop, the season, and where you live.*

seat to creating vegetables and herbs that are more uniform, easier to harvest mechanically, and ship better or store longer. Still, many breeding achievements, such as improved disease resistance and salt tolerance, are a boon to all growers. Available now are hundreds of cultivars that have cast off "normal" habits: peas and other cool-weather crops that can succeed in warm regions; heat-loving crops, such as sweet potatoes, that will tolerate cool conditions; long-season crops that speed to maturity; new colors, shapes, and sizes; and scaled-down offerings—pumpkin plants that cover 6 rather than 25 square feet or pumpkins that weigh 6 ounces rather than 60 pounds—that are a made-in-the-laboratory match for backyard growers.

MAKING SEED SELECTIONS

When you order seeds from a catalog or buy them at your local garden center, be sure to try some brand-new offerings. 'Siam Queen', a Thai basil with extremely large leaves, and 'Cajun Delight', a heavy-yielding okra that bears fruits 3 weeks before most cultivars, are 1997 AAS winners. Or trial 'Spice 'n Easy' cabbage, 'Fourth of July' tomato, or 'The Godfather' sweet pepper, three recent releases from the W. Atlee Burpee & Co., which has won more AAS awards than any other seed company. Then add some "standards," cultivars universally rated as outstanding. Three good candidates are 'Sweet 100' tomato, still the best cherry type, although you'll need a telephone pole to stake it;

'Red Sails' lettuce, a beautiful leaf lettuce that was an AAS winner in 1985; and 'Yukon Gold', a flavorful Canadian potato that immigrated south in 1980.

Don't forget to put a few old-timers, or heirlooms, on your seed list, cultivars like 'Jacob's Cattle' dry bean, 'Eva Purple Ball' tomato, 'Tennis Ball' lettuce, or 'Moon and Stars' watermelon. Heirlooms, loosely defined, are cultivars dating from before 1940 (hybrids became common only after World War II). Most heirlooms have interesting regional histories, and all are open-pollinated, which means you can save their seeds for next year's garden. Increased interest in heirlooms has led many mainstream seed houses to add them to their inventory; for a larger selection, shop with one of the mail-order seed firms or seed-saving organizations that specialize in these edible antiques.

Many heirlooms are also locally adapted, tailor-made for the conditions of a particular place or a place with similar conditions. 'Jackson Wonder' bush lima, a mottled Georgia heirloom, does well in hot climates; 'Stowell's Evergreen' sweet corn, an 8-foot white cultivar developed in New Jersey around 1850, is adapted to the Mid-Atlantic states. Not all regional cultivars are heirlooms, though. 'Permagreen', a sweet pimiento pepper adapted to northern conditions, dates from the 1980s, for example, and breeders are continually producing new cultivars for particular conditions. Gardeners with extreme climates will want to look for a seed company that specializes in cultivars adapted for their area. By dividing your seed order, patronizing more than one company, and supporting businesses and organizations that promote seed diversity, you help keep new, old, and regional selections alive and available.

When you're paging through a seed catalog, take note that many companies treat their seeds to protect them from disease. Hot water baths and inoculations of *Rhizobia* bacteria are beneficial to seeds while not harmful to soil. Don't worry if your seeds have been defuzzed (to keep them from sticking together) or pelleted (coated to make them easier to handle). Finally, many garden catalogs peddle "seed tapes," strips of water-soluble material that contain precisely spaced seeds. Convenient, maybe, but not essential and not recommended.

Fungicide coatings, usually Captan, also protect seeds but are harmful to beneficial organisms in the soil and should be avoided. Catalogs should make clear if the seed being sold has been treated, but another giveaway is a packet filled with seeds that are dyed (a legal requirement when chemical treatments are applied). If being organic is important to you, not only will you want to avoid chemically treated seeds, but you may want to purchase organically grown seeds. Several mail-order companies stock organic seeds.

GERMINATION BASICS

Armed with everything it needs to produce a new plant, a seed germinates, or sprouts, when it receives the proper mix of moisture, oxygen, and warmth. Light, so crucial to plant growth, doesn't affect the germination of most seeds, although the great majority are better off if covered by soil. This is especially true for seeds sown outdoors, where a light covering not only helps seeds retain moisture but also keeps them from blowing or washing away or becoming food for wildlife. Seeds of a few crops do require special handling to germinate, but for most seeds, a covering of warm, damp, well-aerated soil—generally only as deep as the seed is thick—is all that is necessary.

While light doesn't strongly affect germination, time does. If you're using seeds from five seasons ago—or even last year's seeds—proof, or test, them before you plant. (See the individual Plant Portraits for details on seed storage and viability.)

GERMINATION TEMPERATURES

Interestingly, there is a correlation between the best soil temperatures for germination and the best air temperatures for growth for most vegetables and herbs. Watermelon germinates best at a high temperature (95°F), and corn plants need plenty of heat

SPECIAL HANDLING

The great majority of seeds germinate quickly when covered lightly with moist soil. Germinating the seeds of a few vegetables and herbs, however, is aided and/or speeded by special treatment.

Seeds That Germinate Better in Light
Leave these seeds on the soil surface for best germination. Mist or sprinkle them frequently—daily at least—to keep them moist. If you are germinating indoors, a covering of clear plastic suspended above the soil surface by wire hoops eliminates the need for daily misting.

Celery   Lettuce
Dill   Savory

Seeds That Germinate Better in Darkness
Cover the following seeds with enough soil to exclude light.

Coriander   Parsley
Fennel   Tomato

Overnight Soaking
The following seeds germinate best if they are soaked overnight before being sown. Soaking helps hydrate the embryo inside the seed and speeds germination.

Asparagus   Okra
Beet   Parsley
New Zealand spinach Spinach

Inoculating
Legumes, including the plants listed below as well as many cover crops, require special bacteria in order to take nitrogen from the air and fix it in a form that is available to plants. Each requires a different species of bacteria to do its job. Inoculate the seeds below, listed with their specific nitrogen-fixing bacteria, before sowing. Some companies sell pre-inoculated seeds; others sell the inoculant separately.

Bean (*Rhizobium leguminosarum*)
Chickpea (*Rhizobium loti*)
Lima bean (*Bradyrhizobium* spp.)
Pea (*Rhizobium leguminosarum* var. *viceae*)
Soybean (*Bradyrhizobium japonicum*)

(70° to 90°F) to thrive. The optimum soil temperature to germinate spinach seeds, on the other hand, is 70°F, and spinach grows best when daytime air temperatures are cool, between 60° and 70°F.

Many vegetables will germinate well in a wide range of temperatures. Acceptable temperature ranges for germinating some of the most popular vegetables are as follows:

50° to 85°F: beets, cabbages, carrots, cauliflower, celery, Swiss chard, lettuce, onions, parsley, parsnips, peas, radishes, spinach

60° to 85°F: asparagus, snap beans, celery, corn, cucumbers, tomatoes

70° to 85°F: lima beans, okra, pumpkins, watermelons

80° to 95°F: eggplant, melons

Don't worry if you haven't provided the perfect soil temperature for sprouting—seeds are a forgiving lot (turnips are the most forgiving, willing to germinate in soils ranging in temperature from 40° to 105°F). But if the soil is 10 degrees colder than the optimum temperature range, plan on waiting an extra week or two for plants to appear.

GERMINATION TESTING

If you are planting seeds that you've saved from a previous season or from last year's plants, test their germination percentage before planting to make sure you can use them. Place a dozen seeds between damp, but not soppy, white paper towels. Roll or fold up the towels and place them in a warm spot (approximately 75°F) in a loosely closed plastic bag to keep the towels moist but let in air for ventilation. Note how soon the seeds should sprout, based on the specifications given on the seed packet, and begin checking the towels daily for signs of germination on that day. If only six seeds sprout, the germination rate is 50 percent and you should buy new seeds; if the rate is between 65 and 85 percent, use the seeds but sow more thickly than usual. To determine the percentage, divide the number of seeds that germinated by the number tested.

SOWING SEEDS INDOOR

When garden centers overflow with flats of herbs and vegetables each spring, it's logical to ask why anyone should start seeds indoors. There are plenty of reasons, beginning with the constant and close-up access to seedlings growing your own provides. You can watch a tomato's atypical seed leaves unfold, then mark the difference between them and the plant's first true leaves; you'll marvel at the emerging onion seedlings, 1-inch swords with their black seed cases still clinging to their tips. And all without having to get down on your hands and knees on cold, wet soil.

Aside from the pleasure of watching tiny stems break through the surface of the soil and stretch toward the light, gardening indoors may help keep

---

SPROUTING PROBLEMS

If the seeds are fresh, problems with sprouting are likely the result of too much moisture or too little warmth. Soil, indoors or out, needs to be warm and damp, but not waterlogged. Most seeds germinate best in temperatures between 70° and 90°F. They will sprout in colder soil, but they'll take their time. Cabbage seeds, for instance, take 2 weeks to sprout in 50°F soil but will sprout in only 3 or 4 days if the soil is warmed to 85°F. Similarly, parsnips can germinate in soil as cold as 40°F but will take at least 8 weeks. Raise the temperature to 70°F, and you'll have seedlings in 2 weeks. Indoors, you can speed germination by using a heating cable or placing flats in a warm location, but don't overdo it: Extreme heat, like extreme cold, inhibits germination.

If your seeds fail to germinate, the problem may be the result of one of the following:

- Old or nonviable seeds
- Seeds sown too deeply
- Soil not firmed around seeds
- Soil temperature too low or too high
- Overwatering
- Pre-emergent damping-off disease
- Contaminated soil

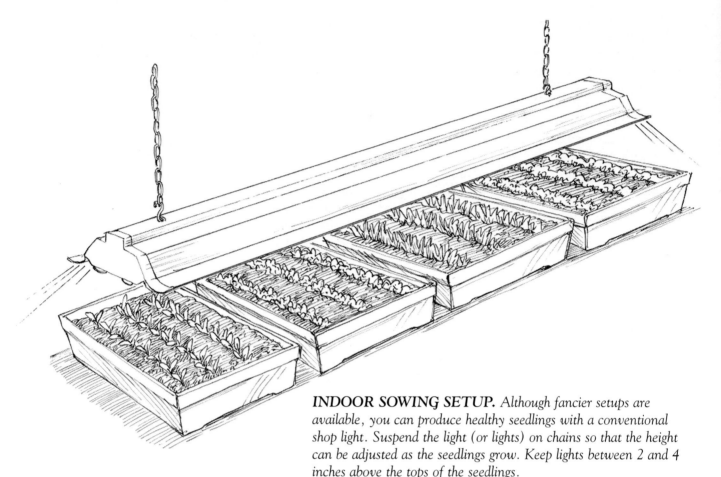

INDOOR SOWING SETUP. *Although fancier setups are available, you can produce healthy seedlings with a conventional shop light. Suspend the light (or lights) on chains so that the height can be adjusted as the seedlings grow. Keep lights between 2 and 4 inches above the tops of the seedlings.*

you from dashing out into the garden 10 weeks before the soil is ready to work. While practicing restraint outdoors, don't forget to be patient indoors. Begin seeds too soon, and your transplants will become leggy and root-bound before you can get them into the garden. Overage transplants—tomatoes and peppers with flowers and fruits, or cabbage-family crops with leathery leaves—will be a disappointment. (See the Plant Portraits in Part Two for specific timing guidelines.)

Supply the conditions seedlings need for good development, and growing your own means stronger and healthier transplants, perfectly timed for *your* garden. Having seedlings ready to go into the ground exactly when you need them makes intercropping and succession planting easier and increases productivity. It gives crops a head start on the weather and on the weeds, which begin sprouting when the soil is tilled. You'll also save money—a packet of seed, which can last for several seasons, costs less than half as much as a six-pack of seedlings. Finally, you'll have access to greater vari-

ety. There will be dozens of flats filled with 'California Wonder' sweet peppers at the local garden center, but you'll probably never find 'Marconi', an Italian heirloom, or 'Chocolate Beauty'.

CONTAINER OPTIONS

Gardeners can start vegetable and herb seeds in almost any container with drainage holes: plug trays, clay and plastic pots, milk jugs, cottage cheese and yogurt containers, Styrofoam and paper cups, peat pots, egg cartons, aluminum cans, wooden boxes, and more. English garden writer Vita Sackville-West remembered having a neighbor who planted in "cardboard dress-boxes tied rough with string to prevent them from disintegrating, and old Golden Syrup tins, and even some of those tall tins that once contained Slug-death. . . . I verily believe that she would use an old shoe if it came handy." You'll want to avoid tins that contained Slug-death, but an old shoe will work—if there are holes in its sole.

To avoid damaging young roots, especially of finicky plants (see "A Room of Their Own" on page

112 for a list of crops that resent root disturbance), many gardeners begin with single containers or segmented flats. Garden centers and mail-order suppliers offer a range of plastic products; with careful handling, most can be reused for several years. Inexpensive plug, or cell, trays are the most common, are easy to use, and come in different sizes. Best are those with a slight conical shape, which guides the young roots down rather than out. Think twice about containers made of peat, which, although highly popular, cannot be reused. They become waterlogged easily (especially the compressed peat pellets); if they dry out, they are difficult to rewet. In the ground, they are slow to decompose, and plant roots can have difficulty penetrating their walls.

And there are better choices. One is the newspaper pot. You can roll your own by using a pot press, which looks like a pepper mill sitting on a matching tray, or by using an aluminum can or drinking glass. Each 2-inch-wide pot is constructed from a 12-by-6-inch strip of newspaper (larger, for a larger pot), which you wrap around the press, leaving about 2 inches extending beyond the bottom of the press. Fold the bottom edges under, and push the press into its base to firm the folds. The result is a newspaper pot that is ideal for vegetable and herb seedlings. Make three dozen, fill them with seed-starting mix, and pack them tightly into a plastic

mesh flat (or a conventional flat with holes in the bottom) to keep them from unraveling. When it's time to move outdoors, make a couple of tears in the damp newspaper to help roots to spread, and set the seedling *still in its pot* in the ground. Nothing could be easier—or more economical.

CONTAINER DOS AND DON'TS

Whatever containers you use to start seeds indoors, observe the following guidelines:

Don't Overpot. Seeds germinate better in small containers. A diameter of 1½ or 2 inches is plenty large for most crops.

Provide Drainage. Make sure each container has drainage holes.

Clean Preused Containers. To prevent problems with fungal diseases such as damping-off, clean any container that has been used previously. First,

---

GERMINATION GUARANTEED

If you're new to starting seeds indoors, begin with plants that are easy and quick to germinate, including those listed below. Remember that once seeds sprout, even "easy" plants need the right amounts of light, water, air, and nutrients to develop normally.

Basil	Chive
Broccoli	Cucumber
Brussels sprout	Leek
Cabbage	Lettuce
Chinese	Okra
cabbage	Onion
Cauliflower	Tomato

BUYING TRANSPLANTS

If you choose to purchase transplants, look for the same qualities you would have pursued if you'd grown your own: lush green color, bushy growth, strong stems. Other caveats for the transplant shopper:

- Choose plants growing in single containers (and only one plant per plug, or cell—that extra tomato is not a bonus) or widely spaced in flats.

- Avoid plants with any signs of disease or insects. Be sure to check under the leaves.

- Reject underfertilized plants: Look for leaves tinged with yellow, red, purple, bronze, or brown.

- Reject overgrown plants, including plants that are in flower or have produced fruits—smaller, less mature plants adjust better to transplanting and quickly outdistance large ones.

A ROOM OF THEIR OWN

Many vegetables and herbs can be transplanted without a hitch, but the plants listed below resent being disturbed. If you start them indoors, use individual containers rather than unsegmented flats. Sow several seeds per container, then thin to one or two plants by cutting extra seedlings down with scissors; do not pull them up, which can disturb the roots. Transplant with care to minimize disturbance.

Bean	Okra
Borage	Melon
Burnet	Mustard
Caraway	Parsley
Carrot	Parsnip
Chervil	Pea
Chinese cabbage	Peanut
Coriander	Radish
Corn	Rutabaga
Cucumber	Squash
Dill	Watermelon

Corn seedling

wash thoroughly, then dip containers in a 10 percent bleach solution (1 cup bleach to 9 cups water). Finally, rinse in clear water.

SEED-SOWING MIXES

To germinate well, seeds must be sown in well-aerated soil that is free of weed seeds and free of pathogens. The quick alternative is to purchase a commercial mix. Most are soilless—a combination

THE NO-CONTAINER CONTAINER

Another top-notch container for starting seeds is no container: soil blocks, which are freestanding cubes of soil. Soil blocks have been around for at least 2,000 years. They are widely used in Europe but are unfamiliar to most home gardeners in this country. That's a shame, for few methods work better. Because the blocks are unconfined, without walls, roots are air-pruned: Rather than circling inside a pot or cell, roots grow to the edge of the soil block and stop. At the same time, gardeners have all the advantages of using a celled container: Each seedling is separate and easy to handle and can go into the garden undisturbed. Once in the ground, soil-block seedlings develop quickly because their roots don't have to push through a biodegradable pot or learn to grow out and down after having grown round and round.

Making soil blocks is easy but requires purchasing one or more soil blockers, metal molds with a spring ejection device. These horticultural cookie cutters are available in several sizes. Begin with a 2-inch model. You'll also need a special soil-block planting mix, a fibrous concoction that hangs together yet drains well. It's available commercially, or you can make your own. (See "Blocking Mixes" for recipes.) Don't be alarmed at the mud-pie consistency of the mix when water is added. The blocks are made by jamming the mold into the mix. They're then ejected into a plastic mesh flat or a conventional flat with holes in the bottom.

Don't cover seeds planted in soil blocks—they germinate better when left uncovered. Keep them moist, watering with a fine rose or misting to prevent erosion. Each soil blocker can be fitted

of sphagnum peat, vermiculite, and ground limestone—and so are sterile, as well as lightweight and water-retentive. Most are also free of nutrients, which is fine at the onset, for seeds have stored all the food they need to germinate. To grow healthy transplants, however, you must move your seedlings into an enriched mix or fertilize regularly.

Commercial mixes are convenient, but it's about as easy to assemble your own. There are scores of recipes—see "Homemade Seed-Starting Soils" on page 114 for recipes to use—or you can sprout seeds in nothing more than vermiculite. You should know that mixes that include soil may also include disease-causing organisms and weed seeds. Compost, too, can harbor diseases and weed seeds, especially if the pile never reached high temperatures. You can "pasteurize" soil (use commercial potting soil or bagged topsoil, not garden soil) or compost by

with a cubic pin so that smaller soil blocks can be fitted into larger ones, the potless version of potting on. If you have only one size blocker and the seedling needs more footroom, place the block in a slightly larger container and add soil.

BLOCKING MIXES

The recipes below include a good balance of nutrients to support seedling growth. Use a 10-quart bucket as the measure for bulk ingredients. Recipes make about 1 bushel of mix.

Mix the black peat and limestone together. Add the other ingredients and mix thoroughly. Then add 1 part water to every 2 to 3 parts of the finished mix to create the mud-pielike consistency necessary for making the blocks.

1 bucket black peat (sometimes sold as
    "Michigan peat" or *terre noire*)
¼ cup ground limestone
1 bucket coarse sand
1 bucket sphagnum, or standard, peat
½ bucket potting soil
½ bucket compost
⅔ cup blood meal
⅔ cup colloidal phosphate
⅔ cup greensand

The following is an alternative, soilless recipe for soil blocks. Mix the ingredients thoroughly.

2 buckets compost
1 bucket sphagnum peat
½ bucket coarse sand
⅓ cup colloidal phosphate
⅓ cup kelp meal
⅓ cup blood meal
¼ cup ground limestone

MAKING SOIL BLOCKS. *To make soil block, mix up blocking mix in a tub or other large container. Add water and mix until the mix sticks together but isn't dripping wet. Jam the metal mold, called a soil blocker, into the mix and then eject the finished "pots" into a flat.*

heating it: Place it in a pan, moisten it thoroughly, and set in a preheated 185°F oven for 45 minutes. Be prepared for the stink! Even this process doesn't guarantee a complete absence of pathogens or weed seeds; moreover, it kills any beneficial organisms living in the soil or compost. Better to take a chance with unpasteurized soil and compost, or fill containers three-quarters full with soil- or compost-based mix, then top them off with milled sphagnum moss or vermiculite. To be 100 percent safe, use a mix that contains neither soil nor compost.

HOMEMADE SEED-STARTING SOILS

Garden soil, which typically contains weed seeds and a rich mix of pathogens, is not recommended for starting seedlings. Instead, purchase a commercial seed-starting mix, or use one of the recipes below, all of which make 1 gallon of mix that is free of weed seeds as well as disease-causing organisms.

This sterile, soilless recipe includes no nutrients:

2 quarts sphagnum peat
1 quart vermiculite
1 quart perlite
1 tablespoon ground limestone

This sterile, soilless mix includes some nutrients:

2 quarts sphagnum peat
2 quarts vermiculite or perlite
2 teaspoons ground limestone
2 teaspoons bonemeal

A simple formula that includes a modest supply of nutrients but, because it contains compost, is not sterile:

2 quarts commercial potting mix
1 quart perlite or coarse sand
1 quart sifted compost

SEED-SOWING GUIDELINES

Once you have containers and seed-starting mix on hand, it's time to sow. Here's a rundown of what you need to do:

Premoisten the Mix. Before sowing, lightly moisten the mix. The easiest way to do this is to place the mix in a large bucket. Then add warm water and stir with your hands until the mixture is about as moist as a damp sponge. If it is wet enough that water drips out when you pick up a handful, add more mix.

Fill the Containers. Fill containers to overflowing, scrape off the excess, and tap the containers lightly on a hard surface to settle the mix. Set them in a flat for easy handling.

Sow. Sow seeds approximately twice as deep as their diameter. Don't sow seeds too thickly—crowding invites damping-off and other problems. If you are using individual containers, sow only two to three seeds per container.

Cover the Seeds. Cover seeds lightly with vermiculite or milled spaghnum peat, and firm gently, leaving $1/2$ inch at the top of the container to allow for watering. Be sure *not* to cover seeds that require light to germinate—see "Special Handling" on page 108 for a list.

Add Labels. Label containers with crop and cultivar names and date. No matter how sure you are that you'll remember what you've planted where, you won't.

Add Moisture. Mist containers until fully moistened; allow any excess water to drain into the flat below, then pour it off.

Ensure Humidity. Cover the containers with glass, plastic, or damp newspaper to maintain moisture. (Don't use newspaper to cover seeds that require light to germinate; for seeds that require darkness, newspaper makes an effective covering.)

Provide Heat. Set containers in a warm spot, such as on top of the refrigerator or water heater, or use heat mats or cables (available from garden-supply companies). If your newly sown containers are covered with a light-permeable cover such as plastic or glass, do not place containers in direct sun. For faster germination, keep soil warm, between 75° and 85°F

Keep the Soil Moist. Keep soil moist but not soggy. Although it is more time-consuming, watering from below is best because it avoids disturbing the seeds and helps prevent damping-off. Fill the flat with water, and let it soak into the soil from below. Drain off any extra water after the containers are thoroughly wet.

Ensure Ventilation. Make sure there is good air circulation by removing covers for several hours *at least* every other day. If you see signs of mold, remove the covers.

CARING FOR SEEDLINGS

The minute small shoots begin elbowing their way through the soil's surface, remove any covers and set the containers in the brightest spot you have. South-facing windowsills catch the most sun, but seedlings set on windowsills rarely receive enough light for sturdy growth. Furthermore, a southern exposure can become too warm during the day and too cold during the night. A better arrangement is to set seedlings under artificial lights—a combination of ordinary "cool white" and "warm white" fluorescent bulbs—keeping the lights between 2 and 4 inches above the seedlings. The inexpensive industrial fixtures available from hardware stores work fine; suspended by chains, they can be raised as the seedlings grow. Keep the lights on between 14 and 16 hours a day—an inexpensive timer will turn them on and off for you. If necessary, turn or move seedling containers to keep plants growing straight.

Strong light is essential to producing stocky, vigorous transplants—too little light, and plants will become tall and spindly—but temperature, moisture, ventilation, and nutrition are important too.

TEMPERATURE

Although they are young, tender, and vulnerable, seedlings don't require the heat that was needed for

---

WHO'S WHAT IN ADDITIVES

Here's a guide to common ingredients found in seed-starting mixes.

Blood Meal. A powder made from dried blood, a good source of nitrogen.

Bonemeal. A powder made from ground bones, a good source of phosphorus.

Greensand. Powdered rock mined from the ocean floor (also known as glauconite), a good source of both potassium and trace elements.

Kelp Meal. The ground form of kelp, a sea plant rich in potassium and trace elements.

Perlite. Volcanic rock that has been heated until its granules explode; it attracts but does not absorb moisture.

Vermiculite. A form of the mineral mica that has been heated until its granules explode, vermiculite is able to retain large amounts of moisture.

PEATS

Black Peat. Also called peat humus, Michigan peat, and *terre noire*. Black peat is made of decomposed plants (mostly sedges) and looks like moist, rich topsoil. It is sold packaged and in bulk.

Sedge Peat. Also called reed-sedge peat. Less decomposed than black peat, reddish brown sedge peat can absorb more water and is slightly acid. It is sold packaged and in bulk.

Sphagnum Moss. Also called floral peat and floral moss. This is undecomposed moss (either hypnum or sphagnum), which is harvested by hand from the tops of bogs and sold in small quantities. It is sold packaged, either milled and unmilled.

Sphagnum Peat. Also called peat, brown peat, standard peat, peat moss, sphagnum peat moss. Partially decomposed, dried sphagnum moss was produced in bogs over many, many centuries; it contains no nutrients, can absorb 15 times its weight in water, and is highly acidic. It is sold packaged, either milled or unmilled.

germination. Most do best in conditions that correspond with their preferences as mature plants. Seedlings of cabbage, leek, and other cold-tolerant crops develop most successfully in cool temperatures, between 50° and 65°F during the day. Seedlings of heat-loving vegetables and herbs, such as eggplant and melon, prefer daytime temperatures between 65° and 75°F. Nighttime temperatures should fall no more than 10 degrees below daytime temperatures. Never let the mercury slide below 40°F, day or night, but if you're going to err, err on the cool side.

MOISTURE

Seedlings need constant moisture, but don't allow soil to become soggy. Water regularly, gently, and thoroughly using warm, but not hot, water, either from the bottom or the top. After 20 minutes, pour off any water that remains in the drainage trays. Wilting, the usual sign of too little moisture, also signals too much water. Soilless mixes can look dry yet still contain plenty of moisture. Feel the soil to determine whether you need to water more or less.

Leaves and stems as well as roots need moisture: Most seedlings do best in 60 percent relative humidity. If your house is dry, mist your seedlings every other day. Some gardeners enclose seedlings in clear plastic (use square hoops made from coat hangers to support the plastic), but this often provides more humid conditions than plants want. If you do create a mini-greenhouse for your plants, watch carefully that they aren't staying too wet. (Closing the ends by loosely folding them over rather than gathering them tightly with a twist-tie is helpful.) Remember, too, that even miniature greenhouses can become overheated in a sunny location.

SEEDLING BASICS

To develop into sturdy garden transplants, seedlings need:

- 14 to 16 hours of strong light daily.

- Air temperatures between 55° and 80°F during the daytime, 10 degrees colder at night

- Moist but not waterlogged soil

- Good ventilation and uncrowded conditions

- Weekly feeding of half-strength compost tea or fish emulsion

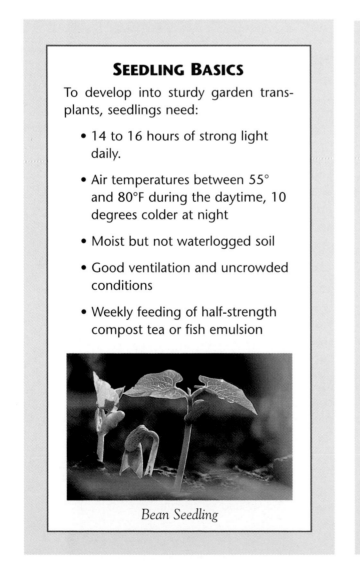

Bean Seedling

DAMPING-OFF

Wake up one morning and find your seedlings lying limp on the soil's surface? Your seedlings have been attacked by damping-off, a common soilborne fungal disease that thrives in high humidity and warm temperatures. There is no cure. All you can do is discard the seedlings and soil, sterilize your containers, and begin again, observing the following guidelines:

- Disinfect containers before filling them with soil.

- Use a soilless seed-starting medium that drains well.

- Cover seeds with a thin layer of milled sphagnum moss, a natural fungicide.

- Give seedlings good ventilation, cool temperatures, and plenty of light.

- Water from below, and do not overwater.

VENTILATION

Whether they prefer warm or cool temperatures, all seedlings need fresh air. Poor ventilation is an open invitation to damping-off and other diseases. Don't set young plants in a draft, but make sure that air is moving freely around them.

Crowding also hinders good air circulation. When the leaves of one seedling bump into a neighbor's, it's time to thin or to transplant. If you thin, don't pull out the discards; instead, use a pair of small scissors to snip off weak or misshapen plants at the soil line, which will avoid disturbing the roots of the seedlings you're keeping.

NUTRITION

A seedling's first true leaves (or $1\frac{1}{2}$ inches of growth in grasslike crops like onions and leeks) signify that the food stored in the seed has been used up. If you used a sterile mix to start seeds, you'll need to feed your indoor farm with a half-strength solution of fish emulsion, compost tea, or other liquid organic fertilizer once a week. (See "Tea Time," right, for directions for making compost and manure tea.) Seedlings growing in a medium containing added nutrients, soil, or compost may have enough available nourishment to hold them until they go into the garden. If their indoor stay is a long one, or if their leaves show tinges of yellow, red, purple, bronze, or brown—signs of undernourishment— water them every 10 days with a half-strength liquid fertilizer. Watch the seedlings carefully. If their leaves begin to curl under, you're overfeeding.

In their first week or two, seedlings don't want much elbow- or footroom, but soon after that, most vegetable and herb plants need larger quarters, above ground and below. Moving a plant to a bigger container—called potting on—stimulates root growth. Plants that grow extremely quickly may have to be potted on more than once.

POTTING ON

Once two sets of true leaves appear, it's probably time to pot on. Potting on also gives you a chance to examine each plant closely—to check its progress and inspect it for problems. Don't be soft-hearted: If a seedling is sickly, toss it out.

Before you move a seedling, fill the new contain-

ers with a moistened soil- or compost-based growing medium that contains the nutrients young plants need to thrive. You can purchase a commercial potting soil that contains fertilizer, or make your own— see "Seedling Mixes" on page 118 for recipes. Either pre-moisten the medium before filling the containers, or water the seedlings thoroughly before moving them. A too-dry medium can damage tender seedling roots. Fill containers to overflowing, then scrape off the excess, and tap them on a hard surface to settle the mix.

TEA TIME

Compost and manure teas are easy-to-make, inexpensive liquid plant fertilizers, and some evidence suggests that they can also help suppress plant diseases. When feeding seedlings, dilute tea to half strength.

To make compost or manure tea:

1. Fill a bucket one-third full of finished compost or well-rotted manure.

2. Add water until the bucket is full.

3. Let mixture steep for 3 or 4 days.

4. Strain the mixture through cheesecloth or a pair of old pantyhose. Add remaining solids to the compost pile or garden.

5. Before using either compost or manure tea, dilute the remaining liquid until it is the color of weak tea.

6. To each gallon of compost or manure tea that is to be used as a foliar feed, add 1/8 teaspoon liquid dish soap or vegetable oil to help it adhere.

Apply compost or manure teas in the morning or on cloudy days.

Take special care when uprooting, or pricking, your seedlings. It's very easy to damage stems and roots at this stage. At worst, it will kill the seedling; at best, it will slow down the seedling's rate of growth. Before transplanting, allow the soil to dry out *slightly*. If the seedlings are growing singly, they are easily removed—simply upend the container, and tap it gently on a hard surface. Seedlings begun in undivided flats should be dug, not pulled. Use a knife to prick them out, holding the plant by its leaves rather than the stem. Or turn the container upside down and catch the root mass as it drops out. Then gently tap it on a hard surface, which will break up the soil and help separate the seedlings. If the plants' roots are hopelessly entangled, use a knife to block the flat: Slice length- and crosswise, as if you were cutting a pan of brownies, then lift the plants block by block.

To successfully transfer seedlings to their new home, use the guidelines that follow.

SEEDLING MIXES

To make a mix for seedlings that need to be moved into larger pots, mix the following ingredients together in a 6-gallon bucket. The recipes below make 5 gallons of mix.

8 quarts compost or potting soil
6 quarts sphagnum peat
6 quarts vermiculite
1/4 cup bonemeal
1/4 cup kelp meal
1/8 cup blood meal.

If you prefer to use a peatless potting mix, combine the following ingredients, also in a 6-gallon bucket.

10 quarts compost
4 quarts potting or garden soil
3 quarts coarse sand
3 quarts vermiculite
1/3 cup kelp meal or greensand
1/3 cup blood meal
1/3 cup bonemeal

Make Room for Roots. Use a pencil or plant label to make a hole in the mix large and deep enough for the transplant's roots—or for the soil block. Don't coil the roots around to fit them into the hole; either make a bigger hole, or start with a larger container. Set the plant slightly deeper than it was growing before. Add additional soil, if necessary, and firm *gently*. Water thoroughly.

Ease the Transition. Set containers in a shady spot for 48 hours to allow seedlings to recover from the stress of transplanting. Then return them to a sunny or lighted location.

Feed. Feed the seedlings every 10 days with a one-third strength compost tea, fish emulsion, or other liquid organic fertilizer until it's time to move plants outdoors.

Water Regularly. Keep the soil evenly moist, but do not allow it to become soggy. Mist plants every other day. If you have had problems with damping-off in the past, watering from below by filling flats with water and pouring off the excess after about 20 minutes is a good idea.

Monitor Temperatures. Keep air temperatures on the cool side, between 60° and 70°F.

TRANSPLANTING SEEDLINGS

Before transplants—either those you've grown or those you've purchased—can go into the garden, they must be prepared for the "real world," a process known as hardening off. By prolonging the trip to the garden, you can reduce the shock of their encountering direct sunlight, cold soil and air, strong winds, and rain. A week before the transplant date, stop fertilizing and cut back on watering. Then set your transplants outside during the afternoon in a sheltered, partially shaded spot for a couple of hours. (Start this process on a weekend if you are away from home during the week.) Gradually increase their stay outside until their move to the garden will be a gentle awakening rather than a rude one. (Alternatively, move your plants to a cold frame, opening its sash a bit farther each day, then shutting it at night. Shade the cold frame with lath or other material the first few days if the weather is sunny.)

TRANSPLANTING BASICS

When your seedlings are hardened off and your garden has warmed to hospitable levels for the crops you're transplanting—2 weeks before the average

TRANSPLANT BASICS. *Before moving seedlings to the garden, harden off plants to let them become accustomed to outdoor conditions. For plants sensitive to cold temperatures, it's a good idea to warm the soil with clear plastic before transplanting.*

frost-free date for cabbages, 2 weeks after the average frost-free date for basil—it's time for the permanent move outdoors. Transplanting is a shocking process for even hardened-off seedlings, and transplant shock can set plants back for days, weeks, or the entire season. To ease their transition into the garden, follow the guidelines below.

Look for Overcast Weather. To protect transplants from hot sun during their move into the garden, pick an overcast day to make the transfer. Misty rain is perfect transplanting weather, and a spell of 2 or 3 days of cloudy weather is ideal. If cloudy weather isn't in the forecast, transplant in late afternoon or evening.

Feed First. Rather than adding fertilizer to the planting hole, soak your transplants in a weak solution of liquid organic fertilizer for 30 minutes before transplanting.

Make Room for Roots. Dig a planting hole that is a little larger than the root ball of the seedling you are transplanting. (See "Speedy Spacing Tip" on page 120 for instructions on making a planting board, which makes it easy to space plants evenly.) You'll want to set transplants slightly deeper than they were growing before (crops, such as tomatoes and broccoli, that send out roots from their stems should be set more deeply than lettuces and other plants that don't root along their stems). Remove transplants from their containers, retaining as much soil around the roots as possible.

Dealing With Root-Bound Plants. If the plant is root-bound—its roots have begun to grow around the bottom and sides of its container—untangle and

---

TROUBLESHOOTING TRANSPLANTS

You want healthy transplants to set in the garden. Watch your plants for these symptoms, then take corrective action.

Symptom: Tall, Spindly Growth
Cause: Too little light, too much water and/or heat.
Solution: Increase light; reduce watering; reduce nighttime temperature; improve ventilation.

Symptom: Poor Growth
Cause: Inadequate fertility.
Solution: Apply liquid fertilizer (at same strength) more often.

Symptom: Poor Root Growth
Cause: Inadequate soil aeration and drainage.
Solution: Repot in lighter soil.

Symptom: Discolored Foliage
Cause: Low fertility.
Solution: Yellow leaves—increase nitrogen; purple leaves—increase phosphorus.

spread the roots before planting, or gently knead the root ball, which stimulates new growth.

Dealing with Peat Pots. If you've used peat pots, tear away any portion of pot that extends above the soil line, and make slits down the sides of the pot so that the roots can grow out.

Settle the Plants in the Soil. Firm the soil around the plant, making sure you've completely covered the root ball. Then water gently with a half-strength liquid fertilizer.

Protect New Transplants. For the first week, give transplants a little protection from sun and wind—use a wood shingle or a square of heavy cardboard propped above them, or use floating row covers or a cloche of some kind. In extremely hot, windy conditions, spray plants with a commercial antitranspirant, which reduces water loss through the leaves and stem, 2 hours before setting them in the garden.

Install Supports at Planting Time. Install any support that the plant will need when it grows taller. This minimizes damage to the roots. (See "Plant Support Systems" on page 80 for options.)

SPEEDY SPACING TIP

A planting board is indispensable for quick, easy, even spacing of transplants and seeds. It's simple to make one from a 4-foot piece of 1-by-4 pine. Cut two sets of notches on the same side of the board:

- Cut 3-inch-deep notches every 12 inches
- Cut 1½-inch-deep notches every 6 inches

To use the board, lay it down in the bed or row and use the notches to guide transplant spacing. For crops that require 6-inch spacing, plant a seedling at every 1½-inch-deep notch, for example. For large crops like tomatoes, use the ends of the board to space plants 4 feet apart.

SOWING SEEDS OUTDOORS

Beginning crops indoors gives gardeners a head start, but seeding directly in the garden is far less work. For many edibles, especially those, like beans and peas, that don't dilly-dally to maturity, there's little to be gained by growing transplants. And if you are succession planting, you may grow transplants of a crop to get an early start on the season, followed by one or more sowings outdoors for later harvest. Once again, the best advice is not to begin too soon. Peas, radishes, dill, and other cold-tolerant vegetables and herbs can be sown once the soil reaches a stable temperature of 45°F. Wait until the soil is 65°F for most other crops, and hold off for a reading of 70°F before you seed the real heat-lovers, such as eggplants, okra, pumpkins, and all melons.

Once the garden plot is prepared—rows measured off, beds made—double-check that the soil is friable, or easily crumbled, to a depth of at least 10 inches. Now give it a final raking to break up any remaining clods and remove stray stones. Tender new roots and shoots have an astonishing ability to penetrate even hardpan, but there's no sense making their job harder. Fine, loose soil is particularly important to carrots, radishes, and other root crops, which will be stunted, misshapen, or damaged if grown in compacted or rocky ground.

If you're planting in rows, the quickest method is to mark the row using string tied between two stakes; next, make a furrow, a narrow, shallow trench, with a hoe. Mechanical seeders, which do save time and energy, are available, but they aren't practical in small gardens. Plant by hand, following the conventional wisdom to set seeds two or three times as deep as their diameter. If the soil is heavy, sow more shallowly; in light, sandy soil that drains quickly, plant slightly deeper. In early spring, when the soil is still cool and wet, sow less deeply. For plantings sown later in the season when the ground has warmed, cover seeds a little more deeply so that they don't dry out.

Not every seed is going to germinate. Try to space the seeds evenly—you may want to use a planting board or mix tiny seeds with sand (1 part seed to 3 parts sand)—but sow more thickly than you'll want once they sprout. Thinning takes less time than reseeding. Use a rake or hoe to pull the right amount of soil over the seeds—or cover them with a soilless growing mix—and firm gently to

SEED-SOWING OPTIONS. *Many crops can be started indoors or out, and the method that's best depends on a variety of factors. For an early start on the season, grow transplants of cool-season crops like cabbage and broccoli indoors. Direct-sowing outdoors, which is less work, is the best method for fast-growing crops, such as peas and beans.*

ensure contact between the seeds and the soil. If you've used a soilless mix to cover the seeds or if the soil is extremely dry, water gently; a watering can with a sprinkling rose attached is ideal for this. Otherwise, there's no need to water. Last, label and date each row. A seed packet stuck over a stake is a garden icon, but packets fade in the sun and blow away in the wind. Instead, use an indelible pen and a wooden or plastic marker. (A pencil on a plastic marker works as well.) And don't forget to record in your garden journal what you've planted and where you've planted it.

Seeds don't have to be plunked down, one by one, in rows or hills. They can be scattered evenly, or broadcast, over a well-prepared, moistened bed or wide row. Take care to make the bed as weed-free as possible; since the seeds fall randomly, there's no

telltale row to make it easier to distinguish the first leaves of ragweed from those of 'Salad Bowl' lettuce or 'Spadona' chicory. The best candidates for broadcasting are green manures and salad greens, especially mesclun mixes. (Mesclun is a salad of mixed greens—herbs and leaf vegetables—which are cut when they are only a few inches tall.) After you've broadcast the seeds, go over the bed gently with the back side of a garden rake. Once the seeds are covered, water the area to firm the soil.

Now take a minute to stand back, catch your breath, and admire your work. Those newly sown seeds still need to be kept moist, and they'll undoubtedly need thinning. There also will be other crops to plant and other problems to solve. But the garden season—the real season, the one outdoors—has begun.

THE BIG PAYOFF. *In summer, all the planning and preparation come to a head. Plants need to be fertilized, weeds pulled, and the main harvest begins to ripen. This harvest of rare winter squash won't be ready until fall.*

CHAPTER SEVEN

CARING FOR THE GARDEN

*Any garden demands as much of its maker
as he has to give. But I do not need to tell you,
if you are a gardener, that no other undertaking
will give as great a return for the
amount of effort put into it.*

ELIZABETH LAWRENCE, *GARDENING FOR LOVE*, 1987

EACH GARDENER IS DIFFERENT. FOR SOME, THE MOST PLEASURE IS IN THE START: sifting through seed catalogs, charting out next year's beds, turning the soil, and planting seeds. For others, it is the finish: pulling beets and carrots, digging potatoes, picking baskets full of plump tomatoes and carrying them into the kitchen, where they will be turned into salads, soups, sauces, salsas, and more. Yet for many—a fact that amazes novices—it is tending the vegetables and herbs that

123

brings the most satisfaction. Not the anticipation, not the culmination, but the work that must be done between the start and the finish. For them, *garden* is a verb first, a noun second.

Wherever you find most joy in the gardening journey, a plot filled with edible plants need not consume every daylight hour. Don't feel you must maintain a blemish-free garden, something precise and sterile like an outdoor operating room. A few weeds won't overwhelm the peas; a slug or two won't devastate the cabbages; not every sweet pepper will succumb to blossom-end rot. "On paper," Eleanor Perényi writes in *Green Thoughts* (1981), gardening "sounds overwhelming—but that is the nature of written directions. The reality is not so onerous."

If you prepared the soil well before planting, if you chose cultivars that are a good match for your region and that have disease tolerance or resistance, you've already reduced the amount of work that a garden can demand. Yet it would be misleading to suggest that growing vegetables and herbs requires neither time nor labor. The care-free garden is an invention of publishers trying to sell books and magazines. And it's a good thing that it is—if gardens didn't require looking after, gardeners would miss half the fun.

The ground is dug, the seeds are sown, the transplants set out. What now?

A sensible approach to caring for the garden begins with inspection tours. Walk among your vegetables and herbs, bend down and take a close look

SIGNS OF NUTRIENT DEFICIENCIES

Undernourished plants don't just look unhealthy, they're also more susceptible to attack by insect pests and diseases. In addition, they tend to grow slowly and yield less produce. As they continue to develop, the lack of one or more of the major elements that plants must have may become evident.

Here are some symptoms to look for:

Too little nitrogen can cause:
- Small leaves
- Pale, yellowing foliage
- Stunted or spindly growth
- Small fruits

Too little phosphorus can cause:
- Reddish purple foliage, especially on leaf undersides
- Reddish purple stems and leaf veins
- Small, dark foliage
- Leaf bronzing and mottling
- Thin stems
- Lush foliage but few flowers and fruits

Too little potassium can cause:
- Gray-green leaves
- Brown leaf edges, curling scorched leaves

- Overall lack of vigor
- Weak stems
- Small, misshapen fruits

Nitrogen, phosphorus and potassium aren't the only nutrients plants need. They also require fair doses of sulfur, magnesium, and calcium, as well as small amounts of seven micronutrients (boron, chloride, copper, iron, manganese, molybdenum, zinc). Interestingly, deficiencies in nitrogen, phosphorus, and potassium, plus magnesium and zinc, tend to show themselves in old foliage located near the base of plants. Deficiencies in the remaining elements are more likely to appear in new growth on the upper half of plants.

Exact diagnoses are difficult. Too little magnesium can produce interveinal chlorosis—yellow leaves with green veins—but so can deficiencies in zinc, iron, manganese, and molybdenum. Rather than overworry about exact causes and remedies, begin with a general-purpose fertilizer. If it doesn't give your plants the lift they need, seek advice about more specific remedies from experienced gardeners in your neighborhood or from the local Cooperative Extension Service.

at their stems and leaves and at the ground in which they grow. Watch for plants that show signs of stress: wilting, yellowing leaves, leaf drop, an overall failure to thrive. Look for insects and insect damage. Turn over leaves and check their undersides. Do you see fine webs stretching between stems or mottling on leaves? (See Chapter 8, "Coping with Garden Problems," for specific disease and pest problems and solutions.) Check the condition of the soil. Do seedlings need watering? Has it become packed and hard? Is there a spot that is always soppy wet? Are your crops spaced correctly, or should they be thinned? Spacing guidelines are listed on seed packets (or check the specific Plant Portraits in Part Two of this book). Daily visits to the garden give you the best chance to catch troubles before they become catastrophes. As the saying goes, "Little children, little problems. Big children, big problems." The same is true for plants.

FERTILIZING

If you prepared the soil well—made sure it was rich in organic matter and had a slightly acid pH level—your crops should flourish without additional fertilizer. Don't give extra food to plants that show no signs of needing it. Too much is as bad as too little. Overfertilized vegetables tend to set fewer fruits, not more. Too much nitrogen is especially nonproductive. It encourages vegetative growth at the expense of flowers and fruits, and the succulent stems and leaves it causes are magnets for sucking insects, such as leafhoppers and aphids. (See "Signs of Nutrient Deficiencies," left, for clues that your crops may need feeding.)

FERTILIZING OPTIONS

If symptoms indicate that your plants need fertilizing, you can feed them by spreading a solid or liquid fertilizer on the soil or by spraying a liquid fertilizer directly on the plants. Solid plant foods, such as compost, dried manures, bonemeal, and rock phosphate, break down slowly. They are nourishment for the underground microorganisms. Solid fertilizers won't provide *immediate* aid to plants, but they are the greatest help over time. To apply a solid fertilizer, use a process called side-dressing. Begin by pulling back any mulch. Then spread the fertilizer in a band alongside or around plants (don't let it touch plant stems or leaves); use a rake or tined hoe

SUDDENLY SUMMER. *Even before the last transplants are in the ground, summertime chores begin. Keep on top of weeds, pest problems, and other plant-care chores by making regular garden inspections.*

to work it into the top 2 inches of soil, and replace the mulch. One side-dressing in midseason should be plenty unless your soil is in really poor shape.

Liquid fertilizers applied to the soil or sprayed on the plant itself provide quicker results. Spraying the soil gives more lasting help; foliar feeding is a lickety-split remedy, the garden version of intravenous feeding. Both compost tea and fish emulsion, which is available as a liquid or a powdered concentrate, are good balanced foods. (See "Tea Time" on page 117 for directions on making compost tea.) Another is kelp, or seaweed, emulsion, which is rich in micronutrients and also contains growth regulators—chemical compounds that stimulate healthy, balanced plant growth. Experts recommend a 50–50 mixture of fish and kelp emulsions as the most effective organic foliar food (follow package directions for diluting). Unless your soil is extremely poor, however, don't overdo things. Apply liquid fertilizers to the soil bimonthly. Spray plants with a foliar food every 10 days. When the symptoms begin to disappear, cut back on feeding. If your plants are thriving, stop altogether.

Many backyard growers, especially those who use every inch of their plots by intercropping and succession planting—an approach called intensive gardening—like to provide an extra meal for plants, even though they don't show any signs of distress. Spraying transplants with foliar fertilizer immediately after setting them out and again in 3 weeks is one common practice. For leaf crops, a foliar feeding every 3 weeks should be plenty in even the most intensively planted gardens. Feed fruit-bearing plants every 4 weeks, or at the times when they most need a nutritional pick-me-up: when they flower, when they set fruit, and when their fruits begin to ripen.

The most likely candidates for fertilizer boosts are crops designated as heavy feeders: artichokes, asparagus, beets, corn, eggplant, rhubarb, and tomatoes, plus vining plants (cucumbers, melons), cabbage and its kin (broccoli, Brussels sprouts, cauliflower), and most leaf vegetables (chard, celery, kale, lettuce, spinach). Herbs are the exception. They do best in average, even thin, soil, so resist the temptation to give them extra fertilizer.

WATERING

Hot summer weather is known as the dog days, but anyone who has read Richardson Wright's description of leaning over a sty fence with a hose and sprinkling his porkers on August afternoons will forever think of them as the pig days. "Their delight and mine," he records in *The Gardener's Bed-Book* (1919), "is enormous." Most gardeners have taken equal delight in aimlessly spraying their vegetables and herbs on still summer evenings, dragging a hose from one bed to another, a slosh here, a swash there. The growing understanding that the world's water needs are outdistancing its water supply has already put an end to this wonderful but wasteful amusement in some regions. Xeriscaping (from the Greek *xeros*, meaning "dry") has entered the gardening vocabulary. Like topsoil, water is something to be conserved, not squandered. In conserving it, there are interesting horticultural lessons to be learned—or recalled.

For instance, clay soils retain water better than

TO SPRAY OR NOT TO SPRAY

Use caution when applying a foliar fertilizer—too much can damage plants. Some crops, including beets, chard, leeks, lettuce, onions, peppers, and spinach, are especially sensitive. Be sure foliar sprays are well diluted, and do not apply them at midday.

sandy ones do, and soils rich in humus retain water better than do those that are not. One estimate is that a 5 percent increase in organic matter quadruples soil's water-holding capacity. Good soil structure, which comes from adding organic matter, encourages large, healthy root systems, the best hedge that plants have against drought. Organic mulches conserve moisture by reducing evaporation. They lower and stabilize soil temperature, reduce compaction, and discourage water-loving weeds; and when mulches break down, they improve the soil's tilth. Plastic mulches also retain moisture.

Water-consciousness calls for maintaining soil pH in the 6.0 to 7.0 range so that nutrients are available to plants, and for being careful not to overfeed plants, especially with high-nitrogen fertilizers that promote excessive vegetative growth. Less growth requires less water. Water-consciousness means harvesting vegetables and herbs the minute they are ripe and removing plants once they have finished bearing. It prescribes more protection from sun and wind—nature's great water thieves—as well as planting drought-tolerant cultivars, particularly open-pollinated heirlooms and strains that typically clamor for less water than hybrids do.

WATERING GUIDELINES

In general, though, plants are a thirsty crowd, losing water—by transpiration through their leaves—even faster than do the gardeners who sweat over them. Plant cells are mostly water—80 percent by weight on average—so moisture is crucial to growing vegetables and herbs successfully. It helps plants obtain nutrients and is indispensable to many biochemical reactions, including photosynthesis. Among edibles, asparagus, artichokes, and celery are water gluttons; tomatoes, beets, and peppers are members of the large group of edibles that make more moderate demands; tepary beans, garlic, sorrel, and many herbs are downright camel-like. Most fruit-bearing plants need more water during flowering and fruit formation than they do early or late in their development; leaf crops need a constant supply of moisture throughout the growing season. (See "What's Thirsty When?" right, for information on when a constant supply of watering is most important.)

The rule of thumb for vegetables is 1 inch of water per week, plus another ½ inch for every 10 degrees above 60°F. Using this formula, 'Honey 'N Pearl' corn wants 2 inches of water during a rainless

WHAT'S THIRSTY WHEN?

Even when there's no drought, you need to pay attention to your garden's water needs. Conditions such as black spots on the bottoms of tomatoes and peppers, split cabbage heads, and tiny cauliflowers are all caused by poor watering practices.

A vegetable garden needs an inch of rain a week, or about 62 gallons of water per 100 square feet. Use a rain gauge to measure the water that falls on your garden. (Try to measure rainfall right after it stops raining; otherwise, some of the water will evaporate, and the reading will be inaccurate.) Don't bother watering if you measure an inch of rain in any week. If $1/2$ inch falls, use half as much water as the table below indicates; if $1/4$ inch falls, use $3/4$ as much, and so on.

Crop	When Water Is Most Important	Water Quantity Per Week

Bean:
    Dried
    Lima
    Snap
	Pollination, pod set, pod growth	$3/4$ gal./ft. of row
		1 gal./ft. of row
		1 gal./ft. of row

Beet	Throughout growing season	$3/4$ to 1 gal/ft. of row
Broccoli Cauliflower	Early in season to prevent "buttoning," or tiny heads; also during head development	1 gal./plant
Cabbage	Head development; after heads develop, too much water will cause heads to split	$1/2$ gal./plant; less after heads develop
Carrot	Throughout growing season	$3/4$ gal./ft. row
Cucumber	Flowering and fruit growth	$1\frac{1}{2}$ gal./plant
Eggplant	Flowering through harvest	$1\frac{1}{2}$ gal./plant
Greens, including Swiss chard	Throughout growing season	1 gal./ft. of row
Herbs	Best flavor with less water; water whenever plants look ready to wilt	$1\frac{1}{2}$ gal./plant

Lettuce:
    Head
    Leaf
	Head development
	Throughout growing season
		$3/4$ gal./ft. of row
		$3/4$ gal./ft. of row

Melon	Flowering and fruit growth	$1\frac{1}{2}$ gal./plant
Onion	Bulb growth; stop watering when tops fall over	1 gal./ft. of row
Peas	Flowering and pod set	1 gal./ft. of row
Pepper	Flowering through harvest	1 pint/plant for young plants; increase to $1\frac{1}{2}$ gal./plant
Radish	Throughout growing period	$3/4$ gal./ft. of row
Squash, summer and winter	Bud development and flowering	$1\frac{1}{2}$ gal./plant
Tomato	Flowering through harvest; an *even* supply of water is best	$2\frac{1}{2}$ gal./plant; more for unmulched, staked plants
Turnip	Root development	$3/4$ gal./ft. of row

Adapted from Penn State Urban Gardening Program, "Water and Your Food Garden"

week of 80°F temperatures. To add that amount to a 1,000-square-foot patch, you'd have to water with a hose that delivers 5 gallons a minute for a little more than 4 hours, or 1 hour four times a week. (See "Water Math," below, for information on calculating how much water to apply to your garden—and how long it will take to apply it.).

Like fertilizer, too much water is as damaging as too little. An overabundance drowns plant roots and washes away nutrients; drought ties up nutrients in the soil and stresses plants, leaving them vulnerable to disease. The general goal is to maintain evenly moist soil. Spotty watering can produce physiological disorders, such as tip burn, blossom-end rot, growth cracks, and sunscald.

In many regions, Mother Nature pretty much supplies all the moisture that plants require, but other sections of the country are less fortunate. The mean rainfall for the mountain states in July is 1.99 inches and 1.43 inches in August. In conditions like these, supplying water becomes the gardener's job. While there is disagreement on how best to water— several moderate waterings each week or one heavy

WATER FOR TASTE. *Many crops, including lettuce, require an even source of moisture for best flavor. 'Lily's' and 'Lollo Rossa' lettuce are planted here with golden and red orach.*

one—there is consensus that superficial sprinkling is of little value. Pleasant for pigs, poor for plants.

Purchase a rain gauge if you don't have one, and keep track of rainfall. Watch plant foliage—wilting is the obvious sign of too little moisture, although some crops will wilt temporarily in brilliant sunshine even though the soil is not completely dry. Another way to measure your garden's moisture is to pull back any mulch, dig down 4 to 5 inches, grab a handful of soil, and squeeze it. If the soil holds together, it has enough moisture; if it doesn't form a ball, you need to water. (Extremely sandy soil won't form a ball but will feel gritty when moist; if its particles are loose enough to flow through your fingers, it's too dry.)

EFFICIENT IRRIGATION

Watering isn't a new horticultural problem. "It behooveth to have a Well or Pump in a garden," Thomas Hill advised in 1577. Hill carried his water in a big-bellied copper pot, but he also wrote about irrigators and gardener-powered sprinklers, which he called "great Squirts." Today's great squirts, oscillating sprinklers, are in danger of going the way of big-bellied copper pots. Compulsory in xerigardens are drip-irrigation systems, mazes of PVC lines equipped with emitters, connectors, pressure regulators, filters, injectors, fittings, even computerized timers. These systems—which aren't inexpensive but can cut water use in half—seep rather than flood and can be designed to deliver water to individual plants, not to the spaces between plants.

WATER MATH

The formula for calculating the number of gallons that equal 1 inch of water to a given area is a simple one. Multiply the square footage of the plot by .083 ($\frac{1}{12}$ of 1 foot), then multiply that product by 7.5 (the number of gallons in 1 cubic foot of water). For a 100-foot-square garden, 1 inch of water would equal a little more than 60 gallons: 100 x .083 x 7.5. If you water by hand with a hose that runs at 3 gallons a minute, it would take about 20 minutes to put down 1 inch of water, or about 5 minutes of watering four times a week.

To determine the water rate of your hose, time how long it takes to fill a standard 6-gallon bucket, then divide the number of minutes by 6 to find the gallon rate per minute.

MULCH BENEFITS. *A layer of organic mulch keeps down weeds, holds in soil moisture, and returns organic matter to the soil. Here, sawdust, which doesn't decompose quickly, is used to keep paths weed-free.*

Drip soakers, either hoses with holes punched in them or porous hoses that ooze water along their length, are less complicated and less costly alternatives to full-scale, permanent drip-irrigation systems. Cheapest of all is a water-filled gallon milk jug with small holes punched in its bottom set among plants that need moisture. In addition to saving water, drip irrigation keeps water off plant foliage, reducing water-related and soilborne diseases, and helps cool the soil. Studies prove that drip irrigation used in combination with plastic mulches increases the productivity of a variety of crops, including peppers, melons, eggplants, squash, and tomatoes.

While drip irrigation is preferable on nearly every score, you don't need to toss out your watering can, hoses, and sprinklers. Watering cans are unsurpassed for some jobs, such as foliar feeding, and belong in every gardener's toolshed. Hoses save trips to the faucet and, fitted with a nozzle, are useful for misting plants and spot watering; or attach a bubbler, lay the hose on the ground, and let the water flood the bed. Sprinklers are good for wetting plants, particularly leaf crops, in torrid weather, and for deep watering if left in place for an hour or more. Much water is lost to evaporation and runoff, though, and sprinklers target an area rather than an individual plant. (One advantage of the more accurate water delivery of drip systems is that you avoid watering weeds growing in paths and areas away from your crops. Sprinklers water these areas along with everything else.) If you use a sprinkler, run it in the morning to reduce evaporation. As you try to conserve water, remember that rainwater can be collected from roofs; graywater—water from laundry and baths—can be used on ornamental plants but is not recommended for edible crops.

MULCHING

Mulching with shredded leaves, straw, or other organic materials is one of the best things gardeners can do for their soil, their plants, and themselves. It not only adds organic matter to the soil but also improves its structure and fertility, reduces soil compaction, conserves soil moisture, and reduces or eliminates the need to cultivate in the process. By improving soil conditions, it encourages root development. A layer of mulch also suppresses weeds, reduces erosion and nutrient leaching, cools and/or warms the soil, and stabilizes its temperature. Additionally, mulch protects biennial and perennial vegetables and herbs from "heaving" in winter, keeps produce clean, and reduces splash and thus the spread of diseases. No wonder mulch is referred to as the gardener's good friend.

If all that weren't a big enough dividend for 30 minutes spent spreading a couple of inches of shredded leaves, compost, or cocoa hulls after the soil warms in spring, organic mulches also can help control soil pH. Heavy use of pine needles, for example, will lower the pH over time; most composts, in contrast, are slightly alkaline and can help to sweeten soil. Mulching saline soil after it has been irrigated to leach out salts will help keep it moist—and fit for growing vegetables and herbs.

While organic mulches contain varying amounts of the major and minor nutrients that are necessary for maintaining healthy soil and growing healthy plants, mulching once a year won't provide all the nutrients your garden needs. Additionally, mulches that have a high carbon-to-nitrogen ratio—typically matter that is brown and dry, such as sawdust, straw, and pine needles—"rob" nitrogen from plants. In fact, the microorganisms working to break down the mulch do the robbing. (See "Compost Ingredients" on page 49 for more on carbon-nitrogen ratios.) If you are carpeting your garden exclusively with carbon-rich materials, spread a little chicken manure, blood meal, or other high-nitrogen fertilizer before you mulch, or mix some high-nitrogen matter, such as fresh grass clippings, with the mulch.

While no-till growers keep a deep layer of

mulch on their garden beds all year long, most gardeners add new mulch in the spring, after the soil has warmed and seedlings are up and established. Be sure to lay down enough mulch to get all its benefits, but don't apply it so thickly that it smothers plants. Three to four inches should be enough of fine-textured mulches, such as sawdust or cocoa hulls. Straw and other loose materials need to be 6 to 8 inches thick to suppress weeds. If you mulch immediately after sowing seeds, apply a thin cover, then add to it once your plants emerge. As the mulch breaks down, add more.

GREAT COVER-UPS

Organic mulches not only conserve moisture and smother weeds but also improve and enrich the soil as they break down. Not all choices are available everywhere.

Bark, Shredded. Readily available; slow to decompose; high in carbon; good water penetration.

Buckwheat Hulls. Not available everywhere; slow to decompose; good water penetration; attractive; expensive.

Compost. Fairly quick to decompose; excellent source of nutrients; good soil conditioner; good water penetration; less good weed suppression; may contain weed seeds.

Cocoa Hulls. Regional availability; moderately slow to decompose; good source of nitrogen; may mat and develop mold; attractive but expensive; easy to handle.

Corncobs/Cornstalks. Regional availability; slow to decompose; should be chopped or ground.

Cottonseed Hulls. Regional availability; fairly rapid decomposition; good source of nutrients.

Grass Clippings. Widely available and inexpensive; quick to decompose; may contain weed seeds; dried clippings high in nitrogen; do not use clippings from lawns treated with herbicides. Also avoid fresh clippings, which can heat up enough to damage young plants.

Hay. Widely available; moderately quick to decompose; adds nitrogen to the soil; contains weed seeds; light color helps keep soil cool.

Leaves. Widely available and inexpensive; moderately quick decomposition; tend to mat unless chopped or shredded; excellent source of micronutrients; good soil conditioner.

Mushroom Compost. Regional availability; good source of nutrients and organic matter; can contain weed seeds. Make sure it hasn't been treated with pesticides.

Newsprint. Widely available; slow decomposition; good weed suppression; unattractive but inexpensive; poor water penetration; cover with other organic matter, such as shredded bark, to weigh down the pages and prevent blowing.

Peanut Hulls. Regionally available; quick to decompose.

Pine Needles/Pine Straw. Widely available; slow decomposition; does not mat; lowers soil pH; weed-free; good water penetration and weed suppression; flammable.

Salt Marsh Hay. Not widely available; slow to decompose; does not mat; weed-seed free.

Sawdust. Widely available; slow to decompose; fresh sawdust can rob soil of nitrogen and lower soil pH; age before using; good weed suppression.

Seaweed, or Kelp. Decomposes slowly; not widely available; excellent nutrient source; may have excessive sodium content.

Sphagnum Peat Moss. Slow decomposition; good soil conditioner; no nutrient value; tends to crust and repel water when dry; not a good choice for mulching.

Straw. Widely available; moderately slow to decompose; free of weed seeds; good soil conditioner; light color helps keep soil cool; flammable.

Wood Chips. Widely available; very slow to decompose; good weed suppression.

Heavy mulching isn't right for all gardens, especially those located in regions where it's soppy-wet or cool year-round. If those conditions sound familiar, wait until late spring or early summer to mulch—when the ground has dried out and warmed—then apply only a thin layer of cocoa hulls or compost, dark-colored mulches that will trap heat. Similarly, if slugs and snails have found their way into your garden, keep mulches pulled back from plants. If mollusks are epidemic, you may need to remove the mulch altogether.

OTHER MULCHING OPTIONS

There are two other mulch possibilities, living mulches and plastic mulches. Living mulches—undersowing crops with a hairy vetch or another green-manure crop—reduce weeds, may increase yields of some crops, and improve the soil when turned under. (See "Using Green Manures" on page 52 for more on cover crops.) On the downside, they are more trouble to establish and maintain than a layer of shredded leaves or grass clippings, and they give the garden an untidy, weedy look that you may not like. Plastic mulches can also be faulted on aesthetic grounds, plus they do nothing to improve the soil. However, they are unsurpassed for warming soil, maintaining soil moisture, suppressing weeds, and keeping fruits clean and safer from soil-borne diseases. (See "Soil-Warming Techniques" on page 101 for more on plastic mulches.)

WEEDING

If you mulch your crops, the time that must be spent on some other garden chores—weeding and cultivating are two—is greatly reduced. Weeds are vigorous and persistent competitors of the crops you want to encourage. Not only do weeds pilfer the water, light, and nutrients that vegetables and herbs need, but they are a haven for diseases and insect pests. Additionally, some weeds, quack grass is one, are allelopathic, which means they contain chemicals that harm garden crops. "Above all," John Evelyn directed his gardener in 1686, "be careful not to suffer weeds … to run up to seed; for they will in a moment infect the whole ground." Evelyn was dead right: A single dandelion flower can produce as many as 300 seeds, the blooms on one lamb's-quarters plant as many as 50,000.

For organic growers, who reject drenching their gardens with long-acting synthetic herbicides, there are still effective approaches to getting the upper hand with weeds. It helps to know what you're dealing with before you plot a control strategy. The local Cooperative Extension Service office can provide detailed information about the common weeds of your region, and before long, you'll be distinguishing purslane from pigweed with ease. The first step, though, is separating the annual weeds from the perennial ones.

Annual weeds, plants that must start anew from seed each year, are easier to wipe out than perennial species, plants like bindweed, which resprout

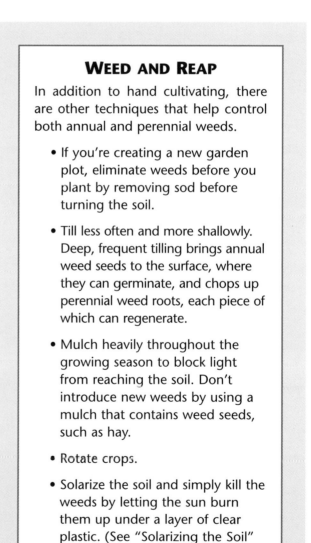

WEED AND REAP

In addition to hand cultivating, there are other techniques that help control both annual and perennial weeds.

- If you're creating a new garden plot, eliminate weeds before you plant by removing sod before turning the soil.

- Till less often and more shallowly. Deep, frequent tilling brings annual weed seeds to the surface, where they can germinate, and chops up perennial weed roots, each piece of which can regenerate.

- Mulch heavily throughout the growing season to block light from reaching the soil. Don't introduce new weeds by using a mulch that contains weed seeds, such as hay.

- Rotate crops.

- Solarize the soil and simply kill the weeds by letting the sun burn them up under a layer of clear plastic. (See "Solarizing the Soil" on page 151 for directions.)

- Cover the garden with black plastic, and leave it fallow for 1 year.

KEEPING WEEDS AT BAY. *Mulch is the first line of defense against weeds, which rob crops of sun, space to grow, and essential nutrients. Pull or cut down annual weeds before they set seed for next year's weed crop. For perennial weeds, regular chopping or hoeing is the best organic control.*

ALLELOPATHIC HELPERS

Many allelopathic plants, such as black-walnut trees, have an adverse effect on vegetables and herbs and should be kept far away from the garden. New studies have determined that other allelopathic species can be garden helpers. When used as mulch, the plants listed below are able to inhibit weeds chemically as well as smother them.

Barley	Red fescue
Cereal ryegrass	Sudan grass
Oats	Wheat

from a permanent root. Hand cultivation—either pulling or cutting them down at the soil surface with a hoe—will drastically reduce annual weeds. The key is never allowing an annual species to form seeds. Be diligent, and in three or four seasons, your garden will be close to free from annual weeds. At least one commercial herbicide is safe to use and effective against annual weeds. Called Sharpshooter, it is a soap-based desiccant, which kills plants by drying them out. The best approach is to spot-spray; if you apply Sharpshooter to an entire site, wait at least 2 weeks before planting it with edible crops.

Eliminating perennial weeds demands a different tack. Pulling is counterproductive for many perennials, because getting out all of their extensive root systems is next to impossible, and each bit of root that is left buried will sprout a new plant. The answer is persistent chopping down, cutting off the plant just below the soil surface. An oscillating hoe is ideal for this work, or use a common garden hoe. Eventually—and it may take a half-dozen efforts—the weed will die. (See "Weed and Reap" on page 131 for other options.) Annual or perennial, don't weed in late afternoon or evening if you can avoid it, or you may find what you thought you'd killed has rerooted by morning. If afternoon and evening are your only options for weeding, gather weeds in a basket, then leave it in the sun to do them in.

CULTIVATING

Gardeners who mulch heavily can pretty much cross "hoe garden" off their list of things to do. Soil remains friable under a protective blanket of organic matter. If you haven't mulched, you'll need to spend some time with a hoe not only to get the upper hand on weeds but to keep the soil surface from crusting, especially after heavy spring rains. Wait until the soil has dried out enough to work—cultivating saturated ground makes things worse, not better. Nothing beats a tined hoe for this job (if you're cultivating and weeding, use an oscillating

---

CULINARY CONTROL

Creating a weed-free garden is the goal of most gardeners, but you may want to leave a few edible weeds—or harvest rather than discard them. Each of the plants/weeds listed below are first-rate when added in small amounts to green salads.

Chickweed (*Stellaria media*)
Chicory (*Cichorium intybus*)
Clover (*Trifolium* spp.)
Dandelion (*Taraxacum officinale*)
Lamb's-quarters (*Chenopodium album*)
Mustard (*Brassica* spp.)
Peppergrass (*Lepidium* spp.)
Pigweed (*Amaranthus retroflexus*)
Purslane (*Portulaca oleracea*)
Shepherd's purse (*Capsella bursapastoris*)

---

hoe). The goal is to disturb only the top 1 or 2 inches of ground. Hoe deeper than 2 inches, and you can damage plant roots and bring deeply buried weed seeds to the surface, where the odds are excellent that they will germinate. Hoeing an unmulched garden exposes its soil to drying, so unless the soil is brick-hard and rain cannot penetrate it, don't over-cultivate in midsummer, especially in hot, arid regions.

THINNING & OTHER TASKS

As you walk around your garden, you'll see other tasks that need doing. Some crops, those like beets, carrots, and lettuces that are easily sown too closely, will need to be thinned, or even thinned for a second time. Pulling or cutting healthy plants seems a profligate act that is inconsistent with gardening, but thinning is like the produce you're growing: It's good for you. Crowding not only invites disease but guarantees spindly plants that give disappointing yields of pint-size produce. Root vegetables especially resent close quarters—leave these underground crops pressed together, and many will develop no edible root at all. If larger, healthier plants and better harvests aren't return enough, remember that you can eat the thinnings of many crops—lettuce and radishes are two. It's also worth trying to transplant some of the extra plants (give them shade and plenty of water for 48 hours after they're moved). But if thinning is still too painful, take the advice of the 19th-century American man-of-letters Charles Dudley Warner. Rather than do the thinning yourself, Warner advised, a gardener "should get his neighbor, who does not care for the plants, to do it."

Installing supports for crops that need a hand to stay vertical should have been done at the same time or shortly after you planted. (See "Plant Support Systems" on page 80 for trellising options.) If yours are in place, the job now is to keep up with new growth by directing, tying, weaving, or tucking—whatever is required. But if the plant has already crawled 5 feet across the garden, leave it there. Trying to hoist a half-grown indeterminate tomato like 'Sweet 100' or to corral 'Lemon', a rambling heirloom cucumber, is a fool's errand. You may get the plant off the ground, but you're likely to do more damage than good in the process. If plants are still small, however, go ahead and put a support in place, taking care to disturb their roots as little as possible.

There are still other midseason chores. Fruits that rest on the ground, even on mulched ground, can develop rot. Slipping a wooden shingle or other moisture barrier under a pumpkin or melon will help avoid this problem. In addition, crops such as potatoes should be hilled. Some crops—cauliflower, celery, endive, and leek are four—must be blanched, or whitened, by covering them to cut off direct light. (See "Turn Off the Light," below, for details.)

PLANNING FOR MIDSEASON PLANTING

Finally, midseason isn't the time for just maintaining a garden. If you're trying to get the most out of your space, it's also the time to plant. Some crops,

BUILT-IN SHADE. *In summer, cool-season plants benefit from the heat protection afternoon shade provides. For late-maturing spring crops and early fall crops, look for a site that will be shaded in the afternoon by vines or tall caged tomatoes.*

such as Brussels sprouts, are best when sown for a fall harvest. The trick with Brussels sprouts and other fall crops is to make sure you don't plant so late that the harvest will be lost to the cold. The formula for calculating planting dates is straightforward: Add the cultivar's days to maturity plus its days to germination plus its days to transplanting, if any. To that total, add two more numbers: 10, the "short-day" factor (crops take more time to mature in late summer and fall because of shorter days and cooler temperatures), and, for frost-tender plants only, 14 (which is included to give the crop at least 2 weeks of productivity before the average first frost).

If you wanted to plant a late crop of 'Decibel', a filet bean from France that takes 50 days to mature, the math would be: 50 (days to maturity) + 7 (days to germination) + 0 ('Decibel' is directed-seeded, not transplanted) + 10 (short-day factor) + 14 (days to first frost) = 81 days. To calculate the latest you should plant, count back 81 days from your average first-frost date. If yours is October 15, you can plant 'Decibel' as late as the third week of July. For 'Beefmaster' tomato, the numbers would be 80 + 7 + 21 + 10 + 14, for a total of 132 days. With an

TURN OFF THE LIGHT

In the kitchen, blanching means dunking vegetables in boiling water or steaming them briefly, then cooling them. In the garden, blanching is caused by preventing light from reaching the portion of the plant that you want whitened. By excluding light, the chlorophyll content that creates the green color is reduced. Blanching also alters flavor—typically making it milder—and reduces vitamin content. Some crops, cauliflower is one, are blanched by tying leaves around the flower head; leeks are blanched by covering them with soil. Other crops, such as asparagus, celery, and endive, are blanched by shading them with boards or other barriers.

October 15 average first-frost date, the latest you could start seeds of 'Beefmaster' would be about June 1.

For crops that tolerate light frosts, such as beets and peas, cut the days-to-first-frost number in half, from 14 to 7; for vegetables and herbs with even more cold resistance, such as cabbage and parsley, change the days-to-first-frost number to 0. (See "Some Like It Hot" on page 82.) The number for 'Ruby Queen', an AAS-winning beet, would be 77 (55 + 5 + 0 + 10 + 7); for 'Lasso', an open-pollinated red cabbage from Denmark, it would be 116 (75 + 6 + 25 + 10 + 0).

Don't forget that having enough days to reach maturity isn't the only consideration when planting in summer. Some cool-weather crops won't survive heat—hold off as long as you can before planting, sow a little deeper than you did in spring, water generously, mulch, and provide afternoon shade if their foliage wilts. (See the Plant Portraits in Part Two for recommended planting schedules.)

HARVESTING & STORING CROPS

The harvest is gardening's big payoff, the pot of gold at the end of the green rainbow. Harvesting seems easy on the surface—pick it when it's ripe. Or as a child might say, "Pick it when it's done." That's good advice for many crops, such as corn and tomatoes, but other vegetables should be handled differently. For the best flavor, most vegetative crops—plants grown for their leaves, stems, stalks, and roots—

HARVEST HELPERS. *Let children help with the harvest. Show them how to pick properly without damaging the plants, but don't worry too much about dropped or damaged produce. Remember, you're growing gardeners too.*

should be harvested when they are still young and tender. Fruit-bearing crops vary. While tomatoes should be left on the vine until they are fully ripe, beans, cucumbers, eggplants, and summer squash taste better if they are picked when slightly immature. Potatoes and peppers are examples of crops that are equally good—but different—whether harvested when immature or mature. Herbs can be harvested throughout the growing season but are their most flavorful just before their flowers open.

PLANTING FOR NEXT YEAR

Gardeners with mild winters are no strangers to planting in fall for harvests in the new year. In areas where it's harsh by Halloween, it's also possible to sow in autumn and reap in winter, spring, and summer, although the rate of success is lower. In the north, short days combined with cold temperatures slow, even stop, plant growth in late December and January.

Among the best candidates for fall planting are garlic and other members of the onion family; mustard-family crops, such as broccoli, cabbage, and cauliflower; hardy leaf crops, including endive, kale, lettuce, radicchio, and spinach; carrots and parsnips; and perennial herbs.

Time seeding so that you have at least a half-mature plant before daytime temperatures linger below freezing. If you've planted in a cold frame—the ideal arrangement—cover it with hay or straw, not only to give added protection from the cold but to block light and force plants into dormancy. If you've planted in the garden, mulch plants with 6 inches or more of straw or shredded leaves secured with a floating row cover. In early spring, when temperatures are in the high 30s, remove the mulch so that light can once again reach your plants.

HARVEST WEATHER

Weather can have an enormous effect on the quality of the vegetables and herbs you grow. For example, cold accentuates color in lettuce, red cabbage, leeks, and other crops, and sun can scald many vegetables, especially as they approach maturity.

Most produce is at its succulent best in the morning and should be harvested early in the day and cooled *immediately*. Leaving vegetables and herbs on the back porch for a few hours will undo all the advantages of harvesting at exactly the right moment. Other weather effects include:

Sun. Lack of sun reduces photosynthesis, reducing the sugar content of corn, tomatoes, and other vegetables and herbs.

Heat. Sunny, hot days make hot peppers like chilies hotter while making lettuce and other greens bolt and become bitter.

Cold. Brussels sprouts, kale, parsnips, and some other crops become sweeter if subjected to periods of frost. Cold nights and warm days produce more sugar in plants, increasing sweetness.

Drought. Drought can produce bitterness in some fruits, such as cucumbers; in contrast, many herbs are more flavorful in dry conditions, when oil concentrations are higher. Drought also reduces sweetness, because water is essential to photosynthesis, which manufactures sugars.

Water. Heavy rainfall during the final stages of development can dilute flavor or swell produce until they crack (tomatoes) or burst (cabbage).

Wind. Windy conditions dehydrate crops and tend to slow photosynthesis, reducing sugar content.

There are many signs of ripeness to watch for. Changes in size, color, and softness, for example. The skin of some produce—including eggplants, edible-podded peas, and summer squash—take on a gloss when they are fully mature. Many root vegetables push up as they grow—the size of their shoulders is a clue to the size of what's underground. Keep your eye on vegetables like summer squash that sprint to overripeness; wait an extra 48 hours, and you'll have a candidate for the giant-vegetable competition at the county fair. Other crops, such as carrots, onions, potatoes, and winter squash, are more forgiving. Another week in the garden won't matter.

When you harvest can make a difference in more than flavor. Surprisingly, harvest time is a last chance to boost your garden's yields. Many crops, such as asparagus, beans, cucumbers, okra, summer squash, peas, peppers, and indeterminate tomatoes, will continue to flower and form fruits if they are picked regularly, especially if the fruits are picked before they are fully ripe. Similarly, a good many leaf crops—basil, lettuce, parsley, and spinach are four—put out new foliage if they are harvested regularly. (See "Harvest How-To," right, for more general guidelines; you'll find harvest guidelines for individual crops in the Plant Portraits in Part Two of this book, beginning on page 175.)

The great advantage of growing your own vegetables and herbs is having garden-fresh produce to enjoy, but unless your garden is the size of a handkerchief, you're unlikely to use each day's harvest immediately. Directions for storing are crop-specific, although a good general rule is not to wash any produce that you won't be eating right away. Most vegetables and herbs should be refrigerated in plastic bags. Exceptions include garlic and other members of the onion family, along with potatoes, squash, and sweet potatoes, which should be stored in a dark location that is dry and cool (45° to 50°F). If your produce isn't quite ripe, leave it at room temperature to mature.

Garlic, onions, peanuts, potatoes, pumpkins, shallots, sweet potatoes, and winter squash are some of the crops that must be cured before they are stored for more than a couple of weeks. (For specific recommendations, see the individual Plant Portraits in Part Two of this book.) If a cold cellar, canning, freezing, drying, or pickling is on your agenda, purchase or borrow a copy of the bible of preserving foodstuff, *Putting Food By*. Detailed instructions for canning and freezing vegetables safely are also available in the *Ball Blue Book: A Guide to Home Canning and Freezing*. (See Reading About Gardening" in the Appendix for more books on the subject.)

SAVING & STORING SEEDS

Saving seeds from this year's garden to plant next year's garden is bonus harvest. Saving seeds will not only save you a bit of money but can supply you with improved cultivars, strains that are tolerant or resistant to disease and better suited to your climate. Cultivars disappear from seed catalogs in a twinkling. Save seeds of one cultivar long enough, and

you may find yourself the sole curator of an heirloom, as M.C. "Radiator Charlie" Byles did. Byles developed a Goliath-size tomato in the 1930s, which he began selling in the 1940s. It was so popular that he was able to pay off the $6,000 mortgage on his house, a feat that also gave the tomato its name: 'Radiator Charlie's Mortgage Lifter'.

When saving seeds, be sure to heed the following guidelines:

- Only save seeds of open-pollinated cultivars, not hybrids.
- Save seeds from the strongest plants and best fruits.
- Watch for special traits, such as disease toler-

HARVEST HOW-TO

In addition to timing the harvest properly, follow these more general guidelines:

- Use shears or a knife to harvest crops like broccoli, cabbage, eggplants, peppers, pumpkins, and squash, which have tough or brittle stems.

- Be gentle. Bruises, punctures, and scrapes reduce the storage life of produce.

- Harvest well before noon, when the sugar content of produce is greatest.

- To avoid spreading diseases, do not harvest when plants are wet.

- Harvest herbs for drying in late morning, when their leaves are dry.

- Leave a portion of stem on crops like peppers, pumpkins, and squash to extend storage life.

- Cool crops immediately after harvesting to prolong storage life.

- Wash only the produce you plan to use immediately.

- Remove tops from root crops to extend storage life.

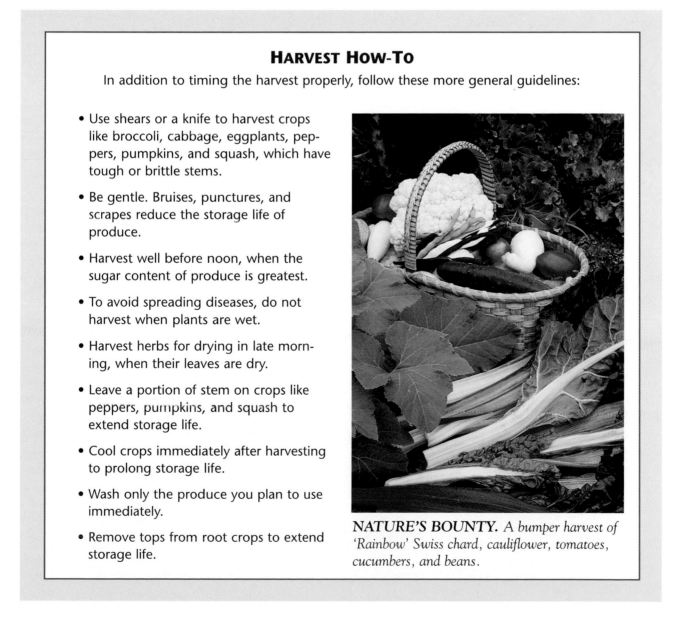

NATURE'S BOUNTY. *A bumper harvest of 'Rainbow' Swiss chard, cauliflower, tomatoes, cucumbers, and beans.*

A BONUS HARVEST. *Saving seeds from a crop from one season to plant the next has its own rewards. You'll save some money, but in the process, you also may find an improved strain of a popular crop or help preserve an heirloom cultivar. For specifics on saving and storing seeds, see the individual entries in Part Two of this book.*

ance, larger fruits or yields, plant vigor, early bearing, or outstanding flavor.

• If you grow more than one cultivar of crops that cross-pollinate, expect that the offspring from saved seeds will differ from their parent.

When collecting seeds,

• Wait until seeds are ripe for dill, fennel, lettuce, onions, members of the cabbage family, and other crops that shatter, or release, their seeds.

• Seeds that are embedded in flesh, such as cucumbers, melons, tomatoes, and peppers, should be harvested when their fruits are slightly overripe.

• Edible seeds, such as beans, corn, and peas, should be harvested when they are dry.

After collecting, cleaning, drying, and labeling (both cultivar name and date), store seeds in an airtight container in a cold (32° to 40°F), dark loca-

---

KEEP YOUR DISTANCE

If you want to save seeds for next year, plant cultivars of vegetables and herbs that are pollinated by wind or insects as far apart as you can to reduce cross-pollination. Wind- and insect-pollinated crops include asparagus, beets, broccoli, all members of the cabbage family, carrots, celery, collards, corn, cucumbers, eggplant, kale, mustard, all melons, onions, parsley, peppers, pumpkins, radishes, rutabagas, spinach, squash, and turnips. (Additionally, some squash and pumpkin cultivars cross-pollinate, as do different cultivars of squash and of corn.)

Even different cultivars of crops that pollinate themselves—beans (snap, lima, soy), chicory, endive, lettuce, peas, tomatoes—may be visited by insects and are best not planted side-by-side.

---

tion. Alternatively, freeze seeds in a sealed container. In either case, enclose with the seeds 1 tablespoon of dried milk (wrapped in a facial tissue), which acts as a desiccant. Before planting, proof your seeds to make sure they're viable. (See "Germination Testing" on page 109 for details; for detailed information about saving seeds of vegetables and herbs, see "Reading About Gardening" in the Appendix.)

EXTENDING & ENDING THE SEASON

The first frost marks the end of the season for most gardeners, but for those who are willing to make an effort, frost is only the beginning of the end. With a little protection, even those who dwell in bone-cold climates can pull beets and parsnips and pick kale and chard for many days after tender plants have fallen victim to the weather. Stretching the garden season in autumn is like pushing it in spring: You use the same solar equipment and techniques, and you work in mittens and a parka.

If you're seeking just an extra 3 or 4 weeks of life for your garden—you're not determined to spend part of New Year's Eve picking peas—floating row covers will supply all the protection necessary. Rather than dashing out an hour after the weather forecaster announces the first frost is imminent, start covering your garden when nighttime temperatures dip into the 30s. Row covers can be laid directly on top of plants, but late in the season, it's better to drape them over hoops or wires to reduce the moisture they trap. Secure their edges to retain heat; and pull them back during sunny days. To obtain even more protection, lay down more than one layer.

All the other plant-protection methods used to get an early start in spring will work too: single-plant cloches like Wall O'Water, paper bags, baskets, plastic caps, domes, and milk jugs. Clear or dark polyethylene gives more frost protection than does spun plastic fabric from which row covers are fashioned, although polyethylene must be vented or removed during the day to let moisture and heat escape. Wrapping polyethylene around a tomato cage or stakes is an easy way to give plants considerable protection from the cold. For even more defense, drape plastic over the top at night, then remove it in the morning to avoid overheating.

One difference between spring and autumn pro-

HOLDING THE HARVEST. *One way to extend the season is to store crops for winter use. Storage time of some crops, such as Chinese cabbage, can be extended by "planting" them in dishpans filled with moist sand. Keep them in a cool (35° to 40°F), moist location, such as a root cellar.*

HERBS FOR WINTER. *Tender herbs, such as lemon grass and rosemary, can be overwintered on a windowsill. For a wintertime taste of summer, try growing parsley, basil, and chives in a sunny window as well.*

tection is that you're covering mature plants now, not only seedlings. As a result, it may be preferable to install continuous cloches that protect groups of plants or entire beds or rows. Tunnels made from sheets of 4- to 6-mil polyethylene suspended on PVC piping or metal half-hoops, or tunnels formed from semi-rigid fiberglass act as temporary greenhouses where the last of the cucumbers or peppers may have an outside chance of ripening. A portable cold frame also can be moved into the garden to protect crops. All these coverings must be vented during sunny days to make sure too much heat is not trapped.

Three more tricks: First, a loose mulch of straw or hay will form an insulating blanket against the cold. The thicker the mulch, the better the protection. Second, research shows that there is a secondary benefit from spraying plants with kelp emulsion—it reduces the water content in the leaf cells, which gives another degree or two of frost protection. To get the best results, begin spraying your plants at least 3 weeks before the first expected frost. Third, if you have water to spare, take a tip from commercial growers faced with an early frost and sprinkle plants with water. Turn on an oscillating sprinkler as soon as the mercury falls below 33°F, and let it run until the morning sun heats the air to 32°F.

None of these efforts is going to protect tender vegetables and herbs, such as eggplants and basil, against repeated frosts or temperatures in the 20s. But you will be able to harvest cold-tolerant crops for many weeks. Really rugged sorts—such as Brussels sprouts, cabbage, endive, kale, radicchio, and spinach—will survive under only a modest cover. Arugula, broccoli, cauliflower, chives, lettuce, mustard, parsley, scallions, Swiss chard, and many Asian greens (bok choy, Chinese cabbage, daikon radishes, and more) are members of the rugged-but-not-impervious clan. Give them more protection. Finally, most of the root crops—beets, carrots, leeks, parsnips, radishes, rutabagas, and turnips, but not potatoes—can be harvested well into winter if they are covered with a thick mulch to postpone the ground from freezing.

SEASON-ENDING TASKS

While it's possible to harvest vegetables and herbs 12 months a year—even in cold climates—most

ROOT-CELLAR STORAGE. *Classic winter-storage vegetables, such as garlic, potatoes, cabbage, winter squash, carrots, onions, and turnips can be kept for winter use in a cool, moist basement or root cellar. Inspect regularly for signs of rot, and use damaged vegetables immediately.*

gardeners are secretly relieved when the first frost arrives. They welcome a break from working in the garden. Shutting down a garden, however, is like shutting a cottage: Good housekeeping when you close down means less work when you open up. Here are some reminders:

Garden Cleanup. Don't leave plant debris in the garden. It's a winter haven for diseases and insect pests. Add it to the compost pile instead.

Toss Diseased Plants. If crops showed any signs of disease, put their debris in the trash, not the compost pile.

Clean and Store Equipment. Gather up any equipment, such as stakes, cages, and trellises. Clean and store it so that it's ready to go for next season.

Season-Ending Tool Care. Clean, sharpen, and oil tools. Also winterize power equipment. (See "Power-Tool Maintenance" on page 36 for details.)

Mulch. Once the ground freezes, mulch perennial crops.

Plant Green-Manure Crops. Turn any remaining mulch into the soil, and plant a green manure; if it's too late to plant a cover crop, mulch the garden with organic matter.

You've put the garden to bed. Now clean the dirt from under your fingernails and put your feet up. Take a few deep breaths, for it's a few weeks at best until your mailbox will be packed with the true garden harbinger: seed catalogs. And if you've caught the gardening bug, the minute you close down this year's plot, you are already thinking about what you want to do next year. A gardener's year never really ends. May it ever be so.

PREVENTING PESTS AND PLAGUES. *Environmentally friendly cultural controls are the first line of defense against insect pests such as tomato hornworms. Physical controls, such as handpicking, are equally safe and effective.*

CHAPTER EIGHT

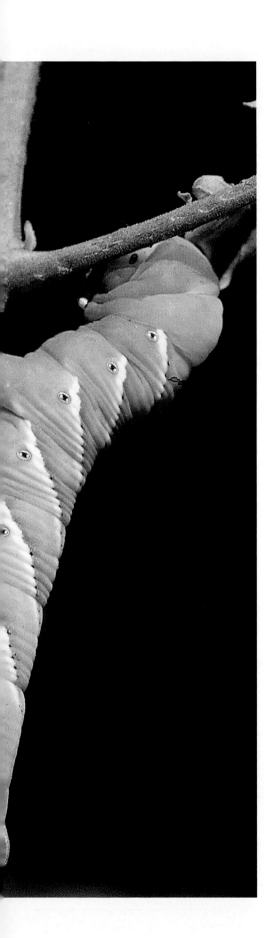

COPING WITH GARDEN PROBLEMS

*From winter, plague and pestilence,
good lord, deliver us!*

THOMAS NASHE,
Summer's Last Will and Testament, 1600

SMART GARDENERS MAY PRAY FOR DELIVERANCE FROM WINTER, BUT FROM PLAGUES AND PESTILENCE, they first take the proverbial ounce of prevention. If prevention fails, they resort to the many solutions to garden problems that are acceptable to environmentally conscious growers. In fact, if there's a need for divine intervention, it's probably not from Japanese beetles or early blight but from American homeowners' overuse of pesticides and other chemicals—sales of

143

more than one billion dollars a year for insect control alone.

Still, there are signs of hope. The sales of chemical fixes to gardeners are decreasing as more and more people resist the lure of a magic-bullet approach to gardening—the belief that a single spray or dust will instantly eliminate all insect and disease problems.

COPING STRATEGIES

Another by-product of late-20th-century concerns about safe food and a safe landscape is IPM, the Integrated Pest Management approach to cultivation, which is a combination of cultural, physical, biological, and chemical practices. Because IPM permits the use of synthetic chemical products, organic gardeners have modified its recommendations, calling their program Organic Pest Management (OPM). The goal of OPM, like that of IPM, is to create a diverse, stable ecosystem in the garden that does not eliminate pests and diseases but keeps them enough at bay to permit satisfactory garden harvests. The OPM strategy, effective for both pests and diseases, is as follows:

Monitor the Garden. Inspect plants weekly for damage, and catch problems in their early stage—while they are still easy to manage. (See "Problem Patrol," below, for symptoms to look for.)

PROBLEM PATROL

Before you can combat pest or disease problems, you have to know what caused them. Here are a few of the most common calling cards left on plant leaves, and the insect pests or diseases that leave them. You'll find more information on these problems in "Controlling Common Pests," page 162, and "Controlling Common Diseases," page 169.

INSECTS

Foliage Symptoms	Pest
Blackened, wilted leaves, & stem tips	Squash bugs
Curled/webbed foliage	Mites, webworms
Distorted foliage	Aphids, leafhoppers, tarnished plant bugs
Foliage with tunnels	Leaf miners
Holes in leaves	Beetles, caterpillars (hornworms, loopers, cabbageworms) grasshoppers, slugs, snails
Spotted foliage	Mites, thrips, tarnished plant bugs
Silver-streaked foliage	Thrips
Sticky foliage	Aphids, slugs, snails, whiteflies

Whole Plant Symptoms	Pest
Stems or entire plants wilt suddenly	Squash vine borers
Seedlings fall over	Cutworms
Seedlings/transplants disappear	Armyworms, cutworms, slugs, snails, wildlife
Stunted, sickly plants that wilt	Borers, cabbage root maggots, mites, rootworms, onion maggots, whiteflies

Identify the Problem. Determine the source of the damage, and learn more about the pest or disease causing it. When is it most vulnerable or easiest to control?

Establish Tolerances. Determine how much damage a crop can endure and still yield an acceptable harvest. Not every infection or infestation must be eradicated.

Use the Least Intrusive Control First. For problems that do need intervention, start with the control that will have the least effect on the garden's overall ecosystem. Cultural controls are the first line of defense, followed by physical and biological controls.

Use Organically Acceptable Sprays and Dusts. Use organically acceptable sprays and dusts only as a last resort, and when you do use them, apply them as carefully as possible.

INSECTS IN THE GARDEN

That insect pests will always be present is a truth so compelling that in her long poem "The Garden" (1946), Vita Sackville-West grimly surrenders for us all:

> *Gardener,*
> *Where is your armistice?*
> *You hope for none.*
> *It will not be,*
> *until yourself breed maggots.*

DISEASES

Foliage Symptoms	Disease
Black mold on leaves	Sooty mold, caused by aphid or whitefly infestation
Curled or distorted foliage	Aster yellows, curly top, tobacco mosaic, or other viral diseases
Red-brown spots on leaves	Rust
Mottled, yellowed or bronzed foliage	Aster yellows, sunscald, tobacco mosaic virus
Yellow or brown spots on foliage	Anthracnose, bacterial blight, bacterial leaf spot, black rot, downy mildew (gray blotches under leaves), early blight, late blight
White or gray spots/patches	Gray mold, powdery mildew
Foliage yellows & wilts	Bacterial wilt, fusarium wilt, verticillium wilt

Whole Plant Symptoms	Disease
Dieback	Anthracnose
Seedlings fall over	Damping-off
Stunted plants with deformed leaves	Aster yellows
Stunted, yellowed plants that wilt	Clubroot, curly top, nematodes, root rot
Stems or entire plants wilt suddenly	Bacterial wilt

MONITOR FOR A HEALTHY GARDEN. *Walking through the garden—daily or at least every few days—looking for problems is the best way to catch them while they're still easily managed. Examine leaves—both tops and bottoms—as well as whole plants for signs of insect damage or diseases.*

But Sackville-West has it wrong. There will be no victory, no wholesale extermination of insect pests, but there can be an armistice, or truce. That's your aim in the garden: not to establish dominion in the Biblical sense—mastery over "every living thing that moveth upon the earth"—but to create an acceptable standoff with pests that are out to feed on your vegetables and herbs.

Thousands and thousands of insects and equal numbers of insectlike bugs exist. Although it may at times seem as if all of them appreciate fresh produce, some are actually beneficial and others are simply benign. Honeybees and ladybugs are probably the best known beneficials, but there are many others. (See "Encouraging Beneficials" on page 153 for more on beneficial insects as well as strategies for encouraging them to make your garden their home.) Insects that are benign may live in your garden, but

they don't affect your plants or your harvests one way or the other.

Before you begin enforcing your part of the great pest standoff, you've got to know what you're dealing with. Inspect your plants carefully, especially their foliage. You may want to invest in a 10x hand lens and a handbook to help with identification. (See "Reading About Gardening" in the Appendix for pest and disease guides, and "Problem Patrol" on page 144 for symptoms to look for.) Make sure the insect you see is a pest and not a beneficial insect already hard at work on controlling it for you—or a benign species that just happens to be in the wrong place at the wrong time.

Identifying which pest you are dealing with is essential, but it is only step one. Since proper timing is important to nearly all controls, understanding a little about insects is crucial to bridling them

KNOW YOUR LIMITS. *One insect does not an infestation make, and a few holes in a plant's leaves won't hurt the harvest. If you spot a potential problem, try to assess the pest population, then look to see whether natural controls, such as parasitic wasps or ladybugs, are already at work.*

in the garden. True insects go through several life stages, or a metamorphosis. Those that undergo complete metamorphosis pass through four stages: egg, larva, pupa, and adult. The larval stage, when insects are in the form of caterpillars or grubs, is often the time when they are most destructive—and most vulnerable. Those that undergo incomplete metamorphosis, such as aphids and grasshoppers, move from eggs to nymphs to adults; nymphs and adults have similar feeding habits. Before you select a control measure, be sure to discover which form of the pest is problematic so that your efforts are productive.

DISEASES IN THE GARDEN

Organic gardeners have fewer options for combating diseases than for battling insect pests. Environmental "diseases," such as blossom-end rot and sunscald,

are the easiest to correct, because they are not really diseases at all—they just look like them. They usually require only an adjustment in soil pH or tilth, or greater or lesser exposure to light or air or amounts of moisture or fertilizer.

Fungal diseases, such as downy or powdery mildew, often show up on plant leaves and spread slowly. Many—but not all—fungal diseases can be kept in check. Removing affected foliage is a physical control that is effective for some diseases; organic fungicides are also available. Bacterial diseases, such as black rot, spread quickly and usually cause plants to rot or wilt. They cannot be cured, so affected plants should be removed and destroyed. Viral diseases, such as curly top, tend to lower the size and quality of the harvest. Like bacterial diseases, they cannot be cured. Affected plants should be removed and destroyed.

COMMONSENSE PLANT CARE. *Cultural controls may be just good plant care, but that doesn't mean they aren't effective. Two controls that are especially helpful in keeping fungal diseases of beans from getting the upper hand are not working among wet plants and being gentle when handling plants.*

CULTURAL CONTROLS

A safe and responsible approach to curbing pests—and especially diseases—starts with good garden practices. Many of these are long-term controls, actions that will have a significant effect but not an immediate one. Good garden practices, like building healthy soil, encourage vigorous plants that are less susceptible to pest and disease problems. Other cultural controls, such as planting resistant or tolerant cultivars, bring immediate results. With time, both types of controls will become second nature—part of your annual gardening routine.

Build Healthy Soil. Repeatedly adding organic matter, including green manures, to improve the soil will lead to vigorous plants that are better able to shrug off pest and disease problems.

Plant at the Proper Time. Seeds sown early or transplants set out too soon are often subject to stress, especially from cold soil and air temperatures. Stress weakens plants, making them more susceptible to diseases and pests.

Provide the Right Conditions. Give plants the amounts of light, moisture, and nutrients they need. This, too, encourages vigorous growth.

Use Foliar Sprays. Sprays made from seaweed extract or compost have disease-fighting properties as well as nutrient value. (For directions on making compost tea, see "Tea Time" on page 117.)

Grow Resistant or Tolerant Cultivars. Plants with resistance to a variety of diseases, including various viruses, wilts, leaf spots, and mildews, are available. Insect-resistant cultivars are also available. Planting locally adapted cultivars is another way to use built-in resistance. That's because plants that thrive in the prevailing conditions—baking summer heat, for example—tend to be more

MULCH FIGHTS PROBLEMS. *A layer of organic mulch helps fight pests and diseases on a variety of fronts. It not only improves the soil and helps provide the right conditions for plants, it also prevents soilborne fungal spores from splashing onto leaves.*

INCREASE CROP DIVERSITY. *Planting schemes that eliminate large blocks of a single crop—intercropping and companion planting are two—help protect plants from pests. Here, leek 'Blue Solaise' is growing with salad crops and sedum 'Autumn Joy'.*

vigorous and thus shrug off more problems than those that aren't adapted.

Practice Good Timing. Adjust planting times so that crops do not coincide with damaging pest cycles. For example, carrot rust flies lay their eggs in spring or early summer. By delaying planting—after June 1 in most areas—you can avoid problems with them altogether. You'll find other timing suggestions in the Plant Portraits in Part Two of this book, beginning on page 175.

Rotate Crops. Moving crops from one location in the garden to another keeps some insects and many diseases from attacking their favored host. (See Chapter 5, "Laying Out the Garden," for information on developing a rotation scheme that fights insects and diseases.)

Increase Crop Diversity. Intercropping, companion planting, and trap cropping are all effective methods for controlling pest populations.

Avoid Wetting Plant Foliage. This is especially important in the late afternoon or evening so that leaves don't remain wet all night long. Many fungal diseases are spread in water droplets, and wet foliage aids their spread.

Don't Work Among Wet Plants. Gardeners become excellent disease vectors when foliage is wet. To avoid transporting fungal spores from plant to plant in water beaded on clothing, tools, and hands, stay out of the garden until foliage is dry.

Be Gentle. Torn leaves, broken branches, and disturbed roots are all invitations for diseases and pests to attack your crops. Handle plants gently when working around them: Cut produce off with a sharp knife rather than yanking it, and try to avoid bruising and tearing leaves when walking down rows.

Don't Introduce Problems. Inspect transplants carefully for signs of insects or disease—be sure to look under leaves before you buy. (If you wear bifocals to read, wear them to inspect plants too.) Also keep tools clean to avoid spreading diseases as you garden.

Use Mulch. Keeping the soil covered with mulch reduces weeds and slows the spread of fungal and bacterial diseases. (A layer of fresh mulch helps prevent soil-dwelling fungi from splashing up onto plant leaves in water droplets.)

Practice Good Housekeeping. Keep the garden

weed-free. Promptly remove plants that are diseased or seriously infested with insects. Clean up plant debris at the end of the growing season.

Encourage the Presence of Natural Enemies. Spiders, beneficial insects such as ladybugs, toads, and birds are more than happy to help control garden pests. (See "Encouraging Beneficials" on page 153 for more on making them feel at home.)

Be Observant. Keep an eye out for incipient problems, and take steps to control them before they get out of hand.

Unfortunately, even the best garden practices are not a warranty against insects and diseases. But there is an assortment of other controls—physical and biological—that will help you to grow healthy vegetables and herbs.

PLANTING A TRAP

Trap cropping—luring bugs away from your vegetables and herbs and to another plant—is a safe approach to insect control. The following list suggests a few of the trap crops that gardeners can plant. Don't forget to remove and destroy the trap crop (or remove the pests from the trap plants) once it is infested.

Pest	Trap Crop
Aphid	Nasturtium
Cabbage looper	Amaranth, celery
Cabbage maggot	Radish, turnip
Colorado potato beetle	Black nightshade, eggplant
Corn earworm	Smartweed
Cucumber beetle	Radish
European corn borer	Sunflower
Flea beetle	Bok choy, Chinese cabbage, radish
Harlequin bug	Mustard, turnip
Japanese beetle	Borage, evening primrose, grape, rugosa rose, white geranium, white zinnia
Leafhopper	Corn
Leaf miner	Radish, lamb's-quarters
Mexican bean beetle	Lima bean
Nematode	Castor bean
Onion maggot	Decaying onions
Slug	Hosta
Squash bug	Radish
Tomato hornworm	Dill
Whitefly	Flowering tobacco (*Nicotiana* spp.)
Wireworm	Pieces of potato

PHYSICAL CONTROLS

After cultural controls, physical controls are the least invasive tactics a gardener can adopt. Physical controls start with the obvious. They get rid of the problem by using heat (solarizing), a blast of water, or a variety of traps.

SOLARIZING THE SOIL

If it's clear that your troubles are soilborne—you're saddled with massive populations of Colorado potato beetles, which overwinter in the ground, or have been laid low by the dirt-dwelling fungi that cause fusarium wilt—it will help to solarize your soil. The process, which raises the soil's temperature to lethal levels (around 150°F), doesn't eliminate all headaches, but it should reduce them markedly. To work, solarization must take place during the hottest time of the year, usually July and August, so you'll likely want to treat your garden piecemeal, beginning with the most problem-vexed section. To solarize, follow the steps below:

1. Clear and till the area to be solarized.

2. Water thoroughly.

3. Cover the area with a sheet of 3- to 6-mil clear plastic, minimizing the space between the ground and the plastic.

4. Seal the edges of the plastic by piling soil along them.

5. Leave the plastic in place for at least 6 weeks, longer in cool regions.

6. Don't cultivate deeply after solarization—soil that is deeper than 6 inches will have been unaffected.

REMOVAL TACTICS

There also are aboveground activities that will help to keep your plants safer from diseases and pests. The first is removal.

Remove Weeds. Weeds not only compete with crops for light, moisture, and nutrients but also harbor pests and diseases.

Remove Diseased and Infected Plants. Either pull up entire plants or remove parts of plants—leaves or stems—that are afflicted. Destroy them; don't add them to the compost pile.

Remove Pests. If insects are causing the dam-

BARRIERS. *Floating row covers and insect netting, as shown here, are very effective at keeping pests at bay. "Tuck in" the edges by piling soil up along them to prevent pests from crawling under them.*

age, a blast of water may be enough to dislodge them. Aphids and thrips are discouraged by the hose, but other pests have to be hand-plucked, bug by bug. It's a time-consuming chore, one that must be repeated daily, and it's not easy for the squeamish. If grabbing a tomato hornworm or a mass of squash vine borer eggs with your fingers is more than you can stomach, use a knife to dislodge them into a can of soapy water. Less sensitive souls can seize and squeeze, but don't drop the remains in the garden or the compost pile—some pests transmit diseases as well as feed on foliage and fruits. One other option is to dislodge them by shaking plants (gently) and gather pests on a sheet spread on the ground.

TRAPS

Installing traps is a less fierce activity than prying worms from the tips of ears of corn or mashing Japanese beetles between your index finger and thumb. Traps, which lure insects to their demise, are used to monitor insect populations as well as to destroy them. If you're trying to check pests through trapping, judge success by the reduced damage to your crops, not by the number of insects killed.

Sticky Traps. Yellow traps seem to attract more insect pests than do other colors, although white, blue, and yellow-orange are also recommended. To make your own sticky trap, paint a 12-by-12-inch square of plywood a bright yellow. Nail it to a 5-foot stake, coat it with a sticky compound, such as

SEASON-LONG BARRIERS. Crops that don't need to be pollinated by insects can be grown under floating row covers, supported here on wire hoops, all season long. Barriers like these are also effective if you are trying to control pollination to save seeds.

Tanglefoot, and place it in the garden. Scrape the board clean and recoat as necessary.

Pheromone Traps. Traps baited with pheromones—chemicals secreted by female insects that lure males of the species—are a mixed bag. Recent research suggests that unless the traps are set out in extremely large numbers throughout a neighborhood, they may attract more insects than they catch. If you decide to use pheromone traps, especially for Japanese beetles, buy more than one and set them well away from the garden—or try to encourage all your neighbors to hang them.

Food Traps. Many insects are attracted by particular foods, especially fermenting foods. Slugs and snails can't resist beer (use tuna cans set in the soil with the can lip slightly above the soil surface, and empty the trap daily). Wireworms, which attack the roots of beets, beans, carrots, corn, lettuce, onions, peas, and many other crops, are attracted to potatoes and carrots. To make a trap, impale a piece of potato or carrot on an 8-inch stick. Bury the traps 3 inches deep throughout the garden, leaving the sticks showing above ground. After 1 week, dig up the vegetable pieces and destroy them.

Shade Traps. Some pests, such as slugs, are attracted by shady, cool locations. Lay grapefruit rinds, boards, or shingles on the bare soil. Check under the trap every morning, remove the slugs, and drop them in a can of soapy water. To help suppress snails, place overturned clay pots in the garden.

Empty them every morning, disposing of the snails in soapy water.

Crop Traps. Setting out a few plants to lure pests away from the vegetable or herb you want to protect is a traditional ploy. A rugosa rose or hollyhock growing 25 feet from the garden may help keep Japanese beetles off the snap beans; two or three eggplants in the potato patch may draw Colorado potato beetles away from the 'Caribe' potatoes; two or three dill plants may attract the hornworms that are heading for the 'Brandywine' tomatoes. Once the trap crops are infested, either handpick the pests, or remove and destroy the trap plants. (See "Planting a Trap" on page 150 for more suggestions.)

BARRIERS

Barriers, which stop pests from reaching their target, are another useful physical control. The keys to success are getting them in place *before* the enemy emerges and making sure there aren't small overlooked openings that pests can enter.

Floating Row Covers. Originally intended as season extenders, floating row covers are excellent barriers against flying insects and are easy to install. Made of spun plastic, they can be laid directly over seedbeds or plants. Be sure to seal all their edges with a mound of soil to keep pests from getting under the cover. (Because clear polyethylene must have ventilation slits to keep plants from becoming overheated, it is not recommended as an insect barrier.) Remove floating row covers from plants that are insect-pollinated, such as squash, when they begin to flower. For other crops, remove covers when the threat is past—for example, when the pest has stopped laying eggs—or after your plants are well established. Many crops—beets, carrots, and onions are three—can remain under floating row covers throughout their season.

Plant Collars. These barriers protect young plants against cutworms. Fashion them out of strips of lightweight cardboard or by cutting a paper-towel or toilet-paper tube into sections. The collars need not be large—about 4 inches high. Set them over transplants, with 2 inches buried in the soil. Or, use a tin can with both ends removed.

Shields. Shields made from tar paper or heavy black plastic will keep pests like cabbage root maggot flies from laying their eggs at the base of vulnerable seedlings, such as broccoli, cabbage, cauliflower, and Chinese cabbage. Punch a small hole in the center of a 6-inch square, then make a slit from the hole to an edge, and slide the shield around each plant.

Diatomaceous Earth. Diatomaceous earth (DE), the ground skeletons of microscopic ocean creatures, can stop soft-bodied pests like slugs by contact. Other pests are stopped by contact and possibly by ingestion (the tiny rough particles scratch their skin, causing dehydration). Apply around the base of plants and on plant leaves and stems. Since DE works best when dry, it must be reapplied after rain.

Wood Ashes. Spread around the stem of cabbage-family transplants, wood ashes can deter root maggots and other pests. Be careful not to get ashes on the plant stem or foliage. Because wood ashes are highly alkaline, do not overuse.

Mulches. Both organic and plastic mulches reduce the spread of bacterial and fungal diseases by preventing water from splashing up from the soil onto plants. Compost—especially compost created by using a passive, or cold, technique—contains substances toxic to some disease-producing organisms and makes a doubly effective mulch.

REPELLENTS

Repellents are another physical control for insects. There are organic products available at garden centers and through mail-order suppliers, or you can concoct your own spray from hot peppers, or chilies. Hot peppers are murder on the eyes—be careful to keep fumes and your hands away from your face. To make a hot-pepper spray, combine 1/2 cup pureed hot peppers (including seeds and membrane) and 2 cups water. Then strain the mixture through cheesecloth. Add 1 teaspoon liquid dish soap to the remaining liquid and mix well. Spray vulnerable plants; reapply after rain.

Garlic sprays are traditional organic pest repellents, but new research indicates that they also kill a goodly number of beneficial insects and microbes. Planting garlic to repel insects, however, is a safe option. Planting any of the supposedly "repellent" plants (see "Naturally Repellent" on page 154 for a list) throughout your garden is another safe option.

BIOLOGICAL CONTROLS

In *Green Thoughts*, Eleanor Perényi succinctly summed up the rationale behind, and benefit of, biological controls: "Every insect has a mortal enemy. Cultivate that enemy and he will do your work for you." Using biological controls is like fighting fire with fire: The good bugs restrain the bad bugs, the good diseases overcome the bad diseases. But using biological controls in the garden requires more than releasing a box of ladybugs—an approach that rarely is effective. Your best bet is to encourage a wide range of beneficial insects and other organisms to remain in your garden by providing a stable, pesticide-free habitat that includes flowering plants and water. To use biological controls against a particular pest, you must first identify that pest and then attract—or purchase—the beneficial organism that will constrain it.

ENCOURAGING BENEFICIALS

With a little encouragement, insects, spiders, toads, lizards, and birds are more than happy to

ENCOURAGING BENEFICIALS. *To recruit free help in the fight against garden pests, fill flower gardens and edible landscapes with plants that attract beneficial insects. This planting features two plants that are popular with beneficials—bronze fennel and rudbeckia 'Goldsturm' interplanted with cabbage and kale, as well as coleus.*

help control garden pests. Snakes may make squeamish gardeners shudder, but they deserve to be included on your list of beneficial species; they are especially effective against mice and voles, but some species also eat insects and slugs. Bats are prodigious consumers of night-flying pests and should be welcomed as well.

A wide range of native beneficial insects—all voracious pest predators—are easy to attract. Native beneficials include aphid midges, assassin bugs, brachonid wasps, fireflies, ground beetles, ichneumon wasps, ladybugs or lady beetles, lacewings, syrphid or hover flies, soldier beetles, spined soldier bugs, tachinid flies, and tiger beetles. In addition to providing them with a pesticide-free place to live, use

the following techniques to attract them and make them feel at home:

Leave Some Weeds, Grow Some Flowers. Although weeds in the garden compete with crops for water, nutrients, and sun, all weeds aren't all bad. The adult forms of many beneficial insects feed on nectar and pollen—either exclusively or to supplement a diet of pest insects. In some species, only the juvenile forms attack pests, while the adults feed on flowers. Weedy areas—or permanent flower gardens—also provide refuge for beneficials for overwintering or when garden areas are being disturbed by activities such as tilling.

Certain plant families are more valuable for attracting beneficials than others. Members of the

NATURALLY REPELLENT

The evidence for insect-deterring plants is largely anecdotal. Asters, calendulas, geraniums, and especially marigolds are believed to deter most insects. Here is a list of other plants and the particular foes they may repel:

Plant	Pest Repelled
Borage	Tomato hornworms
Catnip	Flea beetles
Garlic	Aphids, Japanese beetles
Horseradish	Colorado potato beetles
Marigold	Nematodes, whiteflies
Mint	Aphids, cabbage moths, Colorado potato beetles
Nasturtium	Aphids, squash bugs
Potato	Mexican bean beetles
Radish	Cucumber beetles
Rosemary	Cabbage moths, carrot rust flies
Rue	Japanese beetles
Sage	Cabbage moths, carrot rust flies
Salsify	Carrot rust flies
Tansy	Cucumber beetles, Japanese beetles, squash bugs
Thyme	Cabbage maggots, cabbage moths
Tomato	Asparagus beetles
Wormwood	Carrot rust flies, cabbage loopers, flea beetles

carrot family, Apiaceae, including Queen Anne's lace, dill, fennel, and parsley are effective. Sunflower-family (Asteraceae) and mint-family (Lamiaceae) members are also important sources of pollen and nectar. Sunflower-family plants include goldenrods (*Solidago* spp.), coneflowers (*Echinacea* spp. and *Rudbeckia* spp.), yarrow (*Achillea* spp.), oxeye daisies (*Leucanthemum vulgare*), and feverfew (*Tanacetum parthenium*). Mint-family members include common herbs, such as mints, catnip, lavender, and rosemary, as well as hyssop (*Agastache* spp.).

Provide Water. Insects can find plenty of water to drink when rain is plentiful and frequent, but a supplemental source is helpful during droughts. Fill a shallow container, such as a plant saucer, with rounded rocks, then fill it with water. The rocks, which should partially stick above the water, provide a safe perch for insects to drink from. Replace the water every few days to keep it clean and eliminate mosquito larvae. Installing a water garden with a gradual, stony beach on one side (instead of the steep sides generally used in garden pools) will encourage a variety of wildlife, including toads and frogs. Such shallow-water areas also may double as birdbaths. If rounded rocks poke above the water, beneficial insects may be able to drink from them as well.

Provide Shelter. Hedgerows, shrub borders, mulched flower beds and borders, and weedy areas benefit beneficial insects by cutting down on drying winds and providing protected spaces where they can hide. These areas also are a safe haven when the garden is being disturbed by tilling or other activities.

Live and Let Live. Remember that a healthy garden ecosystem isn't insect-free—in fact, it's teaming with life. Beneficial insects need pests to survive, so it's important to avoid the temptation to zap every last insect with a fast-acting spray or dust—even an organically acceptable one. Instead, try to maintain pest populations at a level that crops can tolerate, using cultural and physical controls as well as the biological controls listed below. Think of remaining pests as a food source for patrolling ladybugs and lacewings.

BENEFICIALS FOR SALE

Beneficial insects and mites are commonly available by mail nowadays, but buying bugs isn't a quick-and-easy solution. For one thing, most don't remain

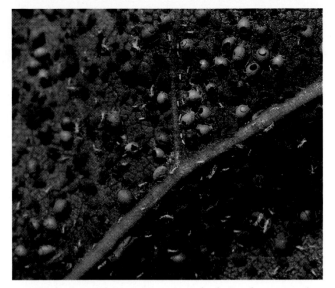

PARASITIC SIGNS. *Learn to look for the signs of beneficial insects preying on pests. If you look closely at this aphid infestation, you'll see parasitic wasps are at work, as evidenced by the tan aphid "mummies."*

WELCOME BIRDS

A wren or bluebird with a hungry brood to feed is one of the most efficient insect predators available. And birds affect insect populations all year long. Woodpeckers, chickadees, and brown creepers spend the winter scouring tree bark for insect eggs; other species sift through leaf litter to unearth overwintering grubs or pupae. (Granted, birds eat some beneficial species along with the pests.) Encourage birds to reside in your yard year-round by providing nesting boxes, food, and a source of clean water, such as a birdbath (use an electric birdbath deicer in winter) or garden pool with a sloping, stony beach that provides safe access to water. Landscaping with shrubs and trees that provide nesting sites and berries to eat is also beneficial.

in your garden. Some of the beneficials commonly available are listed below. When you order a shipment, be sure to follow the directions provided by the supplier for distributing them.

Lacewings. Lacewings (*Chrysoperla* spp.) are native predators with clear lacelike wings. Both adults and larvae eat a variety of soft-bodied insects, such as aphids and small caterpillars. They also will feed on insect eggs. Lacewings, which are shipped as eggs, are suitable for outdoor release but survive shipping poorly. Attract native lacewings by planting sunflower-, mint-, and carrot-family members.

Ladybugs. These well-known beneficials eat aphids, spider mites, and scale insects, but the convergent ladybugs commonly sold are not recommended for outdoor release. They are collected while they are hibernating and generally migrate out of the area as soon as they are released. Attracting native species is a better option. Both adults and their alligator-like larvae are predatory.

Praying Mantids. Hatching out a praying mantid egg case makes an interesting project for a child, but mantids aren't effective for controlling pests, because they eat any insect they can catch—including beneficials.

Predatory Mites. Minute and spiderlike, these predators attack a variety of pest species, especially spider mites; some species feed on thrips. Some commonly sold species are hardy and will become established in gardens. Since different species have different temperature and humidity requirements, most suppliers that sell predatory mites provide a mix of species to ensure control.

Parasitic Wasps. These wasps, which do not sting people, parasitize the eggs or larvae of a wide variety of pests, including corn borers and tomato hornworms. When the wasp eggs hatch, the larvae consume the host from the inside out. A hornworm studded with tiny white, ricelike pupae is a sure indication that parasitic wasps are active in your garden. The doomed host gradually stops eating and then dies. When the young wasps emerge, they fly off to infest a new generation of caterpillars. You can buy parasitic wasps or attract them to your garden by planting pollen- and nectar-rich flowers, such as members of the sunflower, mint, and carrot families.

OTHER BENEFICIAL ORGANISMS

Beneficial insects are by no means the only biological controls available. Beneficial nematodes and a variety of microscopic organisms make excellent biological controls. In addition to the organisms listed below, scientists are developing fungal and viral agents that target pest insects. For best results, always read and follow label directions when applying beneficial organisms.

Bacillus thuringiensis. Perhaps better known as Bt, this is a bacteria that attacks caterpillars but doesn't harm most beneficial insects. Be aware that Bt kills butterfly larvae as well as the larvae of pests such as cabbageworms and tomato hornworms, though, and use it with care. A variety of the bacteria, Btsd (*B. thuringiensis* var. *san diego*), is available that kills leaf-eating beetles such as Colorado potato beetles. Bt is available in a variety of formulations, including sprays and dusts. Follow package directions when applying it. If spray formulations don't stick to leaves, add a small quantity of liquid dish soap to help it adhere.

Milky Disease. This bacterial disease attacks the larvae of Japanese beetles, which commonly feed on lawn-grass roots. Infected grubs spread the bacteria (*Bacillus popilliae* and *B. lentimorbus*) through the soil before they die. Milky disease must be applied over a wide area to have an effect on adult beetles, so enlist your neighbors in the effort if you decide to use it. Since the bacteria can overwinter in the soil, generally only one application is necessary.

Parasitic Nematodes. Nematodes are probably best known as plant pests, not protectors, but parasitic nematodes are effective predators of a wide variety of soil-dwelling insects, especially pests of plant roots, such as grubs, wireworms, and onion maggots. They are also effective against cutworms. Suppliers offer a variety of species and strains, and the nematodes come in a variety of forms. Read the label and apply them according to the suppliers recommendations.

Protozoan Diseases. *Nosema locustae* is a protozoa that infects and kills grasshoppers and crickets, but it is effective only when applied over a large area, since these pests are quite mobile and the disease takes several weeks to kill its host. One application kills several generations.

WHEN TROUBLE STILL STRIKES

Even the best efforts don't prevent all infestations and infections. So you've improved the soil and planted resistant cultivars and watered and pulled weeds and mulched and installed sticky traps and

IMPORTED CABBAGEWORM. *Handpicking is one of the easiest ways to control caterpillars feeding on plant leaves. Bacillus thuringiensis, commonly known as Bt and sold under a variety of brand names, is a bacterial spray that will also control them.*

SQUASH VINE BORER. *The larvae of this adult squash vine moth are borers that tunnel into vines of squash, cucumbers, and other gourd-family crops. Wrapping stem bases with strips of nylon stocking prevents adults from laying eggs.*

plucked Japanese beetles by the bagful, and your crops are still under attack? Rather than resorting to deadly solutions, you might consider forgoing the harvest—a year without producing your own potatoes or basil isn't the end of the world. Or you can bring out the big guns, the last-resort controls.

As you choose weapons to fight diseases and insects, don't forget that all pesticides are toxic. None is entirely safe. Chemical or natural, they can poison beneficial as well as problematic insects, and they can kill mammals, birds, fish, and other wildlife. They can harm you. Environmental friendliness is relative.

That relativity is important, however. The label warning information on registered pesticides in the U.S. is determined from laboratory tests: the oral dose it takes to immediately kill half of the test animals, a measure called the acute oral lethal dose 50,

or LD_{50}, score. LD_{50} scores ranging from 1 to 50 are scored I, "very high" toxicity, and get a skull and crossbones symbol and a "Danger" designation from the Environmental Protection Agency (EPA). Scores from 50 to 500 make up rating II, "high," and carry "Warning" on the label. Substances scoring between 500 and 5,000 are rated III, "medium" toxicity, and come with "Caution" on their containers. Products with scores greater than 5,000, category IV, or "low," are marked "Keep Out of the Reach of Children."

It's a mistake to assume there is a perfect correlation between being natural and being benign. Some green insecticides are more toxic than synthetic products manufactured to treat the same problem. Rotenone, for instance, has a lower LD_{50} score—remember, the lower the LD_{50} score, the *more* dangerous the substance—than either malathion or carbaryl/Sevin. A few natural controls, such as nicotine sulfate, are so unselective and toxic (LD_{50} 50–80) that organic certification organizations have banned their application.

LD_{50} scores can be misleading if taken alone, because they are based on using the pure active ingredient. Most products formulated for home gardeners don't contain only the pure ingredient. The rotenone sold at garden centers is usually a 1- or 5-percent formulation, making it considerably less dangerous than its LD_{50} score suggests. Moreover, acute oral toxicity is only part of the pesticide equation. Important, too, are the other attributes of a substance, including its immediate effects when inhaled or touched, its persistence, its impact when combined with other substances (such as inert and synergistic ingredients, or another pesticide), and its long-term and environmental effects.

Despite legitimate concerns about all pesticides, there's convincing evidence that dusts, oils, soaps, and sprays made from natural substances are safer overall than are synthetic products. Most are less deadly, and most are quicker to break down in sunlight, losing their toxicity in hours or days rather than weeks or months. As a group, they are also slower to show immediate results—less likely to drop bugs in their tracks—but effective in the long run.

All pesticides should be last-ditch treatments, the ultimate tools for protecting vegetables and herbs. They can have a place in the garden, but only a small one. Organic pesticides must be timed carefully to be effective and often must be reapplied. If you choose to use them, educate yourself. Identify the problem first, then seek out the least toxic product that will bring it to bay, one that will have the smallest and briefest impact on the environment. READ THE LABEL. Apply pesticides only on windless days when the humidity is low, and in the late afternoon, when honeybees and other beneficials are less active. (See "Safety First," left, for other important guidelines.)

SAFETY FIRST

All pesticides are toxic to some degree. Use them as a last resort, use them sparingly, and use them carefully.

- Keep pesticides out of the reach of children.
- Read the label carefully and follow its recommendations. Never assume that if a little is good, more is better.
- Mix only the amount of pesticide you need.
- Mix pesticides outdoors.
- Wear protective clothing, including hat, waterproof gloves, goggles, and mask.
- Keep pesticides off your skin and away from eyes and mouth; avoid inhaling.
- Don't drink, eat, or smoke while handling pesticides.
- Do not apply pesticides in windy weather or near water.

- Apply pesticides in late afternoon or even-ing, when beneficial insects are less active.
- Practice spot application—treat specific infestations, plants, or crops rather than the entire garden.
- Wash hands and face carefully after applying pesticides.
- Store all pesticides in their original containers in a cool, dry, dark location. Check labels for specific information about storage and shelf life.
- Dispose of pesticides properly. Contact local authorities for information about disposing toxic wastes.
- Never reuse a pesticide container for any reason.

INORGANIC PESTICIDES AND FUNGICIDES

Elemental inorganic pesticides—technically, controls that don't contain carbon—have been around for decades. Some, such as those containing mercury and lead, are no longer used, but others continue to have a place in the organic garden.

Copper. Copper is often combined with lime to make a fungicide known as Bordeaux mix (named after the French region where it actually was first used to protect grapes from being stolen). Labeled "warning" or "caution," depending on the formulation, Bordeaux mix and other fixed copper-based sprays, such as copper sulfate, help prevent or reduce the damage from a variety of diseases, including mildews, black spot, rust, blights, and leaf spot. Copper-based pesticides are nonspecific and can damage soil microorganisms and beneficial insects. They are highly toxic to aquatic species and should not be used near ponds and waterways.

Sulfur. Available as a dust or in wettable form, sulfur is used as a preventative for and check on black spot, scab, leaf spot, mildews, and other fungal diseases, as well as to curb mites and thrips. While its oral toxicity to humans is only moderate (labeled "caution" in most formulations), it is a strong respiratory irritant, and it can kill beneficial soil microorganisms and beneficial insects. To avoid damage to plants, do not use sulfur in temperatures above 85°F or in combinations with horticultural oils.

Insecticidal Soaps. These are combinations of sodium or potassium salts and oil and have been used as contact insecticides for at least two centuries. Most commercial products are highly specific and virtually nontoxic to humans. Ineffective against beetles and other hard-shelled insects, they are useful in destroying slow-moving, soft-bodied, and sucking pests, such as aphids, spider mites, whiteflies, and thrips. Adding isopropyl, or rubbing, alcohol to an insecticidal soap (½ cup alcohol to 1 quart soap) increases their effectiveness.

Horticultural Oils. Dating back to Roman times, horticultural oils are either refined petroleum or vegetable oil combined with water. They can suffocate infestations of aphids, mites, caterpillars, and other soft-bodied pests; they also help to prevent some fungal diseases. The persistence of horticultural oils is brief, and their toxicity to mammals and beneficials is extremely low. Oils are toxic to fish, however, and some are flammable. Buy products that contain light, highly refined oils with a high viscosity (60 or more). Read the label carefully: Horticultural oils can be used on woody plants when they are dormant or on a wider range of plants during the growing season, and the dilutions are different. Be sure to use a growing-season dilution. To increase the effectiveness of a horticultural oil, add isopropyl alcohol (1 cup alcohol, ½ teaspoon commercial oil, 4 cups water). Do not apply horticultural oils during droughts or when temperatures are above 85°F.

Bleach. More properly known as sodium hypochlorite, this is recommended for disinfecting pots and tools and to prevent fungal and bacterial diseases from spreading. A 2-percent sodium-hypochlorite spray (2½ ounces household bleach to 1 gallon water) can help prevent damping-off.

Antitranspirants. These are products created to reduce moisture loss in plants and may have some fungicidal properties. Do not use during droughts or when temperatures are above 85°F.

BOTANICAL PESTICIDES

Botanical pesticides, or botanicals, come from plants—from the plant material itself, from plant extracts, or from chemicals and chemical compounds isolated from the plant. Hundreds of plants are known to have pesticidal qualities—mostly against insects—and thousands more remain to be discovered. Gardeners have used botanicals for centuries, but don't be assuaged by their long history or their "natural" origins. Botanicals are poisons. Read the label and follow its instructions.

Neem. Also known as azadirachtin, this botanical comes from the seeds of the tropical neem tree, *Azadirachta indica*. While neem and its active

---

SOAP & OIL SPRAY

You can make your own soap-and-oil insecticide concentrate by combining 1 cup vegetable oil and 1 tablespoon liquid dish soap. To use, mix 2 teaspoons of the soap-and-oil concentrate with 1 cup water, and spray.

compounds have long been used in pharmacology in Asia and Africa, its pesticidal qualities are just beginning to be discovered in the West. It affects— as a repellent, a feeding inhibitor, a growth and reproduction inhibitor, and a contact and systemic poison—a wide range of leaf-eating insects, from beetles to caterpillars, yet it is relatively safe for mammals (oral LD_{50} 13,000). It biodegrades in 3 to 7 days in sunlight and remains in the soil for only a few weeks. Preliminary research also shows that bees and some beneficial insects are safe from its toxic effects.

Neem, or azadirachtin, products differ considerably in their formulas, which accounts for the differences in prices, but are typically sold as concentrates. Once diluted with water at the recommended amounts, their strengths are identical.

Pyrethrins. Pyrethrins are the active compounds extracted from the dried flowers of pyrethrum daisies, *Tanacetum cinerariifolium* and *T. coccineum*, that go into pyrethrum, dubbed "the most important insecticide ever developed." One of the safest green insecticides (oral LD_{50} 1,200–1,500), it instantly kills or paralyzes a broad spectrum of pests, including aphids, caterpillars, leafhoppers, and whiteflies. Because of its low toxicity and short persistence—only a few hours in sunlight and temperatures above 50°F—it has been cleared for use on a wide variety of edible crops.

The downside is that pyrethrum is nonselective. It is capable of harming bees, ladybugs, fish, and other cold-blooded animals as effectively as it clobbers garden enemies. Avoid using it in damp weather, which increases its persistence, and do not apply near waterways and ponds. Because they degrade so quickly, pyrethrins are often combined with rotenone and other insecticides or compounds to make them longer-lasting (as well as more toxic). Read the label carefully to make sure what you've purchased.

Stay away from aerosol formulations of pyrethrum, which increase the amount of spray released into the air. Avoid, too, solutions that contain pyrethroids, which are synthetic compounds that resemble pyrethrins. These formulations are more toxic to insects and have greater persistence, 10 days and more, than do products containing only the natural compounds.

Rotenone. One of the most frequently used botanical insecticides, rotenone is also the most potent (oral LD_{50} 75–1,5000). Derived from the roots of several woody leguminous plants, including species of *Derris* and *Lonchocarpus*, rotenone works as both a contact and stomach poison. Nonselective, it is highly toxic to insects, fish, aquatic invertebrates, and birds, and it is moderately toxic to mammals.

Normally applied as a dust, rotenone is an effective—although not instantaneous—killer of aphids, mites, thrips, leaf-eating caterpillars, squash bugs, Colorado potato beetles, and other hard-shelled insects. Death comes in 5 to 13 hours. It persists in the garden for about 5 days. Sold under its own name, rotenone is available in 1- and 5-percent solutions and often is combined with pyrethrins for a double-barrel effect.

Rotenone has been used on food crops for more than 150 years, but it is a wolf is sheep's clothing— more toxic than some synthetic insecticides. As one organic-supply catalog notes, it should be used only "when all other controls have failed."

Ryania. Another contact and stomach poison, ryania doesn't kill insects; it makes them too sick or weak to harm vegetables and herbs. The most selective of the botanical controls—because it is most effective against immature insects—it throttles thrips, cabbageworms, Mexican bean beetles, corn borers, and other pests but has little effect on most beneficial insects. That doesn't mean ryania, which is made from the stems and roots of the tropical plant *Ryania speciosa*, is harmless: Its oral LD_{50} score of 750 to 1,200, which places it in category III, medium toxicity.

Sold under its own name and in combinations with pyrethrum, rotenone, and diatomaceous earth, ryania is somewhat slower to break down in the environment than either pyrethrum or rotenone. Because it is usually applied in powder form but is water-soluble, its long-term effects are decreased.

Sabadilla. Made from the seeds of the tropical lily *Schoenocaulon officinale*, sabadilla is another contact and stomach poison. It is lethal against squash bugs, stinkbugs, corn borers, leaf-eating caterpillars, thrips, cucumber and Mexican bean beetles, and other garden pests. While its oral LD_{50} score indicates its relative safety (LD_{50} 5,000), sabadilla dust is a known respiratory irritant. Wear a mask when applying it—or any other pesticides.

Sabadilla is probably harmful to bees—the data

are inconclusive—but is less a threat to other beneficial insects, and its persistence in the environment is brief, fewer than 24 hours in sunny conditions. Its persistence on the shelf is another matter: If kept in a dry, dark location, sabadilla increases in strength over time.

Quassia. The newest green poison in the garden, quassia's lethal promise is only beginning to be explored. Tests do show that it is capable of killing a wide range of insects in the larval stage, yet appears not to harm honeybees or adult beneficials, and its toxicity to mammals is lower than that of other major botanical insecticides. Moreover, its persistence is brief, about 48 hours.

Quassia is made from the bark and wood of a Latin American tree (*Quassia amara*), a cousin of the ubiquitous tree of heaven (*Ailanthus altissima*), which also has pesticidal properties. Sometimes difficult to find in garden centers and mail-order catalogs, quassia is usually sold in the form of chips or shavings, which must be soaked in water for 24 hours, then brought to a boil and simmered for 4 hours. Strain the liquid, then add 1 tablespoon of liquid dish soap to help it adhere to plant foliage.

Citrus Oils. These are considered nonhazardous, although it's a good idea to keep cats and dogs away from treated plants. Made from the limonene contained in citrus peels, these oils are effective against aphids and spider mites. Largely marketed as products for flea control, the garden applications of citrus oils have only begun to be explored.

COPING WITH WILDLIFE

Like the weather, wildlife will always be part of a backyard gardener's lot. Animals are lured to the garden by fertile, cultivated soil and the vegetables and herbs it produces so generously. While controlling weeds is mindless work, controlling wildlife requires all a gardener's wits—just ask someone who has had deer defoliate his beans, or raccoons harvest her corn. Determining that animals have visited your garden isn't difficult: One moment its plants and fruits are there, robust and healthy, and the next moment they're gone, or trampled, or nibbled so severely, you can see the damage from 100 feet. As the saying goes, animals like gardens as much as gardeners do, and they're better at harvesting them.

One nocturnal visit from a family of wood-chucks, and most gardeners are ready to declare war on anything with legs. There are scores of animal repellents, both commercial products and homemade remedies, that you can try. Many gardeners swear by their efficacy, insisting that bars of soap, bags of human hair, and sprays or dusts containing hot peppers, garlic, putrefied eggs, urine, dried blood, or bonemeal will ward off even the most pesky intruders. Unfortunately, an equal number of gardeners swear these remedies don't work.

Others are convinced sights and sounds, not odors, are the way to keep Thumper and Bambi out of the vegetables and herbs. These gardeners outfit scarecrows, string aluminum pie tins and Mylar scare tapes, inflate plastic scare-owls and scare-snakes, hang out colored balloons, and set up mirrors and reflective sheets of aluminum foil. The truly desperate may invest in a "Crow-Killer Scare-Away," a realistic life-size model of a great horned owl with a crow clutched in its talons, all mounted on a weather vane. The wind not only turns the owl but flaps the doomed crow's wings. Other gardeners set out whirligigs that click and clack as they move in the wind or play loud music. (Some commercial farmers go a giant step farther and install propane cannons that deliver an ear-shattering boom every 2 minutes.)

Rich possibilities, but less rich results. There's some evidence that scare tapes work with birds, but once they stop pulling up seedlings to get at their seeds, birds aren't a major problem in the vegetable and herb garden. As for the effect of these visual and aural devices on animals with four legs, the anecdotal evidence isn't reassuring. Moving apparatus appear to be the most effective in scaring wildlife, but most animals "habituate," or become accustomed, in a week or less. Tapes, scarecrows, or whirligigs, whatever devices you try should be repositioned regularly.

Another approach is to modify your environment to make it less attractive to wildlife: Remove water, shrubs, brush, and mulches that provide cover and food sources, especially plants that the marauders are known to like. While this will help to disinterest animal pests in your garden, it also discourages beneficial wildlife—insects, toads, bats, and insect-eating birds—from taking up residence. What's left? Trapping and fencing.

Trapping animals, although safer than either poisoning or shooting, is a mixed bag. Many gardeners can tolerate killing gophers and voles, but when the mammals get larger and more cuddly, killing gets harder and more distasteful. Using live traps and relocating animals is an alternative to killing outright, but this, too, has a downside. You're eliminating your problem while potentially creating one for someone else. Moreover, some research suggests that many animals that have been trapped and relocated die because they are unable to adapt. Save-a-Life traps may not save a life. Finally, some states and localities have laws against relocating animals off your own land, so check with a local wildlife officer before you invest in a trap.

If you choose to use live traps, take care when handling your captives—most wildlife that hangs around yards and gardens is susceptible to zoonoses, diseases like rabies that can be transmitted from animals to people. Always observe the following precautions:

- Wear gloves.

- Do not touch trapped animals.

- Cover the cage with a drop cloth, and move it gently.

- Choose an appropriate release site that is far away from any houses.

FENCING

Trapping is not an alternative for the neighbor's dog and cat; moreover, for any animal, it is a temporary

HOW FAR IS FAR ENOUGH?

Although the rabbits snacking on your lettuce plants appear to dine exclusively in your garden, many animals that trouble backyard gardens are wide-ranging. If you take the trouble to relocate wild creatures, be sure their new home is far enough away from yours.

Raccoons—10 miles.

Skunks, squirrels—5 miles.

Rabbits, woodchucks, small mammals, and rodents—3 miles.

solution. Remove a woodchuck, and another woodchuck usually moves in. If wildlife are taking a toll on your crops, a fence is the best and most permanent deterrent. Keep in mind that a fence is most effective when installed *before* wildlife know what it's keeping them from. A woodchuck or rabbit accustomed to dining on your delectable vegetables will work harder to get to them than one that hasn't.

Whether the problem is rabbits, raccoons, or deer, the most effective fencing option is an electric fence. Impossible to climb over, an electric fence is powered by household current or batteries and regulated by a controller, or pulser, which measures out current. Newer, safer controllers, called "low impedance" units, send out current pulses that last only a couple of ten-thousandths of a second. That's far too brief to start a fire if the line touches dried grass or leaves—a risk with older models—and current continues to flow through the wires even if they become submerged in vegetation. Be sure your controller has an Underwriters Laboratory tag and that it is properly grounded. Everything you need to install a three-strand fence for a 30-by-60-foot garden, minus the electrical power, should cost about $180. Three strands, one set 4 inches from the ground, one set at 9 inches, and the third set at 30 inches, should discourage short- and long-legged creatures. The electricity needed to run the fence is about the same as that required to power a 25-watt light bulb. For a photovoltaic system, plan on spending an additional $200.

For gardeners who need a more aesthetic option, a picket fence is more attractive, although less effective. Choose a model with tightly spaced pickets, and/or line the inside with chicken wire. To prevent rabbits and other diggers from simply going under it, dig a 1-foot-deep trench around the garden, and line it with chicken wire or hardware cloth; attach the lining to the fence to make a solid barrier. Be sure to electrify the gate as well so that pests can't slip under or around it.

CONTROLLING COMMON PESTS

The first step in any effective pest-control plan is to identify the culprit. Use the descriptions, photographs, and illustrations that follow to identify pests and the damage they cause. Use the techniques listed under "Prevention" and "Control" to keep pest populations in check.

APHIDS. *Aphids, shown here on cabbage, typically cluster on leaf undersides and on stem tips.*

APHIDS

Tiny, pinhead-size, green, pink, or black pear-shaped insects found throughout the U.S., clustering on leaf tips and undersides. They attack nearly all edibles, especially beans, beets, chard, cole crops, peas, rhubarb, and spinach. Aphids cause distorted and yellow foliage. Their sugary secretions may lead to a black sooty fungus on leaves.

Prevention. Install floating row covers in spring to prevent infestations. Reduce nitrogen in soil or fertilizers. Attract or release beneficial insects such as lacewings or aphid midges.

Control. Spray plants with a strong stream of water to dislodge pests. Spray with insecticidal soap, making sure to wet leaf undersides, every 2 days until pests are controlled. Neem is also effective. For serious infestations, use pyrethrum.

ARMYWORMS

The larvae of gray-brown, night-flying moths, armyworms are greenish to green-brown, 1½-inch caterpillars that feed in large groups at night. They eat leaves and stems and can consume entire plants. They often start feeding at the bottom of the plant, making them hard to spot until they have done considerable damage. During the day, they hide under leaf litter or among plant foliage. They eat a wide range of edibles, including beets, corn, peas, peppers, spinach, and tomatoes.

Prevention. Attract native parasitic wasps and flies by planting pollen- and nectar-rich flowers. Cover plants with floating row covers.

Control. Handpick, or spray Bt or neem.

CABBAGE LOOPER

These green, 1½-inch caterpillars move with a characteristic "looping" motion and chew large, irregular holes in leaves. Adults are brownish gray moths with a silvery spot on each wing. Loopers attack cabbage and related plants, such as broccoli, cauliflower, and Brussel sprouts, as well as lettuce, beets, peas, and other vegetables.

Prevention. Install floating row covers to prevent egg laying. Attract native predatory wasps and flies by planting pollen- and nectar-rich flowers.

Control. Handpick. Spray with Bt or neem, or dust plants with diatomaceous earth. For serious infestations, use pyrethrin or sabadilla.

CABBAGE ROOT MAGGOT

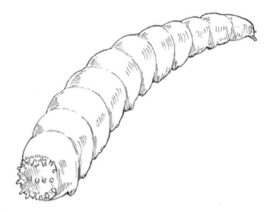

Cabbage Root Maggot

This pest, a legless maggot, is the larva of a ¼-inch fly that emerges from the soil in early spring to lay eggs on early cabbage and broccoli transplants. The maggots also chew tunnels through the roots of other mustard-family crops, including turnips, radishes, Brussels sprouts, and cauliflower, throughout the season. Feeding stunts plants or causes them to wilt, first at midday, then turn yellow and die.

Prevention. Apply parasitic nematodes to soil. Alkaline soil also discourages cabbage flies: Rake ½ cup of wood ashes into the soil around each seedling.

Control. Make shields to prevent egg laying by cutting squares of tar paper or cardboard with a slit to the center and a small hole to accommodate the plant stem. Slip them over transplants at planting time. Or protect plants with row covers. Destroy seriously infected plants; do not compost.

COLORADO POTATO BEETLE

Colorado Potato Beetle

Also called potato bugs, these rounded, ⅓-inch beetles are yellow-orange with black stripes. Their grubs are dark orange with black spots on the sides. Both larvae and adults chew holes in foliage of potatoes, tomatoes, eggplants, and related plants.

Prevention. Plantings of nectar- and pollen-rich plants. Apply beneficial nematodes to the soil.

Control. Handpick; also crush their bright orange eggs, which are laid in dense clusters. Protect plants with row covers. Spray Btsd or Neem. For serious infestations, spray weekly with pyrethrin, sabadilla, or rotenone.

CORN ROOTWORM

Several species of beetles lay eggs on corn, and their thin, wrinkled, grublike larvae, which are whitish with brown heads, tunnel through roots and seeds; seedlings may not germinate, or plants may be stunted. Adults feed on corn tassels and other plants. Adults of northern corn rootworm are ⅓ inch long and yellow-green; southern rootworms, also called spotted cucumber beetles, are yellow-green with black spots.

Prevention. Rotate crops. Plant corn after the soil has warmed up thoroughly in spring, and cultivate soil thoroughly before planting.

Control. Apply parasitic nematodes to the soil.

CUCUMBER BEETLE

These small, ¼-inch-long, yellow-green beetles attack squash-family plants, including cucumbers, melons, and squash. The spotted cucumber beetle, also known as Southern corn rootworm, has black spots; the striped cucumber beetle has black stripes.

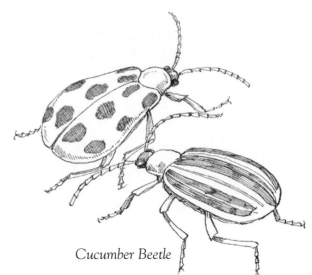

Cucumber Beetle

The grubs tunnel through roots, causing plants to wilt and die. Adults chew foliage of cucumbers, squash, and other gourd-family plants, as well as other vegetables, and transmit serious plant diseases, including bacterial wilt and mosaic.

Prevention. Grow cultivars that tolerate bacterial wilt and mosaic. Destroy, do not compost, crop residue. Rotate gourd-family crops with legumes, especially cover crops such as alfalfa.

Control. Cover plants with floating row covers; remove when flowers appear, or hand-pollinate plants. Apply parasitic nematodes to the soil. For serious infestations, spray adults with pyrethrin, sabadilla, or rotenone as soon as they appear.

CUTWORM

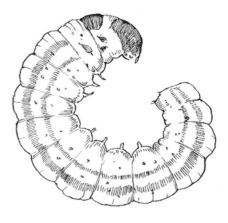

Cutworm

Soil-dwelling, 1- to 2-inch-long cutworms are the caterpillars of several species of brown or gray moths. They will sever the stems of nearly any vegetable seedling or transplant. Generally the top portion of the plant remains untouched, although cutworms will also consume entire seedlings. They feed at night and hide in the soil during daytime.

Prevention. Drench soil with parasitic nematodes a week before planting. Protect transplants with plant collars made from sections of cardboard toilet-paper or paper-towel tubes. Push collars over transplants and about 2 inches into the soil. Dust plants with wood ashes or diatomaceous earth. Beneficial nematodes, parasitic wasps, and soldier beetles are natural predators.

Control. Mix Bt with moist bran and molasses, and scatter over soil.

EUROPEAN CORN BORER

Corn borers are the wormlike, pinkish beige caterpillars of pale yellow to brown, mostly night-flying moths. The 1-inch larvae bore through cornstalks as well as stalks of beans, beets, celery, peppers, and potatoes. Larvae also feed beneath corn husks, eating tassels, kernels, and leaves and chewing tunnels through the tops of the ears.

Prevention. Attract parasitic wasps by planting pollen- and nectar-rich flowers. Rotate crops. After harvest, destroy infested plants, where larvae overwinter.

Control. Spray Bt on leaves and into tips of ears, or dust granular Bt into tips of ears. For severe infestations, spray ryania, rotenone, or sabadilla.

FLEA BEETLE

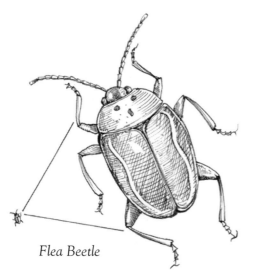

Flea Beetle

These tiny, $1/10$-inch, black or brown beetles jump when disturbed and chew small "shot-holes" in leaves. They are especially problematic in spring and will attack most vegetable crops, especially egg-

plants, peppers, and tomatoes. Flea beetles can kill seedlings; larger plants may survive, but growth is stunted. The adults spread viral diseases as they feed. The larvae, which feed on plant roots, are white grubs.

Prevention. Cover plants with row covers to exclude these pests. Flea beetles prefer full sun, so plant susceptible crops where they will receive some shade.

Control. Dust plants with diatomaceous earth. Spray severe infestations with pyrethrum, two sprays, 3 days apart. Rotenone is also effective.

HORNWORM

Hornworms are large, green caterpillars, up to 4 inches or more in length, with a black horn on their tail. The adults are heavy-bodied, 4- to 5-inch-wide gray moths, sometimes called hawk moths. The larvae eat the foliage, fruit, and stems of tomatoes, peppers, and related plants.

Prevention. Attract native parasites by planting pollen- and nectar-rich flowers.

Control. Handpick. Do not remove any with white, ricelike cocoons sticking out along their backs; these are pupae of native parasitic wasps. Spray caterpillars with Bt when they are small.

IMPORTED CABBAGEWORM

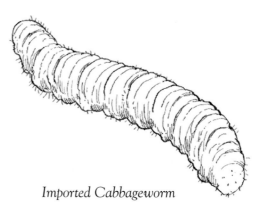

Imported Cabbageworm

The velvety green caterpillars of the imported cabbageworm eat large, ragged holes in the leaves of cabbages and related crops, such as broccoli, kale, and cauliflower. They also soil leaves with their droppings. The adults are white, 2-inch-wide butterflies with black spots.

Prevention. Install floating row covers to prevent egg laying. Attract native predatory wasps and flies by planting pollen- and nectar-rich flowers. Hang yellow sticky traps to catch female butterflies.

Control. Handpick every 2 to 3 days. Spray with Bt or neem. For serious infestations, spray with pyrethrin or sabadilla.

JAPANESE BEETLE

These ½-inch, metallic-blue-black beetles with bronze wing covers will skeletonize or defoliate a wide range of crops and will eat flowers as well. The C-shaped whitish grubs eat plant roots and are primarily a lawn pest.

Prevention. Treat lawns with milky spore disease on a neighborhood-wide basis to control grub populations. Trap adults in commercial traps placed well away from the garden; hanging traps on a neighborhood-wide basis is best.

Control. Handpick adults in early morning by shaking them onto a sheet spread under the plants. Treat serious infestations with sabadilla, pyrethrum, or rotenone.

LEAFHOPPER

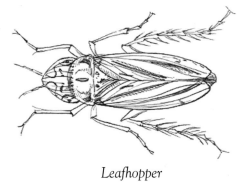

Leafhopper

There are many species of leafhoppers, but most are wedge-shaped, ¹⁄₁₀ to ½ inch long, and green, brown, or multicolored. The larvae resemble the adults but are wingless. Leafhoppers jump rapidly when disturbed. They suck plant juices from stems and leaves and attack most vegetable crops, especially beans, potatoes, celery, and eggplant. Their toxic saliva causes leaves to be distorted, and they also spread viral diseases from plant to plant.

Prevention. Cover plants with row covers to exclude these pests.

Control. Diatomaceous earth and insecticidal soaps will control leafhoppers; use pyrethrum or rotenone for severe infestations.

LEAF MINER

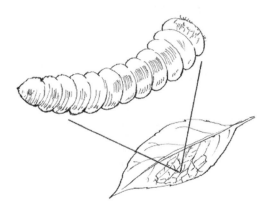

Leaf Miner

Winding whitish to beige tunnels inside plant leaves indicate the presence of leaf miners. Adults are black, ¹⁄₁₀-inch flies that lay eggs on many vegetable crops. The tunneling larvae are pale green, translucent maggots.

Prevention. Cover plantings with row covers. Pick and destroy infested leaves. Attract beneficial insects and parasitic wasps.

Control. Once the larvae are in the leaves, they are beyond the reach of sprays, so prevention is best. Neem sprays will deter adults.

MEXICAN BEAN BEETLE

Mexican Bean Beetle

Skeletonized bean leaves are generally the work of adult or larval bean beetles. The adults are rounded, ¼-inch, yellow-brown beetles with black spots; the larvae are yellow-orange and spiny. Both feed underneath leaves. Defoliation stunts plants and can kill them.

Prevention. Destroy the clusters of oval, yellow-orange eggs. Cover plants with row covers. Clean up plant debris after harvest. Native predators, including spined soldier bugs and parasitic wasps, will help with control. Plant soybeans as a trap crop, and destroy infested plants.

Control. Handpick both adults and larvae daily. Use pyrethrum, neem, rotenone, or sabadilla on severe infestations.

MITES

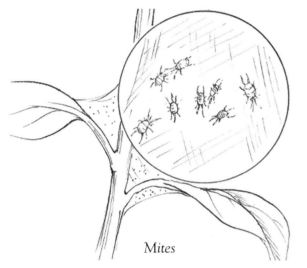

Mites

Commonly called spider mites, these minute ($\frac{1}{50}$ inch) pests attack many vegetable crops. They suck plant juices, feeding underneath leaves and causing yellow speckles or stippling on tops of leaves. Most spin webs on stem tips and under leaves; the webbing is often easier to spot than the mites, which are pale green, yellow, or red. Their feeding causes leaves to drop and weakens and stunts plants.

Prevention. Mites thrive in hot, dry conditions; spray plants with water frequently to discourage them. Attract or release native predators such as ladybugs and lacewings.

Control. Use insecticidal soap; sabadilla, pyrethrum, or rotenone for severe infestations.

ONION MAGGOT

White, $\frac{1}{4}$-inch onion maggots burrow into onions and leeks, killing young plants and stunting older ones. Their tunneling leaves bulbs open to a variety of rot diseases. The adult is a $\frac{1}{4}$-inch gray fly that lays its eggs on the soil near plants.

Prevention. Cover plants with floating row covers, or sprinkle diatomaceous earth around them to prevent egg laying. Plant onions elsewhere in the garden as a trap crop; pull and destroy them 2 weeks after sprouting. Clean up crop refuse at season's end.

Control. Once the maggots have entered the bulbs, they are out of reach of sprays, so prevention is best.

PICKLEWORM

Pale green pickleworm caterpillars are the larvae of a $1\frac{1}{4}$-inch-wingspan moth with brown wing edges and hairy tufts on the end of its abdomen. The larvae chew flowers and bore into stems and fruits of gourd-family plants, especially summer squash, cucumbers, pumpkins, and melons. The pests expel telltale sawdustlike excrement from entry holes in infested fruits and vines.

Prevention. Destroy all gourd-family plants after harvest; tilling plants under is also effective. Plant summer squash as a trap crop. Plant early-maturing cultivars.

Control. The pests are difficult to control once they have entered the plants, so prevention is best.

SLUGS & SNAILS

Slugs & Snails

Slimy, soft-bodied slugs and snails rasp holes in a wide variety of vegetable crops. They can consume entire seedlings and leave slimy trails as evidence of their activities.

Prevention. Set out traps, and check and destroy the pests daily; use shallow cans of beer, boards, grapefruit rinds, or cabbage leaves. Eliminate slugs and snails within a garden bed, and then surround it with copper flashing.

Control. Sprinkle area around plants with wood ashes or diatomaceous earth to keep slugs at bay. Renew after rains.

SQUASH BUG

Squash Bug

These brown-black, flat-topped, $\frac{1}{2}$-inch-long bugs suck plant juices from gourd-family members, especially winter squash and pumpkins. They inject toxins into plant tissue, causing leaves and shoot tips to die back and preventing fruit formation.

Prevention. Cover plants with floating row covers until blossoms appear. Keep garden free of debris; these pests prefer moist hiding places. Attract native beneficial insects by planting pollen- and nectar-rich plants. Train plants onto trellises to keep them out of reach of the pests.

Control. Handpick. For severe infestations, use sabadilla, pyrethrum, or rotenone.

SQUASH VINE BORER

Squash Vine Borer

Summer squash, cucumbers, pumpkins, melons, and other gourd-family members are all attacked by squash vine borers. The adults are 1- to $1\frac{1}{2}$-inch, narrow-winged, olive-green and red moths that lay eggs at the base of squash plants. The larvae tunnel into vines, eventually girdling them from the inside. Afflicted vines wilt suddenly and die.

Prevention. Cover plants with floating row covers until blossoms appear. Or wrap stem bases with strips of nylon stockings to prevent egg laying.

Control. Slit open infested vines, and crush the pests, then cover vines with soil to encourage rerooting. Dust bases of plants with pyrethrum, sabadilla, or rotenone before larvae enter vines.

STINKBUGS

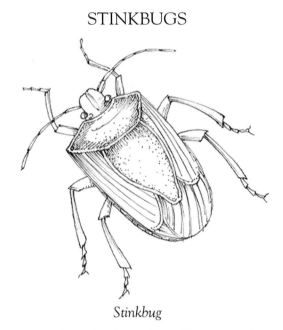

Stinkbug

A variety of shield-shaped stinkbugs attack vegetable crops, especially cabbages and related crops, squash, beans, peas, and tomatoes. The bugs are $\frac{1}{2}$ inch long and brown, green, tan, or gray; harlequin bugs are black with bright red markings. Adults and the similarly shaped nymphs suck plant sap, causing leaves and/or plants to wilt, turn brown, and die. Their feeding also causes catfaced and scarred fruits.

Prevention. Remove weeds and old plant stalks where the pests overwinter. Attract native parasitic wasps by planting nectar- and pollen-rich plants.

Control. Handpick. For severe infestations, use pyrethrum, sabadilla, or rotenone.

TARNISHED PLANT BUG

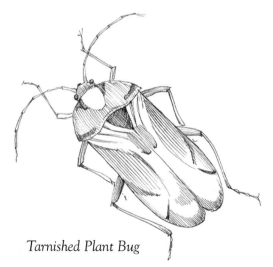

Tarnished Plant Bug

Several species of plant bugs suck plant juices from stems, buds, and fruits of most vegetable crops. The tarnished plant bug is ¼ inch long and green to brown in color; the four-lined plant bug has yellow and black stripes. They inject toxins as they feed, causing deformed, pitted flowers and blackened shoot tips.

Prevention. Hang white sticky traps to catch adults. Clean up plant debris after harvest. Attract native beneficial insects.

Control. Cover plants with row covers. For severe infestations, use rotenone or sabadilla.

THRIPS

Thrips are fast-moving, barely visible (¹⁄₅₀ to ¹⁄₂₅ inch) pests that rasp leaves and flowers of a number of crops, causing silver streaking on damaged tissue. Crops attacked include onions, beans, cucumbers, melons, and tomatoes.

Prevention. Clean up weeds and plant debris. Repel pests with aluminum-foil mulch. Trap them with yellow sticky traps. Attract or release lacewings.

Control. Spray insecticidal soap. In severe cases, use pyrethrum or rotenone.

WEBWORMS

Garden webworms are ¾-inch green caterpillars that spin webs and feed on foliage of a variety of edibles, including beans, beets, corn, and peas. The larvae feed within the webs. Adults are brownish yellow moths with gray and brown markings.

Prevention. Attract native beneficial insects. Install floating row covers to prevent egg laying.

Control. Handpick. Spray Bt. Use pyrethrum for severe infestations.

WHITEFLY

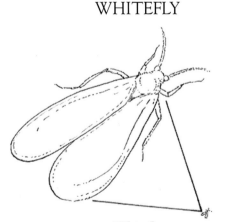

Whitefly

Sometimes called "flying dandruff," whiteflies are tiny white insects that feed underneath leaves and flutter erratically when disturbed. Feeding weakens and stunts plants, and whiteflies also excrete honeydew, which encourages sooty mold, a black fungus on leaf surfaces. Whiteflies can also transmit viral diseases.

Prevention. Many species overwinter in greenhouses and are brought home on transplants; examine transplants carefully before bringing them home. Attract native beneficial insects to act as predators. Catch adults on yellow sticky traps.

Control. Spray with insecticidal soap. For severe infestations, use pyrethrum or rotenone.

WIREWORM

Red-brown wireworms are the larvae of narrow, dark brown "click beetles." While the adults do little garden damage, the larvae bore into root crops such as potatoes, carrots, and turnips. They also consume newly planted seeds and the roots of beans, lettuce, and other crops. They are especially a problem in gardens that were recently converted from lawn.

Prevention. Cultivate the soil frequently to expose pests to predators. Apply parasitic nematodes to the soil before planting susceptible crops.

Control. Trap wireworms in pieces of potato buried in the soil; discard potato traps every other day.

CONTROLLING COMMON DISEASES

Plant diseases are generally harder to identify than pest problems. After all, they don't cause obvious signs, like holes chewed in leaves. But fungi, bacteria, and viruses—along with nematodes, which cause diseaselike symptoms—do cause some readily identifiable symptoms. The list below includes information on common diseases that attack a variety of crops. See "Problem Patrol" on page 144 for common symptoms to watch out for; also refer to the individual Plant Portraits in Part Two of this book for the diseases that attack each crop.

You'll find that preventing diseases is much more effective than controlling them. In most cases, infected plants should be pulled up and destroyed. Do not compost diseased plants unless you maintain a hot compost pile that routinely reaches temperatures in excess of 160°F.

Keep in mind that many of these diseases are

spread by contact—with tools and gardeners. Do not work among plants when they are wet, and avoid working among infected plants and then moving directly to healthy ones without disinfecting tools, washing your hands, and changing clothes.

ANTHRACNOSE

A fungal disease fostered by cool, wet weather; most common in the eastern U.S., anthracnose overwinters in soil and is spread by infected seeds, wind, rain, and contact. Common targets include beans, cucumbers, mint, melons, peppers, pumpkins, rhubarb, squash, tomatoes, and watermelons.

Symptoms. Plants develop dark, sunken patches with pinkish brown centers on leaves, stems, and fruits, followed by dieback.

Prevention. Rotate crops. Plant resistant cultivars and use certified seeds. Thoroughly clean up garden in fall.

Control. Apply a copper- or sulfur-based fungicide every 7 days; if not contained, remove and destroy infected plants.

ASTER YELLOWS

A viral disease spread by leafhoppers found throughout the U.S. Common targets include carrots, celery, cucumbers, endive, lettuce, onions, potatoes, and tomatoes.

Symptoms. Varies by crop, but general symptoms include excessive root growth, stem, and leaf distortion, stunting, and yellowed and bronzed foliage.

Prevention. Cover plants with floating row covers to control leafhoppers. Plant resistant cultivars. Pull weeds that seem infected with the disease.

Control. Infected plants cannot be cured—remove and destroy them.

BACTERIAL BLIGHT

A bacterial disease most common in humid regions east of the Rockies. It overwinters in plant debris and is spread by wind and infected seeds. Common targets include beans and peas.

Symptoms. Large brown blotches bordered with yellow on leaves and fruits; purplish stems.

Prevention. Purchase resistant cultivars and use certified seeds. Do not work among wet plants. Rotate crops.

Control. It cannot be cured—remove and destroy infected plants.

BACTERIAL LEAF SPOT

This bacterial disease is most common in the Northeast and Mid-Atlantic states and overwinters in infected plant debris or on infected seeds. It is spread by seed, soil, rain, and contact. Common targets include mustard-family crops, especially cabbage, Chinese cabbage, cauliflower, and turnips. Young plants are most susceptible.

Symptoms. Small brown or purplish spots on foliage, which yellow and may drop.

Prevention. Rotate crops. Pull up and destroy any seedlings or transplants that develop spots on foliage. Plant resistant cultivars.

Control. Prevention is best—remove and destroy infected plants.

BACTERIAL WILT

A bacterial disease most common east of the Rockies in northern states from the Midwest to the Northeast that overwinters in cucumber beetles, the primary vector. Gourd-family members, including melons, cucumbers, summer squash, and winter squash, are common targets.

Symptoms. Individual leaves wilt first, followed rapidly by entire stems and branches. Infected stems have a thick bacterial ooze inside.

Prevention. Grow resistant or tolerant cultivars. Rotate crops to discourage beetles, which overwinter in soil.

Control. Cover plants with floating row covers. Remove and destroy infected plants.

BLACK ROT

This bacterial disease infects cabbage-family plants throughout the U.S. and is spread by seed, soil, and rain.

Symptoms. V-shaped wedges of yellowed tissue from leaf margins to a vein, followed by blackened veins and leaves that dry and drop.

Prevention. Plant certified seed, or soak seed for 30 minutes in 122°F water before planting. Rotate crops. Plant in well-drained soil.

Control. Remove and destroy infected plants.

BLOSSOM-END ROT

A cultural condition that masquerades as a disease, blossom-end rot is most common in tomatoes and peppers, although gourd-family members are also affected. It is caused by calcium deficiency.

Symptoms. Water-soaked spots on the blossom

end of the fruit. The spots turn brown or black and leathery.

Prevention. Keep soil evenly moist and mulched; wet soil followed by dry conditions affects calcium distribution to the fruit. Avoid excess nitrogen fertilizer and root damage, which also affect calcium levels.

Control. Remove and compost affected fruits.

CATFACING & CRACKS

Misshapen, catfaced fruit can be caused by insect feeding or cultural conditions in a variety of crops; cracked fruit is generally a cultural problem.

Symptoms. Dimpled, gnarled, fruits with or without brown spots result from feeding by insects such as tarnished plant bugs, which inject toxins. Cold damage or incomplete pollination can cause similar symptoms. Cracked fruits, especially tomatoes, that appear otherwise undamaged are a cultural problem caused by dry soil conditions followed by very wet ones.

Prevention. Delay planting warm-season crops such as tomatoes—or cover them with floating row covers—until nighttime temperatures remain above 55°F. Keep soil mulched and evenly moist.

Control. Discard catfaced fruit; harvest and promptly use cracked fruit that is already ripe before disease organisms attack it.

CLUBROOT

This fungal disease attacks cabbage-family crops throughout the U.S. The fungus overwinters in the soil, where it is released by decomposing roots.

Symptoms. Infected plants are stunted, yellowed, and wilt easily. Their roots are gnarled, misshapen, and unable to take up sufficient water.

Prevention. Raise soil pH to 7.2 or above, because the fungus thrives in acid soil. Soil solarization is also effective.

Control. Remove and destroy infected plants.

CURLY TOP

A virus disease spread by leafhoppers, curly top infects beets, beans, carrots, Swiss chard, and tomatoes, as well as mustard- and gourd-family plants.

Symptoms. Deformed foliage that curls upward, turns yellow, and dies. In some plants, the leaves become leathery.

Prevention. Cover plants with floating row covers to control leafhoppers.

Control. There is no control—remove and destroy infected plants.

DAMPING-OFF

Seedlings of all vegetable crops can be afflicted by this fungal disease; plants sown indoors are the most susceptible.

Symptoms. Afflicted seedlings turn brown or black at the soil line and fall over, often overnight. Damping-off can also rot seeds before they emerge.

Prevention. Use clean, sterilized containers (dipped in 1 part chlorine bleach and 9 parts water) and soil-free mix for sowing and potting. Provide well-drained conditions—indoors, water from below by filling flats and draining off excess water after 20 minutes is ideal—along with plenty of light, and gentle air circulation. Dust soil surface with milled sphagnum moss, sand, or perlite.

Control. Seedlings cannot be saved; start over with better cultural conditions.

DOWNY MILDEW

This disease is caused by a variety of fungi that attack a wide range of crops throughout the U.S, especially in cool, moist weather. The fungi are spread on wind, rain, seeds, and beetles; it overwinters in soil in the southern zones. Common targets include lima beans, beets, cabbage, cauliflower, cucumbers, lettuce, onions, peas, and squash.

Symptoms. Irregular yellow spots on the tops of leaves, with corresponding, cottony white or gray blotches under leaves. Leaves eventually turn brown and die. Spots may also appear on fruits and stems.

Prevention. Rotate crops. Don't work among plants when foliage is wet. Space plants properly to provide good air circulation.

Control. Apply Bordeaux mix or a copper-based fungicide to reduce the spread of the disease. Remove and destroy infected plants or plant parts.

EARLY BLIGHT

Tomatoes, potatoes, and other nightshade-family crops are attacked by this fungal disease that is spread primarily by wind and rain. Seeds and flea beetles can also spread the fungus.

Symptoms. Lower leaves are attacked first, forming brown spots with concentric rings. Eventually entire leaves turn brown, die, and drop.

Prevention. Rotate crops. Plant resistant cultivars. Pull up and destroy plants after harvest. Plant certified seeds and seed potatoes.

Control. Spray a copper-based fungicide to prevent the disease from spreading. Remove and destroy seriously infected plants.

FUSARIUM WILT

A fungal disease found throughout the U.S., fusarium wilt overwinters in the soil and infects plants through roots and wounds. The disease can also be spread in water droplets or brought into the garden on transplants. Common targets include asparagus, beets, spinach, Swiss chard, as well as mustard-, gourd-, and nightshade-family crops.

Symptoms. Leaves turn yellow, then brown, and droop, with lower leaves usually affected first. Leaves, and eventually plants, die.

Prevention. Rotate crops, although the fungi can live in the soil for up to 10 years. Plant resistant cultivars. Solarize the soil.

Control. Remove and destroy infected plants.

GRAY MOLD

Also called botrytis, gray mold is a fungal disease found throughout the U.S. It attacks almost all garden plants, especially when humidity is high, temperatures are warm, and air circulation is poor. The fungus, which overwinters in plant debris in the soil, is spread by wind and in water.

Symptoms. Water-soaked spots on leaves, stems, flowers, or fruits develop fuzzy, gray or tan growth. Afflicted plant parts rot.

Prevention. Space plants properly to encourage air circulation and encourage good soil drainage. Clean up crop residue after harvest.

Control. Pick off infected leaves or other plant parts. Remove and destroy seriously infected plants.

LATE BLIGHT

Like early blight, this fungal disease attacks nightshade-family crops, especially tomatoes and potatoes. The fungus overwinters in potato tubers and plant debris. It is especially problematic when cool, moist nights are followed by warm, muggy days.

Symptoms. Water-soaked spots appear on lower leaves, then turn brown. White fungal spores may be visible beneath leaves. Spots also appear on stems and fruits, which rot quickly. Potato tubers are also affected, developing sunken, dry-rotted areas or wet, moldy spots.

Prevention. Harvest all potato tubers, and destroy any that show signs of blight. Plant certified disease-free seed potatoes.

Control. Dig and destroy all infected plants.

LEAF SPOTS

Leaf spots are a symptom rather than an actual disease, since they can be caused by bacteria, fungi, and insects. Bacterial leaf spot causes brownish or purple spots on leaves; downy mildew causes yellow spots on leaves; early blight, brown spots with concentric rings; late blight causes water-soaked spots; mites cause yellow spots or a stippled effect on leaves. See the individual descriptions of these diseases for more information.

NEMATODES

Nematodes are tiny ($\frac{1}{50}$ inch) unsegmented worms that cause diseaselike symptoms. Most live in the soil but attack foliage. Common targets include corn, lettuce, onions, peppers, and potatoes, as well as tomatoes.

Symptoms. Infected plants are stunted, then turn yellow and wilt. Pulling up plants reveals roots with galls, swollen spots, or excessive branching. (Don't mistake the galls caused by root knot nematodes for the nodules on legumes, such as peas and beans, caused by nitrogen-fixing bacteria. Plants with nitrogen-fixing bacteria appear otherwise healthy.) Nematodes on leaves cause distorted growth and galls.

Prevention. Grow resistant cultivars. Rotate susceptible crops with nonsusceptible ones. Solarize the soil. Grow marigolds, and till them into soil at season's end.

Control. Apply chitin, a compound found in shellfish shells, to the soil. The chitin stimulates the growth of microbes that feed on chitin. Since nematodes are also covered with chitin, they are susceptible to the microbes. Add a nitrogen source, such as dried blood, with chiten to supply necessary nutrients. Chitin is available as ClandoSan, which contains a synthetic (not organic) nitrogen fertilizer.

POWDERY MILDEW

A fungal disease common throughout the U.S., it attacks a wide range of vegetable crops, including mustard-, gourd-, and pea-family crops, as well as peppers. The disease thrives in warm conditions when humidity is above 20 percent.

Symptoms. Powdery, white blotches eventually covering entire leaves are a sure sign of this disease. Afflicted foliage turns yellow and brown and shrivels up. The fungus also attacks fruit.

Prevention. Handpick and destroy infected leaves. Prune plants to improve air circulation. Clean up garden debris in fall.

Control. Remove and destroy seriously infected plants.

ROOT ROT

A variety of fungi cause root rot on nearly all vegetable crops, especially in the spring in cool, wet, poorly drained soil.

Symptoms. Afflicted plants turn yellow and grow slowly. Infected seedlings or transplants usually die; larger plants are stunted. Small feeder roots rot first, followed by larger roots.

Prevention. Provide aerated, well-drained soil with plenty of organic matter. Avoid moving transplants to the garden when soil is too cool for rapid growth.

Control. Remove and destroy infected plants, and improve soil conditions.

RUST

Found throughout the U.S., rust diseases are caused by a variety of wind-borne fungi. Common targets include asparagus, beans, beets, carrots, corn, onion, and spinach.

Symptoms. Red-brown patches on leaves—either above or below the leaves—indicate rust. Afflicted plants are stunted and sometimes killed.

Prevention. Plant resistant cultivars. Space plants widely to encourage good air circulation. Clean up and destroy crop residue after harvest.

Control. Remove and destroy infected plants.

SUNSCALD

Diseases that cause leaves to drop can lead to this condition, which is especially common on tomatoes and peppers.

Symptoms. White or pale yellow areas on top of fruit that blister and eventually turn brown.

Prevention. Control leaf diseases. Avoid excessive pruning to maintain foliage cover.

Control. Pick and discard afflicted fruit.

TOBACCO MOSAIC VIRUS

Nightshade-family plants throughout the U.S. are susceptible to this viral disease. In addition to tomatoes, peppers, and eggplants, the disease also attacks beets, some mustard-family plants, and spinach. The disease is carried to plants by contact—by handling tobacco products and on tools and hands, which can move the virus from healthy plants to infected ones. Tomato seeds can also be infected.

Symptoms. Mottled, yellow and green areas on leaves. Plants may be stunted or deformed, and leaves may be puckered.

Prevention. Plant resistant cultivars. Wash hands and sterilize tools after touching infected plants.

Control. It cannot be cured—remove and destroy infected plants.

VERTICILLIUM WILT

This fungal disease, found throughout the U.S., produces symptoms that resemble those of fusarium wilt. The fungi overwinter in the soil and infect plants through roots and wounds. The disease can also be spread in water or on tools or shoes. Common targets include beans as well as gourd and nightshade-family crops.

Symptoms. Leaves turn yellow, then brown, and droop, with lower leaves usually affected first. Leaves eventually die, fruit is small and stunted, and plants die.

Prevention. Use a 4-year crop-rotation scheme. Plant resistant cultivars. Clean up and destroy all infected crop residue at season's end.

Control. Remove and destroy infected plants.

---

*The worst enemyes to gardens
are Moles, Catts, Earewiggs,
Snailes and Mice, and they must
all bee carefuly destroyed, or
all your labor all the year long is lost.*
THOMAS HAMMER,
*The Garden Book
of Sir Thomas Hammer,* 1653

PART II

PLANT PORTRAITS

WHILE A SUNNY SITE, GOOD SOIL CARE, AND ATTENTION THROUGH THE SEASON ARE THE BUILDING BLOCKS OF A HEALTHY GARDEN, meeting the needs of the individual crops you grow—knowing when to plant, providing the right sun and soil conditions, and knowing when to feed, water, or harvest—are also essential keys to success. The Plant Portraits that follow include all the information you need to provide a wide range of vegetables and herbs with ideal conditions, but don't let the information they contain overwhelm you. Vegetables and herbs are a forgiving lot. Most will produce a good harvest with less-than-ideal soil, for example, so go ahead and plant even if you are in the first year of a campaign to transform a morass of clay into a well-drained garden filled with soil rich in organic matter. And if you've done your soil homework well, most crops will be satisfied—it's not necessary to provide special conditions for each and every crop, just as it's not necessary to use season-extension techniques to get the garden planted on the earliest possible date. Do as much or as little as appeals to you—and suits your crops.

If you are a beginning gardener, remember to start small. You'll likely have more success if you plant five rather than ten crops. Once you are comfortable with juggling schedules for five crops, try succession planting to spread out the harvest or make

175

room for more vegetables and herbs in the garden. Another technique to experiment with as you gain experience is intercropping. Depending on your interests, picking the first ripe tomato, growing the largest pumpkin, planting a vegetable no one in the neighborhood has ever heard of, or producing the largest yield in the smallest space can become an enjoyable challenge, one that leads to unending tinkering with scheduling, fertilizers, watering regimes, and more. Another gardener may enjoy spending his or her time figuring out how to incorporate vegetables and herbs in flower beds or borders—or flowers in the vegetable garden. Whatever your goal, you'll find helpful information in the Plant Portraits that follow.

And to ensure success, you may want to appeal to a higher power, perhaps something like the gardener's prayer that appeared in *The Gardener's Year* (1929) by Karel Čapek. He asked only that there be rain every day (but not on the drought-loving plants), sun (but not too much), and "plenty of dew and little wind, enough worms, no plant-lice and snails, no mildew, and that once a week thin liquid manure and guano many fall from heaven." Amen to that.

GROWING TIPS AT A GLANCE

The symbols listed below are used throughout the Plant Portraits in this encyclopedia to highlight growing conditions and special features about each plant.

○ Full sun (more than 6 hours of sun per day; ideally all day)

◑ Partial sun (some direct sun, but less than 6 hours per day)

✻ Cool weather crop

✹ Warm weather crop

✿ Ornamental

▼ Grows well in containers

PLANT PORTRAITS

ADZUKI BEAN

Vigna angularis. Pea family, Fabaceae. Annual.

○ ✹

Adzuki beans, which have been cultivated for several thousand years, are a familiar sight in the Far East, second in popularity only to soybeans. Also known as chi dou and Chinese red beans—they are the basis of red bean paste—Adzukis are nearly as nutritious as soybeans (25 percent protein and high in vitamins and minerals) and are easy to digest. The beans have an unusual, slightly sweet flavor.

There are vining types, but the short-tendril bush form, which grows about 2 feet tall, is more common. A better crop for the South than for the North, adzukis are short-day plants (see "Weather & Day-Length Considerations" on page 99) and won't flower until mid- or late summer above the Mason-Dixon line. Unlike most members of the pea family, which produce white, pink, and purple blossoms, adzukis have yellow blooms. At least one named cultivar is available—'Express'—but most seed catalogs list this bean simply as "Adzuki."

They can be cultivated wherever the garden season is long and warm enough for the crop to mature fully, a minimum of 120 days (USDA Zone 4 and warmer). Although not frost-tolerant, plants will succeed in slightly cooler temperatures than black-eyed peas or asparagus beans can handle. Yields are high, since each 4- or 5-inch-long pod is filled with small, shiny red beans. For a family of four, 20 plants should be enough; if you want to preserve, increase the number.

While adzukis are not especially useful in the landscape, they can be grown in containers. Choose one with good drainage, and fill with enriched potting mix; keep plants well watered, and feed every 3 weeks with compost tea.

HOW TO GROW

Adzuki beans like the same conditions that common green, or snap, beans do: That means full sun and loose, organically rich, slightly acid soil (pH 6.0

to 6.8) that drains well. They can be planted at the same time as bush beans, about a week after the average frost-free date. Gardeners who have abbreviated growing seasons and want to harvest dry beans must begin plants indoors 3 to 4 weeks before the last expected frost. Beans resent transplanting, so use individual containers, harden off fully, and try not to disturb the roots as you move the plants outdoors (when the soil has reached a temperature of 60°F). To have a continuous supply, plant successive crops every week or 10 days.

Alternatively, sow seeds *in situ*, ½ to 1 inch deep, spaced 3 to 4 inches apart, in rows 2 to 3 feet apart. In 68°F soil, germination takes about 7 days (to get a mini-jump on the season, pregerminate seeds indoors on moist paper towels). Adzuki beans are relatively immune to diseases and insects, but installing floating row covers over the planting area will provide insurance against some pests, as well as provide a few degrees of warmth to the emerging plants.

Once plants are established, mulch to suppress weeds and retain moisture. Adzuki beans need an even supply of water, about 1 inch a week; feed plants with compost tea or liquid seaweed when they are 5 inches tall and again when they begin to flower.

HARVESTING

Adzuki beans are normally left in the garden until they are dry, but they can be harvested sooner as "green beans" when the pods just begin to plump but are still tender. Pick at least every third day to keep plants producing.

To harvest dry beans, pull the entire plant. (In Japan and China, dried adzuki beans are ground into flour for making pastries and breads. Adzukis can also be used in soups, casseroles, and salads and for sprouting.) Shell pods if they are fully dry and beginning to split. If they aren't thoroughly dry, hang the plants in a dry place until they are. Shell and store in a sealed container in a cool (50°F), dark place.

Adzuki flowers are self-pollinating, and crossing with other *Vigna* species, such as mung beans, asparagus beans, or southern beans, or with other members of the pea family, is unlikely. Save seeds from the most vigorous and healthy plants. Seeds are viable for about 4 years; store in airtight containers in a dark, cool location.

ANISE

Pimpinella anisum. Carrot family, Apiaceae. Annual.

○ ✳ ❄ ✿

Several herbs taste or smell of anise, but this annual is the one that sets the standard. It has a licorice taste so fresh and clear, the plant was once thought capable of fending off the evil eye; and so pungent, it was considered an aphrodisiac. Anise is one of the most ancient herbs in cultivation, indigenous to Egypt and the Middle East, with a name that derives from early Arabic. Another common name is Sweet Alice.

Anise is a demanding slow-growing herb that doesn't transplant well and needs almost 4 months of warm, frost-free weather to produce a crop of seedlike fruits, the so-called seeds that are the usual plant part harvested. "Annis thrive exceedingly, but Annis Seed … seldom come to maturity," John Josselyn recorded in *Account of Two Voyages to New England* (1673). Although less celebrated, the foliage is edible too and is used fresh in salads or cooked in the manner of many of the plant's herbal relatives, such as chervil and parsley. Anise leaves have two different shapes. Those at the base of the plant resemble flat-leaved parsley, while the leaflets higher up are small and feathery. It can be grown in USDA Zone 4 and warmer.

In late summer, the plant sends up 1- or 2-foot stalks holding lacy, white umbrella-shaped clusters of flowers that look like Queen Anne's lace. These yield the ribbed seeds, actually dried fruits, that are harvested for cooking—in breads, cookies, hard candies, fruit pies, and cooked vegetables—medicine, and cosmetics, and for liqueurs such as anisette,

SWEET ANISE

When buying seeds, don't confuse anise with sweet anise, or Florence fennel, a tall perennial that is grown for its seeds and swollen bulblike stems. (See page 260 for information on growing this herb.)

once prized as an aid to digestion. Similarly, the ancient Romans polished off their huge feasts with anise cakes. Anise tea, another digestive aid, is recommended as well to soothe coughs and nausea. Anise seeds are also used to freshen the breath—and to bait mousetraps.

HOW TO GROW

Anise needs full sun and grows in ordinary well-worked, weed-free soil. A sunny corner of the vegetable garden or a special plot devoted to annual herbs is a good place for anise, which can easily be overshadowed or crowded out by faster-growing plants. Give each plant 6 inches all around. Eight to a dozen plants will provide early greens and a good crop of seeds.

To grow anise in large containers, sow a cluster of seeds and thin to three or four plants. They're attractive as accents behind shorter herbs, such as oregano and lemon basil.

Seeds should be sown directly in the garden when the weather is dependably warm in spring. They germinate at about 70°F. Anise grows slowly. If your growing season is shorter than 120 days, you may not be able to harvest anise seeds at all, because it does not transplant well from an indoor sowing. If you do sow seeds early indoors, use individual pots and transplant carefully to minimize root disturbance. When thinning, be sure to cut seedlings, rather than pull them, to leave their neighbors undisturbed.

Anise, which has no serious disease or insect problems, will not produce seeds if it grows in shade or if the season is too short or too cool. Give it as much warmth and sun as possible.

HARVESTING

Snip off leaves as desired, but do not take so many that the plant is weakened. Seeds ripen unevenly, so when they start to ripen, roughly a month after blooming starts, cut entire plants at the base. To catch the seeds as they fall, gather the plants in bunches and put them inside paper bags with their stems sticking out. Hang the covered bunches upside down in a cool, dry place. Seeds are viable for 3 years; store in airtight containers in a dark, cool location.

ANNUAL MARJORAM. See *Marjoram*
ARTICHOKE, GLOBE. See *Globe Artichoke*

ARUGULA

Eruca sativa. Mustard family, Brassicaceae. Annual.

○ ◑ ❋ ▼

Arugula is a low-growing, cool-weather salad green with a flavor that carries a dash of mustard. It also carries a dash of the medicinal, as it once was prescribed for everything from problems of indigestion to problems of the complexion—"The root and seed stamped and mixed with vinegaer and the gall of an Oxe, taketh away freckles . . . blacke and blew spots, and all such deformities of the face." English herbalist John Gerard, quoting the Roman Pliny, claimed even more for arugula's effect on the skin: "Whoever taketh the seed of Rocket [arugula] before he be whipt, shall be so hardened that he shall easily endure the paine."

Arugula, also called rocket, arrived in North America with the Puritans but gradually sank into obscurity as a garden green. In the past decade, however, it has been rediscovered by gourmets—who often call it by its French appellation, *roquette*—and become a darling of nouvelle cuisine. Its lobed leaves add a cool blue-green hue and peppery taste to salads made in the nouvelle style called "mesclun," a mix of greens picked young and served fresh. (For more on growing these greens, see *Mesclun* on page 301.) In the view of one seed merchant, arugula, "grown well and gathered at the right moment, adds a fullness to salads that will alter history" in your kitchen and in your garden. The

Arugula

words are hyperbolic, but they speak to the current enthusiasm for this versatile green.

DECIDING WHAT TO GROW

Fast-growing arugula—ready to pick about 40 days after seeding—is primarily a spring and fall crop in USDA Zones 3 through 6; in warmer regions, it can be grown through the winter without cover. Because it is ready to use so quickly, arugula can be followed or preceded by other vegetables and herbs or inter-cropped with plants that require more time to mature. While it can be planted in rows, most gardeners choose to broadcast seeds in a bed or add arugula to mesclun.

Four dozen mature plants planted over the season should be enough for a family of four. Arugula, which forms a rosette of deeply lobed leaves, is not an especially pretty plant. It does well in pots and boxes, though, making it a good choice for a container salad garden. Use a container, at least 8 inches wide and 12 inches deep, with good bottom drainage. Fill with enriched potting soil, and keep plants well watered.

There are no named arugula cultivars. Seeds are sold by common name, as arugula, rocket, or roquette.

SITE & SOIL

Arugula is an unparticular green that can survive almost any setting but thrives in soil rich in humus with a pH of 6.0 to 6.8. To keep plants growing quickly, the key to producing succulent and agreeably flavored leaves, make sure they are not stressed by lack of moisture or too much heat. Although rigorously harvesting leaves will slow the process, a spring planting quickly runs to seed with the onset of summer, causing the leaves to become unpalatably hot and bitter.

HOW TO GROW

Arugula seeds sprout quickly, even in cold soil, so there is little to be gained from starting plants indoors. Direct-seed in the spring as soon as the soil can be worked, either by broadcasting seeds in a bed and covering them with a thin layer of compost or by planting them ¼ inch deep, spaced at 1 inch, in rows. Cover the seedbed or row with floating row covers to prevent flea beetles and other insects from reaching the new plants.

When the seedlings are 3 inches tall, thin to 6 inches by pulling individual plants (the culls can be used in mesclun). An early spring crop can be followed in 2 weeks by a second planting; begin planting fall crops at the end of summer, continuing until about 30 days before the average first-frost date.

While arugula needs plenty of water—keep the soil moist—it rarely requires additional fertilizer if sown in moderately fertile soil. If temperatures rise prematurely, shading plants may keep them from bolting. Because arugula is a cool-weather crop, preferring conditions that are too chilly for many insects, it has few pest problems and is rarely bothered by disease.

HARVESTING

Leaves, which are rich in vitamin C and minerals, can be harvested as soon as they reach useful size, usually within 4 weeks of planting. Cut outside leaves at the base of the stem to encourage new growth from the center of the plant. If your plants bolt, harvest their white flowers, light green buds, and unripe seedpods for salads.

Arugula is highly perishable and does not store well. Harvest early in the morning, when temperatures are lower, and refrigerate leaves immediately after picking.

Arugula, which is self-sterile and requires insects for pollination, often self-seeds. It does not cross with other members of the mustard family. To save seeds, which are viable for 5 years, store in airtight containers in a dark, cool location.

ASPARAGUS

Asparagus officinalis. Lily family, Liliaceae.
Perennial.

○ ❊ ❀

People in ancient times not only ate asparagus but used it to cure troubles of the heart, liver, and kidneys, as well as to kill pain, improve eyesight, and even soothe bee stings. Those merits and its perennial habit may account for its early arrival in North America, although its reported ability to "stir up lust" could have had something to do with its importance, the Puritans' reputation for morality notwithstanding. While asparagus immigrated to this country in the 17th century, it wasn't until the 19th century that we unwittingly imported the asparagus beetle and asparagus rust.

Colonial Americans, who called it "sperage," "sparagrass," "sparrow-grass," and just plain "grass," planted asparagus with enthusiasm. Thomas Jefferson grew a cultivar named 'Cooper's Pale Green' and in 1818 wrote a friend that it "come to table" between March 24 and April 14 (the same time that the peach blossoms, house martins, and ticks appeared). Once established on the East Coast, asparagus kept traveling until it reached the West Coast, which now produces more asparagus than does any region of the country. California

allots nearly 30,000 acres to asparagus, more than any other state, but growers in Washington are more efficient. They harvest more spears—82,800,000 pounds a year—on 6,000 fewer acres.

While the medicinal use of asparagus has dwindled, its ornamental qualities—tall, graceful fernlike foliage that turns gold in autumn, and small, bright red berries—are increasingly championed by edible landscapers. Except for extremely warm regions, which don't provide an adequate dormancy period, asparagus can be grown throughout the country (USDA Zone 2 and warmer). Few vegetables are a prettier choice for the ornamental garden.

DECIDING WHAT TO GROW

Asparagus, the only species in the 3,000-member lily family that is cultivated primarily as a food crop, is dioecious: Male flowers are produced on one plant, female flowers on another. For home gardeners, the dioecious cultivar 'Mary Washington' (and a couple of her offspring) have been synonymous with asparagus. Then breeders at Rutgers University in New Jersey introduced a fraternity of asparagus hybrids. In a neat bit of botanical chauvinism, female plants were eliminated, leaving gardeners with nothing but male plants.

Without female plants, there is no crossbreeding and no weak volunteer seedlings that crowd the asparagus bed. Rather than half the plants—the females—expending energy to produce seeds, every plant puts all its resources into producing spears. As a result, yields are far greater, two or three times the size of older, open-pollinated cultivars: In one university trial, 'Jersey Giant' produced nearly 4,000 pounds more per acre than did 'Mary Washington'. Finally, the all-male Jersey hybrids have good tolerance to fusarium crown and root rots, asparagus rust, and cercospera leaf spot, which means fewer controls in the garden. It's no wonder a home-garden Extension Service bulletin from Pennsylvania State University says, "'Washington' types are no longer recommended."

One debate among asparagus growers is how to get started: seeds or the octopus-like crowns? Starting from seeds in a sterile potting mix guarantees plants free from fusarium rots but adds another year of waiting for the first harvest. Certified disease-free crowns are the best way to begin a backyard asparagus patch. Don't waste money on 2- or 3-year-old crowns. Purchase 1-year-old crowns with

ASPARAGUS CULTIVARS

Dioecious cultivars produce both male and female (seed-producing) plants.

'Jersey Giant': all-male hybrid; high yields; especially suited to colder regions; fusarium-crown and root-rot tolerance, rust-resistant; the original Jersey all-male hybrid cultivar.

'Jersey King': all-male hybrid; high yields; widely adapted; performs well in warm climates; fusarium-crown and root-rot tolerance, rust-resistant.

'Jersey Knight': all-male hybrid; high yields; widely adapted; performs well in warm climates; fusarium-crown and root-rot tolerance, rust-resistant.

'Mary Washington': standard open-pollinated home-garden variety; dioecious; some rust tolerance; still popular, but no longer recommended.

'Viking': improved 'Mary Washington' type; dioecious, open-pollinated; rust-tolerant; Canadian cultivar.

'UC 157': hybrid; dioecious; popular commercial cultivar in California and Washington; heat-tolerant; developed at the University of California.

'Waltham': improved 'Mary Washington' type; dioecious, open-pollinated; rust-tolerant; high yields.

fleshy roots, and plant them immediately so that they don't dry out.

If you've chosen one of the Jersey hybrids, 25 plants should be enough for fresh table use for a family of four; double that number if you've picked 'Mary Washington' or another dioecious cultivar. If you want to preserve, increase the planting.

SITE & SOIL

Well-cared-for asparagus plants will produce for 15 years or more, so locate this crop where it won't be disturbed, either in a separate bed or on the edge of the garden. Asparagus will grow in partial sun, but for a generous supply of sturdy spears, full sun is required.

Englishman Thomas Hill declared in 1577 that asparagus "joyeth in a fat, moist, and wel dressed earth." In fact, asparagus will grow in almost any soil that has a pH between 6.5 and 7.0, but plants do poorly in soil with a pH below 6.0. They also do poorly in wet soil, which increases susceptibility to crown and root rot. Recent research shows that asparagus, traditionally pegged as a big water consumer, is far more drought-tolerant than was previously believed. Plants are more likely to drown than to die of thirst. Unless rainfall is scant, supplemental watering is unnecessary. It is important, however, to provide new plantings with adequate moisture—between 1 and 2 inches a week.

At least Hill had part of it right: Asparagus is most productive in "wel dressed earth," soil that is rich in organic matter and amply supplied with phosphorus, especially, and potassium. Because of its extensive root system, asparagus is not recommended as a container plant, though it thrives in raised beds.

HOW TO GROW

Not only has gardeners' choice of cultivars changed but also how they plant them. The common advice was to dig trenches 2 or 3 feet deep and set crowns at least a foot below the soil surface. No more of that. Exhaustive experiments have confirmed that crowns of the all-male hybrids planted deeper than 6 inches will produce fewer spears. Don't crowd plants either: Crowding reduces spear size and encourages diseases.

Asparagus crowns are still planted in early spring (late winter in warm regions), when the soil has warmed to about 50°F. Planting early in cold,

Emerging asparagus shoots

wet soil is no advantage: Crowns won't grow until the soil warms, and the risk of disease is increased. The new planting recommendation is to create 7-inch-deep, V-shaped furrows instead of deep trenches. Spread a handful each of bonemeal and wood ashes, plus a 1-inch layer of compost or well-rotted

---

SECOND COMING

In most regions, you can fool asparagus to produce spears in autumn rather than in spring. When spears emerge in spring, harvest from only half of your bed. Allow the spears in the unharvested section to form brush. Cut the brush after it reaches full size; spears for a second harvest will emerge in autumn.

manure in each furrow. Soak the crowns in compost tea for 10 minutes, then lay them on top of the organic matter, 12 to 16 inches apart, with rows spaced 4 feet apart. Don't worry about spreading out the crowns' roots. Lay them on their sides, and cover with 2 inches of soil.

As the shoots emerge, gradually fill in the furrows—taking care not to cover any foliage—until they are level with the soil surface. Resist temptation: Do not harvest spears from 1-year-old crowns during their first year in your garden. Let each spear "fern out." Keep plants weeded, and mulch heavily after the furrows have been filled in. Mulching—use straw or chopped leaves—reduces soil crusting, helps control weeds and retain moisture, and reduces heaving from freeze-thaw cycles in winter. Side-dress plants with a balanced fertilizer in late summer, and top-dress with an organic mulch in autumn.

Professionals continue to argue over when to remove the tall asparagus stalks, or brush, which develop from spears that weren't harvested—in fall, to prevent pests from overwintering, or in spring, after it's provided winter protection? If you choose to cut the brush down in autumn, wait until after there have been several killing frosts, and mulch the bed after removing it. Or cut down the brush in early spring, before the new spears begin popping through the soil's surface.

In the third year and every year thereafter, spread a layer of compost or well-rotted manure over the asparagus bed in early spring, and apply lime or wood ashes if the soil pH needs adjusting. Keep the bed mulched, and side-dress with a balanced organic fertilizer in late summer. If yields have begun to decrease, spray asparagus foliage (not the spears) with fish emulsion or compost tea every 3 weeks until the first frost.

POTENTIAL PROBLEMS

Unfortunately, even beds of macho all-male asparagus cultivars can't compete with weeds, which steal water, light, and nutrients from plants. Although asparagus tolerates high salinity, the old practice of using salt to kill weeds is no longer recommended, because of leaching and its effect on the soil. Instead, begin with weed-free soil, cultivate when necessary, and mulch heavily, being careful not to use organic matter, such as hay, that contains weed seeds.

To gain protection against the major asparagus

diseases—asparagus rust, fusarium root and crown rots, and cercospera leaf spot—grow disease-tolerant cultivars like 'Jersey Giant'. Purchasing certified disease-free crowns will help avoid importing fusarium rots, as will making sure your soil drains well and has a pH between 6.5 and 7.0.

Asparagus also has several insect foes that attack the plants' foliage, including aphids and mites. (See "Controlling Common Pests" on page 162 for control measures.) Plants can also be plagued by asparagus beetles. If you don't eyeball these 1/4-inch-long blue-black menaces, misshapen spears and defoliation indicate their presence. Install floating row covers in early spring; remove covers when air temperature reaches 65°F. Handpick. For severe infestations, spray with pyrethrum, two applications 3 days apart, and cut down asparagus brush after the first hard freeze.

HARVESTING

Asparagus, which is a good source of vitamins C and B$_6$, folacin, and thiamin, needs plenty of time to settle itself in the garden. To make sure plants are well established, follow the 0-2-4-6-to-8 harvest rule. Harvest for zero (0) weeks the first year the plants are in the garden; harvest for 2 weeks the second year they're in the garden; for 4 weeks the third year; and for 6 to 8 weeks every year thereafter. Keep in mind that these are general guidelines. The length of the harvest season depends on the weather. If the diameter of more than half of the spears is smaller than 3/8 inch, stop harvesting, no matter how many weeks have passed.

Harvest every spear that emerges, even the skinny ones, by cutting it off at the soil line when it is between 7 and 10 inches long and its tip is still tight. (Loose tips, not the diameter of the spear, is the sign of toughness.) Take care not to cut below the soil surface, or you may injure the plant's crown. Many gardeners snap rather than cut spears, but snapping leaves a stub that can harbor pests and diseases. After harvesting asparagus, immediately immerse the spears in ice water until cooled. Drain, seal in plastic bags, and refrigerate.

Asparagus plants cross-pollinate easily. To produce seeds (which are formed only on female plants) that breed true, plant only one nonhybrid dioecious cultivar. Asparagus seeds are viable for 3 years; store in airtight containers in a dark, cool location.

SPECIAL NOTES

White asparagus, a popular culinary treat in France, is not a separate cultivar but the result of blanching by covering to cut off direct light. To blanch asparagus, pull soil up around each spear, or grow under opaque row covers or tunnels.

ASPARAGUS BEAN

Vigna unguiculata var. *sesquipedalis.* Pea family, Fabaceae. Annual.

○ ☀ ▼

Yardlong bean, another name for this species, may be an exaggeration, but this is a vegetable for *Ripley's Believe It Or Not.* Asparagus bean's thin pods really do grow 1 to 2 feet long—3 feet in ideal conditions—making them an attraction for children or anyone else who enjoys the unusual. They've been grown in China for thousands of years, and although they're called beans, they are more closely related to southern cowpeas than to common beans. Gardeners and cooks have argued about their flavor nearly as long, some claiming they taste like asparagus, others that they have a clear "bean" flavor. Everyone agrees that the pods, which are usually harvested before they reach full size and are still immature and tender, taste good, though. Twist an asparagus bean into a pretzel shape, and even your children will be asking for a second helping.

Also known as Chinese long bean, dow guak, and snake bean, asparagus beans are fun to grow, although they can be finicky, sometimes producing small yields for no apparent reason. The plant needs a long, warm growing season (a minimum of 75 days) and a sturdy trellis to climb. The vines have a slightly unkempt look about them—the foliage is less luxuriant than that of runner beans—but the large white and lavender flowers are extremely pretty. Each flower produces two pods. In temperate areas, vine growth is moderate, but in hot regions, plants will twine 8 feet and higher, so locate plants where they won't shade other crops. They do best in USDA Zone 5 and warmer but may succeed in cooler regions if given a southern exposure and protection from the cold. Because they require a tall, sturdy trellis, asparagus beans grown in containers should also be located against a wall or sturdy fence or trellis.

Asparagus bean

Although there are a few named cultivars— 'Orient Wonder', which has 18-inch-long green pods and does fairly well in cooler climates, is the name you're most likely to see—most seed catalogs list asparagus bean by color, either red-seeded or black-seeded. Four plants should be plenty in warm regions where this vegetable thrives.

HOW TO GROW

Asparagus beans, which need a warm site in full sun, are tolerant of thin soil, but they do better when planted in loose, organically rich, slightly acid soil (pH 6.0 to 6.8) that drains well. Like other pea-family members, asparagus beans have the ability to capture nitrogen from the air. For the plants to "fix" nitrogen, certain *Rhizobia* bacteria must be present in the soil. If you haven't added manure or other high-nitrogen material to the garden, coat seeds with an inoculant to make sure the bacteria are present and that your plants can manufacture the nitrogen they need. You can purchase inoculant at a garden center; just before planting, wet the seeds and cover them with the powder.

Direct-sow asparagus beans—1 inch deep with a final spacing between plants of at least 4 inches—1 or 2 weeks after you would common beans or 3 or 4 weeks after the average frost-free date. In 65°F soil, seeds should germinate in about 1 week. Because they are short-day plants (see "Weather & Day-Length Considerations" on page 99), plants won't begin flowering and forming pods until mid- or late summer in northern latitudes. Gardeners with cool or short growing seasons should begin plants indoors 2 to 3 weeks before the last expected frost. Beans resent transplanting, so use individual containers, harden off fully, and try not to disturb the roots as you move the plants outdoors (when both the soil and nighttime temperatures have reached 60°F).

Install a tall, sturdy support—netting, wire trellis, tepees, or heavy strings—for the vines to climb at the same time you sow seeds or transplant. Feed plants every 3 weeks with manure tea, and make sure they receive at least 1 inch of water a week. To retain moisture and suppress weeds, mulch plants once they are established.

Asparagus beans are relatively unbothered by insects and diseases, but seeds can carry viruses. If any plants become infected, remove and destroy them.

HARVESTING

Although asparagus beans can grow 30 inches and longer, don't let them get that large. Instead, pick the pods, which are handled in the kitchen as common snap beans are, when they are still tender, about 10 to 12 inches long. Harvest every day or two to keep plants producing.

Asparagus bean flowers are self-pollinating and not attractive to insects, so crossing is unlikely, even when cultivars are grown next to each other. Save seeds from the most vigorous and healthy plants. Seeds are viable for about 4 years; store in airtight containers in a dark, cool location.

ASPARAGUS LETTUCE. See *Celtuce*
ASPARAGUS PEA. See *Winged Bean*

BASIL

Ocimum spp. Mint family, Lamiaceae. Annual.

○ ◐ ☀ ✿ ▜

Basil is an herb with at least 30 faces and a mixed reputation that has vacillated between evil and sacred. The name basil derives from a Greek term meaning "royal herb," but in Greece, the plant was considered somewhat wicked, needing to be cursed

and reviled in order to grow well. Italians considered it the herb of courtship, calling it *bacia-nicola*, "kiss-me-Nicholas." One species, *Ocimum sanctum*, is consecrated to Vishnu and grown near every Hindu temple in India.

Nicolas Culpeper, a 17th-century English herbalist, said that the plant's disparate roles were causing some consternation: "This is the herb which all authors are together by the ears about, and rail at one another, like lawyers." He wrote, "Pliny and the Arabian physicians defend it," then recorded that an acquaintance of his who had done nothing more than smell the plant "had a scorpion bred in his brain." Concluded the confused herbalist, "I dare write no more of it."

Nowadays, gardeners dare to think a great deal about basil. A foliage herb pretty enough for a flower bed (one cultivar, Thai basil 'Siam Queen', won an All-America Selection award in 1997), basil occupies pages of some herb catalogs. The standard cooking basil has a strong fragrance and flavor of cloves, but there are others that taste of cinnamon, lemon, lime, even camphor. All trace their roots to the tropics, so although basils are strong in fragrance, flavor, and reputation, they are shy about temperature. Even a hint of frost turns the leaves black. Basil goes to flower in summer, thereby ending its season of foliage production.

DECIDING WHAT TO GROW

The standard type, sometimes called sweet basil, grows a foot or two tall, with green foliage the shape of apple leaves. This is the most common cooking basil, but there are many other types. Basil fans could spend their summers in happy experimentation. Any good herb catalog will reveal as many as 30 distinct types, from the common pesto types to basils grown for medicinal use. Some basils have purple leaves, such as 'Dark Opal' and 'Purple Ruffles', which make the most decorative vinegars and jellies. They also are among the most decorative for flower borders.

If you want basil simply for cooking and salads, start out with a cultivar that will produce the highest proportion of leaf to stem, such as 'Large Leaf', 'Lettuce Leaf', or 'Mammoth'. 'Genovese' is another. If you want enough basil for pestos and seasonings year-round, grow at least six plants of a large-leaved type. For dried seasoning alone, three plants of any of these cultivars should do.

Basil 'Opal' and 'Spicy Globe'

Basil 'Green Ruffles'

Basil 'Genovese'

Thai basil 'Siam Queen'

Some of the smaller-leaved types are decorative and also offer good flavor, but your harvest per plant will be reduced. For different flavors, consider the *O. basilicum* cultivars that feature anise and cinnamon flavor. Lime basil (*O. americanum*) and lemon basil (*O. basilicum citriodora*) are excellent with fish. 'Siam Queen' Thai basil has dark green leaves with a spicy anise flavor that is suited to Thai and Vietnamese cooking. It's also an attractive ornamental because of its showy purple flowers. All basils can be grown in USDA Zone 3 and warmer.

Basil can be grown in containers filled with rich soil that is never allowed to dry out. Especially decorative types for containers include any of the purple-leaved cultivars and the topiarylike 'Spicy Bush' or 'Spicy Globe', which forms a neat globe of small leaves about 8 inches high.

HOW TO GROW

Basil needs full sun and well-drained soil, but it should not be allowed to wilt. Soil that has plenty of organic matter will stay damper and help keep plants healthy. Mulch the ground with grass clippings, leaf compost, or hay to conserve moisture. Daily watering may be needed during windy, dry weather. If the site is windy, give basil a windbreak a foot or so tall. This could be nonliving, such as a row of shingles half buried in the ground, or it could be living, such as a row of shrubby annual or perennial flowers. Basil can be grown in the vegetable garden, in an annual herb bed, or in an ornamental setting in containers or in the ground.

Basil is most easily grown from seeds sown directly outdoors in warm soil (at least 60°F) after spring frosts are past. Germination is quick when the soil is warm and moist. Seeds can also be sown indoors 4 to 6 weeks before the last-spring-frost date. Do not transplant outdoors until the nights are warm. Plants should be spaced 6 inches apart.

Basil is prey to various fungal ailments. Cool soil during germination can be an invitation to damping-off. Sow seeds only in warm soil, and water regularly with ambient-temperature water for quick growth. Later in the season, fusarium may cause sudden wilting or defoliation and eventual death. Lemon and purple-leaved basils are less susceptible than are green cultivars. Some seed houses sell seeds selected for fusarium resistance. Basil is susceptible to damage from frost and cold. Cover the plants during long cold spells, or harvest if frost is forecast.

HARVESTING

Pick off fresh young basil leaves whenever you need them, completing the harvest by pinching entire stems before flowers finish blooming. Basil leaves dry quickly, but the stems are fleshy and can be slow. Pinch leaves from stems. Leaves can also be frozen for winter storage. To store leaves on their own, spread them on cookie sheets to freeze, then store them in airtight bags. Or store the leaves minced with olive oil or prepared as pesto; in this case, freezing in ice-cube trays works well.

Basil is pollinated by insects, and all cultivars can cross-pollinate. To ensure seeds that will come true, grow only one cultivar or separate cultivars by at least 150 feet. Seeds are viable for 5 years; store in airtight containers in a dark, cool location.

SPECIAL NOTES

Basil is a favorite companion of tomatoes, not only in the kitchen but also in the garden, where a basil spray is sometimes used to repel hornworms. The ancient Greeks used basil for soothing toothaches and snakebites and still include it in salads of cucumbers, tomatoes, and olive oil. Fresh or dried basil leaves make an excellent vinegar. Lemon basil vinegar is recommended for fruit salads.

BAY

Laurus nobilis. Laurel family, Lauraceae. Perennial.

◑ ✳ ❀ ▰

Bay is much more than a potherb. This is the plant used in ancient Greece to make wreaths for poets and heroes. Its genus name comes from the Latin meaning "to praise," and the species name *nobilis* suggests its regal reputation. Another Latin name, *baccae lauri*, "noble berry," led to the educational term baccalaureate.

Bay is grown to be admired. It is a beautiful, glossy, fragrant evergreen hedge or shrub that can tower to 40 feet in the warm places where it grows outdoors year-round, as in its native Mediterranean countries. Plants that spend summers outdoors may be decorated in early summer with small pale yellow flowers followed by dark purple berries. In cooler places where it must spend winters indoors, it is a lovely container plant, even a full-time houseplant that can be kept easily under 3 feet tall. Bay is reliably hardy to only about 10°F, USDA Zone 8 and warmer.

Nicolas Culpeper, 17th-century herbalist, introduced bay by writing, "This is so well known that it needs no description," then followed with a page and a half of medicinal uses, including curing earaches and relieving "numbness in any part." If beauty is as beauty does, perhaps bay could do even more miraculous things. "Neither witch nor devil, thunder nor lightning, will hurt a man where a bay tree is," Culpeper wrote.

One plant will supply a family of four. There are a couple of cultivated varieties, but they are difficult to locate. One is golden bay, 'Aurea', whose new growth is gold, gradually turning dark green.

HOW TO GROW

Give bay a partly sunny but sheltered position out of strong winds. Bright sun will scorch the leaves. The soil must be well drained but otherwise can be fairly poor. Plants need regular watering in dry weather. Bay does well as a container plant. In areas where it is not hardy, summer plants outdoors in a sheltered location or sink them directly in the garden—pot and all. (Regular watering is especially important for plants in containers, because they dry out more quickly than do specimens growing in the ground.) Before the first frost, bring containers indoors. Gardeners in USDA Zone 7 can try moving plants to a very protected location and burying the pot during the winter or mounding soil around it to keep the roots from freezing. In cold winters, however, this may mean the tops are damaged or die back to the roots.

Bay seeds, which can be sown indoors any time in spring, are viable only when fresh or if kept suitably moist. Generally, this herb is purchased as a seedling or grown from a rooted cutting. In gardens that are mostly frost-free, it can be grown outdoors year-round. Gardeners often remove the plant's lower branches to produce topiary standards.

Indoors, bay can be kept in a pot by a sunny window where temperatures stay above 45°F but don't exceed 80°F. When grown in a container, water just enough to keep the soil from drying out completely. Feed with a complete fertilizer every spring.

You can propagate new bay plants by air layering. In early summer, scrape a small patch of bark from the base of a 6-inch-long branch. Dust the wound with rooting hormone, then wrap with wet sphagnum moss and cover with a square of plastic. Secure the plastic at both ends with twist-ties. Remoisten the moss if it becomes dry. When, in a couple of months, white roots appear, cut off the branch and pot it.

Bay is susceptible to mealybug and scale, especially when grown indoors. Both can be combated with insecticidal soap or rubbing alcohol applied with a cotton swab. Spraying plants with horticultural oil at a growing-season dilution is also effective—add a small quantity of liquid dish soap to ensure coverage. Yellowing leaves can be caused by drought or too much sun.

HARVESTING

Pick off leaves whenever you want them. Since bay is evergreen, and dried leaves have less flavor than do fresh ones, there is no need to dry. However, you can do so if you want to give some away, and dried bay leaves make beautiful wreaths.

Bay leaves added to bins of flours or grains will help keep them free of insect infestations. Add bay leaves to the bath water to relieve the pain in arthritic joints.

BEAN

Phaseolus vulgaris. Pea family, Fabaceae. Annual.

○ ☀ ✿

Beans were grown throughout the Americas for several thousand years before European explorers arrived, a tribute to their nutritional punch and their versatility. A dietary staple of Native peoples—one of the "Three Sisters of Life"—beans can be eaten at three stages, immature, green shelled, or dried. Apparently the Spanish were responsible for introducing *Phaseolus vulgaris* to the Old World, where it was first grown as an ornamental and soon became known as the French bean, or *haricot*. So much for accurate attribution.

Vulgaris means "common." The genus name, *Phaseolus*, refers to the shape of the plant's seeds—as does kidney bean, another common name—which are beautifully colored and varied. "The stocke of kindred of the kidney Beane are wonderfully many," a 17th-century author observed. Stock is wonderfully many still: Today, more than 600 cultivars are available commercially, and several times that number are stored in USDA seed banks and by nonprofit organizations and individual collectors. Beans, more than any other vegetable, are responsible for the current interest in growing and saving heirloom cultivars.

The histories of the old cultivars are fascinating. For example, 'Egg', a bush bean with tan, egg-shaped seeds, can be traced back to the Algonquian Indians. Also called 'Fisher', after the family who preserved it, it is grown for dishes like this 1887 recipe for baked beans:

Boil the beans, until they begin to crack, with a pound or two of fat salt pork; put the beans in the baking-pan; score the pork cross the top, and settle in the middle; add two tablespoons of sugar or molasses, and bake in a moderate oven for two hours; they should be very moist when first put in the oven, or they will grow too dry in baking. Do not forget the sweetening if you want Yankee baked beans.

MEMBERS OF THE FAMILY

After exploring the merits of various snap, shell, and dry beans, consider trying other members of the bean family, including adzuki beans, asparagus beans, chickpeas, favas, lentils, limas, runner beans, and winged beans—all of which have individual entries in this encyclopedia. Southern peas, also called cowpeas and black-eyed peas, are actually beans also and are covered in an individual entry. Adventurous gardeners may want to try even less-known bean crops, such as tepary beans (*Phaseolus acutifolius*), moth beans (*Vigna aconitifolia*), sword beans (*Canavalia gladiata*), rice beans (*Vigna umbellata*), Jack beans (*Canavalia ensiformis*) and hyacinth, or lablab, bean (*Lablab purpurus*). The list goes on and on.

Home gardeners may not be quite as enthusiastic gardeners as was Henry David Thoreau, whose bean rows added together equaled 7 miles. Thoreau recorded in *Walden, or Life in the Woods* (1854) that his beans "attached me to the earth," and that he learned to look out for worms, woodchucks, and frosts. He also learned that he did not want to be like most men he met, who were too "busy about their beans." Gardeners in USDA Zone 3 and warmer are also eligible not to be too busy—or to be too busy—about their beans.

DECIDING WHAT TO GROW

Sorting out different types of beans is like trying to see in muddy water: It's difficult to distinguish clearly. Distinctions can be made on the basis of plant habit, or the color of the pods or seeds, or several other criteria. To complicate matters still more, terms used in cookbooks don't always coincide with terms found in seed catalogs. Nearly every member of the *P. vulgaris* species is a three-in-one vegetable, able to be picked at three stages. Not all are equally good at each stage, however, so assigning cultivars to one of the three—snap, shell, or dry—is the most helpful approach for home growers. All are grown similarly, although they mature at different times.

Snap Beans. Also called string and green beans, snap beans are picked when they are still young and

BEAN ESSENTIALS

- Full sun and a warm location.

- Light, well-drained, slightly acid soil rich in organic matter.

- Sow outdoors after the threat of frost and soil has warmed to at least 55°F.

- Soil and air temperatures of at least 70°F for best growth.

- Use floating row covers for warmth and insect protection.

- Provide about 1 inch of water weekly, but do not overwater.

eaten pod and all. There are both bush and pole cultivars, as well as intermediate types known as half-runners, and green, yellow, or wax, and purple cultivars. *Haricots verts* and "filet" beans are snap beans that are bred to be picked when they are still tiny, about ⅛-inch thick, well before the seeds begin to swell. "Romano" types have broader, flat pods and a strong, rich flavor. Bush types average 50 days to maturity, pole types 65 days.

Shell Beans. Shelly beans, as these are sometimes called, are best when harvested at the half-mature, or green shell, stage, 66 to 75 days. Their seeds have swollen and are still green, but their pods are no longer tender. Also known as horticultural beans and *flageolets*, they can be steamed, boiled, or baked after they are shelled. Both bush and pole cultivars are available, as are green-, yellow-, and purple-podded cultivars.

Dry Beans. Also known as field beans, these are left in the garden until their seeds become hard and/or shrunken and their pods have withered, which takes 90 to 100 days. Available in many seed colors—black, brown, green, mottled, pink, red, white, and yellow—they can be stored for long periods of time and are suited for stewing and baking. Pinto, kidney, navy, and black beans are all members of this group.

Beans are heir to many diseases, which has kept

Bush bean 'Jade'

Bush bean 'Royal Burgundy'

Pole bean 'Rattlesnake'

Pole bean 'Early Riser'

Bush bean 'Wax Romano'

Pole bean 'Fat Goose'

breeders busy producing cultivars with built-in resistance/tolerance. Most seed catalogs supply a code to diseases, the most common being anthracnose (A), two types of bean common mosaic virus (BCMV), curly-type virus (CTV), and bean rust (R). If bean diseases are rampant in your garden, look for cultivars that come armed for such foes.

Finally, before you buy seeds, decide whether you want to go to the trouble to erect some kind of support that climbing, or pole, cultivars require. If trellising doesn't fit into your schedule—or your garden—stick to bush types. Bush beans mature faster than pole types do, but pole cultivars produce two to three times as many beans in the same space. To supply fresh beans for a family of four, 50 bush bean or 30 pole bean plants should be enough; if you want to harvest shell or dry beans, or to preserve, increase the planting.

SITE & SOIL

All common beans want the same conditions: warmth, a sunny location (or partial afternoon shade in extremely hot regions), and light soil that is weed-free, well drained, rich in organic matter, and has a moderately acid pH (5.5 to 6.5). Above all, avoid wet locations, where plants will refuse to set pods, and saline soil. The temperature of both soil and air needs to be at least 70°F for plants to develop well. Beginning too early is likely to cause permanent damage: Your plants may grow, but they won't flourish.

Like peas, beans have the ability to capture nitrogen from the air, so add organic matter and/or fertilizer that contains phosphorus and potassium, rather than materials that are high in nitrogen. For the plants to "fix" nitrogen, certain *Rhizobia* bacteria must be present in the soil. Many gardeners coat bean seeds with an inoculant to make sure the bacteria are present, but that's unnecessary unless you're planting in an area that's never been cultivated before. If yours is a new garden, purchase an appropriate inoculant: Just before planting, wet the seeds and cover them with the powder.

If you're growing pole beans, be sure to locate them where they won't shade more diminutive crops. A bean tepee, constructed from three or more long poles, can double as a hideaway for children. Beans that will be sheltering gardeners-to-be should be planted on the edge of the garden where the to-and-from traffic won't endanger other vegetables

BEAN CULTIVARS

Selecting bean cultivars can be confusing. The list below indicates whether each selection is a pole or bush type and whether it is primarily grown as a snap, shell, or dry bean. Keep in mind that nearly all can be picked at any of the three stages, although not all are equally good at each stage.

'**Black Turtle Soup**': 100 days; green-podded dry; vigorous bush; small black seeds; needs long, hot season; soup cultivar; heirloom.

'**Black Valentine**': 50 days; green-podded snap; bush; also good dried bean; heirloom.

'**Blue Lake**': 60 days; green-podded snap; pole; standard cultivar; heavy yields.

'**Burpee's Stringless Green Pod**': 55 days; green-podded snap; bush; curved stringless pods; heirloom.

'**California Red Kidney**': 100 days; green-podded shell; bush; kidney type.

'**Cherokee Trail of Tears**': 70 days; greenish purple-podded snap; pole; black seeds; also good dried bean; high yields; heirloom.

'**Chevrier Vert**': 65 days; green-podded shell; bush; classic "flageolet" cultivar; can also be harvested at snap or dry stage; heirloom.

'**French Horticultural**': 68 days; red podded (streaked with yellow) shell or dry; vigorous bush; cream-colored seeds striped with red.

'**Goldcrop**': 55 days; yellow-podded snap; vigorous bush ; stringless pods; AAS winner.

'**Great Northern**': 85 days; green-podded dry; bush; small white seeds; good cultivar for North; heirloom.

'**Jacob's Cattle**': 90 days; green-podded dry; bush; white seeds speckled with maroon; traditional New England baking cultivar; good for short seasons; heirloom.

'**Kentucky Wonder**': 65 days; green-podded snap; pole; there are both white- and brown-

and herbs. Pole beans can grow as tall as 15 feet, so make sure your support is large enough to handle the cultivar you plant.

Beans bear heavily but briefly. To extend the harvest, plant successive crops of bush cultivars every 10 days up to 12 weeks before the first expected frost. Beans can be intercropped with vegetables and herbs that are slower to mature, or they can follow cold-tolerant crops, such as radishes, scallions, spinach, and lettuce. Although growing pole beans and corn together is a time-honored tradition, give it a pass unless both crops won't be harvested until autumn. Trying to pick corn while the beans are still developing, or vice-versa, usually damages plants.

Although not as decorative as runner beans (see *Runner Bean* on page 000 for more on this decorative crop), pole beans can be used to cover fences and other vertical surfaces, and as backdrops in ornamental beds and borders. Bush types can be grown in pots and window boxes, although the modest yields—a 10-gallon container will house only two plants—makes beans a less-than-ideal choice for this approach. Landless gardeners who want to cultivate beans should use large containers with good drainage. Fill with an enriched soil mix, water generously, and feed with a diluted liquid fertilizer every 3 weeks.

HOW TO GROW

While the three types of beans are grown similarly, they mature at different rates. Seeds will rot in cold, wet soil, and seedlings won't tolerate frost, so don't sow until a week or two after the threat of frost has past and the soil has warmed to at least 55°F. At that temperature, beans germinate in about 15 days; at 75°F, germination takes between 8 and 10 days. Beans resent transplanting nearly as much as they resent cold; for this reason, beginning plants indoors is not recommended.

Sow seeds 1 inch deep, spaced 2 to 3 inches apart. Thin bush types to 5 to 6 inches in rows spaced 3 to 4 feet apart, pole beans to 6 to 8 inches. If you garden in a humid region, increase the distance between plants to ensure good air circulation. Pole cultivars can be trellised on strings, wires, netting, or tepee-style on poles. Install the supports before or immediately after sowing seeds, so you won't disturb plant roots. Plants are fairly self-sufficient when it comes to climbing, but help guide or secure stems, if necessary.

---

seeded strains; standard cultivar; heirloom; 'Kentucky Wonder Wax' is a yellow form.

'Lazy Wife': 80 days; green-podded shell; pole; small white seeds marked with gray; outstanding flavor; heirloom.

'Navy': 100 days; green-podded dry; dwarf bush; navy type with white seeds; standard commercial cultivar.

'Pinto': 95 days; green-podded dry; vigorous bush; pinto type with pink-buff seeds marked with brown; adapted to hot, dry climate.

'Red Kidney': 95 days; green-podded dry; vigorous bush; kidney type with dark red seeds; standard cultivar.

'Rocdor': 55 days; yellow-podded snap; bush; good cultivar for northern gardens; high yields.

'Roma II': 55 days; green-podded snap; bush; romano type with robust flavor; heavy yields; bush form of 'Romano Pole'.

'Romano': 70 days; green-podded snap; pole; romano type with flat stringless pods; classic Italian bean; also listed as 'Italian Pole'; heirloom.

'Royal Burgundy': 55 days; purple-podded snap; bush; stringless pods; good northern cultivar.

'Sequoia': 58 days; purple-podded snap; vigorous bush; romano type; heavy yields.

'Tenderpod': 50 days; green-podded snap; compact bush; stringless pods; early; widely adapted; AAS winner.

'Trionfo Violetto': 65 days; purple-podded snap; pole; ornamental purple-veined leaves and lavender flowers; good flavor; heirloom.

'Triumph de Farcy': 55 days; green-podded snap; bush; filet type; heavy yields; harvest when pods very small; heirloom.

'Vermont Cranberry Bush': 65 days; green-podded shell; bush; cranberry-colored seeds; can also be harvested at snap or dry stage; heirloom; 'Cranberry Pole' is a pole form.

'Wax Romano 264': 60 days; yellow-podded snap; vigorous bush; romano type; yellow form of 'Roma II'.

Lay floating row covers over bush cultivars to conserve warmth and prevent insects from reaching the plants. As soon as plants develop their second set of true leaves, mulch them with organic matter, such as grass clippings, to suppress weeds and retain moisture.

Beans need an even supply of water—about 1 inch a week, slightly more when pods are developing—but too much is worse than too little. For this reason, take care not to overwater, and don't spray the plants, which can cause blossom drop and encourage diseases. Additional fertilizer is unnecessary if your soil was well-prepared at sowing time, but one or two feedings of compost tea or fish emulsion when plants are small will promote heavy yields.

Once plants have ceased producing pods, till them under or compost to avoid attracting insects, such as bean beetles.

POTENTIAL PROBLEMS

While easy to grow, beans are susceptible to many diseases. Home gardeners can avoid most problems by buying resistant/tolerant cultivars and certified disease-free seeds, planting in well-drained soil in full sun, keeping the garden free of weeds, not working among wet plants, and practicing crop rotation. Many gardeners take the added precaution of soaking bean seeds for 30 minutes in compost tea, which may give plants added protection against diseases. Finally, especially if summer brings high humidity as well as high temperatures, give each bean plant plenty of room. Crowding encourages blights, anthracnose, and other diseases that revel in damp conditions.

Bean rust, which shows up as reddish brown spots on leaf undersides, can be treated with sulfur (spray every 10 days until the problem is eliminated); resistant cultivars are widely available. Cultivars resistant to curly top—look for puckered leaves, or leaves that curl or ball up—are also available. Curly top is a virus and cannot be cured; remove and destroy affected plants. (For specific information about other common bean diseases, including anthracnose, bacterial blight, bacterial wilt, damping-off, and mosaic, see "Controlling Common Diseases" on page 169.)

If the litany of diseases wasn't enough, beans are also beloved by insects. Many, including aphids, cucumber beetles, flea beetles, Japanese beetles, Mexican bean beetles, leafhoppers, leaf miners, and whiteflies, can be controlled by using floating row covers. (For more information about these pests and about cutworms, slugs, thrips, and wireworms, all of which have an affinity for beans, see "Controlling Common Pests" on page 162.)

Despite these potential problems, most home gardeners produce more beans than they can eat. Plants grown well are unlikely to be seriously troubled by insects or diseases.

HARVESTING

Beans are rich in vitamins A, B_1, B_2, and C, calcium, iron, fiber, and protein, although the amounts vary depending on the time of harvest.

Snap beans should be harvested when they are small and tender, before the seeds begin to swell noticeably; keeping plants harvested will encourage them to produce more pods. Harvest shell beans when the pods are plump but before they begin to brown. Dried beans should be left on the plant until the pods are fully dry and the seeds have become hard. If the weather is wet or frost threatens, pull the plants and hang them upside down in a warm, dry location.

Snap and shell beans can be sealed in plastic bags and stored in the refrigerator; store dry beans in a airtight container for up to 1 year.

Beans are self-pollinating—the flowers shed their pollen before they open—but they can be pollinated by bees and other insects that find their way into the unopened blooms. To ensure seeds that will breed true, plant only one cultivar (or plant only one cultivar of the same seed color—if there are crosses, they will be obvious in the new seeds, which can be discarded). Save seeds from the most vigorous and healthy plants; seeds are viable for 5 years if stored in airtight containers in a dark, cool location.

BEAN, ADZUKI. See *Adzuki Bean*
BEAN, ASPARAGUS. See *Asparagus Bean*
BEAN, BROAD. See *Fava Bean*
BEAN, FAVA. See *Fava Bean*
BEAN, GAO. See *Winged Bean*
BEAN, GARBANZO. See *Chickpea*
BEAN, LIMA. See *Lima Bean*
BEAN, RUNNER. See *Runner Bean*
BEAN, WINGED. See *Winged Bean*
BEAN, YARDLONG. See *Asparagus Bean*

BEET

Beta vulgaris, Crassa group. Goosefoot family,
Chenopodiaceae. Biennial grown as an annual.

○ ◑ ❊ ✿

Beets are double-treat vegetables, because both
their vitamin-rich greens and their tender roots are
edible. Yet the Greeks, who gave beets their genus
name, *Beta*, considered them inedible. Rather than
recommending the culinary merits of beets, the
ancients prescribed them for a slew of ailments,
including the nasty effects "of all venomous
Creatures."

Beets were boiled and baked beyond recognition in 17th-century England, where they were
"more often eaten at poor mens tables." Pride
didn't keep American colonists from hauling beet
seeds to New England, though. By the start of the
Civil War, more than 65 cultivars were being
grown, including 15-pound giants destined for
feeding livestock, extracting sugar, or making
borscht for a family of 50.

Widely adapted, beets thrive throughout North
America; in USDA Zone 8 and warmer, they should
be grown as a winter or spring crop. Their foot-tall
green basal leaves, often tinged or veined red, are
pretty enough to make this biennial vegetable a fine
addition to ornamental beds.

DECIDING WHAT TO GROW

For eating fresh, a 30-foot row will yield enough
beets for a family of four; if you want to preserve,
increase the planting. Sow successive crops at 2- to
3-week intervals to spread out the harvest. Most cultivars are ready to pull about 50 days from sowing
seeds, although they can be harvested sooner. If
you're growing beets for their greens, begin harvesting when plants are 6 inches tall.

Both sugar beets and forage beets, or mangels,
can be eaten when still small and tender, but
choose instead from the colorful array of table
beets. They are grouped by root shape: long, or
cylindrical; medium, or semi-globe; and short, or
globe. If your soil is shallow, rocky, or heavy, plant
globe types to avoid deformed or stunted roots. The
leaves of all beets are edible, but 'Early Wonder'
and 'Green Top Bunching' produce especially succulent greens. To stock the root cellar in fall, pick
a storage cultivar, such as 'Lutz Green Leaf'. Newer
hybrids tend to be sweeter than other cultivars are,
and they mature more quickly; and the roots and
greens of nonred beets have a milder flavor than
red cultivars do.

Red is the traditional beet hue, but yellow and
white cultivars are available, although they are considered more difficult to grow and less flavorful. The
striking flesh of 'Chioggia', an Italian heirloom, consists of alternating rings of red and white (which disappear when cooked). Whatever the color or shape,
look for cultivars that are resistant to disease and
bolting. In warm regions, grow a cultivar that
matures quickly, such as 'Kleine Bol', also called
'Little Ball', a true baby beet.

Mixed heirloom beets

Beet 'Chioggia'

Beet greens

BEET CULTIVARS

Beets are grouped by root shape: cylindrical, semi-globe, and globe. Colors indicated below are for skin and flesh.

'Action': red globe; 50 days; hybrid; bolt-resistant; sweet flavor.

'Albina Vereduna': white globe; 60 days; good storage cultivar; mild, sweet flavor; curled, wavy leaves; also called 'Snow-White'.

'Burpee's Golden': gold globe; 55 days; mild flavor; does not bleed when cooked; poor germination in cold soil.

'Chioggia': globe with unusual red- and white-ringed flesh; 58 days; Italian heirloom; extremely sweet; also known as 'Bull's Eye' and 'Peppermint'.

'Crosby's Egyptian': red semi-globe; 58 days; tall tops; sweet flavor; heirloom.

'Cylindra': red cylindrical; 60 days; 6 to 8 inches long; excellent for slicing; good keeper; reddish green leaves.

'Detroit Dark Red': red globe; 60 days; glossy maroon-tinged tops; all-purpose cultivar; heirloom.

'Early Wonder': red semi-globe; 50 days; good for early harvests; tall, superb greens.

'Kleine Bol'/'Little Ball': red globe; 55 days; uniform, smooth skin; true "baby" beet; tender and sweet.

'Lutz Green Leaf': red semi-globe; 80 days; large storage variety for fall harvest; retains flavor and tenderness when mature; lush, chardlike leaves; also called 'Long Season'.

'Monopoly': red semi-globe; 55 days; monogerm cultivar that produces one plant per seed; good bolt resistance; sweet flavor.

'Ruby Queen': red globe; 60 days; uniform; standard home-garden and processing cultivar; AAS winner.

SITE & SOIL

Beets prefer cool, moist weather and full sun, but they tolerate partial shade, especially in hot regions. Locate plants where they won't be shaded by taller crops. They grow best in light, near-neutral soil (pH above 6.5) that is heavily amended with organic matter. To promote healthy root development, make sure the soil is deeply dug—to a depth of at least 10 inches. If you're gardening in heavy clay, situate beets in a raised bed. Because they are fairly cold-tolerant (the roots can withstand prolonged freezing temperatures, but the tops cannot) and quick to mature, beets are a good succession crop for fall harvest. Since they are fast-growing, they are also a good candidate for interplanting.

Beets require medium-size doses of phosphorus and potassium but a smaller amount of nitrogen (lush tops and small roots may indicate too much nitrogen). A potassium deficiency, which results in elongated rather than bulbous roots, can be corrected by side-dressing plants with wood ashes. Internal browning in the root signals a lack of boron, which can usually be corrected by top-dressing with organic matter, such as compost. For severe deficiencies, water with a borax-water solution: 1 teaspoon household borax per 1 gallon water.

Beet seeds can be broadcast or sown in rows. However you plant, expect to thin, because each beet "seed" is actually a dried fruit containing as many as eight seeds. Don't be tempted to space seeds far apart, however: Beets are famous for spotty germination. Some companies sell decorticated seeds, which are single seeds that have been removed from the fruit; there are also monogerm cultivars, such as 'Monopoly' and 'Solo', that produce only one seed per fruit.

Beets' ornamental leaves make them a good patio or deck plant, although they leave a vacant space when cut or pulled. Use a container, at least 8 inches wide and 12 inches deep, with good bottom drainage, and fill with enriched potting soil. Water frequently, and feed every 3 weeks with compost tea.

HOW TO GROW

Although beets can be started indoors in celled flats—they are one of the few root crops that transplant well—most gardeners direct-seed, beginning 2 or 3 weeks before the average frost-free date. Beets can also be sown in summer for autumn harvests (in warm climates, beets are a good winter crop). For better germination, soak seeds overnight in tepid water before planting. Sow seeds 1 to 1½ inches deep, 2 inches apart, with at least 1 foot between rows. Germination occurs in 5 to 8 days in soil in the preferred temperature range of 60° to 80°F but may take 2 or 3 weeks in colder soil. Keep soil moist until seeds sprout.

Immediately after sowing seeds or setting out transplants, cover the area with floating row covers to prevent leaf miners and other insect pests from reaching plants.

Thin plants when they are 2 inches tall. If you're growing cylindrical types or will harvest semi-globe or globe types when they're young and small, thin to 3 or 4 inches apart; for larger roots, thin to 6 inches. If you've planted for greens, not roots, there is no need to thin. Be ruthless when thinning; crowded beets will not develop good roots. Thinnings, which should be cut rather than pulled, can be added to salads. Thin again in 30 days, if necessary.

Even moisture—at least 1 inch per week—and quick growth are the secrets to sweet-flavored beets. In hot, dry conditions, they become tough and stringy, and uneven watering can produce cracked roots marked with interior rings. Once plants are established, mulch with organic matter to help retain moisture and suppress weeds. Side-dress or foliar-feed every 3 weeks with a diluted, low-nitrogen liquid fertilizer to support rapid growth. For lush greens, use a balanced liquid fertilizer.

POTENTIAL PROBLEMS

Beets are troubled by few diseases. To control scab and cercospora leaf spot, ailments that overwinter in plant debris and in the soil, avoid planting beets and their relatives, such as chard and spinach, in the same location. Also keep the soil pH level near to neutral. Annual crop rotations and good air circulation will reduce the threat of downy mildew. A few disease-tolerant/resistant cultivars are available.

Beets are vulnerable to several insects, some of which also carry diseases. Most, including aphids, carrot weevils, flea beetles, leafhoppers, and leaf miners, can be thwarted by installing floating row covers immediately after sowing seed. Discourage mites, which thrive in hot, dry conditions, by spraying plants vigorously with water. For severe infestations, use an insecticidal soap. Lacewings, lady bugs, and predatory thrips are natural predators. Handpick or use beer traps to control slugs and snails, which like to snack on beet leaves.

HARVESTING

You can harvest beets and beet greens whenever you want, although both parts of the plant are best when they are still small and tender. The roots contain vitamin C, folate, and iron and are a source of dietary fiber, but it is the greens that are packed with carotenoids as well as the other nutrients. For greens, harvest the entire plant when leaves are about 6 inches long. Pull or dig beet roots when they measure between 1 and 2 inches across at the soil surface. Remove greens to increase storage life, leaving 1 inch of stem. Place them in plastic bags to help retain their moisture, and refrigerate.

Do not wash beets if you intend to store them long term in sand or sawdust in a root cellar. Fall beet crops can be mulched heavily (1 foot of organic mulch) and left in the garden until the ground freezes.

Because beets are biennials and flower in their second season, saving seeds is difficult. Gardeners in cold climates must dig and overwinter plants, then replant them in the spring; in frost-free regions, carry plants over to a second year. Beet pollen is carried by the wind; all beets (and chards) cross-pollinate. To save seeds, plant only one cultivar. Seeds are viable for 4 years; store in airtight containers in a dark, cool location.

SPECIAL NOTES

If you've never eaten beets that have been roasted—a process that retains their rich, intense flavor—you're in for a treat. Remove stem and rub unpeeled beets with olive oil. Place on a baking sheet, and roast in a 400°F oven until a skewer pierces them easily, about 1 hour. Remove beets from the oven, and let sit until cool enough to handle (but still warm), then scrape off the peel with a paring knife and enjoy.

BEET, LEAF. See *Swiss Chard*
BEET, SPINACH. See *Swiss Chard*
BELGIAN ENDIVE. See *Chicory*
BELL PEPPER. See *Pepper*

Bok choy 'Gourmet Canton'

BOK CHOY

Brassica rapa, Chinensis group. Mustard family,
Brassicaceae. Biennial grown as an annual.

○ ◑ ❄ ❀ ▜

Translated from the Chinese, bok choy means
"white vegetable," a reference to the white, celerylike stems of this mild-tasting Asian green that
resembles a white-stemmed Swiss chard. The thick
stems, which have a crunchy texture, are topped by
rounded dark to pale green leaves. Depending on
the cultivar, plants can range in height from 7 to
almost 20 inches.

Also called pak-choi or pac choy as well as celery cabbage, Chinese white cabbage, and Chinese
mustard cabbage, bok choy is one of the oldest—it's
been cultivated for at least 1,500 years—and most
adaptable greens. It tolerates a range of temperatures and soil conditions, although the plants prefer
cool weather and are well suited for late-spring and
early-fall crops in USDA Zone 6 and colder. In
Zones 7 through 9, bok choy can be set out in the
fall for winter and early-spring harvest. For summer
crops, plant heat-tolerant selections.

DECIDING WHAT TO GROW

Bok choy are fast-growing plants that mature in 45
to 65 days from transplanting. Leaves can be harvested beginning about 15 days before maturity. A
half-dozen small and a half-dozen large cultivars will
provide a family of four with a substantial contribution to salads and stir-fry dishes.

A few cultivars of this versatile green are available. 'Joi Choi', a hybrid selection, is among the
largest bok choy, growing to almost 20 inches. One
of the "Chinese-white pak" types, with white leafstalks and dark green leaves that tend to curl out-
ward, 'Joi Choi' is a fast-growing cultivar—it
matures in 45 days—that is very cold-tolerant yet
also shows some heat tolerance. 'Chinese Pak Choi',
an open-pollinated 65-day cultivar, has thick, glossy
leaves like Swiss chard that are ready to harvest in
30 days.

'Mei Qing', a "green leafstalk" type, is a hybrid
that reaches only 7 inches and is very heat-tolerant.
'Shanghai Pak Choi', another heat-tolerant cultivar, has thick leaves and a greenish cast to its stalks.
Because they can endure considerable summer heat
without losing their flavor and are slow to flower
and set seed in warm weather, 'Mei Qing' and
'Shanghai Pak Choi' are excellent choices for summer cultivation. Both are small plants. Even smaller are "squat," or "Canton," types, such as 'Canton'
and 'Canton Dwarf'. They have slightly savoyed
foliage and white leafstalks and can be harvested as
soon as they are only a few inches tall. Canton types
are extremely heat-resistant but tend to bolt in cool
weather.

A fourth type, "soup spoon" bok choys, are tall
(18 inches) plants with thin white stalks and
cupped, spoonlike leaves. A good cultivar, tolerant
of both cold and heat, is 'Japanese White Celery
Mustard'.

SITE & SOIL

Bok choy thrives in full sun in the cool weather of
spring and fall. For summer crops, afternoon shade
will help delay the bolting. Like its relative cabbage,
bok choy is a heavy feeder. Soil should be high in
organic matter to retain moisture and have a slightly acidic pH, from 6.5 to 6.8. Watering weekly with
diluted manure tea or spraying plants about 4 weeks
after they are set out will provide additional nutrition to keep the crop growing vigorously—bok choy
is best when plants grow quickly.

Spacing depends on the size of the cultivar as
well as the harvest method. Small cultivars can be
spaced every 6 inches, larger ones every 8 to 10
inches. While leaves can be harvested individually,
plants that are spaced every 4 inches can be harvested by cutting them back to 2-inch stubs, then
allowing them to regrow. Vase- or tulip-shaped bok
choy plants are attractive and make fine additions

to spring or fall beds of annuals, such as calendulas, or can be grown in pots. Use a container, at least 8 inches wide and 12 inches deep, with good bottom drainage, and fill with enriched potting soil. Water frequently, and feed every 3 weeks with manure tea.

HOW TO GROW

Seeds for a spring crop can be sown indoors about 4 weeks before the last-frost date. Plant in individual pots or in a divided flat to minimize root disturbance at transplanting. Bok choy is quite sensitive to bolting if the young plants are exposed to several days of temperatures in the low 40s F, so delay transplanting until temperatures are regularly in the 60s during the day. Be sure to harden off plants before moving them to the garden.

Seeds can be direct-sown outdoors when soil temperatures are still in the mid-50s F. Plant seeds ¼ inch deep, one every inch or so. Thin seedlings to 2 inches when they are still small, then to their final spacing. Thinnings can be used in salads.

For fall crops, set plants out 30 to 40 days before the first-frost date. After plants are about 3 inches tall, mulch heavily to maintain soil moisture and suppress weeds. Too little moisture can cause plants to bolt, so water regularly if rainfall is scant. Plants can endure some cold but should be protected from hard frost. With protection, they will continue to grow for several weeks after the first frost.

Early in the season, bok choy is a popular target for flea beetles, which can riddle the foliage with holes. Cover transplants with floating row covers to keep them at bay. (See *Cabbage* on page 204 for information on other pests, including aphids and cabbageworms, that sometimes attack bok choy.)

HARVESTING

You can pick bok choy leaves, which have a hint of mustard, as soon as they reach useful size. Break or cut off the outside leaves at the base of the plant, leaving at least three or four leaves on the plant. New leaves will continue to form at the center of the plant. Alternatively, cut the entire plants back to 2 inches. If you provide water in the form of manure tea, the roots will generate lush new growth. To extend the harvest, cut off flower stalks to delay bolting. If plants do bolt, harvest their flowers and seedpods, both of which are edible.

Because boy choy is a biennial and flowers in its second season, saving seeds is difficult. Gardeners in cold climates must dig and overwinter plants, then replant them in the spring; in frost-free regions, carry plants over to a second year. All members of *Brassica rapa*, including broccoli raab, will cross with each other. To save seeds that will come true, plant only one cultivar. Seeds are viable for about 4 years; store in airtight containers in a dark, cool location.

BORAGE

Borago officinalis. Borage family, Boraginaceae.
Annual.

Decorative enough for a flower bed and beloved by bees, borage has velvety, grayish foliage and beautiful star-shaped flowers, usually deep blue with prominent black anthers. It is an annual, but one of generous size and nature. Where it is content, it can be a dominating plant that needs plenty of space, since it will grow 3 feet high and almost as wide and is apt to self-sow. Its very exuberance could be one reason why the plant was once called "herb of gladness," though it's more likely that the happy label comes from its decorative flowers and its use in curative wines. John Gerard wrote in his herbal of 1597: "Those of our time do use the floures in sallads, to exhilerate and make the minde glad. There be also many things made of them, used for the comfort of

Borage flowers

the heart, to drive away sorrow, & increase the joy of the minde." Because of the color of its flowers, borage was considered a cooling plant, prescribed not only to comfort the heart but also to calm fevers and the raving of lunatics. Even now, cold borage-leaf tea, flavored with honey and lemon and garnished with the blue flowers, is used to soothe the heat of summer. Borage leaves can also be used as a poultice on skin inflammations.

Borage is native to southern Europe and the Middle East. It prefers in cool weather and thrives in USDA Zone 3 and warmer, but will not survive a hard frost. For herbal use, one plant will suffice, but you may want to grow more for decoration. For ornamental effect, look for white or pink flowers as well as the usual blue.

HOW TO GROW

Give borage full sun or part shade in ordinary well-drained soil. This is an excellent herb for containers and flower borders. Once the roots are well established, it is drought-tolerant.

The usual way to grow borage, which doesn't like to be moved, is to sow seeds directly in the garden—don't cover them, as they need light to germinate—in early spring, about a week before the last expected frost. They sprout and grow quickly as the soil warms. Thin seedlings to stand at least 12 inches apart. Seeds can also be sown directly in the garden in late summer, even where winters are harsh. In the manner of biennials, they will form a rosette of leaves the first fall, then reappear in spring to bloom that summer. If you leave some of the flowers unpicked, borage usually self-sows, giving you an ongoing supply. In USDA Zone 6 and warmer, the seeds that fall from borage's summer flowers will mature into a second crop in fall.

As borage is a magnet to both honeybees and bumblebees when in bloom, it should not be grown near playgrounds or where people allergic to bees may come in contact with it.

HARVESTING

Borage leaves, which are mildly diuretic, have a cucumber flavor that complements salads, pickles, and eggs. The leaves are best clipped off as needed and used fresh. Harvesting should be done before blooming begins. The flowers are also edible and can be used as garnishes.

Borage self-sows in most gardens. Seeds are viable for 3 years; store in airtight containers in a dark, cool location.

BRASSICAS. See *Cabbage*
BROAD BEAN. See *Fava Bean*
BROADLEAF CRESS. See *Garden Cress*

BROCCOLI

Brassica oleracea, Italica group. Mustard family, Brassicaceae. Biennial grown as an annual.

○ ✳ ❀

A vegetable of Old World origins, broccoli was slow to gain a wide following among gardeners in the New World. It was even slow to establish its own identity, distinct from its pale-toned cousin cauliflower. Until about 50 years ago, the two vegetables were often listed under the single word "cauliflower," with one described as cauliflower and the other, broccoli, described as winter, or green, cauliflower. Even the *New Yorker* had its say about the broccoli identity crisis in a 1940s cartoon showing a small boy and his mother at the dinner table. "It's broccoli, dear," the mother says. "I say it's spinach," the child replies, "and I say the hell with it."

Indeed, the entire mustard family was something of an outcast in polite gardening society, at least through the early decades of this century. No less a horticultural authority than Norman Taylor, author of *The Garden Dictionary*, damned broccoli with faint praise when he wrote in the 1936 that in cooking, broccoli exudes much less of a "tenement house odor" than does cabbage. His condescending views may have reflected the fact that broccoli

Broccoli 'Love Me Tender'

had been made popular in this country by Italian immigrants.

Broccoli's early partisans, who believed it capable of a vast assortment of cures, should take satisfaction in recent medical research that shows the vegetable to have cancer-fighting qualities. Along with other members of its family, broccoli produces a substance called sulforaphane, which stimulates the body to make enzymes that counteract carcinogens. Due in part to its salubrious status, broccoli is earning space in more and more gardens and is now the second most grown mustard-family member after cabbage. It is a cool-weather crop, most productive with cool nights and daytime temperatures in the upper 60s F, and can be grown in USDA Zone 3 and warmer.

DECIDING WHAT TO GROW

Broccoli is divided into all sorts of categories, most of which are not terribly useful to the home gardener. Although open-pollinated cultivars are still sold—'De Cicco' and 'Purple Sprouting' are two—it

Italian broccoli 'Broccolo Verde Romanesco'

is the hybrid cultivars that dominate. Overall, they have better vigor, tolerance of low and high temperatures, and resistance to diseases and pests. The majority of these modern hybrids are heading types, broccoli that bear large central heads like the ones you find in the supermarket. There are both green- and purple-headed cultivars.

Heading broccoli are also popular with home gardeners, although you may want to look for cultivars like 'Green Comet' and 'Packman' that also send out side shoots after the central head is harvested. Cutting these side shoots, or spears, encourages the plant to produce still more shoots, thereby extending the harvest. Less familiar are sprouting broccoli cultivars, which produce many side shoots and only a small main head. 'Purple Sprouting' and 'White Sprouting' are two well-known cultivars. Sprouting broccoli are also known as Italian, asparagus, or calabrese broccoli.

Even less well known is romanesco broccoli, or summer cauliflower (*B. oleracea*, Botrytis group). It bears a spiral of mild-flavored florets on a thin, conical head that is 4 to 5 inches long. Most mature in about 75 days, and their tapered shape and chartreuse color lend a decorative quality to the garden. Broccoli raab, although not a true broccoli, is frequently listed with broccoli in seed catalogs. Sometimes mistaken for turnip greens, it is grown for its leaves, shoots, and small florets. Also known as rapini and rapine, broccoli raab has a slightly bitter flavor; because it bolts easily, it is usually sown in late summer for an autumn harvest.

Choose cultivars that will succeed in your location. Most hybrids were developed for commercial

---

BUTTON UP, IT'S COLD OUTSIDE

When some broccoli cultivars, such as 'Packman', are exposed to 10 or 12 days of temperatures in the 40s F, they "button," or set small heads prematurely, once the weather turns warm. Sheltering the young plants against the early-season cold with some type of cloche can prevent buttoning.

growers farming in ideal broccoli-growing conditions: the long, cool summers of the Pacific Coast. For spring plantings, look for cultivars that can tolerate cold when they are getting started, mature quickly, and are heat-tolerant. 'Green Comet' and 'Premium Crop' are good choices. For autumn harvests, which are planted in late spring and midsummer, cultivars must be heat-tolerant.

Try growing 'Green Valiant' or 'Waltham 29'.

For eating fresh, between 16 to 24 broccoli plants should be enough to supply a family of four; if you want to preserve, increase the planting.

SITE & SOIL

Broccoli plants thrive in a humus-rich soil with a pH between 6.2 and 7.2. Add compost or well-rot-

---

BROCCOLI CULTIVARS

While most home gardeners are familiar with heading broccoli, romanesco-type cultivars and broccoli raab are less well known. The following list includes hybrid and open-pollinated cultivars for spring and fall harvest and cultivars for overwintering. Broccolis that produce side shoots offer an extended harvest.

'**Bonanza**': 55 days; hybrid with large dark green head; good side-shoot production; good spring crop.

'**Calabrese**': 60 days; open-pollinated sprouting type with medium head; good side-shoot production; heirloom.

'**De Cicco**': 60 days; open-pollinated sprouting type with long cutting period; good spring or fall crop; Italian heirloom.

'**Emperor**': 70 days; hybrid with large green head; good side-shoot production; excellent disease resistance; good spring or fall crop.

'**Green Comet**': 55 days; hybrid with deep blue-green heads on upright, compact plants; heat- and disease-resistant; large main crowns; AAS winner.

'**Green Goliath**': 60 days; hybrid with large blue-green head; good side-shoot production; good spring or fall crop.

'**Green Valiant**': 78 days; hybrid with large heads on compact plants; good side-shoot production; good fall crop.

'**Minaret**': 75 days; open-pollinated romanesco type; green spiral head; good spring or fall crop.

'**Packman**': 55 days; hybrid; good side-shoot production; standard spring cultivar.

'**Paragon**': 75 days; hybrid, an interspecies cross with Chinese Guy Lon, also known as Chinese broccoli; head extends above leaf canopy; good cultivar for humid regions.

'**Premium Crop**': 60 days; hybrid with large blue-green heads on compact plants; few side shoots; disease-resistant; good spring or fall crop; AAS winner.

'**Purple Sprouting**': 210 days; open-pollinated sprouting type with small purple heads; overwintering cultivar for mild climates.

'**Romanesco**': 85 days; open-pollinated romanesco type with spiral-pointed pale green head; good spring or fall crop; favorite commercial cultivar in Italy.

'**Spring**': 55 days; open-pollinated broccoli raab.

'**Super Dome**': 58 days; hybrid with large main head; good side-shoot production; good warm-region cultivar; good spring crop.

'**Violet Queen**': 70 days; hybrid sprouting type with medium purple heads; often listed as a purple cauliflower.

'**Waltham 29**': 75 days; open-pollinated dwarf or compact plant with medium, blue-green head; good side-shoot production; drought-resistant; good fall crop.

'**White Sprouting Late**': 200 days; open-pollinated sprouting type with small white heads; overwintering cultivar.

ted manure to the soil before planting. Plants grow from 2 to 3 feet tall, so pick a location where they won't shade smaller crops. A raised bed or other well-drained site that warms quickly in the spring will give you a head start in spring.

Full sun is recommended for broccoli; it will tolerate light shade, but shade will delay maturity. Since productivity declines as summer temperatures rise, you can replace spring plantings toward midsummer with heat-loving vegetables, such as zucchini or cucumbers. A second fall broccoli crop can be started in flats and set out after the heat of the summer has abated. The plants will endure a few light frosts and continue to make slow growth until the first hard freeze. In USDA Zone 7 and warmer, a fall-planted crop often grows through the winter and into the spring.

How you space broccoli plants in the garden influences their growth. For large central heads, set plants about 18 inches apart. To encourage side shoots, cut the central head when it is about 3 inches across. Spacing plants every 8 to 10 inches will produce smaller central heads but enough side shoots to give you a total per-square-foot yield greater than if you use 18-inch spacing.

A worthwhile yield requires four or more plants, so broccoli is not an ideal container crop. However, two or three plants can be grown in a 5-gallon bucket or other large container that is at least 18 inches deep and will produce a small but steady supply of shoots for salads. All broccoli are ornamental—they are, after all, edible flowers—but for a decorative planting, romanesco types are the best choice. With their bright green color and spiral heads, they will enliven any container or landscape.

HOW TO GROW

To get a jump on the garden season, start broccoli indoors 6 to 8 weeks before the last expected spring frost. Sow seeds ¼ inch deep in cells or individual containers filled with sterile potting soil warmed to about 75°F; germination should occur in 3 to 6 days. Once the seeds sprout, move the plants to a bright, cool location, and feed with compost tea every 10 days. Root-bound transplants will mature slowly in the garden, so pot on if your seedlings outgrow their containers.

Seedlings, after being hardened off, can go into the garden when they are 5 to 6 weeks old, about 2 weeks before the frost-free date. A fall crop can be direct-seeded in late spring or early summer. In warm regions, broccoli can be overwintered; sow seeds directly in the garden 2 weeks before the last expected frost.

Set transplants about 1 inch deeper in the ground than they were growing in their container, up to their first true leaves. A topdressing of compost or well-rotted manure applied when the central head is about 1 inch across will give added nutrients to the soil just as the plant needs the boost. Keep the soil moist by providing between 1 and 2 inches of water a week if rainfall is sparse. Mulch broccoli to retain moisture and suppress weeds, and cover plants with floating row covers to discourage insect pests and provide protection from cold. If broccoli foliage develops a bronze or purplish cast, the plants may be lacking in potassium; a foliar spray of fish emulsion will help correct the deficiency.

POTENTIAL PROBLEMS

Like other mustard-family members, broccoli is particularly susceptible to clubroot. The fungus can be brought into your garden on infected transplants, so growing your own seedlings offers a measure of protection against the ailment. To prevent clubroot and other diseases, choose disease-resistant/disease-tolerant cultivars and avoid planting broccoli, cauliflower, and other members of the mustard family in the same part of the garden for at least 4 years.

Broccoli is targeted by several leaf-eating and leaf-sucking insects, including cabbage loopers, cabbageworms, aphids, and flea beetles. (See "Controlling Common Pests" on page 162 for control measures.) Use floating row covers to prevent pests from reaching plants, and install plant collars to deter cutworms.

HARVESTING

Broccoli heads can be picked as soon as they are large enough to use. Be sure to harvest before the florets show any sign of yellow, which indicates that the tiny flowers are beginning to open. Harvest with a sharp knife, cutting about 2 inches of stem, which is also edible, along with the head. Harvesting side shoots every few days will stimulate the growth of more shoots.

Broccoli is a nutrition Goliath, rich in vitamins A and C, and is also a good source of potassium and fiber. After harvesting, soak broccoli in salt water (2 tablespoons salt per 1 gallon water) for 25 minutes to flush out any worms that may be hiding in the heads. Seal spears in a plastic bag, and refrigerate for up to 1 week.

Because it is a biennial and normally doesn't flower until its second season, saving broccoli seeds is difficult. Gardeners in cold climates must dig and overwinter plants, then replant them in the spring; in frost-free regions, carry plants over to a second year. Broccoli will cross-pollinate with other members of *B. oleracea*, including cabbage, Brussels sprouts, and collards, as well as with other broccoli cultivars. To save seeds that will come true, plant only one *B. oleracea* cultivar. Seeds are viable for 5 years; store in airtight containers in a dark, cool location.

BROCCOLI RAAB. See *Broccoli*

BRUSSELS SPROUTS

Brassica oleracea, Gemmifera group. Mustard family, Brassicaceae. Biennial grown as an annual.

○ ❄

Like other members of the mustard family, including kale, collards, cauliflower, and broccoli, Brussels sprouts descended from wild sea kale, a weedy, loose-leaved herb that grows along the Mediter-

ranean coast. Brussels sprouts—or "hundred headed cabbage," because the sprouts so resemble tiny cabbages—have been cultivated at least since the 16th century, but they've never been terribly popular on either side of the Atlantic.

In the mid-19th century, the golden age of *Brassica* crops, the French nursery Vilmorin-Andrieux listed nothing more than "tall" and "short" Brussels sprouts, while New England market gardener Fearing Burr described only "dwarf," "tall," and "giant." But this vegetable deserves more attention. Before you sow seeds, though, there are two things you should know about sprouts: For best flavor, eat them only fresh from the garden, and don't boil the life out of them.

Gardeners in extremely warm areas (USDA Zones 9 and 10) will have trouble growing sprouts, but those in Zone 5 and colder—gardeners who face frustration trying to ripen large eggplants and red sweet peppers—can find solace in this crop. It shrugs off cold weather, and its flavor is enhanced by a few frosts, a transformation that gardeners in mild climates never know. Sprouts' nutritional value is also greater during a cold spell, when the temperature is at or near 32°F. They are higher in vitamin C than oranges are and have more than twice the vitamin C and three times the vitamin A of cabbage. Brussels sprouts also contain potassium, iron, and fiber.

Brussels sprouts with leaves removed to help sprouts ripen

Brussel sprouts ready for winter storage

One of the oddest-looking vegetables, the plant resembles some prehistoric palm tree. The covering of sprouts on the 2-inch-thick stem gives the appearance of rough bark, while the rosette of large leaves at the top of the stem recreates the fronds. The sprouts themselves, which are actually buds, first appear at the bottom of the plant. They continue sprouting, from bottom to top, until the entire stem is coated. Maturity also follows the bottom-to-top route: As new sprouts, looking like tiny buttons, are popping out above, those below are swelling to maturity.

DECIDING WHAT TO GROW

Brussels sprouts can be grouped in two general categories: short (18 to 24 inches) and tall (24 to 48 inches). While there are exceptions, the shorter types, such as the hybrid 'Jade Cross E', tend to be more cold-hardy and mature earlier. They are good for regions with snowy winters and abbreviated growing seasons. Tall cultivars, such as 'Bedford Fillbasket', ripen more gradually. Many of the tall types were developed in Europe and are better suited for mild climates. Surprisingly, yields for the two strains are similar, because the sprouts are packed more closely on short cultivars than they are on tall ones.

One productive plant will bear about a quart, or between 60 to 100 sprouts. For fresh eating, 12 plants is sufficient for a family of four; increase the number if you want to preserve. Brussels sprouts require from 75 to more than 110 days before they're ready to harvest, depending on cultivar and growing conditions. Don't forget that the days-to-maturity numbers listed in seed catalogs are counted from transplanting, not from seeding.

SITE & SOIL

Brussels sprouts are most at home in cool, humid regions where daytime summer temperatures stay in the upper 60s and low 70s F, but they will grow in a wide range of conditions as long as they are spared extreme heat. Full sun is necessary for plants to bear numerous good-size sprouts. Soil should be well amended with enough humus to retain moisture, and have a pH in the range of 6.5 to 6.8. Plants do best with moderate fertility but overly rich soil, especially an excess of nitrogen, will promote leaf and stalk growth rather than sprouts.

A long-season crop, Brussels sprouts can succeed fast-growing spring vegetables, such as scallions, radishes, or leaf lettuce. Give plants enough room—set them 18 to 20 inches apart—and keep them in the vegetable garden. Brussels sprouts aren't tidy. More bizarre-looking than ornamental, they don't belong in most flower beds or boxes or on most decks or patios, although they can be grown successfully in containers.

BRUSSELS SPROUT CULTIVARS

There are both tall and short hybrid and open-pollinated Brussels sprouts. Remember that days-to-maturity numbers are figured from the transplant date and that plants are generally started indoors.

'Bedford Fillbasket': 96 days; tall, open-pollinated plant with heavy yields.

'Blues': 75 days; short, quick-maturing hybrid; excellent disease resistance.

'Bubbles': 105 days; tall hybrid; some disease resistance.

'Jade Cross E': 88 days; medium to tall hybrid; improved version of heirloom 'Jade Cross'; AAS winner.

'Long Island Improved': 95 days; short to medium, standard open-pollinated cultivar; widely adapted.

'Oliver': 95 days; short hybrid; very quick-maturing; widely adapted.

'Prince Marvel': 90 days; short hybrid; extremely hardy.

'Red Rubine': 85 days; medium open-pollinated cultivar; purple-red sprouts like miniature red cabbages.

'Royal Marvel': 90 days; short to medium hybrid; disease resistance.

'Sheriff': 160 days; medium to tall hybrid; European cultivar; good cultivar for mild-winter regions.

'Valiant': 110 days; tall hybrid; large cylindrical sprouts; standard hybrid cultivar.

HOW TO GROW

The care and cultural requirements of Brussels sprouts are similar to those of most brassicas, but the planting schedule differs. Sprouts should mature at the end of the gardening season. In warm regions, start them in late summer or early fall for a winter to early-spring harvest. In the rest of the country, count backward 3 or 4 months from the first expected fall frost date. If your garden season is a long, cool one, you can direct-seed; otherwise, begin seeds indoors.

To start seeds, indoors or out, follow directions for cabbage. At 75°F, germination takes about 7 days. About 6 weeks after germination, or a month after transplanting, side-dress plants with a balanced fertilizer such as compost, or spray plants with fish emulsion. Keep soil damp during hot weather, mulch to retain moisture and suppress weeds, and install cutworm collars and floating row covers to ward off insect pests.

As sprouts appear, remove the leaves that grow beneath them or any leaves that have yellowed. If the sprout-laden stem threatens to fall over, mound dirt around its base for support. To encourage the plant to ripen a majority of its sprouts all at once, "top" the plant by pinching off the growing point and top leaves. Topping too soon will reduce yields, so wait until the lower sprouts are about ½ inch in diameter before pinching back the top. Plants that have been topped will mature most of their sprouts in about 2 weeks.

Brussels sprouts are a vigorous, enduring crop. Plants that are spared the stress of heat and drought will not be much bothered by the insects or diseases that typically attack other brassicas, such as broccoli and cabbage. To avoid troubles, use floating row covers to deter insects, practice crop rotation, purchase certified disease-free seeds, and grow disease-resistant/disease-tolerant cultivars.

HARVESTING

Brussels sprouts ripen slowly and can be picked over a period of several weeks, depending on the temperature. Begin harvesting as soon as sprouts are large enough to be used, about ¾ inch in diameter, and before they exceed about 1½ inches in diameter.

As the weather cools, sprouts can be "stored" on the plant in the garden, naturally refrigerated for several weeks. They can also be stored briefly in plastic bags in the refrigerator or for longer periods of time in the root cellar (pull or cut the entire plant, leaving the sprouts on the stem). Storing imparts a strong flavor, so remember the first of the two things you should know about Brussels sprouts: Eat them only fresh from the garden.

Because Brussels sprouts are biennials and normally don't flower until their second season, gardeners must overwinter plants in order to save seeds. Plants, which require insects for pollination, will cross with all *B. oleracea* crops, including cabbage, cauliflower, and broccoli. To save seeds that will come true, plant only one cultivar and isolate from other *B. oleracea* crops. Seeds are viable for 5 years; store in airtight containers in a dark, cool location.

BURNET, SALAD. See *Salad Burnet*

CABBAGE

Brassica oleracea, Capitata group. Mustard family, Brassicaceae. Biennial grown as an annual.

○ ◑ ❄ ❀ ▮

The Egyptians, Greeks, and Romans doted on cabbage, but ever since the armies of Julius Caesar carried it to England, its reputation has suffered. Although no one stopped growing or eating cabbage, it was dismissed as having little nutritional value, a gas-producing vegetable fit only for peasants. "Cabbages are extremely windy, whether you take them as Meat or as Medicine; yea, as windy Meat as can be eaten, unless you eat Bagpipes or Bellows," herbalist Nicholas Culpeper observed in 1653.

It may have been the way that cabbage was prepared in Culpeper's day—boiled beyond recognition—that harmed its standing in the kitchen, although a cook in the court of Charles I (1625-49) was more inventive and included a cabbage-goose sandwich in his recipe book.

Cabbage-goose sandwiches didn't catch on, but cabbage continued to be a mealtime staple. It also was valued for its medicinal virtues, credited with the power to cure deafness and colic, to heal bruises and dog bites, and to prevent drunkenness.

Whether for meat or as medicine, cabbages came early to North America, planted in Canada by

Jacques Cartier in the 16th century and in Massachusetts Bay by the Puritans in the 17th. (John Winthrop, Jr., who wrote to England for 8 ounces of cabbage seed in 1631, must have been ordering for the entire colony, since 8 ounces contains about 55,000 seeds.) By the 1880s, more than 50 cabbage cultivars were sold by American seed houses; the W. Atlee Burpee Company alone offered 30 cultivars, including 'Surehead', which was described as "large as a water bucket."

Cabbages didn't begin as large as water buckets. According to the speculations of horticultural historians, they and all their relatives descended from wild sea kale, a scruffy loose-leaved herb that grows along the Mediterranean Coast. Centuries of selection brought about an assortment of related crops (collectively called brassicas because they all belong in *Brassica oleracea*), including broccoli, Brussels sprouts, cauliflower, and kohlrabi. In the case of cabbage, the leaves became larger and thicker and began to wrap around to form heads. Hence the cabbage is part of the Capitata, or "head," group. Although the cabbage no longer looks like its first ancestor, it still favors cool, moist maritime conditions. It can be cultivated almost anywhere, USDA Zone 2 and warmer.

DECIDING WHAT TO GROW

Despite being the Rodney Dangerfield of vegetables, one that "gets no respect," there is a remarkable array of cabbages to choose from. Although there are round, flat, and pointed types, head shape hasn't been an important quality for home gardeners. Color has, though, and there are green, blue-green, and red cultivars to pick among. Or you can decide according to leaf type: smooth-leaved, the usual cabbage form, or savoy. Savoyed cabbages have wrinkled, seersuckerlike leaves and are considered not only the most beautiful but the best-flavored by cabbage connoisseurs.

Timing so that the heads do not develop in hot weather is the trick to growing good cabbages. Largely a spring and fall crop in northern regions, cabbage is a winter crop in the South. Breeders have made timing easier by producing cultivars that mature at different speeds. Early, or spring, cabbages mature in 50 to 60 days; midseason, or main-season, cultivars are also begun in early spring but mature between 70 and 85 days after transplanting. Late-season, or storage, cabbages need at least 85 days in the garden to reach full size and should be timed for harvesting in the fall. Having early, midseason, and late cabbages also simplifies extending the harvest, or you can sow successive crops of the same cultivar every 10 days. Spring cultivars tend to have a milder flavor, good for using fresh in salads and slaws; late-season cabbages are better for sauerkraut and cooking. Remember that the days-to-maturity numbers for cabbages are from transplanting, not from seeding.

Cabbages can be intercropped with scallions, lettuces, radishes, and other vegetables and herbs that mature quickly. Spring cultivars should be succeeded by other crops, such as snap beans. For eat-

Savoy cabbage 'Chieftain'

Green cabbage 'Dynamo'

Red cabbage 'Super Red 77'

ing fresh, 20 heads are enough for a family of four; if you want to preserve, increase the planting.

SITE & SOIL

Cabbages prefer full sun when the weather is cool, but they also do well in partial shade, especially when the mercury rises. They are forgiving about soil, although they prefer fertile, well-drained soil that is extremely rich in organic matter and has a pH between 6.0 and 7.3. Cabbages need a generous supply of potassium; leaf edges tinged with bronze signal a deficiency. Apply a foliar spray of fish emulsion and side-dress plants with wood ashes. Before planting, dust the soil with lime, which helps prevent clubroot, a fungus that affects all brassicas.

As long as you rotate their location each year, cabbages can go almost anywhere in the garden, spaced from 10 to 20 inches apart (small-headed spring cultivars need less room than the larger, late-season cabbages do). When spacing, aim for the leaves of neighboring plants touching, which will shade the ground and suppress weeds. Cabbages have shallow roots, which are easily damaged by hoeing.

CABBAGE CULTIVARS

The best cabbages to grow vary according to season and use. In the list below, the days-to-maturity numbers are from transplanting and indicate the days to full-size heads; you can begin harvesting earlier than that time, as soon as the heads are firm.

'**April Green**': 110 days; open-pollinated; dark green 5-pound heads; late-season storage cultivar.

'**Blue Vantage**': 76 days; hybrid; blue-green ¾-pound heads; excellent disease resistance; midseason cultivar.

'**Chieftain**': 85 days; open-pollinated; blue-green savoy type with 5-pound heads; good heat and cold tolerance; 1938 AAS winner.

'**Dynamo**': 70 days; hybrid; blue-green 2-pound heads; compact; heat-tolerant; good container plant; fusarium wilt-resistant; AAS winner.

'**Earliana**': 60 days; open-pollinated; green 2-pound heads; compact; good container plant; early cultivar.

'**Early Flat Dutch**': 85 days; open-pollinated; green 7-pound heads; heat-resistant; good southern cultivar; heirloom.

'**Early Jersey Wakefield**': 65 days; open-pollinated; green ⅔-pound cone-shaped heads; widely adapted; cracks easily; heirloom.

'**Lasso**': 70 days; open-pollinated; red 3-pound heads; stores well; Danish cultivar.

'**Late Flat Dutch**': 105 days; open-pollinated; green 12-pound heads; extremely hardy; good fall cultivar; excellent keeper; heirloom.

'**Mammoth Red Rock**': 90 days; open-pollinated; red 6- to 7-pound heads; large plant; good storage cultivar; heirloom.

'**Premium Late Flat Dutch**': 100 days; open-pollinated; green 10-pound heads; good storage cultivar; heirloom.

'**Red Rookie**': 78 days; hybrid; red savoy type with 3-pound heads; widely adapted; midseason cultivar.

'**Ruby Ball**': 65 days; hybrid; red 4- to 5-pound heads; early cultivar; AAS winner.

'**Savoy Ace**': 80 days; hybrid; green savoy type with 4-pound heads; fusarium wilt-resistant; good fall cultivar; heat- and cold-tolerant; AAS winner.

'**Springtime**': 200 days; hybrid; green 3-pound heads; overwintering cultivar.

'**Stonehead**': 68 days; hybrid; green 3- to 4-pound heads; fusarium wilt-resistant; AAS winner.

'**Storage No. 4**': 95 days; hybrid; blue-green 5-pound heads; fusarium wilt-resistant; good storage cultivar.

Although cabbages don't do well in greenhouses, they are good plants for pots or window boxes. Choose an appropriate-size cultivar—standard cabbages spread 16 inches or more—and use a container, at least 10 inches wide and 12 inches deep, with good bottom drainage, and fill with enriched potting soil. Water frequently, and feed every 2 weeks with fish emulsion or manure tea.

HOW TO GROW

Cabbages are typically grown from transplants (the days-to-maturity numbers on seed packets refer to the days needed *from transplanting*). Sow seeds ¼ inch deep in flats or in 2-inch containers filled with a sterile medium 4 to 6 weeks before the average frost-free date, and set in a warm location. At 80°F, germination should occur in 4 to 5 days. (Late crops can be seeded indoors, in a cold frame, or an in outdoor seedling bed, or direct-seeded in the garden.) As soon as the new plants emerge, thin to one plant per container and move them to a bright, cool location, 65°F during the day, slightly cooler at night. Keep them watered and feed with diluted compost tea once a week.

Hardened-off seedlings can go into the garden almost as soon as the soil can be worked, 3 to 4 weeks before the last expected frost, or when the soil has reached a temperature of at least 40°F. Space from 10 to 20 inches apart. If you move seedlings outdoors when temperatures are still low, plant them in a shallow trench or set them more deeply than they were growing—up to the first leaf—to protect their stems. Use paper collars to deter cutworms, and cover plants with floating row covers to shield them from cold winds and insects.

A steady supply of water is important to cabbage plants. So is a fertilizer boost: Side-dress with well-rotted manure or blood meal—anything with plenty of nitrogen—3 weeks after transplanting. Mulch plants with a 6-inch-thick layer of organic matter to keep the soil cool, retain moisture, and keep weeds down.

Although cabbages need plenty of moisture while they're developing—periods of drought can cause plants to bolt or to go to flower prematurely—too much moisture when the heads near full maturity can cause them to split. If it rains heavily or if you want to postpone harvesting, either grasp the head in your hands and give it a sharp twist, or use a spade

FLOWERING CABBAGE

With green and red, magenta, pink, or white rosettes, flowering cabbage (*Brassica oleracea*, Acephala group) is at home in either the food or flower garden. These loose-headed ornamental edibles don't develop full color until the short, cool days of autumn. Two hybrid series are widely available. Plants of the Osaka series have wavy-edged leaves that form heads 12 to 14 inches tall. Tokyo-series cabbages, known for good heat resistance, are shorter, 8 to 10 inches tall, and 15 inches across.

Flowering kales are similar to flowering cabbages, but their leaves are thinner and ruffled or fringed rather than smooth-edged. Plants from Nagoya and Peacock hybrid series are widely available and recommended.

CABBAGE ESSENTIALS

- Full sun and cool weather; partial shade in warm weather.

- Fertile, well-drained, humus-rich soil.

- Begin plants indoors, 4 to 6 weeks before last frost.

- Time crops so that heads mature in cool weather.

- Set plants 10 to 20 inches apart; leaves should touch when plants mature.

- Install cutworm collars, and cover transplants with floating row covers.

- Hoeing can damage shallow roots.

and slice into the soil about 6 inches from the stem halfway around the plant. This severs some of the feeder roots and slows growth.

POTENTIAL PROBLEMS

All brassicas are susceptible to the same litany of insect pests, including aphids, cabbage loopers, cabbage root maggots, imported cabbageworms, cutworms, flea beetles, and slugs. (See "Controlling Common Pests" on page 162 for control measures.) Some cabbages stand up to insect pests better than others do, so look for tolerant/resistant cultivars, such as 'Savoy Chieftain', 'Mammoth Red Rock', and 'Red Acre'.

Nearly all brassicas are troubled by the same diseases. Most common is fusarium wilt, or yellows; only infected plants should be pulled and destroyed. Cabbages are also susceptible to clubroot and black rot. To avoid problems, plant resistant cultivars and rotate crops. (See "Controlling Common Diseases" on page 169 for control measures.)

HARVESTING

Raw cabbage has more vitamin C per calorie than orange juice and is a fair source of fiber, potassium, and other minerals. Begin harvesting as soon as heads are firm, even if they are only the size of grapefruits. Use a knife to cut heads, leaving the roots, lower leaves, and as much stem as possible to encourage the production of a second crop of small cabbage heads, or sprouts. Mature cabbages can withstand some frost.

Late-season cabbages store well in cool (32° to 40°F), moist locations, such as root cellars, but early cultivars are not as good for storing. Cabbages for storing should be pulled rather than cut. Warning: Stored cabbages emit a strong odor.

Because cabbages are biennials and flower in their second season, saving seeds requires overwintering plants. All *B. oleracea* crops will cross-pollinate. To save seeds that will come true, plant only one cultivar and separate it from other brassica crops. Seeds are viable for 5 years; store in airtight containers in a dark, cool location.

CABBAGE, CELERY. See *Bok Choy*
CABBAGE, CHINESE. See *Chinese Cabbage*
CABBAGE, CHINESE MUSTARD. See
   Bok Choy
CABBAGE, HAKUSAI. See *Chinese Cabbage*

Cardoon

CABBAGE, NAPA. See *Chinese Cabbage*

CARDOON

Cynara cardunculus. Aster family, Asteraceae.
Perennial also grown as an annual.

Cardoon, a tall, thistlelike Mediterranean native with purple flowers, is a crop for mild regions. Far less popular than its look-alike cousin, the globe artichoke (*C. scolymus*), cardoon was grown by 19th-century American gardeners, although "oftener as a novelty than for use," according to a garden writer of the time. When not grown as a novelty, cardoon was cultivated for its leafstalks and its fleshy root. "Cooked in a delicate way, it is excellent, but with the ordinary cook … is often spoiled," warned the French authors of *The Vegetable Garden* (1885). "The degree of tenderness to which it is boiled should be studied, and the sauce should not be rank with salt and spice after the vulgar fashion."

Although a perennial in USDA Zone 5 and

warmer, cardoon is treated as an annual in colder regions. Even in locations where it can't reach its full height of 5 feet, plants begun indoors well before the frost-free date typically develop tall enough stalks, or leaf petioles, for harvesting. Despite being a tender plant, cardoon needs cool temperatures, 55° to 65°F, to be edible; hot weather produces bitter stalks that even blanching can't cure.

Cardoon, with its arching form and deeply lobed gray-green leaves, is highly ornamental as well as edible, but only a few cultivars are marketed. Among the best known are 'Plein Blanc', a large-leafed French import, and an Italian cultivar, 'Gigante'. In most seed catalogs, it is simply listed as "Cardoon."

HOW TO GROW

Growing cardoon is similar to growing globe arti-chokes (see *Globe Artichoke* on page 267). Organically rich, well-drained soil, a pH between 6.0 and 7.0, plenty of water, and even more room—plants spread to 6 feet—are the prerequisites, plus a growing season of at least 130 cool but sunny days. Locate plants where they won't shade smaller crops.

In warm regions, cardoon can be started out-doors, either from seeds or rooted offshoots. In the rest of the country, sow seeds indoors, one seed per container, about 10 weeks before the last frost. Pot on, if necessary. When the danger of frost has passed, harden off plants and transplant them out-doors, setting them 2 to 4 feet apart. Mulch, keep well watered, and feed monthly with manure tea. Cardoon is rarely troubled by insect pests or disease, although crown rot can occur if the soil is not well drained.

HARVESTING

From 2 to 3 weeks before the end of the growing sea-son, blanch the stalks of cardoon by tying the outer branches together and wrapping the base of the plant—about 18 inches high—with burlap or news-paper. To harvest, cut just below the plant crown and remove the outer leaves. What's left are the large whitened stalks, like an oversize celery, which are usually boiled or steamed, and served with a sauce, preferably not one of "vulgar fashion."

Cultivars cross-pollinate, so grow only one car-doon if you want to save seeds. Seeds are viable for 6 years; store in airtight containers in a dark, cool location.

CARROT

Daucus carota, Sativus group. Carrot family, Apiaceae. Biennial grown as an annual.

○ ❄ ❀

Carrots were once either purple or a faded version of their contemporary selves, their roots off-white or a pallid yellow rather than deep orange. We know about their gradual color change not from plant sci-ence but from art history: A Dutch student studying still-life paintings in European museums document-ed how over the course of 200 years, carrots were rendered in bolder tones, brush strokes of yellow giv-ing way to ever deeper shades of orange. From the Renaissance on, gardeners and breeders selected car-rots for brighter and brighter color. In a happy coin-cidence, they were also promoting carrots with greater nutritional value—a deep orange color indi-cates a high content of beta carotene, a precursor of vitamin A.

Recommending the virtues of eating carrots isn't anything new, of course; old-world physicians and herbalists insisted that they could cure problems of the liver and stomach, heal wounds, and enhance "love-matters," the third claim no doubt connected to their phallic shape. Carrots had long been a sta-ple of the stew pot, but the sweet garden cultivars, which some called "underground honey," also were

CARROT ESSENTIALS

- Full sun and moderate-to-cool temperatures.
- Deeply dug soil free of rocks and debris.
- Direct-sow seeds, and keep seedbed evenly moist.
- Keep seeds and plants covered with row covers.
- Hill up soil to keep tops covered.
- Pulling weeds can disturb roots; cut them instead.

served as dessert, frequently combined with cinnamon, sugar, currants, and nuts. Today's carrot cakes would have been right at home in the 15th century.

With such versatility in the kitchen, it's no wonder that carrots, or "carrets," were early immigrants to North America, arriving in Virginia in 1609. By the time of the Civil War, at least 40 cultivars were being planted in the United States, including 'Early Scarlet Horn', 'Long Orange', and 'Long Red Surrey', three cultivars that are still available. A common crop in American vegetable plots, carrots also slipped over the garden fence and reverted to a wild form, making them the progenitors of Queen Anne's lace on this side of the Atlantic. Like that rugged roadside weed, carrots grow in USDA Zone 2 and warmer.

DECIDING WHAT TO GROW

Breeders have taken carrots in many directions. A search for nutritional value has led to high beta-carotene introductions, such as 'Beta Champ', 'Ingot', and 'Healthmaster'. Also relatively new are finger-size cultivars called fingerlings—'Minicor' and 'Little Finger' are two—and round carrots smaller than golf balls, such as 'Planet' and 'Orbit', all developed for the gourmet trade. Coreless carrots have also been released; these lack the central core most carrots possess, which is tougher and not as sweet as the outer casing of the root.

Think of carrots as a two-season crop, for summer eating and for fall storage. Finger-size and round types gain color quickly and are ready to begin harvesting in 50 days. Larger cultivars are slower to develop but produce a much higher yield per square foot of garden space. Although they may not be fully mature, most large types are ready to pull by the time your planting of small carrots has been harvested. For a fall-storage crop, make a second planting 10 to 12 weeks before the first-frost date. Carrots can be interplanted with faster-maturing crops, such as radishes. For fresh eating, 150 plants should be enough for a family of four; if you want to preserve, increase the planting.

SITE & SOIL

Perhaps more than any other crop, carrots benefit from loose, deeply dug soil that is free of rocks and other debris. Even straw or bits of cornstalk can injure the growing tip of a carrot, causing the root to be stunted or forked. Dig the soil to a depth of at least 12 inches, culling stones and other obstructions as you go. A moderately acid pH (5.8 to 6.8) is ideal. If your soil is heavy, add generous amounts of organic matter to lighten it or grow carrots in a raised bed.

Organic matter benefits sandy soil too by increasing its capacity to absorb water. Soil that remains moist produces carrots that are sweeter and less fibrous. Before sowing seeds, sprinkle wood ashes over the soil to provide extra potassium, but,

Carrot 'Short 'n Sweet'

Carrot 'Orange Rocket'

don't add manure. High nitrogen levels can cause carrot roots to branch. "Hairy" carrots, which are covered with an abundance of small roots, are one sign of soil that is too rich.

While they will tolerate light shade, carrots do best in full sun, which makes frequent watering essential as seeds are germinating. Keep the seedbed moist, watering twice a day, if necessary. Spread a floating row cover over the bed to help retain moisture and warmth and to prevent insects from reaching the seedlings. Lift the cover when the seedlings sprout in order to thin, then replace it.

Carrots, with their frilly, fernlike foliage, are pretty in flower gardens. They also grow well in containers that have good drainage and are at least 12 inches deep. Choose small cultivars, such as 'Oxheart', 'Orbit', or 'Little Finger', for container culture. Fill pots with enriched potting mix, feed with compost tea every 10 days until plants are 6 inches tall, and don't allow the soil to dry out.

HOW TO GROW

Carrots, which are direct-seeded, will germinate when the ground reaches the mid-40s F, but sprouting is sped up when soil temperatures are at least 30 degrees higher. Even in 78°F soil, germination takes a week to 10 days. An early crop can be planted as soon as the ground can be worked, but it's better to wait until about 2 or 3 weeks before the last expected frost. Gardeners in warm regions can plant in fall,

CARROT CULTIVARS

For a varied, long harvest, plant a mix of short-season "baby" carrots and full-size cultivars. The following list includes both hybrids and open-pollinated cultivars in a range of shapes and sizes.

'**Amsdor**': Amsterdam/Nantes cross; 75 days; hybrid; uniform; harvest early for "baby" carrots.

'**Blaze**': Imperator; 68 days; hybrid; good disease resistance; good storage cultivar.

'**Bolero**': Nantes; 75 days; hybrid; fall cultivar; outstanding storage carrot.

'**Canada Gold**': Imperator; 75 days; hybrid; vivid orange color.

'**Danvers Half-Long**': Danvers; 75 days; open-pollinated heirloom; main-crop cultivar; needs light soil; stores well.

'**Imperator Long**': Imperator; 75 days; open-pollinated heirloom; needs light soil.

'**Ingot**': Nantes; 70 days; hybrid; high vitamin A; dark orange.

'**Kinko 4 Inch**': Chantenay; 52 days; open-pollinated; very early; crack-resistant.

'**Little Finger**': Amsterdam/Fingerling type; 65 days; open-pollinated; gourmet "baby" carrot.

'**Minicor**': Amsterdam/fingerling type; 55 days; open-pollinated; widely adapted; early.

'**Nantes Half-Long**': Nantes; 70 days; open-pollinated; nearly coreless.

'**Navajo**': Imperator; 68 days; hybrid; good disease resistance.

'**Oxheart**': Chantenay; 75 days; open-pollinated heirloom; yellow core; good in heavy soil.

'**Parmex**': Paris Market; 50 days; open-pollinated; round; improved form of 'Planet'; good in heavy soil.

'**Royal Chantenay**': Chantenay; 70 days; open-pollinated; standard cultivar.

'**Scarlet Nantes**': Nantes; 70 days; open-pollinated; coreless; very sweet; popular home-garden cultivar.

'**Tamino**': Nantes; 90 days; hybrid; needs light soil; uniform.

'**Tokita's Scarlet**': Chantenay; 75 days; open-pollinated; red core; good fall cultivar.

'**Thumbelina**': Paris Market; 60 days; open-pollinated; round; good for heavy soils; AAS winner.

'**Touchon**': Nantes; 75 days; open-pollinated heirloom; coreless; not heat-tolerant.

A CARROT LEXICON

Amsterdam. Also called Amsterdam forcing, this type grows to the width of a finger and 3 to 5 inches long. Amsterdams are among the first carrots ready for harvest. They are ideal for heavy soils and container growing.

Chantenay. Chantenay carrots are broad-shouldered and chunky, tapering quickly to a blunt end. Ranging in length from 4 to 6 inches, their stout shape makes them well suited for heavy soil.

Danvers. These cultivars, named for Danvers, Massachusetts, where they originated, are almost as broad-shouldered as Chantenay types but longer. They taper slightly to a blunt end, reaching a length of 5 to 7 inches. Danvers are productive and adaptable to a wide range of soils but are not as sweet as Nantes types and, so, not as popular.

Imperator. Imperator carrots are 8 to 10 inches long, tapering to a point. The mainstay of the supermarket produce section, they are less sweet than Nantes types are as well as less crisp, or brittle, which makes them easier to harvest mechanically. Imperators require deep, loose soil, near-perfect growing conditions.

Nantes. Nantes cultivars are cylindrical, 5- to 7-inch-long, cigar-shaped carrots that taper gradually to a blunt end. They are sweet, crisp, and deeply colored, the most popular home-garden carrot.

Paris Market. This is the name given to round or beetlike carrots that reach a diameter of about 1½ inches (the name is taken from market gardeners outside the French capital who popularized spherical carrots in the late 19th century). They're well suited to heavy soil and container culture.

winter, and spring. Presoak seeds in water for 6 hours before sowing to hasten germination.

Although frost-tolerant as seedlings and mature plants, carrots prefer moderate temperatures. Like Goldilocks, they want conditions that are "just right," which means temperatures between 60° and 75°F. No matter when carrots are planted, however, germination is often uneven. Carrot seeds tend to sprout over a range of time, a genetic characteristic. Succession plantings can be made every 2 weeks until midsummer, or until the temperature reaches 80°F.

Make early sowings quite shallow (¼ inch or less) to capture the sun's warmth; sprinkle seeds on the soil surface, tamp them gently, and cover with a thin layer of finely sifted compost. Later in the season, when the soil has warmed, seeds should be planted between ¼ and ½ inch deep. Because germination can be slow, you may want to plant in rows, rather than broadcast seeds in a bed, so that you'll be able to distinguish carrot seedlings from weed seedlings. To maximize productive space, plant seeds in a wide band rather than in a single row.

Carrot seeds are so small—a pinch equals two dozen seeds—that it's difficult to plant at the recommended 1-inch spacing. One solution is to mix seeds with sand (40:60, seeds to sand); another is to purchase pelleted seeds, which have been coated with clay to make them easier to handle. Whatever the approach, carrots will almost certainly have to be thinned. Undertake the job before the leafy tops become entwined, either scissoring off unwanted plants or pulling carefully so as not to disturb the roots of the plants that are to remain in the garden.

Thin carrots to 3 to 4 inches, depending on the cultivar. After thinning, hill soil around any carrots that are exposed to prevent their shoulders from turning green, which gives them a bitter taste. Mulch with compost or grass clippings to suppress weeds and retain moisture. Make sure carrots receive at least 1 inch of water weekly; very dry soil followed by wet soil can cause the roots to crack. Cut back on watering as your plants near maturity. To ensure good growth, spray young plants once with liquid seaweed extract or compost tea.

POTENTIAL PROBLEMS

Carrots are relatively free of insect and disease problems. Install floating row covers to minimize damage from the larvae of the dark brown, yellow-headed carrot rust fly that burrow into plant roots. Row

Carrot 'Thumbelina'

wash carrots that are to be stored. Dry in the sun for a few hours, which encourages the roots to go dormant. One average-size carrot fulfills the RDA requirement for vitamin A and is also a good source of potassium and fiber.

During the height of the summer, carrots should be pulled within a few days of coloring up; in cooler weather, they can be left in the ground for many weeks. To extend the harvest in areas where the ground freezes, mulch plants with 2 feet of straw or leaves. (Roots that freeze will crack and appear water-soaked.) To store carrots, seal in plastic bags to retain moisture and refrigerate. For long-term storage, pack carrots in damp sawdust, and store in a cold (32° to 40°F) location.

Because carrots are biennials and normally don't flower until their second season, saving their seeds is difficult. Gardeners in cold climates must dig and overwinter plants, then replant them in the spring; in frost-free regions, carry plants over to a second year. Carrot cultivars, which are pollinated by insects, will cross-pollinate with each other and with Queen Anne's lace (*Daucus carota*, Carota group). To save seeds that will come true, plant only one cultivar. Seeds are viable for 3 years if stored in airtight containers in a dark, cool location.

covers are also good protection against leafhoppers. To control wireworms, rotate the location of your carrot crop. (See "Controlling Common Pests" on page 162 for more on these two pests.)

Among the diseases that afflict carrots most often are blight, aster yellows, and damping-off. As a defense against blight, choose blight-tolerant cultivars and wait at least 3 years before replanting carrots in the same part of the garden. Row covers protect against aster yellows by controlling the leafhoppers that carry them from plant to plant. (For more on these potential problems, see "Controlling Common Diseases" on page 169.)

HARVESTING

Begin harvesting carrots as soon as they are large enough to be used, or when they develop a deep orange color. Loosen the soil along the row with a garden fork before pulling them up. After harvesting, remove the tops, leaving about 2 inches of stem. Brush off as much soil as you can, but don't

CAULIFLOWER

Brassica oleracea, Botrytis group. Mustard family,
Brassicaceae. Biennial grown as an annual.

○ ✳ ❀ ❚

"Cauliflower is nothing but cabbage with a college education." So goes Mark Twain's often-quoted line from *Pudd'head Wilson* (1894). If college students are a pampered or demanding lot, letting their youthful accomplishments go to their heads, Twain's assessment is true. Cauliflower *is* more demanding than broccoli or cabbage. Garden writers not long after Twain's day characterized raising cauliflower as a horticultural challenge of the first order. "More difficult to grow than any other plant of the cabbage tribe," one observed. "No crop is more likely to go wrong than cauliflower," another cautioned.

Despite difficulties in growing it, cauliflower has long been a popular European vegetable, eaten boiled, baked, pickled, and raw. Its appearance delighted—"hard floures closely thrust together" was an early description. "Of all the flowers in the garden," 18th-century essayist and critic Samuel Johnson wrote, "I like the cauliflower."

While cauliflower does have its quirks, the degree of difficulty in bringing in a healthy harvest can be overstated. Breeders have introduced cultivars such as 'Amazing' with improved tolerance for hot and cold weather so that it can be grown in almost any region, USDA Zone 3 and warmer. Self-blanching types have reduced the need to tie up the leaves to protect the crown, or curd, from sunlight. With proper timing, good fertility, and attentive watering, cauliflower will reward you with handsome large white, purple, or yellow-green heads.

DECIDING WHAT TO GROW

Each cauliflower plant is a one-shot deal. A single head is all you get. Extending the season, means succession planting, and growing a selection of cultivars with a range of maturity dates can also extend the harvest. Keep in mind that the days to maturity can differ widely for the same cultivar, depending on location: 'Snow Crown' may be ready in as few as 50 days in New Jersey but takes more than 60 days to mature in the Pacific Northwest.

When choosing cultivars, look for descriptions of heat and cold tolerance. Resistance to frost is an important characteristic for fall crops but may indicate that the cultivar is a poor choice for early-spring planting. On the other hand, a cauliflower such as 'Snow King', which stands up relatively well in hot weather, can be damaged by frost and should be planted in spring. Gardeners in cool, mild

regions where winter temperatures don't dip below 10°F may want to try an overwintering cultivar, such as 'Purple Cape' or one of the many "Walcherin" strains from Holland. Overwintering cauliflowers, which need about 200 days to form mature heads, are planted out in late summer or early fall and cut the following spring.

White cauliflowers are the most familiar, but breeders have introduced cultivars with purple, yellow-green, and orange crowns. Not only handsome, they are also simpler to grow than are most whites, as they do not have to be blanched. Purple cultivars, which turn green when cooked, are mild-flavored and taste more like broccoli than cauliflower. (The *Brassica oleracea*, Botrytis group family tree is close-knit and complicated, so colored cultivars are often cross-listed in seed catalogs under both cauliflower and broccoli.)

The need to blanch cauliflower heads makes many cultivars inappropriate for the ornamental garden, but the colored types, which are not blanched, are pretty additions to flower beds and borders. Cauliflower also grows well in containers. Set two or three compact plants, such as 'Garant' or 'Snowbaby', in a large container, at least 18 inches

Cauliflower 'Stardust'

Cauliflower 'Purple Head'

deep, and fill with enriched potting mix. Keep the soil moist at all times, and feed with a balanced liquid fertilizer every 3 weeks.

Twenty plants will provide enough cauliflower for fresh use for a family of four; if you want to preserve, increase the planting.

SITE & SOIL

Cauliflower needs plenty of sun for steady growth. If your region is extremely hot in summer, however, a bit of afternoon shade is an advantage. Some cauliflower cultivars are more tolerant of heat than others are, but not one thrives in hot weather. The soil should be fertile and rich in organic matter, with a pH range of 6.0 to 6.8. Cauliflower is a heavy feeder. A purple cast to the top or underside of crowns can indicate inadequate nutrition. Spraying with fish emulsion will help correct the problem.

Because they are large and hungry, cauliflowers need plenty of room. Space plants 18 inches apart in rows 3 feet on center; if planting in a bed, set plants about 24 inches apart. A closer planting, even if given extra moisture and fertilizer, is still likely to produce smaller heads. If garden space is at a premium, set leaf lettuce, scallions, small annual flowers, and other crops between the cauliflowers once the plants are well established.

HOW TO GROW

For spring, or early, cultivars, begin plants indoors about a month before the average frost-free date. Cauliflower is sensitive to transplanting, so use small individual containers or a cell tray. Sow seeds 1/4 inch deep; at 70°F germination occurs in about 6 days. Thin to one plant, move containers into bright light, and let the temperature drop into the mid-60s F. Once plants sprout, move them into bright light.

Transplant to the garden when the soil and air have warmed to at least 50°F, after the danger of frost is past. Set the plants lower than they were growing, almost to their bottom leaves. While cauliflower seedlings are frost-tolerant, they don't thrive in cold weather. Either they sit and do nothing, or, worse, they "button," or form small heads

---

CAULIFLOWER CULTIVARS

While white-headed cauliflowers are best known, green, purple, and even orange-fleshed ones are available.

'Alverda': 90 days; lime green open-pollinated cultivar; do not blanch; demands a long, cool growing season; fall harvest.

'Amazing': 65 days; white open-pollinated cultivar; self-blanching; midseason cultivar for late summer/fall harvest.

'Avalanche': 75 days; white hybrid; self-blanching but benefits from tying in hot, dry weather; large smooth heads.

'Chartreuse II': 65 days; lime green cultivar; do not blanch; demands a long, cool growing season; often cross-listed as broccoli.

'Early Snowball': 65 days; white open-pollinated cultivar; small heads; good small-space cultivar; heirloom.

'Early White Hybrid': 55 days; white hybrid; large heads; very early spring cultivar.

'Fremont': 55 days; white hybrid; self-blanching; uniform maturity; widely adapted.

'Orange Bouquet': 60 days; pale orange hybrid; do not blanch; high vitamin A content.

'Snow Crown': 50 days; white hybrid; good cultivar for early-summer or fall harvest; some frost tolerance; standard home-garden cultivar.

'Snow Peak': 50 days; white open-pollinated selection; early; very heat-sensitive.

'Snowball Self-Blanching': 68 days; white open-pollinated cultivar; self-blanching; good heat resistance; fall harvest.

'Violet Queen': 54 days; purple hybrid; do not blanch; good small-space cultivar.

'White Rock': 95 days; white open-pollinated type; self-blanching; small heads; slow-growing cultivar for areas with long, cool summers.

prematurely once the temperatures rise. Don't be in a rush to get plants outdoors. If you're pushing things a bit, shelter transplants against the cold with some type of cloche or with floating row covers.

To direct-seed for a fall harvest, sow four seeds ½ inch deep in a cluster, spacing the clusters 2 feet apart. When the plants develop their first true leaves, remove all but the strongest seedling from each cluster. Seeds can be sown outdoors at or after the average frost-free date. In 50°F soil, germination will take between 2 and 3 weeks.

Cauliflower is highly weather-sensitive. Extremes of heat or cold can produce browning, ricey (separated) curds, bolting, and buttoning. Staggered plantings are one guarantee of a successful harvest. Another is to avoid stressing plants. Keep the soil evenly moist, providing at least 1 inch of water a week, especially when plants are small and when curds are developing. Adequate moisture also promotes mild flavor. Plants also need a steady source of nutrients: Feed with a balanced liquid fertilizer, such as a mix of seaweed and fish emulsion, when you transplant and every 3 or 4 weeks thereafter.

When a cauliflower head is about the size of an egg, it's time to begin the blanching process that will produce a white, mild-flavored curd. Loop a piece of heavy twine around the foliage, and gently lift up the leaves and tie them so that they cover the curd. Snapping the stems of the largest leaves and draping them over the crown is sometimes recommended as an alternative to tying, but the broken foliage tends to dry and shrivel, providing less shade than tying. Early cultivars benefit most from tying, because the crowns form before the foliage is large enough to wrap them naturally. Self-blanching cultivars can produce good-flavored heads without any help, but tying provides an additional measure of shade. Purple and other-colored cultivars do not have to be blanched.

POTENTIAL PROBLEMS

Cauliflower is susceptible to many of the same insects and diseases as cabbage and other mustard-family members are. (See *Cabbage* on page 204 for a rundown of what problems to watch for.) The most important thing the home gardener can do to prevent problems is to rotate cauliflower plants, making sure that they don't grow in the same location every year and don't follow other members of the mustard family. Good housekeeping—cleaning up

the garden at the end of the season—will prevent overwintering of many diseases and insects, and floating row covers can keep some pests, such as aphids, flea beetles, cabbageworms, and mites, from reaching plants. Making sure plants are not stressed from lack of water or nutrients also helps offset many potential difficulties.

Black leg, a fungal disease that is transmitted in seeds and plant debris, first appears as dark, sunken areas on the stem and gray spots on the foliage. Spray with a fungicide; if plants are badly infected, remove and destroy them. Browning heads and leaf-tip dieback are indications of a boron deficiency in the soil; spray plants immediately with liquid seaweed, repeating every 10 days until the symptoms disappear.

HARVESTING

When heads reach 3 or 4 inches across, begin checking plants daily so that they can be harvested before they pass their peak. Cauliflower, which contains vitamin C, potassium, and iron and shares broccoli's cancer-fighting qualities, should be picked before the curds show a tendency to segment, or become ricey. Cut the crowns, leaving several inches of stem.

Cauliflower can be stored for 2 to 3 weeks if it is kept in a cold (32° to 35°F), humid location. Heads can be stored in the refrigerator in plastic bags, although they rapidly lose some of their flavor.

Because cauliflower is a biennial and normally doesn't flower until its second season, saving seeds is difficult. Gardeners in cold climates must dig and overwinter plants, then replant them in the spring; in frost-free regions, carry plants over to a second year. Cauliflowers will cross-pollinate with each other and other *B. oleraceae* members, such as cabbage and broccoli. To save seeds that will come true, isolate from other *B. oleraceae* cultivars. Seeds are viable for 5 years; store in airtight containers in a dark, cool location.

CELERIAC

Apium graveolens, Rapaceum group. Carrot family, Apiaceae. Biennial grown as an annual.

○ ✳ ❄ ▼

Celeriac is a sibling of celery, much as beets are related to chard. Raised for its crisp, globe-shaped root rather than for its stems or leaves, it looks like a turnip that has sprouted a thin celery plant. Two common names, not surprisingly, are knob celery and turnip-rooted celery. While celeriac offers less eye appeal and versatility in the kitchen than its stalky relative celery does, it is easier to grow and store and somewhat hardier. And its flavor, sweet and mild, is every bit as good as celery's; although usually cooked, thin slices of raw celeriac are a fine salad ingredient.

By one account, gardeners in the service of Persian kings some 4,000 years ago began selecting *A. graveolens* for its root rather than for its top growth, which started celeriac on its way to being a distinct vegetable. More appreciated in Europe than in North America—only two cultivars were widely available in 1865, 'Curled Leaved' and 'Early Erfurt'—celeriac remains a curiosity for many gardeners 150 years later. Seedlings are rarely sold at garden centers, so celeriac is a vegetable that gardeners must start for themselves. It can be grown in USDA Zone 4 and warmer.

DECIDING WHAT TO GROW

A dozen celeriac roots grown to a mature size of 3 to 5 inches will give a household of four plenty of chances to explore its culinary possibilities; if you want to preserve, increase the planting. Most gardeners make do with the species, but there are a few cultivars to choose from: 'Alabaster', a round, smooth-skinned open-pollinated selection; 'Brilliant', an early open-pollinated cultivar that resists pithiness; 'Jose', a very large open-pollinated selection with small tops; and the intensely flavored

Celeriac roots

heirloom 'Giant Prague'/'Large Smooth Prague'. Most celeriacs take between 110 and 130 days to reach maturity. 'Dolvi', a new cultivar recommended for its disease resistance and vigor, takes even longer, 150 days.

HOW TO GROW

Celeriac thrives in the same conditions that celery does—humus-rich soil with a slightly acidic pH and generous amounts of moisture—but it is more tolerant of less-than-ideal settings and is less sensitive to hot, dry weather and to cold. Celeriac prefers full sun and can be closely spaced, 6 to 8 inches between plants. Unlike celery, it makes a good container plant; you can raise several plants in a 5-gallon pot.

Because celeriac is a long-season plant, it must be started indoors 8 weeks before the frost-free date in most climates (although it can be planted in the late summer as a winter and spring crop in USDA Zone 7 and warmer). It is rarely troubled by diseases or insects pests. Although it doesn't require blanching, celeriac is grown as celery is in other respects. (For specific cultural information, see *Celery* on page 218.)

As the roots develop, add soil or mulch to keep them covered. To reduce the number of rootlets that grow from the main root—one writer described a celeriac as looking like a "monstrous millipede of the dinosaur age"—periodically pull the soil or mulch away and prune off the small feeder roots.

Unlike celery, celeriac is not damaged by light frosts; in fact, cold weather will improve the root's flavor by inducing stored starches to convert to sugar.

HARVESTING

Celeriac can be harvested as soon as the rootball reaches about 2 inches in diameter or is large enough to use. Mature plants have a surprisingly tenacious grip on the earth and should be lifted with a garden fork rather than pulled. You can extend the harvest by mulching plants heavily to postpone the ground's freezing. To store celeriac, cut tops off 2 inches above the root, place in plastic bags to retain moisture, and refrigerate. Or store for up to 4 months by burying the roots in damp sand or sawdust in a humid, cold (32° to 38°F) location.

Celeriac is a biennial and normally doesn't flower until its second season. To save seeds, gardeners in cold climates must dig and overwinter plants, then replant them in the spring; in frost-free regions, carry plants over to a second year. Celeriac cultivars, which are insect-pollinated, will cross with each other and with celery. For seeds that will come true, plant only one cultivar. Seeds are viable for 5 years; store in airtight containers in a dark, cool location.

CELERY

Apium graveolens, Dulce group. Carrot family, Apiaceae. Biennial grown as an annual.

○ ◑ ❄

Celery's historic roots are in marshy, rainy regions from Scandinavia east to the Caucus Mountains and the uplands of India, where growing seasons are long, moist, and somewhat cool. Despite its evolution over many centuries from a leafy plant to one with more upright, closely bunched stems and leaves, celery remains most at home in its ancestral conditions, which makes raising a crop challenging for many gardeners. But when it is well grown, celery's taste and texture surpass most supermarket offerings.

Although cultivated since early times—the Roman historian Pliny mentions celery—it apparently was slow to make its way to England and was mostly unknown there until the reign of Henry VIII. By the end of the 17th century, celery, another of those plants whose contribution has changed from medicinal to vegetable, was an acknowledged salad ingredient. Not only its leaves but its blanched stems, when "first peel'd and slit long wise," were eaten with "Oyl, vinegar, Salt, and Pepper." But with one caveat: "CAUTION is to be given of a small red WORM, often lurking in these Stalks."

For all its goodness as a raw vegetable, celery's role is largely a supporting one in soups, stews, and dressings. Sometimes its presence in a cooked dish is overlooked, probably because its crunchy texture is expected. As Ogden Nash observed in what is probably the only celery poem in the English language (*Versus from 1929 On*, 1941),

> Celery, raw,
> Develops the jaw,
> But celery, stewed,
> Is more quietly chewed.

Blanching celery with milk cartons

DECIDING WHAT TO GROW

Celery, which can be grown in USDA Zone 5 and warmer, needs plenty of time to mature, anywhere from 80 days for short-season types like 'Green Giant' and 'Ventura' to 130 or more days for such cultivars as 'Pascal Giant'. Long-season cultivars are rarely practical for gardeners in the crop's northern range, for although celery favors cool conditions, most cultivars do not tolerate frost. An exception to the no-frost rule is a red cultivar, called 'Giant Red' or 'Red Stalk', which not only can stand some frost but requires cold weather to develop its color.

In addition to red, or "trenching," cultivars, most of which were bred in England, there are two other general types: self-blanching, or golden, celeries, and "green" celeries. Self-blanching cultivars, which tend to be more compact, produce less green-pigmented chlorophyll than do green cultivars. Their stems mature to a golden yellow. Green celeries, including the home-garden favorite, 'Tendercrisp', are generally more disease-resistant and have a stronger flavor than the self-blanching kinds do. For fresh use, 20 plants should be plenty for a family of four; if you want to preserve, increase the planting.

SITE & SOIL

If your location can't provide the climate celery needs—daytime temperatures between 65° and 75°F (60° to 65°F at night)—use the garden space for another crop. But if you have a long, cool growing season, celery should thrive. It does best in full to partial sun (at least 6 hours a day) and moist, rich ground with a slightly acid pH in the range of 6.0 to 6.5. Commercial production is often centered in regions with what is called "muck" soil, which is very high in organic matter. Home-garden beds, too, should be enriched with generous amounts of compost or well-rotted manure to hold moisture and keep the plants from drying out. Sprinkle the soil with wood ashes or granite dust to increase its potassium content.

Watch the stalks as they grow. If you see signs of cracking, your soil may be boron-deficient. Water with fish emulsion to correct the problem. Spindly stalks are a sign of a phosphorus deficiency, sometimes a temporary condition due to cold soil. Spray plants with diluted fish emulsion to remedy the problem.

Space plants 6 to 8 inches apart. Because celery takes so long to produce edible stalks, you can make double use of the space it takes by intercropping with fast-growing spring vegetables, such as scallions, radishes, leaf lettuces, and other greens. Plant successively to space harvests. Celery requires such large amounts of nutrients and water that it is not especially suitable for containers or the ornamental garden.

HOW TO GROW

In regions with long, mild growing seasons, celery can be direct-seeded. Otherwise, start seeds in individual containers or cell trays about 8 weeks before the last-frost date. Celery seeds need some light to germinate, so cover them very thinly, to the thickness, as one grower put it, "of a silk scarf." Mist the soil to keep it moist. Germination, which takes 7 to 14 days in 65°F soil, is often uneven. Soaking seeds for 6 hours in compost tea before sowing accelerates sprouting. As soon as germination occurs, move containers to a well-lighted location with temperatures in the mid-60s F. When seedlings have two true leaves, thin to one plant per cell or container. Keep plants well watered, and feed every 10 days with a diluted liquid fertilizer.

Don't be in a rush to move celery outdoors:

Plants exposed to temperatures in the 40s F for 10 to 15 days are likely to bolt prematurely. Transplant hardened-off seedlings to the garden once temperatures are reliably above 50°F. Set them slightly deeper than they were growing previously, and water with a diluted solution of fish emulsion and seaweed extract. Mulch plants heavily to suppress weeds and retain moisture, and install floating row covers to prevent insect pests. Feed monthly with manure tea, and keep

CELERY CULTIVARS

Home gardeners have three types of celery to choose from, conventional green-stalked celery, red-stalked types, and self-blanching, or golden, celeries.

'Giant Pascal': 130 days; green open-pollinated type; large plant; disease-resistant.

'Giant Red'/'Red Stalk': 90 days; red open-pollinated cultivar with strong "celery" flavor; develops deeper color after frost.

'Golden Self-Blanching': 115 days; self-blanching open-pollinated type with thick, waxy yellow stalks; compact plant.

'Green Giant': 75 days; hybrid with thick, pale green stems; very frost-sensitive; first hybrid celery.

'Solid Red': 110 days; red open-pollinated cultivar; vigorous plant; heirloom

'Tendercrisp': 100 days; green open-pollinated cultivar; uniform and upright; favorite home-garden cultivar.

'Utah 52-70 R Improved': 105 days; green open-pollinated cultivar with thick stalks and mild flavor.

'Utah': 100 days; green open-pollinated cultivar; stocky, compact plants; popular home-garden cultivar.

'Ventura': 95 days; green open-pollinated type with tall stalks; widely adapted; good bolt resistance.

the soil damp. Celery, which tolerates wet soil better than do most crops, needs a minimum of 1 inch of water a week if there is inadequate rainfall. Water-stressed plants produce fibrous and bitter stalks.

POTENTIAL PROBLEMS

Many of the insect pests that bother celery, including aphids, cabbage loopers, leafhoppers, whiteflies, and cutworms, can be prevented by using floating row covers and collars. (See "Controlling Common Pests" on page 162 for other control measures.) Instead of harming parsleyworms, which are black-striped green larvae of swallowtail butterflies, move them to nearby Queen Anne's lace plants or an extra patch of parsley or dill. Careful crop rotation and fall cleanup are also effective in reducing insects and diseases, as is planting resistant/tolerant cultivars. To control diseases carried by seeds, such as blights, soak the seeds in hot water (118°F) for 30 minutes before sowing.

Celery diseases are rare in home gardens. (For more information about some of the problems that can affect celery, including damping-off, early and late blight, and fusarium wilt, see "Controlling Common Diseases" on page 169.) Black heart, an environmental disease that shows as browning of leaf tips, can be treated by adding calcium to the soil—good sources are limestone, wood ashes, and bonemeal—and spraying plants with seaweed extract. Pink rot, another celery nemesis, first appears as spots on stalks and a pinkish cottony growth around the plant base. There is no cure; remove and destroy infected plants.

HARVESTING

Although blanching celery was common practice years ago, "green" celery, which contains more nutrients and has a slightly stronger flavor, is now the standard. Self-blanching cultivars are one alternative to blanching. If you want to whiten non-blanching cultivars, begin when plants are about 12 inches tall. There are many techniques: Mound soil or mulch around the stalks; wrap plants with brown paper, and tie loosely with twine; place a metal juice can or piece of PVC pipe over the plant; set 1-foot-wide boards on their edge along both sides of a row, securing them with small stakes, to prevent sun from reaching the stalks. Or you can plant celery in trenches as with leeks, adding compost as the stalks grow. (See *Leek* on page 279 for details.)

Most of celery's meager store of nutrients is in its leaves, although the stalks are a good source of fiber. Begin harvesting plants as soon as they are large enough to use. Either cut off outer stems individually when they develop color, or pull the entire plant and cut away the roots.

Seal celery in a plastic bag, and store in the refrigerator (if the stalks loose their crispness, revive them by recutting the ends and standing them in cold water). For long-term storage, dig celery plants, roots and all, and replant them in boxes of damp sand. Store in a cool, humid, dark location.

Because celery is a biennial and normally does not flower until its second season, saving seeds is difficult. Gardeners in cold climates must dig and overwinter plants, then replant them in the spring; in frost-free regions, carry plants over to a second year. Celery cultivars, which are insect-pollinated, will cross with each other and with celeriac. To save seeds that will come true, plant only one cultivar. Seeds are viable for 5 years; store in airtight containers in a dark, cool location.

CELERY CABBAGE. See *Bok Choy*
CELERY, KNOB. See *Celeriac*
CELERY, TURNIP-ROOTED. See *Celeriac*

CELTUCE

Lactuca sativa, Asparagina group; Sunflower family, Asteraceae. Annual.

○ ❀

Celtuce is an old, relatively obscure vegetable thought to have originated in China and first brought to North America in the late 19th century by missionaries returning from Asia. Few seed merchants even carry celtuce, and there are no named cultivars, although plants sometimes vary. But don't take this lack of popularity as a lack of merit. Celtuce is a versatile vegetable. Its name—believed to be the brainchild of an English horticulturist by some, the concept of the W. Atlee Burpee Seed company by others—represents in syllables the edible qualities of the plant: crunchy, slightly fibrous stalks like celery's and the tender leaves of lettuce.

Despite this nomenclatural merger, celtuce is a type of lettuce, not a cross between celery and lettuce. Nor is it a cross between summer squash and a

Celtuce

generous amounts of organic matter. Starting 2 or 3 weeks before the average last-frost date, sow seeds in the garden ¼ inch deep, spaced at 3 to 4 inches. Celtuce can withstand mild frosts and also will tolerate warm weather. However, cool conditions, temperatures in the low 60s F, produce a more tender, better-flavored harvest and postpone plants from going to seed prematurely. In the North, celtuce is planted throughout the garden season, up to 8 weeks before the first fall frost. In warm regions, it is grown as a spring, fall, and winter crop.

After sowing seeds, cover the bed with a floating row cover to prevent insect pests from reaching the new plants. When seedlings are 2 inches tall, thin to 10 inches and mulch to retain moisture and suppress weeds. Keep celtuce well watered, at least 1 inch a week, which will encourage healthy growth and help prevent bitter-tasting leaves and tough stalks. Uneven watering often causes the stem to crack, so avoid soil that is either too wet or too dry. Water with mature tea when plants are 4 weeks old. Stalks mature in about 85 days, but leaves can be harvested in as few as 40 days.

While many of the same insects and diseases that afflict lettuce can trouble celtuce, if plants are given adequate moisture and spared intense heat, they are generally free of any serious problems.

HARVESTING

Because celtuce is a two-crop vegetable—leaves and stems—harvesting takes place in two stages. Leaves can be picked, starting at the base of the plant, as soon as they are large enough to be used. The stalk should be cut at the soil line before the plant goes to seed, when it is about ¾ to 1 inch in diameter and 12 inches tall. Leave the topknot of leaves on the stalk, and chill immediately in cold water. To store, seal in a plastic bag and refrigerate.

Although gardeners continue to debate the issue, the evidence suggests that *Lactuca sativa* members rarely cross-pollinate, so isolating celtuce is not necessary to produce seeds that will come true. Seeds are viable for 4 years; store in airtight containers in a dark, cool location.

globe artichoke, which is how some describe its flavor ("nutty cucumber" is another). Also known as asparagus lettuce, stem lettuce, and Chinese lettuce, celtuce's young leaves are well suited for salads, but it is for its stem that this plant is grown. Peeled and sliced, it can be eaten raw or cooked.

Celtuce grows upright, sometimes more than a foot tall, with leaves emerging along its greenish white central stalk. It can be grown in containers, although it isn't a pretty plant—harvesting the young leaves results in a bare central stem with a foliage topknot—making it an unlikely choice for the flower garden. Like lettuce, celtuce thrives in USDA Zone 3 and warmer. A dozen plants will provide a productive stand for a family of four; if you want to preserve, increase the planting.

HOW TO GROW

Celtuce succeeds in the same conditions as lettuce: a sunny location with near-neutral (pH 6.5 to 6.8), well-drained soil that has been amended with

CHARD, LEAF. See "Perpetual Spinach,"
    in Swiss Chard
CHARD, SWISS. See *Swiss Chard*
CHERRY, GROUND. See *Tomatillo*

Chervil

CHERVIL

Anthriscus cerefolium. Carrot family, Apiaceae.
Annual.

◑ ❄ ♣ ▮

Chervil, sometimes called sweet cicely, is an exotic and fairly unusual annual herb in the North American garden—it can be grown in USDA Zone 3 and warmer—yet it has a long history of use elsewhere. Flavored of anise, it is considered essential in French sauces and in *bouquet garni* and *fines herbes*. It loves shade and moist soil and is pretty enough for a flower bed, with finely divided, airy, yellow-green foliage that is somewhat parsleylike and grows about 6 inches high. The foliage is topped by umbels of tiny white flowers on stems as tall as 18 inches. When chervil plants are grown in groups, these summer flowers create a lovely misty effect amongst other herbs or flowers.

At one time, chervil was grown not only for its leaves but also for its roots, which were boiled and mixed with oil and vinegar to make a salad or were candied to use for stomachaches. Chervil-root candies were also thought to be a preventative against the plague. And vinegar containing chervil seeds is a folk medicine for hiccups.

For use as a garnish, look for the cultivar 'Crispum', which has curly leaves like those of curled parsley. 'Brussels Winter' chervil is an improved European type that is slower to bolt and grows larger, as tall as 2 feet. Grow at least six plants to use in salads, with chicken, fish, peas, and tomatoes, or in cream soups, omelets, and soufflés.

HOW TO GROW

"It prospers in soil that is dunged and somewhat moist," John Gerard wrote in 1597. Chervil needs ordinary well-drained soil, with watering at least once a week and some shade, perhaps provided by other plants. It grows best in cool weather and is a good container herb for a cool greenhouse or indoors, because it does not need bright light. For indoors, sow several seeds in a 6-inch pot, thinning to three seedlings. Clip back flower stalks to prolong the harvest of leaves. Succession sowings every 3 weeks will yield an ongoing supply of leaves.

Seeds must be fresh for good germination. Obtain a new supply each spring. The usual way to grow chervil outdoors is to sow the seeds directly in the garden in early spring, as soon as the soil can be worked, in the manner of dill. Chervil is difficult to transplant successfully, because it quickly forms a taproot. If you want a steady supply of leaves, plant successive crops about every 3 weeks until early fall. Early crops go to seed around June. The latest sowings provide fresh leaves until the ground freezes. If you allow chervil to go to flower it may self-sow, and self-sown seedlings sometimes survive harsh winters. Thin seedlings to 8 inches apart.

Since the leaves are the part most desired, anything that promotes quick bolting to seed, such as transplanting shock or hot weather, should be avoided if possible. In places where summers are hot, choose slow-bolting cultivars and sow chervil directly where it will grow in early spring while the weather is still cool.

HARVESTING

Pick the leaves as needed any time before the flowers open. Leaves are best used fresh but can be preserved by freezing or, less effectively, by drying. "I use to eat them with oile and vinegar, being first boiled," John Gerard noted, "which is very good for old people that are dull and without courage: it rejoiceth and comforteth the heart, and increaseth their lust and strength."

CHICKPEA

Cicer arietinum. Pea family, Fabaceae. Annual.

○ ✳

Chickpeas are the main ingredient of humus, a dish associated with trendy restaurants in this country. If somewhat new to American menus, chickpeas aren't new to American gardens. Three cultivars— red, white, and yellow—were being grown at the time of the Civil War, although they were "not very digestible," according to 19th-century New England horticulturist Fearing Burr. They were, Burr went on, "largely employed in soups, and for the basis of the *purée aux croutons*, or bread and pea soup, so highly esteemed in Paris." Burr's contemporaries in France, the seed merchants Vilmorin-Andrieux, apparently were less enthusiastic, for they gave less than one page of their 600-page *The Vegetable Garden* to chickpeas. Only *pois chiche blanc*, the white cultivar, "deserves to be considered a table vegetable."

Also known as garbanzo bean, Egyptian pea, Bengal gram, and Indian gram, the chickpea has been cultivated in the Middle East for at least 6,000 years. A lover of sun and heat, plants are remarkably drought-resistant. They grow about 18 inches tall and are bushy, their branches lined with compound leaves, a half-dozen or more pairs of leaflets, and look rather like vetch. The leaves are covered with sticky hairs that exude an acid that may cause an allergic reaction in some people.

The plant's fat pods are only an inch long and nearly as wide; each contains one or two seeds. Large, round, buff-colored chickpeas are the type most commonly found in supermarkets, but cultivars with small, wrinkled seeds are more widely adapted and recommended for home gardeners. That form is the source of the species name, *arietinum*, which means "horned like a ram's head," and is usually listed in seed catalogs as "black-seeded" or "brown-seeded." The cultivar 'Black Kabouli' is especially tolerant of cool temperatures.

To succeed with this high-protein crop, you'll need a sunny location and about 100 warm days, USDA Zone 5 and warmer. Sandy soil is ideal, but any light soil will do. Yields are small—it takes at least two dozen plants to produce enough to make planting worth the space and trouble. Because yields per plant are small, growing chickpeas in containers is not recommended, nor are the plants pretty enough—their flowers are insignificant—to make them useful in the ornamental landscape.

HOW TO GROW

According to Burr's *The Field and Garden Vegetables of America* (1865), "all the culture required is simply to keep the ground between the rows free from weeds." Growing chickpeas is a little more complicated than that, but not much. Sow seeds direct, 1 inch deep, spaced 3 to 4 inches apart, in rows 2 to 3 feet apart, about the same time you would plant common bush beans, 2 weeks after the average frost-free date. In 68°F soil, germination takes 7 to 10 days (to jump-start plants, pregerminate seeds indoors on moist paper towels). Thin plants to 6 inches.

Gardeners with marginal growing seasons should begin plants indoors 3 to 4 weeks before the last expected frost. Beans resent transplanting, so use individual containers, harden off fully, and try not to disturb the roots as you move the plants outdoors. Chickpeas are relatively immune to diseases and insects, but installing floating row covers over the planting area will provide insurance against some pests, as well as extra warmth to young plants.

Once plants are established, mulch to suppress weeds and retain moisture. Chickpeas are more drought-tolerant than most beans and need watering only if there is an extended period without rain (according to folklore, there will be thunderstorms when chickpeas flower). Do not water after the plants have bloomed and set seeds. To ensure a bountiful harvest, feed plants with compost tea or liquid seaweed when they are 5 inches tall and again when they begin to flower.

HARVESTING

Chickpeas, which are typically used like dry beans or peas, can be picked when they are still immature and eaten like a common snap bean. For dried seeds, harvest the entire plant as soon as some of the pods begin to dry. Lay the plants on a cloth or plastic sheeting in the sun until all the pods have dried. Collect the seeds as the pods split.

As with other members of the pea family, chickpea flowers are perfect, but bees and other insects are attracted to the blooms and cross-pollination is common. To ensure that you produce seeds that will breed true, plant only one cultivar. Save seeds from the most vigorous and healthy plants; seeds are viable for about 3 years if stored in airtight containers in a dark, cool location.

CHICORY

Cichorium intybus. Sunflower family, Asteraceae.
Perennial grown as an annual.

○ ◐ ✳ ❀ ▜

Chicory often comes with a warning label in seed catalogs and cookbooks. As one writer cautioned, it is "best when mixed with milder greens." Noted another, chicory "adds bite to cool-season salads." Others employ such phrases as "assertive," a "bit of old-world flavor," or "a bitterness that never quite loses its edge" to describe this hardy crop. Don't let such caveats prejudice you against chicory. Its taste is certainly distinctive, but as part of a salad, it is not overpowering. And not lost in the salad bowl are the beautiful swirling colors of the heading chicories, or radicchios.

Europeans have eaten chicory, or "succory," for centuries. Valued for both its culinary and medicinal attributes, the two qualities were merged by physicians to Queen Elizabeth I, who fed her "succory broth" during her final illness. English herbalists also prescribed chicory for eye problems. It was a predictable recommendation, according to garden historian Ann Leighton: In countries where blue eyes were predominant, blue-flowered plants were believed to be a curative.

European colonists took the trouble to bring chicory seeds to North America in the 17th century. Before long, it escaped to the countryside, and by 1865 was described as "a troublesome weed, in pastures, lawns, and mowing-lands." Thanks to nouvelle cuisine, chicory—in all its forms—is back in favor. It can be grown in USDA Zone 2 and warmer.

DECIDING WHAT TO GROW

Chicories make up a varied genus that includes the biennials endive and escarole. (See *Endive* on page 253.) Although they have somewhat different cultural requirements, all chicories prefer cool weather. In regions where the winter temperature doesn't go below 10°F, chicories can be planted in fall for winter and spring harvests. To make things easy, most seed catalogs divide chicories into three groups: cutting chicory, radicchio, and witloof chicory, or Belgian endive. All are tender perennials but are typically grown as annuals.

Cutting Chicory. Also known as rosette chicories, spring chicories, leaf chicories, and Italian dandelion, cutting chicories are grown for their green or red-tinged variously shaped leaves. Plants that are kept fed and watered will continue to produce new leaves throughout the garden season. Because they mature quickly—in as few as 35 days—cutting chicories are a good green for succession planting as well as intercropping. They can also be included in mesclun. (See *Mesclun* on page 301 for more information on these mixes of salad greens.)

Radicchio. Also called Italian chicory and heading chicory, radicchio is a mainstay of any respectable Italian garden. Most cultivars form small, tight heads, strikingly colored in red and white, but there are also cultivars that are elongated like romaine lettuce. They mature in 75 to 110 days, depending on the cultivar and the climate.

Belgian Endive. This form, also known as witloof chicory, is traditionally grown for its roots (which are ground to make a coffee substitute) but does double duty as a leaf vegetable when "forced" (prompting another common name, forcing chicory). Producing usable roots for forcing takes about 120 days; producing the blanched cylindrical sprouts, which the French call *chicons*, takes another 3 or 4 weeks.

A half-dozen radicchios, another six Belgian endives, and 10 cutting chicories should provide most four-member households with an ample supply of this "old-world flavor."

SITE & SOIL

Chicories do best in moist but well-drained garden soil that is rich in humus and has a pH between 6.0 and 6.8. Plants need full sun in early spring and fall but prefer partial shade in midsummer. Locating them next to a tall or trellised crop, such as corn, pole beans, or cucumbers, is a simple way to provide afternoon screening from the sun.

Perennial cutting chicories tie up garden space permanently, so if you're not growing them as annuals, locate these plants where they won't be disturbed. Radicchio, which is handled as if it were an annual, can be spaced at 10 inches in the food garden and is well suited for ornamental beds and container culture. As the foliage deepens to a burgundy color, the plants become like large edible flowers. Three plants can be grown in a 5-gallon pot. Use a container, at least 8 inches wide and 12 inches deep, with good bottom drainage. Fill with enriched potting soil, and keep well watered.

HOW TO GROW

All chicories seem to do better when direct-seeded (transplanting encourages premature bolting); sow seeds ¼ inch deep, spaced 3 to 4 inches apart. Germination varies by type and cultivar, but in 75°F soil, sprouting should occur in about 8 days. All chicories need an even supply of moisture, about 1 inch of water a week.

Cutting Chicory. Sow cutting chicories in fall, about 3 months before the average first-frost date in northern gardens. Thin plants to about 4 inches. Mulch plants heavily after the first hard frost. Remove the mulch in early spring, and cut plants back to 1 inch above their crowns. If you want to tone down the leaves' bitter flavor—which will also tone down their nutrient content—blanch them by covering them with newspaper or a flowerpot. When plants send up a flower stalk, cut them back and they will resprout.

Radicchio. The stunning color that is the hallmark of radicchio once was obtainable only if plants were cut back and then allowed to resprout in cool conditions. Breeders have made the work of gardeners easier by developing new cultivars that are red

from day one and that form heads without being cut back. Plant traditional cultivars in early spring in the North; warm-region gardeners can sow seeds in summer for a fall or winter harvest. New cultivars that don't need cutting back can be sown in spring, or in summer for a fall harvest. Thin plants to 12 inches, and feed with compost tea; mulch heavily to retain soil moisture and suppress weeds.

Belgian Endive. Whether your harvest is to be chicory coffee or salad greens, producing a good crop of healthy roots is the goal with Belgian endive. Sow seeds early in spring, and thin to 6 inches after the first true leaves appear. Mulch heavily to retain soil moisture and suppress weeds. Cultivate as you would other root vegetables, such as turnips and carrots. Roots can be dug in about 120 days, or after the first fall frost. To store until needed, trim foliage, leaving

Radicchio 'Alto' and 'Augusto' with Chinese cabbage

Chicory flower

Radicchio 'Rossana'

1 inch of stem, and store roots in damp sand or sawdust in a cold (32° to 35°F) location.

To force Belgian endive sprouts, select the best and largest roots from cold storage and rebury them upright in damp sand or sawdust in containers with good bottom drainage. Move containers to a moist, dark location (50° to 60°F) with good air circulation. Keep the soil moist but not soppy. New growth should appear in 3 to 4 weeks.

Given good soil and adequate moisture, chicories are bothered by few insects or diseases. Covering the seedbed with floating row covers will deter flea beetles and other pests.

HARVESTING

Cutting chicory can be harvested when the leaves are large enough to be used, about 4 inches long. Continue to pick individual leaves until the plant sends up a flower stalk, then prune the plant to the ground. It will regrow in a few weeks. To store harvested leaves, seal in plastic bags and refrigerate.

Radicchio can be cut as soon as the head is a useful size (cut 1 inch above the crown, and the plant will resprout in the spring in milder regions). At maturity, the heads, about 4 to 6 inches in diameter, will be firm but not hard. For the most eye-catching color, northern gardeners cut away the green outer leaves about a week before the first fall frost; the cold weather will deepen the burgundy tones of the inner foliage. To store, seal in plastic bags and refrigerate.

Belgian endive is ready to harvest about 3 weeks after the roots sprout. Cut all the sprouts, or *chicons*, then water the roots, and return the container to the dark 50°F location to produce a second or even a third crop. Start new roots as needed. To store harvested roots, seal in plastic bags and refrigerate.

CHICORY CULTIVARS

All chicories are cool-weather greens that add distinctive flavor to salads. The following includes cultivars of all three types: cutting chicory, radicchio, and Belgian endive.

'Alto': radicchio; 60 days; open-pollinated form with improved heat tolerance; does not need cutting back to form head; midsummer or fall crop.

'Biondissima Trieste': cutting; 50 days; open-pollinated; good cultivar for mesclun.

'Castelfranco': radicchio; 85 days; open-pollinated red heirloom with white marbling; does not need cutting back to form head; fall harvest.

'Catalogna Special': cutting; 50 days; open-pollinated cultivar with deeply cut white-ribbed leaves; slow-bolting.

'Early Treviso': radicchio; 80 days; open-pollinated selection of the heirloom 'Red Treviso'; must be cut to encourage heading; fall harvest.

'Flash': Belgian endive; 100 days; open-pollinated cultivar for forcing.

'Giulio': radicchio; 90 days; open-pollinated cultivar with deep burgundy foliage color; does not need cutting back to form head; best for midsummer harvest.

'Grumolo Verde': cutting; 60 days: open-pollinated, very cold-hardy cultivar.

'Nerone di Treviso': radicchio; 110 days; hybrid with elongated heads like romaine lettuce and brilliant red inner leaves.

'Palla Rossa Special': radicchio; 85 days; open-pollinated; does not need cutting back to form head; summer or fall harvest.

'San Pasquale': cutting; 55 days; open-pollinated type with frilly inner leaves; large, vigorous plant.

'Spadona': cutting; 50 days; open-pollinated, very quick-growing cultivar with smooth leaves; very cold-hardy.

'Sugarloaf': radicchio; 90 days; open-pollinated with a pale heart and large romainelike heads; fall harvest.

'Witloof Improved': Belgian endive; 110 days; open-pollinated cultivar for forcing.

'Zoom': Belgian endive; 110 days; hybrid that can be forced without roots being buried.

Chicory flowers are self-incompatible and must be cross-pollinated by insects. As a result, all genus members and cultivars can cross. To produce seeds that will come true, grow only one cultivar or isolate your crop. Seeds are viable for 8 years; store in airtight containers in a dark, cool location.

CHILIES. See *Pepper*

CHINESE CABBAGE

Brassica rapa, Pekinensis group. Mustard family, Brassicaceae. Biennial grown as an annual.

○ ❋ ▼

Chinese cabbage is one of those vegetables that seems bent on confusing gardeners. Botanically, it is closer to mustards and turnips than it is to cabbages. Over the years it has accumulated many names—celery cabbage and hakusai are the most common aliases—and is closely related to and often grouped with bok choy, also called pak-choi, which is also a *Brassica rapa* but a member of the Chinensis group. (For more information, see *Bok Choy* on page 196.) To make things even more difficult, "real" Chinese cabbages come in three forms: barrel-shaped, or hearted, types; tall, cylindrical types; and loose-headed types.

The soft, broad, light green leaves of the barrel types (also known as napa, chiifu, wong bok, or che-foo cabbages) make compact heads that are slightly taller than they are wide. The cylindrical Chinese cabbages (or michihli or chihili types) are about three times taller than wide and have narrower, coarser, and darker green leaves than the barrels'. Loose-leaf, or no-head, Chinese cabbages are the most ornamental; most feature green frilled outer leaves that surround a white core of inner leaves. The good news is that the mild, slightly mustard flavor of all Chinese cabbages is nearly the same, so if the barrel cultivar you planted turns out to be cylindrical or loose-leaf, the mix-up doesn't spell disaster.

All Chinese cabbages can be grown in USDA Zone 2 and warmer. A dozen plants, sown at intervals, should yield enough for fresh table use for a family of four; if you want to store heads, increase the planting. Ready to harvest between 55 and 75 days after planting, they're most at home where the weather is cool, thriving in the spring and fall, when

Chinese cabbage 'Kasumi'

the days are short and air temperatures range between 60° and 70°F. Long days and extended periods of low temperatures in the 40° to 50°F range will cause bolting, or flowering.

HOW TO GROW

Give Chinese cabbages full sun and protection from drying winds, plus moderately rich, well-drained soil amended with plenty of organic matter and a pH between 6.5 and 7.0. Not a crop for xeriscapers, Chinese cabbages have shallow roots and little drought resistance; they need plenty of water and don't do well in arid regions unless irrigation is available. Because plants are always thirsty, it is a high-maintenance vegetable when grown in a pot or a window box. If you do grow them in pots, use a container, at least 8 inches wide and 12 inches deep, with good bottom drainage, and fill with enriched potting soil. Water frequently, and feed every 2 weeks with fish emulsion or manure tea.

Chinese cabbage is at its best when grown as a fall crop, a good succession planting for peas, leaf lettuces, or other cool-weather spring vegetables and herbs that mature quickly. Older cultivars, which bolt easily in long days, do well only when timed to mature in autumn (or winter to spring in mild regions). Modern hybrids have improved bolt resistance, however, and can be sown in the spring. Sow seeds ½ inch deep outdoors (after the last frost, if planting in spring), thinning plants to 12 to 24 inches, depending on the cultivar grown. Small heads tend to have better flavor, so many gardeners crowd plants to keep them from becoming too large.

CHINESE CABBAGE CULTIVARS

Chinese cabbages come in three shapes: barrel, cylindrical, and loose-leaf. All share a mild, mustardlike flavor when grown quickly.

'**Blues**': barrel shape; 55 days; hybrid with medium heads; bolt-resistant; disease-resistant; outstanding for spring/summer crops.

'**Burpee's Two Seasons**': barrel shape; 65 days; hybrid with large heads; bolt-resistant; fall or spring crops.

'**China Pride**': barrel shape; 68 days; hybrid with large heads; disease resistany; good fall-crop cultivar.

'**Jade Pagoda**': cylindrical; 75 days; hybrid; bolt-resistant; good disease resistance.

'**Kasumi**': barrel shape; 65 days; hybrid with medium heads; outstanding bolt resistance; good cultivar for warm regions.

'**Michihli**': cylindrical; 80 days; open-pollinated cultivar with very tall heads; standard commercial cultivar.

'**Monument**': cylindrical; 78 days; hybrid with tall heads; bolt-resistant; excellent disease resistance.

'**Orient Express**': barrel shape; 45 days; open-pollinated cultivar with small, solid heads; excellent bolt resistance; good for warm regions.

'**Round-Leaved Santo**': loose-leaf; 50 days; open-pollinated cultivar with large, medium-green leaves and white ribs; cold-resistant.

'**Serrated-Leaved Santo**': loose-leaf; 60 days; open-pollinated cultivar with serrated leaves; very hardy.

'**Tropical 50**': barrel shape; 55 days; hybrid with small heads; heat-tolerant; good spring/summer-crop cultivar.

Although Chinese cabbage doesn't transplant as well as many crops, you can get an early start by sowing seeds indoors in individual pots 6 weeks before the frost-free date; thin to one seedling per pot, and transplant into the garden 2 weeks before the last frost. Fall crops should be seeded about 3 months before the first expected frost. Mature plants can withstand light frost.

Growing Chinese cabbages successfully means growing them fast. Too little light, water, or fertilizer—anything that stresses the plants—will result in bitter flavor. Side-dress with well-rotted manure or another nitrogen-rich fertilizer, then water with manure tea every 3 weeks. Mulch plants heavily to keep the soil evenly moist, but don't water from overhead, which can encourage disease. Finally, cover plants with floating row covers to exclude flea beetles and other insect pests.

POTENTIAL PROBLEMS

Chinese cabbages are heir to most of the insects and diseases that plague cabbages and other brassicas. Use row covers, and rotate the location of plants each year. To avoid spreading soilborne diseases, remove and discard plant roots rather than composting them. (See *Cabbage* on page 204 for specific problems and solutions.)

HARVESTING

Mature heads are firm and tight—they feel solid when gently grasped—but Chinese cabbages can be harvested as soon as their leaves reach a usable size. Spring plantings should be harvested before hot weather arrives, fall crops before a hard freeze. While you can cut a few stalks at a time, most gardeners harvest the entire plant.

A good source of vitamins A and C and potassium, Chinese cabbages can be stored for short periods of time in the refrigerator or up to 4 months in a cool (35° to 40°F), moist location. Fast-maturing cultivars do not store well.

Since most Chinese cabbages are biennials, flowering normally doesn't occur until the second year, making saving seeds difficult in many regions. All cultivars—as well as many other brassicas—cross-pollinate. To ensure plants that will breed true, plant only one open-pollinated cultivar. Seeds are viable for 4 years; store in airtight containers in a dark, cool location.

CHINESE CHIVE. See *Chive*

CHINESE LETTUCE. See *Celtuce*
CHINESE MUSTARD CABBAGE.
 See *Bok Choy*
CHINESE PARSLEY. See *Cilantro*

CHIVE

Allium schoenoprasum, A. tuberosum. Onion family,
Alliaceae. Perennial.

○ ◑ ❄ ♣ ▜

This familiar *Allium*—no self-respecting restaurant baked potato comes without a dollop of sour cream and a sprinkling of chives—may be the garden's easiest crop. Plant it once, and it will be around forever. In fact, it's been around forever. Known as "cives" in earlier centuries, it was usually grouped with onions, whose history reaches back 5,000 years or more. Despite that, chives didn't receive the glowing recommendation as a healing herb that

Chive

other onions, or alliums, did. Culpeper's *Complete Herbal*, published in the early 1700s, contended that chives were helpful only if "prepared by the act of the alchymist"; if eaten raw, they sent up "vapours to the brain, causing troublesome sleep and spoiling the eyesight."

"Troublesome" isn't a word any knowing gardener associates with chives. Chives are hardy in USDA Zones 3 to 9. In northern locations, the leaves die back in winter, but plants are evergreen in warm regions. Plants develop thick, 8- to 10-inch-tall clumps and have small bulbs as scallions do, characteristic hollow onion leaves, and globe-shaped clusters of tiny flowers. All plant parts are edible, but chives are usually grown for their green leaves. You can graze chives like grass—rather than causing harm, cutting keeps plants healthy, vigorous, and productive, producing new leaves above ground and new bulbs below the soil surface.

Three to five clumps of chives are enough for a family of four; if you want to preserve, increase the planting. Most nurseries and catalogs offer nothing more than "Chives" (*A. schoenoprasum*). Also known as garden and common chives, the species has a mild onion flavor and lavender-pink flowers. The cultivar 'Forescate' has bright rose-red flowers. A new strain, sold under both the cultivar name 'Sterile' and the trademark name "Profusion Chives," produces larger numbers of pinkish purple flowers, which are seedless. Garlic, or Chinese, chives (*A. tuberosum*) taste like garlic and have flat leaves and showy white flowers on 1½- to 2-foot plants. Also called Chinese leeks, garlic chives are widely used in Chinese medicine. They are slightly less hardy than garden chives (USDA Zones 4 to 8) and prefer rich soil; in addition to the white-flowered species, a strain with mauve flowers is available.

Compact, upright, and tidy, both garden and garlic chives are pretty in the flower garden, especially as edging or rockery plants. They also flourish in all types of containers. For farming the windowsill, look for the cultivar 'Grolau', a garden chive from Switzerland bred especially for greenhouse forcing and growing indoors.

HOW TO GROW

Unparticular about their location—sun or partial shade, dry or damp—chives, however, will do best when growing in full sun and moderately rich, slightly acid soil that drains well and has been generously amended with organic matter. Since chives are perennial, plant them with other perennial herbs in a site that won't be accidentally disturbed. You can grow chives from seeds, beginning indoors or out, but germination is slow, 2 to 3 weeks, and it will be a year or more before you can begin serious harvesting. It's far easier and quicker to purchase or beg a small clump (four to six bulbs). Set clumps 8 inches apart.

Chives grow best when temperatures are cool, below 75°F. To keep plants from going dormant, keep the flowers picked. In extremely warm regions, plants may die back in midsummer whatever you do, but most gardeners can harvest chives throughout the growing season. Garlic chives especially are vigorous self-seeders; if you don't want seedlings spreading throughout your garden, be sure to remove spent flowers.

Chives are rarely bothered by insects or diseases. In organically rich garden soil, no additional fertilizer is necessary, but if plants appear to be ailing, water with manure tea. To keep plants vigorous, divide clumps every 3 or 4 years, either in spring or fall.

HARVESTING

Chives can be harvested as soon as the tops grow to 6 inches. Use a sharp knife or scissors, and cut leaves about 2 inches above the ground (don't just snip off the leaf tops). Either harvest selectively by cutting a few leaves from each clump, which will allow you to cut the same clump over and over again, or harvest an entire clump. Clumps that have been cut entirely will take several weeks to regenerate. Stop harvesting 3 weeks before the average first-frost date. To extend the harvest, dig a small clump of chives a month before the first frost and transplant it to a pot. Leave the pot outdoors for at least 3 months, then bring it inside, water, and set it in a sunny location.

While usually propagated from bulbs or divisions, chives can be grown from seeds. They are pollinated by insects, and cultivars cross easily (garden and garlic chives do not cross-pollinate with each other or with other *Allium* species). To produce seeds that will breed true, plant only one cultivar. Seeds are viable for 4 years; store in airtight containers in a dark, cool location.

Chives are best when fresh but can be dried in the microwave or oven for winter use; store in airtight containers.

CILANTRO, CORIANDER
Coriandrum sativum. Carrot family, Apiaceae. Annual.

○ ◑ ✳ ❄ ❁ ▜

Coriandrum sativum is two plants in one. When grown for its leaves, it is called cilantro or Chinese parsley, a staple of Mexican and Asian cooking. When grown for its dried brown fruits, or "seeds," it is coriander, a favorite of British and European cooks. While almost no one objects to coriander, it's thumbs up or down on cilantro. Many adore it, but detractors turn up their noses at the fragrance of the foliage, likening it to the pungent smell of bedbugs, whose Greek name is *koris*, the source of the herb's genus name. Any gardener with cultural flexibility can, of course, harvest both leaves and seeds from the same plant: cilantro in the early season, coriander toward summer's end.

A native of the eastern Mediterranean, coriander is one of the oldest herbs in cultivation, with more than 3,000 years of recorded use. The plant is mentioned in Sanskrit literature, and seeds have been found in the tombs of the Egyptian pharaohs

Cilantro, coriander

and in Grecian ruins dating from the Bronze Age. It sustained the Israelites on their march from Sinai to Paran—"and the manna was as coriander seed"—while European herbalists grew it for its ability to "stimulate the passions."

Coriander, an annual that can be grown in all USDA Zone 3 and warmer, likes a cool, damp spring and a hot, dry summer. Plants develop quickly, in about 60 to 75 days, and reach 1 to 2 feet tall. They have oval leaves on the main stems and feathery leaves on the side branches. The young leaves resemble flat-leaved parsley, with a distinctive, slightly citrus flavor. The pinkish white clusters of flowers form in midsummer on stems as tall as 2½ feet.

DECIDING WHAT TO GROW

The species, sometimes sold as Indian coriander, goes to seed in about 2 months. If you want foliage for a longer period, look for the Chinese, or Long Standing, strain or the cultivars 'Leisure', 'Slo Bolt', or 'Santo'. None of these bolts to seed as rapidly as the common type does.

Other plants given the common name coriander are the tender perennial Vietnamese coriander (*Polygonum odoratum*) and Mexican or Cuban coriander (*Eryngium foetidum*), a Central American native also called culantro, thorny coriander, or *ngo gai*. It is frequently grown where the weather is too hot and humid for success with *C. sativum*. The foliage is tougher but tasty and dries well, unlike other corianders.

SITE & SOIL

Give coriander a sunny or partly shaded position in well-worked garden soil that drains well and has been amended with organic matter. A spot in the vegetable garden is best, although coriander is ornamental enough for a flower bed if grown in clumps of at least three plants. Thin plants to 4 inches apart. Coriander can also be sown directly in large containers filled with an enriched potting mix. Plants can dry out easily, so water regularly.

Six to eight plants should be plenty for a family of four; if you want to preserve, increase the planting.

HOW TO GROW

In spring, after the danger of frost has passed, sow coriander seeds ½ inch deep directly where they will grow (in very mild regions, seeds can be sown in autumn). Germination is slow (2 weeks in cold soil), but once it occurs, plants quickly form a long taproot and should not be transplanted. Mulch to retain moisture and suppress weeds.

For an ongoing supply of leaves until frost, sow succession crops every 3 weeks from spring until late summer. Plants allowed to flower in the garden may self-sow to produce a crop the following spring.

Where summers are hot, anything that will slow bolting equals a longer supply of leaves. Sow the seeds in a partly shaded place in early spring or late summer. Plants are rarely bothered by diseases or insects.

HARVESTING

If you just want foliage, harvest entire plants when they are only about 6 inches high and the leaves are tender. Young leaves can also be pinched off as needed. Most of the flavor of cilantro is lost in drying, so it should be used fresh or preserved by being blended with a small amount of olive oil. Freeze the olive oil-cilantro mix in an ice-cube tray, and then store in the freezer in plastic bags or closed containers. The roots, preferably dug before the plant goes to seed, can be cooked and eaten as a vegetable.

The seeds ripen in late summer or fall, turning light brown and falling to the ground, so if you want to save them, cut the plants off at the base when ripening begins and hang them upside down in paper bags to finish drying. Coriander doesn't cross with any other plant, but cultivars can be cross-pollinated by insects. To save seeds that will come true, grow only one cultivar. Seeds are viable for 5 years; store in airtight containers in a dark, cool location.

SPECIAL NOTES

Cilantro is essential for genuine guacamole and is also an ingredient in Portuguese fish dishes, Indian curries, Chinese soups, and Asian chicken dishes. The seeds, whole or ground, are esteemed in northern European cookies, breads, and custards, as well as sausages. In medieval Europe, coriander seed was used in liqueurs, sweets, and cosmetics such as Carmelite water. The bruised seed applied as a poultice was reputed to relieve the pain of arthritic joints.

CLAYTONIA. *See Miner's Lettuce*

Collard

COLLARD CULTIVARS

Most collard cultivars form a loose mound of large, cabbagelike leaves. Plants tolerate a range of temperatures and soils.

'**Blue Max**': 70 days; hybrid; crinkled blue-green leaves; disease-tolerant; widely adapted.

'**Champion**': 80 days; open-pollinated; blue-green leaves; bolt-resistant; widely adapted.

'**Georgia**': 75 days; open-pollinated; crumpled blue-green leaves; tall, vigorous plant; heat- and cold-tolerant; widely adapted; heirloom.

'**Hi-Crop**': 70 days; hybrid; crinkled blue-green leaves; bolt-resistant; sweet flavor.

'**Morris Heading**': 80 days; open-pollinated; dark green leaves; forms a loose head; heirloom.

'**Vates**': 75 days; open-pollinated; broad dark green leaves; winter-hardy; popular standard cultivar.

COLLARD

Brassica oleracea, Acephala group. Mustard family, Brassicaceae. Biennial grown as an annual.

○ ◐ ❊

Like kale, its first cousin, collards were among the earliest cultivated forms of *Brassica oleracea*. Grown by the Greeks and Romans, they traveled to Britain by 400 B.C., where they were called coleworts and boiled beyond recognition. They were also made into cures for dim eyesight, palsy, animal bites, gout, and more. According to one herbalist, coleworts eaten before the meat course would prevent drunkenness; moreover, the natural antipathy between coleworts and grapes was believed to be so great that if the two plants were grown near each other, "forthwith the vine perisheth and withereth away."

Collards were among the early botanical travelers to North America—first mentioned in 1669—although only a couple of cultivars were being sold by the time of the Civil War. On this side of the Atlantic, they have long been considered a regional crop: Collard greens are a hallmark of southern food gardens, a familiar ingredient in southern cooking and southern literature. Although other mustard-family members are more popular, collards have hung around and are now being rediscovered by American gardeners. And for good reason: A half-cup of collard greens provides a larger dose of nutrients, carotenoids, and fiber than any other vegetable. If you want to be healthy, eat your collards.

Known as "spring cabbages" in Europe, collards can be grown as an annual in all but the hottest USDA Zones; the more hardy cultivars can be overwintered in southern regions. While collards prefer moderate temperatures, they are more tolerant of heat than are most members of the mustard family, including kale. And while far less striking than kale, collards, with their large, wavy, cabbagelike leaves, can be incorporated in ornamental gardens and grown in containers. Plants can grow to 3 feet tall, so use a large container, at least 12 inches deep, with good bottom drainage. Fill with enriched potting soil, feed every 3 weeks with fish emulsion, and keep well watered.

DECIDING WHAT TO GROW

While there are more collard choices today than there were a 150 years ago, when mustard-family crops were at their popularity peak, typical seed catalogs offer only one or two choices. Most cultivars have an open form, but a few—'Morris Heading' and 'Cabbage' are two—form loose heads. Collards need about 75 days to reach full maturity, although you can begin harvesting as soon as leaves are large enough to use. A dozen plants should be plenty for a family of four; if you want to preserve, increase the planting.

HOW TO GROW

Collards will succeed in a wide range of conditions, but for large, succulent leaves, locate this crop in a sunny site that has light, fertile soil rich in organic matter, with a pH between 6.0 and 6.8. Gardeners planning to overwinter collards should be certain that their soil drains well, or plants will rot once the mercury drops. Even, swift growth is the key to good-flavored greens. To make sure plants get all the nitrogen they need, add composted manure or other nitrogen-rich matter to the soil before planting.

Because collards are relatively tolerant of both heat and cold, they can be planted early in spring or in summer for a fall crop. In warm regions, gardeners plant collards in late summer and fall for winter and spring harvests. To get a jump on spring, start plants indoors 8 weeks before the frost-free date; set them outdoors 6 weeks later, 2 weeks before the last expected spring frost, when they are about 3 inches tall.

Or direct-sow collards, 3 weeks before the last expected frost or 70 days before the average first-frost date, setting seeds ½ inch deep, spaced 3 inches apart. In 70°F soil, germination takes about 5 days. Overcrowding will produce spindly plants, so thin plants, first to 6 inches, then to 12 or 18 inches; thinnings can be used in salads. Collards must be kept well watered—at least 1½ inches of water a week. Mulch plants to retain moisture, suppress weeds, and keep the soil cool. Although collards do well in only moderately rich soil, feeding with manure tea every 3 weeks will guarantee larger, more lush greens.

While collards are the potential target of all the diseases and insects that plague cabbage and other members of the mustard family, both they and kale are less susceptible than many of their relatives are. You can avoid most problems by rotating the location of your crop each year and by covering the bed with floating row covers to prevent aphids, cabbageworms, and flea beetles from reaching young plants. (For more information about other potential problems, such as harlequin bugs and downy mildew, see *Kale* on page 275.)

HARVESTING

Collards, whose flavor is improved by a mild frost, can be picked piecemeal—leaf by leaf—or the entire plant can be harvested while still young, half-grown, or mature. Cool leaves immediately after harvesting by immersing them in ice water. To extend the harvest in fall, mulch plants heavily with straw or leaves. To store collards, seal in plastic bags and refrigerate.

Because collards are biennials and normally don't flower until their second season, saving seeds is difficult. Gardeners in extremely cold climates must dig and overwinter plants, then replant them in the spring; in warmer regions, carry plants over to a second year. Collards cross-pollinate with each other and all other *B. oleracea* members, such as broccoli, kale, and cauliflower. To save seeds that will come true, plant only one *B. oleracea* cultivar or isolate your crop. Seeds are viable for 4 years; store in airtight containers in a dark, cool location.

COMMON FENNEL. See *Fennel*
COMMON SAGE. See *Sage*
CORIANDER. See *Cilantro*

CORN

Zea mays, Mays group. Grass family, Poaceae.
Annual.

○ ☀

Before sweet corn was sweet corn, it was grass. Exactly when it made the transition can't be pinpointed, but corn, which is an American native, has been cultivated on this continent for least 3,500 years. Europeans got their first documented look at the plant on October 16, 1492, when Christopher Columbus recorded seeing fields of corn on the island of Hispaniola, little realizing that he had gazed on something far more valuable than the conventional riches Isabella had sent him to find.

Corn was being cultivated throughout the New World when Columbus first caught sight of it—there were thousands of different cultivars prepared differently by different groups of people. According to food historian Betty Fussell, Native Americans roasted, baked, steamed, parched, dried, and pickled

Corn 'Breeder's Choice Bicolor'
'Silver Queen', and 'Breeder's Choice'

Dried heirloom corn

corn. They ate corn in its mature and its "half-ripe, or milky state." They turned it into succotashes, soups, and stews, as well as dumplings, puddings, and breads. They grated and pureed it, cracked and milled it. Corn, one European traveler to the United States wrote, is eaten in "every other way that can be imagined."

The role of corn in American history—how it helped the Pilgrims to survive their first winter—is now the stuff of Disney cartoons, yet corn's status as national food folklore is deserved. In the words of colonial governor William Bradford, the Plymouth settlers "begane to thinke how they might raise as much corne as they could . . . that they might not still thus languish in miserie." The saintly Bradford might have felt differently if he had known that corn would eventually be turned into a high-power liquor (Thomas Jefferson was an early producer). "Here's to Old Corn Likker," one saying goes, "Whitens the teeth, Perfumes the breath, And makes childbirth a pleasure."

The trip from colony-saving staple to ready-to-eat breakfast cereal—Kellogg's sold its first corn-flakes around 1898—was only a matter of 250 years. And for once, America led the gardening world: New England market gardener Fearing Burr listed 28 sweet-corn cultivars in his *The Field and Garden Vegetables of America* (1865), but *The Vegetable Garden* (1885), the French equivalent of Burr's volume, doesn't even mention corn. Years of

bad press in Europe had left their mark: "The barbarous Indians which know not better," one herbalist wrote, "think it is good food; whereas we may easily judge that it nourisheth but little . . . a more convenient foode for swine than for man." Today, the U.S. per capita consumption of sweet corn is 28 pounds. Swine, pigs that they are, eat even more.

DECIDING WHAT TO GROW

Sweet corn, which can be grown in USDA Zone 3 and warmer, is one crop where hybrids have all but

CORN ESSENTIALS

- Full sun and warm soil and air temperatures.

- Rich soil heavily amended with organic matter.

- Direct-seed after the soil has warmed to 55°F (65°F for extra-sweet hybrids).

- Plant in blocks to ensure good pollination.

- Keep soil evenly moist, especially after tassels appear.

eliminated open-pollinated cultivars. Selection—saving inbred seeds for replanting—has a different effect with corn than it has with most vegetables and herbs. Rather than developing an improved strain, casual selection from a small plot is likely to give you a weaker one. In contrast, when different cultivars are crossed, the result is a hybrid that is more vigorous and uniform, one that tends to mature more quickly and produces greater yields. Home gardeners are better off planting hybrids than open pollinated cultivars.

Corn's remarkable ability to cross-pollinate on its own plus the prodigious work of breeders—'Reid's Yellow Dent', the first hybrid, dates from 1847—have produced thousands and thousands of cultivars. Researchers have resorted to using complex "racial complexes" to distinguish corn cultivars, but backyard growers don't need to go much beyond separating "sweet" from "field" corns.

Sweet cultivars are the corns that are eaten "green." Unable to convert all their sugars into starch—a recessive genetic defect called shrunkenness—sweet-corn kernels are wrinkled when dry, unlike field corns, whose kernels are plump. The downside of a sugary flavor for gardeners is that, because their kernels contain less starch, sweet corns germinate less well and are more susceptible to stresses and diseases than field corns are.

Gardeners who limit themselves to sweet corns still have plenty of decisions to make. Open-pollinated or hybrid? Ordinary sweet corn or one of the "enhanced" cultivars? And color—there is a range to choose from. Yellow, white, and bicolor are the familiar hues, but there are also more vivid cultivars, like 'Black Mexican', 'Mandan Red Nueta', and 'Rainbow Inca', a multicolored cultivar from the Southwest. There is no across-the-board relationship between color and flavor, although the brightly painted old-timers tend to be less sweet and tender than modern cultivars and have a more pronounced "corn" flavor.

To ensure success, plant cultivars that have plenty of time to ripen in your location. "Early" corn cultivars require between 55 and 70 days from seeding to produce edible ears; "midseason" types, 71 to 85 days; and "late" cultivars, 86 days and more. Corn needs warmth, from seeding to harvest, so err of the safe side: If your growing season is 100 days long, choose a cultivar well within that limit.

While corn is an efficient plant in using the

Corn 'Silver Queen'

sun's energy—one reason it grows so quickly—it isn't space-efficient. Although some cultivars may produce two ears per plant, the usual math is one plant equals 1½ ears. A family of four needs about 130 plants for fresh eating; if you want to preserve, increase the planting. To spread out the harvest, be sure to stagger your corn crop, either by successive sowings or by planting cultivars that mature at different times. To make better use of space, intercrop corn with vegetables that can be harvested before the cornstalks are tall enough to shade smaller neighbors.

Don't be tempted by the traditional pairing of squash and corn, or pumpkins and corn. That combination only works really well if you're growing corn cultivars, such as dent or flour types, that aren't harvested until the end of the season, when their kernels are hard. Similarly, using cornstalks as supports for climbing crops, such as pole beans, is not a good idea with sweet cultivars, which must be harvested midseason.

SITE & SOIL

Good light, good drainage, and good fertility—corn needs it all. Tall cultivars can reach 6 feet, so locate this vegetable where it will receive full sun but won't

Corn hybrid 'Sunset'

shade smaller plants. Soil for growing corn should be rich—heavily amended with organic matter so that it simultaneously drains well and retains moisture—and have a pH between 6.0 and 6.8. Corn is a big consumer of nitrogen and phosphorus. If leaves begin to yellow, spray with diluted fish emulsion or another high-nitrogen liquid fertilizer.

The traditional practice of grouping several corn plants in a "hill" was a concession to the lack of plows and tillers: It was easier to prepare several dozen hills than to dig a 200-square-foot plot. Whether our ancestors realized it or not, hilling also maximizes pollination, which is dependent on wind. With several plants clustered together, pollen from the tassels is more likely to reach each ear's silks. Instead of sowing one or two long rows, plant a block of five or six short ones.

SWEET TOOTH

The increasing sweetness of sweet corn is a result of three giant steps. The first occurred in the 1950s, when University of Illinois scientist J.R. Laughman identified the recessive gene (shrunken-1, designated *su*, for sugary) that distinguishes sweet corn from field types. Ordinary, or *su*, cultivars, are the most vigorous sweet corns and the most tolerant of cool soil and air. Moderately sweet, they contain 5 to 10 percent sugar, which quickly converts to starch after harvesting. Ordinary sweet-corn cultivars—also called "normally sugary"—do not have to be isolated.

In the 1970s, again at the University of Illinois, a second gene was found. Called the shrunken-2 gene, or sh_2, it could produce crisp kernels that were more than twice as sweet as *su* cultivars. Although containing 20 to 30 percent sugar, sh_2—or "supersweet"—corns are slow to convert it to starch, which means you don't have to run between the garden and the pot of water boiling in the kitchen. However, supersweet plants are less vigorous, unable to cope well with cold and other stresses, and are easily cross-pollinated.

To grow supersweets successfully, you need ideal conditions and a location that is at least 250 feet away from any other corn cultivar (or time plantings so that cross-pollination cannot occur).

In 1980, Illinois researchers hit paydirt a third time by discovering the sugary extender, or *se*, gene. By crossing a *se* plant with a *su*, or ordinary, plant, scientists produced a new group of sweet corns known as "sugar-enhanced" (a common trademark designation is EH, for Everlasting Heritage). Their qualities fall in the middle of the three types: They are sweeter than ordinary cultivars are but not as sweet as supersweets; less tolerant of poor conditions than ordinary sweet corns are but more tolerant than supersweet cultivars; slower than ordinary sweet corns are to convert their sugar to starch but faster than supersweets. In addition to sugar-enhanced corns, there are "sugar-enhanced plus" (*se*+) cultivars, hybrids produced by crossing two se cultivars. Also known as "full se" cultivars, they are somewhat sweeter and more tender than are their parents.

CORN CULTIVARS

In the descriptions below, the terms *su*/ordinary, *sh₂*/supersweet, *se*/sugar extender, and *se+*/sugar-enhanced plus are used to identify the sweetness of hybrid cultivars. See "Sweet Tooth" for more information on these hybrid categories.

'Bodacious': *se*/sugar-enhanced; 85 days; yellow; 8-inch ears; popular home and market cultivar.

'Breeder's Bicolor': *se*/sugar-enhanced; 73 days; bicolor; 8-inch ears.

'Butter and Sugar': *su*/ordinary; 75 days; bicolor; 7-inch ears; good cold tolerance.

'Candy Store': *sh₂*/supersweet; 80 days; bicolor; 7-inch ears.

'Country Gentleman': open-pollinated; 95 days; white; 8-inch ears; kernels irregularly arranged; heirloom.

'D'Artagnan': *se*/sugar-enhanced; 78 days; bicolor; 8-inch ears; vigorous.

'Earlivee': *su*/ordinary; 58 days; yellow; 7-inch ears; short plant; standard early yellow.

'Early Choice': *se*/sugar-enhanced; 66 days; yellow; 10-inch ears.

'Gold 'N Pearl': *se+*/sugar-enhanced plus; 70 days; bicolor; 7-inch ears; good cold tolerance.

'Golden Bantam': open-pollinated; 75 days; yellow; 6-inch ears; one of first yellow cultivars; heirloom.

'Golden Cross Bantam': *su*/ordinary; 85 days; yellow; 8-inch ears; resistant to bacterial wilt.

'Honey 'N Pearl': *sh₂*/supersweet; 78 days; bicolor; 8-inch ears; AAS winner.

'Honey and Cream': *su*/ordinary; 78 days; bicolor; 7-inch ears; popular home-garden cultivar.

'How Sweet It Is': *sh₂*/supersweet; 88 days; white; 8-inch ears; AAS winner.

'Howling Mob': open-pollinated; 80 days; white; heirloom.

'Illini Xtra-Sweet': *sh₂*/supersweet; 85 days; yellow; 8-inch ears.

'Kandy Korn': *se*/sugar-enhanced (Everlasting Heritage, EH); 84 days; yellow; 7-inch ears.

'King Arthur': *se*/sugar-enhanced; 70 days; yellow; 9-inch ears.

'Northern Xtra-Sweet': *sh₂*/supersweet; 72 days; yellow; 8-inch ears; good supersweet for northern gardens.

'Platinum Lady': *se*/sugar-enhanced; 80 days; white; 8-inch ears; tall plant; good disease resistance.

'Precocious': *se*/sugar-enhanced; 70 days; bicolor; 7-inch-long ears; good cold tolerance.

'Pristine': *se+*/sugar-enhanced plus; 75 days; white; 7-inch ears.

'Quickie': *se*/sugar-enhanced; 65 days; bicolor; 7-inch ears; small plants; very early.

'Reward': *su*/ordinary; 82 days; yellow; 9-inch ears; good cold tolerance; many plants produce two ears.

'Seneca Brave': *se*/sugar-enhanced; 72 days; bicolor; 8-inch ears.

'Seneca Horizon': *su*/ordinary; 65 days; yellow; 9-inch ears; good vigor and cold tolerance; good short-season cultivar.

'Silver Choice': *se*/sugar-enhanced; 75 days; white; 8-inch ears.

'Silver Queen': *su*/ordinary; 92 days; white; 9-inch ears; standard white cultivar .

'Skyline': *sh₂*/supersweet; 72 days; bicolor; 8-inch ears; good supersweet for cool soil.

'Snowbelle': *se*/sugar-enhanced; 79 days; white; 7-inch ears.

'Stowell's Evergreen': open-pollinated; 90 days; white; popular home-garden cultivar; heirloom.

'Sugarburst': *sh₂*/supersweet; 80 days; white; 7-inch ears; widely adapted; good cold-soil tolerance.

Cross-pollination occurs between all sweet corns, but it has no effect on flavor except for supersweet (sh_2) cultivars. If you're growing supersweet corn along with other cultivars, isolate it by at least 250 feet. Sweet-corn flavor also can be affected by nonsweet, or field, cultivars, including popcorns. If you're determined to produce cornmeal as well as corn-on-the-cob, be sure to separate the plots.

While corn, topped with a cream-colored tassel like a Christmas tree ornament, is a handsome plant, it's only marginally useful in the flower bed. Its height and low yields also work against this crop's success as container plants.

HOW TO GROW

Corn needs warmth from the start: Seeds planted in cold, wet soil are more likely to rot than germinate. You can push the season a bit by using plastic mulch to warm the soil, by presprouting seeds between sheets of wet paper towels, or by growing transplants, but most gardeners are better off being patient. Unless your growing season is extremely short, wait until at least a week after the frost-free date to sow corn.

Once the soil has warmed to at least 55°F (65°F for extra-sweet hybrids), sow seeds 1 to 1½ inches deep, 4 to 6 inches apart. Don't scrimp when seeding—germination, which should occur in 10 to 14 days, only averages 75 percent. To ensure a steady supply of fresh corn, make successive plantings every 2 weeks, keeping in mind that the same cultivar planted later in the season, when air and soil are warm, will develop more quickly than an earlier planting will.

When plants reach 3 to 4 inches tall, thin to 1 foot. Planting too closely reduces yields and ear size, so be ruthless when you thin. Keep plants weeded, but hoe carefully—as the plants develop, they form new roots *above* the existing ones. Despite a healthy root system, tall cornstalks have a tendency to fall over, a tendency called "lodging." If your crop begins to lean, pull soil around the base of teetering plants to give them additional support.

Once the ground has warmed, mulch to suppress weeds and retain moisture. Feed plants with a balanced liquid fertilizer when they are 10 inches tall, again when they reach 18 inches, and a third time when they tassel. Constant moisture is important, especially to good ear development. Make sure plants receive 1 inch of water a week, beginning when the tassels appear through harvest. To avoid washing pollen away, do not water from above.

The old wisdom was that suckers, the short extra stalks that grow from the main stalk, should be removed. Repeated studies, however, have established that suckers help the plant, so leave them on.

POTENTIAL PROBLEMS

Corn grown in home gardens typically has few disease or insect problems. Earworms, white, green, or red worms that feed on the kernels, can be controlled by spraying with a mixture of horticultural oil and Bt every 2 weeks, beginning when plants are 2 feet tall until the ears are formed. Aphids, cucumber beetles, cutworms, flea beetles, Japanese beetles, thrips, and wireworms also target corn. Many of these insects can be deterred by covering the seedbed with floating row covers. (For more information and specific remedies on these pests, as well as European corn borer, see "Controlling Common Pests" on page 162.)

Most diseases that affect corn can be avoided by cleaning up at the end of each garden season (remove and destroy any stalks from infected plants), rotating crops, and planting resistant/tolerant cultivars. The most common disease problems are bacterial wilt (see "Controlling Common Diseases on page 169) and smut, which appears as white or gray galls, or swellings, on plants. Remove any galls, and spray plants with a sulfur-based fungicide.

More troublesome to corn than diseases and insects is wildlife, especially deer and raccoons. A fence—either electric or 8 feet tall—is the only near-foolproof protection. Barring that, try the following techniques:

- Covering ripe ears with paper bags

- Playing a radio in the garden

- Using a repellent, such as bars of deodorant soap

- Flashing or moving devices, such as aluminum pie pans

- Lights, timed to go on and off

HARVESTING

Most cultivars are ready to harvest about 20 days after the silks appear. Other telltale signs of ripeness are dark green husks, dry brown but supple silks, and full-size kernels to the top of the ear. Try puncturing a couple of kernels—if the ear is ripe, the juice will be milky rather than clear. Pick corn—give the ear a sharp downward twist—in the morning when the ears are still cool, or plunge ears into cold water immediately after picking.

Although the conversion of sugars into starch is most rapid in ordinary sweet corns, all corn, even sugar-enhanced cultivars, is best when used straight from the garden. Ears that cannot be eaten immediately should be husked, sealed in plastic bags, and refrigerated. Corn contains modest amounts of vitamins A and B, potassium, and fiber.

Hand pollinating is the best way to guarantee seeds that will come true if you grow more than one corn cultivar. Because corn is so susceptible to

---

A CORN LEXICON

Although sweet corn is by far the most popular home-garden corn crop, there are other types of corn developed for specific purposes. While most sweet-corn cultivars can be left to mature on the stalk and used to make cornmeal or flour, you'll have better success if you grow a cultivar bred for the purpose. Make sure that the kernels are fully dry before storing (if the kernels are very hard to remove from the cob, they aren't fully dried). Store dried corn in a cool, dry location.

Broom Corn. Although both sweet corn and broom corn are annual members of the grass family, broom corn belongs to a different species, *Sorghum bicolor*. Plants need a long growing season (100 or more days) to produce their colorful sprays of broomlike tops. Recommended cultivars: 'Black Amber', 'Black Kafir', 'Hungarian Black Seeded'.

Dent Corn. Also called field corn, these have a depression, or indentation, on the top of the seed. They contain both hard and soft starch and are used to make cornmeal, flour, corn bread, and hominy, and as roasting ears. Recommended cultivars, all heirlooms: 'Bloody Butcher', 'Blue Charge', 'Hickory King', 'Nothstine Dent', 'Oaxacan Green', 'Reid's Yellow Dent'.

Flint Corn. The kernels of flint corns are so hard that when milled, the result is flour with a granular rather than a powdery consistency. They are used primarily to make cornmeal. Recommended cultivars, all heirlooms: 'Garland Flint', 'Hispanic Pueblo Red', 'Rhode Island White Cap'.

Flour Corn. The kernels of flour corn are soft throughout, making them easy to grind into fine flour. They are cultivated primarily in the Southwest. Recommended cultivars, all heirlooms: 'Anasazi', 'Hopi Blue', 'Hopi Pink', 'Taos Pueblo Blue'.

Miniature Corn. The ears of these cultivars are used in Asian cooking and for pickling. Harvest while still immature, within 1 week of the silks' appearing. Recommended cultivars: 'Baby', 'Baby Asian', 'Candystick', 'Early Arctic', 'Early Sunglow', 'Golden Midget', 'Japanese White Hulless'.

Ornamental Corn. Also known as Indian corn, these come in a rainbow of colors. Most cultivars require at least 115 days to produce mature (dry) ears. Harvest after the kernels are hard, then pull back husks to finish off drying. Any colorful cultivar, such as 'Strawberry', can serve as an "ornamental" corn, but cultivars bred especially for their looks include 'Fiesta', 'Indian Fingers', 'Little Jewels', and 'Seneca Indian'.

Parching Corn. These are red and black types of flour corns that split open when heated. Because they have a sweet flavor, they can also be eaten fresh. Recommended cultivars: 'Hopi Chinmark', 'Parching Lavender Mandan', 'Parching Red Mandan', 'Supai Red'.

Popcorn. See *Popcorn* on page 340 for more complete information on growing this crop in the home garden.

"inbreeding depression," a loss of genetic diversity that produces less vigorous plants, gardeners who wish to save seeds should grow a large stand (200 or more plants) of a single cultivar. Corn seeds are viable for 2 years; store in airtight containers in a dark, cool location.

CORN SALAD

Valerianella locusta, V. eriocarpa. Valerian family, Valerianaceae. Annual.

○ ◑ ❄

Mild-tasting common corn salad is a low-growing, cool-weather salad green with spoon-shaped, slightly nutty-tasting leaves. The plants reach a height of only about 3 inches, but the leaves form an attractive rosette, 4 to 6 inches across. Cultivated since the Middle Ages in Europe—John Parkinson, writing in 1629, observed that "Lambes Lettice" was "wholly spent for sallets [salads], in the beginning of the yeare"—its common names reflect the many countries where it is grown. Mâche, which is pronounced mash, and lamb's lettuce are still frequently used terms for this crop, but it has also been called fetticus, feldsalat, douceur, nüsslisalad, cornell salad, and rapunzel. The term corn salad comes from the plant's habit of growing wild in grain fields.

Massachusetts Bay colonist John Winthrop, Jr., included a half ounce of corn salad seeds on his 1631 order to English grocer Robert Hill. By the 19th century, American gardeners were familiar with three types of corn salad—common, large round-leaved, and large-seeded. But despite its long history as a cultivated plant, this salad green is usually considered a weed, one of many European plants, such as dandelions and chicory, that naturalized in the wild. Still relatively uncommon in home gardens, corn salad's renewed popularity in the past decade, both as a separate crop and as an ingredient in mesclun (see Mesclun on page 301 for more on these salad-green mixes), is changing its status.

DECIDING WHAT TO GROW

Frost does not discourage this easy-to-grow green, which is primarily cultivated as a spring and fall crop in USDA Zones 2 through 6. In fact, chilly nights only sweeten its flavor. With mulch or the protection of a cold frame, a late-summer planting of an overwintering cultivar, such as 'D'Etampes' or

'Gayla', can survive the winter in Zones 5 and 6 and provide fresh greens in the spring. In southern gardens, corn salad is a wonderful fall-planted crop that can be grown through the winter without cover. Plants reach harvestable size in about 50 days from seeds, although some cultivars take as many as 80 days to reach maturity.

Two dozen plants will provide enough tender greens to contribute generously to mixed salads. Corn salad does well in pots and boxes, making it a good choice for a container salad garden. Use a container, at least 8 inches wide and 12 inches deep, with good bottom drainage. Fill with enriched potting soil, and keep plants well watered.

In addition to *Valerianella locusta*, or common (or European) corn salad, there is *V. eriocarpa*, or Italian corn salad. Unlike the short common species, Italian corn salad grows as tall as 16 inches and has larger, slightly hairy leaves.

Greens specialists offer several named cultivars of corn salad, all open-pollinated. 'Verte de Cambrai' has small, roundish leaves and is cold-tolerant, as is 'Coquille de Louviers', which has cupped, deep green leaves. 'Blonde', with small, shell-like leaves is also cold-tolerant. All three are well suited for early spring and fall planting. 'A Grosse Graine' is a relatively heat-tolerant cultivar and is a good choice for late spring and early summer. 'Piedmont', an Italian cultivar that has pale green spoon-shaped leaves is also heat-tolerant. 'D'Etampes', with a compact rosette of large, roundish leaves, and 'Gayla', which has deep green leaves, are both overwintering types.

HOW TO GROW

Corn salad thrives in well-drained soil, rich in humus, with a near-neutral pH of 6.8 to 7.0. Spring-planted crops benefit from full sun early in the season, but partial shade is best with the arrival of summer. Crops planted in late summer and early fall also need partial shade. In hot weather, corn salad quickly goes to seed, but its flavor remains much more palatable than does lettuce or spinach that has bolted.

Sow seeds directly in the garden about 4 weeks before the last frost, either by broadcasting seeds in a bed (cover with a thin layer of soil or sifted compost) or by planting a row (¼ inch deep, spaced 2 inches apart). Seeds take 10 to 14 days to germinate in 65°F soil. Thin plants to about 4 inches. Plants can be spaced more closely if the leaves are picked when small. Adequate moisture is essential to encourage vigorous, tender growth: If weather is dry, provide 1 inch of water a week.

To maintain a supply of fresh leaves, sow corn salad at 2-week intervals until early summer. Begin sowing again in late summer or early fall for fall crops. Corn salad also can be interplanted by broadcasting the seed around onions or garlic and can be followed by a warm-season crop, such as peppers, in a succession-planting scheme. For an extra-early spring crop, you can start seeds indoors in a flat 8 to 10 weeks before the last-frost date. The first sowing, which will be ready to harvest in 50 days, can be left in a flat and moved to a cloche or cold frame rather than transplanted to the garden. Or transplant hardened-off seedlings to the garden, spacing them 4 inches apart.

While corn salad needs evenly moist soil for best growth, it doesn't need fertilizing if sown in moderately fertile soil. If temperatures rise prematurely, shading plants may keep them from bolting. Given rich soil and sufficient water, corn salad is troubled by few insects or diseases. It may be a target of rabbits and deer; erecting a fence is the only reliable solution to an invasion of wildlife.

HARVESTING

Corn salad's leaves are rich in vitamin C, carotene, and iron. They can be harvested individually by picking the larger leaves on the outside of the rosette. New leaves will continue to form at the center. Or harvest entire plants by pulling them up or cutting them off at ground level. Store unwashed leaves in the refrigerator; wash before using.

Common and Italian corn salad cultivars do not cross-pollinate. Named cultivars of each species will cross, however, and wild plants can cross with garden cultivars. If plants, which are insect-pollinated, are allowed to grow into the summer, they will eventually flower and set seed. The plants self-sow freely and can naturalize in the garden if they are not weeded out. To produce seeds that will come true, grow only one cultivar of either species. To save seeds, which are viable for 5 years, store in airtight containers in a dark, cool location.

CREEPING SAVORY. See *Savory*
CRESS, GARDEN. See *Garden Cress*
CRESS, UPLAND. See *Upland Cress*

Burpee hybrid cucumber 'Sweet Burpless'

CUCUMBER

Cucumis sativus. Squash family, Cucurbitaceae. Annual.

○ ✳ ▼

Emperor Tiberius supposedly ate 10 a day; the Roman poet Virgil describes how it "writhes through the grass"; Charlemagne had it planted in the royal garden; Queen Isabella sent it to the New World with Columbus; John Smith planted it at Jamestown; Henry J. Heinz began pickling it in the 1870s; and the Russian cosmonauts grew it in space. Despite its notable history, the cucumber hasn't always been universally loved. According to 18th-century English essayist Samuel Johnson, "a cucumber should be well sliced, and dressed with pepper and vinegar, and then thrown out as good for nothing."

We know that gardeners rejected Dr. Johnson's advice; today, many have also turned their back on the vining plants he knew in favor of modern bush cultivars that take up 2 or 3 rather than 6 or 8 square feet. Sprawling or compact, all cucumbers have large, vaguely heart-shaped leaves with rough margins, prickly stems, and yellow flowers. Vining types grow about 8 inches tall, compact cultivars somewhat taller. Fruits—most pale or dark green, but a few yellow or white—range from 3 inches to 3 feet in length.

Natives of India, cucumbers demand warmth to germinate, grow, pollinate, flower, and fruit. Gardeners living north of USDA Zone 4 may have to use special techniques—planting short-season cultivars, starting seeds indoors, and using cloches, cold frames, and other protective devices—to cultivate them successfully.

DECIDING WHAT TO GROW

For eating fresh, four vining or six compact plants should yield enough fruits for a family of four. Increase the planting if you want to preserve. Cucumbers require between 45 and 75 days to produce mature fruits; to spread out the harvest, plant successive crops at 2- to 3-week intervals. The last sowing should be made about 12 weeks before the first-frost date.

Most cucumbers are monoecious: Each plant produces both female, or fruiting, and male, or nonfruiting, flowers—insects do the pollinating. Newer are gynoecious cucumbers, which produce only female flowers and so must be set near at least one monoecious plant. (Packets of gynoecious cucumbers contain a few pollinator-plant seeds coated with a colored dust for identification. Label them in the garden so that you don't thin them by mistake.) There are also parthenocarpic cucumbers, seedless cultivars that have renounced pollination altogether, but these are best suited for greenhouse cultiva-

---

CUCUMBER ESSENTIALS

- Full sun, warm temperatures.
- Fertile, well-drained, humus-rich soil.
- Sow 1 inch deep, outdoors or in.
- Set vining cultivars 2 to 3 feet apart.
- Keep soil evenly moist.
- Cover seedbed with floating row covers; remove when flowering begins.
- Mulch plants.
- Do not leave mature fruits on the vine.

---

tion. If you have room for only one cucumber plant, make sure it's monoecious.

On monoecious plants, the first blossoms that appear are male, followed by the female blooms, so fruit production is slightly delayed. Gynoecious cultivars, such as 'Conquest', 'Early Pride', and 'Bush Baby', produce earlier and larger crops, making them a good choice for short-season gardeners. Gynoecious cucumbers also tend to set most of their fruits in a short period of time. To lengthen the cucumber season, plant more than one crop or grow both gynoecious and monoecious cultivars. Cucumbers can follow early crops, such as spinach, radishes, and peas.

There are two other decisions to make: Vine or bush? Slicing or pickling?

- Vining cultivars produce more fruits but require far more space.
- Space-saving bush cultivars tend to bear fruit slightly earlier than vining plants do and are easier to tend and harvest.
- Picklers, which have thin, pale green skin, bear fruit earlier than slicing types and concentrate fruiting within a week or 10 days.
- Most slicers produce their dark green fruits a week or so later than do pickling types but continue to set fruit for 4 to 6 weeks.

In case you are second-guessing your cucumber-seed purchase, take heart: You can pickle a slicer—harvest fruits when they're still small—and you can slice a pickler.

SITE & SOIL

Cucumbers need all-day sun and plenty of water, although in hot, dry regions, they may benefit from some afternoon shade. Soil should be high in humus to retain moisture, with a near-neutral pH, and deeply dug and enriched. Cucumbers are heavy feeders. Pale foliage is a sign of too little nitrogen; bronzing indicates a lack of potassium. The short-term solution to both deficiencies is to spray plants with fish emulsion.

You can grow cucumbers in rows—set plants every 3 feet (bush types 18 inches apart) in east-west rows spaced 4 to 6 feet apart; in beds, with a minimum of 3 feet between plants; or in raised hills 3 feet in diameter, three plants per hill, with 6 feet between hills. Gardeners with small plots should

Cucumber 'Lemon'

Cucumber 'Bushy'

CUCUMBER VOCABULARY

Types of cucumbers aren't necessarily in mutually exclusive categories—an Asian cucumber can also be a burpless cucumber—but they are still helpful in sorting out the characteristics you may be seeking.

Asian Cucumbers. Thin, heavily ribbed cultivars like 'Tokyo Slicer', 'China Long', 'Suyo Long', and 'Kyoto Three Feet' that were bred for crisp, sweet flesh, tiny seeds and length (1 to 2 feet and longer); should be trellised to keep fruits from curving.

Beit-Alpha Cucumbers. Smooth, thin-skinned 6- to 8-inch-long cucumbers, such as 'Amira', 'Aria', 'Sweet Alphee', and 'Muncher', with crisp, nearly seedless flesh; also called Middle Eastern cucumbers.

Burpless Cucumbers. Thin-skinned slicing cultivars, such as 'Tasty Green', 'Comet II', 'Big Burpless', and 'Sweet Slice', that were bred to be easier to digest; mild flavor.

Cornichons. Generic French word for small cucumbers; some cultivars, such as 'Vert Petit de Paris' and 'Cornichon de Bourbonne', are touted as cornichon varieties, but pick any cucumber while it's still small, and you have a cornichon.

European cucumbers. Also called greenhouse cucumbers, these are near-seedless cultivars like 'English Telegraph', 'Carmen', 'Corona', and 'Sandra', which are usually grown indoors; a poor choice for backyard gardeners.

Gherkins. True gherkins are not cucumbers but fruits of a different species (*Cucumis anguria*); also a term used for any pickling cucumber.

Lemon Cucumbers. Oval-to-round, yellow, highly productive heirlooms—they are tennis ball look-alikes—that will have your neighbor asking what you're growing; sold under many names—'Lemon', 'True Lemon', 'Apple', 'Apple Shaped', and 'Crystal Apple'—but there is little or no difference between them.

Seed catalogs also may describe cultivars as "white-spined" or "black-spined," a reference to the barbs on small fruits that disappear as the cucumbers mature. There is no difference in flavor between the two types, but the flesh of white-spined types remains white as the fruits age, while the flesh of black-spined cultivars yellows slightly as the fruits mature.

consider trellising vining cultivars. Saving space is only one payoff of trellising: Cucumbers grown vertically have better air circulation, thus fewer disease and insect problems. They also produce straighter fruits and give markedly greater yields.

Choose a location where the vines won't shade other crops, and to avoid damaging plants' shallow roots, erect the support—either a vertical or A-frame trellis covered with 4-inch-square netting—*before* you plant. Set plants 10 inches apart on the windward side of the trellis, and help the young tendrils and vines attach themselves to the support. When vines reach the top of the trellis, cut them back to encourage branching. Trellising cucumbers is not recommended in hot, dry regions.

For container culture, choose a true bush culti-var, such as 'Salad Bush', 'Spacemaster', or 'Bush Champion'. Use a container, at least 8 inches wide and 12 inches deep, with good bottom drainage, and fill with enriched potting soil. Water frequently, and feed every 2 weeks with either fish emulsion or manure tea.

HOW TO GROW

Cucumbers can be direct-sown or, if your garden season is short, started indoors. Being too much of an early bird is no virtue with this crop, however: Cucumbers are unable to endure even light frosts, nor will their seeds germinate in cold soil. Wait at least 2 weeks after the last frost—until the average air temperature is 65°F and the soil has also reached at least 65°F—before sowing seeds or transplanting

---

CUCUMBER CULTIVARS

The following list provides a good cross-section of cucumber cultivars, including both bush and vine types as well as picklers and slicers. Disease resistance is indicated with the following codes: A, anthracnose; Als, angular leaf spot; D, downy mildew; M, cucumber mosaic virus; P, powdery mildew; S, scab; T, target leaf spot.

'Amira': vining F1 hybrid beit-alpha cucumber; 56 days; D, M, P; very vigorous vine; smooth, light green skin and very sweet flavor; monoecious.

'Fanfare': semi-bush F1 hybrid slicer; 63 days; A, Als, D, M, P, S; widely adapted; and performs well under stress; AAS winner; monoecious.

'Jazzer': vining F1 hybrid slicer; 48 days; D, M, P, S; 8-inch long dark green fruits; monoecious.

'Lemon': vining open-pollinated slicer; 65 days; heirloom; very vigorous vines; round, yellow fruits; monoecious.

'Little Leaf H-19': bush hybrid pickler; 55 days; A, Als, D, M, S, T; sets fruits in a wide range of conditions; unusual small leaves; ideal for trellising; very high yields; monoecious/parthenocarpic.

'Marketmore 76': vining open-pollinated slicer; 58 days; D, M, P, S; widely adapted main-crop favorite; monoecious.

'Northern Pickling': semi-bush open-pollinated pickler; 48 days; S; medium green fruits and high yields; standard pickling cultivar; monoecious.

'Poinsett 76': vining open-pollinated slicer; 67 days; A, Als, D, P; excellent variety for southern gardens; dark green fruits; monoecious.

'Salad Bush': compact F1 hybrid slicer; 57 days; D, M, P, S, T; widely adapted; good container plant; AAS winner; monoecious.

'Supersett': vining F1 hybrid slicer; 52 days; A, Als, D, M, P, S; 8- to 9-inch dark green fruits; gynoecious.

'Suyo Long': vining open-pollinated slicer from China; 63 days; P; does well in hot regions; trellis for best fruit quality and yields; very long, thin burpless fruits; monoecious.

'Sweet Success': vining F1 hybrid slicer; 55 days; M, S, T; long, smooth fruits; AAS winner; gynoecious.

'Vert de Massy': French vining open-pollinated "cornichon"; 53 days; S; harvest fruits when tiny; monoecious.

seedlings. If the soil temperature is 80° to 90°F, germination takes as few as 3 days; in cooler soil, it can take up to 10 days. Speed soil warming by creating hills or raised beds and by covering the planting area with clear or black plastic mulch before planting. Sow seeds 1 inch deep.

Indoors, sow seeds no more than 3 weeks before you plan to set the plants outdoors—two seeds per 3-inch pot, thinned to one plant when the first true leaves appear. Use individual pots to reduce disturbing the roots when transplanting, and be sure to harden off plants before moving them to the garden.

Cucumbers are 96 percent water by weight and need a constant supply of moisture, at least 1 inch per week, especially when they are flowering and fruiting. Bitter, misshapen fruit is a sign of water stress. Once the plants are established, mulch the soil or cover it with black plastic to retain moisture and eliminate weeds. Side-dress with a balanced fertilizer, such as compost, or spray plants with fish emulsion about 4 weeks after germination.

POTENTIAL PROBLEMS

Cucumbers are susceptible to a bevy of diseases, such as anthracnose and mosaic, but if you choose resistant cultivars, plant them in full sun, spacing them widely for good air circulation, and rotate the location of your cucumbers at least every 2 years, problems should be few.

Cucumbers are also vulnerable to several insects, including cucumber beetles, aphids, and squash vine borers, some of which also carry diseases. Install floating row covers to prevent these pests from reaching plants, but remove them to ensure pollination. (See "Controlling Common Pests" on page 162 for control measures.)

HARVESTING

Cucumbers, which contain a small dose of vitamin C but otherwise rate low on the vegetable-nutrition scale, mature at the speed of light, so check your plants daily. Pick fruits when they are still moderately sized: picklers between 3 and 4 inches, standard slicers between 6 and 8 inches. Cucumbers left

Cucumber 'Green Knight'

Cucumber 'Salad Bush'

FUN FOR KIDS

Children will enjoy creating the horticultural equivalent of a ship in a bottle by slipping a small cucumber into a small-necked bottle. To keep the fruit from becoming too hot in the garden, cover the bottle with newspaper. Allow the cucumber to mature—don't let it become so large it breaks the container—then cut it from the vine, and bring it indoors to be wowed at.

too long on the vine become seedy and bitter (tinges of yellow or orange at the blossom end are evidence that you've waited too long). Harvesting regularly also keeps your plants producing new fruits—the more you pick, the more you'll get. A month before the first expected frost, begin pinching off blossoms so that plants will channel their energy into maturing the existing fruits rather than producing new ones.

Cool harvested cucumbers immediately by immersing them in cold water. Place them in plastic bags to help retain their moisture, and refrigerate. All types of cucumbers will cross-pollinate. If you wish to save seeds that will breed true, plant only one open-pollinated cultivar, or hand-pollinate and protect the flower from being repollinated by insects by covering it with a small paper bag or keeping the pollinated plant covered with floating row covers. Seeds are viable for 5 years; store in airtight containers in a dark, cool location.

CUTTING CHICORY. See *Chicory*

DILL

Anethum graveolens. Carrot family, Apiaceae.
Annual.

○ ❄ ❀ ▮

Thanks to the best pickle companion a hamburger ever saw, dill is much better known today than many of its herb-garden cousins, such as anise,

coriander, and sweet fennel. All of them look alike, however, and all resent transplanting and share dill's habit of producing fragrant, tasty foliage followed by tall vertical stalks. Atop these stalks are the umbrella-like umbels, or clusters, of yellow flowers. Once the symmetrical umbels, which look like exploding fireworks, have dried, they shatter easily, spilling their pungent fruits, usually called seeds. Dill, which is easy to grow, can reach a stately 3 feet or taller in good soil and sun, although there are shorter cultivars that stay under 2 feet.

A native of the Mediterranean and Black Sea regions, where it still grows wild, dill is much more than a pickle herb. It not only seasons all kinds of foods but has an ancient reputation as an esteemed medicine, prescribed for ailments as diverse as hiccups and insomnia. The latter use may explain the origin of its name—the Norse *dilla*, meaning "to lull" or "put to sleep"—as well as explain an early common name for dill in America, "Meeting-House Seeds."

"Mercury hath the dominion of this plant," wrote Nicolas Culpeper, a 17th-century herbalist with a penchant for astrology, "and therefore to be sure it strengthens the brain." So don't leave the pickle behind when you eat the corned beef on rye.

DECIDING WHAT TO GROW

For cooking and pickling, the usual choice is the species. (Don't confuse it with Indian dill, *A. graveolens* subsp. *sowa*, a more pungent species that is widely cultivated in Asia.) For pickling, grow at least a dozen plants to be sure of plenty of seed heads when you need them. There are several named cultivars as well, most meant for a longer harvest of the feathery leaves, called dillweed. 'Dukat', also known as 'Tetra', and the more recent 'Superdukat' are brighter green with stronger flavor; they are also slower to bolt and therefore offer a longer-lasting supply of dillweed.

Also longer in leaf is the tetraploid cultivar 'Hercules'. The AAS winner 'Fernleaf' was developed specifically to be grown in flower beds. Although it is as edible as any dill, its smaller size, only 18 inches tall, and long-lasting, bushier foliage make it a good choice for any sunny border or container. As with all dills, the seed heads complement flower arrangements. 'Bouquet', another compact cultivar, has especially large seed heads, and 'Vierling,' which is used as a cut flower in Europe,

Dill 'Fernleaf'

Dill flowers

has extra-long stems, ideal for cutting, along with bluish green leaves.

SITE & SOIL

Although it can tolerate a little afternoon shade, dill does best in full sun and in moderate temperatures (extremely hot weather will speed the plant to flower). The ground should be well drained and light, even sandy, and not overly rich. In the vegetable garden, its usual spot, dill can be grown in rows or in beds or scattered amongst other plants, such as cabbages, where it acts as a companion plant. In a flower bed, the tall seed heads are attractive as a background. Dill is a good accent plant in a container of flowers or herbs. For a small container, choose a short cultivar, such as 'Fernleaf'.

HOW TO GROW

Gardeners are more apt to have trouble with dill, which can be grown in USDA Zone 2 and warmer, if they meddle with it than if they scatter the seeds on the soil and let them be. Dill resents transplant-

ing—it has a long taproot—so take advantage of its ability to sprout and grow quickly from seeds sown directly where the plants are to grow.

Sow dill as soon as the ground can be worked in spring. Seeds germinate better when they receive some light, so cover them *very* lightly with soil or compost, just enough to keep them from blowing away. Keep seedbed and seedlings moist; when the young plants are about 2 inches tall, thin to 6 to 8 inches. For an ongoing supply of dillweed, sow successive crops every 3 weeks. Dill seeds can survive fairly harsh winters and sprout when the soil warms in spring, so leave some seed heads in the garden if you want dill to self-sow.

Although its foliage is not dense, dill grows tall and can shade shorter sun-loving herbs or flowers. Locate it where it won't block the sun. Largely free from diseases and insects, dill is one of the host plants of the parsleyworm, more elegantly known as the larva of the swallowtail butterfly. Leave this bright green caterpillar with black stripes in peace. Better to lose a bit of dill than to lose a butterfly.

HARVESTING

Pick dillweed sparingly—no more than one-fifth of the plant's foliage so that the plant is not weakened—as soon as the leaves are large enough to use. The leaves last just a day or two in the refrigerator, so harvest only what you plan to use. Whole leaves can be frozen for longer storage. The flower umbels can be harvested as soon as they are half open. Harvest seeds when they are ripe and brown. Hang bunches upside down in a warm, dry place in paper bags to catch the seeds. Cut holes in the bags to ensure good ventilation.

Although insects will cross-pollinate different cultivars, dill does not cross with other herbs or vegetables. To produce seeds that will breed true, plant only one cultivar. Seeds are viable for 5 years; store in airtight containers in a dark, cool location.

SPECIAL NOTES

Dillweed is requested in many Scandinavian recipes, including those based on cucumbers, potatoes, and salmon. The seeds are used in breads, cheeses, pickles, and sauerkraut. A solution of dill seeds in water can relieve gas pains. Dill umbels can be used to make an attractive vinegar.

EDIBLE FLOWERS

Flowers aren't just for looking at and smelling, they're also for eating. That said, remember the first rule of edible flowers: Not all flowers are edible. Buttercups, daffodils, foxgloves, morning glories, daffodils—they all *look* good enough to eat, but don't be tempted. Each is toxic. Avoid, too, any flowers that have been sprayed with insecticides.

Dozens of blooms can be safely added to salads and other dishes. Some of the best are listed below. Small flowers can be used whole; use large flowers whole as garnishes, or pull them apart and sprinkle the petals over salads and other dishes. (Be sure to pull off woody flower parts, such as stems and calyxes.) Remember, before eating any flowers, be sure you have identified them properly.

ANISE HYSSOP

Agastache foeniculum. Spikes of anise-flavored lavender flowers top this somewhat tender perennial (hardy in Zones 6 to 9), which is also called fragrant giant hyssop. Sow seeds indoors, 5 weeks before the last expected frost, or sow directly in the garden after the danger of frost has passed. To encourage a second crop of blossoms, cut back spikes after its flowers are spent.

CALENDULA

Calendula officinalis. Calendulas, or pot marigolds, are annuals that prefer cool weather. Direct-seed in the garden after all danger of frost has passed, or begin indoors 4 weeks before the frost-free date. Calendula flowers have a distinct tang; their bright orange-yellow petals also add a visual jolt to salads and other dishes.

CULINARY HERBS

The blossoms of all culinary herbs are edible. Among the best choices are the flowers of basil (*Ocimum*

MORE FLOWERS FOR EATING

Many of the following flowers are common in beds and borders. You'll find others, such as peas and squash, in the vegetable garden.

Bee Balm. *Monarda didyma*

Chamomile. *Chamaemelum nobile*

Chicory. *Cichorium intybus*

Chrysanthemum. *Chrysanthemum* spp.

English Daisy. *Bellis perennis*

Honeysuckle. *Lonicera japonica*

Marigold. *Tagetes* spp.

Mustard. *Brassica* spp.

Pea. *Pisum sativum*

Pink. *Dianthus caryophyllus*

Red Clover. *Trifolium pratense*

Rose. *Rosa* spp.

Squash. *Cucurbita* spp.

Sweet Woodruff. *Galium odoratum*

Tulip. *Tulipa* spp.

Edible flowers

spp.), borage (*Borago officinalis*), common and garlic chives (*Allium schoenoprasum, A. tuberosum*), dill (*Anethum graveolens*), fennel (*Foeniculum vulgare*), mint (*Mentha* spp.), rosemary (*Rosmarinus officinalis*), and sage (*Salvia officinalis*). See the individual entries on these herbs for information on growing them. Many vegetables, such as squash, okra, peas, radish, and broccoli, also bear edible flowers.

DAYLILY

Hemerocallis spp. While most edible flowers are used fresh, the unopened buds or the fully opened flowers of this hardy perennial are dipped in batter and deep-fried. The buds can also be added to stir-fries. Any cultivar can be used in the kitchen, but few are better than the common roadside daylily, the tawny *H. fulva*, which escaped from colonial gardens three centuries ago. Daylilies are long-lived perennials that prefer full sun and modestly rich soil. With a few exceptions, each blossom lasts only a day.

NASTURTIUM

Tropaeolum majus. Nasturtiums, which can climb or sprawl, are sun-loving annual flowers that bloom in combinations of yellow, red, and orange. Direct-seed outdoors in a well-drained location after the danger of frost has passed. Both blossoms and leaves have the spicy flavor of cress. Nasturtiums are aphid magnets, so wash the flowers carefully before using.

RUNNER BEAN

Phaseolus coccineus. The colorful flowers of runner beans, a climbing crop that needs support, have a faint bean flavor. Treat this annual as you would any bean: Sow seeds in a sunny location after the danger of frost has passed. To keep the vines producing flowers, harvest beans as soon as they form.

VIOLA, PANSY & JOHNNY-JUMP-UP

Viola spp. All of these spring-blooming violets are popular bedding plants and widely available from local nurseries. Their flowers taste faintly like lettuce, although there is nothing faint about their bright colors—blues, apricots, purples, and more—when they are sprinkled over salads. Grow them in full sun to part shade and give them average to rich soil.

Eggplant 'Black Egg'

EGGPLANT

Solanum melongena. Nightshade family, Solanaceae.
Perennial grown as an annual.

○ ❊ ❀ ▉

Although Thomas Jefferson is credited with being among the first to cultivate eggplants in North America—he first mentions them in his 1809 garden journal—these natives of Asia were slow to take hold on this side of the world. It may have been their nickname "mad apple" and reputation for causing insanity, but more likely, it was their need for a long, hot growing season. Eggplants do best in USDA Zone 5 and warmer, although they can be grown in Zones 3 and 4 if given a giant head start indoors and extra protection outside.

By the middle of the 19th century, eggplant was a regular entry in American cookbooks, although interestingly, as Eliza Leslie noted in *Directions for Cookery* (1837), it was "sometimes eaten at dinner, but generally at breakfast." Leslie had a half-dozen eggplants to choose from, both round and long types, purples and whites, even a striped cultivar, and one "about the size of a hen's egg of a beautiful scarlet." She recommended frying eggplant in fresh butter. Moussaka, parmigiana, and ratatouille were yet to make their way to American shores.

Today's cooks—and backyard growers—have many more eggplant choices, every one lovely enough to find a home with even the most discriminating ornamental gardener. Few vegetables are prettier, beginning with the upright 1- to 3-foot plants covered with large velvet leaves, which are often tinged with purple. Star-shaped flowers, lavender to purple with contrasting yellow stamens, hang gracefully from the stiff stems, then turn into large and small decorative globes, teardrops, ovals, and cylinders colored green, white, yellow, pink, lavender, violet, red-purple, purple, black, multicolor, and more. If there were a beauty contest for edible plants, eggplant would be the odds-on favorite to win. They're nearly too pretty to pick.

DECIDING WHAT TO GROW

Eggplants can be grouped by several categories, such as size, shape, color, or regional origin. Most of the Asian types are longer and thinner than those developed in Europe or North America. They also are somewhat lighter in color and often have such thin skin that they don't need to be peeled. There isn't a great deal of difference in flavor between eggplant cultivars, although some argue that the flesh of white-skinned eggplants is firmer, tastes milder, and is less likely to be bitter. White cultivars also tend to have more seeds.

If the differences in flavor aren't pronounced, there are noticeable differences in the time cultivars need to reach maturity. If your garden season is cool or abbreviated, look for early-maturing cultivars, such as the hybrids 'Orient Express' and 'Tango', which are ready to pick about 60 days after being transplanted outdoors. In contrast, 'Long White Sword' takes 100 days to produce its first fruits and is most successful in regions where summer is hot and fall is long and mild. All eggplants, short-season or long, are retarded by extended temperatures below 50°F, and frost is fatal.

How you use eggplant will dictate what fruit shape to grow. The familiar large oval, or plum, cultivars are best for stuffing, but small cylindrical fruits are easier to slice and are good for frying, grilling, or adding to stewed dishes like ratatouille. There are also cultivars with round or oval fruits only an inch or two in diameter that are used whole or for pickling. Yields vary greatly—southern gardeners can expect nearly twice as many fruits per plants as northern growers can—but six plants should produce enough fruits for a family of four; if you want to preserve, increase the planting.

SITE & SOIL

Eggplants need heat, full sun, and fertile, well-drained soil that is high in organic matter and has a slightly acid pH (5.8 to 6.8). Because they require warm soil as well as warm air, a raised bed is an ideal setting for this Middle East favorite. Blossom-end rot—which creates soft brown spots on the base, or blossom end, of fruits—is sometimes a problem, so make sure soil is not calcium-deficient by liming before you plant.

Eggplants can spread 3 or 4 feet, especially in warm regions, so set standard cultivars 18 to 24 inches apart; large plants may need support to keep fruits off the ground (cylindrical fruits will grow straighter if plants are staked). Compact and dwarf eggplants can be spaced more closely. To speed soil

---

EGGPLANT CULTIVARS

Eggplants come in a range of sizes, shapes, and colors. The best cultivars to choose depend on how you plan to use the fruits. Northern gardeners should select short-season cultivars.

'**Applegreen**': 62 days; open-pollinated; small, oval, light green fruits with tender skin; good cultivar for the North.

'**Baby Bell**'/'**Bambino**': 45 days; hybrid; dark purple, 1-inch oval fruits; prolific; compact; good container plant.

'**Burpee Hybrid**': 70 days; hybrid; classic purple, oval fruits; tall vigorous plants.

'**Casper**': 70 days; open-pollinated; white, cylindrical 6-inch fruits.

'**Dusky**': 63 days; hybrid; medium-size, black-purple, teardrop-shaped fruits; AAS winner; good cultivar for the North.

'**Ghostbuster**': 80 days; hybrid; white, 6- to 7-inch-long oval fruits; vigorous plant.

'**Ichiban**': 66 days; hybrid; dark purple, 10-inch cylindrical fruits; Asian type.

'**Imperial Black Beauty**': 80 days; open-pollinated; purple-black, standard egg-shaped fruits; heirloom.

'**Little Fingers**': 68 days; open-pollinated; purple, 6-inch cylindrical fruits; high yields; Asian type.

'**Louisiana Long Green**': 100 days; open-pollinated; light green, 7-inch cylindrical fruits with green stripes; tall plants; good cultivar for the South.

'**Slim Jim**': 75 days; open-pollinated; lavender-purple, 5-inch cylindrical fruits; compact plant; good container cultivar.

'**Machiaw**': 65 days; hybrid; pink, very thin, 9-inch-long cylindrical fruits with tender skin.

'**Millionaire**': 58 days; hybrid; black, 10-inch cylindrical fruits; Asian type.

'**Morden Midget**': 65 days; open-pollinated; dark purple, plum-shaped fruits; compact plants; Canadian release; good cultivar for the North.

'**Orient Express**': 58 days; hybrid; black, 10-inch cylindrical fruits; good cultivar for the North.

'**Purple Blush**': 65 days; hybrid; lavender, 6-inch oval fruits.

'**Tango**': 60 days; hybrid; white, 7-inch cylindrical fruits; extremely early.

'**Violette di Firenze**': 80 days; open-pollinated; large, lavender, round to oblong fruits striped with white; sprawling plants; needs high temperatures; not recommended for the North.

'**Vittoria**': 65 days; hybrid; purple, 9-inch cylindrical fruits; Italian cultivar; vigorous plants; tobacco mosaic virus-tolerant.

Eggplant 'Asian Bride'

Eggplant 'Purple Blush'

warming, lay down plastic mulch several weeks before the last expected frost. Because eggplants are so tender and thus are outdoor latecomers, you may want to use their space in the garden for an early planting of spinach, mesclun, or other quick-maturing, cold-hardy crop.

While all eggplants do well when grown in containers, those with small or midsize fruits are more in scale with pot culture. There are also dwarf cultivars available— 'Baby Bell'/'Bambino' is one—that are especially appropriate for those who farm in window boxes and on decks and rooftops. Eggplants are heavy feeders and benefit from being fertilized during the growing season. Do not apply high-nitrogen fertilizers, which will delay fruiting.

HOW TO GROW

Tender eggplants, which wither at the rumor of cold, don't rush to produce mature fruits and must be started indoors at least 8 to 10 weeks before the last expected frost. Under ideal conditions—a soil temperature of 85°F— germination occurs in about 7 days. Sow seeds in flats or 2-inch containers filled

with a sterile medium. As soon as the new plants break the soil's surface, move them to a bright, warm location, 70° to 80°F during the day, slightly cooler at night.

Although you need to give eggplants an early start indoors, don't be in a hurry to move them outdoors. Plants that are exposed to cold soil and air temperatures may survive, but they will be stunted and fruit production will be delayed. Moreover, eggplants will not set fruits if nighttime temperatures sink below 60°F. Because they are so temperature-sensitive, it's more important than usual to harden off plants before moving them to the garden.

Transplant eggplants outdoors 2 or 3 weeks after the danger of frost has passed, when the soil temperature has reached 60°F. Add a half-shovelful of well-rotted manure or compost to each planting hole before setting the transplant. Place a paper collar around each seedling to discourage cutworms. To protect new plants from wind, cold, and insects, cover them with floating row covers or cloches. Eggplants are self-pollinating, so covers do not have to be removed when the plants begin flowering.

Heirloom eggplants

Eggplants are somewhat drought-resistant, but they do best when given an even supply of water, about 1 inch a week (water-stressed fruits develop a bitter flavor). After the plants are established and the ground has warmed, mulch with organic matter to retain moisture and eliminate weeds (if you've used plastic mulch to warm the soil, you can leave it in place). Spray with a foliar fertilizer, such as fish emulsion or compost tea, 3 weeks after transplanting. Side-dress plants monthly with a balanced liquid fertilizer.

Three weeks before the first expected frost, pinch back new blossoms so that the plants' energy is channeled into maturing the existing fruits rather than producing new ones. Eggplants are no match to frost, but you may be able to gain an additional week's harvest in autumn by covering plants at night with two or three layers of floating row covers.

POTENTIAL PROBLEMS

Most insects that trouble eggplants can be controlled by using floating row covers. Diseases that bother eggplants, such as verticillium wilt, can be avoided by rotating crops. Never plant eggplants where they grew last year or where their relatives—potatoes, tomatoes, and peppers—grew. Cultivars with resistance to tobacco mosaic virus are available.

HARVESTING

As with many vegetables, bigger eggplants aren't better eggplants. Fruits, which contain dietary fiber and some protein, can be picked as soon as they are large enough to use and until their skin loses its gloss. To double-check whether you've harvested at the right time, examine the seeds in the fruit: If they're brown or hard, the fruit was picked too late. Use a knife or shears to harvest eggplants, leaving a 1-inch piece of stem attached to the fruit. Plants that are kept picked will continue to produce new fruits, thereby extending the harvest.

To save seeds from eggplants, allow the fruits to mature past the edible stage before you pick. Cross-pollination between cultivars can occur but isn't a great danger to producing seeds that will breed true. Seeds are viable for 4 years; store in airtight containers in a dark, cool location.

SPECIAL NOTES

Although no cases of poisoning have been recorded, eggplants contain toxic alkaloids and belong to the nightshade family, which has many members that are poisonous. Do not eat any parts of the eggplant except the fruits.

ENDIVE

Cichorium endivia. Sunflower family, Asteraceae.
Biennial grown as annual.

○ ◑ ❄ ❀ ▼

Endive is a type of chicory (*Cichorium intybus*), its species name derived from the Egyptian word for January, the month when it was eaten in that part of the world. While it may seem this *au courant* green was discovered by upscale restaurateurs in the past

Endive 'Sinco'

decade, endive has been grown for hundreds of centuries. Classical authors, including Horace, Pliny, and Virgil, made little or no distinction between endive and other chicories, recommending them as worthy greens for winter salads. European herbalists in the 16th and 17th centuries also bundled endive with other chicories, believing that they all had "vertue to cool the hot burning of the liver." Endive, according to John Evelyn, "is naturally Cold, profitable for hot Stomachs."

Nor was endive a latecomer to this continent. In 1631, John Winthrop, Jr., sent back to his London supplier for a half ounce of seeds, more than 8,000 by rough count. By the 1850s, 20 or more cultivars were being grown in the United States, including at least two— 'Green Curled' and 'White Curled'—that are still sold today. Yet endive's popularity wasn't universal, New Jersey truck farmer Peter Henderson wrote in 1867. It is "used by few except for German and French population. It is, however, offered now by the wagon load, where a few years ago a few basketfuls would have supplied all the demand." Like all crops grown in small quantities, Henderson went on, "the few that do raise it find it very profitable."

Raising endive, along with its counterpart escarole, remains profitable—if not in the pocketbook, certainly in the salad bowl—and isn't difficult for gardeners in USDA Zone 3 and warmer. However, don't confuse these plants with Belgium endive, also called witloof chicory, which is grown for its roots as well as its forced tops, rather than for its leaves. (See *Chicory* on page 224 for more on this crop.)

DECIDING WHAT TO GROW

Cichorium endivia, which is also a traditional component of mesclun, comes in two forms: curly-leaved and flat-, or broad-leaved. Flat-leaved cultivars, which are called escarole, are the hardier of the two and better suited for fall harvests and overwintering in warm areas. Both types have a bitter flavor, which can be moderated by blanching the plants for 10 days before cutting. Hot weather increases the bitterness of the leaves, so time your plantings to develop when the temperatures are cool. Days to maturity vary widely, anywhere from 45 to 90 days from sowing seeds, and experts contend that the quick-maturing cultivars taste less good.

Plants with curly, finely cut, ragged-edged leaves are known as endive, or frisée. Curly endive

Endive 'Broad-Leaved Fullheart'

forms highly decorative, flat, open rosettes with yellow-white centers surrounded by green outer foliage. Flat-leaved escaroles have thicker leaves and ribs, like lettuce's, that are slightly twisted at the base. Also taller and more hardy than curly endive, escaroles form definite but loose heads with green outer leaves and white hearts.

Curly-leaved endives especially are wonderfully ornamental, their bright yellow-green and ruffled, sternly cut foliage a fine addition to flower beds and borders. Smaller cultivars, such as 'Galia', make exceptional container plants, pretty in window boxes or on decks, rooftops, and patios. Use a container with good drainage. Fill with enriched potting soil, and keep plants well watered.

Twelve plants, a mix of curly and flat-leaved cultivars sown successively, will provide enough endive for a family of four.

HOW TO GROW

Endives, most of which take longer to mature but are cultivated very much like lettuces, need short days and cool temperatures—60° to 65°F—to develop good flavor and avoid bolting, or going to seed. They should be sown in early spring or in summer for a fall harvest; in extremely mild regions, endive can be grown as a winter crop.

Give endives a fertile, humus-rich soil, one that will retain moisture and promote quick growth. While tolerant of pH levels as low as 5.0, slightly acid soil is ideal; plants prefer full sun in cool regions, partial shade in warmer locations.

In northern gardens, begin endive indoors, 6 to 8 weeks before the last expected frost. In 68°F soil, seeds will germinate in about 1 week (seeds germinated in cold soil tend to bolt prematurely). After hardening off, seedlings can be planted outdoors as early as 2 weeks before the frost-free date. To avoid rot, set plants so that their crowns are above the soil surface and protect them from the cold and from insects with floating row covers.

Alternatively, sow seeds outdoors, ¼ inch deep, spaced 6 inches apart. Thin to about 12 inches, depending on the cultivar, but don't crowd plants, which encourages rot. (See *Mesclun* on page 301 for information on spacing and care in mesclun plantings.) Make successive sowings every 2 weeks, stopping once temperatures start to rise. Fall plantings, which are preferred by many gardeners because light frost tempers the leaves' bitter flavor, should be made starting about 15 weeks before the first expected frost.

Once plants are established and thinned, mulch with organic matter, such as compost or grass clippings, to suppress weeds and retain moisture. Feed with manure tea every 3 weeks. Make sure plants receive plenty of water, a minimum of 1 inch a week, which will help prevent bolting and leaf ends from browning. If temperatures turn hot, higher than 75°F, shade plants.

When grown in cool conditions, endive is rarely troubled by diseases; aphids and most other insect pests can be warded off by using floating row covers. (For information about potential problems, see *Lettuce* on page 284.)

Although some gardeners like its bite, most growers blanch, or exclude light from, endive to moderate its bitterness. About a week before harvesting, either gather up the outer leaves and tie them with twine, a technique that is especially easy with flat-leaved cultivars, or cover plants with a flowerpot or bucket.

HARVESTING

Harvest endive as soon as its leaves are large enough to be used, beginning about 50 days after seeding. Pick individual leaves, or allow heads to mature and cut the entire plant at ground level.

Endive, which contains vitamin A, iron, potassium and fiber, is best if eaten immediately after being picked. For short-term storage, about 10 days, seal leaves in plastic bags and refrigerate. If leaves become limp, set them in a bowl of ice water for 1 hour to recrisp them.

Endive flowers open at dawn and close by noon and are self-pollinating. While they do not cross with chicory cultivars (although chicory can be pol-

ENDIVE CULTIVARS

For a mix of salad greens, plant successive crops of both curly- and flat-leaved endives, which are commonly called escarole.

'Broad-Leaved Batavian': flat-leaved; 90 days; large heads; standard escarole cultivar; also listed as 'Full-Heart Batavian'; heirloom.

'Coral': flat-leaved; 50 days; medium heads; very early; widely adapted.

'Florida Deep Heart': flat-leaved; 85 days; 12-inch, upright plants; good southern cultivar.

'Galia': curly; 45 days; very small rosettes; finely cut leaves; matures quickly.

'Green Curled Ruffec': curly; 85 days; extremely large rosettes; good cold tolerance; heirloom.

'Moss Curled': curly; 90 days; small rosettes; highly cut leaves; heirloom.

'Neos': curly; 45 days; extra-frilly leaves with mild flavor; very early; also listed as 'Très Fine'.

'Perfect': flat-leaved; 80 days; medium-green ruffled leaves; very hardy.

'President': curly; 80 days; deeply cut and frilled leaves; very hardy.

'Salad King': curly; 70 days; large leaves and rosettes; heat- and cold-resistant; good fall cultivar.

'Très Fine': curly; 60 days; small rosettes; standard frisée cultivar; heirloom.

'White Curled': curly; 80 days; pale yellow-green leaves; harvest when young and tender; heirloom.

linated by endive), insects can cross-pollinate different cultivars. Because endives are biennials and flower in their second season, saving seeds is made more difficult. Gardeners in cold climates must dig and overwinter plants, then replant them in the spring; in frost-free regions, carry plants over to a second year. To save seeds, plant only one cultivar. Seeds are viable for 6 years; store in airtight containers in a dark, cool location.

ENDIVE, BELGIAN. See *Chicory*

EPAZOTE

Chenopodium ambrosioides. Goosefoot family, Chenopodiaceae. Annual.

○ ❄

Finding epazote in a North American garden book is a testament to the popularity of California and Southwest cuisine, for until recently, this herb was better known to those who cure than to those who cook. It was the oil from the seeds and flowers that was used as a vermifuge and gave rise to one of the plant's common names, wormseed. Also known as Mexican tea, the herb is potentially dangerous—its use as a medicine is restricted in some countries—and can cause dizziness, convulsions, even death. It should not be prescribed carelessly.

Most home gardeners grow epazote for its leaves, however, which can be safely used to season Mexican dishes—corn, fish, and especially beans, in which it reputedly prevents flatulence. Many describe epazote's flavor as resinous, somewhat reminiscent of oregano; others call it camphorlike. No one disputes its pungency. A hardy annual, native to the American tropics, it can be grown throughout North America; in warmer regions, where it has naturalized, plants reseed easily. "Weedy if given free rein," warned one seed catalog.

Epazote can grow tall, its striped stalk rising 3 feet or more, a bushy, treelike plant that can't be called ornamental. It can be grown in containers. The leaves are long and serrated; spikes of tiny flowers appear in late summer. One plant should be plenty for a family of four. There are no cultivars—look for the common name epazote or the botanical name, *Chenopodium ambrosioides*, in the herb section of seed catalogs.

Epazote

HOW TO GROW

Epazote isn't difficult to cultivate, nor is it particular, but it does best when growing in full sun and moderately rich soil that drains well, contains plenty of organic matter, and has a near-neutral pH. Plants may benefit from afternoon shade in extremely warm regions. Begin seeds indoors—in 75°F soil, they will sprout in about 10 days—sowing them shallowly in individual pots (four to six seeds per container) at least 8 weeks before the last expected frost. In warm regions, epazote can be sown outdoors in autumn. Epazote seedlings grow very slowly, about 2 inches in 6 weeks, but can be moved outdoors as soon as the danger of frost has passed. After hardening off plants—still unthinned—transplant them to the garden, setting them 10 to 12 inches apart. Once the young plants are established, thin each planting to one plant. Pinch back stems to encourage bushy growth.

Water plants every 3 weeks with manure or compost tea or fish emulsion, and mulch to suppress weeds and retain moisture. Epazote is rarely troubled by diseases or insects, although covering transplants with floating row covers will prevent aphids and other pests from feeding on the plants while they are still young and vulnerable.

To prevent epazote from self-seeding, uproot plants in late summer or early fall, before they go to seed.

HARVESTING

Begin harvesting individual leaves as soon as they are large enough to be used. To dry epazote, cut stems and hang them upside down in a dry, dark location; store dried leaves in sealed opaque containers.

It is unlikely that epazote will cross with other *Chenopodium* species. Seeds are tiny—more than 150,000 per ounce—and are viable for 3 years; store in airtight containers in a dark, cool location.

ESCAROLE. See *Endive*
ESTRAGON. See *Tarragon*

Fava Bean

Vicia faba. Pea family, Fabaceae. Annual.

○ ❋

Favas, or fabas, are one of the oldest cultivated vegetables, "brought into culture at some remote period of antiquity" according to the French seedsmen Vilmorin-Andrieux. Favas are mentioned in the Bible and were grown by the Egyptians, Greeks, and Romans, who carried them to England where they were—and are—called broad beans. Although "beans eaten are extremely windy meat," the 17th-century astrologer-physician Nicholas Culpeper warned, their medicinal virtues were many, and "if after the Dutch fashion, when they are half boiled you husk them and then stew them...they are wholesome food."

Indeed they are a first-rate source of protein, vitamins A, B_1, B_2, and C, iron, potassium, and dietary fiber, although they were served as often in the barn as in the dining room in 18th- and 19th-century America. Their use as fodder gave rise to another common name for the fava, horse bean. Fearing Burr called it "garden-bean of the English" and noted that the crops required a "moist, strong soil, and a cool situation" in *The Field and Garden Vegetables of America* (1865).

While called beans, favas are more like peas in that they prefer cool temperatures. They can be grown in USDA Zone 3 and warmer and are often planted as a lima bean substitute in cold regions. Bushy, upright, and tall, 2 to 4 feet, the square-stemmed, blue-green-leafed plants need support so that they won't topple over as their pods develop. And, movie buffs, they do go well with a good Chianti.

DECIDING WHAT TO GROW

Both Burr and Vilmorin-Andrieux describe nearly two dozen favas, including several—'Broad Windsor', 'Green Windsor', and 'Johnson's Wonderful'—that are still sold, or, in 19th-century language, "still unflinchingly maintain their position." There are both short-podded (holding about four seeds) and long-podded (holding between six and eight seeds) favas, but taste differences are minimal. Cultivars with pale seeds, such as 'Express', may have a slightly milder flavor.

Scores of named favas are available in Europe and England, but North American seed catalogs tend to list little more than the generic "broad bean" or "fava bean." A few companies do carry fava cultivars, however. Gardeners in areas where summer comes early and hot should look for 'Express', 'Loreta', or 'The Sutton', all of which mature in about 80 days. Most cultivars need at least 90 days to produce full-size seeds.

'Jumbo', which has three huge seeds per pod, was bred for fresh shelling; 'Aprovecho Select' also has large seeds. 'Imperial Green Longpod' and 'Aquadulce' are standard cultivars with 8- to 12-inch pods filled with six to eight seeds. The heirloom 'Aquadulce Claudia' is particularly cold-tolerant, a good choice for overwintering in mild climates. Another heirloom, 'Masterpiece', matures in about 90 days and is widely adapted.

Many gardeners grow fava beans as a green manure, broadcasting seeds in spring or early summer and turning the plants under after they're killed by frost (in warm regions, sow seeds in fall and winter, and turn under when plants begin to flower). 'Bell', a small-seeded fava that is tolerant of a wide range of soils, is a popular cultivar for cover cropping.

SITE & SOIL

The most hardy of all the beans, favas can be sown in mild areas in fall and overwintered or, in cooler parts of the country, planted early in spring or late summer if the garden season is long enough. They need a sunny location—partial shade if temperatures rise—and organically rich soil that drains well. Like other pea-family members, favas have the ability to capture nitrogen from the air. For the plants to "fix" nitrogen, certain *Rhizobia* bacteria must be present in the soil. If you haven't added manure or other high-nitrogen material to the garden, coat seeds with an inoculant to make sure the bacteria are present so plants can manufacture the nitrogen they need. You can purchase inoculant—one developed for favas and other vetch crops—at a garden center; just before planting, wet the seeds and cover them with the powder.

Tall cultivars, such as 'Imperial Green Longpod', have a tendency to flop over and should be supported. Many gardeners use 3-foot-long sections of branched brush from trees or sturdy shrubs. Sharpen the butt end of each piece, and stick it in the ground among the plants. An even better technique is to encircle, or cage, the plants with twine. Stake the perimeter of the row or bed, and run two or three parallel lines of twine around the 4-foot posts, beginning 1 foot from the soil surface.

Their height makes favas a less-than-ideal choice for container culture, but the plants have pretty flowers—there are both red and white cultivars—and can be incorporated in an ornamental bed or border. To spread out the harvest, sow both spring and fall crops, and follow spring plantings with midseason crops, such as common green beans. Fifty plants should be adequate for a family of four; if you want to preserve, increase the number.

HOW TO GROW

Grow favas as you would peas (see *Pea* on page 326 for details). Because they are cold-tolerant, there's little advantage to beginning indoors, but sow seeds as early as your soil allows: Plants that mature their beans in hot weather are susceptible to insects. Germination occurs in about 2 weeks in 50°F soil. Set seeds 1½ inches deep (deeper still in warm regions or in light, sandy soils), 3 to 4 inches apart, in double rows or beds, and install supports immediately so that plants don't fall over as they develop. Once the plants are established, when they are about 3 inches tall, thin to 6 inches and mulch with compost, grass clippings, or other organic matter to retain moisture and suppress weeds.

Young plants need only about ½ inch of water a week, so watering is usually unnecessary unless there is an extended drought. Once plants begin to flower, the need for water increases to 1 inch a week. Plants growing in moderately fertile soil shouldn't require fertilizing, but feeding twice with liquid seaweed or compost tea will help ensure heavy yields.

POTENTIAL PROBLEMS

Fava beans, if grown in cool, moist conditions, are largely untroubled by diseases or insects, but once the the mercury rises, they do less well. Plants will drop their blossoms in temperatures above 75°F. Temperatures above 75°F also encourage insects, especially aphids and bean beetles. Using floating row covers can prevent many pests from reaching plants. (For more information about identifying and controlling these pests, see "Controlling Common Pests" on page 162.)

HARVESTING

Like most beans, favas are a three-in-one vegetable. Pick when the beans are still small and tender—and when their flavor is most mild—and you can eat the entire pod, as you would a snow pea or common snap bean; or pick when the pods are half-mature, then shell and use the seeds as you would English peas or limas; or allow the pods to dry on the plant, then shell and use as you would any dry bean. Flavor grows stronger as the seeds mature.

Extremely large fava bean seeds may need to be skinned before they are eaten. To remove skins, quickly immerse cooked beans in cold water, which will cause the skins to slip off easily.

Although fava beans are self-pollinating, their flowers are frequented by bees and other insects, which can result in crosses between cultivars grown within 1 mile of each other. To ensure producing seeds that will come true, plant only one cultivar. Seeds are viable for 5 years; store in airtight containers in a dark, cool location.

SPECIAL NOTES

Mature fava beans cause a serious allergic reaction (called favism) in some people, especially males of southern European ancestry. Soaking the seeds in hot water before using (discard the water) will decrease the danger, but if you've never eaten favas before, begin with a small helping.

FENNEL

Foeniculum vulgare, Azoricum group. Carrot family, Apiaceae. Perennial grown as an annual.

○ ❄ ❣ ▼

Fennel is a Mediterranean native, grown and eaten—leaves, stems, and seeds—by the Egyptians, Greeks, and Romans. It was one of the nine favored healing herbs of the Anglo-Saxons. In ancient China, where it was called *Hui-xiang*, fennel was used to soothe the digestive organs and cure snakebites. In the 17th century, Nicolas Culpeper recorded that fennel seed "boiled in wine and drunk, is good for those that are bit with serpents, or have eat poisonous herbs, or mushrooms." Colonial Americans called fennel seeds "meetin' seeds," because they could dull the appetite if chewed during long meetings. More recently, the emphasis has been on fennel's culinary merits. It has become something of an *herbe célèbre* during the 1990s, served with panache in many a fine restaurant.

There are two distinct forms of fennel. The first is sweet (or common, or Roman) fennel, *Foeniculum vulgare*, Azoricum group, a dramatic perennial hardy to USDA Zone 6 that looks like dill's big brother. Sweet fennel grows as tall as 8 feet, and it has the flavor of anise. It has escaped to roadsides from Connecticut to Florida and is a weed in warm places like California. In colder regions, it is grown as an annual. The beautiful green, feathery foliage—inspiration for the genus name *Foeniculum*, which means "small hay"—is used mostly as an herb in fish dishes and to make a soothing, digestion-enhancing tea. Sweet fennel has hollow, bright green stems that can be used as drinking straws for cool summer drinks. The flat umbels of golden flowers that bloom from July until October are edible and beautiful in leafy or fruit salads. The small, dried fruits of the plant, commonly called seeds, are prized herbal ingredients in meat dishes, liqueurs, European rye breads, cheeses and sauerkrauts, as well as with vegetables, especially beets, cabbage and potatoes. In India, the seeds are chewed after a meal to sweeten the breath and improve digestion.

The second type of fennel, *F. vulgare*, Dulce group, is quite different from sweet fennel in size, shape, and habit. Called Florence fennel, or finocchio, it is more vegetable than herb, although its foliage, which also has a delicate anise flavor, can be used as a seasoning. (See *Florence Fennel* on page 260 for more information.)

The majority of gardeners grow the species, which is the only sweet fennel available from most seed houses. There are a couple of named cultivars, however, including 'Berfena', which is taller than the species and has a slightly stronger flavor. There also is a bronze-red cultivar, listed as copper fennel or 'Rubrum' or 'Purpureum', which is highly decorative but can be used in the kitchen as the green types are. One or two plants are enough for a family of four, even if you want to preserve.

HOW TO GROW

Sweet fennel does best when growing in a sunny location in well-drained soil with a near-neutral pH, but it is a forgiving plant and will tolerate less-than-ideal conditions. It can be grown as a specimen plant at the back of a sunny perennial flower border, as the centerpiece of an herb garden, as part of a vegetable bed, or in containers. Give each plant 1 foot all around.

Start sweet fennel from seeds, sowing directly in the garden in spring in cold regions or in autumn in southern gardens. Seeds germinate best at 60° to 65°F, although germination can occur at soil temperatures as low as 45°F. Install floating row covers over the seedbed to prevent insects, such as leafhoppers and carrot rust fly, from reaching the young plants. Mulch to retain moisture and suppress weeds, and stake plants if your site is a windy one.

Sweet fennel is rarely troubled seriously by diseases or insects. Like all members of the carrot family, it attracts swallowtail butterflies and their bright green larvae. Leave the caterpillars in peace to make more butterflies.

HARVESTING

Begin cutting sweet fennel leaves as soon as they are large enough to be used. Collect seeds after they become dry but before they fall from the flower heads or shatter. (Plants will frequently self-seed; thin them out if they become weedy.) All types and cultivars of fennel cross-pollinate, so grow only one cultivar if you want to produce seeds that will come true. Seeds are viable for about 3 years; store in airtight containers in a dark, cool location.

FENNEL, FLORENCE. See *Florence Fennel*
FINOCCHIO. See *Florence Fennel*

Fennel 'Fino Florence'

FLORENCE FENNEL

Foeniculum vulgare, Dulce group. Carrot family,
Apiaceae. Perennial grown as an annual.

○ ❄ ♣ ▮

Florence fennel, although relatively unknown among home gardeners, was recently chosen as Plant of the Year by a national horticultural organization. None of the attention would have surprised Thomas Jefferson, who was absolutely ga-ga about fennel, writing that it "is beyond every other vegetable, delicious . . . there is no vegetable equals it in flavour. It is eaten at dessert, crude, and with or without dry salt, indeed I preferred it to every other vegetable, or to any fruit."

Don't confuse Jefferson's favorite vegetable with the herb sweet fennel, *Foeniculum vulgare*, Azoricum group. Florence fennel, although also designated *F. vulgare*, is part of the Dulce group and is quite different in size, shape, and habit from the herb. Known as finocchio in Italy, Florence fennel stems

look rather like celery. They form a bulb at their base—"varying in size from that of a hen's egg to that of the fist," according to a 19th-century authority—and are topped by fernlike blue-green foliage.

Able to withstand only light frost, Florence fennel is usually grown as an annual in the vegetable garden, where its feathery foliage adds a decorative touch. Its artful form also makes it a first-rate choice for the ornamental garden or for container culture. Use a container, at least 8 inches wide and 12 inches deep, with good bottom drainage, and fill with enriched potting soil. Water frequently, and feed every 3 weeks with compost tea.

All parts of the Florence fennel plant are edible, although the parts most used are the broad, tender leafstalks and the crisp bulb. Raw or cooked, this vegetable has a delicate anise flavor like sweet fennel's. It can be grown in USDA Zone 3 and warmer.

Most seed racks offer nothing beyond "Florence fennel," but there are several cultivars with European names, indicating the popularity of this plant overseas. In trials at Purdue University in Indiana, the best-yielding cultivar was 'Zefa Fino'. 'Romy' is a fast-growing Italian heirloom that produces a large bulb. Grow half a dozen plants the first time to find out if you like it.

HOW TO GROW

In addition to full sun and plenty of water, Florence fennel needs rich, light, well-worked and well-drained soil with a pH between 6.5 and 7.0. It does best where summers are moderate, as weather too hot or cold, or soil too dry, makes for tough plants and early bolting to seed.

Florence fennel takes 90 to 115 cool but frost-free days to produce bulbs. Where summers are short, it should be started indoors 6 weeks before the average last-frost date, then hardened off and transplanted outdoors when the danger of frost has passed and the soil has reached a temperature of 65°F. In more moderate regions, sow seeds ¼ inch deep directly outdoors in spring or summer. Thin plants to 1 foot, and water them with manure tea every 4 or 5 weeks to ensure large, tender bulbs.

When the aboveground bulb reaches the size of an egg, pull soil or mulch around it to blanch the lower stems. Mulching also conserves moisture, suppresses weeds, and helps ensure steady growth. Remove any seed stalks so that plants put all their energy into producing stems and bulbs.

Like all carrot-family members, Florence fennel attracts swallowtail butterflies and their bright green larvae. Leave the caterpillars in peace to make more butterflies. It is bothered by few other insects or diseases but has a tendency to bolt to seed in hot summer weather or after transplanting. In places where winters are warm, fennel can become weedy, so self-sown seedlings should be ruthlessly thinned.

HARVESTING

Florence fennel, which is low in calories and contains small amounts of vitamin A and C but a good serving of fiber, is seldom available in supermarkets because it is somewhat demanding to grow and needs gentle handling at harvest time.

Leaves can be picked once plants have reached 18 inches tall. The rest of the plant should be harvested when the greenish white bulb is firm and the size of a clenched fist, about 3 inches in diameter. Don't leave Florence fennel in the ground too long—delaying the harvest will yield tough, woody bulbs and stems. To harvest, cut off the ferny leaves, then dig the whole plant. Remove and discard any roots. The quality of Florence fennel deteriorates quickly after harvest. Use it immediately, or store in plastic bags in the refrigerator—but only for a few days.

All types and cultivars of fennel cross-pollinate, so grow only one cultivar if you want to produce seeds that will come true. Seeds are viable for about 4 years; store in airtight containers in a dark, cool location.

FLOWERING CABBAGE. See *Cabbage*
FLOWERS, EDIBLE. See *Edible Flowers*
FRENCH TARRAGON. See *Tarragon*
FRISÉE. See *Endive*
GAO BEAN. See *Winged Bean*
GARBANZO BEAN. See *Chickpea*

GARDEN CRESS

Lepidium sativum. Mustard family, Brassicaceae.
Annual.

○ ◑ ❋ ▼

This cool-weather salad green has much to recommend it, not the least of which, if the Greek proverb is correct, is that eating cress makes one witty.

Garden cress growing with red orach

Moreover, garden cress is fast-growing, the perfect plant for instant gratification. It can be planted long before the last expected frost in spring and harvested as soon as 10 days after sowing. Blink twice, and this speed-demon annual has flowered—tiny white blossoms—and is already producing its reddish brown seeds, 19,000 to the ounce.

Garden cress's peppery flavor—some say pepper with a dash of mustard—gives rise to the plant's best-known common names, peppergrass, pepper cress, and mustard cress. A native of western Asia, garden cress has naturalized throughout Europe and in parts of North America. According to novelist/playwright Alexandre Dumas (Dumas *fils*), who also wrote a *Dictionary of Cuisine* (1869), garden cress is "the healthiest of the *fines herbes*."

In fact, garden cress contains only small amounts of vitamin C and A and a bit more calcium, but it is the easiest of all cresses to grow and is widely adapted, USDA Zone 2 and warmer.

DECIDING WHAT TO GROW

There are three types of annual garden cress, but all are similar in flavor. The most common is broadleaf cress, considered by many as the best cress for salads. It has bright green leaves, some as large as 4 inches long and 2 inches wide, and is usually listed in seed catalogs simply as broadleaf. A few specialists carry named cultivars, such as 'Reform', 'Victoria', and 'Cressida'.

Curly cress—also known as cresson—resembles parsley or chervil. Usually darker green than broadleaf types, it has thin, branching stems and lacy foliage. Normally sold in catalogs as curly cress, it may be listed as curled cress, curlicress, fine curled cress, moss curled cress, or extra-curled cress.

The third type of garden cress—and available only through seed cooperatives and exchanges—is a golden-leaved form, sometimes called Australian cress. If you can find seeds, it creates a nice contrast in the salad bowl. Broadleaf, curly, or golden, a bed 1 foot square, successively planted, will produce enough garden cress for a family of four.

Garden cress does well in pots and boxes, making it an excellent crop for a container salad garden. It can also be grown indoors on a windowsill for a ready source of winter greens (Dumas observed that "children and old maids amuse themselves by growing . . . cress on dampened cotton"). Indoors or out, use a container with good bottom drainage, and fill with enriched potting soil. Sow seeds thickly, and water thoroughly. Once the seeds sprout, move the container to a sunny or partially shaded location. Keep the soil moist. Garden cress seeds can also be sprouted. (See *Sprouts* on page 380 for details.)

HOW TO GROW

The secret to growing good garden cress is to plant it often, grow it quickly, and harvest it when the plants are still young. Cress's time is fleeting: Plants loose their agreeable flavor with the arrival of hot weather and become inedibly pungent. For this reason, it is primarily an early-spring and fall crop; in warm regions, it can be grown through the winter.

Moist, fertile, humus-rich soil that has a slightly acid pH (6.2 to 6.8) is the best home for garden cress. Full sun is the usual recommendation, but plants will tolerate light shade, so they can be grown beside taller crops, such as peas. Keep the soil evenly moist, but not soggy.

Sow seeds as soon as the soil can be worked, as early as 6 weeks before the last-frost date. Seeds will germinate in about 14 days in soil as cold as 45°F, but they sprout much more quickly—often in 48 hours—when soil temperatures are near 70°F. While you can sow seeds ¼ inch deep in rows, most gardeners broadcast cress seeds, covering them very lightly with soil or finely sifted compost. Because cress is harvested so soon after planting, thinning is unnecessary.

Garden cress can be interplanted with other crops, such as carrots, radishes, and leaf vegetables, or add it to a mesclun bed. (See *Mesclun* on page 301 for information on spacing and care in mesclun plantings.) For a continuous supply of young, succulent plants, succession-plant every 2 weeks. Stop sowing when hot summer weather threatens, then begin again in early fall. Provide young summer-planted seedlings with extra moisture and shade until they are established.

Heat and drought are garden cress's greatest adversaries. Given moderate temperatures and/or partial shade and adequate moisture, plants are rarely troubled by insects or diseases. The most common insect pest, flea beetles, can be controlled by covering the planting area with a floating row cover. (See "Controlling Common Pests" on page 162 for more information and for other control measures.)

HARVESTING

Although you can pull individual plants, garden cress is best treated as a cut-and-come-again crop. Begin harvesting plants when they are about 2 inches tall by cutting stems and leaves back to ½-inch stubs. Plants will regrow and can be recut another three or four times before they go to seed. In hot weather, provide shade and extra water until foliage is reestablished.

There is little information about cross-pollination between different garden cresses, but crossing is possible. To ensure seeds will breed true, plant only one form or cultivar. To save seeds, which are viable for 5 years, store in airtight containers in a dark, cool location.

GARDEN PURSLANE. See *Purslane*

WILD CRESSES

Although garden cress has escaped into the countryside in North America, gardeners who like to forage can also find two native cresses for grazing: cow-cress (*Lepidium campestre*) and poor-man's-pepper (*L. virginicum*). Similar to each other and to garden cresses in flavor, the leaves of poor-man's-pepper are toothed, while those of cow-cress are entire. Both plants flourish on waste ground.

Hardneck garlic 'Rocambole'

GARLIC

Allium sativum, Sativum and Ophioscorodon
groups; Onion family, Alliaceae.
Perennial grown as an annual.

How can a gardener not grow garlic, a plant that, according to a Mohammedean legend, sprang up from Satan's left footprint as he stepped out of the Garden of Eden? A plant that helped Ulysses escape being changed into a pig? A plant able to ward off vampires? And to "expelleth wormes," "taketh away black and blew spots," and "helpeth the griefs of the lungs"? One that ensures you will win every race you enter? That has its own association (Lovers of the Stinking Rose), newsletters (*Garlic Times*, *Garlic Press*, *Fresh Garlic News*), and an annual festival (in Gilroy, California)?

If these aren't enough reasons to join the garlic bandwagon, consider the words of Stanley Crawford: ". . . if you grow good garlic, people will love you for it." Crawford, a 5,000-pounds-a-year commercial grower and author of *A Garlic Testament: Seasons on a Small New Mexico Farm* (1992), goes on to say, "You can grow even fair garlic or even rather cosmetically inferior garlic, and people will still compliment you for your pains, more so than perhaps for any other vegetable." The reason, he explains, is the world of difference between fresh garlic and supermarket garlic. Once you taste that difference, the "stinking rose" may leapfrog to the top of your plant list.

This isn't to say garlic doesn't have its detractors, as John Harrington observed in *English Doctor* (1609).

*Sith Garlicke then hath power
to save from death,*

*Beare with it though it makes
unsavory breath;*

*And scorne not Garlicke,
like to some that think,*

*It only makes men winkle,
and drinke, and stinke.*

But with garlic, there is far more to like than dislike, both in the garden and in the kitchen. It is easy to grow, although it requires a long season, and remarkably productive. Under good conditions, 1 pound of cloves will produce 10 pounds of bulbs. In the kitchen—well, as one French chef wrote, "It is not really an exaggeration to say that peace and happiness begin . . . where garlic is used in cooking."

Rather than hollow leaves like the onion's, garlic has solid, thin bladelike leaves, between 1 and 2 feet long; underground, it produces a rounded sheathed bulb, or head, that is divided into cloves. One of the most hardy members of the *Allium* species, it can be grown in USDA Zone 2 and warmer. Like some of its cousins, garlic is sensitive to day-night lengths (see the discussion of photoperiodism under "Weather & Day-Length Considerations" on page 99) and to temperature, wanting short, cool days in the beginning, when it is producing foliage, and long, warm days to produce sizable bulbs. Fall-planted garlic takes about 8 months to mature; in mild regions, garlic begun in January or February can be harvested in late summer or early autumn.

DECIDING WHAT TO GROW

Nearly all garlic reproduction is vegetative, meaning that plants are reproduced by dividing and replanting the bulbs. In the past decade, scientists have discovered how to produce garlic seeds, but they are not widely available. Some plants produce flowers, but they are usually sterile, while others have lost the ability to flower altogether. Each garlic is a clone, an exact copy, of its parent. That does not mean that a garlic clove is a garlic clove is a garlic clove, however. There are several hundred garlic landraces, or ancient clones, each with its own flavor, color, and shape. Exactly when and how they developed is yet to be discovered, a horticultural how-did-they-do-it.

A CLOVE (OR MORE) A DAY

While few plants have the medicinal effects alleged by early physicians and herbalists, garlic may be an exception. Granted, it won't "cureth the bite of venemous things," as 16th-century gardener Thomas Hill believed, but preliminary studies by American researchers indicate that the ancients were on to something. Among the early findings are that garlic

- Lowers the risk of stomach cancers.

- Reduces harmful LDL cholesterol and triglycerides.

- Lowers blood pressure.

- Reduces blood clotting.

- Protects cells against industrial pollutants, such as heavy metals.

Better still, health-conscious gardeners don't have to smell like the "stinking rose" they consume: Cooked and deodorized garlic appear to be more effective than fresh garlic.

Sorting out different garlics isn't easy, but for gardeners, a good general distinction is between softneck and hardneck types. (Researchers at the University of Wisconsin have discovered that in cold climates, softneck garlics "become" hardnecks after several years. Why this happens is not yet understood.) Softnecks (*A. sativum*, Sativum group), which include silverskin and artichoke garlics, are the types most often found at the supermarket. Also called common garlics, they are widely adapted, have pliable stems, and store well. Hardnecks, or top-setting, garlics (*A. sativum*, Ophioscorodon group) have a stiff central stem that twists and curls at the top. They're divided into purple-striped, porcelain, and rocambole types. While more cold-hardy than softnecks are, they store less well.

If you purchase generic garlic, you can examine the bulb to see what you have. Hardneck bulbs have a woody stem encircled by a single layer of cloves; softnecks lack a woody stem, and their cloves are overlapped, like artichoke scales. For fresh use, 24 plants should be enough for a family of four; if you want to preserve, increase the planting.

SITE & SOIL

Garlic likes what other members of the onion family like, only more of it: full sun and deeply dug, light, organically rich soil that drains well while retaining moisture. While this herb will tolerate a wide pH range (5.0 to 8.0), slightly acid soil (6.2 to 6.8) is best. Begin in a weed-free location: Because garlics have grasslike tops rather than large leaves, they don't shade the soil as squash or cucumbers do, and plants can be easily overtaken by weeds. If your garden remains soppy after a rainfall or if the soil is compacted, grow garlic in a raised bed.

Garlic is typically direct-planted, although in cold regions, it can be started indoors 4 or 5 weeks before setting out in early spring or late fall (See *Onion* on page 313 for specifics.) Most gardeners plant outdoors in autumn, about 6 weeks before the soil freezes. Planting in spring will yield fewer and smaller bulbs, or "rounds," meaning bulbs that aren't segmented. You can scatter plants throughout the garden, interplanting with other crops, but because garlic takes so long to mature, grouping plants in a single area reduces the chances of unwittingly spading into dormant bulbs.

The combination of somewhat scraggly foliage, an extremely long growing season, and the need for

Garlic braid and harvested cloves

plants to die back before harvesting means that garlic isn't a great choice for flower gardens. It does do well in deep containers, however. Choose one with good bottom drainage, and fill with enriched potting soil. Water frequently, and feed every 3 weeks with manure or compost tea.

HOW TO GROW

Garlic is grown from cloves rather than from seeds. Don't be tempted to plant garlic from the supermarket produce department. It may carry diseases or have been treated to prevent sprouting. Instead, purchase garlic from a local nursery or mail-order supplier. After harvesting your first crop, save some of the best cloves for replanting. Garlic strains adapt to local conditions over time, so in 5 or 6 years, your

---

READY-TO-USE GARLIC

A convenient way to store garlic is to seal peeled cloves in a glass container filled with olive oil. Be *absolutely* sure to keep the jar refrigerated: Potentially lethal bacteria from garlic can thrive in oil that is warmer than 50°F.

---

selection should be nicely in tune with your garden's location.

Plant only the largest cloves from the bulb—if they haven't been treated, you can use the smaller ones in the kitchen—and discard any cloves that are pitted or touched with blue-green, signs that the bulb is infected with mold. To plant, set unpeeled cloves, pointed end up, 2 inches deep, spaced 5 inches apart (3 inches deep and 10 inches apart for elephant garlic). Top-dress the planting area with compost, and mulch to retain moisture and discourage weeds. Fall-planted garlic should be mulched a second time after the ground freezes to protect the plants from the cold and prevent them from heaving. Pull back the mulch in spring to allow the sun to warm the soil, then remulch when the temperatures have warmed and new growth begins.

Garlic needs an even supply of water, 1 inch per week, to produce good-size bulbs. Cease watering once the plant foliage begins to yellow or fall over. If your soil is rich in organic matter, you may not need to fertilize, but spraying plants one or two times with liquid seaweed extract or compost tea in spring will help ensure they produce large bulbs. Cut back any flower stalks to keep all the plant's energy directed toward developing bulbs.

POTENTIAL PROBLEMS

More troubled by lack of water and weeds than by diseases or insects, garlic should not be grown where it or other members of the onion family grew the previous 2 or 3 years. (For potential problems, see *Onion* on page 313.)

HARVESTING

You can harvest and use garlic leaves as you would chives. (Garlic leaves have a delightful, mild garlic flavor but are stronger-tasting than chives. Chop them on garlic bread, or add them to stir-fries, soups, or pasta dishes.) Begin cutting as soon as they are large enough to use. Cut entire leaves, but don't remove more than ¼ of any plant's foliage, or you'll compromise bulb size. If you find yourself using lots of leaves, consider planting a separate, permanent patch of garlic for leaf production only. Locate it in an out-of-the-way spot, where you won't accidentally disturb the plants when they are dormant. The plants will gradually form a clump that returns each year. Plants grown in this manner will have small cloves.

Bulbs are ready to begin harvesting when three-quarters of the tops have yellowed. Dig one or two plants to start. If their bulbs aren't well segmented and the cloves easy to separate, your crop needs more time in the ground. If garlics haven't begun to wither by autumn, root-prune by slicing under the plant on one side with a spade, keeping in mind that this treatment may shorten the bulbs' storage life. (If you want to braid garlic, harvest while the leaves are still semi-green and pliable.) Dig carefully: Bulbs that are bruised rot quickly when stored. Garlic that must be harvested but still has green tops will not store well and should be used straightaway.

Like onions, garlic must be cured before it can

be stored. Spread bulbs, with tops and roots attached, in a single layer on a screen or some other surface (or tie into bundles and hang) in a very warm, dry, airy location that is out of the sun. After 2 or 3 weeks, when the bulbs are completely dry—the wrappers should be paperlike—remove excess dirt, roots, and tops, leaving 1 inch of stem, and store whole bulbs in mesh bags in a dry, cool (40° to 50°F) location. Immediately use any bulb that sprouts. Save a few large bulbs from your most vigorous and healthy plants for replanting. If you live in a warm area, refrigerate bulbs for 2 weeks before planting.

Garlic can be propagated either from the under-

GARLIC TYPES AND TERMS

There are two general kinds of garlic, hardneck and softneck; each is divided into several types.

Silverskins. Softneck. Also known as Italian garlics, silverskins typically have all-white wrappers, between 10 and 20 pinkish cloves per head. They are the favorite of braiders and store better than other types—6 months and longer. Late to mature, they need mild winters and long growing seasons. Look for 'Mild French', 'Silverwhite', 'Silverskin', 'Burgundy', 'Rose du Var', and 'Locati'.

Artichokes. Softneck. Also known as "Italian Red" garlics, although most are neither from Italy nor red. Noted for their overall vigor, most produce large bulbs (8 to 20 cloves) encased in off-white or purple-blotched wrappers. Artichokes store well and are the easiest garlic to cultivate. 'California Early' and 'Early Red Italian' are early types; 'California Late' and 'Inchelium Red' are midseason strains; and 'Mucdi', an import from the Republic of Georgia, is a late-season garlic.

Purple-Striped. Hardneck. These are garlics that live up to their name, having heads and cloves (8 to 12 per bulb) marked with purple lines, stripes, and marbling. Popular types include 'Chesnok Red', 'Persian Star', 'Red

Rezan', 'Brown Tempest', and 'Metechi'.

Porcelain. Hardneck. Not widely known in the U.S., porcelains have smooth white bulb wrappers, three to six fat, purple-streaked cloves per bulb and store well. Names include 'Leningrad' and 'Romanian Red'.

Rocambole. Hardneck. Rocamboles have distinctive flower stalks that have tight loops at the top and produce off-white aerial bulbils. Heads, encased in blotchy purple wrappers, average between 6 and 10 plump, brownish, easy-to-peel cloves. Rocambole has become the favorite of many cooks because of its full-bodied flavor, but it stores less well than do softneck types. Early types are 'Purple Rocambole' and 'French Rocambole'; midseason choices include 'Spanish Roja' and 'German Red'; 'Carpathian' and 'Killarney Red' are late-maturing rocamboles.

Elephant. Also called great-headed garlic (*A. ampeloprasum*, Ampeloprasum group), elephant garlic is actually a different species from other garlics, closely related to the leek. It produces extra-large white bulbs—close to 1 pound given ideal conditions—and has a modestly pungent flavor, mild enough to use raw in salads. Considerably less hardy than other garlics are, it is not a good choice for overwintering in very cold regions.

ground bulbs or from the top-setting bulbils. Most gardeners prefer the bulbs, because the smaller bulbils can take 2 years to produce good-size bulbs. After curing, store bulbs for replanting in a cool (35° to 40°F), dark location.

SPECIAL NOTES

Garlic, like other members of the onion family, is reputed to keep insects and fungal diseases at bay. While the jury is still out on garlic sprays, you may be able to ward off some problems by growing clumps of garlic throughout your garden.

GARLIC CHIVE. See *Chive*

GLOBE ARTICHOKE

Cynara scolymus. Sunflower family, Asteraceae.
Perennial also grown as an annual.

○ ❋ ♣ ▜

Globe artichokes give hollandaise sauce a reason for being—and vice versa. "The green and gold of my delight," the turn-of-the-century American journalist Thomas Daly called this aristocratic combination. Not a bad fate for a thistlelike plant from the Mediterranean, a handsome but prickly perennial with deeply cut silver-green leaves that grows 4 or 5 feet tall and nearly as wide.

When the artichoke shows its fragrant flowers—"a tufte of blewish purple thrummes or threds, under which growe the seed, wrapped in a great deal of dounie substance," wrote a keen-eyed 17th-century admirer—its culinary value has passed. But not the plant's other virtues, according to early English herbalists who touted its ability to "procure bodily lust" and calm the liver, qualities that surely increased its planting among the fun-loving.

The culinary value of the globe artichoke lies not in its seeds, flowers, fruits, stalks, leaves, or roots, but in its flower bud—in the bracts, or modified leaves, that grow at the base of flowers along with the tender heart, or choke, they surround. The large, brilliant red "petals" of the poinsettia are actually bracts; in the artichoke, the bracts are the fleshy scalelike parts, sometimes tinged with purple, that form what looks like a pinecone.

Globe artichokes do best in damp, mild coastal regions, USDA Zones 8 to 9, although they can be

Globe artichoke flower

grown as annual plants as far north as Zone 4 if begun early enough indoors. Dramatic, lovely-looking plants, they make fine additions to the ornamental garden. They can also be grown in a container, at least 12 inches wide and 18 inches deep, with good bottom drainage. Fill with enriched potting soil, water frequently, and feed every 2 weeks with compost tea.

DECIDING WHAT TO GROW

Gardeners who live in a region where globe artichokes are at home, such as northern California, can pick among the commonly available cultivars, fewer than 10 in all. 'Green Globe', a longtime commercial favorite, has been replaced by 'Green Globe Improved', the standard choice for gardeners with long, mild growing seasons. Where conditions aren't so ideal, look for cultivars that mature more quickly, such as the elongated, purple-budded 'Violetto'. 'Texas Hill' is a low-chill cultivar adapted for the conditions of the Southwest: high heat,

Globe artichoke 'Green Globe'

alkaline soil, and warm winters. The 3-foot 'Imperial Star', a University of California cultivar, was bred to be grown as an annual and is the best bet for short-season gardeners. 'Grande Beurre', a French cultivar, is also recommended for regions with brief summers.

If your growing season is long and mild—most cultivars take at least 125 days—eight plants should be enough for fresh table use for a family of four. If you want to preserve, increase the planting. Artichokes take a good deal of room. If you haven't grown them before, you may want to experiment with two or three plants before you give over all the space that eight plants require.

SITE & SOIL

Except in regions where the mercury regularly hits 80°F and protection is welcome, globe artichokes need full sun. Choose a site where the plants won't shade smaller crops and where, if you're growing them as perennials, they won't be disturbed.

For the best results, grow artichokes in rich, well-drained soil, deeply dug and heavily amended with organic matter that is rich in phosphorus and potassium. The soil's pH should be slightly acid. Because plants are wide as well as tall, leave at least 3 feet between plants, in rows at least 5 or 6 feet apart.

HOW TO GROW

Although its best to begin globe aartichokes from divisions, it's possible to grow them from seeds. Start seeds indoors, 8 to 12 weeks before the last spring frost (before sowing, soak seeds in water for 8 hours, then refrigerate them in a jar filled with slightly moist sand for 2 weeks to promote early flowering). Sow ½ inch deep in 3-inch containers filled with a soilless mix, and set in a warm location; seeds should germinate in about 12 days. Once the seeds sprout, move the plants into bright light. Fertilize with a half-strength solution of fish emulsion or other liquid fertilizer every 10 days. When the first true leaves form, thin to one plant. After 1 month, transplant each seedling into a 5-inch pot.

After hardening off and the danger of frost has passed, move artichoke transplants to the garden. Set each plant so that its crown is just above the soil surface. When they are growing as annuals in cold regions, set plants deeper and cover with straw mulch and floating row covers until the air temperatures warm. Water well.

Feed plants monthly with fish emulsion or manure tea. Keep plants mulched and well supplied with water during the growing season—at least 2 inches a week—especially when temperatures rise above 75°F.

In late autumn in mild regions, cut plants being grown as perennials to the ground, and mulch. In areas where the ground freezes only lightly, cut plants back to 1 foot, hill with soil, and mulch the hill with manure and straw. Gardeners in extremely cold regions should treat artichokes as an annual crop, starting new plants early each spring. If you want to try to overwinter plants, cut them back to 5 inches above the crown. Dig the roots, removing any soil, and store in mesh bags in a cool, damp frost-free place. Plant roots in pots indoors in spring, 1 month before the frost-free date. Transplant outside after the danger of frost has passed.

Although they are perennials, most artichoke plants lose vigor after 4 or 5 years. When that occurs, remove them and replant.

POTENTIAL PROBLEMS

Globe artichokes grown in the home garden are little bothered by diseases. Keeping plants vigorous by providing sufficient moisture, nutrients, air circulation, and light is the best defense against disease pathogens. Botrytis, or neck rot, a fungal disease that sometimes strikes in humid regions, forms a gray mold on leaves. It cannot be cured; remove and destroy infected plants.

Plants are occasionally troubled by aphids,

which are discouraged by installing floating row covers in spring. To control snails and slugs, handpick or use beer traps. (For more specific remedies, see "Controlling Common Pests" on page 162.)

HARVESTING

Without the hollandaise, artichokes are low in calories; they contain fair amounts of vitamin C, folacin, and magnesium and a lesser amount of potassium. Harvest buds while the bracts are still green and tight, before they begin to open or separate. Use a knife to harvest, leaving 2 or 3 inches of stem attached to the choke. The central bud is usually ready to harvest first, followed by the smaller buds that form on side shoots. After harvesting the central stem, cut it back to 1 foot to encourage side shoots. To store artichokes, seal in plastic bags and refrigerate.

Globe artichokes, which cross-pollinate with enthusiasm, rarely come true from seeds and are best propagated from divisions. Artichoke seeds remain viable for 6 years.

GREEK OREGANO. See *Oregano*
GREEN PEPPER. See *Pepper*

GREENS

Leaf lettuce, spinach, beet greens, collards, and kale are just the tip of the iceberg when it comes to the crops collectively referred to as greens, all of which are grown for their leaves or leafy stems. Plenty of crops, traditionally referred to as potherbs, can be added to soups and stews or simply steamed or boiled and served as cooked vegetables. And in recent years, gardeners have discovered there's much more to salads than 'Iceberg' lettuce—arugula and radicchio are just a couple of the exotic-sounding ingredients that are common salad fare today, and mesclun, a mix of young greens, has become *de rigueur* in upscale restaurants. Herbs such as chervil, parsley, and cilantro can also be used as salad greens. Even some weeds can be added to the salad bowl. (See "Culinary Control" on page 133 for a list.)

But while cooks divide greens into potherbs and salad greens, gardeners divide them into cool- and warm-weather crops, a distinction that summarizes when and how they are grown.

Green orach with pansies

COOL-WEATHER GREENS

Typical cool-weather greens—spinach, arugula, and kale are three—thrive in cool conditions and are grown as spring and fall crops in most regions. In areas with cool summers, such as the Northwest, they can be grown from spring to fall. In the South, cool-weather greens are often planted in fall and grown through the winter.

Cool-weather greens are typically sown 3 or 4 weeks before the last spring frost. They require fertile soil, even moisture, and cool conditions for fast growth—and good flavor. Most can be planted until late spring, with crops timed to mature before summer's heat causes them to bolt, or go to seed. Fall crops can be started beginning in late summer up to about a month before the first fall frost.

The following crops can be grown as cool-weather greens and have individual entries in this encyclopedia: Arugula, Beet, Bok Choy, Celtuce*, Corn Salad*, Endive and Escarole, Garden Cress, Kale, Lettuce*, Mesclun*, Miner's Lettuce, Mizuna*, Mustard, Orach*, Radicchio, Spinach, Swiss Chard*, Upland Cress, Turnip. Crops marked with an asterisk (*) can also be grown in warm weather with careful selection of cultivars and/or special attention to growing conditions.

WARM-WEATHER GREENS

For filling the salad bowl or soup pot in summer, look to warm-weather greens—Malabar Spinach,

New Zealand Spinach, and Purslane have individual entries in this encyclopedia. In general, these crops thrive in warm weather and fertile soil that is kept evenly moist. But they aren't the only option for warm-weather growing. Many cool-weather crops will also tolerate warm temperatures in constantly moist, rich soil; providing shade during the hottest part of the day also helps them grow despite warm summer temperatures. For summer crops of cool-weather greens, plant heat-tolerant cultivars.

GROUND CHERRY. See *Tomatillo*
HAKUSAI CABBAGE. See *Chinese Cabbage*

PERENNIAL GREENS

Most greens are grown as annuals, but perennial good King Henry (*Cheno-podium bonus-henricus*) will produce crops of fleshy, arrow-shaped, dark green leaves for years with minimal attention. The spring shoots can also be harvested and eaten like asparagus. As a member of the goosefoot family, it is related to spinach, thus the common names wild and perennial spinach. It has also been called allgood, fat-hen, goosefoot, and mercury.

For the best results, grow good King Henry in full sun in deep, evenly moist soil that is rich in organic matter. Plants can also tolerate average to poor soil and partial shade. Select a site away from the vegetable garden, or at least to one side of it, to avoid disturbing this permanent crop accidentally when tending more conventional annual crops.

In spring, sow seeds 1 foot apart, cover lightly with compost, and keep them moist until germination. Clumps will eventually be a foot or more in diameter. Harvest in spring, beginning in the second year from seeds, by cutting the young leaves.

HAMBURG PARSLEY

Petroselinum crispum, Tuberosum group. Carrot family, Apiaceae. Biennial grown as an annual.

○ ◑ ❄

Hamburg parsley—also known as turnip-rooted or large-rooted parsley—is grown much the same way as its better-known relative, leafy parsley, but the favored part of this plant is its tender, off-white root. The roots taste like a mild blend of celery and parsley and vary in size according to cultivar, from a few inches to almost a foot long. Ready to harvest 2 or 3 months after outdoor sowing, the root can be cooked like any root vegetable, in soups and stews or on its own. The leaves, resembling those of flat-leaved parsley in appearance and flavor, are also edible. Mixed in stews and soups, according to a 19th-century source, "they impart a pleasant, aromatic taste and odor."

Although Hamburg parsley is a biennial, only the first year's growth has any culinary value. While it is very hardy, to about USDA Zone 3, the plant goes to seed in its second spring, causing the root to become tough and unpalatable. For practical purposes, unless you want to harvest the seeds, it is a hardy annual and must be replaced every year.

Hamburg parsley was once called Dutch parsley, so it may have been developed in that country. According to Vilmorin-Andrieux (*The Vegetable Garden*, 1885), "this plant is not one of the old-fashioned vegetables, but, like the bulbous-rooted Chervil, was taken in hand and introduced into cultivation at a comparatively recent date." It was only briefly accepted in Britain and has never become well known in North America, but it remains popular in Holland, France, Germany, and eastern Europe. Before you brag about your harvest, though, remember that all parsleys are reputed to grow better for the wicked than for the good.

DECIDING WHAT TO GROW

There are several cultivars available to home gardeners. 'Hamburg Half Long' has wedge-shaped roots, about 6 inches long; 'Hamburg Long' is 9 or 10 inches long and is more slender, the preferred shape in western Europe. 'Early Sugar' has very sweet, triangular roots, only 3 inches long, and is a good choice for heavy or shallow soils. The cultivar 'Bartowich Long' has the reputation of having the best flavor of all the Hamburg parsley cultivars.

Grow a dozen plants the first year if Hamburg parsley is unknown to you, then judge the size of future crops accordingly.

HOW TO GROW

Because the root is the harvest, the condition of the soil is especially important to growing Hamburg parsley. Soil should be loose and deeply dug, especially if you choose a long-rooted type. Only moderate fertility is needed: Too much nitrogen can cause excessive top growth and root branching. Plants, which need substantial amounts of water, do best in moderately acid (pH 6.2 to 6.8) soil enriched with compost or another organic additive. Best grown in the vegetable garden in full sun or partial shade, where harvesting won't disturb neighboring plants, Hamburg parsley doesn't make a particularly good container crop. If you do attempt to grow it on your patio or deck, use a large container, one at least 18 inches deep.

In spring, around the time of the last expected frost, sow the seeds ¼ inch deep directly where they will grow in rows 10 to 12 inches apart. In warm regions, Hamburg parsley can be planted in autumn for a spring harvest. To speed germination, soak seeds overnight and keep them watered after planting. Thin seedlings to 4 inches. Or sow seeds indoors, 4 to 6 weeks before the frost-free date, in individual pots. Transfer hardened-off plants to the garden while they are still small, before their roots become crowded. Keep young plants well watered, and mulch to retain moisture and suppress weeds. Once plants are established, little care is required.

Parsleyworms, which can be handpicked, are about the only problem that bothers Hamburg parsley, but since they are the larvae of swallowtail butterflies, you may want to leave them undisturbed—or move them to other carrot-family plants, such as Queen Anne's lace. Disturbance during transplanting and hot weather can cause plants to bolt prematurely.

HARVESTING

It takes about 90 days to form a good-size fleshy root. Roots can be dug as soon as they are large enough to use, but they taste best after the first fall frosts. In cold regions, dig all roots before the ground freezes. Hamburg parsley can be dug all winter if the soil does not freeze (mulch plants heavily to extend the harvest in the North). Greens can be harvested throughout the growing season, but don't remove more than two or three stems from any plant.

Remove the tops of harvested roots, and clean off excess dirt. For short-term storage, seal in plastic bags and refrigerate. Hamburg parsley also can be stored in damp sand for up to 3 months in a cold (32° to 40°F) location or root cellar.

Because Hamburg parsley is a biennial and flowers in its second season, saving seeds is difficult. Gardeners in cold climates must dig and overwinter plants, then replant them in the spring; in frost-free regions, carry plants over to a second year. All parsley cultivars, including leaf types, will cross-pollinate with one another. To save seeds that will breed true, keep crops well separated or plant only one cultivar. Seeds are viable for 3 years; store in airtight containers in a dark, cool location.

HARDY MARJORAM. See *Marjoram*
HEADING CHICORY. See *Chicory*
HOLLAND GREENS. See *Turnip*

HORSERADISH

Armoracia rusticana. Mustard family, Brassicaceae. Perennial.

○ ◑ ☀ ❄ ▮

The word *horse* in this plant name means "coarse," and indeed, this member of the mustard family is coarse in almost every way. A hardy perennial that can be grown in USDA Zone 3 and warmer, horseradish forms foot-tall clumps of rough, bright green, lobed or toothed, foot-long leaves topped by clusters of small white flowers, each with four petals. Grown for its thick, pungent roots, horseradish can overpower your sinuses, your kitchen, and even your garden. "It is a most pernicious weed where it intrudes, on account of the multitude of vital germs with which its root stock abounds, and by which it is rendered a sort of vegetable polypus, every inch of it being capable of developing a growing bud," according to a 1874 British encyclopedia. On the positive side, horseradish is a plant that you can count on: Once planted, it will thrive despite neglect.

Horseradish, a native of Europe and Asia, was a common roadside plant in this country by the early 1800s, but it seems to have only one role in modern

Horseradish

America—the roots are ground and added to vine-gar to make a condiment for roast beef. Despite that limited use, the plant has a rich medicinal history, extending back to classical times. In addition to mustard oil (allylisothiocyanate) and vitamin C, the roots contain an antibiotic substance. Ground roots mixed with water were once used to make a poultice to generate heat and relieve pain. The roots were also used as a diuretic and to reduce fevers. Today, the average amount of horseradish used per person a year is less than 2 ounces; more than half the American demand can be satisfied by just 1,000 acres of western Illinois farmland, where conditions suit it perfectly. The roots from one plant will make about a half-pint of sauce, so plant accordingly. Horseradish cultivars exist—'Bohemian' and 'Maliner Kren' are the best known—but most seed companies sell only the species, which they list as "horseradish."

Keep horseradish away from the vegetable gar-den. The roots spread vigorously, and any small piece left in the soil will grow into a new plant.

Tilling a clump may leave you with horseradish from one end of the garden to the other. Plant this crop in a corner of the yard where it can grow undis-turbed. Horseradish also can be grown in contain-ers, one plant in a deep pot at least 18 inches wide, or pots can also be sunk in the soil, as with mint, to control the plants' spread. Horseradish is not attrac-tive enough to be included in ornamental plantings.

HOW TO GROW

American vegetable authority Fearing Burr observed in 1865 that few crops were as neglected as horseradish, which was usually "planted in some obscure corner of the garden." And for good reason: Horseradish will grow almost anywhere, sun or shade, wet soil or dry, poor or rich. Only in deep shade or constant wetness is it likely to suffer. Deep soil, rich in organic matter and free of rocks and other obstructions, produces the straightest, fattest roots and makes harvesting easier. Too much nitro-gen fertilizer can cause excessive top growth and root branching.

Horseradish is grown from roots or plants, rather than from seeds, and roots are generally planted in spring, although fall planting is also suc-cessful. Prepare the soil at least a foot deep before setting plants or roots 1 foot apart. Water thorough-ly. After that, plants can be left to their own devices, although mulching, which will help retain moisture and suppress weeds, is a good idea.

To propagate horseradish, divide the crowns or take 6- to 8-inch-long root cuttings that are ½ inch wide. Make sure each cutting has at least one bud, and mark the top (the end nearest the soil surface) of each cutting. Then remove any side roots. Plant the cuttings right side up (root cuttings planted upside down won't grow), and water. In regions with extremely long growing seasons (at least 150 days), horseradish can be harvested in its first year; other-wise, begin harvesting in the second year.

Few pests or diseases trouble horseradish. The roots can become infected with fungal diseases, causing the roots to rot. Plant healthy roots that show no signs of rot in a site with well-prepared, well-drained soil. If a planting becomes infected, remove and destroy it. Replant with disease-free stock in a location where horseradish has not been grown within 4 years. Flea beetles also attack the foliage in early spring, but healthy plants quickly outgrow the damage.

HARVESTING

Dig horseradish roots anytime from midsummer onward, although yields will be greatest and the flavor best if the harvest is delayed until after the first fall frosts. The roots, which can grow as long as 2 feet, have brittle offshoots that break off in harvest; when left in the soil, these will grow into new plants. Taking time to loosen the soil and remove the side shoots reduces breakage and helps control the spread of the plants.

After harvest, trim off the plant tops and the side roots, and scrub. Grate only as much as you'll use in the month so that it will remain pungent and fresh-tasting in the refrigerator. Whole roots will retain their flavor for up to 3 months if stored in damp sand in a cool location or in perforated plastic bags in the refrigerator. Keep roots out of bright light, or they will turn green. In areas where the ground does not freeze deeply, store roots in the garden by mulching plants with straw in fall. Dig roots as needed throughout winter.

SPECIAL NOTES

Be careful when grating horseradish: It irritates the eyes even more than chopped onions. Ruth Stout, author of *The Ruth Stout No-Work Garden Book*, wrote, "I would rather do almost anything than grate it, so I don't grow it." Keep in mind, too, that large amounts of horseradish can cause inflammations of the lining of the throat and stomach.

HUSK TOMATO. See *Tomatillo*
ITALIAN DANDELION. See *Chicory*
ITALIAN OREGANO. See *Oregano*
JALAPEÑO. See *Pepper*
JAPANESE PARSLEY. See *Parsley*

JERUSALEM ARTICHOKE

Helianthus tuberosus. Sunflower family, Asteraceae.
Perennial.

○ ✳ ❄ ❀

The Jerusalem artichoke is an example of names imposed upon plants by people who have no knowledge of them, John Gerard grumbled in his 1633 herbal. "For this plant hath not similitude in leafe, stalke, root or manner of growing with an Artichok . . . neither came it from Jerusalem." Gerard was cor-

Jerusalem artichoke

rect. *Helianthus tuberosus*, Jerusalem artichoke, is a North American plant, a relative of the sunflower that was carried to Europe by the French explorer Samuel de Champlain. Its edible part, its tuber, must be dug. No wonder John Parkinson, official botanist to King Charles I, called it "Potatoes of Canada."

Jerusalem artichokes grow in USDA Zones 2 to 9, although they produce smaller yields in extremely warm regions. Rangy, with broad, coarse leaves, and tall—they can reach 12 feet or more—they're topped by 3-inch, all-yellow daisylike flowers that bloom in late summer.

DECIDING WHAT TO GROW

Ten plants should yield enough tubers for a family of four, although yields vary greatly, depending on the cultivar grown. Many gardeners may argue that "cultivar" is too fine a term for the Jerusalem artichoke, which has tended to be a plant exchanged among neighbors and friends rather than one pur-

*Jerusalem artichoke tubers 'Red Fuseau',
'Golden Nugget', ' Garnet', and
'French Mammoth White'*

chased from a seed house or nursery. In most catalogs, it is listed simply as "Jerusalem Artichoke." The generic plant produces knobby brown-skinned, white-fleshed tubers, about 3 inches long, 1½ inches wide, similar to fingerling potatoes.

In fact, there are nearly 100 named cultivars available, mostly from nonprofit organizations like Seed Savers Exchange, including a large number of red-skinned tubers ('Red Fuseau', 'Garnet', 'Boston Red', 'Gurney's Red', 'Dave's Shrine'), as well as pink, purple, rose, and gold types, all with white flesh. 'Street Survivor' is adapted to heat and drought; 'French Mammoth White' produces a cluster of knobby tubers under the plant, which makes them easy to find; 'Clearwater' sends out long tubers with few knobs; medium-size 'Sugar Ball' is another near-knob-free cultivar; 'Skorospelka', collected in Russia by the USDA, yields large crops of fat, knobby tubers concentrated under the plant.

SITE & SOIL

Sunchoke, another common name for the Jerusalem artichoke, suggests the primary requirement for this vegetable, although partial shade in the afternoon is desirable in extremely hot locations. Most soils will do—this is a common roadside plant—but moderately rich loam will produce larger tubers.

Be sure to locate plants on the north edge of the garden, where they won't shade smaller crops and can be left year after year. They are fine additions to the back of a large ornamental border but do not make good container plants. Like a bad habit, Jerusalem artichokes are easy to start and hard to get rid of. As well as being a perennial species, they spread easily. The best bet is to plant them in a bed of their own, separate from your vegetable and herb garden. If you find yourself with too many plants in the spring, cut them back with a hoe.

HOW TO GROW

Since most seeds produced by Jerusalem artichoke plants are sterile, begin new plants from tubers—make sure each piece has at least two eyes. Plant in spring, after the last expected frost, or in autumn, a month before the average first-frost date. Set tubers 3 to 5 inches deep, at least 18 inches apart, and mulch with straw or another organic material to retain moisture and suppress weeds.

Keep plants weed-free, and provide extra water during periods of drought; tubers planted in organically rich soil need no additional fertilizer during the growing season. Top-dress plants in spring with compost or well-rotted manure at least every 2 years.

Jerusalem artichokes have no serious disease or pest problems.

HARVESTING

Although frequently likened to potatoes, Jerusalem artichokes contain no starch; instead, their carbohydrates are stored in the form of inulin, which is converted in the digestive tract to fructose, not glucose, making this vegetable a good choice for diabetics as well as for people who must reduce starch and calories in their diet. The tubers can be steamed, parboiled, braised, stir-fried, or eaten raw, sliced thinly in salads, or served as an appetizer.

Be patient when harvesting Jerusalem artichokes: Their nutty flavor improves tenfold after the first killing frost. Wait until the plant stalks brown, then cut down the entire plant and use a spading fork to dig the edible tubers. No matter how many tubers you collect, a few will elude your fork and produce next year's crop.

The ground is the perfect storage place for this tender-skinned crop, so remove only as many tubers as you can use. Mulch the bed heavily, then harvest additional tubers as needed. Seal in plastic bags for refrigerator storage.

KALE

Brassica oleracea, Acephala group. Mustard family, Brassicaceae. Biennial grown as an annual.

○ ◑ ✳ ❄ ❀ ▮

A traditional Scottish story tells of a young doctor looking for a town in which to open his practice. "If you see kale growing in the gardens, move along," he was advised. "They won't be needing your services there." Kale may not be a complete substitute for health insurance, but it is one of our most nutritious cultivated greens. It has slightly less iron than spinach does but three times the vitamin C, more vitamin A, more B vitamins, and more calcium, potassium, and protein.

Its garden history is equally impressive. Probably the first cultivated form of *Brassica oleracea*, kale was grown by the Greeks and Romans, then traveled to northern Europe and Britain and, in the 16th century, on to North America with the French explorer Jacques Cartier. Over time, cabbages replaced kale in garden and culinary popularity—the botanical name for kale means "cabbage without a head"—but kale has hung on, especially in the South, where it has acclimatized itself to warm weather and become a home-garden staple.

Kale can be grown as an annual in all but the warmest USDA Zones. The hardiest cultivars, if given some protection, can be harvested all winter in southern regions. Given its druthers, though, kale prefers cool weather, and its flavor is sweetened when the leaves are touched by frost.

DECIDING WHAT TO GROW

Botanically, kales are identical to collards, although devotees of these two crops would claim there is a world of differences between them. There are also differences among kales. One type, known as Scotch kale, or borecole, has curled leaves that are reminiscent of parsley. Siberian kale, in contrast, has smooth leaves, often with frilled or feathered margins. Both open-pollinated and hybrid cultivars are available; hybrids tend to mature more quickly and are marginally more productive.

Finally, there is a handful of ornamental kales. Although these cultivars are edible—and they have become a standard restaurant garnish—their preeminent value is their ability to add intensely colored and interestingly formed foliage to the flower garden or a container planting. While considerable overlap exists, ornamental kales are sometimes

Heirloom kale

SEA KALE

Don't confuse kale with sea kale, *Crambe maritima*, a hardy perennial (USDA Zone 4 and warmer) that is grown for its shoots rather than for its leaves. Cultivated much as asparagus is, sea kale can be started from seeds or divisions and is harvested beginning in its third year. Cover plants in late winter with a basket or pot to blanch. Cut shoots when they are large enough to use, about 6 inches.

divided into flowering cabbages, which have a rounded form and leaves, and flowering kales, which are characterized by fringed or feathery leaves.

Twenty plants will provide enough kale for a family of four.

SITE & SOIL

Kale likes full sun in the early spring; later in the season, especially in areas with hot summers, it benefits from partial shade. Like cabbage, broccoli, and other mustard-family members, it does best in slightly acid (pH 6.5 to 6.8), humus-rich soil, but it is more forgiving about growing conditions than are most other family members. Be moderate: Too much fertilizer, especially too much nitrogen, will produce super-succulent plants that are more susceptible to insects and disease. Don't be moderate about moisture, however. Kales must have an average of 1 inch of water a week; if plants are not adequately irrigated, their leaves will become fibrous and off-flavored.

Ornamental kales were meant for flowerpots and boxes, but all cultivars make good container plants. Use a container, at least 8 inches wide and 12 inches deep, with good bottom drainage, and fill with enriched potting soil. Keep well watered, and feed every 3 weeks with fish emulsion. Ornamental cultivars are wonderful additions to deck or patio, and to flower gardens, where they will remain colorful well after the first fall frosts.

Kales reach their full height in 55 to 70 days from seeds, depending on cultivar and growing conditions, and thus are good candidates for succession planting and for undercropping with vegetables that don't mature until much later in the season.

HOW TO GROW

Kale is very hardy and easy to grow, one of the really self-sufficient home-garden vegetables. For an early crop, start seeds indoors 6 to 8 weeks before the average last-frost date. Or direct-seed outdoors as soon as the soil can be worked, sowing seeds $\frac{1}{4}$ to $\frac{1}{2}$ inch deep, spaced at 4 inches. In 70°F soil, ger-

KALE CULTIVARS

Ornamental kales have become a common sight in fall flower gardens, but even conventional kale cultivars, with their frilled and curled leaves, are attractive. The following list includes both types.

'Dwarf Blue Curled Vates': 55 days; open-pollinated; small, low-growing plant with finely curled bluish green leaves; very hardy; also listed as 'Vates'.

'Dwarf Green Curled': 55 days; open-pollinated; extremely curled yellow-green leaves on small, low-growing plants; very cold-hardy; heirloom.

'Lacinato': 62 days; open-pollinated; thick, crinkled dark blue-green leaves; also called 'Black Cabbage'; heirloom.

'Red Russian'/'Russian Red': 60 days; open-pollinated; oak-leaf-shaped foliage with dark red to purple stems and leaf veins; color deepens after frost.

'Redbor': 50 days; open-pollinated; ornamental with dark mahogany-red foliage and stems; 18 to 24 inches tall.

'Siberian': 50 days; open-pollinated; frilly dark green leaves form a rosette 24 inches in diameter; very hardy.

'White on Green': 65 days; open-pollinated; ornamental with fringed green-and-white leaves; not heat-tolerant.

'Winterbor': 60 days; hybrid; curled blue-green leaves; 2 to 3 feet tall; good bolt resistance; good cold tolerance.

Peacock Series: 70 days; hybrid; ornamental; deeply cut, fringed leaves on compact plants; red and white forms available; frost-hardy.

Tokyo Series: 70 days; hybrid; ornamental; smooth, wavy-edged leaves; pink, red, and white forms available; heat-resistant.

mination takes about 5 days. Thin plants to 12 inches. About 2 weeks before the last frost—after hardening off—move plants begun inside to the garden, setting them slightly deeper than they were growing in their containers. Direct-seed fall crops of kale about 8 weeks before the average first frost. In southern gardens, sow very early in spring and again in late autumn for winter and spring harvests. To overwinter kale in mild climates, cover plants with leaves or straw when the ground freezes; remove the mulch in the spring.

Cover the seedbed or transplants with a floating row cover to suppress weeds and to prevent insects, such as flea beetles and cabbageworms, from reaching the crop. Mulch heavily to retain moisture and keep soil damp. Beginning when plants are 5 inches tall, feed every 3 weeks with fish emulsion or manure tea.

POTENTIAL PROBLEMS

Kale is much less troubled by insects and disease than are broccoli and other members of the mustard family, but it is susceptible to the same problems, including aphids, cabbageworms, cabbage loopers, and flea beetles. (See "Controlling Common Pests" on page 162 for control measures.) Keeping plants from being stressed, using floating row covers, and rotating crops regularly should prevent nearly all the problems kale is heir to.

HARVESTING

For fresh salads, begin picking kale leaves when they are 3 inches long. Use a knife, and cut each stem at the base of the plant, starting from the outside. New foliage will grow from the top of the plant. Or cut the entire plant when it reaches about 1 foot. Cool leaves immediately after harvesting by immersing them in ice water. To extend the harvest in fall, mulch plants heavily with straw or leaves. To store kale, seal in plastic bags and refrigerate.

Because kale is a biennial and normally doesn't flower until its second season, saving seeds is difficult. Gardeners in extremely cold climates must dig and overwinter plants, then replant them in the spring; in warmer regions, carry plants over to a second year. Kales cross-pollinate with each other and all other *B. oleracea* members, such as broccoli, cauliflower, and kohlrabi. To save seeds that will come true, plant only one *B. oleracea* cul-

tivar or isolate your crop. Seeds are viable for 4 years; store in airtight containers in a dark, cool location.

KNOB CELERY. See *Celeriac*

KOHLRABI

Brassica oleracea, Gongylodes group.
Mustard family, Brassicaceae.
Biennial, grown as an annual.

○ ◑ ❄ ❀

Alice B. Toklas, partner of author Gertrude Stein, cookbook author, and mother of hashish fudge, wrote that kohlrabi has "the pungency of a high-born radish bred to a low-brow cucumber." In fact, kohlrabi is a cross between a cabbage and a turnip. Young tops can be steamed and eaten as greens, but the real attraction of this plant is its cabbage-flavored swollen stem, which is often referred to as a "bulb."

Gardeners have been cultivating kohlrabi for at least 1,500 years—Charlemagne reportedly had it planted as cattle feed—yet any mention of this vegetable is met with at least a few blank stares. Certainly its pincushion look is bizarre. The swelling of the stem, the French nursery firm Vilmorin-Andrieux noted in 1885, "commences close to the surface of the ground, [and] takes the shape of an almost regular ball, the size of which in some varieties does not exceed that of an average-

Kohlrabi

sized orange, while in others it nearly equals that of a man's head." From the surface-sitting swollen stem, colored either white to pale green or purple, emerge long stems, topped with turniplike leaves.

Kohlrabi is a fast grower, ready to cut in about 8 weeks, and can be followed by—or follow—other crops. Planted as both a spring and fall crop (or winter vegetable in warm regions), it can be grown in USDA Zone 3 and warmer. Although it is oddly ornamental, kohlrabi has a deep root and doesn't thrive in containers. Make succession plantings to extend the harvest. Each plant produces one stem; for eating fresh, 24 plants are enough for a family of four. If you want to preserve, increase the planting.

HOW TO GROW

Like other *Brassica* species, kohlrabi prefers full sun and organically rich soil that drains well yet still retains moisture. A pH between 6.0 and 6.8 is best. Despite preferring cool temperatures, kohlrabi does well when the weather warms as long as plants get plenty of water. Although kohlrabi transplants fairly well, it grows so quickly that most gardeners begin outdoors. Sow seeds ½ inch deep, 3 inches apart, about 4 weeks before the frost-free date; thin to at least 6 inches to make sure plants get enough light. In 70°F soil, germination should occur in about a week. Mulch heavily to preserve moisture and suppress weeds.

Cover the seedbed or transplants with floating row covers to ward off aphids, cabbage maggots and worms, flea beetles, and other insects that trouble members of the mustard family. To keep kohlrabi growing quickly, apply a foliar spray every 3 or 4 weeks and make sure plants receive at least 1 inch of water a week.

POTENTIAL PROBLEMS

Kohlrabi is heir to all the insects and diseases that trouble cabbages and other brassicas, but most problems can be avoided by using floating row covers, keeping the soil pH above 6.2, and rotating crops each year. Stems will become woody and hot-flavored if plants don't receive enough water or if they are allowed to grow very large.

HARVESTING

Young kohlrabi leaves can be cut for greens. Harvest stems, which contain moderate amounts of vitamins C and A, calcium, and potassium, when they are young and tender, about 1½ inches in diameter, by cutting an inch or two below the soil surface. For short-term storage, seal stems in plastic bags and refrigerate. Kohlrabi can be stored for up to 3 months in a cold (32° to 40°F) location or root cellar.

Because kohlrabi is a biennial and flowers in its second season, saving seeds is difficult. Gardeners in cold climates must dig and overwinter plants, then replant them in the spring; in frost-free regions, carry plants over to a second year. Kohlrabi cultivars will cross-pollinate with each other and with all other *B. oleracea* crops. To save seeds that will breed true, keep crops well separated. Seeds are viable for 4 years; store in airtight containers in a dark, cool location.

KOHLRABI CULTIVARS

Both open-pollinated and hybrid kohlrabies are available, with white to pale green or purple "bulbs." Generally, both taste the same.

'Early Purple Vienna': 65 days; open-pollinated purple heirloom.

'Early White Vienna': 55 days; open-pollinated white to pale green dwarf heirloom cultivar.

'Giganté': 130 days; open-pollinated white to pale green Czechoslovakian heirloom with huge stems; stores well.

'Grand Duke': 50 days; hybrid pale green cultivar; good tolerance to heat and cold; AAS winner.

'Kolibri': 50 days; hybrid purple German cultivar; heat-tolerant.

'Lauko': 60 days; open-pollinated purple cultivar; hardy; good fall crop.

'Purple Danube': 50 days; hybrid purple cultivar; early.

'Waldemar': 60 days; hybrid pale green Austrian cultivar.

'Winner': 45 days; hybrid pale green early cultivar; heat-tolerant.

LAMB'S LETTUCE. See *Corn Salad*
LEAF BEET. See *Swiss Chard*
LEAF CHARD. See *"Perpetual Spinach" in Swiss Chard*
LEAF CHICORY. See *Chicory*

LEEK

Allium ampeloprasum, Porrum group. Onion family, Alliaceae. Biennial, grown as an annual.

○ ◑ ✳ ❄

The leek, another *Allium* that is overpriced in the supermarket and easy to grow in the backyard, had its 15 minutes of fame as a boutonniere in 640 A.D. According to legend, the Britons were victorious over the Saxons because they wore leeks and thus could tell friend from foe. The vegetatively deprived Saxons, "from want of such a distinguishing mark, frequently mistook each other, and dealt their fury among themselves." The leek is the emblem of Wales and is still worn on St. David's Day, March 1. (Growing Goliath-size leeks is a Welsh pastime. The current champion, the result of a twice-weekly high-nitrogen diet, weighed in at a little over 12 pounds.)

First carried to England by Roman legions, leeks quickly became a stew-pot staple, a popular cure for venomous bites, ulcers, poor eyesight, nosebleeds, headaches, drunkenness, coughs, toothaches, and several dozen other ills, as well as an enhancer of

Leek 'Giant Winter Wila'

fertility. "The Welsh, who eat them much, are observ'd to be very fruitful," John Evelyn, the 17th-century English diarist and garden writer, observed.

Leeks are grown for their enlarged stems as scallions are. Stem size varies, from 1 to 3 inches thick, 6 to 12 inches long. Topping the stem is a fanlike sheath of long, flat, blue-green or yellow-green leaves. Many cultivars are extremely hardy and will tolerate below-freezing temperatures; they can be grown in USDA Zone 2 and warmer.

In order to make them more tender and mild-flavored, leeks are blanched, or "made white," in the garden by drawing soil around their stems. While not unattractive, their use in ornamental beds is limited, and they are not well suited to container growing.

DECIDING WHAT TO GROW

There are two groups of leeks: nonhardy cultivars like 'Titan' that mature in about 70 to 90 days; and hardy types, such as 'American Flag', that take 100 days or more to reach full size. Nonhardy cultivars, which are harvested in summer and fall, have a milder flavor, don't store well, and tend to be tall and thin with lighter green leaves. Hardy leeks can be stored for many weeks; many hardy cultivars have blue-green foliage, a characteristic associated with cold tolerance.

Leeks can be interplanted with quick-maturing crops, such as lettuce and radishes. Nonhardy cultivars, because they mature more quickly, can be succeeded by other crops. Even if you have a weakness for vichyssoise or cock-a-leekie, 40 plants should be enough for a family of four; if you want to preserve, increase the planting.

HOW TO GROW

Leeks prefer pretty much the same conditions that onions like—near-neutral soil (pH 6.2 to 7.0) that is well-drained yet moisture-retentive, as well as moderately fertile and rich in organic matter, such as compost and manure. If your ground drains slowly, try growing leeks in a raised bed. Leeks will tolerate some shade but do better in full sun.

If your growing season is extremely long or mild, you can direct-seed leeks, but most northern gardeners begin seeds indoors at least 10 weeks before the average frost-free date. Sow seeds thickly, ½ inch deep, in flats filled with a damp sterile mix. In 70°F soil, germination should occur in about a week.

LEEK CULTIVARS

Both nonhardy and cold-hardy leeks offer advantages. Nonhardy types mature quicker and are grown for summer or fall harvest. Hardy types take longer to mature and store better. They can be "stored" in the garden after the first frost if protected with a thick layer of mulch.

'**Alaska**': 125 days; thick stalk; extremely cold-hardy; disease-tolerant; good heat resistance ('Arkansas' is an improved form of 'Alaska').

'**American Flag**': 130 days; large, thick stalk; cold-hardy; standard home-garden cultivar.

'**Bleu de Solaise**': 125 days; medium stalk; tops turn blue-violet in cold; very cold-hardy; heirloom ('St. Victor', 145 days, is a reselected strain of 'Bleu de Solaise').

'**Broad London**'/'**Large American Flag**': 120 days; large, thick stalk; cold-hardy; standard cultivar.

'**Durabel**': 125 days; medium stalk; very cold-hardy; good heat resistance; upright foliage.

'**Falltime**': 90 days; very long stalk; for summer harvest; not cold-hardy.

'**Kilima**': 80 days; long, medium stalk; mild flavor; not cold-hardy.

'**King Richard**': 75 days; long, medium stalk; not cold-hardy.

'**Musselburgh**': 130 days; large, thick stalk; vigorous; very cold-hardy; also known as 'Scotch Flag'; heirloom.

'**Titan**': 80 days; long, medium stalk; fast-growing; not cold-hardy; very early.

'**Varna**': 85 days; very long, slim stalk; fast-growing; not cold-hardy.

'**Winter Giant**': 120 days; large, long stalk; cold-hardy heirloom.

When the seedlings are 3 inches tall, transplant to celled containers or pots that are at least 6 inches deep, and set them in a bright, cool (60° to 65°F) location. Fertilize weekly with a diluted solution of fish emulsion and liquid seaweed. Commercial growers trim their seedlings several times to encourage stockiness, but tests now indicate this practice has little effect; if you use undivided containers, however, modest root trimming, which won't hurt the plants, may be necessary. Seedlings should be hardened off before going into the garden.

About the time of the last spring frost, when seedlings are about the thickness of a pencil, transplant seedlings to the garden, setting them from 4 to 8 inches apart, depending on what cultivar you're growing. To encourage thicker stems, space plants farther apart; for long, thin stems, grow plants closer together. You have several alternatives when planting, all of which blanch the stem and encourage it to elongate.

Dibble Method. Using a dibble or the handle of a hoe, make a hole deep enough to leave only the top inch of the transplant exposed. Place one transplant in each hole, and water, which will wash enough soil around the plant for it to take root.

Hilling Method. Using a hoe, create a shallow furrow, and set out transplants in rows, burying them deeply. Hill soil around the plants as they develop.

Trenching Method. Set plants in a trench, 12 inches deep, 6 inches wide, covering all but the top inch of each plant with soil. As the leeks grow, fill in the trench with soil.

Piping Method. Set plants in the garden, and surround each with a 6-inch-long section of clay or plastic pipe. As the plant grows, fill the bottom pipe with compost and add another 6-inch piece of pipe on top of the first one.

Mulch leeks to help control weeds. Also make sure the plants receive plenty of water—at least 1 inch a week—to keep stems from becoming tough. Side-dress with manure tea once a month.

POTENTIAL PROBLEMS

While leeks are potential targets of all the diseases and insect pests that bother garlic, onions, and other alliums, they are normally trouble-free if not planted where other family members were grown the season before. (For potential problems and solutions, see *Onion* on page 313.)

HARVESTING

Begin harvesting leeks, which contain modest amounts of calcium, potassium, and vitamin C, as soon as they are large enough to be used. (Young plants can be used fresh in salads and other dishes.) Plants with 1½-inch-diameter stems are ideal. To harvest, first loosen the soil with a spading fork, then pull the plant. Remove all but 2 inches of leaves, seal in plastic bags, and store in the refrigerator. For long-term storage, bury in damp sand in a cold (32° to 40°F) location, such as a root cellar.

The harvest of hardy cultivars can be extended long after the first frost by mulching plants heavily with organic matter, such as straw. Leeks that are overwintered should be dug early in the spring, before they begin growing.

Because leeks are biennials and normally don't flower until their second season, saving seeds is difficult. Gardeners in cold climates must dig and overwinter plants, then replant them in the spring; in frost-free regions, carry plants over to a second year. Leeks, which are insect-pollinated, do not cross-pollinate with other *Allium* species. To produce seeds that will come true, plant only one leek cultivar. Seeds are viable for 3 years; store in airtight containers in a dark, cool location.

LEMON BALM

Melissa officinalis. Mint family, Lamiaceae.
Perennial.

○ ✳ ❄ ◼

Lemon balm is a somewhat weedy-looking plant that resembles a small-leaved nettle, but touch one of its leaves, and this herb's identity will be as obvious as your own nose. The foliage and the stems of this herb smell like lemon—with a hint of mint. Also called balm, sweet balm, honey flower, and bee balm, which is the common name generally used for another mint-family herb, *Monarda didyma*, lemon balm grows 2 or 3 feet tall. The fragrant green leaves are oval to heart-shaped with jagged edges. The plant's four-sided stems mark it as a member of the mint family.

Small clusters of pale yellow to white flowers that attract bees appear in summer. Lemon balm honey—the genus name *Melissa* is Greek for "honeybee"—is delicious. Early beekeepers also recorded

Variegated lemon balm

Lemon balm

that the fragrance of the foliage seemed to keep honeybees from swarming and that bees were less likely to sting hands rubbed with lemon balm leaves. If that preventive didn't work, a poultice of leaves soothed insect bites. John Parkinson wrote in 1629 that balm was used "to make baths and washings for mens bodies or legges in the Summer time, to warme and comfort the veines and sinewes, to very good purpose and effect." Lemon balm was chosen as the medicinal plant of the year in 1988 in Europe, where its essential oils are prescribed as a sedative, as well as a treatment for spasms and for cold sores. In North America, however, its contemporary use as a medicinal plant is minimal.

Today, lemon balm is better known as a culinary or tea herb. Its flavor is light—for strong lemon flavor, look to other herbs, such as lemon verbena, lemongrass, and lemon basil—so it can be used without overwhelming foods with which it is combined. Lemon balm adds flavor to fish dishes, and the fresh leaves can be added to green or fruit salads. It makes a good tea, hot or cold, that is still used as an herbal remedy for colds, headaches, and insomnia. Because the leaves retain their scent after drying, they can be used in potpourris.

Gardeners on USDA Zone 4 and warmer can grow this useful herb, originally native to southern Europe but now naturalized in parts of the United States, as a perennial. Two plants will probably provide all the lemon-flavored foliage you need.

LEMON AIDS

If you're wild about lemon, don't stop at *Melissa officinalis*. There are lemon basils—look for a cultivar called 'Mrs. Burns' Lemon'—as well as lemon-flavored thymes, lemon catnip (*Nepeta cataria* 'Citriodora'), lemon bergamot (*Monarda citriodora*), lemon geraniums (*Pelargonium crispum* 'Frensham Lemon'), and the mild-flavored 'Lemon Gem' marigold, too pretty to be overlooked. There are even lemon lilies (*Hemerocallis lilio-asphodelus*), which are old-fashioned hemerocallis that initiate the daylily season with a citrus scent.

Nearly as valuable as lemon balm are lemon verbena and lemongrass. The former, lemon verbena (*Aloysia triphylla*), is a tender shrub originally from South America. It has narrow, 4-inch-long lemon-scented leaves and bears clusters of tiny pale lavender to white flowers in summer. In USDA Zones 9 through 11, where it is a hardy evergreen, plants can reach 10 feet; farther north, lemon verbena is most commonly grown as an annual or pot plant.

Lemongrass (*Cymbopogon citratus*) is the only grass welcome in the herb garden. Native to India and Sri Lanka, this 3-foot-tall clump-forming plant has been used to add a strong, distinct lemon flavor and fragrance to a variety of dishes in Asian cuisine for centuries. Plants, which seldom flower in cultivation, are hardy in USDA Zones 9 to 11 and grown as annuals or container plants in the colder regions.

It's easiest to start both lemon verbena and lemongrass from plants rather than from seeds. Grow them in a site with full sun and moderately rich, evenly moist soil. To grow plants on a deck or patio, use a container that is at least 12 inches wide and fill it with enriched potting soil that will stay moist yet drain freely. Feed plants monthly with fish emulsion or manure tea. Set containers outside during the warm months, bringing them indoors well before the first frost (cut lemon verbena plants back first). Overwinter plants indoors in a sunny, cool spot. (Lemon verbena plants may drop their leaves when brought indoors, but they will regrow.) Regular misting helps control spider mites, which often attack overwintered herbs.

Lemongrass

Although plain lemon balm is generally best kept in the herb garden because it is too weedy-looking for ornamental plantings, more attractive yellow- and variegated-leaved cultivars are available. 'All Gold', which has bright yellow foliage, should be located in a site with midday to afternoon shade to prevent the leaves from scorching. 'Aurea' has green-and-yellow variegated leaves. Lemon balm is well suited to containers, one plant to a pot at least 6 inches wide. The herb can also be grown on a kitchen window ledge, in which case, it stays about a foot tall. It needs a sunny, not-too-hot window, where the temperature hovers around 60°F.

HOW TO GROW

Lemon balm thrives in well-drained, ordinary soil and can be grown in full sun or partial shade. Since plants prefer somewhat cool conditions, a site that is shady from noontime on is a good idea in warm climates. Shady conditions also encourage larger, more succulent leaves. Plants tolerate a wide range of soil pH, from slightly acid to slightly alkaline (pH 6 to 7.8). Although somewhat drought-tolerant, established plants grow best when they receive ½ inch of water each week. Clumps spread gradually—lemon balm is not as invasive as its mint cousins—but plants may self-sow excessively where conditions suit them. Remove flowers after they have gone by if you want to prevent them from setting seeds.

Sow lemon balm seeds in spring, indoors or directly in the garden, after the danger of frost has passed. Since germination may take as long as 3 weeks, many gardeners opt for the quicker route of buying a seedling or cutting, or propagating by dividing existing plants. Set plants or thin seedlings 18 inches apart.

Lemon balm is sometimes attacked by aphids, especially when grown indoors. A strong spray from the hose is often all that is required to control infestations. (For information on dealing with serious infestations, see "Controlling Common Pests" on page 162.)

HARVESTING

To harvest lemon balm, either clip leaves and stem tips back as needed or cut the entire plant back to about 2 inches about the soil, then allow it to resprout. Morning is the best time to harvest, when the foliage is cool and succulent. Like most herbs, lemon balm is most flavorful before plants begin to flower. Fresh leaves have the most flavor, but they can be preserved by drying. If not dried quickly, leaves often turn black and lose their flavor altogether. To dry, spread the leaves and stems on screens in a hot (90° to 110°F), dark place.

LEMON BASIL. See *Basil*

LENTIL

Lens culinaris. Pea family, Fabaceae. Annual.

○ ☀ ❄

While the identity of some plants mentioned in the Bible is a matter of interpretation, there's no question about the lentil. It first appears in the Book of Genesis in the story of Esau selling his birthright to his brother Jacob for food: "Then Jacob gave Esau bread and pottage of lentils . . . ." An important crop in the ancient world—archaeological records indicate it was cultivated as early as 6700 B.C.—lentils are not only rich in protein but, like other members of the pea family, can be consumed green or dried and stored.

Like many foods, lentils also had purported medicinal uses. Ground and "mixed with honie," according to one 16th-century English herbal, they could "clense corrupt ulcers and rotten sores, filling them with flesh againe." More often, however, lentils were added to soups and stews and ground into flour to make bread. They were, a French authority noted in 1885, "a capital addition to our food supplies."

Lentils are vetchlike plants. Nicholas Culpeper, the 17th-century physician-herbalist, described them accurately when he wrote that they have "many long-winged leaves . . . with claspers at the end of the leaf." The bushy 12 to 16 inch plants produce tiny white or mauve flowers, followed by small flat pods that contain one or two seeds, variously colored gray-green, yellow, orange, red, or brown (Jacob used red lentils to trick his brother out of his inheritance). The few seed catalogs that carry this bean typically designate cultivars only by seed color.

Although they are native to the Near East and southern Europe, able to withstand heat and drought, lentils can be grown in cooler climates, USDA Zone 5 and warmer. They need a long season—a place in the garden for at least 110 days, which makes succession planting impossible for most growers—and full sun. While tolerant of poor soil, lentils do better in light, organically rich ground that is well-drained and has a pH between 6.0 and 6.5.

Too weedy to make good landscape plants, lentils are not productive enough to justify container planting. Forty plants should be enough for a family of four; increase the size of the planting if you want to preserve.

HOW TO GROW

Sow seeds direct, about the time of the average frost-free date, 1 inch deep spaced 3 inches apart; germination takes about 10 days in 68°F soil. To get a slight head start, pregerminate seeds indoors on moist paper towels. While lentil plants have tendrils, they do not need to be trellised but do need good air circulation to avoid mildews and other problems, and should be thinned to about 5 inches. The crop is relatively immune to diseases and insects, but installing floating row covers over the planting area will provide insurance against some pests as well as provide a few degrees of warmth to the emerging plants. Weevils, which are small beetles, are the bean's most common foe and can be controlled with pyrethrum or sabadilla. Beneficial nematodes released in early spring are also a deterrent. If weevils are present in your garden, remove and destroy infested plants in autumn and rotate crops.

Once plants are established, mulch to suppress weeds and retain moisture. More tolerant of drought than most beans, lentils need watering only if there is an extended period without rain. Do not water after the pods have begun to dry. To ensure a bountiful harvest, feed plants with compost tea or liquid seaweed when they are 5 inches tall and again when they begin to flower.

HARVESTING

Lentils are typically used like dry beans or peas, but can be picked when they are still immature and prepared like a common snap bean. For dried seeds, pick the pods when they have matured completely and the seeds are hard. The pods shatter easily, so harvest with care. Unlike most dried beans, lentils are better left unshelled until they are to be used. Freeze pods for 12 hours to kill any insects, then seal in air-tight containers and store in a cool, dry place.

Like other members of the pea family, lentil flowers are perfect and apparently unattractive to bees and other insects, so isolating cultivars is unnecessary. Save seeds from the most vigorous and healthy plants; seeds are viable for about 3 years if stored in airtight containers in a dark, cool location.

LETTUCE

Lactuca sativa. Sunflower family, Asteraceae. Annual.

A rose may be a rose, but lettuce is a sunflower—or at least a member of the sunflower family, the descendant of a weed called prickly lettuce or compass-plant (*Lactuca serriola*), which travelers once used to find due north. Lettuce's bitter wild progenitor was unappetizing, "bycause underneath the leafe the middle sinewe or ribbe is set full of sharpe prickles." Before long, however, the ancients civilized lettuce, even erected statues to it (after a lettuce tonic reputedly cured Augustus Caesar). The "sharpe prickles" were bred out, and Americans have been eating it—about 26 pounds per person a year—ever since colonial times, despite the 16th-century warning that children born of lettuce eaters "do become idle foolish and peevish persons."

Despite Caesar's endorsement, the medicinal uses of lettuce—mainly as a sedative—have fallen

LETTUCE ESSENTIALS

- Full sun and cool conditions.

- Fertile, evenly moist but well-drained soil.

- Before sowing, remove rocks and soil clods, and sow seeds shallowly.

- Use row covers for protection against insect pests.

- Keep the soil evenly moist for fast, succulent growth.

away, and gardeners have focused on cultivating lettuce as food. It is, John Evelyn observed in *Acetaria: A Discourse of Sallets* (1699), "the principal foundation of the universal tribe of Sallets." It's safe to say that the foundation is sturdy: About 500 cultivars are available for purchase today, including the small butterhead 'Tennis Ball', an English heirloom that Thomas Jefferson grew at Monticello. Hundreds more are protected in the USDA gene bank in Salinas, California. When it comes to lettuces, the home grower's cup runneth over.

Happily, gardeners in all USDA Zones can grow lettuce, although not all gardeners can grow all types of lettuces well. Be warned that marauding wildlife may have you identifying with Mr. McGregor rather than with those drug-savvy little bunnies, who knew that lettuce was soporific (a fact also known in the classical world, where Venus threw herself on a bed of lettuce to cool her ardor after the death of Adonis). Exactly what libidinous thoughts Flopsy, Mopsy, Cottontail, and Peter were dampening is unrecorded—although the procreating proclivities of the species is well known—but you may want to plant an extra "rabbit row" to

ensure that your salad bowl is ever filled with sweet, fresh green and red leaves. The bunnies won't complain either.

DECIDING WHAT TO GROW

Lettuce does best in cool, sunny conditions, so it is typically planted in spring, midsummer, and/or early fall. Modern lettuce breeding has focused on producing disease- and bolt-resistant cultivars, which has made more lettuces possible for more gardeners, as well as on ever more intricate leaf shapes and colors. All lettuces are open-pollinated, which means you can save seeds for next year's crop; however, some cultivars are "protected"—usually designated in catalogs as PVP—which means you can't sell the seeds you've saved.

Start by deciding what kind of lettuce you want to grow (see "Lettuce Leagues" on page 287 for an overview of the selections), keeping in mind that slow-maturing types, such as a crisphead like 'Great Lakes', require a long, cool garden season. Romaine lettuces also need a fair amount of time to form their upright heads, but they are heat-resistant; slow to bolt, they can be grown in regions with moderately

Lettuce 'Royal Red'

Lettuce 'Blondo Lisle'

Lettuce 'Red Riding Hood'

Lettuce 'Tempora'

Leaf and butterhead lettuce mix

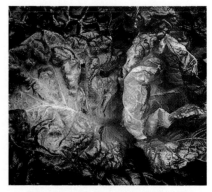
Heirloom lettuce 'Red Head'

hot summers. Butterheads and summer crisps fall into the middle ground: Ready to pick about several weeks before crispheads are but less heat-tolerant than the romaines, they are typically sown in early spring or late summer. Quick-maturing leaf lettuces, which can be planted in early spring or fall, are a good choice for gardeners who have long, sweltering summers; many bolt-resistant cultivars are available.

Once you've settled on a type—or types—of lettuce, diversify further by choosing cultivars with contrasting colors, leaf shapes, and textures. Rather than create a large bed of 'Parris Island Cos', the standard green romaine cultivar, divide the space into thirds and add 'Rouge d'Hiver', a red, and 'Red Leprechaun', a miniature romaine with savoyed red leaves. Or for an even prettier garden, interplant the three cultivars.

Lettuce is not as susceptible to diseases as some crops are, but it can encounter trouble. Gardeners who know that lettuce mosaic or other infections are common in their region should look for seeds that have been tested for the virus and/or cultivars that are disease-tolerant, such as the dark green leaf/crisphead cross 'Centennial'. Careful watering—keeping the soil moist but not soggy—will help plants stay vigorous and healthy, making them unlikely to succumb to diseases. For a family of four, 80 plants, timed to mature throughout the growing season, should provide enough lettuce.

SITE & SOIL

Although lettuce can be grown on a wide range of soils, it prefers fertile, slightly acid (pH 6.0 to 6.8) soil that retains moisture but drains well. Add plenty of organic matter before sowing seeds or setting out transplants. Many gardeners manure their lettuce beds in autumn to provide the nitrogen that plants need to grow quickly.

Lettuce seeds are small, so be sure to prepare the planting area well by removing stones and other debris and breaking up clods that may hinder germination and root development. In cool regions, full sun is recommended, but in hot areas or for summer crops, partial sun is preferable. Using taller vegetables, such as corn, pole beans, or tomatoes, to shade lettuce is an easy way to give plants the protection they require. Set plants well apart—8 to 16 inches, depending on the cultivar—because crowding and poor air circulation encourage diseases and insect problems.

Remember, too, that the harvest time for lettuces is brief, often no longer than 10 days. By planting spring and fall crops, choosing cultivars that mature at different times, and sowing successive crops every 10 days, you can avoid the feast-or-famine scenario and keep your salad bowl filled from spring until the snow flies. Choose bolt-resistant cultivars for late-spring plantings, cold-resistant lettuces for cutting in the fall. Lettuce, especially leaf cultivars that mature quickly, is also a good crop for interplanting with long-season vegetables such as tomatoes.

Lettuces rank high on the most-beautiful-vegetables list, especially when different forms and colors are combined. They can be planted in ornamental beds—they make elegant edging plants—and grown in pots, tubs, and window boxes, where a mix of cultivars looks rather like a bouquet of red and green roses. Or combine lettuce with other crops to create a salad garden. Fill the container with an enriched potting mix, keep plants well watered, feed every 2 weeks with compost tea or a diluted mix of liquid seaweed and fish emulsion,

Red romaine lettuce
'Roman' with 'Curly' and 'Liller'

Lettuce 'Iceberg'

Lettuce 'Biondo'

and provide partial shade, especially if the weather turns hot.

With lettuce, timing is almost everything. Like most leaf crops, it must grow fast to grow well, and it should mature when temperatures are still cool, between 60° and 65°F. Seeds will sprout in near-

LETTUCE LEAGUES

Home gardeners faced with hundreds of cultivars should begin by deciding which of the main types of lettuce they want to grow. The groups are based on growth habit, or the degree to which the plants head up, and are listed below, ranging from leaf lettuces, which do not form heads, to tight-headed crispheads. But while clear differences exist between a leaf lettuce and a crisphead lettuce, the distinctions in the middle of the continuum—between butterheads, buttercrunches, summer crisps, Batavias, and other crosses—are less obvious.

Leaf Lettuce. Also known as cutting and looseleaf lettuce, leaf cultivars are the easiest type to grow. Nonheading and quick to mature—from 45 to 60 days—they can be harvested leaf by leaf or as whole plants. The group includes three forms: those with leaves that are wavy with curly margins, such as the popular old-timer 'Black Seeded Simpson'; those that have deeply lobed leaves, such as 'Oakleaf'; and those with very frilly leaves, such as red-edged Italian cultivar 'Lollo Rosso'.

Romaine Lettuce. Supposedly popular with the Romans—thus the name romaine—lettuces in this group have loose upright heads of thick, elongated leaves with heavy, stiff midribs. There are both red and green cultivars, some as tall as 20 inches; most mature in about 70 days. Cos, another common name for romaine lettuce, comes from the name of the Mediterranean island. Romaine is essential to Caesar salads, but that reference is not classical. The Caesar of Caesar salad is Caesar Cardini, the brother of Italian flying ace Alex Cardini, who originated the salad in his Tijuana, Mexico, restaurant after World War I. Among the most popular

romaines are two heirlooms, 'Paris White Cos' and 'Rouge d'Hiver'.

Butterhead Lettuce. The largest and best-flavored group of lettuces, butterheads—which may also be listed as bibb, Boston, or loosehead lettuce in seed catalogs—form a loose head of soft, succulent, almost oily leaves that are green or brown-red on the outside, creamy white inside. Easier to grow than crisphead cultivars, butterheads take from 55 to 75 days to mature. Included in this group are the burgundy 'Merveille des Quatre Saisons'/'Four Seasons', perhaps the most beautiful of all lettuces, and 'Burpee Bibb' and 'Juliet'.

Summer Crisp Lettuce. **Sometimes called French cri**sp lettuce, this is an intermediate group, halfway between butterheads and crispheads. Most catalogs also stick French Batavia lettuces, such as 'Canasta', and buttercrunch lettuces in this group. Many of these cultivars, blessed with crisp, juicy leaves, have an open form when young, then mature to a compact head. Leaves can be harvested early, as with leaf lettuces, or you can wait and cut the entire head. Most mature in 50 to 75 days. Good cultivars include 'Red Grenoble', 'Buttercrunch', 'Centennial', and 'Sierra'.

Crisphead Lettuce. The most difficult to grow are crisphead, or iceberg, lettuces, which have firm, compact heads of crisp leaves. They require a long, cool season (about 75 days to mature) and constant attention; any stress, and plants will head prematurely—and badly—or bolt. Bred to be uniform and durable, crispheads last longer than any other lettuces in the refrigerator. The first cultivar, 'Iceberg', was released in 1894 and is still widely cultivared.

freezing soil (although they take about 50 days to do so), and seedlings can tolerate mild freezes, so this crop can be begun early. In 50°F soil, germination occurs in about 7 days; in 70°F soil, 48 hours.

HOW TO GROW

Sow seeds very shallowly—they need light to sprout—in spring as soon as the soil can be worked, as early as a month before the frost-free date; in extremely warm regions, lettuce should be sown in fall and winter. For fall crops, count back from the average first-frost date to calculate when to plant (see "Planning for Midseason Planting" on page 134 for more information about timing fall crops). Mature plants are more sensitive to freezing temperatures than transplants are, so don't wait too long to begin a fall crop. (If necessary, you can use floating row covers to protect plants in autumn or mulch with a light material such as straw). For spring or fall crops, remember to succession-plant at 10-day intervals to spread out the harvest. Lettuce seeds won't germinate in temperatures above 80°F, so you may need to shade the planting bed or sow seeds in a cool location indoors to start plants in summer.

Alternatively, begin lettuce indoors, about a month before the expected transplantation date. Sow seeds shallowly in plug trays or in flats, and set in a moderately warm location. Once germination occurs, move the containers to a bright, cool (50° to 60°F) location. Thin plants if they become crowded. Keep the soil evenly moist, and water every 10 days with a diluted (¼ strength) liquid fertilizer.

Lettuce plants can go outdoors as soon as nighttime temperatures stay above 30°F. To reduce stress,

LETTUCE CULTIVARS

The list below provides a cross section of lettuce cultivars that represent all of the types available. To grow attractive and tasty salads, plant cultivars with a mix of colors and leaf shapes.

'**Black-Seeded Simpson**': leaf; 45 days; wavy lime-green leaves; extremely early; heat-resistant; heirloom.

'**Brune d'Hiver**': butterhead; 60 days; medium green heads tinged with brownish red; very hardy; bolts easily; heirloom.

'**Burpee Bibb**': butterhead; 75 days; loose dark green heads tinged with brown; slow to bolt.

'**Buttercrunch**': summer crisp; 70 days; compact medium green heads; good heat resistance; AAS winner.

'**Centennial**': summer crisp; 55 days; large green heads; cold- and heat-tolerant.

'**Cerise**': crisphead; 65 days; medium red heads with blanched centers; widely adapted; good home-garden cultivar.

'**Crispino**': crisphead; 57 days; large green heads; widely adapted; does well in less-than-ideal conditions; good home-garden cultivar.

'**Dark Green Boston**': butterhead; 75 days; large dark green Boston type; resistant to tipburn; popular home and market cultivar.

'**Deertongue**': leaf; 55 days; slightly savoyed green leaves; extremely slow to bolt; also listed as 'Matchless'; a red form is also available; heirloom.

'**Esmeralda**': butterhead; 70 days; medium green Boston type; bolt- and tipburn-resistant.

'**Grand Rapids**': leaf; 48 days; wavy dark green leaves; vigorous; bolt-resistant.

'**Great Lakes**': crisphead; 85 days; medium dark green heads; popular home and commercial cultivar; AAS winner.

'**Green Ice**': leaf; 45 days; crisp, savoyed, glossy green leaves; superior heat resistance.

'**Green Salad Bowl**': leaf; 48 days; medium green lobed leaves; good heat resistance; a red cultivar, 'Red Salad Bowl', is also available.

'**Iceberg**': crisphead; 75 days; compact medium light green heads; good heat tolerance; heirloom.

'**Juliet**': butterhead; 65 days; medium-size green heads with red blush; widely adapted.

'**Little Caesar**': romaine; 70 days; small heads; good home-garden cultivar.

'**Lollo Biondo**': leaf; 50 days; yellow-green ruffled leaves; very ornamental; excellent cut-and-come-again cultivar.

transplant the hardened-off seedlings in the late afternoon, then water immediately with a diluted liquid fertilizer. Be careful when cultivating—lettuce plants have many shallow roots—and mulch to suppress weeds, to keep the soil cool, and to retain moisture. (Gardeners with severe problems with slugs should not mulch lettuce but should keep plants weeded and well cultivated.) Install floating row covers to protect plants from very cold temperatures and insect pests, such as aphids, leaf miners, and flea beetles. (Row covers, suspended on hoops, also can be used to shade lettuce in warm weather.)

Lettuce must be evenly watered—never let the soil dry out—but avoid wetting plant leaves in the evening, which can encourage diseases. To maximize yields, feed plants every 3 weeks with a liquid fertilizer, such as seaweed extract or compost tea.

POTENTIAL PROBLEMS

A short life saves quick-maturing lettuces from most insects and diseases; cultivars that take longer to develop are more susceptible to problems. Some insect pests, such as aphids, leaf miners, and leafhoppers, can be controlled by using floating row covers. (See "Controlling Common Pests" on page 162 for more information about cabbage loopers, cutworms, slugs, and wireworms, which also can damage lettuce plants. For information about most common lettuce diseases—damping-off, downy mildew, mosaic, and fusarium—see "Controlling Common Diseases" on page 169.)

Plants that are subjected to hot weather or drought will bolt and/or become bitter-tasting, but keeping plants unstressed should ensure a trouble-free harvest. Take care to choose appropriate

---

'Lollo Rosso': leaf; 55 days; bicolor red-and-green cultivar; moderate heat resistance; extremely beautiful.

'Merveille des Quatre Saisons'/'Four Seasons': butterhead; 65 days; red-and-green-bicolored heads; extraordinarily beautiful.

'Mighty Red Oak': leaf; 50 days; large, finely lobed red leaves; high yields; slow to bolt.

'Mini Green': crisphead; 75 days; miniature dark green grapefruit-size heads; small cream-colored hearts; tolerates heat.

'Oakleaf': leaf; 48 days; light green lobed leaves; 'Red Oakleaf' is a similar red cultivar; resists bolting; heirloom.

'Parris Island Cos': romaine; 75 days; tall green heads; widely adapted; standard romaine cultivar, named after Parris Island, South Carolina.

'Red Grenoble': summer crisp; 55 days; red-tinted Batavia type; excellent resistance to cold and heat.

'Red Riding Hood': butterhead; 65 days; large red Boston type; good heat and drought resistance.

'Red Sails': leaf; 45 days; bronze-red savoyed leaves; extremely dependable and beautiful; widely adapted AAS winner.

'Rouge d'Hiver': romaine; 65 days; large green heads tinged with red; good cold and heat tolerance; heirloom.

'Ruby': leaf; 48 days: extremely dark red savoyed leaves; heat-resistant; AAS winner.

'Salad Bowl': leaf; 48 days; lobed lime-green leaves; heat- and tipburn-resistant; 'Red Salad Bowl' is a red cultivar.

'Sierra': summer crisp; 50 days; wavy puckered green leaves with red tinges; bolt-resistant; good spring, summer, or fall cultivar.

'Simpson Elite': leaf; 48 days; wavy light green leaves; extremely heat-resistant; popular home-garden cultivar.

'Summer Bibb': butterhead; 62 days; small to medium green bibb type; very slow to bolt.

'Summertime': crisphead; 70 days; medium pale green heads; heat-tolerant; resistant to tipburn; good home-garden cultivar.

'Tango': leaf; 45 days; dark green, deeply serrated endivelike leaves; bolts easily.

'Tennis Ball': butterhead; 50 days; miniature medium green heads; cold-hardy; bolts very easily; probably synonymous with 'Tom Thumb'; heirloom.

'Winter Density': romaine; 65 days; large green heads; a cross between romaine and crisphead; both heat- and cold-resistant; good fall cultivar.

cultivars—select heat-tolerant ones for late-spring crops. Also plant, water, and fertilize lettuce correctly; and practice crop rotations.

HARVESTING

Begin harvesting leaf lettuces as soon as they are large enough to be used, cutting from the outside of the plant (which will encourage the inner leaves to develop); alternatively, let leaf types grow to maturity, and cut the entire plant. Heading lettuces, crisphead, romaines, and summer crisps should be harvested when their heads are firm and fully formed; use a knife, and slice them off at ground level. Always pick lettuces in the morning, when their leaves are most crisp and succulent.

Lettuce is best if used immediately. To store lettuce, seal in a plastic bag and refrigerate for up to 3 weeks (crisphead cultivars can be stored the longest, butterhead and leaf lettuces the shortest). Crisphead lettuces are the least nutritious of all types, but no lettuce is a health powerhouse: Ninety percent water, lettuce does contain small amounts of minerals and vitamins A, B, and C.

Lettuce flowers open only once—some for as little as 30 minutes—and cultivars are unlikely to cross-pollinate. Crossing is possible, however; to ensure seeds breed true, separate cultivars by 25 feet. Seeds are viable for 4 years; store in airtight containers in a dark, cool location.

LETTUCE, ASPARAGUS. See *Celtuce*
LETTUCE, CHINESE. See *Celtuce*
LETTUCE, MINER'S. See *Miner's Lettuce*
LETTUCE, STEM. See *Celtuce*

LIMA BEAN

Phaseolus lunatus. Pea family, Fabaceae. Annual and perennial grown as an annual.

○ ✳ ✿

A tropical South American native, the lima bean is one of the botanical treasures that Spanish explorers hauled back across the Atlantic Ocean. The species name, *lunatus*, means shaped like a crescent moon and alludes to the form of the seeds. The common name, lima, comes from the Peruvian capital, but this bean was cultivated long before that city was founded in the 16th century. Although the beans soon were planted throughout the warmer

Pole lima bean 'Burpee's Best'

parts of Europe and in Africa, they apparently didn't reach North America until introduced by the English colonists in the 17th century.

As with most vegetables, there are many heirloom cultivars with interesting stories. 'Carolina', a pole cultivar, dates from pre-Columbian times and was grown by Thomas Jefferson at Monticello; 'Hopi', a strain selected by the Hopi Indians, has small orange seeds with maroon markings and was used to make flour. Most remarkable, however, is 'Dr. Martin's', which may be the only vegetable cultivar that has its own seed company: Fern Hill Farm in New Jersey, which is not too far from West Cape May, New Jersey, the self-proclaimed "Lima Bean Capital of the World."

Developed in the 1920s by Dr. Harold Martin, a Pennsylvania dentist, this cultivar has enormous vines—extending as far as 20 feet—and enormous pale green seeds. It's only a slight exaggeration to say that one 'Dr. Martin's' bean is a mouthful, one pod a meal. Despite their size, the seeds are sweet and tender.

Limas can be grown in USDA Zone 5 and warmer; gardeners who live in areas with moderate temperatures or shorter seasons should plant cold-adapted cultivars, such as 'Geneva', and may have to use special heat-enhancing techniques to be successful with this crop.

DECIDING WHAT TO GROW

While all limas are designated *Phaseolus lunatus*, not all limas are alike. For starters, there are two types of plants: bush and pole. Bush cultivars, which tend to have smaller seeds, also bear more quickly, beginning about 80 days after planting. For a good harvest, you'll need about 100 warm days. Pole limas, which usually have larger seeds and can climb as high as 10 or 12 feet, take longer to produce, usually 90 or more days. They also give larger yields— 'nearly double that of bush cultivars—and have a reputation for better flavor.

In addition to different plant habits, lima bean come in two sizes: small-seeded and large-seeded. Small-seeded limas, which are also called butter beans, sieva beans, Madagascar beans, and Carolina beans (look for the term "baby limas" in seed catalogs), originated in Mexico and are annuals, setting pods for only a certain length of time. Large-seeded limas, or potato limas, are the type usually found in the dried-bean section of supermarkets. They are perennials in tropical climates, but most home gardeners treat them as annuals; plants will continue bearing until the first frost.

If your growing season is brief, choose a small-seeded bush cultivar, but if your climate is close to providing 130 warm, frost-free days, grow pole limas. Two dozen plants should be enough for a family of four if you've planted a pole cultivar, 75 if you've chosen a bush lima. Increase those numbers if you want to preserve.

SITE & SOIL

Although limas need more warmth than common snap beans, they prefer the same conditions: a sunny location (or partial afternoon shade in extremely hot regions) and light soil that is weed-free, well drained, rich in organic matter, and moderately acid (5.5 to 6.5). Avoid wet or saline soils.

Like other pea-family members, limas have the

LIMA CULTIVARS

The following list of both bush and pole limas includes large- and small-seeded cultivars. Pole limas out-produce bush types.

'Baby Fordhook': small-seeded bush; 70 days; 2- to 3-inch pods with 3 to 4 seeds; compact plants.

'Burpee's Best': large-seeded pole; 95 days; vining version of 'Fordhook 242'.

'Carolina': small-seeded pole; 80 days; 3-inch curved pods with 3 to 4 light green seeds; also listed as 'Sieva'.

'Dr. Martin': large-seeded pole; 90 days; vigorous vines; huge pods with 2 to 3 very large pale green seeds; heirloom.

'Eastland': small-seeded bush; 75 days; 3- to 4-inch pods with 3 greenish white seeds; excellent short-season cultivar.

'Excel': large-seeded bush; 75 days; large plants; broad pods with 3 to 4 greenish white seeds; best cultivar for cool regions.

'Florida Butter': small-seeded pole; 90 days; tolerant of hot, humid climates; 3-inch pods with 3 to 4 speckled buff seeds; also listed as 'Calico Pole' and 'Florida Speckled'.

'Fordhook 242': large-seeded bush; 80 days; 4-inch curved pods with 3 to 4 beans; standard cultivar; AAS winner.

'Henderson': small-seeded bush; 68 days; 3-inch pods with 3 to 4 green seeds; small, erect plants; heirloom.

'King of the Garden': large-seeded pole; 90 days; broad 5-inch pods with 5 to 6 white seeds; good pole cultivar for northern gardens; heirloom.

'Packers': small-seeded bush; 80 days; an improved form of 'Geneva'.

'Prizetaker': large-seeded pole; 95 days; clustered 6-inch pods with 3 to 4 extremely large seeds.

'Thorogreen': small-seeded bush; 70 days; 3-inch pods with 3 to 4 green seeds; heat-resistant; AAS winner.

ability to capture nitrogen from the air. In order for the plants to "fix" nitrogen, certain *Rhizobia* bacteria must be present in the soil. If you haven't added manure or other high-nitrogen material to the garden, coat seeds with an inoculant to make sure the bacteria are present. You can purchase inoculant at a garden center; just before planting, wet the seeds and cover them with the powder.

Because they cannot be planted until the air and soil warm, limas can follow radishes, green onions, or other cold-tolerant crops in regions with extremely long growing seasons. If you're growing pole cultivars, make sure you locate plants where they won't shade neighboring crops. Pole limas make good ornamental backdrops. Try the 15-foot heirloom 'Willow Leaf', introduced by W. Atlee Burpee in 1891, which has dark glossy willowlike green leaves and short, dark green pods.

Bush types can be grown in pots and window boxes. Be sure to use large containers that have good drainage. Fill with an enriched soil mix, water generously, and feed with a diluted liquid fertilizer every 3 weeks.

HOW TO GROW

Lima bean plants cower at the threat of frost, so don't be in a rush to get started in spring. Seeds planted in cold soil won't germinate, and marginal air temperatures will retard growth, even cause permanent damage. If the mercury is slow to rise, begin lima beans indoors. Sow seeds in individual containers to avoid disturbing plant roots, and be sure to harden off seedlings fully before moving them to the garden.

Otherwise, sow seeds—eye down—outdoors, 1 to 2 inches deep, spaced 3 to 5 inches apart, when the soil temperature reaches at least 65°F (70°F is even better), about 2 to 3 weeks after the last expected frost. Germination occurs in 5 to 7 days at that temperature. (Because lima seeds are susceptible to soil fungi and bacteria, many gardeners pregerminate seeds indoors on damp paper towels to give them a head start.)

After plants emerge, thin to 6 inches for bush types, 8 inches for pole cultivars. If you've planted pole types, handle them like other pole beans and install a tall, sturdy support—netting, wire trellis, tepees, heavy strings—for the vines to climb at the same time you sow seeds or transplant.

Feed plants, especially pole cultivars, which

need more nutrients than bush types, every 3 weeks with manure tea, and make sure they receive at least 1 inch of water per week. To retain moisture and suppress weeds, mulch plants once they are established. Cover young plants with floating row covers to retain heat and prevent insect infestations.

POTENTIAL PROBLEMS

Limas suffer from the same diseases and insects that trouble common snap beans. Home gardeners can avoid most problems by buying certified disease-free seeds, planting in well-drained soil in full sun, keeping the garden free of weeds, not working among wet plants, and practicing crop rotations. Give each plant plenty of room: Crowding encourages blights, anthracnose, and other diseases. Either cold and wet weather or extremely hot, dry conditions can cause flower blossoms to drop, which reduces yields. (For specific information about the insects and diseases that may attack lima beans, see *Bean* on page 187).

HARVESTING

Limas can be left in the garden and harvested as dried beans, but most gardeners pick this crop at the shell, or green-mature, stage when its flavor is fresh and there isn't a hint of starch. Begin harvesting when the pods are plump and bright green, before they begin to dry. Limas grown to the dry stage shatter easily, so pick carefully. If weevils are common in your region, freeze dried seeds for 48 hours before storing.

Green-mature limas, which are high in protein and contain vitamins A, B, and C (and are also higher in calories than fresh snap beans), can be sealed in plastic bags and refrigerated. To store dry beans place them in an airtight container for up to six months.

Although lima beans are self-pollinating, their flowers are attractive to bees and other insects, and crossing between all cultivars (bush and pole, large- and small-seeded) is common. To ensure you produce seeds that will come true, plant only one cultivar or separate cultivars by at least 1 mile. Save seeds from the most vigorous and healthy plants; seeds are viable for 3 years if stored in airtight containers in a dark, cool location. (Seeds for extremely large-seeded cultivars, such as 'Dr. Martin's', are viable for only 1 year.)

LOVAGE

Levisticum officinale. Carrot family, Apiaceae.
Perennial.

○ ◑ ✳ ❈ ✿

Lovage is a little-known perennial herb that looks like a celery plant that didn't know when to stop growing. Established clumps can reach 6 feet and 3 feet across and produce a bounty of long, thick, hollow stems topped with plenty of celerylike foliage. Leaves, stems, and seeds, which follow the umbels of small yellow flowers in summer, taste like celery as well. "The whole plant and every part of it smells strong and aromatically," the 17th-century herbalist Nicolas Culpeper wrote. "It takes away the redness and dimness of the eyes if dropped into them; it removes spots and freckles from the face. The leaves bruised, and fried in hog's lard, and laid hot to any blotch or boil, will quickly break it."

Once primarily grown as a medicinal herb, lovage is also called loveache or lovache, a name derived from its use as an aphrodisiac. Today, this Mediterranean native is better known as a cooking herb. Although it tastes like celery, its flavor is much stronger, perhaps in keeping with its toughness, hardiness, and size. A few leaves can overpower a delicately flavored dish. On the other hand, a few leaves are just right to season tomato and mixed vegetable juices. The hollow stems can be used as drinking straws—an especially appropriate use for cold, tomato-based summer drinks.

Since it is perennial, lovage is best grown with other perennial vegetables and herbs in a location where it won't be disturbed. Hardy in USDA Zone 4 and warmer, plants die back each fall but return in early spring. Lovage is attractive enough to be part of ornamental plantings, but because of its height, situate it in the rear of flower borders, or use it as a focal point at the center of an herb planting. One plant is sufficient for a family of four.

HOW TO GROW

In one regard, lovage differs from celery: It is easy to grow. Plants prefer full sun but will grow in partial shade in warm regions. They are unparticular about pH, tolerant of anything from 5.5 to 7.5, but benefit from being in moist, fertile, well-prepared soil that is slightly acid. Even in poor, droughty soil, though, lovage is likely to hang on year after year. Regular watering and a topdressing each fall with well-rotted manure or compost are all the care this herb needs to flourish.

Lovage can be grown from seeds, but since most families will want only one plant, buying a plant or acquiring a division from a friend is a better way to start. Lovage seeds germinate and grow slowly, so while they can be planted outdoors as soon as the soil can be worked, about 4 weeks before the last expected frost, sowing indoors is a better option. Use individual pots, beginning about 8 weeks before the frost-free date. After hardening off, transplant the seedlings outdoors while the soil is still cool, spacing them 2 feet apart. The clumps do not spread rapidly but will self-sow, albeit modestly.

Lovage is vigorous and undemanding, seldom troubled by pests or diseases. In fact, its flowers attract beneficial wasps, which prey on cutworms and other pests. Although the plant also attracts parsleyworms, they are best left to grow into swallowtail butterflies. Aphids, which sometimes gather

Lovage

on the seeds, and leaf miners can be controlled by using floating row covers in spring.

HARVESTING

Cut stems and leaves as needed before plants flower, beginning in the second year. To gather the seeds, cut the seed heads just as the small fruits open, then hang them in small bunches in paper bags to catch the seeds. Lovage leaves freeze well, and both leaves and stems can be dried by hanging them in small bunches in a warm, dry place. Dried lovage turns yellow when exposed to light, so store in tightly sealed, opaque containers.

To propagate new plants, divide lovage clumps in early spring or late autumn, when the plant is dormant, making sure that each root division has at least one bud, or eye. The viability of seeds is brief, 1 year; store in a sealed container in the refrigerator.

MÂCHE. See *Corn Salad*

MALABAR SPINACH

Basella alba. Basella family, Basellaceae. Perennial grown as annual.

○ ✳ ❄ ❀ ▼

Despite its large, dark green, spinachlike leaves, Malabar spinach is decidedly unlike its namesake in both culture and habit. This warmth-loving green, also known as Indian and Ceylon spinach, takes its name from a region of India's southwest coast, where the discouraging word "frost" is seldom heard. It thrives in conditions where cool-weather greens, like spinach or lettuce, wilt. The mere mention of frost is enough to send this tropical plant, a vigorous climbing vine, into decline. In USDA Zone 6 and warmer, it can easily climb 6 feet on a trellis or fence during the course of a season; in colder zones plants reach 4 to 5 feet during the course of a season. It is a rampant vine in Zones 10 and 11.

Malabar spinach—known as late as the mid-19th century by the ominous name of Malabar nightshade, although there's no relation to the nightshade family—is grown for its thick, roundish leaves, which have a mild flavor. Young foliage is most palatable, and is used fresh in salads or steamed like spinach, but larger, older leaves become mucilaginous.

Seed companies usually list just the species, but one reddish purple-stemmed cultivar, 'Rubra', is recognized. Once believed to be a separate species, it has deep green leaves. Sometimes both forms are included in the same package, so when thinning seedlings, examine the stems to ensure that the final stand will include both types. Four or five plants will contribute generously to salads and steamed greens for many weeks, even in a large household.

SITE & SOIL

Malabar spinach thrives in hot weather, full sun, and well-drained soil that is rich in organic matter and has a slightly acid pH (6.5 to 6.8). It can withstand dry periods, but growth is most vigorous, and new leaves most tender, if plants receive at least 1 inch of water a week. Skyrocket temperatures in the mid-90s F only make it happy.

Like any twining vine, Malabar spinach requires a trellis, fence, or other support on which to climb—the taller the better in warm regions, where plants can cover a pergola in a single season. A 4-foot-tall tomato cage or trellis is adequate in cooler parts of the country, or use a south-facing fence, which provides plants with support and with the heat they crave. Training plants to a support not only keeps them off the ground and spares the foliage from being splashed with soil but also saves space and keeps the vines from overwhelming neighboring crops. As horticulturist Fearing Burr noted in *The Field and Garden Vegetables of America* (1865), if not trellised, Malabar spinach vines "will twist themselves about other plants, or whatever objects may be contiguous." Be sure to site plants where they won't shade smaller neighbors.

Given its luxuriant foliage and vining habit, Malabar spinach makes a fine addition to edible landscapes, where it can be trained on trellises at the back of flower borders. It also is attractive in a large container—at least 3 gallons for two plants—with good drainage. Fill the container with enriched potting soil, water frequently, and feed every 3 weeks with manure tea. The vines trail over the sides of the container and will set small flowers in clusters late in the season.

HOW TO GROW

In USDA Zone 7 and warmer, seeds can be sown directly in the garden in midspring, or about 2 weeks after the last-frost date. Northern growers should start seeds in pots indoors about 6 weeks before the last frost. Maintain a soil temperature of about 70°F for germination, which can take up to 3 weeks. To speed sprouting, scarify the seeds, which are encased in black berrylike cases, by lightly sanding them with a nail file, or nick them with a sharp knife.

In Zone 6 and colder, wait for the soil to warm before transplanting this heat-loving crop to the garden, at least 3 weeks after the last frost. (Transplants can be set out even later in the season as well, since they grow quickly.) Malabar spinach transplants can follow an early crop of peas, with the double benefit that plants can be allowed to climb the same trellis after the peas begin to languish in the summer heat. Space plants every 12 inches.

In warm regions, the plants grow very quickly and will be ready to harvest in about 4 weeks. In northern gardens, growth will be slow until daytime temperatures are above 80°F, after which plants seem to leap up a trellis or fence. Mulch plants with organic matter to retain moisture and suppress weeds, and feed plants midway through the season by spreading an additional 1-inch layer of compost around the their base. If well grown—given adequate moisture and fertile soil—Malabar spinach is a largely trouble-free plant.

HARVESTING

Pick leaves, which "are put forth in great profusion," according to a 19th-century source, as soon as they reach 2 to 3 inches across or are large enough to use. As the plants mature, the upper leaves will be the smallest and most tender. Harvest in the morning, when the temperatures are cool. To store greens, seal in plastic bags and refrigerate.

Malabar spinach is self-pollinating and does not cross with any other garden crop. Seeds are viable for 4 years; store in an airtight container in a cool, dark location.

MARJORAM

Origanum majorana. Mint family, Lamiaceae.
Perennial grown as an annual.

○ ✳ ❀ ▼

Like a delicate version of its cousin oregano—both are members of the genus *Origanum*—sweet marjo-

ram is frost-tender and has a more subtle flavor. Its oval, gray-green leaves are fuzzier than those of oregano (*O. vulgare*), and in summer, it is covered with short, dense terminal spikelets of tiny white or pale pink flowers, each with an oval bract below it. The unopened clusters resemble knots, hence an old name for marjoram, knotted marjoram.

Although usually grown as an annual—it is sometimes called annual marjoram—sweet marjoram is actually a tender perennial, native to northern Africa and southwestern Asia, now naturalized in southern Europe. In areas where it is hardy, USDA Zone 9 and warmer, it can become a small shrub as tall as 2 feet. The name *Origanum* means "joy of the mountains," from the Greek *oreos*, for "mountain," and *ganos*, "joy." The Greeks planted marjoram on graves, believing it would ensure that the dead slept in peace, and Greeks and Romans alike, because the herb was associated with Venus, made crowns of marjoram for newly married couples. Sweet marjoram was a favorite medieval herb for perfumes and potpourris, desirable "in all odoriferous waters and powders that are for beauty and delight."

Sweet marjoram was recommended as a "remedy against cold diseases of the braine and head" in the 16th century; today, it is almost exclusively used as a culinary herb. An essential ingredient in authentic German potato soup, it is often used in sausage and meat loaf and to season peas, mushrooms, and summer squash. It complements lamb, veal, pork, and chicken as well as most soups and omelets. Fresh young leaves can be added to salads.

In addition to sweet marjoram, there is the so-called hardy marjoram, sometimes called Italian oregano, which is a sterile cross, probably between *O. majorana* and *O. vulgare*. It looks and tastes much like sweet marjoram, forms a 14-inch mound of gray-green foliage that is covered in white flowers in early summer, and is a little more cold-tolerant, perhaps as far north as Zone 7. Pot marjoram, *O. onites*, has a taste that combines marjoram and oregano and can be used as a substitute for either herb, although its flavor is slightly bitter. Also called Cretan or Greek oregano, it also is hardier than sweet marjoram—to Zone 8—but may survive in more northern locations with protection.

Because they are fast-growing and frost-tender, all these marjorams are commonly grown as annuals in areas where they aren't hardy. They are easy to accommodate in either the vegetable or the herb garden when treated as annuals. Sweet marjoram is especially attractive and bushy—well suited to flower borders and other ornamental plantings. Golden marjoram, *O. onites* 'Aureum', has wrinkled yellow-green leaves that are more mildly scented than are sweet marjoram's. For a family of four, two or three plants of any type will provide an adequate supply.

Marjorams also are suitable for container culture outdoors but tend to do less well indoors than do some herbs. Grow one plant per 6-inch-wide pot with good drainage that has been filled with light potting soil. Water regularly, and feed monthly with diluted compost tea.

HOW TO GROW

Although marjorams have a more delicate constitution than oregano does, they are nevertheless easy herbs to grow. Plant them in moderately rich, well-drained soil in a sheltered place in sun. Neutral to alkaline soil is preferable—pH 7.0 to 8.0—but they will grow in slightly acid soil as well. Given warm weather, plants will grow quickly even in poor, dry soil.

Seeds can be sown directly in the garden in late spring, after the last spring frost. For an early start—germination can be slow in cool soil—many gardeners sow marjoram indoors a month or 6 weeks before the last-frost date. Or propagate from cuttings or divisions, especially when growing named cultivars. Transplant hardened-off seedlings or cuttings to the garden, spaced 6 inches apart, after all danger of frost is past. Prolonged cold weather and/or wet soil will encourage diseases, so keep marjoram plants warm and on the dry side.

To overwinter marjoram, pot up entire plants in fall or take cuttings in summer and root them. Or grow marjoram in containers year-round either on a sunny terrace or deck or in pots sunk to the rim in the soil. Grow plants over winter in a sunny, cool spot, then move them back to the garden after all danger of frost has passed. Pinch back the foliage to discourage legginess, and keep an eye out for aphids and other houseplant pests, which have a special fondness for marjoram.

HARVESTING

The leaves can be picked as soon as they are large enough to be used; flavor is best before the plant's

flowers open. Store harvested leaves in plastic bags in the refrigerator, or dry marjoram in a warm, dark place, either spread on screens or hung in small bunches. In cooked dishes, add marjoram just before serving; otherwise, the oils responsible for the flavor will dissipate.

MARJORAM, WILD. See *Oregano*

MELON

Cucumis melo, Cantaloupensis, Inodorus, and Reticulatus groups. Gourd family, Cucurbitaceae. Annual.

The first cultivated melons—both the Egyptians and the Romans were enthusiasts—were small, probably no larger than oranges, and not nearly as sweet as the melons eaten today. Over time, gardeners' careful selections boosted both size and flavor, but it wasn't until the French rediscovered melons in the 15th century that they received their due. "O precious food! Delight of the mouth!/Oh, much better than gold, masterpiece of Apollo!/O flower of all the fruits! O ravishing melon!" the French poet Marc Antoine de Saint-Amant wrote. Melons, or

MELON ESSENTIALS

- Full sun and a warm, protected location.

- Light, fertile soil mulched with black plastic.

- Use floating row covers for warmth and insect protection.

- Remove row covers when flowers appear.

- Provide 1 inch of water weekly until fruits are tennis-ball size; reduce watering after that for best-quality fruits.

Melon 'Ambrosia'

Canary melon 'Sweet Thing'

"millons," were, Englishman John Evelyn declared with stereotypical British restraint, "the noblest production of the garden."

Melons—probably green-fleshed types—were being grown on this continent at least by the 16th century, culinary luxuries to accompany the beets, pumpkins, squash, cabbages, and other mustard-family crops that were the garden mainstays of the no-nonsense European colonists. Thomas Jefferson cultivated several types of melons at Monticello, including 'Early Roman', a cultivar that has disappeared from gardens, probably because it was susceptible to disease. However, some heirloom melons, such as 'Golden Beauty', 'Jenny Lind', 'Nutmeg', and 'Rocky Ford', are still grown and enjoyed.

Melon vines produce three kinds of blossoms: perfect, or hermaphroditic, which have both male and female parts; male, which have only male parts; and female, which have only female parts. This anatomy has led to scores of cultivars, both intentional and unintentional. More than 150 open-pollinated cultivars are commercially available, plus another 50 or so hybrids. Native to tropical Africa and Asia, melons continue to prefer the warm conditions of their original homes. They can be grown in USDA Zone 4 and warmer, although gardeners on the northern edge of that designation may have to grow short-season cultivars and use heat-enhancing techniques to realize a crop.

DECIDING WHAT TO GROW

Nearly all melons that home gardeners grow are members of the same species, *Cucumis melo*, but commonly grown cultivars belong to three different groups: Cantaloupensis, Reticulatus, and Inodorus.

Cantaloupensis includes the "true" cantaloupes, or rock melons, superbly fragrant fruits with a hard, rough, warty rind. Although cantaloupe is an often-used term, true cantaloupes are rarely cultivated in North America. What most gardeners actually grow are muskmelons, members of the Reticulatus group. Reticulata means "netted," a reference to the net-like markings on the skins of these fruits, which can have salmon, white, or green flesh. Melons in the Inodorus group—the name comes from their lack of fragrance—include honeydews, casabas, and Crenshaws. Also known as winter melons, these are more susceptible to diseases and are slower to mature, usually taking 100 days or more. (See "Melon Terms" on page 300 for a rundown on types and terms you may encounter while deciding what to grow. See *Watermelon* on page 415 for information on this popular crop.)

Season length is the most important consideration for home gardeners when growing melons, which take anywhere from 70 to 140 days from seeding to ripen. If you live in a region with short or cool

Honeydew melon 'Venus Hybrid'

summers, stay away from winter melons; instead, try quick-maturing muskmelon cultivars, such as 'Sweet 'n Early'.

Ripening on melon plants is uniform—all fruits mature about the same time. If your season is long enough, plant successive crops to have a steady harvest or grow cultivars that take different lengths of time to mature. One plant produces between two and five melons. Ten plants will give a family of four a reasonable supply of melons. However, keep in mind that in determining overall yield, pollination is more important than the cultivar you are growing. Yields can vary depending on how successfully insects, such as bees, pollinate the flowers in any given year. If conditions are poor—rainy and cold, for example—there will be few bees, and yields will be down.

MELON CULTIVARS

When deciding which melons to grow, select cultivars that will reliably produce mature fruit in your climate. For example, in Helena, Montana, with an average 122-day freeze-free season, short-season types are the best choice; gardeners in Sacramento, California, with an average 289 freeze-free days can grow even the longest-season winter melons.

'Ambrosia': hybrid muskmelon; 90 days; round 4-pound fruits with salmon flesh; prolific vines; disease-resistant.

'Ananas': open-pollinated muskmelon; 110 days; oval 5-pound fruits with white flesh; vigorous vine; disease-tolerant.

'Athena': hybrid muskmelon; 80 days; oval 4-pound fruits with orange flesh; good disease resistance; widely adapted.

'Banana': open-pollinated muskmelon; 90 days; cylindrical 3-pound fruits with salmon-orange flesh; heirloom.

'Burpee Hybrid': hybrid muskmelon; 80 days; oval 4-pound fruits with deep orange flesh; high yields; widely adapted; popular market and home cultivar.

'Chaca': hybrid cantaloupe; 70 days; round 2-pound fruits with extremely sweet orange flesh; early; good cool-region cultivar.

'Charentais': open-pollinated cantaloupe; 80 days; 2-pound globe-shaped fruits with extremely sweet orange flesh; also known as 'Vedrantais'; heirloom.

'Crenshaw': open-pollinated winter (Crenshaw) melon; 110 days; oval 5-pound fruits with salmon-pink flesh; needs long, warm season.

'Delicious 51': open-pollinated muskmelon; 85 days; round 3-pound fruits with orange flesh; disease-resistant.

'Earli-Dew': hybrid winter (honeydew) melon; 80 days; round 2-pound fruits with lime green flesh; widely adapted; vigorous vines; disease-resistant; early.

'Earli-Sweet': hybrid muskmelon; 70 days; round 3-pound fruits with salmon flesh; disease-resistant; early.

'Early Crenshaw': hybrid winter (Crenshaw) melon; 95 days; oval 8-pound fruits with salmon flesh; vigorous vines.

'Galia': hybrid muskmelon; 65 days; round 2-pound fruits with light green flesh; disease-resistant; good home-garden cultivar.

'Golden Beauty': open-pollinated winter (casaba) melon; 110 days; oval 7-pound fruits

SITE & SOIL

Melons, children of the tropics who refuse to cooperate when it's cold, want a sunny location and light, even sandy, well-drained soil that is fertile and has a near-neutral (6.5 to 7.5) pH. Choose a protected spot. For success, both soil and air must be warm, the latter between 70° and 80°F during the day, no lower than 60°F at night. Although plants need plenty of moisture, the best melons are produced when the weather is sunny, hot, and dry. If summers are humid in your area, make sure the soil doesn't remain overly wet and space plants generously. Good air circulation will help prevent foliar diseases.

You can grow melons in rows—set plants every 3 feet (bush cultivars 2 feet apart) in rows spaced 6 feet apart—or in beds, with 4 or more feet between plants, depending on the cultivar. Traditionally, though, gardeners have planted melons in raised hills, which helps keep soil warm and well drained; in this case, grow three plants per hill with at least 5 feet between hills.

If you have only a small plot, consider trellising cultivars with small fruits, such as 'Jenny Lind'. Saving space is only one payoff of trellising: Melons grown vertically have better air circulation and more access to sunlight and thus tend to have fewer disease and insect problems. Choose a location where the vines won't shade other crops, and erect the support—either a vertical or A-frame trellis covered with 4-inch-square netting—*before* you plant to avoid damaging plants' roots. Set plants 18 inches apart on the windward side of the trellis, and help the young tendrils and vines attach themselves

---

with white flesh; disease-resistant; needs long, warm climate; heirloom.

'**Green-Fleshed**': open-pollinated winter (honeydew) melon; 110 days; oval 5-pound fruits with green flesh; needs long season; disease-resistant.

'**Haogen**': open-pollinated muskmelon; 80 days; round 3-pound fruits with pale green flesh; vigorous vines.

'**Hearts of Gold**': open-pollinated muskmelon; 90 days; round 4-pound fruits with orange-salmon flesh; popular Midwest cultivar; heirloom.

'**Honey Ice**': hybrid winter (honeydew) melon; 80 days; round 3-pound fruits with near-white flesh; disease-resistant; good cultivar for the North.

'**Honey Rock**': open-pollinated muskmelon; 85 days; globular 3-pound fruits with salmon flesh; popular home-garden cultivar; AAS winner; heirloom.

'**Honeyshaw**': hybrid winter (Crenshaw) melon; 85 days; oval 8-pound fruits with pinkish orange flesh; early.

'**Iroquois**': open-pollinated muskmelon; 90 days; round 5-pound fruits with deep orange flesh; disease-resistant; widely adapted.

'**Jenny Lind**': open-pollinated muskmelon; 75 days; 1½-pound fruits with sweet, aromatic,

light green flesh; disease-resistant; heirloom.

'**Minnesota Midget**': open-pollinated muskmelon; 65 days; globular 2-pound fruits with golden flesh; dwarf vine; disease-resistant; extremely early.

'**Musketeer**': open-pollinated muskmelon; 90 days; round 2-pound fruits with pale orange flesh; short vines; good container cultivar.

'**Passport**': hybrid winter (honeydew) melon; 75 days; round 5-pound fruits with green flesh; early; fruits slip when ripe.

'**Rocky Ford**': open-pollinated muskmelon; 90 days; round 2-pound fruits with green flesh; popular commercial and home cultivar; also called 'Eden Glen'; heirloom.

'**Sungold**': open-pollinated winter (casaba) melon; 85 days; round 6-pound fruits with greenish white flesh; short vines; good northern cultivar.

'**Sweet 'n Early**': hybrid muskmelon; 75 days; oval 3-pound fruits with salmon flesh; disease-resistant; productive; early.

'**Sweet Bush**': hybrid muskmelon; 75 days; round 2-pound fruits with orange flesh; compact plants; early.

'**Sweetheart**': hybrid cantaloupe; 75 days; oval 2-pound fruits with reddish flesh; good short-season cultivar; extremely sweet.

to the support, if necessary. You'll also have to provide support for each melon—mesh bags or cloth slings tied to the trellis are the usual methods. Pinch back the vines' tips when they reach the top of their support.

Alternatively, grow a compact cultivar, such as 'Musketeer' or 'Minnesota Midget'. If you choose a short-vined melon, thin to two fruits per plant so that a good leaf-fruit balance is maintained. Melons can be grown on rooftops, decks, and patios too. Use a container, at least 24 inches deep, with good bottom drainage, and fill with enriched potting soil. Water frequently, and feed every 2 weeks with fish emulsion or manure tea.

HOW TO GROW

To help prevent disease, begin by soaking seeds in compost tea for 20 minutes before planting. In warm regions with a long growing season, direct-sow melons as soon as the soil reaches 65°F, no earlier than 2 weeks after the last expected frost. You can speed soil warming by creating hills or raised beds and by covering the area with plastic mulch. Germination takes about 10 days in 68°F soil, 3 days at 90°F.

Gardeners in other parts of the country should begin indoors, 1 or 2 weeks before the last expected frost. Plant seeds ½ inch deep in individual containers, two seeds per 3-inch pot. As soon as the seedlings break the soil's surface, move them to a warm location that receives bright light; thin to one plant when the first true leaves appear. Be sure to harden off plants before moving them to the garden, 3 weeks after the average frost-free date.

Home gardeners have discovered, as have commercial growers, that melons mulched with black plastic do markedly better than do plants grown without it. The plastic mulch warms the soil, retains moisture, keeps down weeds, and protects the fruits as they develop. When it's time to transplant the seedlings, slit the plastic and set the plants—about 1 inch deeper than they were growing—in shallow holes that have been amended with compost. Water

MELON TERMS

Ananas Type. These are oval melons weighing between 2 and 4 pounds, typically with yellow-orange rinds and white flesh, although there are also orange-fleshed cultivars available.

Canary Type. Also known as Spanish-type melons, these are large, averaging about 4 pounds, and typically have thick yellow rinds and white/pale green or yellow flesh.

Cantaloupe. True cantaloupes have hard, rough, warted rinds, either gray-green or yellow-tan, and orange or salmon-orange flesh. Fruits, which are round, oval, or globe-shaped, average 2 pounds.

Casaba. These large winter melons have ribbed, rough, yellow-rinded fruits with greenish flesh—an average weight is 5 pounds.

Charentais Type. Descendants of the "true" French cantaloupe, these melons are usually globe-shaped, weighing 2 pounds or less, with a smooth gray-green rind. Their deep orange flesh is extremely sweet and fragrant.

Crenshaw. These are large, oval winter melons with smooth yellow-green skin. Flesh is usually pale green or salmon, and average weight is 6 pounds.

Galea Type. These especially aromatic melons, which originated with Israeli breeders, have netted green-gold rinds and green flesh. They average 2 or 3 pounds in size.

Honeydew. Honeydews are winter melons that bear round fruits averaging about 3 pounds and have smooth, white rinds. The fruits can have green, white, orange, or pink-orange flesh.

Muskmelon. Round, globular, or oval fruits with relatively smooth yellow-tan netted rinds, muskmelons can have salmon, white, or green flesh. Fruits, which are sometimes ribbed, average 2 or 3 pounds.

Persian Type. These are large—as much as 7 or 8 pounds—nearly round melons with yellow-orange netted rinds and orange flesh.

well with compost tea, and cover immediately with floating row covers, which will protect the young plants from cool winds and temperatures as well as from insect pests. Be sure to remove the covers when the plants begin to flower, because they depend on bees and other insects for pollination.

Melon plants need at least 1 inch of water a week in their early stages but less as the fruits begin to mature, when excessive moisture can produce cracking and bland flavor. Unless there is a prolonged drought, stop watering once the fruits are the size of a tennis ball. To ensure good growth, spray plants with fish emulsion or compost tea when they begin to set fruits. If you haven't used plastic mulch, lay down an organic mulch once the plants are established and insert a shingle or board under each fruit when it is half-grown to prevent rotten spots.

POTENTIAL PROBLEMS

Melons are susceptible to all the pests and diseases that trouble the many members of the gourd family, but most can be avoided by not permitting plants to be stressed—choose a sunny, warm location, and give plants plenty of room. Growers who complain about a lack of sweetness in the melons they raise should look at several possible causes: poor fertility, cool temperatures, excessive rain, inappropriate cultivar, too little foliage.

Purchase disease-resistant cultivars to avoid powdery mildew, downy mildew, alternaria leaf spot, anthracnose, and fusarian wilt, the most common ailments. (See "Controlling Common Diseases" on page 169 for more information and for controls.)

Cucumber beetles are melons' primary foe. They not only damage plants but carry bacterial wilt, which can devastate melon plants. Use row covers to protect plants from cucumber beetles, as well as from aphids, squash bugs, and flea beetles, three other potential pests. (See "Controlling Common Pests" on page 162 for more information and for control measures.)

HARVESTING

Most true cantaloupes, honeydews, casabas, and Crenshaws must be cut from the vine. Signs of ripeness include softness at the blossom end, but for honeydews and most other types of melons, the skin color is the best indicator—it turns either creamy gold or white. Muskmelons, the melons most frequently grown in home gardens, "slip," or separate, from the vine by themselves when they are fully ripe. Rather than wait for the fruits to do the work—and avoid overripening your melons—harvest at the "half-slip" stage (about 2 days before "full-slip"), the point when just a little pressure on the stem separates it from the fruit.

Like most sweet corns, muskmelons start losing their sweetness as soon as they are picked. If you can't use the harvest immediately, store unwashed melons in the refrigerator. Rather than being refrigerated, honeydew, casaba, and Crenshaw melons should be stored out of direct light in a cool (45° to 50°F), humid location.

All melons, which are a good source of vitamins A and C, are insect-pollinated. They cross freely, although watermelons do not cross with members of the *C. melo* species. To save seeds that will breed true, plant only one cultivar. Seeds are viable for 5 years; store in airtight containers in a dark, cool location.

MESCLUN

Mesclun isn't one crop, it's many crops. The word itself, which is French for "mixture," says it all. Long popular in Europe, mesclun consists of an amalgamation of colorful leaves that are cut when they are only a few inches high, still young and tender. The first *salade de mesclun* undoubtedly was made up solely of wild greens; the traditional recipe from Provence in France calls for one part arugula, two parts chervil, one part curly endive, and four parts lettuce. In today's spirited and competitive gourmet food world, however, anything goes.

Mesclun, which is grown in all USDA Zones, can be simple or complicated, mild-tasting or zesty. Its common denominator is that it consists entirely of leaves—perhaps garnished with edible flowers such as violets—and that it pleases the eye as much as the palate. The rest is up to you—an opportunity to create a mix of greens that contains exactly the right flavors, colors, and shapes for your salad bowl.

DECIDING WHAT TO GROW

There are dozens of possible mesclun ingredients, but your mix needs to work together in the garden as well as in the salad bowl. The most logical cultural approach is seasonal: mescluns for early harvest, for midseason picking, and for fall. A spring mesclun garden, for example, might contain leaf lettuce, spinach, arugula, bok choy, radish, and mustard. For a midseason harvest, there is chervil, onion, lamb's lettuce, borage, arugula, parsley, lettuce, and beet. A fall mesclun salad could contain mustard, garden cress, chive, lettuce, onion, radish, and chicory.

Another approach is culinary, a mix of either mild or tangy greens—or of both. Among mellow-flavored plants are lettuce, orach, Good King Henry, purslane, perpetual spinach, and miner's lettuce, or claytonia. To add zip to your mesclun, plant and harvest crops such as arugula, broadleaf garden cress, chicory, kale, endive, radish, and mustard.

MESCLUN CROPS

Arugula, chervil, endive, and lettuce are the classic ingredients, but any edible leaf can be used in mesclun. Listed below are some of the vegetable, flower, and herb possibilities—both cultivated and wild. When choosing what to grow, look for contrasting colors, forms, and textures as well as flavors (many seed companies now offer premixed packets of "Mesclun" seeds). While your salad mélange can be made up of two dozen plants, the best result may be produced by combining only three or four greens. The usual dressing for mesclun is a simple vinaigrette made from white-wine vinegar, olive oil, and Dijon mustard. In the list below, an asterisk (*) indicates that the plant has an individual entry in this encyclopedia.

Anise hyssop, *Agastache foeniculum*

Arugula or rocket/roquette, *Eruca sativa**

Basil, *Ocimum basilicum**

Beet, *Beta vulgaris*, Crassa group*

Bok choy, *Brassica rapa*, Chinensis group*

Chervil, *Anthriscus cerefolium**

Chicory, *Cichorium intybus**

Chive, *Allium schoenoprasum, A. tuberosum**

Corn salad, or mâche, *Valerianella locusta, V. eriocarpa**

Dandelion, *Taraxacum officinale*

Endive, *Cichorium endivia**

Fennel, *Foeniculum vulgare,* Azoricum group*

Garden cress, or peppergrass, *Lepidium sativum**

Good King Henry, *Chenopodium bonus-henricus*

Green onion, *Allium cepa*, Cepa group*

Johnny-jump-up, *Viola tricolor*

Kale, *Brassica oleracea*, Acephala group*

Lamb's-quarter, *Chenopodium album*

Leaf lettuce, *Lactuca sativa**

Lovage, *Levisticum officinale**

Miner's lettuce, or claytonia, *Montia perfoliata**

Mizuna, *Brassica juncea*, Japonica group* (see *Mustard*)

Mustard, *Brassica juncea*, various groups*

Nasturtium, *Tropaeolum majus*

New Zealand spinach, *Tetragonia tetragoniodes**

Orach, *Atriplex hortensis**

Parsley, *Petroselinum crispum*, Crispum group*

Plantain, *Plantago major*

Purslane, *Portulaca oleracea**

Radicchio, *Cichorium intybus** (see *Chicory*)

Radish, *Raphanus sativus*, Radicula group*

Salad burnet, *Sanguisorba minor*

Sorrel, *Rumex acetosa, R. scutatus*

Spinach, *Brassica perviridis**

Sweet cicely, *Myrrhis odorata*

Swiss chard, *Beta vulgaris*, Cicla group*

Tyfon, *Brassica rapa*

Violet, *Viola odorata*

Watercress, *Nasturtium officinale**

Harvesting endive for mesclun

(See *Greens* on page 269 for more on these leafy plants, most of which also have individual entries in this encyclopedia.)

Among these plants are leaves of every shade of green, plus reds, purples, and near yellow; leaves that are entire, lobed, wavy, frilled, and savoyed; leaves that are large, small, and midsize. The grower's task is to balance what will be handsome and tasty at the table with what will grow under the same conditions and at about the same rate in the garden—or in a container, since mesclun is a good crop for patios, decks, and roof tops. Use a container, at least a foot wide and deep, with good bottom drainage, and fill with enriched potting soil. Keep well watered, and feed every 3 weeks with compost tea. Although mesclun plantings are highly ornamental, they don't fit well into the ornamental garden, since they are harvested while still small.

HOW TO GROW

Like all leaf crops, mesclun plants prefer full sun; fertile, weed-free soil that has been heavily amended with organic matter; and plenty of moisture. The soil pH should be slightly acid, 6.5 to 6.8. (For general instructions, see *Greens* on page 269, or see the entries on individual crops.)

Mesclun is direct-seeded, beginning 2 to 3 weeks before the last expected frost. You can grow individual mesclun crops in rows—the plants' different colors, forms, and textures make a pretty effect, especially when set out in designs—but many gardeners prefer to broadcast a mix of greens that mature at the same time in small beds, 3 feet by 3 feet, say. Row or bed, plant successive crops—every 7 or 10 days—and sow seeds thickly. Because you'll

be harvesting plants when they're still small, they won't need room to spread, so there's no need to thin. Quick growth is essential, though, so keep the plants well watered, the soil damp but not soppy.

Mixing several crops in one bed discourages insects and disease by not providing a single target. For additional protection from pests, such as flea beetles, cover the entire planting bed with a floating row cover.

HARVESTING

Like voting in Chicago, "early and often" is the rule with harvesting mesclun. As soon as plants are 4 or 5 inches tall—about 6 weeks—use scissors to cut them about an inch above the ground, then water the bed with manure tea. Many crops will resprout in about 20 days and can be cut again. After about three harvests (two for some greens), the stress of being cut back will kill most of the plants, and the bed can be dug and replanted with another crop of mesclun or some other vegetable or herb. Alternatively, harvest entire plants as soon as they are large enough to be used, and then replant the bed.

Harvested greens, which contain vitamin A, potassium, and calcium, should be immersed in cold water, then dried between soft towels. To store mesclun, seal in plastic bags and refrigerate.

MEXICAN OREGANO. See *Oregano*
MEXICAN TARRAGON. See *Tarragon*

MINER'S LETTUCE

Montia perfoliata. Purslane family, Portulacaceae.
Annual.

○ ◑ ❄

Miner's lettuce is a cool-weather salad green native to North America that has only recently begun to gain recognition in its own land. Plants first bear lance-to-kidney-shaped leaves, 2 inches or more across, that sit atop thin 4- to 6-inch stems. The succulent foliage is delicate, easily bruised in handling, and mild-flavored. As the plant matures, it bears small white edible flowers that open in the cones formed by pairs of round leaves.

The name miner's lettuce originates from the time of the California gold rush, when miners, eager for fresh greens of any sort, picked the leaves of this wild plant. European gardeners have championed the plant for some years, yet miner's lettuce is carried by only a few seed houses in North America. Despite its limited following, it has acquired enough common and botanical names to keep gardeners confused about its real identity. The genus name *Montia* is derived from the name of Italian professor of botany Giuseppe Monti, but miner's lettuce was once classified as *Claytonia perfoliata* and is still sometimes listed under that name or as *C. montia*. (*Claytonia*, which commemorates early American botanist John Clayton, is the genus of spring beauties, *C. virginica* and *C. caroliniana*, beloved early-spring wildflowers.) Common names for miner's lettuce abound as well—winter purslane and claytonia are still used, but the plant, native from British Columbia to Mexico, has also been called Indian lettuce and Cuban spinach.

There are no named cultivars of this mild, almost bland, green. Small sowings in spring and fall—two dozen plants is sufficient for a family of four—can be used to blend with other greens of greater personality. It can also be included in mesclun. (See *Mesclun* on page 301.) One of the plant's best qualities is its cold tolerance. It easily overwinters unprotected in parts of USDA Zone 6 and south. It will flourish as a winter crop in Zone 7 and parts of Zone 8. For northern gardeners, miner's lettuce can be planted in early spring and late summer or can be grown as a winter crop with the protection of a cloche or cold frame.

HOW TO GROW

Miner's lettuce thrives in full sun when temperatures are cool but prefers partial shade once the weather heats up. Give it humus-rich, evenly moist soil with a near-neutral pH of 6.8 to 7.0. Seeds can be sown 5 to 6 weeks before the last-frost date, either broadcast in a bed or spaced every inch or so in a row. Sow seeds ¼ inch deep. Germination takes about 10 days. If they are part of a mesclun planting, thin seedlings sparingly to 2 to 3 inches; or, to harvest leaves individually from each plant, space plants every 6 inches.

In Zone 5 and colder, sowings can be made every 2 weeks from early spring to early summer. A second crop can be planted in early fall. In warmer regions, sow seeds in late fall for a winter and spring harvest. With good soil and adequate moisture, miner's lettuce is troubled by few insects or diseases.

HARVESTING

Plants mature in about 60 days from seeds, but

Harvesting spearmint

leaves can be harvested 30 to 35 days after sowing, as soon as they are large enough to be used. Allow plants to grow to about 6 inches, then harvest by cutting them back to about 1 inch in height. With adequate moisture, plants will regrow and can be cut back again. Or pick leaves individually from the outside of the plant.

The flowers of miner's lettuce are perfect and self-pollinating, and plants do not cross-pollinate with purslane or other crops. They do self-sow freely, however, and can naturalize in the garden if they are not weeded out. To save seeds, which are viable for 5 years, store in airtight containers in a dark, cool location.

MINT

Mentha spp. Mint family, Lamiaceae. Perennial.

○ ◑ ✳ ❄ ▮

Most mints are vigorous plants with unusual square stems that grow as tall as 2 feet and spread just as far; their lance-shaped leaves, which can be smooth, hairy, crinkled, and variegated, are typically sharply toothed. Spikes of tiny flowers—white to pinkish purple—appear in midsummer. The best-known mints are widely adapted (USDA Zones 4 to 9), but the handsome variegated pineapple mint (*Mentha suaveolens* 'Variegata', the tiny mosslike Corsican mint (*M. requienii*), and a few others are hardy only to Zone 6 or 7.

Today, most gardeners plant mint for culinary uses—in addition to flavoring fresh and cooked dishes, both savory and sweet, fresh and dry mint leaves are often used in teas and other drinks—but

Pineapple mint

mint also has a long history as a medicinal herb. The Greeks, who started the Saturday-night-bath ritual, emerged from their classical tubs and rubbed their arms with mint, while the Romans believed that mint "does stir up the minde and the taste to a greedy desire of meate." English herbalists of the 16th and 17th centuries recommended mint for scores of ills, everything from the "bitings of mad dogs" and "watering eies and all manner of breakings out on the head" to weak stomachs and "Nervous Crudities." Victorian ladies, who believed mint signified "warmth of sentiment," used it to make tussie-mussies. Contemporary herbalists prescribe mint tea for nausea, indigestion, flatulence, and headaches.

Take two dozen species of mint, add centuries of botanical promiscuity, and the result is more than 500 species and cultivars, each more or less different from the other. And while apple mint, ginger mint, grapefruit mint, basil mint, lemon mint, lime mint, orange mint, pineapple mint, and even chocolate mint have their merits, peppermint (M. x *piperita*) and spearmint (M. *spicata*) are the most widely cultivated. Of the two, spearmint is the essential culinary herb. One or two plants of the species is all the spearmint you'll ever need, but some gardeners may want to try M. *spicata* 'Crispa', which has round, crinkled leaves and a milder flavor. Julep makers can look for M. x *cordifolia* 'Kentucky Colonel', the product of crossing spearmint and apple mint.

The Romans brought spearmint to England, where it became a staple (as "spere *mynte*" in medieval gardens; from there, it traveled to America with the early colonists. In time, spearmint jumped the fence and naturalized so widely that it became known simply as garden mint. Today,

depending on its grower's culinary tastes, it is also called lamb mint, green mint, gum mint, mackerel mint, fish mint, and pea mint.

HOW TO GROW

Mints flourish in full or partial sun and in moderately rich, moist, slightly acid soil but will tolerate almost any setting. Because they spread by creeping along the soil surface, they can do double duty as ground covers. You may want to place a plant near a walkway, where you will brush it—and release its fragrance—when you pass. Mint grown in containers, which is the only no-fail method to keep it from spreading, should be divided every 2 or 3 years. Container plants must be watered regularly and fertilized with fish emulsion monthly in order to grow vigorously..

Most mints spread by rhizomes, or underground stems. Seed germination is erratic and varietally unpredictable, so buy plants or propagate in early fall by division, or in spring or fall by stem-tip or rhizome cuttings (which will root in water or damp sand). Most types of mint should be set 12 to 18 inches apart. Plant cuttings shallowly, just beneath the soil surface. Once established, as herbalist John Gerard writes, mints "continue long, and remaine sure and fast in the ground." To keep plants bushy, pinch the stem ends in spring and prune back plants vigorously when the garden season ends. Top-dress with compost in the fall.

Mints are immune to most diseases and pests but are pushy plants, completely without manners. Grow them in a separate bed, where they won't overwhelm their companions, or, to restrain them in the garden, plant them in 10-inch-deep bottomless containers, such as pots or clay drainage tiles, that have been set in the soil. The rhizomes can still escape over the lip of the container, but it's easy to see them and stop their getaway.

HARVESTING

You can pick mint throughout the growing season (country wisdom advises harvesting in the light of the moon), but it is most flavorful just before the plant comes into flower. Cut the top half of young stems rather than single leaves.

MITSUBA. See *Parsley*
MIZUNA. See *Mustard*
MOUNTAIN SPINACH. See *Orach*
MULTIPLIER ONION. See *Shallots*

MUSTARD

Brassica spp. Mustard family, Brassicaceae. Annual.

○ ◑ ❄ ❀ ▰

There are scores of mustards—bamboo shoot, curled, involute, wide petiole, white-flowered, long petiole, tuberous-rooted, tillered, flowerlike leaf, brown, black, red, small leaf, strumous, swollen stem, and penduncled are only some of them—so keeping the members of this Asian clan straight is no mean task. All are *Brassica* species, however, and all are annuals that are fast to mature, fairly tolerant of heat yet hardy—they can be grown in USDA Zone 2 and warmer—and willing to put up with inattention.

The illustrations in John Gerard's famous herbal (1597) give only vague hints of which mustards were being grown at that time, although all types were considered curatives for coughs, epilepsy, and melancholy, even for removing splinters, improving the memory, and clearing the throats of singers. "Water of mustard seeds distilled," according to a 1577 garden book, "Amendeth Ulcers of the Gummes . . .[and] heateth the marrow in the bones."

Mustard's role in heating the marrow in the bones may have disappeared, but not so the role John Evelyn described in *Acetaria, A Discourse of Sallets*, the first book on salads, published in 1699. Mustard, Evelyn wrote, was "so necessary an Ingredient to all cold and raw Salleting, that it is rarely if at all to be left out." The Chinese were using mustard greens as early as 200 B.C., but American salad makers, who apparently don't have *Acetaria* in their libraries, have been slow to discover mustard's peppery merits. Although North Americans have cultivated leaf mustards, or mustard greens, since colonial times, it's the recent popularity of mesclun and Asian cuisine that has inspired interest in this crop.

DECIDING WHAT TO GROW

While the leaves of all mustards are edible, the major distinction that is normally drawn is between those grown primarily for their seeds, which are ground, mixed with white wine and cream, and turned into the familiar condiment, and those cultivated mostly for their foliage. For many years, the traditional seed-mustard was *Brassica nigra*, or black mustard. It is still used, but several forms of *B.*

Mustard 'Red Giant'

Mustard 'Osaka Purple'

juncea, which are better suited to mechanical harvesting and have a milder flavor, are now more widely employed. Good cultivars are 'Burgonde' and 'French Brown', which take from 65 to 85 days to mature. 'Tilney', which was developed by the English firm of Colman Foods, Ltd., is the source of seeds used to produce the yellow mustards Americans use to smother hot dogs.

Most home gardeners grow mustards for their greens, not their seeds. Flavor ranges from the mild mizuna to types that will have you reaching for a 10-ounce glass of water. Pungency also varies within each plant: The fire in some mustards is in the stems; in others, the leaves. Plants taste less peppery when they are young and small and grow hotter as they mature, especially after they flower.

Most of the mustard greens available to home gardeners belong to the species *B. juncea*, which is divided into 17 groups. Seed catalogs tend to be

Mustard 'Tai Sai Giant'

Mixed mustards

indifferent to the taxonomic distinctions—perhaps because they are complicated, confusing, and constantly changing—so expect all mustards to be grouped together, despite differences between plants. Below are the most common types available in North America.

Broad-Leaved Mustards. Also called big mustards, these are large, handsome plants with heavy stalks and big leaves that are often crinkled or savoyed and as long as 20 inches. Both stalks and leaves are edible. Leaf color ranges from deep green to purple (some cultivars have striking green leaves with purple veins). Plants grow from 12 to 18 inches tall and are heat-tolerant and cold-hardy, sown both in early spring and in late summer for an autumn harvest (or overwintered in frost-free regions). The most widely available cultivars include 'Red Giant', 'Osaka Purple', 'Red Chirimen', 'Green Chirimen', 'Miike Giant',

'Savanna', and 'Florida Broadleaf'.

Wrapped Mustards. These have leaves that fold inward to create heads or hearts. Used almost exclusively in Asian cooking, these plants are large, do well in warm conditions, and are normally planted in summer for an autumn harvest. In warm areas, sow seeds in fall. The best-known cultivars are 'Big Heart', 'Swatow', and 'Wrapped Heart'.

Curled Mustards. Most curled mustards have handsome, stiff, extremely curled or frilled leaves. Hardy and easy to grow, these types can be planted in spring or summer and can be overwintered in extremely warm regions. Among the most popular cultivars, many of which have been developed in this country, are 'Southern Giant Curled', 'Green Wave', and 'Fordhook Fancy'.

Common Mustards. Also called leaf mustards, these have dark green serrated leaves, either long or rounded. Stalks are light green and ridged, and plants grow to 1 foot. Also known as Chinese mustard and little mustard, these types bolt quickly when planted in spring. They mature in about 40 days and are usually sown in late summer for a fall harvest. A good cultivar is 'South Wind'.

Green-in-the-Snow Mustards. These have either deep or pale green lobed leaves and grow about 12 inches tall. Vigorous, quick to mature, and hardy—the name is a giveaway—green-in-the-snow types are very pungent, especially after plants begin to flower, and are usually cooked rather than used raw. Sow in summer for an autumn crop. 'Green-in-the-Snow' is the cultivar listed most often in North American seed catalogs.

Swollen-Stem Mustards. As their name indicates, these mustards have enlarged, or swollen, stems that feature a half-dozen or more bulges. They are grown for pickling. Slower to mature than most mustards—90 to 125 days—they prefer a cool, humid climate. Popular in Asia but largely unknown in North America, they are sold under the common name swollen stem.

Mizuna. For a mild-tasting mustard that is also one of the most attractive greens you can grow, try mizuna (*B. juncea*, Japonica group). Its 6- to 10-inch-long, deeply cut, ferny leaves, held on short white stalks, form a dense, 12-inch-wide, glossy dark green rosette. A native of China but often considered a Japanese vegetable, adaptable mizuna—it is both heat- and cold-tolerant—is also called kyona, Japanese greens, and Japanese mustard. Seeds are

Mizuna

usually sold under the name mizuna; the most common cultivars are 'Tokyo Beau' and 'Tokyo Belle'.

Mibuna. A mustard with murky origins, mibuna is a relatively new introduction to North America. Known also as mibu, after the Japanese town where it has been cultivated for centuries, mibuna has long, narrow, unlobed leaves, either dark or light green, and forms an upright clump as large as 18 inches across. Slightly stronger-flavored than mizuna but still a "mild" mustard, mibuna is a cool-weather plant, intolerant of both hot and very cold weather. There are early and late cultivars of mibuna, which is typically listed under its generic name; 'Green Spray' is a cultivar found in some catalogs.

Twenty plants, sown in spring and summer, should provide plenty of mustard greens for a family of four; if you want to harvest seeds, increase the planting.

SITE & SOIL

Most mustards prefer moderate conditions—not too hot, not too cold—yet can survive light frosts and are willing to put up with considerable heat, more so than spinach or lettuce do, for example. Plants thrive in full sun early and late in the garden season but benefit from partial shade during the summer. Moderately fertile soil, well tilled and heavily amended with organic matter, that has a moderately acid pH (5.8 to 6.8) is ideal for cultivating mustards, although plants will tolerate ground that is as sweet (alkaline) as 7.5. Because of their shallow roots, mustards are more susceptible to drought than to excessive rain, but water-stressed plants develop hotter flavor, so be sure plants receive at least 1 inch of water a week.

Mustards are more likely to bolt, or flower prematurely, when planted in spring than in midsummer (scientists continue to argue whether the bolting is caused by the long days or by high temperatures). Experienced growers delay sowing mustard until mid- or late summer; in frost-free regions, mustards can be seeded in autumn and overwintered. Spring plantings are recommended, however, if you are growing mustard as a mesclun crop and harvesting when plants are young and small. (See *Mesclun* on page 301 for information on spacing and care in mesclun plantings.)

Mustards rush to maturity—most cultivars are ready to harvest in about 50 days—and need the soil to have plenty of nitrogen. Supply it by digging in well-rotted manure or another high-nitrogen material before planting. Mustards quick growth make them good plants for intercropping with long-season vegetables and herbs. To extend the harvest, sow seeds in both early spring and midsummer.

Most mustards make themselves at home in ornamental gardens and are good container crops, especially the prettier types, such as mizuna. Use a large container with good drainage, and fill with enriched potting soil. Keep plants well watered, and fertilize every 3 weeks with compost or manure tea.

HOW TO GROW

In spring, sow seeds outdoors 2 to 3 weeks before the last-frost date, ¼ inch deep, 1 inch apart, or in midsummer for an autumn crop. For a winter or spring harvest in warm regions, plant in late autumn, about 8 weeks before the first expected frost. Mustard seeds germinate quickly, about 5 days in 68°F soil. Thin seedlings to 5 to 18 inches apart, depending on the cultivar; thinnings can be used in salads. If mustard is to be cut for mesclun, try broadcasting seeds in beds rather than sowing in rows.

Mulch seedlings with compost or other organic material to preserve moisture and suppress weeds, and cover the area with floating row covers to prevent insects from reaching plants. Water every 10 days with manure tea or fish emulsion, beginning 2 weeks after seeds germinate, to stimulate lush leaf growth.

Overall, mustards are remarkably problem-free. Plants are sometimes troubled by flea beetles, whiteflies, and aphids, which can be controlled by using floating row covers. (See "Controlling Common

Pests" on page 162 for more information and for control measures.)

HARVESTING

Mustards, which are rich in vitamins A and C, calcium, phosphorus, and iron, can be harvested as soon as the leaves are large enough to be used, beginning about 3 or 4 weeks after germination. Plants can be allowed to mature and harvested entire, cut leaf by leaf (start at the base of the plant taking outside leaves first—new growth will emerge from the center of the plant), or treated as a cut-and-come-again crop, sheared back to 2-inch stubs, which will regrow.

In time, all mustards become too bitter-tasting to be used fresh. Rather than remove the plants from the garden, allow them to mature, enjoy their beauty, and harvest their yellow blossoms and immature seedpods, both of which are edible. Or add zip to a winter salad by sprouting mustard seeds indoors. To harvest seeds, cut the pods after they turn brown but before they shatter.

Mustard greens don't store well and should be harvested as needed. All members of *B. juncea*, whatever the group or subspecies, will cross-pollinate. To produce seeds that will come true, grow only one cultivar. Seeds are viable for 4 years; store in airtight containers in a dark, cool location.

MUSTARD CRESS. See *Garden Cress*
NAPA CABBAGE. See *Chinese Cabbage*

NEW ZEALAND SPINACH

Tetragonia tetragoniodes. Carpetweed family, Aizoaceae. Perennial grown as an annual.

Blistering weather that sends true spinach and lettuce into a terminal decline is no match for New Zealand spinach. According to one garden writer earlier this century, this heat-tolerant crop not only "thrives in hot weather which spinach cannot stand, but gives repeated cuttings all summer long, and having more open growth does not collect as much sand and require as much washing as spinach." Strong praise for a crop that earned its passage to England from its native New Zealand in 1771 by helping keep the crew of Captain James Cook's vessel free of scurvy. New Zealand spinach,

sometimes listed as *T. expansa*, had been discovered by the ship's botanist, Sir Joseph Banks, and plants were gathered to take aboard the *Endeavor* for the long return voyage. Back in England, it was grown for years as a potted houseplant, despite its legacy as a nutritious green.

Gradually, salad gardeners in England, France, and eventually North America came to appreciate the heat tolerance of this low-growing plant, which will spread over several feet and reach a height of more than 1 foot. It produces the most spinachlike leaves of the warm-weather spinach substitutes—Malabar, perpetual, and New Zealand spinach. The succulent, triangular or slightly oval leaves are pale green with a slight gray cast and 2 to 4 inches long. Some foliage has a glistening quality, which apparently gave rise to the crop's other common name, New Zealand ice-plant. Plant breeders have shown little interest in "improving" New Zealand spinach, so plants grown today are largely unchanged from the species collected more than 200 years ago. 'Maori', with upright growth and dark green triangular leaves, is the named cultivar most often mentioned, but most seed catalogs list the crop simply as New Zealand spinach.

With hospitable growing conditions, three or four plants are adequate for a family of four. While New Zealand spinach can be grown in the vegetable garden, it is attractive enough to be grown as an edging or temporary groundcover. Or try it in hanging baskets, window boxes, or containers, where it will trail over the edges. Two plants can be grown in a 5-gallon pot, five in a 10-gallon tub.

HOW TO GROW

While New Zealand spinach grows well despite heat and lack of rainfall, it actually prefers moderate conditions and tastes best when grown with plenty of moisture. Plant it in a spot with full sun and humus-rich soil with a near-neutral pH of 6.8 to 7.0. Summer crops benefit from a partially shaded spot—afternoon shade is most beneficial—especially in the warmest zones. Although it does not trail as vigorously, New Zealand spinach is best planted in hills, like squash, spaced about 2 feet apart. While the plants can tolerate considerable drought, the leaves are more tender and flavorful if they receive about 1 inch of water a week. Mulching plants will help retain moisture.

New Zealand spinach is much more frost-sensitive than true spinach is, and planting or transplanting should be delayed until after the last-frost date. In USDA Zone 6 and warmer, sow seeds directly in the garden—¼ inch deep, three seeds per hill. Thin to the strongest plant. In Zones 4 and 5, start seeds indoors 3 weeks before the last-frost date, and set transplants out at about 6 weeks, or 3 weeks after the last frost. Either way, soak seeds overnight in water before planting to speed germination.

Plants mature in about 50 days but will continue to grow vigorously for many more weeks, barring cold weather. Even a mild frost will kill the crop. If given good soil and adequate moisture, New Zealand spinach is bothered by few insects or disease.

HARVESTING

Harvest young leaves and tender tip growth, which are the most palatable parts of the plant—old leaves become tough and bitter. Regularly harvesting the new leaves and pinching off branch tips encourages new, bushier growth and keeps the plants productive.

Flowers are perfect but plants can cross. Grow only one cultivar to ensure seeds will come true. Seeds are encased in hard fruits, which occur along the length of the vines. They are viable for 5 years if stored in an airtight container in a dark, cool location.

OKRA

Abelmoschus esculentus. Mallow family, Malvaceae. Annual.

○ ✻ ❀

There's little debate over the good flavor of okra, which one gardener described as "a mix between green beans and oysters," yet cooks tend to be thumbs up or down about this heat-loving vegetable. Either they mind its slimy texture when cooked—mucilaginous is the nice word for it—or they don't. Never wildly popular in Europe, okra caught on "in the colonies," the Vilmorin-Andrieux plantsmen commented with only slightly concealed snobbery in 1885. "The young and tender seed-vessels are very extensively used as a table vegetable."

Okra's long association with the American South is an accident of history and geography. A

Okra 'Star of David'

native to northern Africa, it made its way to North America in the middle of the 17th century, a by-product of the slave trade. The name okra derives from the Ashanti language, spoken in West Africa; another common name, gumbo, comes from the Bantu language of South Africa. The story of the okra's origin also comes from Africa.

According to legend, the man in the moon invited a starving woman and her child to join him in the sky. The woman's husband, wildly jealous, made a rope from vines and climbed up to retrieve his family. As the couple struggled, the child fell to the earth. Before she landed, the man in the moon changed her into the okra plant. He "was almost too late," Vernon Quinn wrote in *Vegetables in the Garden and their Legends* (1942), "for a splotch of her crimson blood still shows in the yellow-ghee flower; and in the gumbo's slender pods, you can see her small arms, uplifted toward her mother, the Woman in the Moon."

Gardeners can't help but like okra. It's relatively easy to grow, and it's pretty. Handsome foliage and flaring yellow bell-like flowers with red centers

Okra 'Thick Pod Red'

and decorate the plants, which range from compact cultivars like the 3-foot 'Blondy', an AAS winner, to the 6-foot heirloom 'Cow Horn', a cultivar that 19th-century New England horticulturist Fearing Burr knew as 'Giant'. The blooms are reminiscent of hollyhock and hibiscus flowers—okra's previous botanical name was *Hibiscus esculentus*—and a few plants would be perfectly at home in an ornamental bed or border. Okra pods, which are sought after for dried flower arrangements, grow upright. Most older cultivars' pods are heavily ribbed; when sliced, they look like stars.

Although a tropical crop, okra can be grown in USDA Zone 4 and warmer, but yields will be smaller in colder regions, and gardeners may have to use special heat-conserving techniques to succeed with this vegetable.

DECIDING WHAT TO GROW

Most okras take at least 70 warm days to produce edible pods, but recent breeding successes have given commercial and backyard gardeners compact cultivars that mature even sooner, in as few as 50

OKRA CULTIVARS

Both hybrid and open-pollinated okras are available. Gardeners in cooler zones should choose early cultivars for best results.

'Annie Oakley': 45 days; hybrid; more spiny than most cultivars; very early; widely adapted; good cultivar for the North.

'Blondy': 48 days; open-pollinated; compact 3-foot plant; early; good cultivar for the North; AAS winner.

'Burgundy': 55 days; open-pollinated; red-maroon pods on 4-foot plants; AAS winner.

'Cajun Delight': 50 days; hybrid; high yields; good cultivar for the North; AAS winner.

'Clemson Spineless': 55 days; open-pollinated; 4-foot plant; the standard okra cultivar; AAS winner.

'Cow Horn': 65 days; open-pollinated; spiny 6-foot plants with pods twisted like a cow's horn; heirloom.

'Dwarf Green Long Pod': 55 days; open-pollinated; compact 3-foot plant; widely adapted.

'Emerald Green': 55 days; open-pollinated; 5-foot plants with round pods.

'Gold Coast': 75 days; open-pollinated; 5-foot plants with good drought and heat resistance; sustained yields; widely adapted.

'Louisiana Green Velvet': 60 days; open-pollinated; round-podded 6-foot plant; popular commercial cultivar.

'North & South': 52 days; open-pollinated; good yields; widely adapted; good cool-weather tolerance.

'Red Velvet': 70 days; open-pollinated; 4-foot plants with red pods that turn green when cooked.

'Star of David': 65 days; open-pollinated; highly productive; unusual strong flavor; Israeli heirloom.

days. The household name in okra is 'Clemson Spineless', an old-timer that is as popular today as it was when it won an AAS award in 1939. (The "spineless" in 'Clemson Spineless' refers to the spines on the leaves, which can cause skin rashes. No cultivar is truly spineless, but 'Clemson Spineless' comes pretty close to living up to its name.) The new okras, such as 'Blondy', a 1986 AAS winner, are a result of breeders trying to develop a commercial cultivar that could be harvested mechanically. In the process, they provided home gardeners with cultivars that are more flavorful and more widely adapted.

In addition to the traditional okras, such as 'Clemson Spineless', which have ridged pods, there is a group of round-podded cultivars. Also known as smooth-podded okras, most are unknown to home gardeners. Their pods can be allowed to grow longer, 4 to 8 inches, before harvesting, and they have the advantage of holding their shape when sliced and cooked. One widely available cultivar is 'Emerald Green'.

A dozen plants is plenty for a family of four; if you want to preserve, increase the planting.

HOW TO GROW

Okra does best when planted in light, fertile soil that has been tilled to at least 8 inches and been generously amended with organic matter that is rich in nitrogen, such as well-rotted manure. Soil pH can range from 6.0 to 8.0. Full sun is essential. Unless you choose a compact cultivar, plants are tall, so locate them where they won't shade shorter neighbors. If you have an especially warm, protected spot in your garden, reserve it for okra. Because of its height, okra is an ungainly plant to grow in a container, but it is a superb addition to an edible-landscape design.

To aid sprouting, soak seeds overnight in water before sowing. In the South, many gardeners freeze seeds for several days, which breaks the seed coat, before planting them. In mild climates, direct-seed okra 1 inch deep, spaced 3 inches apart, as soon as the weather has settled and the soil's temperature reaches 65°F. Plant when the soil is cold, and seeds will rot; at 65°F, germination should occur in a week to 10 days. Germination takes only 5 days at 75°F. In colder regions, or for an early crop, start seeds indoors, 4 to 6 weeks before the last expected frost. Okra resents having its roots disturbed, so use indi-

vidual containers or celled trays. Once seeds sprout, move plants into bright light and feed with diluted fish emulsion.

Set hardened-off okra plants outdoors, spaced 12 to 16 inches apart, 2 or 3 weeks after the danger of frost has passed, when the soil temperature has reached 65°F (to help raise soil temperature, cover the planting bed with black plastic). Add a half-shovelful of compost or bonemeal to each planting hole before setting the transplant.

To protect transplants from wind, cold, and insects, cover them with floating row covers or cloches. If you want to lay down an organic mulch, wait until the soil has warmed. Adequate moisture is necessary for good yields; make sure plants receive at least 1 inch of water a week.

Other than cold temperatures, the most common problems encountered when growing okra are nematodes, blight, and fusarium wilt (for specific remedies, see "Controlling Common Diseases" on page 169), but plants are generally free from insects and diseases. Rotating the location of the crop each year will help avoid most problems.

HARVESTING

Like large summer squash, large okra pods, which become fibrous and inedible, belong on the compost pile. Pick daily—or every other day—when pods are still soft and small, about 2 or 3 inches long, about 4 days after the flowers fade. (Because okra leaves give some people a rash, you may want to wear long sleeves and gloves when harvesting.) You should be able to snap off the pod, although some cultivars are tough and may need to be cut with a knife or shears. Picking regularly not only ensures a good harvest, it means a larger harvest: The more pods you pick, the more pods you'll get.

Okra, which is a good source of calcium and fiber, doesn't store well. Any pods that can't be used immediately should be spread out in a cool location and sprinkled lightly with water.

Okra flowers are perfect, meaning they have both stamens and pistils and can self-pollinate, but because they attract bees and other insects, cross-pollination between cultivars is common. To produce seeds that will come true, plant only one cultivar. Pods that contain ripened seeds are dry and hard on the hands—wear gloves when handling. Seeds are viable for 5 years; store in airtight containers in a dark, cool location.

Onion sets for 'Red Hamburger', White Bermuda', and 'Yellow Globe'

ONION

Allium cepa, Cepa group. Onion family, Alliaceae.
Biennial grown as an annual.

○ ◑ ✳ ❄ ❀ ▮

Cooked or raw, onions may be the most versatile of all vegetables in the kitchen, where they can find a place in nearly any dish, from haute cuisine to left-overs. It's difficult to imagine cooking without them. No wonder the per capita onion consumption in the United States is a hefty 18.2 pounds (surpassed only by potatoes and head lettuce)—and the 18.2 figure doesn't include onions grown in home gardens. Not bad for a vegetable that makes the eyes run and the air and breath rank. "Happy is said to be the family which can eat onions together," Charles Dudley Warner wrote in *My Summer in a Garden* (1871).

Onions have been cultivated for at least 5,000 years, making them one of the oldest as well as most popular vegetable-garden crops. The Egyptians, Greeks, and Romans all ate onions. They were an essential food in the Middle Ages; by the Elizabethan period, their medicinal powers were as well known as their culinary virtues. They were "cherished everie where in kitchen gardens," the English herbalist John Gerard pointed out, and were used to treat stuffy heads, mad-dog bites, gout, and burns. "The juice anointed upon a pild or bald head

Onion plants ready to harvest

in the Sun," Gerard added, "bringeth the haire againe very speedily."

The first European settlers in North America found and ate an assortment of native onion relatives, collectively called alliums, including wild garlic and ramps, but they preferred the globe onions that they had known in England. John Winthrop, Jr., ordered a pound of "new onyon seed" in 1631—around 150,000 seeds—which indicates how important onions were to the colonists. By the time of the Civil War, at least 60 cultivars were being grown, although New Englander Fearing Burr observed that "many kinds succeed only in warm latitudes."

Although he didn't know it, Burr was identifying onions' sensitivity not only to warmth but to day length, a phenomenon called photoperiodism that was not understood until the 20th century. (See "Weather & Day-Length Considerations" on page 99 for more on photoperiodism.) Onions can be grown in all USDA Zones, but different cultivars require different amounts of light and dark to form bulbs. "Long-day" onions require at least 14 hours of sunlight to set bulbs; "intermediate-day" cultivars, between 12 and 14 hours of sun; and "short-day" onions, only 11 or 12 hours of daylight. Southerners, who grow onions as a winter crop, plant short-day cultivars. In regions where onions are sown in late winter for summer harvest, inter-mediate-day cultivars are used. In the North, where onions are seeded in spring, gardeners should choose long-day onions.

DECIDING WHAT TO GROW

"Knowing your onions" is an apt phrase for being an expert, because, with more than 400 *Allium* species, knowing your onions is no simple matter. In addition to leeks, chives, garlic, shallots, and other first

cousins, there are any number of bulbing onions and at least five ways to classify them: color, flavor, shape, day length, and use. (See *Leek*, *Garlic*, and *Shallot* for more on these popular crops; for information on multiplier onions, see *Shallot*.)

Onion colors are white, yellow, and red. Flavors, which are affected by growing conditions, are sweet, mild, and pungent. Shapes are globe, flattened, or torpedo. Day lengths are short, intermediate, and long. Perhaps use—storage; slicing; pearl, used for pickling; and green, grown for their stalks and tops—is the most helpful distinction for home growers.

Storage Onions. 'Spartan Sleeper', 'Early Yellow Globe', and other storage onions tend to have darker color, thicker skins, and more pungent

ONION CULTIVARS

How you want to use your onion crop, where you live, and when you plant will all help determine which cultivars to plant. The following list is divided by use into bulbing, pearl, and green onions/scallions. Day-length requirements are provided for bulbing cultivars.

Bulbing Onions

'Ailsa Craig': 110 days; intermediate-day; large, sweet, yellow-skinned globe; stores well; English heirloom.

'Burgundy': 120 days; short-day; large red-skinned flattened type with very sweet flavor; some disease tolerance; poor keeper.

'Copra': 105 days; long-day; medium-size yellow-skinned globe with mild flavor; excellent storage; hybrid.

'Early Yellow Globe': 100 days; long-day; medium-size, mildly pungent yellow-skinned globe; stores well; widely adapted.

'Fiesta': 110 days; intermediate-day; mid-size yellow-skinned globe with slightly pungent taste; poor keeper; hybrid.

'Red Granex': 165 days; short-day; large, sweet, flattened bulb with red skin; hybrid.

'Red Torpedo': 120 days; intermediate-day; very large red-skinned, torpedo-shaped onion with sweet flavor; some disease tolerance.

'Red Wethersfield': 105 days; long-day; large, pungent, flattened bulb with red skin;

widely adapted; stores fairly well; heirloom.

'Redman': 105 days; long-day; medium-size red-skinned globe with slightly pungent taste; stores well.

'Southport Red Globe': 110 days; long-day; medium-size red-skinned globe with very pungent flavor; stores fairly well.

'Southport White Globe': 90 days; long-day; medium-size white-skinned globe with pungent taste; stores well; good scallion cultivar.

'Spartan Sleeper': 110 days; long-day; medium-size yellow-skinned globe with pungent flavor; outstanding storage onion; hybrid.

'Stockton Early Red': 180 days; intermediate-day; large red-skinned onion with flattened shape and mildly pungent taste; excellent bolt resistance; some disease tolerance.

'Sweet Sandwich': 110 days; long-day; large yellow/brown-skinned globe with slightly pungent flavor; drought-resistant; hybrid.

'Texas Grano 438': 180 days; short-day; very large yellow-skinned onion with flattened shape and slightly pungent flavor.

flavor, and they keep for long periods of time. Most mature in 90 to 150 days from seeds.

Slicing Onions. Slicing types, such as 'Red Torpedo' and 'Walla Walla', have lighter color, thinner skins, and a sweeter flavor than do other types; they do not store well. Also known as Bermuda and Spanish onions, most mature in 90 to 150 days from seeds.

Pearl Onions. These, such as 'Crystal Wax', have small bulbs and mild flavor and are intended for pickling. Also known as cocktail onions, most pearl onion cultivars are ready to pull in about 65 days from seeds.

Green Onions. Also called scallions, bunching onions, spring onions, Welsh onions, nebuka onions, Japanese bunching onions, and salad onions, green onions, such as 'Evergreen White Bunching', have little or no bulb and are grown for their stalk and tops. Most are perennials and belong to a different species, A. *fistulosum*, or are crosses between A. *fistulosum* and A. *cepa*, but any onion cultivar can be pulled prematurely and called a scallion. They mature in 65 to 75 days from seeds.

For fresh use, 125 bulbing onions, 50 scallions, and 25 pearl onions should provide enough for a family of four; if you want to preserve, increase the planting.

SITE & SOIL

Like other underground crops, onions want near-neutral soil (pH 6.0 to 7.5) that is well-drained yet moisture-retentive, moderately fertile and rich in

---

'**Texas Supersweet**': 175 days; short-day; large, very sweet yellow-skinned globe; disease-resistant.

'**Vidalia**': 170 days; short-day; large, flattened yellow-skinned globe with extremely sweet flavor; hybrid.

'**Walla Walla Sweet**': 125 days (300 days overwintered); long-day; large yellow-skinned onion with flattened shape and extremely sweet flavor; poor keeper; heirloom.

'**White Bermuda**': 90 days; short-day; medium-size white-skinned type with flattened shape and very mild flavor; poor keeper.

'**White Sweet Spanish**': 100 days; long-day; large, mildly pungent white-skinned globe; stores fairly well.

'**Yellow Granex**': 165 days; short-day; large, very sweet yellow-skinned onion with flattened shape; bolt-resistant; some disease resistance; standard southern cultivar; hybrid.

'**Yellow Sweet Spanish**': 110; long-day; large, mild-flavored yellow-skinned globe; good home-garden cultivar.

Pearl Onions
'**Barletta**': 70 days; uniform, nearly round white bulb with mild flavor.

'**Crystal Wax**': 60 days; flattened white bulb with very mild flavor; some disease resistance.

'**Pompeii Perla Prima**': 65 days; flattened white bulb with mild flavor.

'**Purplette**': 60 days; purple bulb; hybrid.

'**White Portugal**'/'**Silverskin**': 100 days; large, flattened white bulbs with mild, sweet flavor; good cultivar for scallions; heirloom.

Green Onions/Scallions
'**Beltsville Bunching**': 65 days; white stalk and green tops with very mild taste; widely adapted; drought-resistant; hardy; some disease resistance.

'**Evergreen White Bunching**': 65 days; white stalk and long green tops with mildly pungent taste; extremely hardy; moderate disease resistance.

'**He-Ski-Ko**': 65 days; white stalk and green tops; mild flavor.

'**Hikari**': 65 days; white stalk and green tops with mild flavor; good fall cultivar.

'**Ishikura**': 65 days; thick white stalk with green tops and mildly pungent taste; very hardy.

'**Red Welsh**': 70 days; red stalk with green tops and very pungent taste; very hardy.

'**Tokyo Long White**': 68 days; long white stalk and green tops with mildly pungent taste; not hardy; good disease resistance.

organic matter. If your ground drains slowly, grow onions in raised beds. To make forming bulbs easy, dig the ground to a depth of 8 inches and begin in weed-free soil. Because onions produce grasslike tops rather than large leaves, they don't shade the soil as cucumbers or beans do, and young plants are easily overtaken by weeds. Many gardeners sprinkle soil with wood ashes or lime to ensure it isn't excessively sour (acid). Apply parasitic nematodes to control onion maggots and cutworms before planting.

Onions are suitable for both succession planting and underplanting. Combine scallions with vegetables and herbs that will be in place most of the growing season, such as tomatoes, peppers, and basil. Plant bulbing cultivars with quick-maturing spring crops, such as leaf lettuce. Locate onions where they receive at least 6 hours of sun daily. All types do well in containers, but not all types belong in the ornamental garden. Storage onions, which must stay in the ground until their tops die back, are a poor choice for a flower bed, but the staunchly vertical tops of tightly spaced green onions are striking in ornamental beds, window boxes, and other containers. Use a container, at least 8 inches wide and 12 inches deep, with good bottom drainage, and

---

ONION ESSENTIALS

• Full sun and cool, but not cold, temperatures.

• Near-neutral, well-drained soil that retains moisture.

• Weed-free soil dug to 8 inches deep.

• Before planting, apply parasitic nematodes to soil to control onion maggots and cutworms.

• Water regularly, and mulch to control weeds and retain soil moisture.

• Stop watering when tops turn yellow or fall over.

---

fill with enriched potting soil. Water frequently, and feed every 3 weeks with compost tea.

HOW TO GROW

Onions like cool temperatures (55° to 75°F) in the beginning, then need more warmth to mature their bulbs. Don't be in too much of a hurry to plant, though. While most young onion plants are able to stand up to a couple of late frosts, their development may be delayed by extended periods of temperatures in the 30s and 40s F.

Except in very warm regions, where they are grown as a winter crop, onions usually are planted in spring. Onions are planted as seeds, as sets, which are dime-size dormant bulbs, or as transplants, which are small plants grown in the fall or winter in warm regions. Sets and transplants are easier than seeds are to care for in the beginning and also mature more quickly, both of which are important factors for gardeners with brief garden seasons. However, onions grown from sets, especially large sets, are more likely to bolt, producing seed stalks rather than bulbs, than are onions started from seeds or transplants. They also tend to store less well. Transplants, which must be bought in bulk, are not available in many regions, and both transplants and sets are often labeled simply "white," "red," or "yellow." Both are more expensive than seeds are. If your garden season is long enough, grow onions from seeds. That way, you'll know what you're growing, and you'll have access to cultivars that are perfect for your taste and location.

Starting From Seeds. To produce good-size bulbs, most gardeners need to begin seeds indoors 8 to 10 weeks before the average frost-free date (in warm regions, onion seeds can be sown in autumn). Soak seeds in compost tea for 15 minutes to reduce the threat of damping-off, then sow thickly, ½ inch deep, in flats filled with a damp sterile mix. In warm soil (65° to 85°F), germination should occur in 5 days. Once seeds have sprouted, thin or transplant to a spacing of 1 inch, and move containers to a bright, cool (60° to 65°F) location. Fertilize weekly with a diluted solution of fish emulsion and liquid seaweed.

Seedlings, after being hardened off, can go into the garden 2 to 3 weeks before the last expected frost; warm the soil before transplanting by covering it with plastic. Remove plastic mulch, and set plants slightly deeper than they were growing, spaced 2 to

6 inches apart, depending on the size of the cultivar's mature bulb. For scallions, space plants 1 inch apart.

To direct-seed outdoors, plant seeds 3 to 4 weeks before the last frost; or plant in fall in warm regions. Warm soil with plastic mulch before sowing, then remove the plastic and sow seeds thickly, ½ inch deep. When the plants are 5 inches tall, thin to 2 to 6 inches apart, depending on the size of the cultivar's mature bulb. For scallions, thin to 1 inch.

Starting From Sets. Buy small dormant sets, no larger than ¾ inch in diameter (if you're growing scallions from sets, choose white types). Presoak sets in compost tea for 15 minutes. Speed soil warming by laying down plastic mulch several weeks before planting. When the soil temperature reaches 40°F, or 4 weeks before the last expected frost, remove the

Onions 'Copper', 'Mambo', and 'Ailsa Craig'

plastic mulch and push the sets (pointed end up) into the ground, about ½ inch below the soil surface. Space 2 to 6 inches apart, depending on the size of the cultivar's mature bulb. For scallions, space sets 1 inch apart.

Starting From Transplants. Buy only green, healthy plants that haven't been allowed to dry out. Keep transplants cool. Before planting, submerge them in compost tea for 15 minutes. Speed soil warming by covering the soil with plastic mulch several weeks before the expected planting-out date. When the soil reaches 40°F, remove the plastic mulch and set the transplants in the garden, 1 to 2 inches deep. Space them 2 to 6 inches apart, depending on the size of the cultivar's mature bulb. For scallions, space transplants 1 inch apart.

Care Through the Season. Cover the seeds, sets, or seedlings immediately after planting with floating row covers to prevent onion maggot flies from laying eggs. Except in humid, wet regions, mulch plants when they are still small to retain moisture. Keep plants well weeded, taking care not to disturb their roots. Side-dress with compost tea 3 weeks after planting, again when the tops are 6 inches tall, and a third time when bulbs begin to swell. Do not feed with high-nitrogen fertilizers, which will result in massive tops and small bulbs.

Onions have a shallow root system. Once established in the garden, they need an even supply of water—about 1 inch a week. When the onion tops begin to yellow or collapse, signs that the bulbs are reaching maturity, stop watering.

YOU'RE THE TOP

Top-setting, or Egyptian tree, onions (*Allium cepa*, Proliferum group) are perennials. They produce clusters of small bulblets at the top of their stalks in addition to dividing underground. They're also called walking onions, because a single bulb not only produces a cluster of 6 or more underground bulbs, but the aboveground bulblets (which sometimes sprout shoots that are topped with yet more bulblets) fall to the soil in midsummer and produce new plants. Mulch plants in winter to prevent them from heaving.

Hardy top-setting onions, which are rarely bothered by diseases or insects, are pungent—many find the small underground bulbs too strong except when harvested in early spring. Young tops taste like scallions but become increasingly strong-flavored as they mature. 'Moritz Egyptian', an heirloom with deep maroon bulbs, is the most widely available cultivar; 'Catawissa Onion' is an heirloom cultivar from France by way of Canada.

Bulbing onions have a tendency to heave, or push out of the ground. Rather than hill up the bulbs, as you would leeks, cover them lightly with mulch to prevent sunscald. Once the tops begin to wither, pull back any mulch to encourage bulbs to dry.

POTENTIAL PROBLEMS

Commercial growers battle all sorts of onion diseases and insect pests, but backyard gardeners normally encounter few problems. Prevention is the best way to keep possible plagues at bay, so be sure to grow cultivars that are suited to your region, warm the soil before planting, change the location of your onions every year, and use floating row covers to control onion maggots and other insects.

Onions are attacked by a few common pests and diseases, including onion maggots, thrips, wireworms, damping-off, and downy mildew. (See "Controlling Common Pests" and "Controlling Common Diseases" on pages 162 and 169 for control measures.) One serious disease is pink root, which stunts onion roots, turning them pink or red. Infected plants cannot be cured; remove and destroy them, and rotate crop location. Purchase tolerant/resistant cultivars, such as 'Burgundy',

HOMEGROWN SETS

Growing your own sets from seeds allows you to choose from the wide range of onions available yet still benefit from the advantages of starting from sets. You have to begin a year ahead to grow your own onion sets. Good yellow cultivars include 'Yellow Globe Danvers', 'Stuttgarter', and 'Turbo'. Sow seeds thickly in summer, but do not thin them. After 2 months, knock the tops over to force small bulbs to form. When the tops are dry, pull the bulbs and cure them as you would full-size onions. Remove the tops, leaving ½ inch of stem. Store over winter in mesh bags in a cold (35°F), dry, well-ventilated location, then plant in spring.

'Red Torpedo', 'Tokyo Long White', 'Red Granex', and 'Yellow Granex'. Smut causes dark, thickened patches on onion seedlings; affected plants should be removed and destroyed. Protect young plants by applying an organic fungicide. 'Beltsville Bunching' and 'Tokyo Long White' are resistant to smut.

HARVESTING

For scallions, or green onions, keep in mind that flavor becomes stronger as the plants grow larger; begin harvesting as soon as the tops are about 6 inches tall. To harvest bulbs, which are a good source of potassium, begin pulling as soon as they are large enough to use. (Remove any onions that have bolted, and use them immediately.) Pull or dig carefully: Bulbs that are bruised rot quickly when stored. Bulbs are fully mature when their tops turn yellow and fall over. Although it will shorten their storage life, you can speed the process by knocking the green tops down with a hoe or rake. Onions that must be harvested but still have green tops will not store well and should be used right away.

Because onions are biennials and flower during their second season, saving seeds is difficult. Gardeners in cold climates must dig bulbs in the fall, overwinter them, and replant them in the spring; in frost-free regions, carry plants over to a second year. Onions are easily cross-pollinated by insects. To save seeds that will come true, plant only one cultivar. The standard wisdom is that onion seeds are viable for only 1 or 2 years, but newer information from the U.S. Department of Agriculture suggests that if seeds are properly stored—in airtight containers in a dark, cool location—they remain viable for at least 5 years.

SPECIAL NOTES

To store onions for any length of time, they must first be cured. After harvesting, spread onions in a single layer (off the ground). Leave them outdoors for 2 to 10 days to dry, or dry them in an well-ventilated indoor location for about 2 weeks. When the bulbs' outer skins are dry and the tops have withered completely, remove the tops, leaving 1 inch of stem. Store in mesh bags in a cool (35° to 40°F), dry, well-ventilated location. Check stored onions frequently, and immediately use any bulb that sprouts.

ONION, MULTIPLIER. See *Shallot*

Red orach

ORACH

Atriplex hortensis. Goosefoot family,
Chenopodiaceae. Annual.

○ ❄ ✿ ▆

"It is an herb so innocent that it can be eaten in the leaf salad," the 17th-century English physician-astrologer Nicholas Culpeper wrote. The mild, slightly astringent flavor of young orach leaves has earned this cool-weather salad green a comparison with spinach, another member of the goosefoot family. Orach, also spelled orache, produces broad, arrow-shaped leaves that range from pale green to dark red. The branching, upright 4- to 6-foot-tall plants are quite unlike spinach in appearance, however. They produce long, intriguing flower and seed spikes. Still, as Bernard M'Mahon, one of North America's earliest garden writers, noted 200 years ago, orach can be "sown at the same time and treated in every respect like spinage .... Some persons," he continued, "prefer it."

Like other cool-weather greens, such as arugula, orach is fast-growing and best if picked when the leaves are young. Harvesting can begin about 40 days after seeding and continue until plants begin to flower. Although orach retains its flavor later in the season than does spinach, it, too, is an annual and will lose its salad quality and run to seed before the summer is over.

You may have trouble finding orach seeds—some catalogs list the plant under herbs—but more than a dozen orachs were sold in the 19th century, including a pale purple cultivar that was tinged with green and had the intriguing name of 'Lurid'. Today, there are really only three choices, each based on leaf color. Green-leaved orach, which is usually listed simply in seed catalogs as orach or under its botanical name, *Atriplex hortensis*, is sweeter-tasting than red-leaved forms. Red orachs, which may be listed as 'Red', 'Purple', 'Crimson Plum', or 'Rubra' in catalogs but are all probably the same plant, are more ornamental than green forms are, and they retain their color when cooked. Yellow orach—variously listed as 'Yellow', 'Golden', 'Blonde', and 'Belle Dame'—grows as tall as green and red types, but its pale yellow leaves are smaller. Widely cultivated in France, it is considered by many as the sweetest and most tender form.

Orach can be grown as a spring to summer crop and sown again as a fall crop in USDA Zones 3 through 6; in warmer regions, it can be grown through the winter without cover. A half-dozen plants or a thickly planted 10-foot row harvested mesclun-style should provide plenty of leaves for salads and steamed greens for a family of four. A half-dozen plants can be raised in a 5-gallon pot, 15 in a 10-gallon tub, if they are cut back periodically. Red orach is an especially decorative container crop, particularly if plants are allowed to reach mature height and bloom, and form plume-like seed heads. If you plan to let your orach blossom and set seed, grow one plant per 5-gallon pot, three to a 10-gallon tub. A combination of both red and green cultivars adds color to ornamental beds and borders.

SALTBUSH

Orach is sometimes called saltbush, although that name rightfully belongs to a cousin, *Atriplex patula*. The leaves of saltbush are edible, fresh or cooked, like spinach; Native Americans mixed the plant's ground seeds with meal corn for steaming.

HOW TO GROW

Orach has been cultivated for perhaps 4,000 years, and its many common names —mountain spinach, sea purslane, butter leaves, and French spinach among them—suggest the plant's cultural adaptability and broad climatic range. A site in full sun with well-drained soil that is high in organic matter and has a near-neutral pH (6.8 to 7.0) is ideal. However, orach is one of few vegetables that will grow in slightly saline soil, and the species has naturalized widely in coastal areas. To keep the flavor and texture of the foliage palatable water attentively about 1 inch a week.

Seeds can be sown directly in the garden, ¼ inch deep, 2 to 3 weeks before the last-frost date, or when the soil temperature has risen above 50°F. Germination can be spotty and takes 10 to 12 days, depending on soil temperature. Remember that orach is a tall plant if allowed to mature, so locate your crop where it won't shade other vegetables or herbs if you let it reach its full height.

Orach can be raised in various ways. The seeds can be thickly sown, and the young plants, thinned to a few inches apart, sheared when they reach 5 to 6 inches in height. There will be some regrowth, which can be recut. Another option is to sow seeds every 2 weeks from midspring to midsummer to maintain a constant supply of young leaves. Still another method is to sow seeds in midspring, thin plants to 18 inches, and harvest young leaves as needed for salads and steamed greens. Pinch back the tops to keep plants to a height of about 3 feet. Remove any flowers that emerge, and the plants will continue to bear mild-flavored leaves for several more weeks.

Orach is occasionally troubled by aphids, which damage the growing tips of the plants and can transmit disease (for specific information, see "Controlling Common Pests" on page 162); otherwise it is largely trouble-free.

HARVESTING

For salad greens, pick young leaves, 3 to 4 inches long, or shear entire plants when they are about 6 inches tall and allow them to regrow. Larger leaves can be used for steamed greens.

Orach's small flowers are wind-pollinated. To ensure seeds that will come true, plant only one cultivar. Seeds are viable for 6 years if stored in airtight containers in a dark, cool location.

Oregano flowers

OREGANO

Origanum vulgare. Mint family, Lamiaceae.
Perennial.

○ ✳ ❄ ❀ ▼

Oregano and its close relative marjoram share a tangled web of names that tests even the most patient of gardeners. There's even an ancient but ongoing debate about which plant is the *true* culinary oregano. In fact, according to Steven Foster in *Herbal Bounty* (1984), "Oregano more properly refers to a flavor rather than one particular plant." When garden books and seed catalogs refer to oregano, however, they're usually talking about *Origanum vulgare.*

Also known as wild marjoram, *O. vulgare* is an attractive, shrubby perennial native to Eurasia that is hardy in USDA Zone 5 and warmer. The plants produce gray-green, 1½-inch-long, oval leaves and loose clusters of purplish pink flowers in summer.

Oregano plants, even those labeled as *O. vulgare*, are often variable. Bees love the plants, but the foliage may or may not be aromatic. It's a problem that becomes apparent when gardeners grow oregano from seeds, because seed-grown plants frequently have no flavor whatsoever.

In the past, oregano has been prescribed for snakebites—between oregano "and adders, there is a deadly antipathy," herbalist Nicholas Culpeper wrote in 1653—for toothaches, and for "wambling of the stomacke." Today, it cures wamblings of stomach as the indispensable flavoring of Italian cuisine, an essential herb of pasta sauces and pizza.

The best culinary oregano, which has white flowers, is listed botanically as O. *vulgare* spp. *hirtum*, or as O. *heracleoticum*, and is sometimes sold as "Greek" or "Italian" oregano. Flavor still varies from plant to plant, so taste before you buy. A number of ornamental cultivars—most of which also can be used in cooking—are also available as well. Variegated oregano, O. *vulgare* 'Variegata', has leaves marked in white and yellow. 'Compactum' grows only 2 to 3 inches tall and has strong-flavored ½-inch leaves. 'Nanum' is another dwarf cultivar; it spreads easily and has purple flowers. Golden creeping oregano, 'Aureum', grows to 6 inches. Its golden leaves have a mild flavor. 'Aureum Cripsum', a newer gold-leaved cultivar that may be listed as 'Gold Crisp' oregano, has rounded crinkled leaves and an ascendant habit, making it a fine addition to window boxes and hanging baskets. 'Album' is a small, bushy cultivar, 10 inches high with white flowers.

Since oregano is a perennial, it's best kept out of, or at least at the edges of, the vegetable garden. Instead, grow it with other perennial herbs or in ornamental plantings. Once established, most oreganos are vigorous plants that make attractive, weed-smothering groundcovers. Dwarf and creeping cultivars—including 'Compactum', 'Nanum', and 'Aureum'—are especially good plants for sunny slopes or for the crevices of a rock garden. Pot culture is also an option. Plant one plant per 6-inch pot, or combine oregano with other herbs that thrive in well-drained, slightly dry soil for a container herb garden. Good drainage is essential: Fill containers with a light, somewhat sandy mix that drains well.

HOW TO GROW

Full sun and well-drained average soil are the secrets

Oregano leaves

to success when growing oregano. Plants prefer somewhat alkaline conditions, but they succeed in a wide range of conditions—pH 6.5 to 8.0, almost anything except constant wetness.

NEARLY OREGANO

In addition to *Origanum vulgare*, there is a host of oregano taste-alikes, everything from the trailing *O. rotundifolium* 'Kent Beauty' to Syrian oregano (*O. maru*) and Turkestan oregano (*O. tyttanticum*). Best known of these near-oregano plants is *Lippia graveolens*, or Mexican oregano, which is a tender shrub with aromatic leaves and small white flowers. The oblong, 2½-inch-long leaves have a spicy oregano-like flavor and are considered essential for traditional southwestern-style chili. Hardy only in USDA Zone 9 and warmer, where it can attain a height of 5 to 6 feet, Mexican oregano also is easy to grow in a pot. Plant one plant per 12-inch-wide container filled with light potting soil. Grow plants outdoors in full sun in summer, taking care to keep the soil evenly moist. In fall, bring them indoors before frost, and overwinter them in a cool, sunny window.

If possible, start with plants that were propagated asexually either by division or from cuttings. Before you buy, rub and taste a leaf to determine whether you like the flavor. Alternatively, oregano can be grown from seeds sown outdoors in late spring or indoors 6 to 8 weeks before the last expected frost. At 70°F, seeds should germinate in about 4 days. Plan on growing plenty of seedlings, then select the most fragrant plants, and rouge out, or discard, the others. Set hardened-off seedlings outdoors after the last frost, spaced 1 foot apart. Oregano self-sows, usually yielding flavorless offspring, so be sure to weed plantings regularly.

In full sun and well-drained soil, oregano seldom is affected by pests or diseases. Plants can be killed by an extra-cold winter or by a wet, cold spring. Dig entire plants, or take cuttings in summer to overwinter oregano in areas where it is winterkilled; move plants back outside in spring once the weather is warm at night.

HARVESTING

Oregano leaves are most flavorful before plants flower. Pick individual leaves as soon as the plant is large enough to be harvested. Alternatively, cut back entire plants when they are about 6 inches tall, again just before they begin to flower, and a third time in late summer. Store fresh oregano in plastic bags and refrigerate. To dry oregano, cut and hang stalks in a warm, airy location. When completely dried, store in a sealed jar.

Saving seeds is not recommended.

ORIENTAL CUCUMBER. See *Cucumber*
ORNAMENTAL KALE. See *Kale*
OYSTER PLANT. See *Salsify*
PAK-CHOI. See *Bok Choy*
PAPRIKA. See *Pepper*

PARSLEY

Petroselinum crispum, Crispum and Neapolitanum groups. Carrot family, Apiaceae.
Biennial grown as an annual.

○ ◑ ❄ ❀ ▓

Parsley has become such a humble herb in the 20th century, merely a green leafy sprig to understudy fried eggs or sandwiches, that its noble, even dan-

Parsley 'Italian Broadleaf'

Curley-leaved parsley

gerous past is hard to fathom. This European native was once the herb of hell and death, dedicated by the Greeks to Persephone, Queen of Hades. Wreaths of it were placed on tombs, and so strongly was it associated with tragedy that it was never brought to the table.

Well known for its ability to sweeten the breath, one 16th-century garden writer recommended it to "young maidens and widows to deceive their wooers." Parsley also calms the stomach. Or at least one stomach: "First he ate some lettuce, and some broad beans, then some radishes," Beatrix Potter wrote in *The Tale of Peter Rabbit* (1902), "and then feeling rather sick, he went to look for some parsley." More recently, parsley has become better appreciated as a high-vitamin ingredient in salads, soups, and sandwiches.

Parsley is a biennial, which means it grows a crop of leaves in its first year, then, if the root is allowed to overwinter, it shoots up seed stalks late the following spring, bearing umbels of flowers, then seeds. Gardeners usually grow parsley only for its foliage, however, so it can be considered a hardy annual, tolerant of spring and fall frosts; it can be cultivated in USDA Zone 2 and warmer, reaching its full size in about 80 days. As it stays bright green all summer, parsley is as nice to look at in the garden as it is on the edge of a plate. It grows about a foot tall and wide, or a bit larger and is well suited to bordering flower beds or herb gardens, filling out containers, even shady window boxes, or occupying a bed in the vegetable garden.

DECIDING WHAT TO GROW

There are two forms of standard parsley, curly-leaved and flat-leaved. Curly-leaved, a member of the Crispum group, is the type used commonly for garnishing. Several cultivars exist, including the standards 'Champion Moss Curled', an heirloom, and 'Triple Curled'. Newer are 'Forest Green', 'Green River', and 'Krusa', an import from Holland. 'Sherwood' is a vigorous cultivar with excellent heat resistance. In tests in the 1980s, curly parsley was found to have more flavor-producing compounds than plain-leaved types.

Flat-leaved parsley, also called single or Italian parsley, belongs to the Neapolitanum group and has leaves that look much like those of celery. It is more palatable and is preferred by cooks, because the leaves are flat, not curly. Most taste tests give the edge to flat-leaved parsleys, which are sweet with a hint of spice, despite having fewer "flavor-producing compounds." The usual cultivars are 'Dark Green Italian', which is often listed simply as 'Italian' or

JAPANESE PARSLEY

Japanese parsley (*Cryptotaenia japonica*) is another carrot-family member that is almost unknown in North America. (A relative sometimes called white or wild chervil, *C. canadensis*, grows wild from eastern Canada to Texas.) Also called mitsuba, Japanese parsley forms foot-tall clumps and looks much like flat-leaved parsley in leaf shape but differs chiefly in its stronger flavor and its perennial disposition. It is hardy to USDA Zone 5 with mulching and elsewhere can be potted up and moved indoors for the winter. Leaves can be harvested from its first year. The flower stalks shoot up in summer and are topped by umbels of small white flowers followed by 1/4-inch seedpods. Although it sometimes self-sows, save some of the seeds for next year if you grow mitsuba as an annual, for the plant is rarely included in seed catalogs.

Like other types of parsley, this crop does best in rich, moist soil that is close to neutral (pH 7.0), so is most commonly grown in the vegetable garden. Plants prefer a spot in partial shade; the leaves turn pale in full sun (afternoon shade is especially beneficial). One or two plants should provide enough for a family of four.

Plants are seldom available, so Japanese parsley must be grown from seeds. The usual route is to sow seeds anew every year, treating this crop as an annual. Tolerant of light frost, seeds can be sown directly outdoors, 1/2 inch deep, as soon as the soil can be worked in spring, in the manner of regular parsley. Unlike regular parsley, the seeds germinate quickly, provided the soil stays moist. Thin plants gradually until they are about 6 inches apart. Alternatively, seeds can be started early in peat pots indoors, then hardened off before they go outdoors around the last-frost date. In warm regions, seeds can also be sown in early fall. In Japan, plants are generally blanched by hilling to produce tender, pale stalks.

Use leaves and leafstalks as needed, anywhere you might use parsley but especially in Japanese dishes, such as those including tofu, fish, vegetables, or noodles. The roots can be cooked and eaten on their own or in soups or stews.

"Plain," and 'Neapolitan', or 'Gigante d'Italia'. 'Catalogno', which has very large leaves, and 'Sweet Italian', a new cultivar with a sweeter flavor but less stiff stems, are other names to look for.

Six plants of either type will provide summer garnishes and enough surplus to dry or freeze for winter. The first leaves will be ready to pick as soon as plants are established. Plants mature 2 to 3 months from sowing.

SITE & SOIL

Parsley should have fertile, organically rich, well-worked soil and full sun, although plants will tolerate partial shade. Soil should be slightly acid (pH 6.0 to 6.8). Plants also can be grown in large containers, one plant to a pot at least 1 foot wide and deep, or they can be carefully dug in fall and transplanted into large containers to be brought indoors for fresh use in winter. Put the pot near a cool, bright window, and do not allow the soil to dry thoroughly.

HOW TO GROW

Parsley is easy to grow from seeds, but germination is slow, taking as long as 3 weeks in 70°F soil. (Folklore claims that parsley seeds go seven times to the devil and back before they sprout.) To speed germination, soak seeds overnight in water, then sow indoors in individual containers 7 to 10 weeks before the last spring frost. After the seedlings have been hardened off, transplant outside while the weather is still cool, a week or two before the frost-free date. Parsley has a long taproot and resents being moved, so take care to retain soil around the root ball when you transplant.

For a later but easier crop, sow seeds directly in the garden as soon as the soil can be worked. Mix a few radish seeds, which will sprout quickly, with the parsley seeds to mark their location. Thin plants to 8 inches. Parsley growth is best in cool soil. Where summers are hot, give the plants partial shade, water in dry weather, and mulch the ground to moderate the temperature around the roots, retain moisture, and suppress weeds. Where summers are cool, parsley prefers full sun. Water with compost or manure tea in midseason to keep plants vigorous.

Parsley is a largely trouble-free herb, although hot weather or transplanting disturbance may cause plants to bolt to seed in their first year. To avoid crown rot, keep mulches an inch or two away from plants and do not overwater. Insect pests can be discouraged by covering young plants with floating row covers. Parsleyworms, green caterpillars that can be handpicked, are fond of parsley, but since they are the larvae of swallowtail butterflies, you may want to leave them undisturbed—or move them to other carrot-family plants, such as Queen Anne's lace.

HARVESTING

Begin harvesting parsley leaves, which are rich in iron and vitamins A and C, as soon as they are large enough to be used. Use leaves whole or chopped in salads, vegetable dishes, and stews. Blend parsley with garlic and butter to make garlic bread. The roots can also be dug and used in the manner of Hamburg parsley (see the entry on this crop on page 270).

Keep harvesting by cutting, not pulling, the outside leaves, which will keep plants producing new, tender growth. In mild regions, overwintered plants will resprout in spring. Once parsley flowers, however, the leaves' flavor becomes bitter.

Store fresh parsley in plastic bags or closed containers in the refrigerator, where it will keep for several weeks. It can be stored longer if dried or frozen.

Because parsley is a biennial and flowers in its second season, saving seeds is difficult. Gardeners in cold climates must dig and overwinter plants, then replant them in the spring; in frost-free regions, carry plants over to a second year. Parsley pollen is carried by insects, and all parsleys, including wild species, crossbreed. To save seeds, plant only one cultivar or isolate your crop. Seeds are viable for 3 years; store in airtight containers in a dark, cool location.

PARSLEY, CHINESE. See *Cilantro*
PARSLEY, HAMBURG. See *Hamburg Parsley*
PARSLEY, TURNIP-ROOTED. See *Hamburg Parsley*

PARSNIP

Pastinaca sativa. Carrot family, Apiaceae. Biennial grown as an annual.

○ ◐ ❄

It's hard to reconcile the delicate flavor of parsnips with their rugged constitution. Not only are the

Parsnip 'Hollow Crown'

roots able to withstand a winter underground, they are sweetened by low temperatures. "For they are not so good in any respect," the 17th-century French botanist Joseph Tournefort wrote, "till they have been first nipt with Cold." Tournefort's advice runs counter to the old wives' tale that parsnips become poisonous if left in the ground until spring. That belief was buttressed by enough "poison" victims to lead the U.S. Department of Agriculture to investigate. The culprit turned out not to be parsnips and cold but water hemlock (*Cicuta maculata*), which resembles the parsnip and is toxic. The moral of the story is *never* dig a "wild" parsnip.

In contrast to this darker side, the parsnip, which is a cousin of the carrot, has been prescribed for a variety of ailments since Roman times. It has been recommended as a cure for snakebites, ulcers, colic, pain, consumption, and even psychological ills. "It profiteth the Melanchollicke," an early herbalist wrote. The reputed benefits of parsnip wine—boiled parsnips, sugar, and yeast—have carried into the 20th century, and it continues to be recommended as a spring tonic as well as a treatment for fever and jaundice.

Most gardeners will be more interested in the parsnip as food than as medicine. A European native, it is one of the hardiest of all biennial crops, easily grown throughout North America, USDA Zone 2 and warmer. Flavor differences between cultivars are minimal; differences in shape—long and slender versus blocky—are more pronounced. If your soil is heavy or rocky, avoid a long-rooted cultivar like 'Tried & True', which set a record in England at nearly 145 inches, and choose a short-rooted parsnip, such as 'Fullback'.

Because parsnips take their time to mature—as many as 150 days—they need a space in the garden

PARSNIP CULTIVARS

Since parsnip cultivars differ very little in flavor, use soil type as the determining factor when deciding what to grow. In heavy, rocky, or shallow soil, choose short-rooted types.

'All America': 110 days; open-pollinated; slender 12-inch root; stores well.

'Andover': 120 days; open-pollinated; slender root; canker resistant.

'Fullback': 95 days; open-pollinated; short, blocky root; good for shallow soils.

'Gladiator': 110 days; hybrid; canker-resistant; first hybrid parsnip; British cultivar.

'Harris Model': 120 days; open-pollinated; medium, tapered root; standard cultivar.

'Hollow Crown': 120 days; open-pollinated; long, tapered root; good storage cultivar; heirloom.

'Javelin': 110 days; hybrid; slim, tapered root; canker-resistant.

'Tender & True': 105 days; open-pollinated; very long, tapered root; canker-resistant; heirloom.

all season long, although they can be interplanted with quick-maturing spring crops, such as radishes or green onions. For a family of four, 40 plants should yield enough parsnips; if you want to preserve, increase the planting. Because of their long root, parsnips are not a suitable crop for container gardens.

HOW TO GROW

Parsnips often slip over the garden gate and naturalize, evidence of their unparticular nature. Almost any soil will do, but near-neutral (pH 6.2 to 7.2) ground that is dug to at least 18 inches—24 for long cultivars—and rich in organic matter ensures good root development. To speed germination, soak seeds overnight. Sow seeds thickly early in spring, as soon as the soil can be worked (in warm regions, sow seeds in early fall for a spring harvest), ½ inch deep, in rows 18 inches apart. In 50°F soil, germination will take between 3 and 4 weeks. Thin seedlings to 4 inches, and mulch to retain moisture and suppress weeds. Be ruthless when thinning; crowded plants will fail to develop good roots. In midseason, spray with compost tea and/or side-dress with wood ashes or compost to promote growth. Keep plants well watered, at least 1 inch per week, or the roots will become tough.

Parsnips, which contain modest amounts of vitamin C, potassium, and fiber, are seldom bothered by insects or diseases. To prevent problems, cover the seedbed with floating row covers and rotate their location in the garden.

HARVESTING

You can begin digging parsnips as soon as they are large enough to be used, but it's better to wait until after the first few frosts, which will improve their flavor. Mulching heavily will extend the time roots can be dug in cold regions. Roots left in the ground over winter should be dug before new growth begins in spring. Some gardeners are allergic to the juice contained in the foliage and stems of parsnips. Keep your hands away from your face when working around plants.

For short-term storage, place roots in plastic bags to retain moisture and refrigerate. Parsnips can be stored for up to 6 months in damp sand or sawdust in a cold (32° to 40°F) location.

Parsnips are biennials and normally don't flower until their second season. In extremely cold regions, plants must be overwintered indoors and replanted in the spring; in warmer parts of the country, carry plants to a second year. Plants are insect-pollinated, and cultivars cross easily. To save seeds that will come true, plant one cultivar. Seeds are viable for only 1 year; store in airtight containers in a dark, cool location.

PEA

Pisum sativum subsp. *sativum*. Pea family, Fabaceae. Annual.

○ ◑ ❄ ❀

Peas have been cultivated for such a long time that their origin is a mystery, so believing the European legend that they came from Thor, the god of thunder, may be as good an explanation as any. (Ironically, Thor had punishment in mind when he sent peas to earth to foul the humans' wells, but a few seeds dropped on the ground and rooted.) Whatever their native home—scientists speculate it was western Asia—peas were a staple by the Middle Ages and were among the first crops planted by

Pea 'Snappy'

American colonists. Recommended supplies to keep a settler going for a year in the New World included "three paire of Stockings; sixe paire of Shooes; one gallon of Aquavitae; one bushell of Pease."

Success with peas on this continent was immediate. John Josselyn, in his 1672 account of native and introduced plants in New England, recorded that he found "Pease of all sorts" in American gardens, "and the best in the World; I never heard of, nor did see in eight years time, one Worm eaten Pea." Although peas had little medicinal value— several herbalists noted that they were without "effectuall qualitie"—they weren't without worth but were a "dish of meate for the table of the rich as well as the poore," according to John Parkinson, botanist to King Charles I.

More than 175 cultivars were being grown in the United States by the middle of the 19th century. "New sorts are yearly introduced," Fearing Burr reported in 1865, "and it would be injudicious not to give them a fair trial." More than 200 cultivars are commercially available today, which should be enough, even for a crop that can be grown almost everywhere in North America, USDA Zone 2 and warmer, yet new cultivars continue to be introduced. Because hybrid peas are difficult to produce

PEA ESSENTIALS

- Full sun, cool weather, and good air circulation.
- Light, moderately fertile soil that drains well.
- Sow seeds 3 inches apart, or 5 to 6 inches in double rows.
- Install strings or other supports at planting time.
- Thinning isn't necessary.
- Mulch plants when 3 inches tall.
- Pinch or cut pods from plants; regular harvesting increases yields.

on a large scale, all available cultivars are open-pollinated. The most prominent new cultivar in the past 20 years was 'Sugar Snap', the first snap pea. The result of a cross between a garden and a snow pea, snap peas combine the best of both types: plump, sweet seeds and tender pods.

DECIDING WHAT TO GROW

There are several questions facing the gardener who wants to grow peas, but the place to begin is which pea? Those that are shelled, or *mangetout* peas, and those eaten entire—pod and all.

Garden Peas. Also called English or green peas, these are the traditional crop—the type of peas that are shelled or that come in a can. Only the seeds are eaten. In addition to the standard garden-pea cultivars, there are two subclasses. First are small-seeded, or *petit pois*, types, which are considered by many as the best-flavored of all peas. They are bred to have small seeds and are often labeled as "baby peas" when canned. (Picked early, any garden pea becomes a *petit pois*.) Second are dry, or soup, peas. These cultivars are typically left on the vine to mature fully, rather than picked at the green stage as standard garden peas are. The ingredient of Mother Goose's "Pease porridge hot,/Pease porridge cold,/Pease porridge in the pot/Nine days old," they're also known as pod and field peas.

Snow Peas. Also known as Chinese, sugar, and edible-podded peas, these types are harvested when the pod reaches full size but before the seeds become enlarged; both pod and seeds are edible.

Snap Peas. Developed in Idaho by plant breeder Calvin Lamborn, snap, or sugar snap, peas are picked when both the pod and its seeds are green-mature. 'Sugar Snap', the first snap cultivar and perhaps the most popular vegetable cultivar of the past 25 years, was released in 1979 and won an AAS award. Both pod and seeds are edible.

When deciding what to grow, you'll also want to take height and days to maturity into consideration. Cultivars can be as short as 1 foot and as tall as 8 and can take anywhere from 55 to 85 days to mature. If you don't want to erect trellises, choose a dwarf cultivar, such as 'Petit Pois', while keeping in mind that even compact plants benefit from a little support. The last word in nonclimbing, no-support peas are the semi-leafless, or half-leaf, cultivars, such as 'Novella' and 'Novella II', which have a mass of vigorous tendrils that hold the plants off the

PEA CULTIVARS

When selecting pea cultivars, consider days to maturity as well as type—the list below includes garden peas, which must be shelled, along with edible-podded snow and snap peas.

'Alaska': garden pea; 58 days; 2½-foot vines; good cold resistance; extremely early; standard canning cultivar; heirloom.

'Austrian Winter': dry- or soup-type garden pea; 80 days; use as soup pea or for sprouting.

'Burpeeana Early': garden pea; 65 days; 2-foot vines; high yields; good for freezing; early.

'Carouby de Maussane': snow pea; 65 days; 4-foot vines; highly ornamental.

'Cascadia': snap pea; 60 days; 2-foot vines; good disease resistance; early.

'Dwarf Gray Sugar': snow pea; 68 days; 2½-foot vines; widely grown; good midseason cultivar; heirloom.

'Green Arrow': garden pea; 65 days; 2½-foot vines; disease-resistant; good yields; standard main-crop cultivar.

'Holland Brown': dry- or soup-type garden pea; 80 days; use as soup pea or for sprouting; heirloom.

'Knight': garden pea; 60 days; 2-foot vines; good disease resistance; early; standard home-garden cultivar.

'Lincoln': garden pea; 68 days; 2-foot vines; also known as 'Homesteader'; high yields; good cultivar for the North; heirloom.

'Little Marvel': garden pea; 65 days; 1½-foot vines; high yields; popular home-garden cultivar; heirloom.

'Maestro': garden pea; 60 days; 2- to 3-foot vines; disease-resistant; heavy yields; early.

'Mammoth Melting Sugar': snow pea; 75 days; 4-foot vines; vigorous plants; high yields.

'Multistar': garden pea; 70 days; 4-foot vines; heat-tolerant; disease-resistant; good late cultivar.

'Novella II': garden pea; 65 days; bush vines; semi-leafless, or half-leaf, cultivar; plant closely.

'Oregon Giant': snow pea; 60 days; 2-foot vines; disease-resistant; high yields; early.

'Oregon Sugar Pod II': snow pea; 68 days; 2-foot vines; heavy yields; widely adapted; disease-resistant.

'Petit Pois': garden petit pois-type pea; 60 days; 1½-foot vines; good cold tolerance.

'Petit Provencal': garden petit pois-type pea; 60 days; 1½-foot vines; very hardy.

'Snappy': snap pea; 65 days; 6-foot vines; disease-resistant.

'Snowbird': snow pea; 58 days; 1½-foot vines; heavy yields; good short-season or fall cultivar.

'Sugar Ann': snap pea; 55 days; 2-foot vines; very early; AAS winner.

'Sugar Daddy': snap pea; 68 days; 2-foot vines; stringless pods.

'Sugar Snap': snap pea; 68 days; original snap pea; 6-foot vines; widely adapted; not disease-resistant; AAS winner.

'Super Sugar Mel': snap pea; 70 days; 2½-foot vines; high yields.

'Super Sugar Snap': snap pea; 65 days; 5-foot vines; improved form of 'Sugar Snap'; disease-resistant.

'Tall Telephone': garden pea; 75 days; very vigorous 6-foot vines; also known as 'Alderman'; heirloom.

'Thomas Laxton': garden pea; 65 days; 2- to 3-foot vines; very high yields; named for famous 19th-century pea breeder; good maritime cultivar; heirloom.

'Utrillo': garden pea; 71 days; 3-foot vines; plant in summer for fall harvest.

'Wando': garden pea; 70 days; 2½-foot vines; widely adapted; heat- and cold-resistant; heavy yields; standard home-garden cultivar.

'Waverex': garden petit pois-type pea; 65 days; 2-foot vines; small pods; good cultivar for cool climates.

ground. Although bred with the commercial grower in mind—and somewhat less sweet than standard garden-pea cultivars—they fit nicely in backyard gardens, because they don't need trellising and can be grown in blocks rather than in rows.

SITE & SOIL

Plant peas in light, moderately fertile, slightly acid (pH 6.2 to 6.8) soil that drains well and is rich in organic matter. Like beans, peas have the ability to capture nitrogen from the atmosphere, so add only organic matter and/or fertilizer with moderate amounts of phosphorus and potassium, rather than materials, such as fresh manure that contain high levels of nitrogen.

For the plants to "fix" nitrogen, *Rhizobia* bacteria must be present in the soil. Many gardeners coat pea seeds with a *Rhizobia* inoculant every year to make sure the bacteria are present, but that's unnecessary unless you're planting in an area that's never been cultivated before. If it is a new garden, purchase inoculant at a garden center. Wet the seeds, and coat them with the powder just before planting.

Because peas can be started so early in the garden season, soil drainage is crucial. Pea seeds can tolerate cold—they will germinate, albeit slowly, in 40°F soil—but they won't tolerate soil that is both wet and cold. If your garden is slow to dry out in spring or if the soil is extremely heavy, grow peas in raised beds or on a slope with southern exposure, locating them so that they won't shade other plants. Wherever they are placed, make sure they have full sun and good air circulation.

Most peas, even dwarf cultivars, benefit from having some sort of support as they develop (see "Plant Support Systems" on page 80 for options). Getting the vines off the ground increases their access to light and fresh air. Pea tendrils, which need something thin, such as string, to grasp, are fragile; to avoid breaking stems, install your trellis at the same time you plant and make sure the support is as tall as your cultivar is supposed to grow. A traditional alternative to strings or mesh fencing is supporting peas with 3- or 4-foot branched brush from sturdy shrubs. Sharpen the butt end of each piece of brush, and stick it in the ground along the row.

Most pea cultivars are ready to pick in about 70 days from sowing. To spread out the harvest, stagger plantings of the same cultivar every 10 days as long as weather permits, or grow several cultivars that

Edible podded pea

mature at different times. Peas can also be intercropped with other vegetables, such as radishes and spinach, and followed by different crops, such as leeks, potatoes, or squash. Between 100 and 150 plants, successively cropped, should provide an ample harvest for a family of four; if you want to preserve, increase the planting.

Peas have pretty flowers, either white or lavender, and good-looking blue-green foliage. Tall cultivars create living screens and make handsome backdrops for ornamental plantings. Because they require a sturdy support, peas are only moderately good container plants. One solution is to set a tomato cage in a half-barrel and sow seeds around the base of the cage. Keep the soil barely moist, and feed with diluted compost tea twice during the growing season.

HOW TO GROW

A frost-hardy, cool-weather vegetable, peas do best when planted early in spring, or in late summer for a fall harvest. In extremely warm regions, grow peas as a winter crop. Because they are cold-tolerant, there's no advantage to beginning indoors. Gardeners in England sow peas on St. David and St. Chad's days, March 1 and 2, but that may be too early for your location. Instead, direct-seed in spring

Pea 'Little Marvel'

Pea 'Super Sugar Snap'

as soon as the soil can be worked, from 5 weeks before the last expected frost. Seeds will germinate in 13 days in 50°F soil, in 9 days if the soil is 60°F.

Set pea seeds 1 inch deep, 3 to 4 inches apart (deeper in warm regions or in extremely light, sandy soils), in bands or double rows 5 to 6 inches apart, with 3 to 4 feet between each pair of rows. To speed planting, make an extra-wide furrow with your hoe and sow both rows at one time. Or plant in single rows, spaced 30 inches apart. Semi-leafless cultivars can be broadcast in beds. Be sure to tamp the rows or bed so that there is good contact between seeds and soil. After planting, erect any support system along the row, or down the middle of the double

WRINKLED OR SMOOTH?

Most garden-pea seeds are wrinkled, thanks to Englishman Thomas Knight, who made the crosses in the 1780s that first produced them. If your packet contains seeds that are round and unwrinkled, you've purchased a cultivar—'Alaska' is one example—that has a high starch content. Most smooth-seeded cultivars are extremely hardy, but they are also less sweet. While round cultivars can be eaten when still green, they are often allowed to dry on the vine and used in soups as split peas.

row, and guide the vines as soon as they are long enough to climb. Peas don't resent crowding, so there is no need to thin; once plants are established, when they are 3 inches tall, mulch with compost, grass clippings, or other organic matter to retain moisture and suppress weeds.

Fall crops of peas should be sown about 10 weeks before the first expected frost. To give seedlings protection from midsummer heat, sow seeds in 6-inch-deep trenches and cover with 2 inches of soil. As the young plants appear, gently cover them with soil or compost until the trench is filled.

Young pea plants need only about ½ inch of water per week (1 inch when grown in extremely sandy soil), so watering is usually unnecessary unless there is an extended drought. Once plants begin to flower, the need for water goes up to 1 inch per week. Plants growing in moderately fertile soil don't require fertilizing, but feeding twice with liquid sea-weed or compost tea will help ensure heavy yields. Overfeeding, especially with a high-nitrogen fertil-izer, will produce lush foliage and reduce yields.

POTENTIAL PROBLEMS

Because peas do most of their growing during early spring, before most insects arrive, home gar-deners usually have few problems. The bad news is that peas that are trellised cannot be easily protect-ed with floating row covers. (For specific informa-tion about likely pests—aphids, cabbage loopers, cucumber beetles, thrips, and wireworms—see "Controlling Common Pests" on page 162.)

Most diseases that attack peas, including bacte-rial blight, fusarium wilt, powdery mildew, and root rot, can be avoided by planting resistant cultivars and by not allowing plants to be stressed. Time crops to coincide with cool weather, rotate the location of peas and related crops each year, and, in cold regions, make sure that plants have a sunny location.

Heat and birds may be the worst enemies of a good pea crop. Time sowing seeds—plants prefer temperatures that range between 55° and 75°F. If plants die for no apparent reason or if yields are poor, hot weather may be the cause. Birds are extremely fond of peas and pull up seedlings to get at the seeds. The best control is netting.

HARVESTING

Peas, which are extremely low in calories and contain vitamins A and C, folate, iron, and protein (snow and snap peas are also a good source of fiber), should be ready to pick about 3 weeks after the plants begin to flower. The pods on the lower part of the plant mature first. Don't yank on the pods, which can stress or damage the plant; instead, hold onto the stem and pinch off the pod, or use scissors.

Garden cultivars should have filled out the pods, which ought still to be bright green, not dull. Snow peas are ready to pick as soon as the pod is full-size, when the seeds are visible but before they begin to swell. Harvest snap peas after the seeds fill out but before they become overlarge and hard. Harvesting daily will keep plants producing.

Like sweet corn, the sugar in peas starts turning to starch as soon as they are harvested. They can be refrigerated in plastic bags for up to 5 days, but it's better to use or process them immediately after picking. For dried peas, allow the pods to wither and turn brown on the vine; pick, shell, and dry peas in a warm location for about 3 weeks, or until dry. Store out of direct sunlight in sealed jars.

SPLITTING PEAS

Split peas aren't a special cultivar. Rather, they are dried peas that have been halved by gently crushing them—a mortar and pestle work well—until the two halves separate. If necessary, winnow to get rid of any seed coats.

Peas, which do not cross with other members of the pea family, are self-pollinating. While there is little chance of crossbreeding among pea cultivars, to ensure seeds that will come true, plant only one cultivar, or separate cultivars by at least 50 feet. Seeds are viable for 3 years; store in airtight containers in a dark, cool location.

PEA, ASPARAGUS. See *Winged Bean*

PEANUT

Arachis hypogaea. Pea family, Fabaceae. Annual.

○ ✳ ❀

If you spent all summer in the garden watching peanut plants grow, you might think they had a brain. For after the small flowers appear around the base of the tidy, 18-inch-tall cloverlike plants, their runners, or pegs, somehow know to bend downward and burrow into the ground. There, in darkness, the edible seeds, incorrectly called nuts, are formed. Or, as a 19th-century author expressed it, the "blossoms . . . insinuate their ovaries into the earth; beneath which, at the depth of several inches, the fruit is afterwards perfected." The species name, *hypogaea*, is Greek for "burying one's head."

Although traditionally associated with Africa, the peanut is native to South America, where it has been cultivated for thousands of years. Southerners have grown peanuts since colonial times, mostly as food for livestock. And as food for slaves, who brought the plant from Africa to Virginia—the regional name goober peas is a corruption of *nguba*, a Bantu word for "ground nuts."

Peanuts moved north after the Civil War, partly a by-product of the new popularity of baseball ("Buy me some peanuts and cracker-jacks . . . ," the 1908 song goes) but more because of the research of George Washington Carver. A former slave, Carver discovered hundreds of ways to use peanuts, including making peanut butter. "Course, we don't get meat as often as our forefathers," Will Rogers wrote in his autobiography, "but we have our peanut butter and radio."

While some cultivars can be grown well north of the Mason-Dixon line, peanuts remain a hot-weather crop and do best in USDA Zone 7 and warmer. Gardeners in Zones 5 and 6 who take advantage of heat-conserving techniques may produce small harvests.

DECIDING WHAT TO GROW

Peanuts are divided into two types, runner and erect. Runner peanuts, which includes the Virginia types, typically have large seeds, two to the pod, take longer to mature, and require more space. Erect types include Spanish and Valencia cultivars. Their seeds are somewhat smaller, but Valencia types average three per pod. Spanish peanuts need the fewest days to mature—around 120—and are the best choice for home gardeners who don't live deep in the heart of Dixie. All types can be used for confections, salting, or roasting in the shell.

Be sure to purchase seeds from a seed company: Peanuts that have been roasted won't sprout. Spanish-type cultivars include 'Early Spanish', 'Spanish', and 'Improved Spanish'. 'Virginia Jumbo' grows 18 inches tall and 36 inches wide and is widely adapted, maturing in about 130 days. 'Jumbo', which also has large seeds, is another Virginia type that does well outside the South, as does 'Tennessee Red', a Valencia peanut with small seeds, three to four per pod.

Cultivars vary, but under good conditions, a single plant produces about 50 pods; yields will be smaller in USDA Zone 6 and colder.

SITE & SOIL

Although peanuts will grow on thin soils, the best harvest comes from plants that are cultivated in very light, humus-rich soil. Because peanuts are legumes, they can take nitrogen from the air, but the gardener needs to supply phosphorus, potassium, and calcium. Bonemeal and wood ashes, applied about a month before planting, are good sources of all three elements. The soil also needs to drain well, be well dug, and have a slightly acid pH (6.0 to 7.0). Locate plants where they will receive full sun; in northern areas, a sheltered, south-facing slope is ideal.

Because peanuts take so long to produce a crop, they don't lend themselves to succession plantings. However, their neat appearance and pretty yellow flowers (in addition to the small flowers around their base, plants produce larger blossoms on their upper portion) make them an interesting choice for ornamental beds and borders.

They also make good container plants—when they are situated on deck or patio, it's easier to watch the plants' pegs reach down and pierce the soil. Make sure the container is broad and deep enough to handle the underground crop, at least 18 inches wide and 24 inches deep, and has good drainage. Fill with light, enriched potting soil; keep soil loose and water frequently until the pegs root themselves, moderately thereafter; and feed every 3 weeks with compost tea.

HOW TO GROW

While peanuts can be started indoors in individual containers 4 weeks before the last frost, they resent transplanting. Unless your growing season is brief or cool, wait until the soil has warmed to 65°F and all danger of frost is past and direct-sow. Germination takes between 7 and 14 days. In warm regions, sow unshelled peanuts, 3 to 4 inches deep, 5 inches apart; to speed germination in short-season areas, shell peanuts (but do not remove the skins) before planting 2 inches deep, 5 inches apart.

Once plants are established, thin to 18 inches for erect types, 2 feet for runner plants, and hill each plant by pulling additional dirt around it, as you would for potatoes. Keep the hilled soil well cultivated so that the pegs can root themselves without difficulty; once the pegs have rooted, mulch plants with straw or compost to suppress weeds.

Home gardeners who practice good crop rotations rarely encounter pest or disease problems when growing peanuts.

HARVESTING

Take note of when your plants bloom, because their seeds will be ready to dig about 60 days after that date. Yellowing foliage is another sign that the crop is ready to harvest (gardeners without the long season that peanuts prefer should wait until after the first few light frosts). Don't try to pull plants. Use a spading fork, and begin by digging around the plants. Collect a few pods: If the peanuts are mature, the inside of the shell will be brown and the seed skins papery, unwrinkled, and pinkish. If the crop is ready, harvest the entire plant, leaving the peanuts attached to the plant.

Peanuts, which contain vitamins B and E plus a healthy dose of protein and other nutrients, must be cured, or dried, before they can be stored or used. Either hang the entire plant in a warm, dry location, or spread the pods in a single layer on a screen and set in a warm, dry location for about 3 weeks. Seal cured peanuts in plastic bags, and freeze until you're ready to use them.

Peanuts are self-pollinating, but their flowers are also pollinated by insects. To ensure seeds that will come true, plant only one cultivar. After curing pods that are to be kept for replanting, store them in a dry, cold (35°F) location. Under cold conditions, seeds remain viable for 3 years. Pods stored in warmer conditions are viable for 1 year.

PEPPER

Capsicum spp. Nightshade family, Solanaceae.
Perennial grown as an annual.

○ ✳ ✿ ▼

Black pepper, *Piper nigrum*, was one of the spices Christopher Columbus was looking for when he shoved off to find a new route to the Indies. He found neither, although he did go home with peppers—red peppers, *Capsicum annuum*, which had been cultivated in South America for at least 6,000 years. Despite the similar common names, red peppers aren't even distant cousins of black pepper.

In time, peppers made their way back from European gardens, where they were reputed by some to have "a certayne hidden evyll qualitie," to the American colonies. Cultivated peppers also reached North America by a more direct route: Hot-blood-

ed botanical migrants known as chilies crossed the border from Mexico into the American Southwest.

The home gardener's legacy from this long history of pepper cultivation by many cultures in many locations is a boon of hot and sweet cultivars. Most peppers start out green and turn red or orange when they mature. They are produced on multistemmed plants from 1 to 3 feet tall, with dark green, shiny,

---

PEPPER ESSENTIALS

- Full sun, warm temperatures.

- Moderately fertile, well-drained, humus-rich soil.

- Begin plants indoors, 6 to 10 weeks before last frost.

- Set plants 12 to 18 inches apart; support tall cultivars.

- Keep soil evenly moist.

- Cover transplants with floating row covers.

- Mulch plants.

- Keep plants picked to extend the harvest.

Pepper 'Jalapeño'   Pepper 'Long Yellow Cayenne'   Pepper 'Hot Chiltepin'

oval leaves and white flowers. There are also yellow, purple, and brown cultivars—even a green one, 'Permagreen', which is green in both its immature and mature stages.

All peppers prefer warm weather. Gardeners living north of USDA Zone 4 may have to use special techniques to cultivate them successfully: planting short-season cultivars, such as 'Gypsy', 'Ace', 'Long Slim', and 'Hungarian Yellow Wax Hot'; starting seeds very early indoors; and using cloches, cold frames, and other protective devices. If, in contrast, you live in blazing-hot conditions, look for peppers with "NuMex" or "TAM" in their name. These cul-

tivars have been bred to set fruit in extremely high temperatures.

DECIDING WHAT TO GROW

A dozen sweet cultivars and six hot cultivars per person should produce all the peppers a family of four can use; if you want to preserve, increase the planting. Most peppers, sweet or hot, require at least 70 days from transplanting to reach the edible "green" stage. For the peppers to reach full maturity, add still another 3 or 4 weeks. Remember that the days-to-maturity numbers on seed packets are based on ideal conditions. It may take only 70 days to pro-

Pepper 'Puerto Rico'

Pepper 'Bulgarian'

Pepper 'Sunnybrook Pimento'

Pepper 'Golden Bell'

Pepper 'Corno Di Turo'

Pepper 'White Bullnose'

duce a perfect 'Hungarian Sweet Wax' in the warmth of California's Sacramento Valley, but it can take 100 days in Portland, Oregon. Be careful to choose a cultivar that will thrive in your location. Gardeners in wet, humid regions should look for cultivars with disease tolerance; gardeners with abbreviated summers should look for a selection that matures quickly.

Since there are sweet as well as hot jalapeños, and hot as well as sweet bells, specialists divide peppers—nearly all members of the species C. *annuum*—not by heat but by their pod shapes. Heart-shaped anchos and pimentos, blocky bells, long, thin cayennes and pasillas, skinny del arbols, round cherries, tapered cubans and waxes, and more. Two of the hottest peppers belong to different species: fiery habañero peppers (C. *chinense*), which look like small misshapen bell peppers, and Tabasco peppers (C. *frutescens*), inch-long fruits that are most familiar in a liquid form.

Pepper heat comes from flavorless chemical compounds called capsaicins, which are concentrated in the fruit's membrane, especially around the seeds. The level of fire, measured in Scoville Heat Units, ranges from zero for a sweet bell pepper to more than 200,000 units for an eye-watering habañero. Jalapeños weigh in at about 3,500 units, but not all jalapeño cultivars are equally hot. Pepper heat is also affected by climate: Hot weather produces hotter peppers. Next time you break into what pepper aficionados call a "gustatory sweat" after consuming a hunk of habañero, don't reach for a glass of water to put the fire out. Instead, try milk, yogurt, or another dairy product to stop the burning.

SITE & SOIL

Pepper plants need a steady supply of water, full sun, and well-drained soil that is high in organic material, with a near-neutral pH (6.7 to 7.0). Because they require warm soil as well as warm air, a raised bed is an ideal setting. Peppers don't need rich soil—they are modest feeders—but narrow leaves with a gray

continued on page 138

A PEPPER LEXICON

Peppers are classified by the shape of their pod rather than by being sweet or hot. The following are most of the commonly cultivated types, as designated by Dr. Paul Bodland from the University of New Mexico. All except habañero are members of the species *Capsicum annuum*.

Ancho/Poblano. Pendant, conical pods, 3 to 6 inches long, 2 to 3 inches wide.

Bell. Pendant, blocky, 3- or 4-lobed, bell-like pods.

Cayenne. Pendant, slender pods, up to 10 inches long and 1 inch wide; pods are often wrinkled.

Cherry. Erect, round pods, 1 to 2 inches wide.

Cuban. Pendant, slender, tapered pods, 2 to 10 inches long and up to 2 inches wide.

Exotics. A catchall group; most have erect, elongated pods, 2 to 3 inches long and ½ inch wide.

Habañero (C. *chinense*). varies; pendant, flattened, bell-shaped pods, some elongated with a pointed end, others flattened at the end.

Jalapeño. Pendant, conical pods about 3 inches long and 1 inch wide.

Mirasol. Erect or pendant, elongated, pointed pods, 3 to 5 inches long and ¾ inch wide.

New Mexican. Pendant, elongated pods, bluntly pointed, 4 to 12 inches long.

Paprika. European cultivars; pod shapes vary.

Pasilla. Pendant, cylindrical pods, 6 to 12 inches long and 1 inch wide.

Pimento. Pendant, heart-shaped pods, 2 to 5 inches long and 2 to 4 inches wide.

Piquin. Erect, round, or oblong pods, ¼ to ½ inch long and wide.

Seranno. Erect or pendant, bluntly pointed pods, 1 to 4 inches long and ½ inch wide.

Wax. Vary greatly; erect or pendant, conical pods tapering to a blunt point, 2 to 8 inches long.

PEPPER CULTIVARS

Peppers are divided into types by the shape of their fruits. Most pepper types are represented by the cultivars below.

Days to maturity, listed immediately after the type, are the number of days it takes a 6-week-old transplant to produce a usable pepper. The high end of the range indicates full maturity.

Ripening progression of the fruit is indicated with arrows—green → red, for example.

Flavors are rated as follows: sweet → mild → moderate → hot → very hot → VERY hot.

Disease tolerance is indicated with the following codes: TMV, tobacco mosaic virus; PVY, potato virus Y; TEV, tobacco etch virus; BLS, bacterial leaf spot; Stip, stip.

'**Ace**': bell type; 60 to 80 days; hybrid; bushy 1- to 2-foot plants; blocky small- to medium-size green [AR] red fruits; sweet; best short-season hybrid sweet bell.

'**Ancho**': ancho/poblano type; 90 to 135 days; open-pollinated; 3-foot bushy plants; large, heart-shaped, green → red → brownish red fruits; mild; warm-climate cultivar; good for stuffing.

'**Bajio**': pasilla type; 80 to 110 days; open-pollinated; TMV; 2- to 3-foot plants; slender, 7-inch green → red → brown fruits; mild/moderate; smoky flavor; used for making mole.

'**Big Bertha**': bell type; 75 to 95 days; hybrid; large 2-foot plants; blocky, jumbo-size green → red fruits; sweet; requires ideal growing conditions.

'**Biscane**': cuban type; 65 to 85 days; hybrid; 2-foot plants; tapered, 7-inch lime green → yellow → red fruits; sweet; excellent for roasting and frying; harvest when yellow-green.

'**Cherry Sweet**': cherry type; 75 to 95 days; open-pollinated; bushy, upright, 1½-foot plants; round, 1-inch green → red fruits; sweet; good pickler.

'**Chiltepin/Tepin**': piquin type (*C. annuum* var. *aviculare*); 150 to 200 days; open-pollinated/wild cultivar; large plants; round, ¼-inch green → red fruits; VERY hot; frost-free regions only; also called bird peppers.

'**Cubanelle**': cuban type; 70 to 90 days;

open-pollinated; tapered, 6-inch yellow-green → orange-red fruits; sweet; excellent for roasting and frying; harvest when yellow-green; standard cultivar; widely adapted.

'**Early Jalapeño**': jalapeño type; 70 to 90 days; open-pollinated; stocky 2-foot plants; conical, 3-inch green → red fruits; hot; widely adapted; harvest in green stage.

'**Española Improved**': New Mexican type; 70 to 90 days; open-pollinated; vigorous 2-foot plants; elongated, 5-inch green → red fruits; moderate; good for Southwest.

'**Golden Bell**': bell type; 70 to 90 days; hybrid; vigorous 2-foot plant; blocky, medium-to large-size light green [AR] golden-yellow fruits; sweet; highly productive.

'**Gypsy**': bell type; 65 to 85 days; hybrid; TMV; spreading 1½-foot plants; blocky, elongated, medium-size yellow → orange-red fruits; sweet; early-maturing; AAS winner.

'**Habañero**': habañero type (*C. chinense*); 100 to 140 days; open-pollinated; tall, large-leaved plants; wrinkled, bell-like, 2-inch green → orange-red fruits; VERY hot; also known as 'Scotch Bonnet'; requires long, hot season.

'**Hungarian**': paprika type; 80 to 110 days; open-pollinated; 2-foot plants; slightly wrinkled, 5-inch-long green → red fruits; mild; flavorful; grind dry fruits to make paprika.

'**Hungarian Yellow Wax Hot**': wax type; 70

to 95 days; open-pollinated; stocky 2-foot plants; conical, tapering, 4- to 6-inch pale green → yellow → red fruits; moderate; widely adapted.

'Hungarian Sweet Wax': wax type; 70 to 90 days; open-pollinated; 2-foot plants; cylindrical, 5- to 6-inch pale green → yellow → orange-red fruits; sweet; also called 'Sweet Banana' and 'Yellow Banana'; widely adapted.

'Ivory': bell type; 70 to 90 days; hybrid; TMV, PVY, Stip; erect plants; blocky, medium-size white → pale yellow → orange fruits; sweet.

'Jalpa': jalapeño type; 70 to 90 days; hybrid; compact plants; conical, 3-inch green → red fruits; hot; harvest in green stage.

'Jingle Bells': bell type; 65 to 85 days; hybrid; TMV; compact 1-foot plants; blocky, tiny green → red fruits; sweet; good container plant.

'Key Largo': cuban type; 70 to 90 days; hybrid; TMV; 2-foot plants; tapered, 6-inch lime green → orange fruits; sweet; excellent for roasting and frying; harvest when yellow-green.

'King Arthur': bell type; 75 to 90 days; hybrid; TMV, PVY, TEV, BLS; upright plants; blocky, large green → red fruits; sweet; outstanding disease tolerance; widely adapted.

'Lilac': bell type; 70 to 90 days; hybrid; 1- to 2-foot plants; blocky, medium-size lavender → red fruits; sweet.

'Long Slim': cayenne type; 75 to 95 days; open-pollinated; vigorous spreading plants; slender, wrinkled, 6-inch green → red fruits; very hot; heavy yields.

'Mirasol to Mexican Improved': mirasol type; 80 to 100 days; open-pollinated; sturdy 2-foot plants; elongated, 4-inch green → red fruits; mild to medium; fruits borne upright.

'NuMex Joe E. Parker': New Mexican type; 80 to 100 days; open-pollinated; 2-foot plants; 6-inch green → red fruits; mild; excellent, all-around southwestern-type chili.

'Orabelle': bell type; 75 to 95 days; hybrid; TMV, PVY; bushy 1- to 2-foot plants; blocky, medium-size green → yellow fruits; sweet.

'Pimento L': pimento type; 80 to 100 days; open-pollinated; TMV; vigorous 2-foot plants; large, heart-shaped, green → red fruits; sweet; widely used for canning.

'Purple Beauty': bell type; 70 to 95 days; open-pollinated; compact plants; blocky, medium-size green → purple → red fruits; sweet.

'Red Cherry Hot': cherry type; 80 to 100 days; open-pollinated; upright 2-foot plants; round, 1- to 2-inch green → red fruits; moderate to hot.

'Ring-O-Fire': cayenne type; 85 to 120 days; open-pollinated; 2- to 3-foot plants; smooth, thin, 4-inch green → red fruits; very hot.

'Seranno': seranno type; 85 to 110 days; open-pollinated; gray-green, fuzzy-leaved 2- to 3-foot plants; cylindrical, 2-inch green → orange → orange-red fruits; VERY hot; heavy yields.

'Super Cayenne II': cayenne type; 75 to 95 days; hybrid; TMV; 2½-foot plants; thin, 6-inch green → red fruits; very hot.

'Sweet Chocolate': bell type; 65 to 90 days; open-pollinated; 1- to 2-foot plants; blocky, medium-size green → brown fruits; sweet; tolerates cool nights.

'Thai Dragon: exotic type; 68 to 80 days; hybrid; 2-foot plants; 2½-inch green → red fruits; very hot; early cultivar.

'Thai Hot': exotic type; 75 to 96 days; open-pollinated; bushy, dwarf 8-inch plants; tapered, 1½-inch green → red fruits; very hot; good container plant.

'Valencia': bell type; 70 to 90 days; hybrid; TMV, Stip; 1- to 2-foot plants; blocky, green → orange fruits; sweet.

'Yankee Bell': bell type; 65 to 85 days; open-pollinated; bushy 1- to 2-foot plants; blocky, medium-size green → red fruits; sweet; good short-season open-pollinated sweet bell.

cast are a sign of too little phosphorus. To correct the problem, spray the plants with diluted fish emulsion and side-dress plants with wood ashes. To make certain plants receive enough magnesium, side-dress with Epsom salts, 1 teaspoon per plant.

Almost any pepper cultivar can be grown in a pot, but compact plants, such as 'Gypsy', 'Jingle Bells', or 'Thai Hot', are the best candidates. Use a container at least 8 inches wide and 12 inches deep, with good bottom drainage, and fill with enriched potting soil. Water frequently, especially during fruit set, and feed every 2 weeks with fish emulsion or manure tea. Make sure your container is heavy enough that it won't overturn, and provide support for cultivars taller than 1 foot.

HOW TO GROW

Peppers, unlike radishes or cress, aren't an overnight crop and must be started indoors to mature before the garden season is over. Under ideal conditions—a soil temperature of 85°F—germination occurs in about 10 days, but some peppers, such as habañeros, take far longer. Sow seeds in flats or 2-inch containers filled with a sterile medium 8 to 10 weeks before

Heirloom sweet pepper collection

Pepper 'Orange Bell'

Pepper 'Bell King'

Ornamental peppers 'Candlelight' and 'Marbles'

Pepper 'Lipstick'

Pepper 'Ring-of-Fire'

your average frost-free date. As soon as the new plants break the soil's surface, move them to a bright, warm location, 70°F during the day, 65° at night.

Although you need to give peppers an early start indoors, don't rush to move them outdoors. Plants that are exposed to cold temperatures may survive, but they will never recover fully and will produce meager harvests of small fruits. Because peppers are so temperature-sensitive, it's even more important than usual to harden off plants before moving them to the garden.

Transplant peppers outdoors 2 or 3 weeks after the frost-free date, when the soil temperature has reached 60°F. Set plants 14 to 16 inches apart in the garden, closer for small ornamental cultivars, such as 'Super Chile', 'Jigsaw', and 'Fiesta'. Place a paper collar around each seedling to protect against cutworms, and protect them from chilling winds, cold, and insects by covering them with floating row covers or cloches. Providing support for tall cultivars will keep them from falling over. Staking also produces earlier and larger harvests. To avoid damaging their shallow roots, install the support—a 4-foot stake or a tomato cage—at the same time you set your plants in the garden.

Peppers need a constant supply of moisture, 1 inch a week, especially as the fruits develop. Once the plants are established and the ground has warmed, mulch with organic matter or cover the soil with black plastic to retain moisture and eliminate weeds. Side-dress when plants flower and again in 3 weeks with a balanced fertilizer such as compost. Avoid supplying too much nitrogen, which will produce giant plants and very few fruits.

Peppers cannot withstand frost, but you may be able to eke out an additional week's harvest in autumn by covering plants at night with two or three layers of floating row covers.

POTENTIAL PROBLEMS

Peppers are susceptible to several incurable diseases, such as tobacco mosaic virus and bacterial leaf spot. Choose tolerant or resistant cultivars, plant them in full sun, spacing them widely for good air circulation, and rotate the location of your pepper plants. Peppers also are subject to blossom-end rot and sunscald. (For more on these potential problems, see "Controlling Common Diseases" on page 169.)

Several common insects also attack peppers, including aphids, flea beetles, cutworms, and tomato hornworms. (See "Controlling Common Pests" on page 162 for control measures.)

HARVESTING

With peppers, the more you pick, the more you get. They can be picked at the immature, or "green," stage or when they have matured fully and their vitamin A and C content is highest. Harvest immature sweet peppers as soon as they are large enough to use; harvest mature sweet peppers when they are two-thirds colored. Hot peppers can be picked when they are green, but their full heat and flavor increase if they are allowed to color. Pepper stems are brittle—use scissors to cut fruits from the plant. If frost is forecast, pick all remaining fruits.

You can store fresh sweet peppers in a cool (50° to 55°F) place—not in the refrigerator, which is too cold—for up to 2 weeks. Hot cultivars should be dried or pickled. Pick chilies for drying when they are just beginning to turn red (pull the entire plant and hang it upside down, or string individual fruits). Warning: To avoid burns, wear rubber gloves when working with hot peppers, and keep your hands away from your eyes.

All pepper flowers are perfect but cross pollination by insects is common. For seeds that will come true, plant only one cultivar. Pepper seeds are viable for 2 years; store in airtight containers in a dark, cool location.

SPECIAL NOTES

To make long *ristras*, or strings, of cayennes or other elongated chilies, use freshly picked peppers that are just starting to turn red or are red. Using string, create clusters by tying three pods together by their stems. Attach a strong length of twine to an overhead support. Make a loop at the end of the twine to keep the peppers from slipping off. Then, starting at the bottom, braid the clusters around the twine, using the twine as one strand and strings from two clusters of pods as the other two strands.

PEPPER CRESS. See *Garden Cress*
PEPPERGRASS. See *Garden Cress*
PEPPERMINT. See *Mint*
PERPETUAL SPINACH. See *Swiss Chard*
PICKLING CUCUMBER. See *Cucumber*
PIMENTO. See *Pepper*

POPCORN

Zea mays, Praecox group. Grass family, Poaceae.
Annual.

○ ✳

Only a backyard grower is likely to know that there is a rainbow universe of popcorn: red, brown, blue-black, and multicolored ears, as well as the familiar white and yellow. It's not surprising that many popping corns retain the bright hues of ancient strains, for popcorn is one of the oldest corns grown and a not-so-changed descendant of cultivars planted thousands of years ago.

Early American settlers made limited used of popcorn—they ate it, sweetened with maple syrup, for breakfast—but its popularity didn't soar until the late 1800s, when steam-powered popcorn wagons began appearing on the streets of American cities. One vendor, Frederick William Ruckheim, mixed molasses and peanuts with popcorn and called it Cracker Jack. About the same time, popcorn began finding a place in mail-order seed catalogs. The W. Atlee Burpee Company listed two cultivars in 1887, 'Queen's Golden' and 'Silver Lace': "Ears, 10 cts. each, or 3 for 25 cts., by mail. Shelled, 10 cts. per pkt.; 40 cts. per pint; 75 cts. per quart, postpaid."

Today, more than 1 billion pounds of popcorn is sold each year in the United States, which multiplies out to nearly 19 billion quarts of popped corn, 70 percent of which Americans pop themselves. Neither 'Queen's Golden' nor 'Silver Lace' are sold any longer, but more than 50 cultivars are available, although most are carried only by seed-saving organizations. Only a handful of popcorns, which can be grown in USDA Zone 4 and warmer, are listed in commercial seed catalogs.

DECIDING WHAT TO GROW

Popcorn is an extremely hard strain of flint corn, high in protein and starch. The most common cultivars are hybrids, yellows such as 'Creme-Puff', 'Iopop 12', and the various 'Robust' strains, and whites like 'Snow Puff', 'White Cloud', and 'Peppy'. If you want to grow an open-pollinated popcorn, try the yellow cultivars 'South American' or 'Tom Thumb', or 'Japanese Hulless', a popular white cultivar with 4-inch ears. For the record, "hulless" popcorns have hulls—popcorn couldn't pop without them—but their hulls are more tender than average.

If you're after color, try heirlooms like 'Black', 'Strawberry', or 'Seneca Mini Indian', a multicolored old-timer that produces two or three small ears per stalk. 'Robust Red S-100' is a modern hybrid derived from 'Strawberry' with 5-inch ears, red kernels, and a slightly nutty flavor. What's outside isn't inside, however. Whatever the color of the kernel, when it pops, it will be either white or pale yellow.

To grow even early popcorns, 90 frost-free days is the minimum season length necessary. Most cultivars require at least 115 days to mature, so if your garden season is brief and cool, you're probably better off letting Orville Redenbacher grow your popcorn for you.

HOW TO GROW

Like sweet corn, popcorn needs a sunny location and organically rich, fertile soil in which to grow. In addition, it needs a much longer growing season, since "maturity" now means dry, hard ears. (For culture, see *Corn* on page 233.)

HARVESTING

The most difficult thing about growing popcorn is curing it, making sure it has the 13- to 14-percent moisture content required for good popping. Allow ears to remain on the stalks until they are dry and hard. Once full maturity has been reached—and before the first frost—harvest the ears. Remove the husks, and spread the ears in a single layer (or hang them in mesh bags) in a cool, well-ventilated location to cure.

After 3 weeks, try popping a few kernels. If they crack but don't explode, your corn needs more time to dry. If the kernels won't pop at all, they are too dry. Shell the ears, and place the kernels in a glass jar. Add 1 teaspoon water, let sit for 2 hours, and retest. Once popcorn is properly cured—8 out of 10 kernels should pop—store it in a sealed glass container in a cool location.

SPECIAL NOTES

Native Americans once warned that there was a demon living inside each corn kernel and that when it was heated, he became so angry, he exploded. It's a nice story, but actually it's water that makes popcorn pop. As the kernels are heated, the moisture in their starch vaporizes; when the pressure is great enough, the outer hull gives way and the kernels burst, turning themselves inside out.

Heirloom potatoes, including 'Purple Peruvian', 'Red Erik', 'Cariboo', 'Caribe', and 'Blue Isle'

POTATO

Solanum tuberosum. Nightshade family, Solanaceae.
Annual.

○ ❋

Banned in parts of France as a cause of leprosy, shunned in Scotland as a sinful aphrodisiac, the potato had a rocky reception in the 16th century, when it was introduced to Europe from its native South America. There were rumors, spread by the clergy, that the potato was the forbidden fruit that grew in the Garden of Eden. It took almost 200 years before the merits of the tuber overcame the exorbitant allegations in Europe—when the peasantry from Ireland to Siberia adopted the potato as part of its basic diet, making it the first crop in the world to become a food staple outside its native region.

Early on, potatoes were most often sweetened and turned into pies and puddings. "Ye Best Potatoe Pudding," an English recipe dating from 1694, called for a pound of potatoes, boiled and strained, 1 pound of melted butter, 10 eggs, ½ pound of sugar, and a healthy dose of nutmeg. "Mix them together & put it in a quick Oven. One hour will bake it. So serve it up to Table."

By one famous account, potatoes arrived in the United States from Europe in 1719, traveling with an Irish family who settled in New Hampshire. In fact, there is evidence that potatoes made their way to North America much earlier than 1719, for the English herbalist John Gerard included a chapter entitled "Of Potato's of Virginia" in the 1633 edition of his *Herball.* Americans were slow to appreciate potatoes, however, considering them a third-rate foodstuff: "Let us eat potatoes and drink water; let us wear canvas, and undressed sheepskins," John Adams wrote to his wife Abigail, "rather than submit [to British tyranny]."

By the middle of the 19th century, American gardeners were up to their ears in potatoes—Fearing Burr listed nearly 70 cultivars in *The Field and Garden Vegetables of America* (1865), while

Potato plants

noting that "foreign authors" enumerated "upwards of five hundred varieties." In time, potatoes were recognized for the nutritional mother lode they are, filled with protein, fiber, carbohydrates, magnesium, zinc, iron, copper, iodine, and vitamins B and C, but neither fat nor cholesterol. Today, they are the world's fourth most important food crop. Americans alone consume more than 5 billion pounds just in the form of French fries, which, alas, is a food that negates the potato's claim to being a low-calorie—100 calories for a medium-size tuber—vegetable.

Potatoes favor a relatively cool growing season—when temperatures reach 85°F, tubers pretty much stop growing, because the plants consume

POTATO ESSENTIALS

- Full sun and cool to moderate temperatures.

- Light, well-drained soil rich in organic matter.

- Plant seed-potato pieces.

- Mulch to retain soil moisture and suppress weeds.

- Provide 1 to 1½ inches of water a week.

carbohydrates as quickly as they are produced. They can be grown in USDA Zone 3 and warmer. For a family of four, 40 plants spread over the growing season should provide enough potatoes.

DECIDING WHAT TO GROW

Part of a huge plant family that includes 2,000 species, there are hundreds of *Solanum tuberosum* cultivars, ranging in size from baking potatoes weighing a few pounds each to tiny "fingerlings," and in color from white and yellow to red, purple, and rose. There are even 'Gemchip' and 'Chipeta', bred especially for making potato chips, and genetically engineered cultivars designed to fend off diseases and insects as well as withstand the bumps and bangs of mechanical harvesting are already being trialed. (You'll have to order from a potato specialist, such as Ronniger's Seed Potatoes in Idaho, for access to this enormous variety.) The great appeal of potatoes is that most cultivars keep for weeks in storage and are remarkably versatile in the kitchen. Gardeners can plant as many potatoes as their garden will accommodate, and the crop will not go to waste.

Potatoes are usually classed by their maturation time: early, which are ready to dig after about 65 days; midseason, which mature starting 80 days after planting; and late potatoes, which mature in 90 days or more. Early potatoes are at their best eaten soon after harvest, while midseason and late potatoes are better keepers. In regions with extremely hot summers, early-season cultivars are most successful. Fingerlings, despite their small size, tend to be slow to mature and, for the most part, are classed as midseason and late cultivars.

Potato plants are started from small whole potatoes or pieces of potato, called seed potatoes, rather than from seeds, which would add many more weeks to producing a harvest. Most seed suppliers sell "B-size" seed potatoes, which weigh about 1½ ounces and should be planted whole. Don't waste time planting potatoes from the supermarket, which mostly sell tubers that have been treated with a growth inhibitor to prevent them from sprouting. (Some supermarkets carry true seed potatoes for gardeners in spring.) Do purchase seed potatoes that are certified disease-free, however. One pound of seed potatoes will yield anywhere from 3 to 10 pounds of potatoes, depending on the cultivar and growing conditions.

SITE & SOIL

Potatoes thrive in full sun—although they don't like intense heat—and light soil that drains well, is high in organic matter, and rich in potassium and phosphorus. Compost and/or cover crops will build up the soil's humus content (go easy on adding manure, which may encourage potato scab, or any high-nitrogen fertilizer, which will encourage foliage at the expense of tubers and delay maturity). Greensand and phosphate rock are good sources of potassium and phosphorus. Don't overfeed potatoes: Hollow heart, a cultural problem that leaves tubers with a cavity at their center, can be produced by too much fertilizer. Make sure soil is well cultivated, to a depth of 12 inches; if drainage is poor in your garden or if your soil is extremely heavy, grow potatoes in a raised bed.

Knowledgeable growers recommend an extremely acid soil, primarily because a pH below 5.5 discourages scab, a disease that pits a potato's skin but doesn't affect its flavor. Soil with a pH of 6.5 to 6.8 may produce potatoes with a touch of scab, but the vines will be vigorous and the ground better suited for most crops that may follow.

Potatoes aren't an ideal crop for ornamental beds or containers, although they aren't as space-inefficient as commonly believed: A square yard of garden can produce as many as 20 pounds of tubers. Planting all three types—early, midseason, and late cultivars—will ensure an extended harvest. Space plants at least 12 inches apart, 14 inches for fingerling types, in rows at least 2 feet apart.

HOW TO GROW

Although potato foliage is frost-tender, potatoes can be planted in USDA Zone 6 and colder in early spring, once the soil has reached 40°F, 2 to 4 weeks before the average frost-free date. In very warm regions, potatoes are typically planted at the end of September and harvested in December and January. In between, Zones 7 and 8, potatoes can be planted from early February into March. Successive crops can be planted, except in very hot regions, up to 3 months before the first expected frost in fall.

Small seed potatoes (1½ ounces or less) should be planted whole; larger tubers can be cut into pieces about the size of a hen's egg, making sure that each piece has two "eyes," or buds (each eye will produce a stem). Some fingerling potatoes, including 'Purple Peruvian', have dozens of eyes and can be cut into very small pieces for planting. Traditional wisdom was to let the pieces "cure" for several days before planting, but recent research suggests planting within a few hours from when you cut up the tubers.

Seed pieces can be planted in a number of different ways, depending on how the plants will be tended. Potatoes form on underground stems, or stolons, and must be protected from light, or they will develop a green cast, a telltale sign of an excess of a bitter, toxic alkaloid called solanine. Tubers can be covered with soil or mulch, which encourages

POTATO TERMS

Fingerling Potatoes. Also called German potatoes, fingerlings are any of the small, usually oddly shaped and colorful cultivars with a waxy texture, such as 'Purple Peruvian' and 'Russian Banana.'

Idaho Potatoes. Not a cultivar but simply a potato that was grown in Idaho; similarly, Maine potatoes are potatoes grown in the Pine Tree State.

Irish Potatoes. A generic term for white potatoes.

New Potatoes. Rather than a special type, new potatoes are simply tubers that are harvested when relatively small and used immediately after being dug.

Red Potatoes. Potatoes with red skin, such as 'Red Norland', usually with white flesh.

Russet Potatoes. Potatoes with a high starch content and mealy texture; excellent for baking, mashing, and for making French fries.

White Potatoes. Potatoes with off-white or buff-colored skin and white flesh, such as 'Irish Cobbler' or 'Kennebec', that have a medium starch content and are all-purpose in the kitchen.

the main stems to grow taller, giving them more length along which to send off underground shoots. Three planting styles are common:

Hilling. In the hilling method, favored by most commercial growers, seed pieces are set 3 inches deep, cut side down, every 12 inches in trenches. It will take between 2 and 3 weeks for shoots to emerge when planted at this depth. When the plants are 6 to 8 inches tall, hoe soil up around the stems within ½ inch of the lower leaves. Reshape and raise the hill throughout the season to encourage more stem growth and the development of underground stolons.

Mulching. In the mulching method, plant seed

POTATO CULTIVARS

Planting early, mid-, and late-season potatoes is an easy way to spread out the harvest. Fingerling types generally are mid- to late-season.

'All Blue': late-season; oblong tubers with blue-purple skin, blue-purple flesh; stores well.

'All Red': mid/late-season; oblong tubers with red skin, pink-red flesh; good yields; also known as 'Cranberry Red'.

'Anoka': very early; medium to large tubers with tan skin, white flesh; scab-resistant; good heat tolerance.

'Austrian Crescent': fingerling; tan skin, yellow flesh; heavy yields.

'Caribe': early; medium tubers with bluish purple skin, white flesh; high starch content; widely adapted; stores well.

'Carola': late-season; buff skin, yellow flesh; high yields; all-purpose; stores well.

'Dark Red Norland': early; medium to large tubers with red skin, white flesh; excellent disease resistance.

'Desiree': mid/late-season; large tubers with pink-red skin, yellow flesh; good disease resistance; all-purpose cultivar.

'Frontier Russet': midseason; large, high-starch tubers with russet skin, white flesh; excellent disease resistance.

'German Yellow': fingerling; gold skin, yellow flesh; low starch; prolific; good keeper.

'Green Mountain': late-season; tan skin, white flesh; widely adapted, high-starch content; heirloom.

'Irish Cobbler': early; tan skin, white flesh; widely adapted; good heat tolerance; heirloom.

'Kennebec': mid/late-season; light tan skin, white flesh; medium starch; good heat tolerance; standard all-purpose cultivar from Maine.

'Norgold "M"': early; russet skin, white flesh; heat- and drought-tolerant; high starch; stores well.

'Norland': early; medium-size tubers with light red skin, white flesh; all-purpose cultivar; stores well.

'Pontiac': early; red skin, white flesh; widely adapted all-purpose cultivar; stores well; also known as 'Red Pontiac'.

'Purple Peruvian': fingerling; purple skin, purple flesh; large tubers for fingerling.

'Red Gold': midseason; medium tubers with red skin, yellow flesh; good heat tolerance; all-purpose cultivar; outstanding flavor.

'Red Norland': very early; medium-size tubers with red skin, white flesh; standard red cultivar.

'Russet Burbank': midseason; russet skin, white flesh; scab-resistant; standard Idaho cultivar; high starch; stores well.

'Russian Banana': fingerling; buff skin, yellow flesh; high yields; disease-resistant; all-purpose cultivar.

'Yellow Finn': mid/late-season; yellow skin, dark yellow flesh; high starch; stores well.

'Yukon Gold': early/midseason; yellow skin, yellow flesh; good heat tolerance; all-purpose cultivar; stores well.

pieces 2 to 3 inches deep. When the stems are 6 to 8 inches tall, pull a thick blanket of mulch around the plants, leaving the foliage exposed to light. Continue mulching as the plant grows (a layer almost a foot thick will be needed). Leaves, straw, or hay, cut before it sets seed, make good mulches.

Deep Planting. In the deep-planting method, set seed pieces 7 to 8 inches below ground. The stems will work their way to the surface, forming underground stolons along their length. A small amount of hilling may also be done to encourage more top growth. Deep planting makes good use of garden space and requires little maintenance. However, this method is not well suited to early planting in areas with a cold, damp spring, because the soil at that depth is slow to warm. Also, harvesting is more laborious with this method, because the tubers are deeper than are those of mulched or hilled plants and more difficult to dig.

Whichever method you use, cover the seedbed with floating row covers to help prevent insect pests, such as flea beetles and Colorado potato beetles, from reaching plants. Mulching young plants with straw after they emerge will help suppress weeds and retain moisture.

Like the human body, potatoes are roughly 80 percent water. They thrive on a steady supply of moisture, between 1 and 1½ inches a week. Potatoes grown in fertile soil probably won't require additional nutrients during the growing season. To make sure plants aren't stressed, spray them with fish emulsion or compost tea at 1 month and again when they flower.

POTENTIAL PROBLEMS

Potatoes are susceptible to a number of insects and diseases, although home gardeners have many fewer problems than do commercial growers. The best defenses against all of them is to keep plants well watered, carefully weeded, and growing vigorously. Raising plants from certified disease-free seeds, keeping the soil pH low, using floating row covers, and rotating crops so that potatoes are not grown in the same ground each year (or in ground that hosted other members of the nightshade family, such as tomatoes) also helps to reduce the incidence of most ailments.

Early and late blights, mosaic virus, and fusarium and verticillium wilts can all affect potatoes. (See "Controlling Common Diseases" on page 169 for descriptions and information on controls.) Keeping the soil moist and the pH below 6.3 will discourage common scab; many cultivars, both old and new, are scab-resistant. Black heart, which produces gray, purple, or black areas in tubers, is caused by compacted, waterlogged soil. It cannot be cured, but it can be avoided by growing potatoes in humus-rich soil that drains well.

The most common pests to trouble potatoes are flea beetles, aphids, European corn borer, cucumber beetles, cutworms, Japanese beetles, leafhoppers, wireworms, and, of course, Colorado potato beetles. Many can be controlled simply by using floating row covers and handpicking. (For more information, see "Controlling Common Pests" on page 162.)

HARVESTING

Early potatoes can be harvested when still small, as soon as 7 to 8 weeks after planting. Harvest main crops about 2 weeks after the tops have died back but before a hard frost. Dig potatoes with a garden fork (or with your hands, if the soil is loose) when the soil is relatively dry, working carefully to reduce the likelihood of damaging tubers. It is usually better to dig an entire plant than to try to pluck a few potatoes from several plants, which often disturbs the roots.

Brush away excess dirt with your hand—don't use a brush, which can damage the skin—and allow the potatoes to air in a shaded location for several hours to harden their skin. Inspect the harvest for damage. Eat bruised or split potatoes immediately.

STARCH STATUS

Want to know whether your potato is high or low in starch? Cut the potato in half, rub the cut surfaces together, and stick them together. If they adhere, it is a high-starch potato. Potatoes with a high starch content have a mealy texture and are excellent for baking and mashing. Low-starch potatoes, which include fingerlings, are good for boiling and for making potato salad and au gratin dishes.

Potatoes that are to be stored—mid- and late-season cultivars store best—should be cured by spreading them in a single layer in a dark, cool (50°F) location for 2 weeks. After curing, store in a dark, humid, cold (33° to 40°F) place.

Save some of the best tubers to use as seed potatoes in next year's garden. Do not plant any tubers that have signs of disease, such as spots or sunken areas.

SPECIAL NOTES

Greenish skin, which is often produced by light, is a sign that your potatoes contain an excess of solanine, a natural chemical that can be toxic in great amounts. Removing the peel will eliminate any danger. Potato sprouts also contain high levels of solanine and should not be eaten; if the potato has grown a lot of sprouts, discard it.

POTATO ONION. See *Shallot*
POT MARJORAM. See *Marjoram*

PUMPKIN

Cucurbita spp. Gourd family, Cucurbitaceae.
Annual.

○ ❋ ▐

The phrase ought to be "As American as pumpkin pie," since pumpkins, not apples, are American natives, originating in Central America and cultivated as early as 4,000 B.C. Because *Cucurbita* is a mixed-up genus, early references to pumpkins—such as Captain John Smith's observation that "Amongst their Corne, they [the Indians] plante Pumpeons"—may have been a reference to hard-shelled squash.

Whatever their classification—they both grow on trailing vines and have bright yellow flowers—there's no debate that pumpkins quickly became a staple in the colonial America diet, a fact made clear by an anonymous poet in 1630:

If fresh meat be wanting to fill up our dish
We have carrots and pumpkins and
turnips and fish;
We have pumpkins at morning and
pumpkins at noon;
If it was not for pumpkins, we
should be undone.

Hull-less or naked-seeded pumpkin with seeds

In what is perhaps the first recipe for "pumpion-pye"—dating from 1673—the pumpkin is in the crust, not the filling. Instructions called for sliced pumpkin to be mixed with thyme, rosemary, marjoram, cinnamon, nutmeg, pepper, cloves, sugar, and eggs, and fried like a pancake, then topped with apples, currants, and sugar and baked. Stuffing pumpkins with fruits and meats and baking them whole was also common colonial practice.

Pumpkins also had nonculinary uses and were recommended for removing freckles and "spottes," for expelling worms, curing snakebites, and "female ills." It wasn't until the 1840s, however, that the pumpkin became the symbol of Halloween in this country. The tradition of the jack-o-lantern is a contribution of Irish immigrants, who brought with them the tale of Jack, a stingy but clever man barred from both heaven and hell and condemned to carry a lantern—originally made from a turnip and a burning coal—and walk on earth until Judgment Day. Without the bounty of native pumpkins, Americans might be carving turnips on October 31.

Pumpkin 'Zorba'

Pumpkin 'Rouge Vif d'Etampes'

Pumpkin 'Long Pie'

Jack-o-lanterns, pies, stews, puddings, cakes, breads, dwellings for nursery-rhyme wives, and carriages for fairy-tale stepdaughters: There isn't much a pumpkin can't do. Fortunately, this versatile native grows throughout most of North America, in USDA Zone 3 and warmer.

DECIDING WHAT TO GROW

Centuries of promiscuity among the huge mix of crops that belong to the gourd family, including squash, gourds, melons, and cucumbers, have turned the pumpkin's family tree into a genealogical jungle. Taxonomists depend on the characteristics of the stems, leaves, flowers, and seeds to classify pumpkins, which now fall into four species: C. argyrosperma, C. maxima, C. moschata, and C. pepo. Rather than identify the species—normally a sensible practice—most gardeners look for familiar cultivar names, such as 'Connecticut Field' and 'Small Sugar'. As the experts at the National Garden Bureau observed: If it looks like a pumpkin, tastes like a pumpkin, and carves like a pumpkin, it is a pumpkin.

For the record, most pie types are C. moschata and have sweet, thick, finely grained flesh and weigh between 5 and 10 pounds. Pumpkins destined for jack-o-lanterns are bred to be symmetrical, usually belong to the species C. pepo, weigh 8 to 20 pounds, and have moderately thick flesh. (For a truly ghostly effect, try a white cultivar like 'Lumina'.) If, like Peter, you have a spouse that needs housing, grow one of the giant cultivars. Most belong to C. maxima and can weigh more than 500 pounds. 'Atlantic Giant', bred by Canadian Howard Dill, is considered the top of the type. The current record holder—1,061 pounds—is large enough for Peter, his wife, and two or three offspring.

Two newer trends in the pumpkin patch are mini pumpkins and pumpkins with hull-less, or naked, seeds. Minis, such as 'Jack Be Little', run as small as 2 inches in diameter. While the fruits are tiny, the vines of mini pumpkins may be full-size:

'Jack Be Little' wanders 8 feet and more. Hull-less seeded pumpkins—'Baby Bear' and 'Triple Treat' are two—don't actually lack a hull; instead, the seed coat is parchment-thin and has a faintly nutty flavor. Breeders have developed cultivars like 'Autumn Gold' that bear fruits that color early in the season, rather than at its tail end.

Once you've decided on what kind of pumpkin you want to grow, make sure to pick a cultivar that fits your climate and garden. Pumpkins are a long-season crop, taking anywhere from 90 to 130 days, and they are space hogs. Vining cultivars amble 15 feet and more, and even semi-bush pumpkins can travel 5 feet. Six plants should supply a family of four with plenty of pumpkins; if you want to preserve, increase the planting.

SITE & SOIL

Like most other gourd-family members, pumpkins need full sun and light, very rich soil that drains

---

PUMPKIN CULTIVARS

Whether you're making pies, carving jack-o-lanterns, or growing a champion, there's a pumpkin cultivar for you—some can be used for more than one purpose. Unless otherwise noted, all of the cultivars below have typical pumpkin-orange skin and flesh.

'**Atlantic Giant**': 120 days; open-pollinated; 200+ pounds; exhibition type bred for size.

'**Autumn Gold**': 100 days; hybrid; 10 to 15 pounds; fruits color early; vigorous vines; AAS winner.

'**Baby Bear**': 105 days; open-pollinated; 1 to 3 pounds; edible semi-hull-less seeds; disease-resistant; AAS winner.

'**Baby Boo**': 95 days; open-pollinated; miniature 6-ounce fruits; white skin and flesh; stores well.

'**Big Max**': 115 days; open-pollinated; 75+ pounds; good cultivar for pies and carving; rough, bright orange skin.

'**Big Moon**': 120 days; open-pollinated; 150+ pounds; exhibition type; vigorous vines.

'**Bushkin**': 95 days; open-pollinated; 8 to 10 pounds; semi-bush plants.

'**Connecticut Field**': 115 days; open-pollinated; 15 to 25 pounds; traditional Halloween pumpkin; heirloom.

'**Frosty**': 95 days; hybrid; 15 to 20 pounds; semi-bush; good pie cultivar; stores well.

'**Ghost Rider**': 115 days; open-pollinated; 10 to 25 pounds; good for cooking and carving.

'**Howden**': 115 days; open-pollinated; 15 to 25 pounds; stores well; uniform fruits; disease-tolerant; good Halloween cultivar.

'**Jack Be Little**': 95 days; open-pollinated; miniature 3- to 6-ounce fruits; heavy yields; susceptible to virus diseases.

'**Jack 'O Lantern**': 110 days; open-pollinated; 10 to 15 pounds; good for cooking and carving.

'**Lumina**': 100 days; open-pollinated; 10 to 20 pounds; white skin, orange flesh; good Halloween cultivar.

'**Prizewinner**': 120 days; hybrid; 50 to 100 pounds; large seeds; large pie cultivar.

'**Rouge Vif d'Etampes**': 110 days; open-pollinated; 10 to 15 pounds with orange-red skin; also listed as 'Cinderella'; heirloom.

'**Small Sugar**': 110 days; open-pollinated; 4 to 10 pounds; very sweet pie cultivar; stores well; also listed as 'New England Pie'; heirloom.

'**Sweetie Pie**': 95 days; open-pollinated; miniature 6-ounce fruits; deeply ribbed; stores well.

'**Trick-or-Treat**': 105 days; hybrid; 8 to 12 pounds; semi-bush plants; hull-less seeds.

'**Triple Treat**': 110 days; open-pollinated; 6 to 10 pounds; all-purpose cultivar; hull-less seeds.

well and has been heavily amended with organic matter, such as well-rotted manure and compost. Their roots spread nearly as far underground as the vines spread above ground, so dig wide as well as deep when you prepare the garden. Soil pH should be slightly acid, between 6.0 and 6.8.

Be sure to give pumpkins plenty of room. Crowding encourages disease, especially in humid regions, and will mean fewer and smaller fruits. If your garden is small, allow the vines to trail into the lawn. Mini cultivars can be trellised on either a vertical support or an A-frame. Choose a location where the vines won't shade other crops, and erect the support *before* you plant to avoid damaging plants' roots. Set plants on the windward side of the trellis, and help the vines attach themselves to the support, if necessary. You'll also have to provide support—mesh bags or cloth slings tied to the trellis are the usual methods—for each pumpkin. Pinch back the vines' tips when they reach the top of their support.

If planting in rows, space semi-bush pumpkins between 1 and 3 feet apart, vining types 3 to 5 feet, with at least 8 feet between rows for viners, 4 feet for semi-bush pumpkins. If planting in hills—a technique that helps warm the soil—thin to three plants per hill.

As long as there is room for the vines to ramble, pumpkins can be grown in containers. Use a large container, at least 10 gallons, for each plant. Fill with an enriched soil mix, keep well watered, and feed every 2 weeks with manure tea. Pumpkins' sprawling vines don't lend themselves to ornamental beds and borders, but plants could serve as an effective groundcover on a sunny slope.

HOW TO GROW

You can begin pumpkins indoors, about 3 weeks before the last expected frost. In 75°F soil, seeds will germinate in about 7 days. Don't begin too early, as seedlings grow quickly and are finicky about transplanting. Sow seeds 1 inch deep in 12-inch containers, thinning to one plant per container. After germination, move the plants to a bright, warm (75° to 85°F) location until it's time to transplant; harden off plants before setting them in the garden.

If your growing season is long and warm, sow seeds direct, 1 inch deep. Pumpkins won't germinate in soil temperatures below 60°F, so delay direct-seeding until the soil warms (use plastic mulch to speed the process). Once plants are established,

mulch with organic matter to help retain moisture and suppress weeds, and cover with floating row covers to conserve heat and prevent pests. Don't forget to remove the covers when the first flowers appear or if temperatures rise. Pumpkins are greedy, so feed plants every 2 or 3 weeks with compost tea or seaweed extract, and make sure they have plenty of water, between 1 and 2 inches a week, especially when the plants are blooming and the fruits are being set.

Once the vines have set fruits, it's safe to pinch them back to limit their growth. Occasionally, rotating pumpkins will help keep them symmetrical, and placing a board or shingle under large fruits will help avoid rot.

GROWING GIANTS

If you have an eye on a blue ribbon, follow these guidelines from Howard Dill, king of giant pumpkins. And line up 10 strong friends to get your pumpkin from the patch to the fair.

- Choose a cultivar bred for size, such as 'Atlantic Giant'.

- Begin seeds indoors.

- Prepare the soil—50 square feet per plant—by adding at least 5 bushels of rotted manure or compost.

- Sow three seeds, and thin to a single plant.

- Hand-pollinate by picking a male blossom (the flowers held on long, thin stalks) and brushing its pollen around the inside of a female flower.

- Thin to one fruit per plant.

- Feed every 2 weeks with a high-nitrogen fertilizer.

- Keep plants well watered, about 50 gallons a week.

POTENTIAL PROBLEMS

While less bothered than some members of the gourd family, pumpkins are potential targets for all the insect pests that can prey upon that large group of vegetables. Use floating row covers to prevent insects from reaching plants. (For specific information about dealing with aphids, squash vine borers, squash bugs, and striped cucumber beetles, the four most common pumpkin pests, see "Controlling Common Pests" on page 162.)

Anthracnose, bacterial wilt, and downy and powdery mildew are the most likely diseases to attack the pumpkin patch. Rotating the location of your pumpkin patch, using drip irrigation rather than overhead watering, spacing plants generously, providing adequate nutrients and moisture, and preventing aphids and other disease-carrying insects from reaching plants will prevent most infections. (See "Controlling Common Diseases" on page 169 for more information and for control measures.)

HARVESTING

There's no great rush to harvest pumpkins, which can be left to sun themselves in the garden until the vines yellow and die (the exception are white cultivars, which should be cut when their skins are still streaked with green). Light frosts won't harm these fruits, but a hard freeze will. Once the rind, or skin, is hard and fully colored, use pruners to cut the pumpkins from the vine, leaving a 5-inch stem.

If you want to store pumpkins for more than 1 month, first cure them by subjecting them to 85°F temperatures and high humidity for 10 days. To reduce surface molds, wipe fruits with a bleach/water (1:4) solution. For long-term storage, place blemish-free pumpkins in a well-ventilated, cool (50°F) location.

Three-quarters of a pumpkin's nutrition lies in its seeds, which have good-size doses of protein and unsaturated oil, plus potassium, iron, phosphorus, calcium, and vitamins A and C. The pumpkin's low-calorie flesh is not without merit, however, and contains vitamin A, potassium, and calcium, as well as smaller amounts of vitamin C and fiber.

Male and female pumpkin flowers are borne on the same plant and are pollinated by bees and other insects. Plants, pumpkins or squash, within the same species cross easily, and crossing between species

may occur. To produce seeds that come true, plant only one cultivar of each species. Seeds are viable for 6 years; store in airtight containers in a dark, cool location.

PURPLE BASIL. See *Basil*

PURSLANE

Portulaca oleracea. Purslane family, Portulacaceae. Annual.

Mild-tasting purslane is a warm-weather salad green that has evoked strong sentiments from gardeners and plant explorers for several hundred years—some celebrating its "moist and cooling qualities," others condemning it as "perhaps the most notorious weed in the world." In the 17th century, Englishman John Evelyn claimed purslane "quickens Appetite, asswages Thirst, and is very profitable for hot and Bilious tempers," while in the 19th, his countryman William Cobbett called it "a mischievous weed that Frenchmen and pigs eat when they can get nothing else."

Whatever its history, purslane's lemony flavor and crunchy texture make it an unquestionably positive contribution to any midsummer salad. Moreover, plant breeders have helped reconcile these

Purslane

polarized purslane positions by developing domesticated, or garden, purslanes—both green and golden forms— that are more respectable than are their weedy cousins. Where wild purslane creeps along the ground, domesticated types are taller and more upright—domesticated plants can reach 12 to 16 inches in height and have thicker, more succulent, and milder-flavored leaves than their wild cousins do. The oval to fan-shaped leaves can be almost 2 inches across at their top and form an attractive rosette at the tip of each branch.

A native of India—and possibly the Americas—purslane has naturalized throughout the temperate world. It can be grown successfully in USDA Zone 3 and warmer.

DECIDING WHAT TO GROW

Both green- and golden-leaved purslanes are available. Golden-leaved types have pale yellow leaves that are larger and thicker than are those of green types. 'Goldgelber' and 'Goldberg' are two yellow-leaved cultivars. Green types are sold as well—'Garden Purslane' and 'Erect Large Leaf' are two. All are open-pollinated and mature in about 60 days from direct-seeding.

Early in the season when growth is slow, 18 to 20 plants may be needed to provide a plentiful supply of leaves and tip growth. As the plants begin to spread, however, they can be thinned to reduce the stand to a dozen plants, which is plenty for a family of four. Plants will contribute generously to salads, especially during the hottest part of the summer, when greens such as lettuce and spinach have expired.

HOW TO GROW

Purslane will grow almost anywhere, but it thrives in full sun and humus-rich soil with a near-neutral pH of 6.8 to 7.0. Plants do less well in cool, moist conditions. Sow seeds directly in the garden a week or two after the last-frost date. Seeds can be sown ⅛ inch deep every 1 inch in a row or broadcast in a bed and covered with an extremely thin layer of soil or compost. Keep the soil moist until germination occurs, about 8 days in 65°F soil. In USDA Zone 6 and colder, an early- or late-season crop can be grown in flats protected under a cloche or cold frame.

Thin plants as they grow, first to every 2 inches, then to every 4 inches, until they stand 10 to 12 inches apart. The best spacing depends on the method of harvest: Grow plants 4 inches apart, and harvest by shearing back entire plants; or thin to 10 to 12 inches, and pick leaves and tip growth from individual plants. If your climate is damp and cool, be sure not to crowd plants, which will encourage disease. For container plantings, three plants can be raised in a 5-gallon pot, eight in a 10-gallon tub. Fill with enriched planting mix, and keep plants well watered, but don't allow the soil to become waterlogged. In the ground or in containers, water plants with manure tea or fish emulsion when plants are 4 to 5 weeks old.

Even though purslane has been domesticated, it retains the aggressive self-sowing quality of its weedy cousin. Pinch off flower buds, or keep plants cut back to prevent it from popping up next year in unwanted numbers or places.

If the weather is cool and damp, purslane will languish and may be prone to various fungal diseases. However, with hot weather and occasional watering, less than 1 inch a week, purslane is largely immune to insect and disease problems.

HARVESTING

Like the wild strain, domesticated purslane is rich in vitamins C and E. And it has a higher concentration of Omega-3 fatty acids, linked to reducing heart disease, than does any other plant growing on land. Like spinach, it also contains oxalic acid, which prevents the body from absorbing all the calcium the plant has.

Their upright growth makes domesticated purslanes easy to harvest and less gritty than low-growing weedy forms are. Begin picking tip growth as soon as the leaves are a useful size, usually within 30 days of sowing. Or grow plants in a dense stand, and shear them back to 2-inch stubs when they reach a height of 5 to 6 inches, then allow them to regrow. Purslane doesn't store well, even when refrigerated, so pick only as much as you can use.

Purslane, which is self-pollinating, has been so rarely studied that little is known about crossing between cultivars or between domesticated and wild forms. To be safe when saving seeds, grow only one form. If wild purslane is common, cover your crop with floating row covers to prevent possible cross-pollination. Seeds are viable for 6 years; store in airtight containers in a dark, cool location. Purslane sprouts can be added to salads, so you may want to try sprouting some of the seeds you save.

PURSLANE, SEA. See *Orach*
PURSLANE, WINTER. See *Miner's Lettuce*
RADICCHIO. See *Chicory*

RADISH

Raphanus sativus, various groups; Mustard family, Brassicaceae. Annual and biennial grown as an annual.

○ ◑ ✳ ▼

Radishes are another of the garden's underground treasures, minor surprises to be unearthed and enjoyed. Many would emphasize the adjective minor, casting this nippy but nutrition-poor root in the role of garnish—to be made into rosettes to decorate plates filled with more substantial foods. Perhaps the radish's obscure origin is part of the problem—no indigenous *Raphanus sativus* has even been found. Yet its cultivation is ancient, dating at least to the Egyptians, whose pharaohs supposedly fed huge quantities of radishes to their pyramid-building slaves.

Early on, radishes were more at home in the medicine cabinet than in the kitchen, recommended to cure a host of ills, including poisonous bites, kidney and bladder stones, colic, rheumatism, and insanity. They would remove warts, freckles, scars, pimples, and corns (if applied when the moon was on the wane), and a compound of radish roots, honey, and dried sheep's heart would make hair grow. On the other hand, radishes "eaten before or after meat . . . dulleth the braine, eyes, and reason," according to 16th-century Englishman Thomas Hill.

Despite their mixed press, radishes landed in North America with the first European settlers. Thomas Jefferson cultivated a rainbow of radishes at Monticello, including red, white, black, salmon, and violet types. His salmon radish, which has disappeared, was probably 'Long Salmon', a cultivar that is scarlet at the top, salmon in the midsection, and white at the bottom of the root. By 1865, more than 50 radish cultivars were available in the United States, including the pear-shaped 'Black Spanish', which is still widely grown.

Jefferson's garden diaries record that he nearly always sowed radishes on March 1. The planting date may be different in Fairbanks, Alaska, or San Diego, California, but gardeners in all USDA Zones can grow radishes.

DECIDING WHAT TO GROW

For a vegetable labeled "minor," there are an astonishing number of radishes available—well over 250 cultivars—and many ways of grouping them. Although their shapes, colors, and flavor vary, the most helpful distinction for home gardeners may be the number of days a cultivar takes to mature. Most spring radishes (*Raphanus sativus*, Radicula group) are small and ready to pull in a month or less, about the time of the first brood of robins. They can also be planted in late summer for an autumn harvest.

Long-season, or winter, radishes, a loose group that includes all the Asian radishes (also known as daikon, Oriental, Japanese, Chinese, and lobok

Radish 'French Breakfast', 'Cherry Belle', and 'White Icicle'

radishes, *R. sativus*, Daikon group), usually have much larger roots and take more time to reach full size, 2 months or more. Long-season radishes store better than spring cultivars do, but bigger doesn't mean hotter. Most daikons, including the heirloom 'White Chinese', which has an 8-inch cylindrical root, lack pungency, while 'Snow Belle' and 'Crimson Giant', two spring types, have enough zip to please most hotheads.

Not all radish zip is in the root: Leaves and seed-

RADISH CULTIVARS

The sprinters of the vegetable garden, spring radishes go from seed to table in under a month. Long-season cultivars take somewhat longer—between 1½ and 2½ months—but come in more shapes, sizes, and colors than spring types do.

'April Cross': long-season; 65 days; long, tapered white root; hybrid.

'Black Spanish': long-season; 60 days; extremely large, oblong, purplish black root; heirloom.

'Burpee White': spring; 25 days; white, round or globe-shaped roots; also called 'Snowball'.

'Champion': spring; 24 days; red globe-shaped root; AAS winner.

'Cherry Belle': spring; 23 days; round red root with short tops; AAS winner.

'Cherry Bomb': spring; 25 days; round red root; good bolt resistance.

'China Rose': long-season; 55 days; elongated rose-colored root with pungent flavor; good cultivar for sprouts; heirloom.

'D'Avignon': spring; 21 days; cylindrical red-white bicolor root.

'Easter Egg': spring; 28 days; round multicolor (white, red, purple, pink, violet) root; hybrid.

'Flamboyant': spring; 28 days; cylindrical red-white bicolor root; French cultivar.

'French Breakfast': spring; 25 days; oblong red-white bicolor root; heirloom.

'Hailstone': spring; 28 days; round white root.

'Little Tokyo Round': long-season; 40 days; white root the shape and size of a turnip; spring or fall crop; hybrid.

'Long Scarlet': spring; 25 days; cylindrical red root; heirloom.

'Misato Rose': long-season; 65 days; large, round root with green skin and pink flesh; stores well; hybrid.

'Nero Tondo': long-season; 50 days; large, round black root; good bolt-resistance.

'Purple Plum': spring; 28 days; globe-shaped purple root with short tops; widely adapted.

'Red Meat': spring; 50 days; large, round root with green skin and pink flesh; for fall crop only.

'Round Black Spanish': long-season; 55 days; large, round purplish black root; heirloom.

'Sparkler': spring; 25 days; round/oblong red-white bicolor root; widely adapted cultivar.

'Spring Song': long-season; 60 days; long, tapered white root; good bolt resistance; unusual spring-crop daikon; hybrid.

'Summer Cross No. 3': long-season; 45 days; long, tapered white root; hybrid.

'Tae-Baek': long-season; 70 days; large, blunt white root; good disease resistance; fall crop; hybrid.

'Valentine': spring; 25 days; round green-white bicolor with red flesh.

'Violet de Gournay': long-season; 70 days; long, cylindrical purple root with pungent flavor; stores well; fall crop; heirloom.

'White Chinese': long-season; 60 days; long, cylindrical white root with mild flavor; also called 'Celestial'; heirloom.

'White Icicle': spring; 30 days; cylindrical white root; heat-tolerant.

pods also contain a bit of fire and are first-rate salad ingredients. Rat-tailed radishes (*R. sativus*, Caudatus group) are grown specifically for their immature seedpods. They're difficult to find except from seed-saving organizations; fortunately, the pods and leaves of all radish cultivars are edible. Between 100 and 150 plants, successively cropped, should provide enough fresh radishes for a family of four.

SITE & SOIL

Spring radishes are ready to pull so quickly that many gardeners don't give them their own space. Instead, they interplant them with crops that mature more slowly. Radishes and carrots are a traditional pairing, but you can interplant with nearly any vegetable or herb. Gardeners often mix radishes with crops that germinate slowly, such as parsley, to mark rows, and use them as a trap crop to attract insects away from other plants.

If your radishes are more than guideposts to find the parsnips or decoys to protect the peppers from aphids and flea beetles, be sure to sow them where they'll get at least 6 hours of sun each day. They grow best in light, well-aerated soil that is slightly acid (pH 5.8 to 6.8). Avoid adding any high-nitrogen fertilizer, such as fresh manure, immediately before seeding; the result will be large, lush tops and undersize roots. Undersize and/or misshapen roots are also caused by compacted soil, stones, or other debris, so make sure the planting bed is well dug—to a depth of at least 6 inches for spring radishes, at least twice that deep for winter types.

Spring radishes are excellent container plants, good companions for basil, lettuce, spinach, and other vegetables and herbs, as well as for edible flowers, such as marigolds and nasturtiums. Use a container with good bottom drainage that is at least 10 inches wide and 12 inches deep. Fill with enriched potting soil, keep watered, and feed once with compost tea.

HOW TO GROW

The word radish comes from the Latin for "easily reared," a tip-off to its culture. Begin spring cultivars outdoors 4 to 6 weeks before the last expected frost, sowing seeds ½ inch deep, 1 inch apart. Make successive sowings every 7 to 10 days, stopping when the average air temperature reaches 65°F. Resume sowing when temperatures fall in autumn. Radishes germinate quickly, in a week or less in soil warmer

than 50°F. (In warm climates, grow radishes as a winter crop.) Long-season radishes can be planted in spring or summer, depending on the cultivar. True winter-storage types, such as 'Black Spanish' and 'Violet de Gournay', should be planted so that their harvest coincides with the first fall frosts, which improve the roots' flavor and texture. Sow seeds ¾ inch deep. For larger radishes, sow seeds deeper, up to 1½ inches.

Thin spring radishes to 2 inches, winter cultivars to 6 inches, and mulch to retain moisture and suppress weeds. Be ruthless when thinning (you can use the discards in green salads); crowded plants won't develop good roots. Cover all radish plantings with floating row covers to discourage flea beetles and other insects.

Good flavor and texture depend on fast growth and cool temperatures, so time plantings accurately and keep the soil moist. Stressing radish plants with uneven watering or heat (the ideal growing temperature is 60° to 65°F) will result in bitter, tough roots or push plants prematurely toward flowering rather than forming roots.

POTENTIAL PROBLEMS

Radishes aren't heavy feeders; soil rich in organic matter should provide all the food they need. If you find dark spots on and in radish roots, your soil has a boron deficiency, which should be corrected by top-dressing with compost. (For severe deficiencies, water with a borax-water solution: 1 teaspoon household borax per 1 gallon water.)

Radishes are rarely troubled by disease, but growing them in the same place several years in a row invites clubroot; rotate their location annually. The most common insects that prey on radishes—cabbage root maggot, imported cabbageworm, and flea beetles—can be controlled by using floating row covers. (See "Controlling Common Pests" on page 162 for more information on these pests.)

HARVESTING

No one grows radishes for their nutritional content, although they do contain about 10 percent of the recommended daily amount of vitamin C plus lesser amounts of vitamin B and iron. It's their nippy flavor and crunchy texture that gardeners are after, both of which are compromised if harvesting isn't timed correctly. Begin pulling spring radishes as soon as they are large enough to use—once they are full-size, their quality declines immediately. To produce edible pods, let a few spring cultivars go to seed and pick them when they are immature. You can also let the pods dry, collect the seeds, and use for growing sprouts.

Winter types also can be harvested as soon as they are large enough to use, but mild frosts improve their quality. Harvest all roots before the first hard freeze. To store winter radishes, cut tops off 2 inches above the root, place in plastic bags to retain moisture, and refrigerate; or store for longer periods of time in damp sand or sawdust in a cold (32° to 40°F) location.

Although some winter radishes, such as 'Black Spanish' and 'China Rose', are biennials, spring cultivars are annuals and flower in their first year as temperatures warm and the day length increases in midsummer. Radishes are pollinated by insects, and all cultivars will cross. To produce seeds that will come true, plant only one cultivar. Seeds are viable for 5 years; store in airtight containers in a dark, cool location.

RAPINI, RAPINE. See *Broccoli*

RHUBARB

Rheum rhabarbarum. Buckwheat family, Polygonaceae. Perennial.

○ ❊ ❀ ▮

Culinary rhubarb suffers from an identity crisis. Although designated as a species, *Rheum rhabarbarum*, all our rhubarbs are actually hybrids, the result of centuries of cross-pollinating. Worse still, although technically a vegetable—defined as any crop in which the leaf, stem, or root is eaten—rhubarb is usually treated as a fruit in the kitchen. Vegetable-cum-fruit. (Botanical bafflements aren't limited to rhubarb: Tomatoes, cucumbers, and peppers are three "vegetables" that technically are fruits.)

The Chinese, using different *Rheum* species from the one we now eat, turned rhubarb roots into medicines nearly 5,000 years ago. According to Gerard's *Herball* (1633), the roots were good for all "griefes" of the stomach, a view that carries over today, when a dish of culinary rhubarb is still thought to be the traditional spring cathartic. "The

first rhubarb of the season is to the digestive tract of winter-logged inner man what a good hot bath with plenty of healing soap is to the outer [man] after a bout with plough and harrow," cookbook author Della Lutes wrote in 1938. Exactly when people began eating rhubarb's leafstalks, or petioles, is unclear, but its popularity soared in 1815, when the trick to forcing rhubarb was accidentally discovered in the Chelsea Physic Garden in England.

One of the garden's few perennial vegetables, culinary rhubarb is also an immigrant. Unlike most botanical aliens, it landed not on one coast but on two—carried by 18th-century Europeans to New England and the mid-Atlantic colonies and by 18th-century Russian fur traders to Alaska. Despite this dual invasion, rhubarb wasn't widely planted until the end of the Civil War, when its merits—superb tart flavor and easy cultivation—elevated it from the exotic to the everyday, from *Rheum rhabarbarum* to "pie plant." Locate an abandoned homestead from the last century, and you're also likely to

Rhubarb 'Chipman's Red'

find a gnarled lilac, an overgrown apple tree, and a healthy clump of rhubarb.

Early settlers may have concentrated on rhubarb's value in the kitchen, but no gardener today will overlook this long-lived plant's tall, colorful stalks and oversize, crinkled, red-veined leaves. Wonderfully decorative—2 or 3 feet tall and 4 feet across—and adapted to USDA Zone 8 and colder, rhubarb is a plant for all gardens.

If medicinal, culinary, and ornamental merit weren't enough, rhubarb also has environmental significance. Chemists at Yale University have discovered that stockpiles of ozone-depleting CFCs can be safely and inexpensively destroyed by passing them through sodium oxalate, which is found in rhubarb leaves. It's the stuff of bumper stickers: SAVE THE WORLD • PLANT RHUBARB!

WINTER RHUBARB

You can extend the rhubarb harvest by forcing, or manipulating a plant to grow or flower out of season. To force rhubarb, dig a medium-size plant in late autumn, after it is dormant but before the ground freezes. Replant it in a large container filled with an enriched mix, with the buds 1 inch below the soil surface. Water and place the container outdoors for at least 8 weeks of temperatures below 40°F. After the cold treatment, move the container indoors, setting it in a cool, totally dark location (or cover the container with a box or basket). Keep the soil moist, and in about 6 weeks, you'll be cutting winter rhubarb. Its flavor will be identical to stems cut in spring, but it will look different: red stalks topped with small, crinkled yellow leaves. Many gardeners discard plants that have been forced, but they can be replanted outdoors in spring. Allow them a year to recover before harvesting them again.

DECIDING WHAT TO GROW

In 1772, Ben Franklin sent rhubarb seeds from Scotland to John Bartram, who was busy creating America's first botanical garden near Philadelphia, but today, only curious gardeners seeking new strains should grow rhubarb from seeds. All of the approximately 100 culinary rhubarb cultivars are hybrids of some kind and do not come true from seeds.

The obvious difference between rhubarb cultivars is color: leaf stems of green, pink, or red. Green and pink cultivars give greater yields, but not great enough to be important to a home grower. In addition to yield and color, breeding has focused on eliminating the tall seed stalks that rhubarb plants send up once the weather warms. As for flavor, the differences are too subtle to be noticeable.

Good cultivars for home gardeners are 'Canada Red'/'Chipman', 'Valentine', and 'Cherry Red', all of which are red outside and in; 'Strawberry' and 'Sutton' are widely adapted pink rhubarbs. Avoid 'Victoria', an heirloom with green stalks that turn brown when cooked, unless you plan to force plants (when forced in total darkness, 'Victoria' produces red stalks). Commercial growers in southern California plant 'Cherry Giant', a good warm-region cultivar that is triggered into dormancy by drought rather than by cold.

Rhubarb buds begin to open as soon as the mercury moves into the mid-40s F, making it one of spring's first crops. Stems will survive mild frosts, but a hard freeze may damage them. If they are injured by the cold, cut them off to promote new growth. Four to six large plants should yield enough rhubarb for fresh use for a family of four; if you want to preserve, increase the planting.

SITE & SOIL

Rhubarb prefers cool conditions and is most productive in regions where winter temperatures fall below 40°F and summer temperatures average 75°F. (Most cultivars need temperatures below 40 in order to break dormancy and stimulate production of petioles and leaves.) Once the mercury rises above 80°F, stem growth declines as plants pour all their energy into producing seed stalks, which are 5 feet tall and topped with tiny greenish white flowers.

Well-fed rhubarb plants will produce for 20 years or longer, so locate this vegetable where it won't be disturbed, either in a separate bed or on the

Rhubarb in flower

Each set should include a fist-size piece of root with at least two buds and should be kept cool until planted to prevent sprouting.

Dig a hole at least 18 by 18 inches for each set, then partially refill it with a 50-50 mixture of soil and well-rotted manure or compost. Plant the set so that the buds are 1 to 2 inches below the soil surface (deeper in sandy soil); cover and firm the soil. As soon as the first shoots emerge, mulch heavily with shredded leaves, grass clippings, or other organic matter to control weeds and retain moisture. Keep new plants well watered, at least 1 inch a week. In late autumn, after the plant has died back, top-dress with well-rotted manure or compost. Top-dress again the following spring and each spring and fall thereafter.

Once plants produce seed stalks, their production of petioles declines, so remove the seed stalks as soon as they appear. Do not harvest rhubarb during the first year, and harvest sparingly the second season. Beginning in the third year, you can "gather with freedom," as a 19th-century American gardener put it. Begin picking as soon as stalks are large enough to use, about the width of a finger.

After 8 or 10 years, rhubarb plants may become crowded and produce smaller and thinner stalks. To rejuvenate plants, dig them up in early spring—don't worry about severing the deep roots—while they are still dormant. Using a spade or knife, cut the crown (the fleshy upper part of the underground plant) into several doughnut-size pieces, making sure each division contains at least

edge of the garden. Rhubarb will grow in partial sun, but for a generous supply of sturdy stems, full sun is required. Fertile, well-drained soil is also necessary—rhubarb crowns planted in heavy clay can rot. Amend it generously with organic matter, such as compost or well-rotted manure. Slightly acid soil (pH 6.0 to 6.8) is ideal, but rhubarb is not particular and can tolerate a pH as low as 5.3. Set plants 4 feet apart.

Rhubarb is a handsome plant for deck or patio. Use a large container, at least 24 inches deep, with good bottom drainage, and fill with organically rich potting soil. Water frequently, and feed every 2 weeks with manure or compost tea.

HOW TO GROW

The second best thing about rhubarb—the first best thing is its tart flavor—is that once it's established, little care is required. Container plants are available at some nurseries, but most gardeners propagate rhubarb in early spring from sets, or root divisions.

PULL OR CUT?

Traditionally, gardeners have pulled rather than cut rhubarb, believing that cutting the petioles opened plants to diseases and insects. However, research has shown that cutting rhubarb is just as safe as pulling it. So you can either grip the stalk's base and twist it slightly while pulling gently, or use a sharp knife to cut the stalk just above the soil line. Trim the stem bottoms, and discard the leaves.

one bud. If you can't replant immediately, store the divisions in the refrigerator, then rehydrate them by soaking them in water for at least 6 hours before planting.

POTENTIAL PROBLEMS

Rhubarb is close to problem-free. Keep new plants heavily mulched to prevent them from being overtaken by weeds. Weeding also discourages two potential pests, rhubarb curculio and potato stem borer. Mites, which suck on plant leaves and thrive in hot, dry conditions, can be controlled by spraying plants vigorously with water. For severe infestations, apply an insecticidal soap. Lacewings, lady bugs, and predatory thrips are natural predators.

Phytophthora crown rot, which attacks the plant crown and causes stalks to rot at their base, is rhubarb's most common ailment. It's normally a problem only in poorly drained soils, and it cannot be cured. Affected plants should be removed and discarded.

HARVESTING

Home gardeners usually harvest rhubarb selectively, stalk by stalk, for a 4- to 8-week period. (In contrast, commercial rhubarb producers harvest all the stalks at one time. If you're making pies for the entire neighborhood, don't be afraid to cut every stalk.) As the weather warms the production of new leafstalks slows. In autumn, if rainfall increases, rhubarb plants will send up new petioles that can be cut for a second harvest. In cool regions, you may be able to keep plants producing throughout summer by harvesting regularly, removing all seed stalks, and making sure plants have plenty of water.

Rhubarb contain vitamins A and C, calcium, and potassium; low in calories, it is good source of fiber. After harvesting rhubarb, immerse the stems in ice water until cooled. Drain, seal in plastic bags, and refrigerate.

Planting from seed is not recommended.

SPECIAL NOTES

Rhubarb leaves are toxic and should never be eaten under any circumstances.

ROCKET. See *Arugula*
ROMANESCO BROCCOLI. See *Broccoli*
ROMAN FENNEL. See *Fennel*
ROQUETTE. See *Arugula*

Rosemary foliage

ROSEMARY

Rosmarinus officinalis. Mint family, Lamiaceae.
Perennial.

Rosemary is a tender evergreen shrub with gray-green needlelike leaves and pale lavender-blue to white summer flowers. Both flowers and foliage are aromatic—the fragrance is due to a volatile oil that smells something like a combination of pine, mint, and ginger. A close look at the flowers reveals the tiny two-lipped blooms that mark rosemary as a relative of mint, sage, and thyme. Plants grown outdoors in mild climates where rosemary is hardy can reach 4 to 6 feet in height; in colder regions, rosemary must be brought indoors each winter, and plants remain much smaller.

Centuries ago, rosemary was valued more for rituals than for cooking. An old name for it, coronaria, arises from its use in the weaving of ceremonial garlands and crowns. Shakespeare's "There's rosemary, that's for remembrance" alludes to a tradition that dates back to at least Grecian times, when students wore rosemary garlands to improve their memory while taking examinations. In addition to remembrance, rosemary also represents friendship, loyalty, and love and was used to symbolize those sentiments at both weddings and funerals. It's not hard to imagine how this herb gained such a reputation, for brushing against the foliage releases a distinctive fragrance that, in the manner of all perfumes, compels memories in an instant.

Rosemary flowers

Rosemary is native to the slopes that border the Mediterranean Sea—its genus comes from the Latin *ros*, "dew," and *marinus*, "of the sea." The name indicates more than the plant's native habitat, however. It also describes the maritime conditions this herb likes: well-drained soil and humid air. Both demands can't be met consistently in most gardens, but as long as rosemary is kept from freezing or resting in water, it can be surprisingly resilient, growing into a stately woody shrub in a few years in warm climates. Amenable to clipping into hedges or topiary shapes, it is an excellent hedging plant where it is hardy, and trailing types can be used as groundcovers in herb gardens.

DECIDING WHAT TO GROW

Most rosemaries are reliably hardy only in USDA Zone 8 and warmer. The cultivar 'Arp', which has pale gray-green leaves and nearly white, lemon-scented flowers, is considered the hardiest and reportedly can withstand temperatures to –10°F if it

has some protection, making it a possible plant for Zone 7 gardens.

Although botanists differ on whether or not more than one species in the genus *Rosmarinus* exists, there's no doubt that a good supply of cultivars is available to choose from, with specialist catalogs offering a dozen or more. In addition to extra-hardy 'Arp', 'Miss Jessup's Upright', which has a vigorous vertical habit, 'Salem', and 'Alba', which has white blooms, are thought to be somewhat hardier than the species. 'Blue Boy' is a creeping dwarf plant, to 1 foot, with dense growth and small leaves that make a fine container specimen. 'Huntington Carpet', which originated at California's Huntington Gardens, is another creeping cultivar. 'Golden Rain', also called 'Joyce Debaggio', has golden streaks on its new foliage. Other well-known cultivars include 'Blenenden Blue', 'Majorca Pink', 'Tuscan Blue', and 'Rex', all upright cultivars.

One healthy plant will provide plenty of leaves for a family of four.

HOW TO GROW

The traditional wisdom is that "Rosemary grows well only when the mistress is master." In addition, it prefers a near-neutral soil (pH 6.5 to 7.0) that drains well. While the soil should never be allowed to dry out completely, it also should never be wet—roots that sit in wet soil are sure to rot. Average or even thin soil is fine for this herb; an excess of fertilizer will produce succulent stems and leaves that are easy prey for diseases and insects. In areas where rosemary is hardy, select a permanent location in full sun or one with very light afternoon shade, because plants resent disturbance and do better if they aren't moved. Make sure plants have good air circulation by giving them plenty of room, 2 feet of space all around.

The species can be grown from seeds sown indoors in pots, but germination and growth are slow, and only fresh seeds germinate reliably. The best, quickest route—and the only good route when growing a named cultivar—is to start with purchased plants or cuttings. In areas where rosemary isn't hardy, most gardeners treat rosemary as if it were an annual, beginning with new plants each year.

Although a challenge, rosemary can be grown year-round in a container. Use a clay pot, at least 12 inches across and 12 inches deep, with plenty of drainage holes, and pot on as necessary. Fill pots with a light potting soil—cactus soil with perlite added is one recommendation. Feed plants monthly in spring and early summer with compost tea. Water regularly, but never let the soil stay wet. After hardening off, set potted plants outdoors in late spring (if they dry out too quickly on a deck or patio, sink the pots to the rim in the garden). Bring the plants back indoors in late summer, well before the threat of frost, and set them in a bright but cool spot, about 45°F. Water cautiously, but don't allow the soil to dry completely, and mist plants at least twice a week with tepid water.

The only other care rosemary requires is an occasional pruning. Pinch stem tips to encourage bushiness, or remove branches to attain a desired shape. If, despite pruning, your plant becomes woody and lanky after 3 or 4 years, take cuttings and then discard it. Four-inch cuttings, taken in mid- to late summer, also are a good way to propagate plants to bring indoors for the winter. Dip the stems in rooting hormone powder, and stick them in a 4-inch pot filled with a damp mix of half vermiculite and half perlite. Roots should form in about 3 weeks.

Scarlet runner bean

Rosemary is troubled by few pests and diseases. Plants subjected to drought, drowning, or frost will drop their needlelike leaves. Wet soil, especially in winter, will cause root rot. Plants grown indoors are susceptible to aphids, spider mites, and other houseplant insect pests.

HARVESTING

Clip leaves or stem tips as needed. Store leftover fresh rosemary in plastic bags or closed containers in the refrigerator. For longer-term storage, try freezing branches of rosemary; remove the frozen leaves from the stems on an as-needed basis. Rosemary also can be dried by hanging bunches in a warm, dark, dry place. Do not use heat to dry rosemary, as the fragrant oils are volatile.

RUNNER BEAN

Phaseolus coccineus. Pea family, Fabaceae. Perennial grown as an annual.

It's no contest in the pea-family-flower beauty contest: Runner beans are the hands-down winners. Seventeenth-century gardeners like the herbalist John Gerard wrongly believed that their colors depended on the soil—"the floures, that do vary and differ in the colours, according to the soile where they grow"—as those of hydrangeas do. In fact, the showy blooms—red and white, plus 'Sunset', an unusual pink cultivar, and 'Painted Lady', an heirloom bicolor—are a result of selection. Held well above the dark, dense foliage, the blossoms are irresistible lures to hummingbirds, butterflies, bees, and a host of other insects.

Runner beans are also known as painted ladies because of their colorful flowers. Native to Mexico and Central America, they are tender perennials—their foliage dies back with the first frost—with dahlialike tuberous roots. Plants climb from 8 to 12 feet high when grown as annuals and need a sturdy trellis to support their winding travels. The large seedpods are always green, but seed colors vary: Most common is blackish purple stippled with maroon or, depending on your perspective, maroon stippled with blackish purple.

Gardeners in USDA Zone 3 and warmer can grow runners, but those tilling in the coldest regions will want to begin plants indoors. The runner bean, as a 19th-century source put it, "requires the whole season for its perfection." Most cultivars need at least 90 warm days to produce edible pods, another 30 days to produce a good-size harvest. Yields are heavy, so two to three dozen plants should be enough for the neighborhood hummingbirds and a family of four. If you want to preserve, increase the planting.

SITE & SOIL

Runner beans want a sunny location, or partial shade in extremely hot climates. They prefer well-prepared, well-drained soil that is rich in humus and slightly acid pH (6.5 to 6.8). Better able to deal with cool temperatures than many beans, runners are not frost-tolerant. Even if your season is a long one, however, don't postpone planting too long in spring. Plants that are subjected to high temperatures—above 90°F—rarely set pods. If summers are cool in your garden, give plants a home out of the wind and a southern exposure.

Except for dwarf types, all cultivars need something to climb—trellises made from sheep fencing or wood laths work well, as do pole tepees. Lightweight strings and plastic netting are less successful. The vines twine from right to left, so if you help them get started climbing, make sure you head them in the correct direction. Install the support when sowing seeds or transplanting seedlings so that plant roots aren't disturbed.

Locate runner beans where they won't shade smaller neighbors. Many gardeners plant borage nearby to attract the bees and other insects that trigger pollination.

Runner beans are unsurpassed among climbing vegetables in the ornamental landscape. Two plants will blanket a trellis 10 feet tall and 4 feet wide with dark green foliage punctuated by colorful blooms. Dwarf runners, such as 'Hammonds Dwarf', are a first-rate choice for pots and window boxes. Use a large container with good bottom drainage. Fill with enriched potting soil, keep well watered, and feed every 3 weeks with compost tea.

HOW TO GROW

Runner beans are cultivated as common snap (pole) beans are—see *Bean* on page 187 for details. Direct sow seeds 1 to 2 inches deep, spaced at 6 inches, as soon as the danger of frost has passed and the soil

has warmed to at least 60°F. In 65°F soil, germination takes about 13 days, but it takes only 2 to 3 days at 85°F. Make one sowing of this long-season crop, and cover the seeds lightly, making sure that the soil remains moist and friable. Runner beans produce their first leaves underground, so any crust that forms can prevent emergence. Once plants are established, thin to 12 inches.

Alternatively, start runner beans indoors, sowing seeds in individual containers, two seeds per

---

RUNNER BEAN CULTIVARS

Whether they have white, red, or bicolor flowers, runner beans make attractive—and productive—additions to both vegetable and flower gardens.

'Butler': 70 days; red flowers; 12-inch stringless pods.

'Enorma': 95 days; red flowers; thin 18-inch pods; purple seeds with black streaks; high yields.

'Hammonds Dwarf': 65 days; red flowers; 18-inch non-climbing cultivar; 7-inch pods.

'Painted Lady': 100 days; red and white bicolor flowers; 10-inch pods; brown-black and white seeds; does well in cool regions; heirloom.

'Prizewinner': 95 days; red flowers; 20-inch pods; purple seeds with black streaks; brilliant flower color.

'Scarlet Runner': 90 days; red flowers; large black seeds mottled with maroon; most famous of all runner beans; heirloom.

'White Dutch Runner': 95 days; white flowers; 12-inch pods; white seeds; vigorous vines, 10 feet or more; heirloom.

'White Dwarf Aztec': 65 days; white flowers; long, curved pods; white seeds; short, 3-foot long runners; heirloom.

container (thin to one when plants are 2 inches tall). Beginning indoors can aid gardeners with short growing seasons, but be prepared for plants to sulk for a week or 10 days after they are transplanted. Pregerminating seeds indoors on damp paper toweling is another way to get a head start.

In areas where there are frosts but the ground doesn't freeze, vines will regrow from the roots. Vines started from roots bloom earlier than those grown from seed. Gardeners in regions where the ground freezes may want to try digging plant roots in autumn, overwintering them in damp sand, and then replanting them in spring after the danger of frost has passed.

Keep runner beans well watered, at least 1 inch per week, and mulch to retain moisture and suppress weeds. Additional fertilizer is unnecessary if your soil was well-prepared when you planted, but one or two feedings of compost tea or fish emulsion when plants are small will promote fast growth and heavy yields.

Although runners can be troubled by the same insects and diseases that trouble other *Phaseolus*

HYACINTH BEAN

If runner bean flowers win the blue ribbon, hyacinth bean flowers deserve the red. Like runners, hyacinth beans *(Lablab purpurus)* are twining plants, Asian natives that have naturalized in the Deep South. Leaves are purple-green, the perfumed flowers purple, red, pink, or white. The shiny purple to maroon pods are handsome as well. Short-lived perennials in warm regions, they are willing to put up with poor soil and meager rainfall.

Primarily grown as an ornamental, hyacinth, or lablab, beans are edible—and strongly flavored. Dry beans can cause an allergic reaction in some people, but soaking the seeds in hot water before using (discard the water) should eliminate any danger.

---

species, they usually grow undisturbed. If you keep the vines harvested, they will continue to flower until they are killed back by the first hard frost.

HARVESTING

Most gardeners cultivate runners solely as ornamentals, but their seeds are edible at any of three stages: snap, shell, or dry. Like other beans, they are an outstanding source of protein. Treat young pods, which should be sliced before cooking, like common snap beans, and harvest when the pods are still flat. For shell, or half-mature, beans, begin harvesting when the pods have filled out but before they begin to change color; for dried beans, allow the pods to mature fully on the vine.

If frost threatens before the seeds are fully mature, pick the pods, spread them in a single layer in a warm location out of direct sunlight, and let them dry. To store dried beans, shell and seal in an airtight container. The large flowers are also edible and have a distinct bean flavor.

Runner bean flowers are perfect but require insects' help—called "tripping"—to self-pollinate. While runners don't cross with other species of beans, the hummingbirds, bees, and other insects that ensure self-pollination visit many flowers, and cross-pollination between cultivars is common. To ensure that your seeds will come true, plant only one cultivar (or separate cultivars by at least ½ mile). The seeds, which are easy to shell, are viable for 3 years if stored in airtight containers in a dark, cool location.

RUTABAGA

Brassica napus, Napobrassica group. Mustard family, Brassicaceae. Biennial grown as an annual.

○ ❄

Rutabagas, which are also called Canadian turnips, Russian turnips, Swedish turnips, swedes, and yellow turnips, are frequently described as "big turnips." It's a practice that rutabaga lovers resent. After all, did the poet Carl Sandburg, whose works include *Rootabaga Stories* (1922) and *Rootabaga Pigeons* (1923), name two books after turnips? Did Frank Zappa sing "Turrrrrniiiip?" No, the refrain is "Rooooootabaaaaga."

The confusion about rutagabas is long-standing. Nineteenth-century American agriculturist Fearing

Burr wrote that they were "analogous to the Kohl Rabi." Across the Atlantic, the nurserymen Vilmorin-Andrieux listed it as "turnip-rooted cabbage" in *The Vegetable Garden* (1885) and noted that it liked "a stiff and moist soil." But in most garden books, even today, the commentary under rutabaga is "See Turnip."

Yet there are some important differences between these two vegetables: Not only are rutabagas larger than turnips, they have yellow rather than white flesh. Rutabagas also take longer to mature—1 month on average—and store longer—up to 6 months. Finally, rutabaga fans would add, their flavor is sweeter than turnips'.

Still, when most gardeners think rutabagas, they think turnips and well they should, because both can be grown in USDA Zone 2 and warmer, and their culture is almost identical.

Gardeners will find a few rutabaga cultivars to choose from in catalogs. 'Altasweet', which takes 90 days to mature, forms a very large, globe-shaped root that is exceptionally sweet. 'American Purple Top' is a widely adapted globe-shaped heirloom that matures in 100 days. 'Gilfeather', 75 days, which may be a turnip-rutabaga hybrid, produces egg-shaped roots. 'Laurentian' is a standard globe-shaped cultivar that matures in 105 days. 'Marian' is an 80-day globe-shaped cultivar that shows good disease resistance. 'York' is a 105-day Canadian globe-shaped cultivar and is resistant to clubroot.

Rutabaga 'Purple-Top Yellow'

All of these cultivars above are open-pollinated purple-yellow bicolors.

HOW TO GROW

Rutabagas are typically grown as a fall crop, sown from seeds 3 to 4 months before the average first-frost date. For a family of four, 35 plants should be adequate; plant more if you want to store roots. Like turnips, rutabagas prefer full sun and moderately rich, near-neutral (pH 6.8 to 7.5) soil that is well-drained and has been amended with humus. To promote healthy root development, make sure the soil is well dug to a depth of at least 14 inches. Sow seeds ½ inch deep, 1 inch apart; thin seedlings to 8 inches, and mulch heavily to keep the soil cool, preserve moisture, and suppress weeds. Be ruthless when thinning; crowded plants will fail to develop good roots.

No fertilizing is necessary during the growing season, but make sure plants receive an even supply of water, about 1 inch a week. Rutabagas are rarely bothered by insects or diseases. Practice crop rotation, and install floating row covers over the planting bed to avoid problems.

Rutabagas can be grown in large containers, although they leave a space when harvested. Use a container with good bottom drainage, and fill with enriched potting soil. Water frequently, and feed every 4 weeks with compost tea.

HARVESTING

Rutabagas can be pulled as soon as they are large enough to use, beginning when they are about 3 inches in diameter. Small roots are more tender than large ones are, but most gardeners postpone harvesting until after the first frost, which improves both taste and texture. The waxy blue-green rutabaga tops, which are a good source of vitamins A, C, and E, should be picked when they are young and small. Don't remove more than several leaves from each plant, however, as foliage is essential to root production.

Mulching heavily will extend the time roots can be left in the ground. To store rutabagas, cut tops off 2 inches above the root, place in plastic bags to retain moisture, and refrigerate. Rutabagas store extremely well if kept in damp sand or sawdust in a cold (32° to 40°F) location but will shrivel without enough humidity. To extend their storage life, dip each root in a pan of warm water to which a small amount paraffin has been added before storing.

Because rutabagas are biennials and normally don't flower until their second season, saving seeds is difficult. Rutabagas cross-pollinate with each other and with other *B. napus* members, such as Siberian kale and rape. To save seeds that will come true, plant only one cultivar. Seeds are viable for 4 years; store in airtight containers in a dark, cool location.

SAGE

Salvia officinalis. Mint family, Lamiaceae. Perennial.

○ ◑ ✳ ❄ ♣ ▼

Common sage is a hardy perennial herb, a Mediterranean native with aromatic gray-green leaves chock-full of volatile oils and tannins. Merely rubbing against the foliage releases its characteristic fragrance, a beguiling mix of lemon and camphor. Like many of its *Salvia* relatives, sage is a handsome plant that could be grown for ornament alone. It forms a loose, somewhat woody, 1½- to 2-foot-tall shrub covered with velvety, 1½- to 3-inch-long leaves that have a puckered or wrinkled texture. Plants are topped in summer by spikes of purple, pink, or white two-lipped flowers that attract both hummingbirds and butterflies.

Although primarily used as a culinary herb today—as a seasoning for stuffing, sausage, meat loaf, and bread, or to rub on pork, veal, or lamb before roasting—sage has an ancient reputation for

Sage 'Icterina'

Sage 'Purpurea' with salvia 'Berggarten' and other culinary sages

medicinal use. Its genus name, *Salvia*, is from the Latin, "to save or heal." Centuries ago, sage was among the most important medicinal herbs, dedicated by the early Greeks to Zeus and by the early Romans to Jupiter. People throughout the ancient world believed it could cure nervous disorders, stop bleeding, mend broken bones, aid conception, and extend life. It could even dye the hair black—another, if more ephemeral, way to prolong youth. "How shall a man die," the Arabic proverb goes, "who has sage in his garden?"

An early import to North American gardens—cultivated at least by 1631, when John Winthrop, Jr., ordered ½ ounce of seeds to be sent from England—sage was prescribed for migraine headaches by Captain Lawrence Hammond, a 17th-century South Carolina resident known for his "Physical Receipts." His cure required "Mugwort and Sage, a handful of each, Camomel and Gentian a good quantity, boyle it in Honey, and apply it behind and on both sides ye Head very warm, and in 3 or 4 times it will take it quite away."

Sage is hardy in USDA Zones 4 through 8 and semi-evergreen to evergreen in warmer zones, from about Zone 7 southward. Wet conditions are frequently a more limiting factor for this herb than are cold temperatures. Waterlogged soil in winter or spring can kill plants in areas where they normally are quite hardy.

DECIDING WHAT TO GROW

While common sage has gray-green leaves, several cultivars with handsomely variegated leaves are also available. All are aromatic and can be used just like common sage, although most are less hardy and somewhat more difficult to grow. 'Aurea', commonly called golden sage and sometimes sold as 'Icterina', has leaves variegated in green and yellow. 'Kew Gold', a compact 18-inch-high sage, has yellow leaves, some marked with green. 'Purpurea' or 'Purpurascens', purple sage, has gray-green leaves marked with purple, and 'Tricolor' features leaves variegated with cream, purple, and green. 'Nana' is a dwarf cultivar that stays under 1 foot tall yet spreads to 2 feet. 'Holt's Mammoth' has larger, rounder leaves than the species' and grows to 3 feet. 'Berggarten' has round, broad leaves—the largest of any of the cultivars—but reaches only 18 inches in height and has a compact habit.

Because it is a perennial, sage is best grown outside of or at the edge of the vegetable garden proper, where it could be disturbed accidentally. All sages make handsome additions to the herb garden and can be included in sunny flower beds and borders. They also make fine container plants. For best results choose a large container, at least 12 inches across and 12 inches deep, that has plenty of drainage holes, and fill it with light potting soil. In the northernmost limits of sage's hardiness, bury the pot to the rim for the winter, or insulate it with soil or straw. If you're gardening in Zone 4 or colder, overwinter container-grown plants indoors in a bright but cool spot, about 45°F. One or two plants is sufficient for a family of four, although you may want to have more, simply because they are so pretty.

HOW TO GROW

Sage does best in full sun, although it will tolerate light afternoon shade in warm regions. Average soil that is slightly acid to slightly alkaline and not too rich suits it. Good drainage is essential. If your soil is heavy or wet, locate sage plants in a raised bed or on a slight slope to help ensure good drainage.

Although the species can be grown from seeds, the cultivars must be propagated asexually—by cuttings, layering, or division. For this reason and because it takes 2 years to produce good-size plants from seeds, most gardeners begin with plants. To start from seeds, sow outdoors in early spring about 6 weeks before the last-frost date or sow indoors 8 weeks before the last frost. Germination takes 2 to 3 weeks. Space plants or thin seedlings to 1½ to 2 feet

THE OTHER SAGES

While most salvias are grown strictly for their ornamental value, common sage is not the only member of the genus used as an herb. Clary (*Salvia sclarea*) is a biennial that bears heart-shaped leaves and spikes of pale pink or purple two-lipped flowers. Both foliage and flowers have a balsamlike fragrance and can be used like sage.

Pineapple sage (*S. elegans*, also listed as *S. rutilans*) is a tender perennial with pineapple-scented leaves and striking scarlet flowers that appear in late summer and fall. One cultivar sold as "honeydew melon sage" has melon-scented foliage. Both add fruity flavor to a variety of foods and can be used in jams and jellies. (*S. dorisiana*, or fruit-scented sage, adds a similar flavor to foods.) Take cuttings of these frost-tender perennials in late summer, and overwinter them indoors.

If you buy sage at the supermarket, you're likely getting Greek sage (*S. fruiticosa*, also listed as *S. triloba*), which has distinctive gray-green leaves with fuzzy white undersides. Chefs consider this species to be less flavorful than common sage, but it has the advantage of adapting well to indoor cultivation.

apart—or as close as 1 foot if you are using sage as an edging plant. Water well until plants are established; once they have a good foothold in the garden, plants are relatively drought-tolerant.

Cut sage plants back by one-third each spring to promote new growth. Once plants become woody, begin anew by taking cuttings, layering, dividing vigorous new growth on the outside of the clumps, or simply buying new plants. Sage plants need to be renewed every 3 or 4 years.

Given full sun and well-drained soil, sage is seldom bothered by pests and diseases. In poorly drained conditions, however, plants will succumb to root rot.

Starting from seeds is not recommended.

HARVESTING

Pinch leaves off as needed, especially until the flowers, which are edible, open. Cut back the flower stems after blooming to encourage more leaf growth. Stop harvesting in early fall to harden off plants for the winter. To store harvested leaves briefly, seal them in plastic bags and refrigerate; for long-term storage, dry by spreading leaves in a single layer in a dry location out of direct sunlight. When completely dry, seal in a glass jar and store in a dark place.

SALAD BURNET

Sanguisorba minor. Rose family, Rosaceae.
Perennial.

○ ◑ ✳ ❄ ❀ ▜

Some 400 years ago, salad burnet was as common in salads and cool drinks as celery, but today, few gardeners have tasted the leaves of this perennial green. A bushy perennial herb, it forms a 1½- to 2-foot mound of divided, silver-green fernlike leaves with oval, toothed leaflets. Newly picked young foliage has a pleasant, cucumberlike flavor and fragrance. Although grown primarily for its new leaves, the bottlebrush-like purple-pink flowers, borne in summer above the foliage, are also edible and can be used in salads or as garnishes. In Germany, it is known as *wiesenknop*, or meadow button, an allusion to the buttonlike flowers.

Botanists reclassified salad burnet from *Poterium sanguisorba* to *S. minor*, thus reuniting it with the medicinal herb great burnet (*S. officinalis*) and a bloody heritage. The name *sanguisorba* is from the Latin, *sanguis*, meaning "blood," and sorbeo, "to absorb." Great burnet has been used as an herb for at least 2,000 years, and both species were believed to stop internal bleeding and used to treat a variety of skin ailments. They were also incorporated in ointments used to treat wounds. On a more positive note, "the leaves of burnet steeped in wine and drunken, comfort the heart, and make it merry," according to a 16th-century authority.

Salad burnet is a handsome ornamental often recommended as an edging plant in herb gardens. (Sir Francis Bacon recommended it be planted in pathways, because the plants emit a pleasant fragrance when stepped on.) It makes an attractive addition to flower gardens as well and can be grown in USDA Zone 3 and warmer.

HOW TO GROW

Grow salad burnet in full sun to partial shade. Unparticular and accommodating, it will tolerate a wide range of conditions as long as the soil is well-drained. Average soil that is slightly acid to neutral is fine, but plants will also grow in alkaline soil. Since it is a perennial, a site away from the vegetable garden is best so plants will not be disturbed accidentally. No cultivars are available.

You can begin salad burnet from nursery plants, which are available in spring, or from seeds, beginning either indoors or out. Soak seeds in warm water for an hour or two to spur germination, then sow outdoors, spacing them 6 inches apart. Thin the seedlings to 15 inches, slightly closer—about 12 inches—if you are planting an edging. Indoors, begin seeds in individual containers 4 to 6 weeks before the last expected frost. Set hardened-off plants in the garden when the danger of frost has passed. Once established, salad burnet needs little care and has few problems with insect pests or diseases. Keep the flowers picked off to encourage the production of new leaves and control self-seeding. In autumn, top-dress plants with compost, and mulch to keep plants from heaving.

HARVESTING

Pick the youngest, most tender leaves to keep plants in production. Alternatively, harvest salad burnet by cutting back entire plants with scissors, then allowing them to regrow.

Salad burnet is easy to propagate by division—

simply dig the clumps in spring, cut them apart with a sharp spade, and replant. Self-sown seedlings can also be lifted with a trowel and moved to where they are wanted. To save seeds, which will remain viable for 3 years, allow the plants to flower, and collect seeds in late summer.

SALSIFY

Tragopogon porrifolius. Sunflower family, Asteraceae. Biennial grown as an annual.

○ ❀

What root vegetable is thinner than a parsnip and has the flavor of an oyster? The answer is salsify. But ask most gardeners what salsify is, and the answer may be, "It's what you do when you dip tortilla chips into salsa." That wouldn't have been the response a century ago, when salsa wasn't chic and salsify was.

Cultivated at least since the 13th century, salsify is grown for its roots, which do taste slightly like oysters and give rise to the common names of oyster plant and vegetable oyster. Young shoots, flower buds, and flowers are also edible, and sprouted salsify seeds are good in salads and sandwiches. The plant's rose-purple flowers close at midday and have earned salsify yet another common name, John Go to Bed at Noon—and a place in floral clock plantings. Its grasslike leaves also fit comfortably in the ornamental landscape.

Salsify, which can be cultivated in USDA Zone 3 and warmer, grows slowly, a minimum of 100 days from seeds to harvestable roots. In the past 50 years, it has received as little attention from breeders as from gardeners. Many seed catalogs list this 2-foot vegetable simply as "salsify"; the heirloom 'Mammoth Sandwich Island' is the only widely available cultivar. (Don't confuse cultivated salsify with its yellow-flowered relative *Tragopogon pratensis*, which is too weedy for the edible garden.)

HOW TO GROW

Salsify needs a spot in full sun and light, loose, rich soil with a slightly acid pH (6.0 to 7.0). Make sure the ground is deeply dug—a minimum of 16 inches—and heavily amended with humus. Sow seeds in early spring, as early as 2 weeks before the last expected frost, $\frac{1}{2}$ to 1 inch deep, 1 inch apart, in rows 18 inches apart. In extremely mild areas, sow seeds in autumn for harvesting the following spring. Thin seedlings to 4 inches. Be ruthless when thinning; crowded plants will fail to develop good roots. For eating fresh, 20 to 30 plants should yield enough for a family of four; if you want to preserve, increase the planting.

Salsify is a trouble-free crop, not seriously bothered by diseases or insects. Mulch plants to maintain moisture and reduce weeds.

HARVESTING

Gardeners can begin digging roots after the first frost—which greatly improves their flavor—and continue harvesting as long as the ground remains unfrozen. Salsify stores better in the garden than in the refrigerator, so dig as needed. To extend the salsify season, mulch heavily to delay the soil from freezing.

Roots can be stored in damp sand or sawdust in a cold (32° to 40°F) location. Leave an inch or two of stem attached to the root to reduce dehydration. Because salsify is a biennial and doesn't flower until its second season, saving seeds is difficult. Gardeners in cold climates must dig and overwinter plants, then replant them in the spring; in frost-free regions, carry plants over to a second year. Seeds are

---

SCORZONERA

Scorzonera (*Scorzonera hispanica*), or black salsify, is also a member of the sunflower family, a perennial relative of salsify. Scorzonera has a black-skinned root, wider leaves, and yellow flowers, but otherwise is similar to salsify. It takes 120 days to produce edible roots. All parts of the plant—root, leaves, shoots, and flowers—are edible. 'Black Giant Russian', or 'Geante Noire de Russie', is the best-known cultivar, but two new scorzoneras from European breeders, 'Gigantia' and 'Duplex', are also available from a few mail-order seed companies.

viable for 4 years; store in airtight containers in a dark, cool location.

SALTBUSH. See *Orach*

SAVORY

Satureja spp. Mint family, Lamiaceae.
Perennial, annual.

○ ◐ ✳ ❄ ♣ ▜

This culinary herb isn't one plant, it's two—winter savory (*Satureja montana*) and summer savory (*S. hortensis*). Both are spicy, peppery-flavored plants native to the Mediterranean region that have been used for more than 2,000 years both in cooking and in medicine. Until black pepper (*Piper nigrum*) and other spices were brought from India to Europe, the savories were the strongest-tasting herbs available to Europeans. They made their way early to North America too and were growing in New England as early as 1630. While the common name savory simply means "tasty," the genus name, *Satureja*, refers to another use for this long-cultivated herb: It is derived from the word *satyr*, because savory was considered a stimulant and aphrodisiac.

Winter savory is a shrubby perennial, hardy from USDA Zones 5 to 9, that ranges from 12 to 15 inches in height. Its narrow, 1-inch-long dark green

Winter savory

leaves are semi-evergreen to evergreen and are less sweet and more strongly flavored than those of summer savory. Summer savory, a fast-growing annual, has narrow, 1-inch-long leaves that are gray-green in color. Although started from seeds each spring, it grows in the warm weather of summer with nearly weedlike speed to form a delicate-looking shrub about 18 inches tall. The erect stems of aromatic leaves are topped in summer by clouds of small pink flowers.

Summer and winter savory are used in much the same manner, whether in the kitchen or in the medicine cabinet (one exception is as an aphrodisiac, summer savory supposedly enhanced the sex drive, while winter savory diminished it). Summer savory is one of the herbs in the classic *herbes de Provence* (along with rosemary, thyme, and oregano). Also called the bean herb, it is used ceaselessly to flavor beans, peas, and lentils, a culinary combination probably resulting from the herb's being ready to pick about the time the beans come in. (John Parkinson wrote in 1629 of the savories that they were "effectuall to expel winde," an appropriate role for a bean herb.) Winter savory is more strongly flavored than summer is, but both can be used in salads, soups, dressings, sausage, and bean dishes.

Two or three plants of either type of savory should be enough for a family of four. Annual summer savory is easy to accommodate in the vegetable garden but is pretty enough for flower beds and borders, and, of course, for an herb garden. Winter savory is best grown with other perennial herbs or at the edge of the vegetable garden where it won't be disturbed. Also effective in ornamental plantings or as an edging in herb gardens, winter savory is a traditional plant in formal knot gardens.

Twelve-inch-tall dwarf or pygmy winter savory (*S. montana* 'Nana') is especially effective in ornamental plantings, and its leaves, although smaller than the species', can be used just like its full-size parent's. Creeping savory (*S. spicigera*, also listed as *S. repandra*) is a good choice for a low groundcover or in rock gardens. Plants, which grow 2 to 3 inches tall, produce white flowers in summer; their leaves are somewhat more strongly flavored than those of summer or winter savory.

There are also a handful of unsavory savories, *Satureja* species that don't taste like savory. Two worth trying are lemon savory (*S. biflora*) and thyme-leaved savory (*S. thymbra*).

SITE & SOIL

Winter and summer savory both thrive in full sun and require well-drained soil. Neither will survive for long in moist soil, so if you're in doubt about drainage, grow these herbs in a raised bed or on a slight slope that faces the sun. Both prefer slightly alkaline conditions, but they will grow in slightly acid to neutral soil as well. For winter savory, poor, even sandy, soil is best; summer savory prefers light but fertile soil that has been enriched with humus. Winter savory needs occasional watering; summer savory tolerates drier conditions. Both are good herbs for containers and can be planted singly, one plant per 6-inch pot, or combined in pots or tubs with other dry-soil herbs, such as thyme. In USDA Zone 5, bury containers of winter savory to the rim in fall to protect the roots over winter; in Zone 4 and colder, bring pots indoors to spend the winter in a cool, sunny window.

HOW TO GROW

Although it's easier to start with plants if you want to grow winter savory, it's possible to grow it from seeds. Sow seeds indoors 6 to 8 weeks before the last-frost date. Do not cover the seeds, as light is necessary for germination, which is variable and can take 2 to 3 weeks or more. Move hardened-off seedlings to the garden after the last frost, spacing plants 12 to 15 inches apart. Mulch plants in late fall after the ground freezes where winters are harsh and snow cover is poor. Like sage, winter savory becomes woody and less productive after a few years. Renew plants every 2 or 3 years by taking cuttings in summer or by dividing plants in spring.

Since summer savory does not transplant well, sow it directly in the garden where the plants are to grow after the last-spring-frost date. Germination takes about 1 week. Do not cover the seeds, as light is necessary for germination. Thin seedlings to 8 inches apart. Sow new crops every 3 weeks for an ongoing harvest of leaves.

HARVESTING

Snip off leaves, which contain vitamin A, and young shoots as soon as plants are large enough to be used; flavor is better before flowering begins. Flowers are also edible. Clipping back the flower stems encourages leaf growth and helps keep plants more compact.

Store fresh savory in plastic bags in the refriger-

ator. Although the leaves of winter savory become very hard when dried and are best used fresh, summer savory dries well. To dry, cut stalks when plants are in bud and hang them in a cool, dry place, then rub off the leaves and buds, and store them in sealed containers in a dark location.

SEA PURSLANE. See *Orach*

SHALLOTS

Allium cepa, Aggregatum group. Onion family, Alliaceae. Perennial also grown as an annual.

○ ◑ ▼

Shallots are the crème de la crème of the onion family—a status unmistakably reflected in their inclusion in scores of gourmet recipes and their elevated price at the supermarket. If you haven't tried shallots, in either the kitchen or the garden, you should.

Shallots

Their delicate flavor, often described as a blend of onion, scallion, and garlic, is unsurpassed, and they're as easy to grow as any of their cousins.

Like other members of the onion family, shallots have a rich history as well as a rich flavor. They supposedly originated near the ancient Palestine city of Ascalon, which is the source of their common name. The Romans carried them to England—they were typically eaten raw in "sallets"—but it was the French who turned shallots into aristocrats, taking advantage of their lovely color and tenderness in sauces and other dishes. In a bit of 19th-century Gallic one-upmanship, Vilmorin-Andrieux noted that "the plant commonly sent in quantities to the London market is not the True Shallot, but a small roundish Onion with a rich brown skin. The True Shallot has a pale-gray skin, and is elongated in shape."

A gray shallot—still considered "the True Shallot" by many connoisseurs—is available under the name 'Grey'. Today, however, "French" shallots are characterized by pinkish brown skin and pinkish purple flesh. Cultivars include 'French Red', 'Hative de Niort', 'Prince de Bretagne', and 'Atlas', a hybrid that can be grown from seeds. "Dutch" shallots are larger than French types and have orange-yellow skin and a slightly stronger flavor; look for 'Dutch Yellow' or 'Atlantic'. Larger still is 'Frog's Leg', a Mideastern type, shaped like its name, with sweet, mild flavor. The differences between these cultivars aren't giant ones, which makes it bearable that most seed catalogs list nothing other than "Shallot."

All shallots are a type of multiplier onion, hence the group name Aggregatum. Rather than producing one large bulb as most onions do, they produce a cluster of eight or more small bulblets, or sets (called cloves in the kitchen), that are joined at the base. Hardy and perennial, they can be grown in all USDA Zones and are well suited for container culture. Twenty-five plants should provide enough shallots for a family of four; if you want to preserve, increase the planting.

HOW TO GROW

Shallots are grown from sets or transplants, started 2 to 4 weeks before the frost-free date in northern gardens, or in autumn in the South. They like the same conditions that onions do and are grown similarly. Space plants 6 to 8 inches apart. Do not rebury bulblets that have pushed out of the ground. Like onions, shallots need a continuous source of nutrients and moisture, or the harvest will be scant. Feed with compost tea every 3 weeks, and make sure plants receive about 1 inch of water a week until the tops begin to yellow, when watering should be curtailed.

Shallots are susceptible to the same diseases and pests that onions are. To minimize problems, don't plant shallots in soil where other *Allium* species have grown, and use floating row covers after planting to prevent insects from reaching plants. Plants are hardy except in extremely cold regions that lack good snow cover; to ensure successful overwintering, mulch in late autumn.

HARVESTING

Begin harvesting shallot tops as you would scallions when they are tall enough to be used, about 30 days after planting. Green bulblets can be dug about 45 days after planting, mature shallots in 90 to 120 days, or as soon as the tops wither. Harvest and handle like onions, storing in mesh bags in cool, dry conditions.

Shallots rarely produce seeds and are propagated by dividing and replanting bulblets. Choose the largest and best clumps. After their tops wither, dig and save bulblets for replanting immediately or for storing and replanting in spring. For the best-quality shallots, replant each year.

ONE TIMES TWO IS...

The potato onion, another type of multiplier onion and *A. cepa*, Aggregatum group member, also divides underground to form a cluster of small- to medium-size bulblets, or sets. Also known as hill onion, pregnant onion, nest onion, and mother onion, it was widely planted in the 19th century but now is grown mostly in the mid-South. Its culture is similar to shallots'. Most seed catalogs list only "Potato Onion," but specialists offer red, white, and yellow cultivars, all heirlooms. Propagate each year from sets—in the spring in the Far North and in spring or fall in other regions.

SKIRRET

Sium sisarum. Carrot family, Apiaceae. Perennial often grown as an annual.

○ ☀

Although it is rarely seen in gardens today, skirret has been cultivated for more than a thousand years. Carried to Britain by the Romans—the historian Pliny (A.D. 23-79) observed that skirrets grew best in cool climates—they were a popular vegetable in medieval times, boiled, stewed, roasted, even baked in pies, and made into fritters. Their sweet flavor was especially welcome in an era when only the wealthy could afford to purchase sugar. "They doe help . . . to procure bodily lust," John Parkinson, botanist to Charles I. wrote in the 17th century. "Any way that men please to use them they may finde their taste to be very pleasant, far beyond any Parsnep."

What's used are the bunches of thin, 6-inch-long, cylindrical white roots that lie beneath the 3- to 4-foot-tall plants, which are perennial in USDA Zone 5 and warmer. You're unlikely to find skirret on local seed racks, although seeds are available from seed-saving organizations; there are no cultivated varieties. If you want to try something different that is, according to one authority, "delicious when mashed with potatoes, served with a cheese sauce, or dressed in a vinegar marinade," skirret is worth tracking down. For eating fresh, 6 to 10 plants should be enough for a family of four; if you want to preserve, increase the planting.

HOW TO GROW

Skirret likes full sun and light, rich soil that retains plenty of moisture and has a pH between 6.5 and 7.0. If beginning from seeds—skirret also can be propagated from root divisions—sow seeds as soon as the ground can be worked or begin indoors in individual pots, 8 to 10 weeks before the average frost-free date. Gardeners in mild regions can plant in autumn for harvest the following year. When started from seeds, skirret requires about 120 days to produce usable roots.

The ground should be deeply dug to avoid misshapen roots and amended with organic matter. Outdoors, sow seeds 1 inch deep, 4 inches apart; thin to at least 12 inches. Be ruthless when thinning; crowded plants will fail to develop good roots.

Like parsley, skirret is slow to germinate—it takes a minimum of 10 to 21 days. Mulch plants to retain soil moisture and suppress weeds, and stake if necessary. If rainfall is scant, water regularly, at least 1 inch a week. Skirret has no significant disease or insect problems.

HARVESTING

Begin digging roots, which taste like parsnips, as soon as they are large enough to be used (save a few roots for replanting). Like many root vegetables, skirret's flavor improves after frost. Large, old roots may have a tough central core that should be removed after cooking, but young roots are tender throughout. Mulching plantings heavily will extend the time roots can be dug in cold regions. For short-term storage, place roots in plastic bags to retain moisture, and refrigerate them. Skirret can be stored for longer periods of time in damp sand or sawdust in a cold (32° to 40°F) location or left in the ground.

Skirret normally doesn't produce its characteristic clusters of white flowers until its second year. Seeds are viable for 8 years; store in airtight containers in a dark, cool location.

SORREL

Rumex acetosa, R. scutatus. Buckwheat family, Polygonaceae. Perennials also grown as annuals.

○ ◑ ☀ ❄ ❀

Sorrel is a perennial green grown for its slightly sour, tangy-tasting, arrow-shaped leaves. The tang is compliments of oxalic acid, a compound in the leaves to which some people are allergic. Two species are commonly grown: *Rumex acetosa*, garden sorrel, and *R. scutatus*, French sorrel. A third species, *R. acetosella*, which is known as common, or sheep, sorrel, is edible only when the leaves are small and is usually gathered from the wild rather than cultivated. (Don't confuse sorrel with members of the genus *Oxalis*, which are commonly called wood sorrels and have cloverlike foliage.)

Sorrel's history reaches back to the Romans. Earlier generations used it as a medicine to "attempter and coole the bloud," but it was also popular in the kitchen. It was "much used in sawces [and] . . . It is divers waies dressed by Cookes, to

French sorrel

Gardeners in Zones 5 to 9 can grow either species as a perennial, but plants generally are short-lived and need to be renewed by division every 3 to 4 years. In USDA Zones 9 and colder, sorrel can also be planted in spring and grown as an annual.

As perennials, sorrels are best planted outside the vegetable garden proper, to avoid disturbing them accidentally. They can be incorporated in herb gardens or even in flower beds, where they can be interplanted with annuals, or grown in containers.

HOW TO GROW

Grow both types of sorrel in full sun or partial shade. Moderately rich, acid soil (pH 5.5 to 6.8) that is evenly moist but well drained is best, although plants will tolerate a wide range of conditions. Root divisions are the most common method of establishing sorrel. If beginning from seeds, sow in spring, ½ inch deep. To grow sorrel as an annual crop, thin to 4 inches apart. To grow it as a perennial, thin to 1½ feet. Plants will produce leaves of harvestable size in about 2 months. Side-dress plants each spring with compost or well-rotted manure. A mulch of compost or other organic matter will help retain soil moisture and suppress weeds.

Perennial plantings will need to be replaced every 3 or 4 years, either by sowing new seeds or by digging the plants in spring and replanting younger divisions from the outside of the clumps. Since sorrels are dioecious, meaning they bear male and female flowers on separate plants, it's possible to propagate only male plants by division and develop a planting that will not set seed. Once sorrel is established in your garden, it is undemanding and rarely bothered by pests and diseases.

HARVESTING

Begin harvesting leaves, which contain generous amounts of vitamin C as well as other minerals, 10 weeks after sowing seeds, by picking them individually as soon as they are large enough to be used. Sorrel can be harvested over a long season, provided the flower stalks are removed as they emerge to encourage new leaves to continue forming. Another option is to cut the plants down entirely and let them regrow.

All sorrel cultivars will cross-pollinate with each other. Since plants are easily divided, vegetative propagation is recommended.

please their Masters stomacks," according to John Parkinson. Colonial American gardens also included sorrel—Thomas Jefferson recorded a crop failure in 1809—in their kitchen gardens, mostly choosing to eat rather than prescribe this tart green.

Garden sorrel, also called sour dock, has a more acidic taste than milder, lemony French sorrel, which should be your first choice. Both produce a rosette of leaves and red-brown flowers, but common sorrel is a larger, more erect plant than French, reaching 2 feet or more with 5-inch-long leaves. True French sorrel is low-growing—under 1 foot—with glaucous or gray-green leaves. 'De Belleville', which produces large, broad 10- or 12- inch-long leaves that have a lemon tang, and 'Blonde de Lyon', which also has thick broad leaves and does well in warm regions, are the usual cultivars found in seed catalogs. The leaves of both species are used raw, but sparingly, in salads and also can be cooked like spinach or added to sauces for a lemony flavor, as herbs are. Sorrel is a common ingredient in mesclun.

SOUTHERN PEA

Vigna unguiculata subsp. *unguiculata*. Pea family,
Fabaceae. Annual

○ ✳

Southern peas are more beanlike than pealike, a heat-loving crop native to India and Africa. One of the foods that were introduced to North America through the slave trade, southern peas were right at home in hot climates of the southern colonies. They have remained largely a regional crop despite having a distinctive, hearty flavor. Like other beans, they can be used at any stage—snap, shell, or dried—and they don't have to be cooked with slabs of fat pork and swim in grease. Even if you don't grow southern peas, eat them on New Year's Day to guarantee yourself a year of good fortune.

Southern peas are also known as field peas and cowpeas—they are fed to livestock and used as a green manure. Many seeds have a distinctive black eye that marks the hilum, or seed scar, and gives rise to the name blackeyed pea, the best-known southern pea (others have maroon, purple, pink, red, or brown eyes). The three other types of southern peas are crowder, which have the most robust flavor (the term crowder comes from the seeds being "crowded"

Southern pea

in the pod); cream, or conch, peas, which have the mildest flavor; and purple-hull peas, named for the color of their pods. Depending on the cultivar, plants can be upright, sprawling, or even vining. None are especially attractive, although climbing types can be used to cover fences or trellises, and bush cultivars can be grown in containers. Use a large container with good bottom drainage. Fill with enriched potting soil, water frequently, and feed every 3 weeks with compost tea.

Gardeners in USDA Zones 5 and warmer can grow southern peas without difficulty. Those living in slightly colder regions may also cultivate this crop, although they may not be able to produce dried beans, but should choose cultivars that will germinate in cooler temperatures and mature more quickly. Gardeners in the South should look for cultivars that are disease resistant, such as 'Mississippi Purple' and 'Colossus'. Most cultivars need a minimum of 75 warm days to produce edible pods; 100 plants should be enough for a family of four, but increase the number if you want to preserve.

HOW TO GROW

Southern peas, which want full sun, will grow in nearly any well-drained soil. Moderately acid (pH 5.8 to 6.5) ground that has been amended with organic matter is ideal, but don't overdo it: High fertility results in large plants but few pods. Like other members of the pea family, southern peas have the ability to capture nitrogen from the air, so add organic matter and/or fertilizer that contains phosphorus and potassium, rather than materials that are high in nitrogen. In order for the plants to "fix" nitrogen, certain *Rhizobia* bacteria must be present in the soil. Many gardeners coat bean seeds with an inoculant to make sure the bacteria are present, but that's unnecessary unless you're planting in an area that that's never been cultivated before.

Sow seeds direct, 1 inch deep, spaced at 4 inches, 2 weeks after the last expected frost, when the soil has reached a temperature of at least 65°F. Southern peas are heat-tolerant, so continue to sow crops every 2 or 3 weeks. Germination takes about 2 weeks in 65°F soil. Thin bush cultivars to 6 to 8 inches apart, sprawling types to 18 inches. Provide vining cultivars with a strong support, installing it at the same time you sow seeds in order to avoid disturbing plant roots.

If conditions in your garden are marginal for

this hot-weather crop, start seeds indoors, sowing them in individual containers, two seeds per container (thin to one when plants are 2 inches tall). Pregerminating seeds indoors on damp paper toweling is another way for northern gardeners to get a head start.

Once plants are established, mulch to suppress weeds. Southern peas are remarkably tolerant of hot and dry conditions; watering is unnecessary unless there is an extreme drought. Additional fertilizer is rarely necessary either, although one or two feedings of compost tea will give plants a boost, especially if they are growing in thin soil.

The pea curculio, a beetle that eats into the immature pods, is the great enemy of Southern peas. It and many other insects, such as aphids, can be prevented from reaching plants by using floating row covers. If possible, avoid planting in soils known to harbor nematodes or fusarium wilt. (See "Controlling Common Diseases" on page 169 for more information). To help avoid potential difficul-

ties, rotate crops regularly, use floating row covers, purchase certified seeds, and plant disease- and insect-resistant cultivars.

HARVESTING

High in protein, Southern beans can be picked when they are immature and used as common snap beans are, picked when they are half- or green-mature for shell beans (harvest before the pods turn yellow), or allowed to mature fully and used as dried beans. Because their seeds are small, Southern peas dry more quickly than most beans. To store dried beans, shell and seal in an airtight container.

Southern peas do not cross with other beans or peas. Their flowers are perfect and normally self-pollinate before they open, although bees can cause crossing between cultivars. To be sure that you produce seeds that will come true, plant only one cultivar. Save seeds from the most vigorous and healthy plants; seeds are viable for 5 years if

SOUTHERN PEA CULTIVARS

All four types of southern peas can be harvested when immature, as snap beans are, just before the pods turn yellow as shell beans, or as dry beans.

'Brown Crowder': crowder type; 65 days; bushy plants bearing cream seeds with brown eyes.

'Calico Crowder': crowder type; 80 days; vining plants bearing buff seeds with maroon markings; cultivar for warm regions only; heirloom.

'California Blackeye No. 5': blackeye type; 75 days; tall, vigorous plants with heavy yields; good disease-resistance; standard blackeye cultivar.

'Colossus': crowder type; 85 days; sprawling plants with large brown seeds; excellent flavor.

'Knuckle Purple Hull': crowder type; 70 days; bushy, erect plants with large brown seeds.

'Magnolia': blackeye type; 70 days; bushy, erect plants; extremely high yields;

very good disease-resistance.

'Mississippi Purple': crowder type; 75 days; erect plants with large brown seeds; high yields; good disease-resistance.

'Mississippi Silver': crowder type; 85 days; bushy plants with tan seeds and high yields; good in hot, humid conditions.

'Pink Eye Purple Hull': purple-hull type; 70 days; sprawling plants bearing maroon-eyed seeds; two crops per season in warm regions; high yields.

'Queen Anne': blackeye type; 70 days; compact bushy plants with high yields; extremely dependable cultivar.

'Running Conch': cream type; 95 days; sprawling plants; hard to shell; heirloom.

'Zipper Cream': cream type; 75 days; bushy plants with large white seeds; pods are insect-resistant; easy to shell.

they are stored in airtight containers in a dark, cool location.

SOYBEAN

Glycine max. Pea family, Fabaceae. Annual.

○ ☀

Although the soybean isn't a common backyard vegetable, it unarguably is the most widely grown and protein-rich member of the pea family and one of the major crops of worldwide agriculture. Called "Great Treasure" in the Far East, where it has been cultivated for at least 3,000 years, the soybean did not reach North America until it was brought from China to Georgia by a merchant seaman Samuel Bowen in the mid-1770s. Benjamin Franklin was another early importer.

It took 100 years for soybeans to catch on in this country, but once American farmers discovered the crop's value, they adopted it in a big way: The U.S. now produces nearly 2.5 billion bushels a year, more than any other nation. Although soybeans are still used as fodder, the oil they contain is extracted before they reach the feedlots. More than three-fourths of the oil goes to the food industry; the remainder is used to make an astonishing array of nonedible products, including printing inks, caulking compounds, pesticides, cardboard, glues, paints, and more. (Interestingly, Henry Ford, who was one of the soybean's early champions, financed the development of soybean plastic, hoping it would allow America to "grow cars rather than mine them.")

The same horticultural qualities that make soybeans a good commercial crop—they're easy to grow, tolerant of poor soil and drought—also make them a good backyard crop. They can be cultivated anywhere common snap beans can—USDA Zone 3 and warmer—although there may not be enough time in short-season areas to produce dried beans. Plants range between 12 and 24 inches tall; most cultivars are bushy and upright, but a few are sprawlers. Yields are heavy, so 60 plants should be enough to supply a family of four; if you want to preserve, increase the planting.

DECIDING WHAT TO GROW

The USDA seed banks contain more than 10,000 soybean cultivars, everything from seeds the size of BBs to seeds the size of large kidney beans. Colors range from black through gray, along with brown, green, and yellow to white—many with contrasting stripes, spots, or streaks. The most common field cultivar is yellow and has a black eye, or hilum (a scar from where the seed was attached to the pod). Whatever the color of the seeds, soybeans pods are pretty much the same: Produced in clusters of three to five, they are green and furry, each containing from 2 to 4 seeds.

Seed catalogs typically use the word "edible" in listing soybean cultivars, but it is a misleading term since all soybeans are edible. While the so-called edible kinds tend to mature more quickly and have larger seeds, differences in flavor between them and field cultivars are difficult to detect. In the Far East, green-seeded types are considered the most tender and best flavored; black-seeded beans are the first choice for drying; yellow-seeded cultivars are used primarily to make soy (or soya) milk, curd, and flour.

The trick to soybean success is to choose a cultivar that is suited to your growing season. Soybeans are sensitive to day length (see the discussion of photoperiodism under "Weather & Daylength Considerations" on page 99), but breeders have

Soybean 'Butterbeans'

made life easy by developing both short-day and long-day cultivars. The minimum number of days to produce green shell beans is about 75; dried beans, 100 or more. While soybeans are high-yielding enough to make them good container plants, they are not exceptionally attractive and are rarely grown in pots or the ornamental garden. They do make a fine green-manure crop, however.

SOYBEAN CULTIVARS

The following list, which includes black-, green-, and yellow-seeded types, features just a sampling of the 10,000 soybean cultivars available.

'Black Jet': 105 days; field type; 2-foot plants with thin-skinned black seeds; good dried cultivar; widely adapted.

'Butterbeans': 90 days; edible type; bushy, 2-foot plants with green seeds; superb flavor.

'Envy': 75 days; edible type; upright, 2-foot upright plants with green seeds; extremely heavy yields; short-season cultivar good for northern areas.

'Fiskeby V': 70 days; edible type; small yellow seeds; exceptionally hardy and early maturing; easier to digest than many yellow cultivars.

'Hakucho Early': 75 days; edible type; dwarf, 14-inch plants with yellow-green seeds; reliable; short-season cultivar; not day length-sensitive.

'Maple Amber': 110 days; field type; 30-inch plants with yellow seeds; developed in Canada.

'Panther': 120 days; field type; black seeds; also listed as 'Kuromame'; best cultivar for dried seeds.

'Prize': 85 days; edible type; erect plants with green seeds; widely adapted; good cultivar for sprouting.

HOW TO GROW

Somewhat more cold-tolerant than many beans—although not frost-tolerant—soybeans need a sunny location and light, well-drained soil that is only moderately rich in organic matter and has a pH between 6.5 and 7.0. Like other members of the pea family, soybeans have the ability to capture nitrogen from the air. In order for the plants to "fix" nitrogen, certain *Rhizobia* bacteria must be in the soil. Many gardeners coat soybean seeds with an inoculant to make sure the bacteria are present. If you do use an inoculant, be sure it is specific for soybeans.

Sow soybeans 1 inch deep, spaced 4 inches apart (6 inches for sprawling cultivars), about 1 week after the danger of frost has passed and the soil has reached a temperature of at least 60°F. Germination can be slow—2 weeks or longer in 65°F soil. If your growing season is short, begin soybeans indoors in individual containers; move transplants outdoors after hardening off, about 2 weeks after the last expected frost. Soaking seeds overnight or pregerminating seeds on damp paper toweling are other ways for northern gardeners to get a head start. Inoculating seeds can also speed growth, as well as increase yields.

Once plants are established, mulch to suppress weeds and retain moisture. Soybeans are reasonably tolerant of hot and dry conditions, making watering unnecessary unless there is an extreme drought (water is most critical when plants are flowering). Additional fertilizer is necessary only if plants fail to thrive.

Soybeans grown in home gardens are rarely troubled by diseases or insects; rotating their position in the garden each year will help avoid potential problems, as will covering young plants with floating row covers. Also, avoid working among plants when they are wet. (Some home growers use soybeans as a target crop for rabbits, chipmunks, and other wildlife and plant one or two rows on each side of their garden.)

HARVESTING

Soybeans are a first-rate package of nutrients, one filled with protein, fiber, and an assortment of chemicals that help reduce cholesterol and may offset some cancers. They can be eaten at either the shell (half-mature) or dry stage, or as sprouts.

For shell beans, pick when the pods are plump but still green and soft. Fresh soybeans lose their flavor quickly, so use them immediately after picking (to make hulling easier, steam or boil the pods for 5 to 10 minutes). Most pods ripen at the same rate, so you may want to pull the entire plant. For dry soybeans, harvest entire plants once their foliage has yellowed, and hang them upside down in a warm, airy place. (Soybean pods shatter easily, so don't wait too long to pull plants.) Once the pods are entirely dry, shell and store seeds in airtight containers in a cool location.

Soybeans are another example of a plant with perfect flowers that fertilize themselves before they open. As a result, cross-pollination between cultivars in unlikely. Save seeds from the most vigorous and healthy plants; seeds are viable for 3 years if stored in airtight containers in a dark, cool location.

SPECIAL NOTES

Soybeans contain trypsin inhibitors, chemicals that indirectly prevent the digestion of proteins, and should not be eaten raw. If you sprout soybeans—which are delicious—boil the sprouted beans for at least 5 minutes before eating.

SPEARMINT. See *Mint*

SPINACH

Brassica perviridis. Mustard family, Brassicaceae.
Annual.

○ ◑ ❋ ❀ ▼

Spinach-lover Popeye had the right to boast that he was "strong to the finish"—sort of. That's because spinach, rich in oxalic acid, which reduces the body's ability to absorb the iron and calcium it contains, doesn't have much to make you strong. But spinach is loaded with nutrition, second on the *Nutrition Action Healthletter* list of most beneficial vegetables. Nutrition drops, however, when it is boiled "to a Pult," as John Evelyn recommended in 1699. No wonder that most 17th- and 18th-century gardeners repeatedly wrote that "spinedge" was "almost without taste" and "yeeldeth little or no nourishment at all." As the American humorist George Ade put it, "One man's poison ivy is another man's spinach."

Despite the poor press, spinach was an early traveler to New England, arriving at the start of the

Spinach 'Sigmaleaf'

17th century. It didn't attract much attention among horticulturists, although Peter Henderson, who described himself as "Gardener, Author, Merchant," wrote in 1884 that spinach, "which certainly requires no more labor in raising than a crop of Potatoes, continues to give a profit of at least three times as much per acre." The D. Landreth Seed Company, the oldest continuing seed house in the U.S., was responsible for 'Bloomsdale' spinach, a progenitor of 'Bloomsdale Long Standing', today's most widely grown cultivar. (Landreth's, which opened its doors in 1784, also can boast of former customers named George Washington, Thomas Jefferson, and James Monroe.)

DECIDING WHAT TO GROW

When deciding on which spinach to grow, first think about your location. If mosaic virus and/or downy mildew are problems, look for disease-resistant cultivars, such as 'Melody'. Remember, too, that spinach is one of the light- and heat-sensitive crops. (See the discussion of photoperiodism under

"Weather & Day-Length Considerations" on page 99.) Long days—defined as days that have more than 12 or 13 hours of sunlight—will cause plants to bolt, and spinach that has been exposed to extremely high or low temperatures will bolt even sooner. In hot regions, gardeners should pick an early-maturing cultivar, such as 'Tyee', that is resistant to heat and bolting. The choices for gardeners blessed with cool summers are nearly unlimited.

The other spinach decision is whether to plant smooth or savoyed. Smooth-leaved cultivars, most of which come to American gardeners from Asia, have thin, tender, sweetly flavored leaves. Savoy-leaved spinaches, which have broader, thicker, crinkled leaves, hold up better when cooked. These cultivars, because of the texture of their foliage, are more difficult to clean. Clearly they were the types grown by the ancients, who ordered that each leaf should be washed 12 times before it was cooked: Eleven times in water, once in human tears.

Spinach, which will survive light frosts, can be grown in all USDA Zones; it can be cultivated as a winter crop in regions where temperatures rarely fall below 25°F. Sixty plants, successively cropped, should be plenty for a family of four; if you want to preserve, increasing the planting.

SITE & SOIL

Because it matures quickly and revels in the cool parts of the growing season, spinach is a good crop for succession planting. Early sowings can be followed by tomatoes, beans, and other heat-loving vegetables and herbs; late plantings for a fall harvest can follow crops that are harvested in midsummer. To extend the harvest, plant a succession of spinaches, beginning with cold-tolerant cultivars

SPINACH CULTIVARS

The following list, which includes both smooth- and savoy-leaved cultivars, also includes heat-tolerant types for southern gardeners along with disease-resistant selections.

'**America**': savoy-leaved; 45 days; open-pollinated; mild flavor; heat-resistant; AAS winner.

'**Bloomsdale Long Standing**': savoy-leaved; 45 days; open-pollinated; heat-tolerant; vigorous, upright plants; highly popular home and commercial cultivar; heirloom.

'**Correnta**': smooth-leaved; 48 days; hybrid; extremely bolt-resistant; mild flavor.

'**Denali**': smooth-leaved; 38 days; hybrid; upright plants; good disease resistance; widely adapted.

'**Hybrid 612**': savoy-leaved; 45 days; hybrid; high yields; good fall cultivar; widely adapted, good disease resistance.

'**King of Denmark**': semi-smooth-leaved; 50 days; open-pollinated; very hardy; bolt-resistant; heirloom.

'**Melody**': savoy-leaved; 40 days; hybrid; bolt-resistant; disease-resistant; widely adapted; AAS winner.

'**Norfolk**': savoy-leaved; 50 days; open-pollinated; extremely cold-tolerant; spring or fall cultivar; heirloom from Canada.

'**Popeye**': smooth-leaved; 40 days; hybrid; tall, upright growth.

'**Skookum**': semi-savoy-leaved; 42 days; hybrid; vigorous plants; excellent disease resistance.

'**Sohshu**': smooth-leaved; 40 days; open-pollinated; tall, upright growth; heat-tolerant; good spring cultivar.

'**Space**': smooth-leaved; 42 days; hybrid; bolt-resistant; spring or fall cultivar; high yields.

'**Tyee**': savoy-leaved; 50 days; hybrid; upright growth; cold-hardy; extremely bolt- and heat-resistant; disease-resistant.

'**Virginia Savoy**': savoy-leaved; 40 days; open-pollinated; cold-tolerant; good fall cultivar for warm regions; disease-resistant.

'**Winter Bloomsdale**': savoy-leaved; 45 days; open-pollinated; cold-tolerant; good fall cultivar; disease-resistant.

like 'Tyee', followed by 'Indian Summer' or 'Sohshu', which are heat-resistant.

Spinach does well in full sun in cool conditions or in partial sun in warm regions. Southern gardeners may want to locate spinach next to taller crops that will provide afternoon shade. For the best yields, soil should be fertile, rich in organic matter, and have a near-neutral pH (6.5 to 7.5). Liming in autumn will sweeten acidic soils, as will applying wood ashes in spring. Poor germination and yellow or brown leaf margins and tips are signs that the soil is too acid. A fall cover crop or application of manure will improve the soil's structure and increase its nitrogen content—nitrogen is essential to producing large, healthy leaves.

Spinach, although it is normally harvested after fewer than 50 days, is a pretty addition to flower gardens, its dark green savoyed leaves a welcome sight in early spring. It also can be grown in pots and window boxes, perhaps as part of a container salad garden. Use a container, at least 10 inches wide and 8 inches deep, with good bottom drainage, and fill with enriched potting soil. Keep the soil evenly moist—a total of about 1 inch of water every 10 days—and feed plants every 10 days with manure tea.

HOW TO GROW

Soak spinach seeds in water or compost tea for several hours before sowing either directly in the garden, 4 to 6 weeks before the average frost-free date, or indoors in celled flats (spinach resents transplanting, so handle seedlings carefully). Spinach germinates well in cold—about 10 days in 50°F soil—so unless your garden is extremely wet in spring, starting seeds indoors is of little advantage.

Sow seeds ½ inch deep, 2 inches apart, in wide rows (for a nonstop harvest, sow every 2 weeks for up to 45 days before daytime temperatures average 75°F). When seedlings are 4 inches tall, thin to 6 inches, saving the discards for salads. If you plan to harvest the entire plant, you can set plants more closely. Research indicates that crowded plants are more likely to bolt, however, so don't try to scrimp on space. Cover the planting area with floating row covers to prevent insects from reaching the leaves; once plants are well established, mulch with compost to help the soil stay damp, cool, and weed-free. To keep plants growing quickly, make sure the soil remains moist, and water with manure tea or fish emulsion every 10 days until plants are 6 inches tall.

The productivity of fall crops, which will have a longer harvest period because of cooling temperatures and shorter days, can be prolonged even further in the North by mulching plants with straw or by growing in a cold frame.

POTENTIAL PROBLEMS

Spinach is a relatively trouble-free green. Planting disease-resistant cultivars, rotating crops, and making sure plants mature when the temperatures are cool are three ways to avoid problems with the most common spinach diseases—blight, downy mildew, and fusarium wilt. (For specific information and remedies, see "Controlling Common Diseases" on page 169.)

Floating row covers will prevent most insects from reaching spinach leaves, including aphids, flea beetles, leafhoppers, and leaf miners, the most common spinach pest. Unless the mercury climbs above 70°F or you want to produce seeds, the row covers can remain on the plants until they are ready to be harvested. (For more information about specific pests, see "Controlling Common Pests" on page 162.)

HARVESTING

Spring spinach, which is more likely to bolt, is usually harvested by cutting the entire plant. Plants that begin to bolt also should be cut entirely. Fall crops are typically harvested selectively by home gardeners. To harvest selectively, cut individual leaves from the outside of the plant as soon as they are large enough to be used. The inner leaves will continue to grow. Pick spinach in the morning, or plunge leaves into cold water immediately after harvesting to cool them. Drain completely before storing. Store spinach for up to 1 week by sealing it in plastic bags and refrigerating.

Because spinach is dioecious and wind-pollinated, gardeners who want to save seeds should attempt to grow two female plants to every one male plant. Unfortunately, the sex of plants is difficult to determine until the seed stalks appear, but most seed packets contain a good mix. All spinaches will cross; to produce seeds that will breed true, plant only one cultivar. Seeds are viable for 2 years; store in airtight containers in a dark, cool location.

SPINACH BEET. See Swiss *Chard*
SPINACH, MOUNTAIN. See *Orach*
SPINACH, PERPETUAL. See *Swiss Chard*

SPROUTS

Various species

Sprouting seeds is a time-honored practice in the Far East but relatively new to Americans. Backyard gardeners busy growing vegetables and herbs outdoors in summer tend to think of sprouts as a winter crop only, something to do when the ground is frozen and the price of iceberg lettuce soars to $1.95 a head. Landless gardeners are wiser. They cultivate sprouts throughout the year, winter or summer. In 3 days and in less than a square foot of counter space, they grow the stuff of salads, sandwiches, stir-fries, and snacks. No sun or soil required.

DECIDING WHAT TO GROW

Producing sprouts, which is nothing more than germinating seeds, is simple; the most difficult part of this form of farming is deciding which "crops" to grow. Mung beans and alfalfa are usual suspects, the sprouts most often found in supermarkets, but many other possibilities exist, everything from cabbage, clover, and cress to parsley, peanuts, and pumpkin. All vegetable and herb seeds "sprout," of course, but some, such as corn, have seeds that are too hard to be used unless cooked.

Once you get started, you may want to mix and match, combining different kinds of seeds rather than sprouting just one. You can buy sprouting mixes or create your own. Just remember that mingled seeds need to germinate at the same time. Alfalfa and peas are a good combination, as are mung beans and radishes.

All sorts of special sprouters are available (multi-compartment multi-level plastic devices, bamboo baskets, linen bags, and more), but all you need to sprout seeds is a wide-mouthed clear-glass jar, a piece of cheesecloth, and a rubber band. If that's too complicated, you can forgo the cheesecloth and rubber band and leave the jar open.

HOW TO GROW

If you're a first-time sprout gardener, don't invest in any special equipment. Even when you use an old

---

SEEDS FOR SPROUTING

Sprout seeds separately to assess flavor, then try combining seeds you like to custom-blend your own mixes. Remember to mix only seeds with similar sprouting times.

Adzuki/aduki (*Vigna angularis*): 3 to 5 days; mild flavor; cousin of the mung bean.

Alfalfa (*Medicago sativa*): 5 to 7 days; mild flavor; rots easily in warm conditions; wait for leaf before harvesting.

Cabbage (*Brassica oleracea*, Capitata group): 3 to 5 days; remove hulls.

Chives (*Allium schoenoprasum*, *A. tuberosum*): 10 to 14 days; onionlike flavor.

Clover (*Trifolium pratense*, *T. incarnatum*): 4 to 6 days; wait for leaf before harvesting; flavor has a slight bite; pretty leaf.

Fennel (*Foeniculum vulgare*): 12 to 14 days; zesty anise flavor.

Fenugreek (*Trigonella foenum-graecum*): 6 to 8 days; wait for leaf before harvesting; bitter flavor; tall; likes cool temperatures.

Garbanzo (*Cicer arietinum*): 2 to 4 days; steam if eating in quantity.

Kale (*Brassica oleracea*, Acephala group): 5 to 6 days; wait for leaf before harvesting.

Lentil (*Lens culinaris*): 3 to 5 days; steam if eating in quanity.

Mung beans (*Vigna radiata*): 3 to 5 days; mild flavor; no need to remove hulls.

Mustard (*Brassica nigra*): 3 to 5 days; peppery flavor; use black, not yellow, mustard; wait for leaf before harvesting.

Peas (*Pisum sativum*): 5 to 7 days; mild flavor; avoid seeds that have been treated.

Radish (*Raphanus sativus*): 3 to 5 days; peppery flavor; wait for leaf before harvesting.

Sunflower (*Helianthus annuus*): 6 to 10 days; mild flavor; tall; use black, or oil, types; keep well drained to avoid mold; wait for leaf before harvesting.

Turnip (*Brassica rapa*, Rapa group): 3 to 5 days; wait for leaf before harvesting.

canning or mayonnaise jar, sprouting is pretty much no-fail as long as you follow the steps below:

1. Wash the jar, and rinse with boiling water.

2. Fill the jar with water, and soak seeds for 6 hours.

3. Pour off the water, and rinse and drain the seeds, removing any chaff.

4. Either cover the jar opening with cheesecloth and secure it with a rubber band, or leave it open.

5. Turn the jar on its side, making sure the seeds are spread evenly in a single layer (don't overcrowd: 1 tablespoon of mung beans will produce enough sprouts to fill a quart jar).

6. Place the jar in a cool spot, about 70°F, where there is good air circulation and indirect light (sprouts, such as cress, that develop shoots and leaves rather than just a root, need slightly more light in order to turn green; if you want blanched sprouts, set the jar in a dark location).

7. Rinse and drain seeds twice a day—keep them damp but not waterlogged.

HARVESTING

Once you can see more sprouts than seeds—the time varies from 3 or 4 days for mustard to 12 or 13 days for chives—it's time to harvest your crop. (With some crops, such as clover, mustard, and radish, wait for the leaf to appear before "harvesting.") While the hulls of many sprouts are so inconsequential that there's no reason to spend time picking them out, you'll want to remove the hulls of large seeds, such as sunflower, before eating. The hulls are unpalatable and tend to develop mold. Since most hulls float in water, you can get a head start by removing them each time you rinse the seeds/sprouts.

Dehulled sprouts store better than those with hulls do, but even in an airtight container, most sprouts keep less than a week in the refrigerator (the rule of thumb is storage time equals sprouting time). Sprouts aren't nutritional giants, but many are a respectable source of vitamins B and C, calcium, iron, and protein.

Seeds for sprouting should be kept in an airtight container and stored in a cool, dark place for up to 3 months, or in the refrigerator or freezer for up to 8 months.

SPECIAL NOTES

Purchase only seeds that are designated for sprouting. Many seeds intended for garden planting have been treated with chemicals.

SQUASH

Cucurbita spp. Gourd family, Cucurbitaceae.
Annual.

All the early explorers to North America—Columbus, de Soto, Coronado, Cartier, Champlain—noticed and described native squash, although they sometimes mislabeled them as melons or gourds. Squash was one of the staples of Native American gardens, interplanted with beans and corn in a symbiotic trinity, one of the "three sisters of life." The combination was mutually beneficial: The beans provided nitrogen for the corn, the

Zucchini 'Embassy'

*Yellow summer squash
'Early Summer Crookneck'*

Zucchini 'Ronde de Nice'

Squash 'Golden Scallop'

Squash 'Bush Spaghetti'

*Winter squash 'Red Chestnut',
'Large Yellow Paris', and 'Hubbard'*

Squash 'Winter Cushaw'

corn provided supports for the beans, and the spiny squash vines provided protection for everyone.

European colonists quickly came to see squash as part of God's bounty to their new land, one of "New-England's Rarities Discovered," to borrow the title of John Josselyn's 1672 book. There were all

kinds of squash, Josselyn noted, "some of these are green, some yellow, some longish like a Gourd, others round like an Apple, all of them pleasant food boyled and buttered, seasoned with Spice."

Squash were viewed less enthusiastically in Europe, where they were served in the barn as often as in the dining room. Even by the middle of the 19th century, Europeans were growing far fewer squash—which they often listed as pumpkins—than were Americans, who were already familiar with acorns, crooknecks, cashews, marrows, hubbards, Turk's caps, pattypans, sweet potato squash, and more. The prolific zucchini became popular only in the 20th century, after being reintroduced from Italy. It is, according to horticultural humorists Henry Beard and Roy McKie, "the only garden vegetable with its own ZIP code."

Although frost-tender, squash can be grown in almost all ZIP codes, USDA Zone 3 and warmer; winter squash, which jog rather than sprint to maturity, may require special growing techniques in regions with cool or abbreviated garden seasons.

DECIDING WHAT TO GROW

Squash are another of those superfriendly genera whose members border on the promiscuous. Most squash are members of one of four species— *Cucurbita argyrosperma, C. maxima, C. moschata,*

SQUASH ESSENTIALS

- Full sun and warm, fertile, well-drained soil.
- Use black-plastic mulch to maximize yields.
- Don't plant until soil and air have warmed up in spring.
- Feed with compost tea every 2 to 3 weeks.
- Protect plants with row covers, but remove them when flowers appear.
- Provide 1 inch of water weekly.

and C. *pepo*—but even "authoritative sources" disagree on who belongs where, and interspecific crosses are common. Fortunately, taxonomic ignorance is bliss for home gardeners, who need only know that there are summer squash and winter squash—and that within those mansions, there are many rooms (see "Squash Scorecard," below).

Mild-flavored summer squash, which are picked when they are still immature and their skins are tender, mature in about 50 days. They cannot be stored for long periods of time. Most summer squash plants are bushy rather than vining, and they are astonishingly productive. Six plants, a mix of types planted successively, should be more than enough for a fam-

ily of four; if you want to preserve, increase the planting.

Winter squash are left on the vine until they are fully ripe, 85 days and more. (Many winter squash—the acorn 'Cream of the Crop' is a good example—can be harvested when immature and eaten as a "summer squash.") Although breeders are creating more and more bush cultivars—'Bush Table Queen' is one—most winter squash grow on sizable vines and require plenty of room in the garden. The variety among winter types—shapes, sizes, colors, flavors—is mind-boggling, but all are grown in the same way, and most can be stored for several months. Four plants will provide enough squash for

---

SQUASH SCORECARD

It pays to know the players when you are trying to decide from among the many summer and winter squash cultivars offered. Here's a rundown of types you'll encounter.

Summer Squash

Cousa, or Mid-East. Blocky, tapered fruits, most with pale green skin.

Scalloped, or Pattypan. Disk-shaped fruits with scalloped edges; skin colors from bright yellow through gray-green to cream.

Yellow Summer. Cylindrical yellow fruits, either smooth and straightneck or warty crookneck.

Zucchini. Club-shaped fruits with various skin colors, from dark green through yellow to near-white.

Winter Squash

Acorn. Ribbed, acorn-shaped 2- to 4-pound fruits, most with yellow flesh and black-green skin.

Buttercup. Rounded or blocky 2- to 5-pound fruits, most with green skin and orange flesh; many cultivars have a "button" on the blossom end.

Butternut. Mostly cylindrical 2- to 8-pound fruits with a bulbed end, most with tan skin and orange flesh.

Delicata. Slightly ribbed, elongated or rounded 2- to 3-pound fruits with green-striped or flecked yellow skin and pale yellow-orange flesh; edible skin; does not need curing before storage; also called sweet dumpling or sweet potato squash.

Hubbard. Round to oval, variably ribbed, bumpy 8- to 16-pound fruits with a neck at the stem end, most with orange flesh and gray-green skin.

Kabocha. Flattened-round 2- to 6-pound fruits, most with green or orange skins and orange flesh; some cultivars have "buttons" at the blossom end.

Spaghetti. Oblong, football-like 2- to 6-pound fruits, most with buff-colored skin and yellow-orange flesh that magically separates into spaghettilike strands when cooked.

Others. These include pear-shaped cushaws ('Green Striped Cushaw', 'Golden Cushaw'); flattened cheeses ('White Cheese', 'Long Island Cheese'); round cubans ('La Primera Calabaza'); vividly striped Turk's turbans ('Turk's Turban'); globular vegetable marrows ('Boston Marrow'); huge bananas ('Pink Banana Jumbo'); and many more regional types. There is hardly a color or shape that has not found a home in the squash family.

a family of four (if you're growing giants like 'Blue Hubbard', reduce the number); if you want to preserve, increase the planting.

SITE & SOIL

Both summer and winter squash need full sun and moderately fertile soil that is rich in organic matter and has a pH between 5.8 and 6.8. Incorporate compost, well-rotted manure or other organic matter into the planting area in spring before sowing seeds or setting out transplants. Winter squash are heavier feeders than summer types are, so make sure that the soil where they will grow is especially rich.

Squash, like cucumbers and other gourd-family members, prefer warm soil that drains well, so many gardeners plant this crop in hills, hilled rows, or raised beds. Set summer squash in hills spaced 3 to 4 feet apart, two plants per hill; for winter types, grow two plants per hill, and separate the hills by at least 5 feet. Be sure to give squash plenty of room.

SQUASH CULTIVARS

The list below provides a cross section of both summer and winter squash cultivars to try. In addition to bush- and vine-type plants, there are also semi-bush and semi-vining plants. These latter two terms indicate plants that fall between compact bush types and sprawling vines. The term semi-bush is used for large bush types that produce some vining growth; semi-vining plants are even larger, but not as large as full-fledged vines.

Summer Squash

'Benning's Green Tint': scallop; 55 days; open-pollinated; medium bush; fruits have pale green skin, pale green flesh; home-garden favorite; heirloom.

'Burpee Hybrid': zucchini; 50 days; hybrid; bush; fruits have medium green skin, white flesh; heavy yields.

'Costana Romanesco': zucchini; 55 days; open-pollinated; large bush; ribbed fruits have gray-green flecked skin, white flesh; Italian cultivar; moderate yields.

'Gold Rush': zucchini; 50 days; hybrid; bush; fruits have yellow skin, white flesh; AAS winner.

'Goldbar': yellow summer straightneck; 60 days; hybrid; bush; fruits have gold skin, cream-yellow flesh; long harvest season; high yields.

'Peter Pan': scallop; 50 days; hybrid; bush; fruits have light green skin, pale green flesh; productive; widely adapted; AAS winner.

'Pic-N-Pic': yellow summer crookneck; 50 days; hybrid; bush; fruits have yellow skin, cream flesh; high yields; early.

'Roly Poly': zucchini; 50 days; hybrid; semi-vining plant; fruits have pale green skin, white flesh; unusual round shape.

'Ronde de Nice': zucchini; 50 days; open-pollinated; large bush; spherical fruits have light green skin, white flesh; heirloom.

'Saffron': yellow summer straightneck; 50 days; hybrid; bush; fruits have yellow skin, cream flesh; high yields.

'Scallopini': scallop; 55 days; hybrid; semi-bush; fruits have dark green skin, pale green flesh; productive; AAS winner.

'Sunburst': scallop; 55 days; hybrid; semi-bush; fruits have yellow skin with a green pattern, white flesh; AAS winner.

'Sundance': yellow summer crookneck; 55 days; hybrid; bush; fruits have yellow skin, cream flesh; widely adapted; popular home-garden and commercial cultivar.

'Sweet Gourmet': cousa; 50 days; hybrid; bush; fruits have light green skin, cream flesh; disease-tolerant.

'Yellow Crookneck': yellow summer crookneck; 60 days; open-pollinated; large bush; fruits have bumpy yellow skin, cream flesh; good yields.

'Zahra': cousa; 48 days; hybrid; bush; fruits have pale green skin, cream flesh; very early.

Winter Squash

'Ambercup': kabocha; 100 days; open-polli-

Crowding encourages diseases, especially in humid regions. If your garden is small, you can allow vining cultivars to trail onto the lawn.

Vining squash that have small fruits, such as 'Sweet Dumpling', can be trellised, on either a vertical support or an A-frame. Choose a location where the vines won't shade other crops, and erect the support *before* you plant to avoid damaging plants' roots. Set plants on the windward side of the trellis, and help the vines attach themselves to the support, if necessary. You'll also have to provide support—mesh bags or cloth slings tied to the trellis are the usual methods—for each squash.

Both summer and winter squash can be grown in containers (vining types will need room to ramble). Use a large container, at least 10 gallons, for each plant, and fill with an enriched soil mix. Keep well watered, and feed every 2 weeks with manure tea. Vining squash aren't good choices for ornamental beds and borders, but they can be used as a

---

nated; vine; fruits have streaked orange skin, orange flesh.

'Blue Ballet': hubbard; 95 days; open-pollinated; vine; fruits have blue-green skin, orange flesh; sweeter and smaller (4 pounds) than most hubbards; stores well.

'Blue Hubbard': hubbard; 100 days; open-pollinated; vine; fruits have bumpy green skin, yellow flesh; traditional New England cultivar.

'Bush Table Queen': acorn; 85 days; open-pollinated; bush; deeply ribbed fruits have dark green skin, orange flesh; widely adapted.

'Butter Boy': butternut; 80 days; hybrid; vine; fruits have buff skin, red-orange flesh; heavy yields.

'Buttercup': buttercup; 105 days; open-pollinated; moderate vine; fruits have striped green skin, orange flesh; excellent flavor; standard cultivar.

'Chicago Warted Hubbard': hubbard; 105 days; open-pollinated; vine; fruits have dark green skin, orange-yellow flesh; stores well.

'Cream of the Crop': acorn; 85 days; hybrid; bush; fruits have unusual near-white skin, cream flesh; AAS winner; stores well.

'Delicata': delicata; 100 days; open-pollinated; vine; elongated fruits have flecked and striped cream skin, orange flesh.

'Early Butternut': butternut; 85 days; hybrid; semi-bush; fruits have orange skin, orange flesh; early; AAS winner.

'Hasta La Pasta': spaghetti; 75 days; open-pollinated; semi-bush; fruits have orange-yellow skin, orange flesh; high yields.

'Hokkori': kabocha; 95 days; hybrid; vine; fruits have green skin, orange flesh; extremely sweet.

'Jersey Golden Acorn': acorn; 65/85 days; open-pollinated; vine; fruits have yellow skin and flesh; dual-purpose cultivar that can be harvested as a summer or winter squash; AAS winner.

'Sweet Dumpling': delicata; 100 days; open-pollinated; medium vine; teacup-shaped fruits have ivory skin flecked and striped with green and orange flesh; rich flavor.

'Sweet Mama': buttercup; 100 days; hybrid; semi-bush; fruits have striped green skin, yellow flesh; some disease resistance; AAS winner.

'Table Ace': acorn; 80 days; hybrid; semi-bush; fruits have black-green skin, orange flesh; early; standard commercial cultivar.

'Table King': acorn; 80 days; open-pollinated; large bush; fruits have green skin, yellow-orange flesh; stores well; standard home garden cultivar; AAS winner.

'Tivoli': spaghetti; 100 days; hybrid; bush; fruits have pale yellow skin, yellow-orange flesh; AAS winner.

'Turk's Turban': Turk's turban; 110 days; open-pollinated; vine; orange-, red-, and green-striped skin, light orange flesh; edible but mostly used for ornament; heirloom.

'Vegetable Spaghetti': spaghetti; 100 days; open-pollinated; vine; fruits have ivory skin, yellow-orange flesh; heirloom.

'Waltham Butternut': butternut; 95 days; open-pollinated; vine; uniform fruits have tan skin, orange flesh; stores well; AAS winner.

Bush winter squash 'Emerald Buttercup'

groundcover on a sunny slope. Bush types, with their large ivylike leaves and showy yellow flowers, look as if they were made for the flower garden.

Summer squash, which mature quickly, can follow spring crops, such as radishes, spinach, leaf lettuce, or peas. Succession plantings will spread out the harvest and keep it manageable, as well as save space. To lengthen the harvest period of winter squash, grow types and cultivars that mature at different times, such as 'Table King' acorn, which is ready in about 80 days, and 'Green Hubbard', which matures in about 110 days.

HOW TO GROW

Squash are among the easiest crops to grow, which explains why baskets of zucchini and acorns with a FREE sign attached are a common feature of the American landscape during the garden season. Both summer and winter types require warm soil and air to prosper—soil temperatures between 75° and 85°F; air temperatures between 70° and 85°F during the day, 65° to 75°F at night—so don't rush to get this crop in the ground. Tests show that using black plastic mulch when growing squash can speed up maturity by as much as 2 weeks and increase yields.

Two or three weeks after the last expected frost, when the soil is at least 60°F, direct-sow seeds, 1 to 2 inches deep (before planting, soak seeds in compost tea for 15 minutes to help prevent diseases). Germination should occur in about 7 days in 65°F soil. Alternatively, begin squash indoors, 3 to 4 weeks before the transplant date. Indoors, sow seeds no more than 3 weeks before you will set the plants outdoors—two seeds per 3-inch pot, thinned to one plant when the first true leaves appear. After germination, move the seedlings to a bright, warm (75° to 85°F) location until it's time to transplant; harden off plants before setting them in the garden.

Cover the planting area with floating row covers to reduce insect problems and to protect young plants from cold temperatures and wind. Once plants are established, mulch with organic matter, such as straw, to retain moisture and suppress weeds. Don't forget to remove the row covers when the first flowers appear—squash depend on insects to pollinate their flowers—or if temperatures rise.

Squash are heavy feeders, especially winter types. Fertilize plants every 2 to 3 weeks with compost tea or seaweed extract. Don't use high-nitrogen fertilizers, which will encourage leaves at the expense of fruits, but if you're going to err, err on the generous side. Squash won't tolerate being put on a diet. And do make sure plants have plenty of water, 1 inch a week, especially when they are blooming and fruits are being set.

POTENTIAL PROBLEMS

Floating row covers should prevent aphids, cucum-

GOURDS

While many gourds are suitable only for making wren houses and ladles, a few can be eaten—they're prepared like summer squash—when the fruits are young and tender. Among the edibles are bitter gourds (*Momordica charantia*); bottle gourds (*Lagenaria siceraria*); fluted gourds (*Telfairia occidentalis*); luffa, or loofah, gourds (*Luffa acutangula, L. aegyptiaca*); snake gourds (*Trichosanthes cucumerina, T. cucumeroides*); and pointed gourds (*T. dioica*). While their culture is similar to that of squash, many gourds are finicky and require a long growing season (95+ days), very warm conditions, and trellising.

ber beetles, leaf hoppers and squash bugs from reaching your plants. If squash vine borers, which are particularly fond of summer squash, are a problem in your garden, mound soil around the base of each plant, covering the bottom 6 inches of stem to discourage adults from laying eggs. Traditional wisdom, albeit anecdotal, recommends interplanting radishes with squash. Don't harvest the radishes, which are reputed to repel squash pests of all sorts. (See "Controlling Common Pests" on page 162 for more information and for control measures.)

Similarly, crop rotation and good cultural practices—providing adequate nutrients, water, and space, choosing an appropriate location, and selecting proper cultivars—should prevent most diseases from infecting your plants. (For specific information about the diseases that may affect squash, including anthracnose, bacterial wilt, downy and powdery mildew, mosaic, and scab, see "Controlling Common Diseases" on page 169.)

HARVESTING

Although summer and winter squash are grown in much the same way, the similarity ends when it comes to harvesting. Use the guidelines that follow to bring in your harvest.

Summer Squash: Begin picking zucchini, cousa, and yellow squash as soon as the fruits are large enough to be used, when they are about 6 inches long. Their skin should be glossy, not dull, and be easily punctured by a thumbnail. Scalloped cultivars should be harvested before they turn cream-colored, when they are about 4 inches in diameter. Pick summer squash, which contain vitamin A and potassium, every 2 or 3 days to keep plants producing new fruits. Leaving a short piece of stem on fruits will extend their storage life. Summer squash can be sealed in plastic bags and refrigerated for about 7 days.

Winter Squash: Knowing when to harvest is about the most difficult part of growing winter squash. The standard advice is to look at the stem, which should have begun to shrivel, and to test the skin with your thumbnail—when it is so hard that it can't be scratched, the fruit is mature. An even better indicator may be color. Fruits that are full-colored, which can be anything from ivory through orange-red to green-black, are ready to be picked. Fortunately, most winter squash are unfazed by an extra week or two on the vine, but don't allow them

to stay in the garden if a hard frost is predicted (if your garden is hit by an unexpected freeze, you can still harvest fruits, but use them immediately). Be sure to leave a 2-inch piece of stem attached to squash that you want to store. Winter squash, which is higher in starch and calories than summer squash, contains moderate amounts of vitamin A and potassium and in addition is a fair source of vitamin C and calcium.

Winter squash that have been harvested with the stem attached and cured can be stored in a dry location (temperature 50° to 60°F). The exceptions are acorn, spaghetti, and delicata squash, which should not be cured and are stored at slightly cooler temperatures, about 45° to 50°F.

Cure winter squash by subjecting them to 85°F temperatures and high humidity for 10 days—if the weather is warm and sunny, cut them from the vine and leave them in the garden for 10 days. To reduce surface molds that may develop during storage, wipe fruits with a bleach/water (1:4) solution.

On both summer and winter squash, male and female flowers occur on the same plant and are pollinated by bees and other insects. Different species of squash are unlikely to cross, although crossing does occur, but cultivars of the same species cross easily. To produce seeds that will come true, separate cultivars of the same species by at least ½ mile, or plant only one cultivar. Seeds are viable for 6 years; store in airtight containers in a dark, cool location.

STEM LETTUCE. See *Celtuce*
STRAWBERRY TOMATO. See *Tomatillo*
SUMMER SAVORY. See *Savory*
SUMMER SQUASH. See *Squash*
SUNCHOKE. See *Jerusalem Artichoke*

SUNFLOWER

Helianthus annuus. Sunflower family, Asteraceae.
Annual.

○ ✳ ❀

Sow a packet of 'Mammoth Grey Stripe', and you'll understand why Henry David Thoreau was moved to write, "I have great faith in a seed. I am prepared to expect wonders." The wonders are patent with sunflowers, especially 12-footers like 'Mammoth Grey Stripe', although some garden writers have

Sunflower

criticized them as too big, gaudy, and crude. Not for Vincent van Gogh, of course, who began painting sunflowers in the 1880s. Not for Paul Gauguin, who painted van Gogh painting sunflowers. And not for merchandisers, who plaster sunflowers on everything from sheets to shirts, or for flower stylists, who make room for sunflowers in nearly every bouquet.

Status as contemporary chic might be heady stuff for some plants, but the sunflower is used to being in the spotlight. Native Americans singled it out centuries ago, placing high value on all its assets—culinary, medicinal, and ornamental. They ground the seeds into meal for making breads, puddings, and soups and extracted its oil to season food and make paint. Sunflower infusions were brewed to treat snakebites and chest pains; juice from the plant stems was applied to wounds.

No part of the sunflower went unused, and more than 60 North American species were available to exploit. Spanish, English, and French explorers sent them back to their homelands, where their size and colors dazzled: the sunflower, by one 16th-century

account, was "the most perticulars that ever hath been seen, for it is greater than a greate Platter of Dishe, the whiche hath divers coulers . . . it showeth marveilous faire in Gardens."

Think sunflower, and that image—a sky-high stalk carrying a 4-inch-wide disk with golden rays—comes to mind. No wonder it was called "Hearbe of the Sunne" at least a century before Linnaeus got around to designating the genus *Helianthus*, from the Greek *helios*, or "sun," and *anthos*, or "flower." Named cultivars are typically offspring of the common sunflower (*H. annuus*) or interspecific crosses, usually with the smaller beach sunflower (*H. debilis*). Nearly all the popular garden cultivars are annuals and thrive in USDA Zone 3 and warmer.

DECIDING WHAT TO GROW

There is a vast collection of annual sunflowers, which begin blooming from 50 to 95 days after sowing seeds. Most cultivars have their origins in Russia. An early breeding success, 'Mammoth Russian', was brought to North America in the 1870s, where it was planted without wide enthusiasm. (Kansans, however, felt differently and adopted the sunflower as their state flower in 1903. Some years later, in an effort to protect its soybean crop, next-door neighbor Iowa threatened to declare the sunflower a noxious weed. Kansas retaliated by threatening to declare Iowa's state bird, the eastern goldfinch, "bothersome and raucously noisy." Neither resolution was adopted, and the flower-and-feather feud faded.)

When planting sunflowers primarily for seeds, choose a "confectionery" type, such as 'Sundak', 'Mammoth Russian', 'Giant Grey Stripe', 'Jumbo', or 'Mammoth'. All have large, gray-and-white-striped seeds, and their colossal flower heads are so heavy—an average 'Mammoth' contains about 1,000 seeds—they hang down like a chastened dog's. In contrast, "oilseed" sunflowers have small black seeds, which are edible but are the devil to shell. Multiflowered cultivars, such as 'Italian White' and 'Lemon Queen', are excellent for cut flowers but yield far fewer seeds.

If skyscraper plants with huge seed heads are your pleasure—perfect for impressing neighbors and providing backdrops—look to the large, single-stem confectionery cultivars like 'Giant Grey Stripe'. But don't stop with the big, bold bright classics. Thanks mostly to the recent work of breeders in Japan and Europe, there are scores of other sunflower possibilities.

Semi-Dwarf. Bred for cut-flower growers, some semi-dwarf sunflowers are sterile, but most deliver a modest seed crop on scaled-down plants measuring between 4 and 8 feet tall. Good choices are 'Arrowhead', 'Sunrich Lemon', and 'Peredovik', all with full-size yellow-gold blooms with dark center disks.

Multi-Stem. Also called branched sunflowers, these bear many smaller flowers rather than a single large blossom. There are both tall ('Primrose Yellow', 'Henry Wilde') and semi-dwarf ('Sunrise', 'Valentine') cultivars, all bearing gold or yellow flowers. 'Vanilla Ice' is a fine ivory cultivar, similar to—and better than—the heirloom 'Italian White'.

Doubles. In double sunflowers, such as 'Sol d'Or', 'Teddy Bear', and 'Sun Gold', the ray flowers have disappeared, leaving a dandelion-like bloom made up solely of elongated disk flowers. They're great, unless you want a sunflower that looks like a sunflower.

Dwarf. Some of these sunflowers are no taller than 18 inches. 'Big Smile', 'Sunspot', and 'Zebulon' are the three good performers. Despite their diminutive height, each produces a single full-size bloom. Some gardeners think them distressingly disproportionate, but most 5-year-olds, able to look their flowers in the eye, feel quite differently. Also good is 'Music Box', a multi-stemmed 2-footer bred in Holland, which is covered with bicolored flowers of yellow, gold, and mahogany.

Colors. Today, there are more colors in the sunflower paint box—shades of yellow, orange, red, and purple—to consider as well. Don't go without the traditional golden orbs—'Peredovik', a commercial oilseed variety, and 'Sunbeam', supposedly the model for van Gogh, are superb—but the yellow tones of 'Sunrich Lemon' and 'Moonwalker' are also glorious. Bolder are 'Velvet Queen', 'Color Fashion Mixed', and 'Autumn Beauty', which add red, purple, and brown to the sunflower garden, the chrysanthemum colors of fall. Some cultivars, such as 'Inca Jewels' and 'Evening Sun', have two or three bands of contrasting hues. 'Sunset' has mahogany rays tipped with gold.

Sunflowers with whitish green foliage are also available. 'Silverleaf', a 6-foot, multi-stemmed cultivar with yellow rays and a chocolate disk, is a striking plant without its flowers. As the name suggests, its foliage is markedly different from the large green heart-shaped leaves of most sunflowers.

HOW TO GROW

Growing healthy sunflowers is uncomplicated, as the herbalist John Gerard observed 400 years ago:

A BOUQUET OF ONE

As members of the large sunflower family, Asteraceae, sunflowers are cousins of asters, chrysanthemums, marigolds, and other daisylike plants. Each sunflower is many flowers, a botanical *e pluribus unum*. The bloom's so-called petals are actually sterile ray flowers, designed to lure pollinating insects; the center eye is made up of hundreds of fertile disk flowers. When you pick a single sunflower, you pick a bouquet.

Left behind, when the disk flowers have faded, are the seeds, arranged in a mathematically precise conical pattern. It is, English herbalist John Gerard observed, "as though a cunning workeman had of purpose placed them in very good order, much like the honiecombes of Bees."

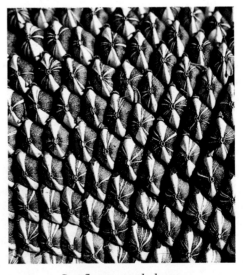

Sunflower seed cluster
'Mammoth Russian'

"These plants grow of themselves without setting or sowing." Sunflowers will tolerate less-than-ideal conditions, but to produce sturdy, healthy plants, you'll need full sun and moderately rich soil with a near-neutral pH (6.8 to 7.0). What sunflowers don't like is heavy, wet ground, although small plants need plenty of water.

Gardeners with extremely short seasons should grow short-season cultivars, such as members of the hybrid Sun series ('Sunbeam', 'Sunbright', 'Moonbright'), and can begin seeds indoors 3 weeks before the frost-free date. Use 4-inch pots, and keep the seedlings under artificial light so that they don't develop spindly stalks. Transplants tend to mature more quickly than direct-seeded plants do.

In other regions, start sunflowers outdoors after the danger of frost has past. Sow seeds 1 inch deep, 6 inches apart, in rows 18 to 24 inches apart. If the soil temperature is between 45° and 50°F, germination occurs in about a week. Rather than sowing all at once, plant a new row of sunflowers every 2 or 3 weeks. Sunflower blooms aren't long-lived, so successive crops will give you a continuous supply of bouquets and seeds.

Thin plants to 18 to 24 inches; the thinnings, although they wilt instantly, can be transplanted elsewhere. (All this is good advice if you want Goliath flowers or if a seed crop is the goal. But if you want smaller blooms, a better fit for vases, use the method of cut-flower growers: Reduce the spacing between plants to 6 inches).

Be sure to locate tall sunflowers on the north side of the garden so that they won't shade smaller plants. Run rows east and west to take advantage of the sun. William Blake and Percy Bysshe Shelley are among the poets who seized on the sunflower's affinity for the sun, how it turns "where he turns, and all his motions trace." In fact, sunflowers respond to light as all plants do, but once their ray flowers open, they cease to bend toward the sun, and most heads will face east.

Once established, sunflowers are relatively drought-tolerant, exactly what you'd expect of prairie natives. Mature plants need watering only in extremely hot, dry regions; however, mulching with straw or other organic matter helps retain moisture and discourage weeds. Unless they have been sown in extremely thin soil, sunflowers do not need to be fertilized, but 6-foot cultivars will need support. Looping three or four stalks together is one solution.

Insects may munch a few holes in the leaves, but serious problems with diseases or pests are rare. For container culture, choose a small cultivar, such as 'Big Smile', 'Sunset', or 'Sunspot'. All sunflowers look good in the ornamental garden or anywhere in the landscape.

HARVESTING

Sunflowers don't rush to ripen their seeds—it takes about 85 to 95 days for even quick-maturing cultivars to ripen. To prevent birds from beating you to the harvest, cover the maturing seed heads with netting or a paper bag. To harvest the seeds, cut the flower heads—leaving a 2-foot stalk attached—as soon as their backs begin to brown. Hang the heads in a dry, airy place until the seeds are completely dry. To bring the flowers indoors for arrangements, cut them in the morning, just as they begin to open, and remove all but two or three leaves.

Rubbing the dried seeds off the head is easy, but hulling takes more time. Don't use the hulls as mulch—like the husks of black walnuts, they are phytotoxic and will stunt the growth of other plants (this characteristic explains the bare spot under the bird feeder).

Sunflowers both self-sow and cross-pollinate. To produce seed that will breed true, plant only one cultivar. Seeds are viable for 6 years; store in airtight containers in a dark, cool location.

SWEET BASIL. See *Basil*
SWEET BAY. See *Bay*
SWEET CICELY. See *Chervil*
SWEET CORN. See *Corn*
SWEET FENNEL. See *Fennel*
SWEET MARJORAM. See *Marjoram*
SWEET PEPPER. See *Pepper*

SWEET POTATO

Ipomoea batatas. Bindweed family, Convolvulaceae.
Perennial grown as an annual.

○ ✳ ♣

The sweet potato is one of the chunks of botanical gold that European explorers discovered in the New World. This vining member of the bindweed family, a cousin of the morning glory, was found in parts of Peru and Ecuador and in Central America, thriving in the tropical heat of lowland regions. "Batata," the name some indigenous people used for the plant,

Heirloom sweet potatoes 'Miller', 'Gold Nugget', 'Bermuda Pink', 'Korean Purple', 'Continental Red', 'Southern', and 'Frazier White'

eventually influenced English explorers and horti-culturists, who applied the slightly mispronounced term "potato" to both *I. batatas* and to the Irish, or common, potato, *Solanum tuberosum*.

Each year around Thanksgiving time, the confusion about sweet potatoes and yams is renewed. Although the terms are often used interchangeably, sweet potatoes and yams actually are two quite different vegetables, members of two separate plant families and dissimilar in growth habit, appearance, and flavor. True yams (*Dioscorea* spp.) are of West African and Asian origin and are dry and starchy compared with the moist, sweet flavor of most sweet potatoes. And unlike Irish potatoes, which develop on swollen underground stems, or stolons, sweet potatoes are actually roots that thicken as the plant stores a rich supply of carbohydrates and sugars.

Once far more popular than they are today, sweet potatoes were cultivated by American colonists at least by 1648. George Washington grew them at Mount Vernon, Thomas Jefferson at Monticello. Jefferson, while serving as the American Ambassador to France, wrote to a friend in Virginia in 1787, asking for "seeds of the common sweet potato (I mean the real seeds and not the root which cannot be brought here without rotting) . . ." to plant in his Paris garden. How Jefferson's crop fared is unrecorded, but he may have been disappointed. A century later, Vilmorin-Andrieux noted that, "As the Sweet Potato requires a rather long time to complete its growth, it is difficult to cultivate in the climate of Paris without the aid of artificial heat."

Sweet potatoes thrive where the growing season

SWEET POTATO CULTIVARS

Sweet potatoes are distinguished by the type of flesh—moist or dry. For northern gardens, look for short-season cultivars.

'**Beauregard**': 95 days; moist-fleshed; red-orange skin, orange flesh; high yields; widely adapted.

'**Boniato**': 120 days; dry-fleshed; reddish skin, white flesh; also known as 'Cuban Sweet Potato'.

'**Bush Porto Rico**': 110 days; moist-fleshed; copper skin, reddish orange flesh; superior flavor; short-vine type; heirloom.

'**Centennial**': 110 days; moist-fleshed; bright copper skin, deep orange flesh; widely adapted; standard home-garden cultivar.

'**Georgia Jet**': 90 days; moist-fleshed; reddish purple skin, deep orange flesh; moderate to good yield in northern gardens; early-maturing.

'**Jewel**': 100 days; moist-fleshed; copper skin, medium orange flesh; good disease resistance; stores well; standard commercial cultivar.

'**Nancy Hall**': 110 days; moist-fleshed; yellow skin, deep yellow flesh; stores well; heirloom.

'**Southern Delite**': 100 days; moist-fleshed; rose to dark copper skin, orange flesh; superior insect and disease resistance; stores well.

'**Vardaman**': 110 days; moist-fleshed; golden skin, orange flesh; short-vine type; widely adapted.

'**White Yam**': 120 days; dry-fleshed; white skin, white flesh; also known as 'Southern Queen' and 'Choker'; heirloom.

'**Yellow Jersey**': 120 days; dry-fleshed; orange skin, yellow flesh; resistant to nematodes; widely adapted.

is long and hot. Gardeners north of USDA Zone 6 may find it difficult to grow sweet potatoes, although the development of quick-maturing, cold-tolerant cultivars at least means that Yankees, unlike Parisians, don't have to resort to artificial heat.

DECIDING WHAT TO GROW

For home gardeners, the choice is between dry- and moist-fleshed sweet potatoes. Dry types usually have yellow or white flesh and are more mealy and starchy but less sweet than moist types are. Dry-fleshed sweet potatoes, which are not widely available, tend to do well in cooler climates. Moist-fleshed sweet potatoes, which convert most of their starches to sugar when they're cooked, have soft, very sweet flesh, usually colored dark yellow or orange-red. This more popular type tends to grow better in the South, although 'Georgia Jet', a cultivar that does well as far north as Canada, is an exception to that rule.

Sweet potato plants take up a good deal of room, not unexpected with a vine, but breeders have developed short-vine cultivars—'Vardaman' is one of the most popular—for gardeners who are short on space. If you have room on your patio or deck for a sweet potato to roam, one or two plants will provide handsome foliage, although not a huge harvest. Use a barrel-size container with good bottom drainage, and fill it with enriched potting soil. Water generously when plants are young, and feed every 5 weeks with compost tea.

Sweet potatoes can easily yield 3 pounds of potatoes per plant and often produce more than 5 pounds (between 4 and 12 potatoes). For a family of four, 25 plants should be plenty.

SITE & SOIL

Full sun and at least 100 warm days and warm nights are a prerequisite for growing sweet potatoes well. Even a light freeze will kill these sensitive vines. Soil doesn't have to be rich, but it should be light and acid (pH 5.5 to 6.5). Make sure it drains well and has been dug to at least 10 inches. Avoid walking on or otherwise compacting the soil.

Set plants, which require about the same amount of space as winter squash does, every 12 to 18 inches in hilled rows or mounds (8 inches high and 1 foot wide at the base) spaced 3 feet apart. Hilling the soil helps keep it warm and encourages

Sweet potatoes 'Gold Nugget' and 'Frazier White'

good drainage. Gardeners in colder regions should lay down plastic mulch to raise the soil's temperature. Close spacing favors smaller but more numerous potatoes; spacing plants farther apart will produce fewer but larger roots.

HOW TO GROW

Sweet potatoes are normally begun from slips, or rooted sprouts, rather than from seeds. You can buy slips from local nurseries or mail-order suppliers (to avoid creating problems in your garden, purchase only certified disease-free slips), or you can grow your own from sweet potatoes overwintered from your own or a neighbor's garden. (Don't try growing slips from supermarket sweet potatoes, which are treated to prevent sprouting.) To grow slips, begin about 3 months before they will be transplanted outdoors by setting a sweet potato in a glass that is half-filled with water (about one-third of the tuber should be submerged). Leave it in a warm (75°F), sunny location where it will sprout. When the sprouts are at least 6 inches long, pull them off the potato and set them in water or damp sand until they develop roots.

Hardened-off slips can go outdoors once the weather has warmed, about 2 weeks after the frost-free date. The soil should be at least 60°F and nighttime temperatures above 60°F. Set the hardened-off slips deeply, to the first leaves. (In cold regions, leave the plastic mulch in place, and plant through it, then cover transplants for at least 2 weeks with floating row covers to preserve heat.) Top growth may be slow initially as plants develop deep feeder

Harvesting sweet potatoes

roots; once plants are established and daytime temperatures stay above 70°F, vine growth is rampant. Weed assiduously when plants are small.

Once vines develop, cultivate under them or lift the vines to keep them from establishing secondary roots that will compete with the main roots, which form the potatoes. Otherwise, sweet potatoes are surprisingly self-tending. Established plants need little irrigation unless drought is prolonged (too much moisture will cause the roots to crack). Extra fertilizer isn't essential either, although you can give plants a boost by watering them with compost tea or side-dressing with wood ashes 5 weeks after transplanting (avoid a high-nitrogen food, which will promote leaf rather than root development).

POTENTIAL PROBLEMS

Home gardeners, unlike commercial growers, are rarely troubled with insects or diseases when growing sweet potatoes. Rotating crops to avoid planting sweet potatoes in the same soil for 4 years and keeping the soil pH acid will discourage fungal and bac-

teria problems. Buying certified disease-free plants is always prudent, as is planting disease-resistant cultivars. Use floating row covers to discourage flea beetles, which may attack plants in northern gardens. In the South, crops can be afflicted by nematodes and weevils that bore into the roots. Nematodes disfigure tubers and reduce plant vigor. Sweet potato weevils do not lower plant yield but, like a worm in an apple, reduce the culinary value of the tubers. Weevils overwinter on plant material. Cleaning up the garden in the fall will help to reduce the weevil population.

HARVESTING

Gardeners can begin harvesting as soon as the potatoes, which are rich in vitamins A and C as well as potassium and fiber, are large enough to use. For the best flavor, allow plants to grow until they are killed by a light frost or daytime temperatures drop into the 50s F. Once frost has killed the vines, harvest the crop immediately. Dig tubers carefully with a garden fork. Potatoes that are bruised won't store well and should be used first.

Before they are stored, sweet potatoes should be cured by allowing them to sit in the sun for a day, then in a warm (80°F), humid location out of direct sun for 2 weeks. Store in a dry, cool (55°F) location for up to 5 months.

SWISS CHARD

Beta vulgaris, Cicla group. Goosefoot family, Chenopodiaceae. Biennial grown as an annual.

○ ◐ ✳ ❄ ❀ ▬

Chard, grown for its large leaves and crisp leafstalks, or petioles, and beets, valued for their roots, are siblings in the goosefoot family. Chard is by far the older of the two, but age counts for less than sweetness in the horticultural world, so beets are the better known and loved of the pair. Europeans had been eating chard greens (*beta* means "greens" in Latin) for centuries before gardeners began to select plants for root size and developed the beet as a separate vegetable. Contemporary seed catalogs celebrate the colorful foliage of ruby chards as if they were a novelty, but the red leaves were well known in Aristotle's day (circa 350 B.C.).

Also known as spinach beet and leaf beet, chard

has less sugar than beets do, but its greens are lower in oxalic acid and have a mild flavor. It is also widely adaptable—it can be grown in USDA Zone 2 and warmer. And although it prefers cool temperatures in the 60s F, it is far more heat-tolerant than are lettuce and many other leaf crops.

Nevertheless, chard has never come near the top of most-popular-vegetable lists in this country either, although it has been around since colonial times—George Washington grew chard at Mount Vernon. The status of chard hasn't changed much since 1867, when one garden writer observed that it was "cultivated to some extent in private gardens only." Unintentionally anticipating the edible-landscape movement, he went on: "Its handsome foliage is as attractive as many of our prized flower-garden 'leaf plants,' and no doubt it would be much valued if we could only regard it without the idea that it is only a Beet."

DECIDING WHAT TO GROW

Chard is generally grouped into two types: Swiss chard and leaf chard, also called perpetual spinach. (See "Perpetual Spinach" on page 396 for more on leaf chard.) Swiss, or stem, chard, has large succulent leaves and thick, crisp stems. Some cultivars have attractively crinkled, or savoyed, leaves. There are basically two types of Swiss chard to choose from: red cultivars, such as 'Rhubarb' and 'Charlotte', and white-stemmed plants like 'Fordhook Giant' and 'Lucullus'.

A dozen plants will provide enough chard for a family of four; if you want to preserve, increase the planting. Most cultivars produce harvestable leaves in 5 weeks and reach full size in 50 to 60 days. Although it matures quickly, chard can be harvested for many months, but you'll still want to make two or three plantings at 2-week intervals to maintain a steady supply of tender young leaves. Chard can be planted throughout the growing season—it tolerates both heat and frost—making it a good succession crop.

SITE & SOIL

Chard plants, which grow to 2 feet tall, aren't finicky and do reasonably well in almost any setting. Given the choice, however, they prefer full sun (partial shade in hot regions) and well-drained soil that is rich in humus and has a pH between 6.0 and 6.8. Working composted manure into the soil will boost its nitrogen level, which is essential to good leaf development.

White or red, all Swiss chard plants are a wonderful blending of form and function, making them fine for ornamental and container gardens as well as for the vegetable patch. Use a container, at least 8 inches wide and 12 inches deep, with good bottom drainage, and fill with enriched potting soil. Water

---

CHARD CULTIVARS

To create a handsome planting that produces a steady supply of mild-tasting greens, plant a mix of cultivars with variously colored stalks. All of the cultivars listed below are open-pollinated.

'Argentata': 55 days; silvery-white stalks with deep green savoyed leaves; tall, vigorous plants; heirloom.

'Broadstem Green': 60 days; white midribs and stems with large green leaves.

'Charlotte': 59 days; deep red stalks and leaf veins with green leaves; highly ornamental.

'Fordhook Giant': 55 days; cream-colored ribs with medium green leaves; heirloom.

'Joseph's Coat': 55 days; orange, pink, yellow, red, and white stalks with green leaves; heirloom.

'Lucullus': 55 days; white stalks with extra-large yellow-green leaves; huge yields; popular home-garden cultivar; heirloom.

'Paros': 55 days; thick white stalks with medium-green savoyed leaves; popular French market cultivar.

'Rhubarb': 59 days; scarlet stalks and dark green leaves veined with red; may bolt if exposed to spring frosts; highly ornamental; heirloom.

'Silverado': 55 days; broad white stalks with dark green savoyed leaves on compact plants; bolt-resistant.

Swiss chard 'Rhubarb'

Swiss chard 'Silverado'

frequently, and feed every 4 weeks with compost tea.

HOW TO GROW

Chard can be direct-seeded 1 to 2 weeks before the last expected frost (in mild regions, it also can be planted in autumn for winter and early-spring harvests). Sow seeds ½ inch deep, spaced every 4 inches—germination takes about a week in 60°F soil. Like beets, a chard "seed" will sprout several plants, so thinning is necessary. Culls can be used in the kitchen or replanted elsewhere in the garden. When plants are 6 inches tall, thin to 8 to 12 inches, or slightly closer if you intend to pick leaves regularly and space is at a premium. Mulch plants to retain moisture and suppress weeds.

To promote vigorous leaf growth, side-dress chard with a light application of blood meal or water plants with manure tea at 4 weeks. Even more than extra fertilizer, chard needs a constant supply of moisture, 1 inch a week, especially as the weather turns hot. Drought-stressed plants are more likely to bolt, and their leaves and stalks will be fibrous

and bitter. If a flower stalk does appear, remove it to prolong the harvest.

Given good soil and adequate moisture, chard is rarely troubled by insects or diseases. Flea beetles, aphids, leaf miners, and leafhoppers occasionally feed on the leaves; to prevent them and other insect enemies from reaching plants, cover the seedbed with floating row covers. (For more information about leaf spot and downy mildew, which sometimes strike chard plants, see "Controlling Common Diseases" on page 169.)

HARVESTING

Begin harvesting individual leaves when they reach a length of 5 or 6 inches or are large enough to use. Break off the outer leaves at their base, taking care not to damage inner leaves. Plants that are harvested regularly will continue to produce new growth from the center of the plant. Protect plants with floating row covers to keep them producing after the first frost in cold regions.

Swiss chard is near the top of the nutrition

chart, bettered only by collard greens, spinach, and kale. All cultivars contain generous amounts of vitamin C, calcium, potassium, and iron; red cultivars also contain a good-size dose of vitamin A. To store Swiss chard, seal in plastic bags and refrigerate.

Because Swiss chard is a biennial and flowers in its second season, saving seeds is difficult. Gardeners in cold climates must dig and overwinter plants, then replant them in the spring; in frost-free regions, carry plants over to a second year. Pollen is carried by the wind—as far as 5 miles—and all chards and beets cross-pollinate. To save seeds, plant only one cultivar or isolate your crop. Seeds are viable for 4 years; store in airtight containers in a dark, cool location.

TARRAGON

Artemisia dracunculus var. *sativa*. Sunflower family, Asteraceae. Perennial.

Tarragon is among the most esteemed herbs in *haute cuisine*—you can't make bearnaise or hollandaise without it—so you might expect that it would be difficult to grow. Quite the opposite. Although contemporaries of 17th-century herbalist John Parkinson speculated that tarragon arose from flax seeds inserted into onions—a notion Parkinson dismissed as "an absurd and idle opinion"—this delicate-tasting, licorice-flavored herb is actually an *Artemisia*, making it a relative of tough, tolerant wormwood and sagebrush. In fact, tarragon has enough of the constitution of a prairie weed to make it one of the best perennial herbs for gardens in USDA Zone 4 and warmer. Plants will grow in the far South, but they do best in regions where there is a dormant period in winter. There, they return each spring to lend their cordon bleu flavor to the most finicky sauces and the most subtle salad dressings. A single plant, renewed every few years, can mean a lifetime of satisfying quantities of delicate-flavored leaves.

Despite the many medicinal claims of other members of the *Artemisia* genus, tarragon's history is

PERPETUAL SPINACH

Chard's lesser-known sibling, perpetual spinach, has been grown for its large, tender leaves since classical Greek times. As its name suggests, the slightly savoyed bright green foliage resembles spinach. Like Swiss chard, perpetual spinach prefers cool weather but tolerates warm temperatures and retains its mild flavor through most of the summer in USDA Zone 6 and colder. In southern gardens, it can be raised as a spring and fall crop. It is also called sea spinach, because it tolerates slightly saline soils and is acclimated to coastal areas.

Grow perpetual spinach as you would Swiss chard, but space plants closer—about every 8 inches. A dozen plants is sufficient for a family of four. 'Erbette', with smooth-textured green leaves, is the most common named cultivar, but most seed houses sell the crop by its generic name. Plants mature in about 50 days from seeds, but you can begin to harvest individual leaves as soon as they are large enough to use. Pick leaves from the outside of the plant, allowing new growth to fill the center. Plants can also be harvested by shearing them back to about 3 inches in a cut-and-come-again fashion.

Tarragon

almost entirely culinary. There are few references to curative qualities. Even John Gerard was reduced to conclude that although it was "not to be eaten alone in sallades, but joyned with other herbs . . . neither do we know what other use this herbe hath." Contemporary herbalist Steven Foster comes to the same judgment, writing in *Herbal Renaissance* (1993) that tarragon's "medicinal possibilities are very limited."

Because it is a perennial, tarragon is best kept out of the vegetable garden, unless it can be planted in an out-of-the-way spot where routine tilling won't disturb it. Combine it with other perennials in the herb garden instead. Although not showy, tarragon can be included in flower borders or containers. Plant one plant in a pot that is at least a foot wide, or grow tarragon in larger containers with other dry-soil perennial herbs, such as thyme and savory. In Zones 4 and 5, bury the pot to its rim to protect the roots over winter. One or two plants will be enough for most families.

DECIDING WHAT TO GROW

Also called French tarragon and estragon, this native of Europe and southern Asia has relaxed stems with narrow, 1- to 2½-inch-long green leaves. Plants range from 1½ to 3 feet in height. Tight clusters of small, greenish white flowers appear in summer, but they do not open and do not produce viable seeds. This is a crucial fact to know before you plant. True French tarragon (A. *dracunculus* var. *sativa*) is only propagated asexually—by division or cuttings—never from seeds.

When shopping for tarragon plants, smell and taste before you buy. True French tarragon has a distinctly warm, anise/licorice fragrance and flavor with a hint of mint. Russian tarragon (A. *dracunculus* subsp. *dracunculoides*), which can be grown from seeds, is a larger plant than French tarragon—as tall as 5 feet—and has paler, willowy leaves. Most important, it has a pungent and less pleasing flavor. Seed-grown tarragon is inevitably Russian, not French.

HOW TO GROW

A site with well-drained soil is important for French tarragon—root rot is inevitable in sites where the soil remains moist. Moderately rich soil with a pH range of 6.2 to 7.0 suits it perfectly, although it will tolerate soil as sweet as 8.0. Plants are remarkably drought-tolerant, and a sloping site, even if the ground is rocky or sandy, is suitable—as is a raised bed. While willing to put up with some afternoon shade, tarragon does best in full sun.

As with many herbs, care is minimal when growing tarragon. Space plants about 1 foot apart at planting time. To encourage more leaves to form, cut plants back in summer when they begin to flower. In late fall, after the ground freezes, mulch tarragon with a loose covering of cut evergreen branches, straw, or a similar material that will not compact.

After 3 or 4 years, the roots of tarragon become hopelessly crowded and tangled, reducing plants' vigor. Renew your planting by digging the clumps as soon as the shoots emerge in spring. Gently break off 2-inch pieces of root with shoots attached and replant. Discard the old, woody portions of the clumps.

MEXICAN TARRAGON

Tarragon grows best in areas with relatively cool summers, but southern gardeners need not despair. Instead, consider growing Mexican tarragon (*Tagetes lucida*), an herb used as a tarragon substitute in Latin America, where the climate is too hot for French tarragon. Also called pericon or sweet-scented marigold, Mexican tarragon is a tender perennial marigold native to Central America. It is generally grown as an annual for its anise-scented leaves, which are used for both seasoning and tea. Start the seeds, which germinate slowly, indoors 6 to 8 weeks before the last-spring-frost date, and transplant hardened-off seedlings after the frost date, once the soil has warmed up. Mexican tarragon requires a long, warm season to bloom. In USDA Zone 5, it produces its clusters of yellow blossoms only at the close of the growing season, but it is still a useful foliage herb, with or without flowers.

HARVESTING

Begin picking tarragon leaves, which are best flavored before the flowers begin blooming, as soon as the plant is well established. Use leaves fresh, or preserve their flavor in a vinegar. For short-term storage, seal fresh tarragon in plastic bags, and refrigerate. Although tarragon, which contains small amounts of vitamin A and other minerals, can be preserved by drying, some flavor will be lost.

THAI BASIL. See *Basil*

THYME

Thymus spp. Mint family, Lamiaceae. Perennial.

○ ◐ ✳ ❄ ✿ ▼

Thymes, like basils and mints, are a delightfully varied group of herbs. Not only do they offer a variety of flavors and fragrances, but growth habit, hardiness, and appearance also vary. Despite their differences, all are woody-based perennials that have small (¼ to ½ inch), pungent leaves on slender stems. In summer, small dense clusters of tiny, two-lipped white, lilac, or pink flowers appear. The flowers, once thought to attract fairies, are favorites of bees and make delicious honey.

Mediterranean natives, thymes have been associated with courage and energy for centuries. Athletes in ancient Greece rubbed thyme oil into their skin to encourage them to act bravely. The genus name may be derived from the Greek *thymos*, "courage," although another interpretation is that it is derived from the Greek verb "to fumigate," because thyme branches were once burned to keep away insects. The Roman Pliny dissolved thyme in vinegar and honey to cure hypochondria and melancholy, and the herb was also recommended as a cure for stomachaches, asthma, and worms. In fact, the oil in thyme has antiseptic properties and was used to clean wounds as late as World War I.

Thyme is still an ingredient in several phytomedicines in Europe, mainly as a treatment for the symptoms of bronchitis, and is contained in a number of creams and lotions sold in North America. Its leaves contain vitamin A, niacin, potassium, calcium, and iron, but thyme's reputation has always been more culinary than medicinal or nutritional—it is the perfect herb to complement

Thyme

vegetables, such as onions, carrots, and beets, and to flavor stuffings and soups, and to use in fish and in beef dishes.

DECIDING WHAT TO GROW

There are many different thymes, a situation confused by species names that keep changing and cultivar names that may be inaccurate. As one herb expert put it, the genus is a "taxonomic Pandora's box . . . . There are about four hundred species—or a hundred species with four hundred names." The best route is to taste before you buy rather than depend on a label. And there's plenty to taste, as herb specialists often offer several dozen cultivars, with flavors from coconut and orange to nutmeg and menthol.

Begin with common, or English, thyme (*Thymus vulgaris*), the most frequently grown species and a favorite of cooks and gardeners alike. Hardy in USDA Zone 4 and warmer, it is a shrubby plant, ranging from 12 to 18 inches in height, with gray-green leaves. A number of cultivars are available, all of which can be used in cooking, including 'Argenteus', with leaves edged in white, and 'Orange Balsam', a 10-inch-tall plant with orange-scented leaves. Ten-inch-tall 'Narrowleaf French' has narrower, stronger-flavored leaves than does the species, while 8-inch 'German Winter' is more compact still.

Restricting an herb garden to just a planting of common thyme is like eating only vanilla ice cream: No matter how good it tastes, there are other flavors to try. Foot-tall lemon thyme (*T.* x *citriodorus*) produces leaves with a pungent lemon scent and pale lilac summer flowers. It is hardy in Zone 5 and

Silver thyme

warmer. 'Aureus' has lemon-scented, yellow-edged leaves. 'Golden Creeping' is only 4 inches tall, with shiny, lemon-scented leaves variegated in gold and lavender flowers. Caraway thyme (*T. herba-barona*) is a diminutive, 4-inch-tall species with pale purple-pink summer flowers and minute leaves that smell of caraway. It is hardy in Zone 6 and warmer.

Two other species are most commonly grown as ornamentals but have aromatic leaves that can be used as common thyme. Creeping thyme (*T. prae-cox*), hardy in Zone 5 and warmer, is a mat-forming, 2-inch-tall plant with pink to purple flowers and tiny leaves. Wild thyme (*T. pulegioides*) is another mat former that ranges from ½ to 3 inches in height and is hardy to Zone 4. Formerly—and wrongly—called *T. serpyllum*, wild thyme has naturalized in North America, the only species to do so.

HOW TO GROW

Thymes do best in full sun and dry soil. They are among the best groundcovers for herb gardens and make handsome additions to rock gardens and flower gardens—provided the soil is well drained. Grow one or two plants of as many varieties as you can manage to find room for. Although they all look delicate and hard to grow, they are actually quite tough. The tiniest of them can survive for years, growing in the spaces between paving stones or carpeting a dry, sunny slope. When brushed or stepped on, they release their characteristic heady fragrance.

Shrubbier thymes can be used to cascade over a stone wall or the edges of a raised bed. They also are fine subjects for container culture: Fill pots with a somewhat sandy soil mix, and make sure drainage is adequate. Grow one plant per 6-inch pot, or combine them with other dry-soil-loving herbs in large tubs and containers. If you intend to leave pot-grown thymes in the garden over the winter in Zone 5 or colder, bury the container to the rim in fall and protect it with evergreen boughs or another loose mulch that will not compact.

While all thymes require light and well-drained soil, they will tolerate a wide pH range—from 6.0 to 8.0. If in doubt about soil drainage, grow thyme in raised beds, and/or work plenty of organic matter deeply into the garden before planting. A site in full sun is best, although plants will tolerate some shade, provided the soil remains on the dry side.

Some thymes can be grown from seeds, but it's better to begin with purchased plants. Not only is germination inconsistent and growth slow, but most thyme cultivars do not come true from seeds. Start with a transplant whose fragrance and flavor you like, which will grow so much faster that it can produce three times the yield of direct-sown thyme in its first year. Set new thyme plants 6 to 12 inches apart. Cut plants back after they flower in summer to encourage bushiness. Mulch thyme over the winter if you are not certain of a particular cultivar's hardiness. After 3 or 4 years, thyme becomes woody and less productive and should be renewed.

There are three ways to renew thyme—or to propagate new plants. The easiest is to divide plant clumps, either in spring or fall. Carefully dig the clumps, which can have very deep roots, and replant the youngest, healthiest portions. Water new transplants deeply.

The second option is to take cuttings from young, new growth in spring to early summer, before the plants bloom, and root them in wet sand. They should root in 2 to 3 weeks.

The third approach, best used with bushy thymes, is mound layering. In late spring, mound loose soil, sandy soil, or shredded bark mulch mixed with compost several inches high in and around the plant, leaving 3 to 4 inches of shoot tips exposed. Keep the mound slightly moist throughout summer, replacing the mulch as necessary. In fall, check for roots at the base of the buried branches. The rooted shoots can be cut off and planted. If roots aren't apparent, however, remulch and check again in spring.

HARVESTING

To harvest thyme, clip foliage and flowers as needed. Don't be shy about cutting plants—back-shearing promotes new growth.

Thyme dries easily. When plants are blooming, cut entire branches with flower clusters and hang to dry. Strip off leaves and flowers, and store in plastic bags or lidded containers.

TOMATE. See *Tomatillo*

TOMATILLO

Physalis spp. Nightshade family, Solanaceae. Annual.

○ ☀

Tomatillos are an ancient crop from Central and South America that has recently been rediscovered by North Americans hungry for Mexican dishes. Aficionados don't stop at salsa verde—the Mexican equivalent of Italy's tomato sauce—but add tomatillos to soups and sauces and turn them into appetizers, even desserts and jams. Tomatillos are the source, experts say, of the "piquant" flavor in authentic Mexican cuisine.

Husk tomato, the plant's common name, is wonderfully descriptive, since each tomato-like fruit (actually a berry) ripens within a papery husk. The 1- to 2-inch-diameter fruits are produced on sprawling plants with oval, 3-inch-long leaves that have slightly toothed margins and small, nodding, bell-like flowers. Pollinated flowers form a husk—technically a bladderlike calyx—which is gradually filled, and often splits open, with the fruit that grows inside it.

A first look at the genus *Physalis* reveals a confusing array of common names. Perhaps the best-known member of the genus, *P. alkekengi*, is usually called Chinese-lantern plant, but it's also known as strawberry tomato and winter cherry. Although it bears edible red fruits, it is most often grown in perennial beds and borders and used in dried-flower arrangements for the showy, bright orange husks, or lanterns, that surround them. *P. ixocarpa* is the traditional green tomatillo or tomate, also called jam-

Ground cherries in husks

berry and Mexican husk tomato, and grown for its sweet-tart fruits that resemble small green tomatoes once the husk is removed. 'Toma Verde' is the most common cultivar and has golf-ball-size fruits that can reach 2½ inches in diameter. Plants range from 2 to 3 feet in height and can spread from 3 to 4 feet. 'Indian Strain' has a more compact habit and sweeter-tasting fruits. *P. philadelphica*, called both wild tomatillo and purple ground cherry, produces yellow to purple fruits. Its cultivar 'Purple de Milpa' has large purple-streaked husks and dark purple and green fruits that are sweeter than green tomatillos are. Plants reach 3 to 4 feet across and 4 feet or more in height.

Ground cherries, *P. pruinosa* and *P. pubescens*, both native to North America, are close relatives of tomatillos. They yield sweet, cherry-size fruits on 2- to 3-foot-wide 1- to 2-foot-tall plants; fruits ripen from green to golden yellow inside husks that turn from green to straw-colored. The berries of these two species—also called strawberry tomato, husk tomato, and dwarf cape gooseberry—are thought to have been collected from the wild or treated as encouraged weeds long before they were brought into cultivation. 'Goldie' has golden orange berries; 'Cossack Pineapple' bears pineapple-flavored fruit. Cape gooseberry (*P. peruviana*), a similar, slightly larger plant with sweet yellow fruit, is native to the Andes of South America, despite the common name, which was attached after seeds were carried from South America to South Africa to New South Wales.

Tomatillos and ground cherries can be grown in

Ground cherry

Tomatillos

USDA Zone 3 and warmer and begin bearing fruits from 60 to 80 days after transplanting. Although they are a warm-weather crop, they tolerate cool temperatures well and will continue bearing, despite weather that would slow down tomatoes. Neither is ornamental enough to be used outside the food garden, although they can be grown in containers. For a family of four, two to four tomatillo plants and the same number of ground cherries should provide a plentiful harvest; if you're a devotee of south-of-the-border cooking, increase the planting.

HOW TO GROW

Tomatillos and ground cherries require full sun, much like their better-known relatives tomatoes, but unlike tomatoes, they grow best in average soil that is not too rich. Amend the soil with humus to make sure that it drains well and has a near-neutral pH.

Except in areas with extremely long growing seasons, start plants indoors between 6 and 8 weeks before the last expected frost. Sow seeds, ¼ inch deep, in cell packs; bottom heat speeds germination, which occurs in about 7 days in 70°F soil. When plants have at least one set of true leaves, transplant to 3-inch pots. As the frost-free date approaches, harden off your seedlings, then move them to the garden once nighttime temperatures remain above 50°F. Set them slightly deeper than they were previously growing—like tomatoes, their stems will sprout roots. In areas with long, warm seasons, direct-sow seeds after the danger of frost has past and the soil has warmed. Don't rush—beginning outdoors too early will delay plant development.

Spacing depends on whether you plan to cage plants or let them sprawl. Space plants that will be caged 2 feet apart, 3 feet apart if you don't cage. Install cages or other support at planting time—the ordinary tomato cages available in garden centers, which are generally too small for most tomatoes, are fine for tomatillos. Pinch off the tips of the branches to control spread. In healthy garden soil, no additional fertilizer is necessary, although occasional watering with compost or manure tea will keep the plants vigorous. Water if the weather is dry, and apply a loose mulch to retain moisture and suppress weeds.

Although some of the pests and diseases that attack tomatoes will attack tomatillos and ground cherries, these are problem-free crops for the most part. Handpick tomato hornworms and Colorado potato beetles. Crop rotation will control most diseases—do not plant tomatillos where nightshade-family crops, including tomatoes and peppers, have been grown for at least three seasons—and floating row covers, installed early in the season, will prevent insects from reaching plants.

HARVESTING

In general, tomatillos and ground cherries, which contain vitamins A and C and niacin, are ready for harvest when the fruits fill out the husks and the husks begin to break open. (In some cases, the fruits won't break open the husk, and you have to feel the fruits for firmness.) Ripe tomatillos turn from green to pale yellow; 'Purple de Milpa' ripens to dark purple. Ground cherries ripen from pale green to golden yellow. Papery, straw-colored husks are another sign of ripe fruits, which become sweeter but more seedy as they enlarge. Harvesting keeps the plants bearing until frost kills them, so check your plants every day or two: Fruits left too long on the vine are bitter and don't store well.

Harvest the fruits, husk and all. If you are using them right away, remove the husks and wash the sticky fruits. Leave the husks in place to store the fruits. Both tomatillos and ground cherries can be stored for up to a month in the husks, but don't seal them in plastic bags or airtight containers. Instead, treat them as you would onions: Store them in a cool (55°F), well-ventilated spot in mesh bags.

Tomatillos are generally cooked (simmer 5 to 10 minutes in water) or roasted (in the broiler until the skin blackens slightly) to bring out their full flavor before adding them to salsa or other recipes. Ground cherries, on the other hand, are eaten fresh, used as a dessert fruit, or added to sauces, preserves, salads, or pies.

Tomatillos and ground cherries have perfect flowers and normally do not cross-pollinate, so saving seeds won't require limiting yourself to only one cultivar. In warm regions, however, they do self-seed, so if you don't want hundreds of volunteers, keep plants harvested. Be sure to choose the best fruits from the most vigorous and healthy plants. Seeds are viable for 3 years; store in airtight containers in a dark, cool location.

TOMATO

Lycopersicon esculentum. Nightshade family, Solanaceae. Perennial grown as an annual.

○ ✳ ❀ ▆

Love apple, Moor's apple, stinking golden apple, amorous apple—whatever apple you call it, it's still a tomato and still America's favorite vegetable. Its most sinister name, wolf peach, comes from the long-held belief that the tomato was poisonous. As one 17th-century cookbook declared, while it was safe but "not advisable" to eat a cooked tomato, eating a raw fruit would cause instantaneous death. Although erroneous, the accusation of being lethal was long-lived, lingering until the early 1800s.

In fact, people were eating tomatoes without fatal consequences well before Spanish conquistadors carried them from South America to Europe in the 1500s. Tomatoes soon flourished in Mediterranean gardens, and southern Europeans didn't waste any time taking culinary advantage of the tomato: The first cookbook to contain tomato recipes was published in Naples in 1692. Other Europeans were less enthusiastic, the English herbalist Gerard noting that they "yeeld very little nourishment to the body, and the same naught and corrupt."

American colonists, English to the core, not only brought tomatoes back to this continent but also imported most of the popular prejudices about them. While a few adventuresome gardeners grew tomatoes—Thomas Jefferson, who first mentions planting them in 1809, is the most prominent—they were not widely cultivated in this country until after 1830.

If the controversy over the tomato being toxic or benign weren't burden enough, an additional debate centered over whether the tomato was a vegetable or a fruit. The issue was settled legally in 1887, when the United States Supreme Court ruled that although "botanically speaking tomatoes are

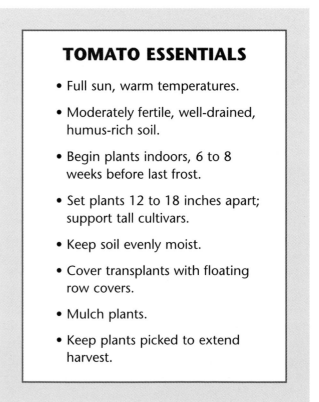

TOMATO ESSENTIALS

- Full sun, warm temperatures.

- Moderately fertile, well-drained, humus-rich soil.

- Begin plants indoors, 6 to 8 weeks before last frost.

- Set plants 12 to 18 inches apart; support tall cultivars.

- Keep soil evenly moist.

- Cover transplants with floating row covers.

- Mulch plants.

- Keep plants picked to extend harvest.

the fruit of a vine," they were vegetables "in the common language of the people."

Fruit or vegetable, plant breeders have been changing the tomato ever since it cleaned up its sinister reputation. More than 40,000 *Lycopersicon esculentum* accessions are held in gene banks worldwide—10,000 in the U.S. alone—although USDA scientists suggest that redundancy is high and that the true number of tomato cultivars is about 25,000. The latest breeding achievement—or mischief, some would say—is 'Flavr Savr', a commercial culti-

var with tweaked genes that remains firm when ripe. It can be grown in USDA Zone 3 and warmer, as can most tomato cultivars.

DECIDING WHAT TO GROW

A mix of 15 to 20 cultivars should provide enough tomatoes for a family of four; if you want to preserve, increase the planting. And what an assortment there is. There are a good many ways to sort tomatoes, including fruit color (red, orange, pink, yellow, bicolor, and more), fruit shape (large, small, round,

Heirloom tomato 'Black Krim'

Cherry tomato 'Sweet Gold'

Cherry tomato 'Ruby Cluster'

Tomato 'Celebrity'

Tomato 'Lemon Boy'

Tomato 'Viva Italia'

Tomato 'Striped Cavern'

Heirloom tomato 'Brandywine'

Paste tomato 'Super Italian'

flattened, elongated), and use (all-purpose, salad, slicing, canning, paste/sauce, juice, stuffing). The most common method combines size, shape, and use. From large to small, the usual classes are: beef-steak and/or very large; medium or standard; paste, including plum and pear; and cherry. Other tomato characteristics to consider before you start digging include:

Hybrid or Open-Pollinated. Tomatoes are self-pollinating when left to their own devices (and desires). Scores of fine open-pollinated selections and hybrids are available, each type with its own merits. In addition to coming true from seeds, many open-pollinated tomatoes have the advantage of being locally adapted, or suited to a particular region. They may have adjusted to the environmental conditions, such as drought or cold, where they

were developed or have multi-resistance to common diseases of their locale. Hybrids, which do not produce seeds that come true, have the advantage of better-than-average vigor and earlier, more uniform, and higher yields. Moreover, many hybrids, such as 'Celebrity', have been bred with outstanding disease resistance/tolerance.

Indeterminate or Determinate. The tomato's wild progenitor is a viney, sprawling plant, a heritage still seen in a vigorous indeterminate cultivar like 'Sweet 100'. Indeterminate tomatoes continue to grow until they are halted by frost, and they produce earlier and more—and some argue better-tasting—fruits than determinates do. As long as the conditions are hospitable, indeterminate cultivars will continue to set fruit. In contrast, determinate tomato plants are compact and only moderately tall,

Tomato 'Georgia Streak'

Tomato 'Burpee Big Boy Hybrid'

Tomato 'Tumbler'

Tomato 'Burpee 650'

Heirloom tomatoes

bred to have a finite size and to mature their fruits in a concentrated period, usually 6 weeks or less. Most determinates require no support, while most indeterminates do, but some cultivars, called semi- or vigorous determinates, may need help staying upright. At the other end of the determinate spectrum are dwarfs, cultivars ideal for container culture, and miniatures, such a 'Minibel', scaled-down cultivars with short stems and marble-size fruits that are usually grown as ornamentals, not edibles.

Days to Maturity. Most tomato cultivars are designated simply as "early" (up to 65 days), "midseason" (66 to 79), and "late" (more than 80 days). Keep in mind that these are figured from the date transplants go into the garden. When scheduling crops and sowing times, don't forget to add the time it takes to produce a transplant—about 6 to 8 weeks—to these approximate numbers. Remember, too, that regional conditions affect the time it takes to produce mature fruits. Plants are slowed by cool weather (tomatoes like daytime temperatures in the high 70s and low 80s F), by an excess of cloudy days, and a host of other environmental factors. A midseason cultivar like 'Principe Borghese' may be ready to pick in 75 days in central Missouri but may need as many as 90 days to mature fruits in a cool, coastal location.

Disease Resistance/Tolerance. Tomatoes are heir to a more-than-generous array of diseases, including anthracnose, botrytis fruit rot, bacterial canker, bacterial spot, bacterial wilt, curly top, damping-off, early and late blights, fusarium wilt, mosaic, septoria leaf spot, and tobacco mosaic. Because many of these maladies—bacterial and fusarium wilts and tobacco mosaic are three—cannot be cured, choosing disease-resistant/tolerant cultivars is important, especially in hot, humid regions, where infections hit hard and fast. Fortunately, there is a good-size collection of cultivars that have been bred to resist or tolerate diseases to pick from (see "Tomato Cultivars" for a list).

SITE & SOIL

Tomatoes like warmth, so find a protected spot in full sun with organically rich soil (pH 6.0 to 7.0) for your plants. This vegetable is a heavy feeder and requires a generous and balanced supply of the three major soil elements, but don't overdo the N in the N–P–K package. An excess of nitrogen produces lush foliage but a meager crop of fruits. On the other hand, small, pale, yellowing leaves are a sign of too little nitrogen. A phosphorus deficiency makes itself known by foliage that takes on a reddish purple cast and delayed flowering; too little potassium slows growth and reduces yields. All three deficiencies are corrected by spraying plants with diluted fish emulsion or compost tea.

Tomatoes, which are set out about the time of the last spring frost, can be intercropped with fast-maturing vegetables, such as scallions and leaf lettuce. If you grow early-season determinate cultivars, they may finish bearing in time to be succeeded by a fall crop of radishes or kale. To ensure you'll have tomatoes for the table from midsummer until the first frost, plant cultivars that ripen at different times.

While any tomato can be grown in a pot, a small determinate cultivar or miniature is the best choice. Use a large container—at least 10 gallons—that has good drainage, and fill with an enriched potting mixture. Provide plenty of moisture—tomatoes are 94 percent water—and feed every 3 weeks with a low-nitrogen liquid fertilizer.

Tomato Pruning and Training. While tomatoes in hot, arid, windy regions do better when kept close to the soil surface, most cultivars benefit from getting off the ground. There are good reasons for keeping plants erect rather than allowing them to sprawl. It gives them better exposure to the sun, makes them easier to maintain and harvest, and saves space. Tomatoes that have been staked (and compact cultivars) can be planted as close as 2 or 3 feet apart; large plants that are allowed to wander need twice that space. Staking plants and pruning them by removing some shoots and foliage can also mean an earlier harvest of cleaner fruits and can reduce some disease and insect problems, such as rotting, blight, and damage from slugs. In addition to these cultural advantages, neatly staked tomatoes are enormously attractive.

Among the best alternatives for supporting tomatoes are staking, caging, weaving, and stringing (see "Plant Support Systems" on page 80 for details). Propping—giving plants a horizontal platform on which to grow—is another technique, one more useful for vigorous determinates than for tall indeterminates. This method takes up more space in the garden but is especially suited to windy regions, where plants are likely to become diseased if left on the ground. A sturdy Quonset made from 4-foot-wide concrete reinforcing wire is an easy prop to make. Cut the wire to whatever length you need—enough to cover one tomato or an entire row—then arch it over your transplants (see the bottom of page 81 for a photograph). Alternatively, set a wooden trellis or section of concrete reinforcing wire parallel to the ground on top of 1-foot posts.

Most tomatoes that are either staked, caged, or trellised are also pruned, but not all. As a rule, determinate tomato plants should not be pruned, especially in hot, arid regions where sunscald is a problem, but pruning goes hand in hand with staking large indeterminate cultivars. By removing some shoots and foliage, pruning encourages the growth of the central stem and increases fruit production. It also helps prevent diseases by improving air circulation. Severe pruning occurs most often when plants are staked or trained to a single or double string.

For a single-stem plant to be staked or trained to a string, remove the leafy sprouts, or suckers, that grow in the joints between the central vertical stem and each horizontal leaf stem. If you live where tomatoes need all the sun they can get, pinch out the entire sucker; otherwise, cut the sucker just beyond the second or third leaf. (If you want a two-stem plant, let the first sucker arising from the main stem of the plant grow out, then prune the other suckers as you would for a one-stem plant.)

Be sure that whatever support system you select is hefty enough to handle the cultivars you're growing, and install it when the plants are still small to avoid damaging their roots. If you've chosen weaving or another method that requires periodic maintenance, be sure you keep up with the plants' growth. Long, heavy stems that should have been tied or threaded 3 weeks earlier are nearly impossible to redirect. As you work with plant stems, be careful not to crush them by tying them too tightly.

HOW TO GROW

Although there are pitfalls—beginning too early is probably the biggest—growing tomatoes is easy and straightforward. Except in locations with extremely long growing seasons, tomatoes must be begun indoors, between 6 and 8 weeks before the last expected frost. Don't rush—in the garden, large, spindly, root-bound seedlings are quickly surpassed by smaller, younger plants. (Similarly, if you buy transplants, look for stocky plants with dark green foliage that have *not* begun to flower.)

Sow seeds ¼ inch deep in celled flats—two seeds per cell—filled with a sterile potting mix. At 75°F, seeds will germinate in about 1 week. Move the flats into bright light. When the seedlings have grown their first true leaves, remove the weaker plants by cutting them off with scissors. To encourage early fruiting, keep the daytime temperature at 65°F, nighttime 10 degrees cooler. Fertilize weekly using a diluted liquid fertilizer, such as a seaweed/fish-emulsion mix. As the seedlings begin crowding one another, transplant them into larger and larger containers. Each time you pot on, set the plant deeper than it was growing—at least up to the first set of leaves—to encourage new roots, which will form along the stem.

As the frost-free date approaches, harden off your seedlings. When planting day arrives—nighttime temperatures should remain above 50°F—dig a basketball-size hole for each tomato. Incorporate a shovelful of compost and a handful of crushed eggshells (for extra calcium) in each hole, and set plants deeply, up to within four branches from their top, to encourage new roots. Install collars to discourage cutworms, and cover transplants with floating row covers to protect them from wind, cold, and insects. When the weather has warmed and your tomatoes are fully acclimated to the outdoors, remove the row covers, mulch the soil, and install whatever supports the plants will need as they grow larger, taking care not to disturb plant roots.

If your garden soil is healthy and rich with organic matter, no additional fertilizer will be necessary. To ensure bumper yields, however, spray your plants with compost tea or seaweed extract 2 weeks after transplanting, after the first flowers appear,

SEEDLING SECRETS

You'll produce more sturdy seedlings if you brush your plants for 1 or 2 minutes twice a day by running your hand gently along the tops of the seedlings. If your plants are getting too large, install a small fan: Research indicates that if plants are exposed to a slight breeze their growth rate is slowed.

when the fruits reach the size of golf balls, and after the first tomato ripens. Ensure, too, that your plants get plenty of moisture, between 1 and 2 inches of water every week.

POTENTIAL PROBLEMS

Cool weather can play havoc with growing tomatoes, delaying their ripening and harming their flavor, even stopping fruiting altogether. Using floating row covers at night will help retain heat; remove them during the day. Catfacing, tan scars on the fruits' skins, is the result of the stresses from extremely high or low temperatures, wind, or drought. Cracking of fruits is caused by uneven watering—periods of drought followed by heavy rainfall. Be sure to grow cultivars that are suited to your conditions. Make sure your plants are mulched, and provide additional moisture during dry spells as well as protection from winds and, in very hot regions, from excessive sun. (For more information about two other stress-related tomato troubles, sunscald and blossom-end rot, which resemble diseases, see "Controlling Common Diseases" on page 169.)

Disease is the greatest threat to growing toma-

CURRANT EVENT

Currant tomatoes, members of the species *Lycopersicon pimpinellifolium*, are scaled-down versions of their popular cousins. Their intensely flavored fruits are tiny, about ½ inch in diameter, which explains another common name for the plant, German raisin. All currant tomatoes—here are both red and yellow cultivars, usually listed simply as 'Red Currant' and 'Yellow Currant'—are open-pollinated and mature in midseason. Plants, which produce large crops characteristic of indeterminate tomatoes, are compact and make good candidates for container culture. They are also disease-resistant. The grape-size fruits are susceptible to cracking, however, and must be picked frequently.

toes successfully, but most gardeners can outwit potential infections by rotating the location of their tomatoes each year, carefully cleaning up the garden in fall, and growing disease-resistant/tolerant cultivars. If soilborne diseases appear to have invaded your tomato plot, solarize the soil (see "Solarizing the Soil" on page 151). (For specific solutions for dealing with the diseases that most often affect tomatoes—anthracnose, bacterial leaf spot, bacterial wilt, damping-off, early blight, fusarium wilt, late blight, and tobacco mosaic—see "Controlling Common Diseases" on page 169.)

Holes in tomato foliage are a pretty good sign that you have at least tomato hornworm, a 3-inch-long green caterpillar with white strips and a horn on its rear end, in your garden. Large enough to see easily, hornworms can be handpicked. (For more information about controlling other insects that are attracted to tomato plants, including aphids, Colorado potato beetles, cutworms, flea beetles, mites, slugs, and whiteflies, see "Controlling Common Pests" on page 162.)

HARVESTING

"Vine-ripened" is the epitome of tomato perfection, a fruit left to grow until its color is even and glossy, its texture perched between firm and soft. Tomatoes picked too early are hard and less sweet and juicy, but wait too long, and the tomato skin becomes tough, its flavor flat. Watch the fruits carefully, especially the bottom of tomatoes, where ripening begins. Many tomatoes, especially large heirlooms, are fully ripe before they become fully colored. If the skin appears to be losing its waxy smoothness, go ahead and harvest, even if the fruit's shoulders have yet to turn red, pink, purple, or golden yellow.

About 1 month before the first-frost date, pinch off all new flower clusters, or top the plant. These are blossoms that will never have time to mature into edible fruits. By removing them, your plant will put all its energy into ripening existing fruits.

For all their popularity, tomatoes don't lead the vegetable nutrition list, although they do contain vitamins A and C, as well as potassium and iron. Store tomatoes at room temperature, refrigerating only those that are overripe (temperatures below 55°F slow ripening). To ripen green tomatoes, place on a rack so that the fruits are not touching and set in a warm location (65° to 70°F) away from

continued on page 410

TOMATO CULTIVARS

When it comes to tomatoes, there is a wealth of cultivars to try. The ones on these pages are some of the best and include different sizes, shapes, and colors. Early tomatoes take up to 65 days to produce fruit from the time transplants are set out into the garden; midseason cultivars, 66 to 79 days; late, 80 or more days.

Disease resistance is summarized with the following abbreviations: A, alternaria (early) blight; As, alternaria stem canker; F, fusarium wilt, race 1; F_2, fusarium wilt race 2; L, gray leaf spot; N, nematodes; T, tobacco mosaic virus; V, verticillium wilt.

'**Abraham Lincoln**': Indeterminate; open-pollinated red heirloom beefsteak with solid 12-ounce fruits and bronze-green foliage; late; not for short-season regions.

'**Beefsteak**': Indeterminate; open-pollinated red beefsteak with meaty, faintly ribbed 1-pound fruits; late; classic beefsteak cultivar.

'**Bellstar**': Determinate; open-pollinated red paste with large, firm, plum-shaped, meaty 4-ounce fruits; midseason; good canner.

'**Better Boy**': Indeterminate; hybrid large red standard bearing large crops of 12-ounce fruits with fine flavor; midseason; widely adapted; good leaf cover; (VFNAs).

'**Big Beef**': Indeterminate; hybrid red beefsteak with good-flavored, meaty 10-ounce fruits; midseason; exceptional disease resistance; widely adapted; AAS winner; (VFF$_2$AsLNT).

'**Big Rainbow**': Indeterminate; open-pollinated large multicolor heirloom slicer with $1\frac{1}{2}$-pound fruits; late; needs long season to mature; heirloom; (AAs).

'**Brandywine**': Indeterminate; open-pollinated dark pink heirloom standard with rough 10-ounce fruits; midseason to late; no disease resistance; potato-leaf foliage; widely considered best-tasting tomato available.

'**Caro Rich**': Determinate; open-pollinated orange standard with high vitamin A content, low-acid, 5-ounce fruits; midseason; does well in cool climates.

'**Celebrity**': Vigorous determinate; hybrid red standard with heavy yields of 7-ounce globe-shaped fruits; midseason; widely adapted; outstanding disease resistance; AAS winner; (VFF$_2$AsNLT).

'**Dona**': Indeterminate; hybrid red standard with glossy, fine-flavored 6-ounce fruits; midsea-son; French home-garden favorite; (VFF$_2$NT).

'**Earlirouge**': Determinate; open-pollinated red standard with 6-ounce fruits; early; reliable home and market cultivar; widely adapted.

'**Early Girl**': Indeterminate; hybrid red standard with high yields of rich-flavored 4-ounce fruits; early; home-garden favorite; (V).

'**Evergreen**': Indeterminate; open-pollinated green heirloom standard with meaty 4-ounce fruits that are green when ripe; midseason.

'**Floramerica**': Determinate; hybrid red standard with 8-ounce fruits; early to midseason; excellent disease resistance; AAS winner; (VFF$_2$NLAs).

'**Green Grape**': Vigorous determinate; open-pollinated yellow-green cherry bearing clusters of 1-inch bicolored fruits with green flesh and sweet-tart flavor; midseason to late.

'**Heatwave**': Determinate; hybrid red standard with tasty, uniform 8-ounce fruits; early to midseason; heat-tolerant cultivar suited for the Southeast; (VFF$_2$).

'**Husky Gold**': Indeterminate; hybrid yellow-orange standard with mild, sweet 7-ounce fruits with orange flesh; midseason; AAS winner; red and pink forms also available; (VF).

'**Hybrid Ace**': Determinate; hybrid red standard with mild-flavored 6-ounce fruits; late; adapted for the West.

'**Ida Gold**': Determinate; open-pollinated orange standard with low-acid 2-ounce fruits; early; bred for cold regions.

'**Jetstar**': Indeterminate; hybrid red standard with high yields of firm, meaty, low-acid 8-ounce fruits; midseason; does best when staked and pruned; (VF).

'**Lemon Boy**': Indeterminate; hybrid yellow standard with mild 7-ounce globe-shaped fruits;

midseason; widely adapted; (VFN).

'**Marglobe**': Vigorous determinate; open-pollinated red standard with sweet 6-ounce fruits; popular old home and commercial cultivar; midseason; susceptible to cracking; (F).

'**Mountain Pride**': Determinate; hybrid red standard with smooth 7-ounce fruits; midseason; disease-resistant "Mountain" series bred for hot, humid regions; (VFF$_2$AsL).

'**Oregon Spring**': Determinate; open-pollinated red standard with 6-ounce seedless globe-shaped fruits; early; adapted for regions with short, cool summers; (V).

'**Oxheart**': Indeterminate; open-pollinated large rose-pink beefsteak bearing fleshy, mild-flavored 1-pound heart-shaped fruits; late; do not prune ('Yellow Oxheart' is also available).

'**Pixie**': Determinate; hybrid red cherry bearing 1¾-inch fruits with excellent flavor; early; compact 16-inch plants suited to container growing ('Orange Pixie' is also available).

'**Porter**': Indeterminate; open-pollinated pink-red heirloom cherry type with egg-shaped, meaty 1-ounce fruits; midseason; Texas cultivar that thrives in heat and drought.

'**Principe Borghese**': Indeterminate; open-pollinated red heirloom cultivar with 1-ounce plum-shaped fruits for sun-drying; midseason.

'**Pruden's Purple**': Indeterminate; open-pollinated pink-purple heirloom standard with flattened, meaty 1-pound fruits; midseason; potato-leaf foliage.

'**Quick Pick**': Indeterminate; hybrid red standard with heavy yields of meaty 5-ounce fruits; early to midseason; (VFF$_2$NTA).

"**Roma VF**": Vigorous determinate; open-pollinated red paste bearing fleshy, plum-shaped 2-ounce fruits for paste and sauce; midseason to late; disease-resistant form of 'Roma'; (VF).

'**Rutgers**': Vigorous determinate; open-pollinated red standard bearing high yields of 8-ounce fruits with mild flavor; late; widely adapted favorite; (F).

'**San Marzano**': Indeterminate; open-pollinated red heirloom paste bearing clusters of mild-flavored 3-inch-long fruits; late; also known as 'Italian Canner'; good for drying.

'**Siberia**': Determinate; open-pollinated red standard with 3-ounce fruits with fair flavor; early; Siberian cultivar that sets fruit at extremely low temperatures; good high-altitude cultivar.

'**Solar Set**': Determinate; hybrid red standard with uniform 8-ounce fruits; midseason; bred to set fruit at high temperature; (VFF$_2$A).

'**Stupice**': Indeterminate; open-pollinated red standard bearing large crops of 2-ounce fruits; early short-season cultivar from Czechoslovakia; compact vines with potato-leaf foliage.

'**Sub-Arctic Maxi**': Determinate; open-pollinated red standard with 2½-ounce fruits; early; bred for extremely cold climates; best of the Canadian Sub-Arctic series.

'**Sungold**': Indeterminate; hybrid gold cherry bearing long trusses of superbly flavored, crack-resistant 1-inch fruits; early; heavy yields; (FT).

'**Sweet 100**': Indeterminate; hybrid red cherry bearing huge crops of 1-inch fruits in grapelike clusters; early; best of the red cherry cultivars; should be staked and pruned.

'**Taxi**': Determinate; open-pollinated yellow standard with firm 5-ounce fruits; early to midseason; compact vine requires no staking; widely adapted.

'**Tiny Tim**': Determinate; open-pollinated red cherry with ¾-inch fruits; early; dwarf cultivar (13-inch vine) with rugose (wrinkled) foliage; often grown as an ornamental; does best in pots or hanging baskets; (As).

'**Tumbler**': Determinate; hybrid red cherry with sweet 1-inch fruits; early; bred for hanging baskets and pots.

'**White Beauty**': Indeterminate; open-pollinated white heirloom standard with fleshy, sweet-flavored 8-ounce fruits; late; also listed as 'Snowball'.

'**Whopper**': Indeterminate; hybrid red standard with heavy yields of 12-ounce fruits; midseason; favorite southern cultivar but widely adapted; (VFNT).

'**Yellow Bell**': Indeterminate; open-pollinated yellow heirloom paste bearing clusters of sweet, rich 3-inch-long fruits; early; adapted to cool conditions.

continued from page 407

sunlight. To slow the ripening of green tomatoes, store in a cooler location, 50° to 55°F.

Most tomatoes do not cross-pollinate, so saving seeds doesn't require limiting yourself to only one cultivar. Be sure to choose the best fruits from the most vigorous and healthy open pollinated plants. Seeds are viable for 4 years; store in airtight containers in a dark, cool location.

TOMATO, HUSK. See *Tomatillo*
TOMATO, STRAWBERRY. See *Tomatillo*

TURNIP

Brassica rapa, Rapa group. Mustard family, Brassicaceae. Biennial grown as an annual.

○ ◐ ❋ ▮

If you read cookbooks from 50 years ago—"Boil until tender and serve with a white sauce made of milk boiled til it thickens, into which has been stirred a little butter" is a standard recipe—you won't be surprised to learn that the turnip has slipped off the list of favorite vegetables and disappeared from many seed catalogs. Yet turnips once were widely admired and grown.

In the 16th century, cooks carved them into cathedrals and ships, vegetative centerpieces for the dinner tables of aristocrats. Although prepared less ingeniously, they also were a staple of the early American dinner table. In a 1637 letter to his wife,

---

TRY TYFON

Tyfon, or Holland greens, is a lesser-known *Brassica rapa*, Rapa group member, a cross between a turnip and a Chinese cabbage. Planted for its mild-flavored tops, which can be used in salads or for cooked greens, tyfon's cultural requirements are identical to the turnip's. Named cultivars are not available.

John Winthrop, the first governor of the Massachusetts Bay colony, reports on his health, prays for peace on his family, sends kisses and affection, and closes with a reminder to gather the turnips. By the middle of the 19th century, more than 85 different turnips were being grown in the United States and Canada, including giant cultivars that averaged 35 pounds. (The *Guiness Book of World Records* gives the modern record to a 51-pounder grown in Alaska.)

While turnips are a cool-weather vegetable—Alaska's world's record proves that—they can be cultivated successfully throughout North America; however, they're usually grown as a winter crop in warm areas. Most cultivars have deeply lobed, rough-textured leaves and the visual bonus of red or white roots breaking the soil surface, but their ornamental value is limited.

DECIDING WHAT TO GROW

Turnips are traditionally divided on the basis of root shape: flat, globe, egg-shaped, or cylindrical. They could be just as well divided by color: bicolor (purple/red and white, green and white), white, red, yellow, and black. Turnip aficionados may argue about subtle differences in flavor, but most gardeners, even keen ones, won't detect the distinction. Another option is to choose on the basis of the harvest: Roots, greens, or both? While the leaves of all cultivars are edible, several turnips bred exclusively for their greens—called "foliage turnips"—have tough, fibrous roots that cannot be eaten.

Turnips mature quickly. The tops are ready to pick in less than a month after sowing, roots in between 30 and 60 days. Plant successively at 2-week intervals—both spring and fall crops—to spread out the harvest, timing plantings so that roots mature when the temperatures are still cool. Spring turnips can be interplanted with other crops, such as tomatoes, peppers, cucumbers, and squash. For eating fresh, a 30-foot row should produce enough turnips for a family of four; if you want to preserve, increase the planting.

SITE & SOIL

No prima donnas, turnips are willing to grow under almost any conditions. But give them ideal conditions—full sun and moderately rich, near-neutral (pH 6.8 to 7.5) soil that is well-drained and has been amended with humus—and you'll shorten the time between sowing and harvesting, which means larger, more succulent greens and roots. Because turnips prefer soil on the sweet side, sprinkle a handful or two of wood ashes over the seedbed before planting.

To promote healthy root development, make sure the soil is well dug to a depth of at least 1 foot. Beware of adding high-nitrogen amendments, which will produce lush tops but small roots, but be generous with phosphorus—contained in bonemeal and rock phosphate—which will support good root development. Make sure turnip plants receive an even supply of water, but the soil should be moist, not waterlogged.

Like other small roots crops, turnips do well in containers, although they leave a space when harvested. Use a container, at least 8 inches wide and 12 inches deep, with good bottom drainage, and fill with enriched potting soil. Water frequently, and feed every 4 weeks with compost tea.

HOW TO GROW

The trick to growing sweet, crisp turnips is making sure they mature quickly when the weather is cool. Hot, dry conditions cause roots to be off-flavored, small, and woody. In spring, sow seeds as soon as the ground can be worked; fall crops should be planted in mid- or late summer, timed to harvest around the average first-frost date. In 50°F soil, germination takes between 5 and 7 days.

Sow seeds ¼ inch deep, 1 inch apart, with 12 inches between rows. If you're growing turnips only for their tops, don't bother to thin; for turnip roots, thin plants to 4 inches. Be ruthless when thinning; crowded plants won't develop good roots. The thinnings, which should be cut rather than pulled, can be used as greens. Once plants are established, mulch with organic matter to help keep the soil cool, moist, and weed-free. Turnips are light feeders and do not need to be fertilized during the growing season.

POTENTIAL PROBLEMS

Turnips are potential heirs to most of the insect pests and diseases that attack brassicas such as broccoli and cabbage, but plants that are not stressed by heat or drought tend to be problem-free. To protect against the most common insects, such as aphids, flea beetles, and cabbage root maggots, cover the planting bed with a floating row cover immediately

TURNIP CULTIVARS

Turnips, which tolerate almost any conditions, are grouped by the shape of their roots. A few cultivars have been bred soley for their nutritious greens

'All Top': 40 days; hybrid; grown exclusively for its greens; bolt-resistant.

'Di Milan': 35 days; open-pollinated; flat purple-white bicolor; can be pulled as "baby" turnip; French heirloom; standard home-garden cultivar.

'Golden Ball': 55 days; open-pollinated; yellow globe with yellow flesh; spring or fall cultivar; heirloom, also known as 'Orange Jelly'.

'Hakurei': 38 days; hybrid; flat white root; root or greens are good for fresh use; early.

'Hinona-kabu': 45 days; open-pollinated; cylindrical purple-white bicolor; bolts easily; Japanese cultivar.

'Just Right': 55 days; hybrid; fattened white globe; spring or fall cultivar; AAS winner.

'Longue de Caluire': 55 days; open-pollinated; cylindrical black root with white flesh; French cultivar.

'Presto': 30 days; open-pollinated; small white globe; very fast-maturing; good pickling cultivar; dislikes extreme heat or cold.

'Purple-Top Milan': 45 days; open-pollinated; flat purple-white bicolor; excellent for storage; heirloom.

'Purple-Top White Globe': 55 days; open-pollinated; purple-white bicolor globe; heirloom; standard cultivar.

'Scarlet Ball': 55 days; open-pollinated; red semi-globe with white flesh; attractive red-veined stems and foliage.

'Tokyo Cross': 40 days; hybrid; white semi-globe; disease-resistant; good spring or fall cultivar; AAS winner.

after sowing seeds. A good crop-rotation scheme will prevent most diseases that attack turnips. (For specific problems and remedies, see *Cabbage* on page 204.)

HARVESTING

Begin pulling roots when they are still small (1 to 2 inches in diameter), crisp, and sweet; greens can be cut as soon as they are large enough use, as many as 3 weeks before the roots are ready. If you want to harvest both greens and roots, leave at least five or six leaves on each plant so that its root will continue to develop.

Make sure you harvest some turnip greens, since that's where the nutrient wallop of this vegetable lies. The leaves are rich in vitamins A, B$_2$, C, and E, plus calcium, potassium, and iron; the roots, in contrast, contain one-sixth as much vitamin C as the leaves do. Light frosts make turnip roots sweeter, which is why most gardeners grow them as a fall crop, but repeated hard freezes will kill the tops and damage the roots. Mulching heavily will extend the time roots can be left in the ground. To store turnips, cut the tops off 2 inches above the root, place in plastic bags to retain moisture, and refrigerate. Turnips can be stored for longer periods of time in damp sand or sawdust in a cold (32° to 40°F) location.

Because turnips are biennials and normally don't flower until their second season, saving seeds is difficult. Gardeners in cold climates must dig and overwinter plants, then replant them in the spring; in frost-free regions, carry plants over to a second year. Turnips will cross-pollinate with each other and other *B. rapa* members, such as Chinese cabbage. To save seeds that will come true, plant only one *B. rapa* cultivar. Seeds are viable for 4 years; store in airtight containers in a dark, cool location.

TURNIP-ROOTED CELERY. See *Celeriac*
TYFON. See *Turnip*

UPLAND CRESS

Barbarea verna. Mustard family, Brassicaceae.
Biennial grown as an annual.

○ ◑ ❄ ▯ ▮

Easy-to-grow upland cress is a cool-weather green with a flavor similar to watercress. When young,

Upland cress with chrysanthemum greens

both plants have a similar spicy flavor, although as upland cress matures, its leaves communicate more of its mustard-family heritage. Fortunately, upland cress is much easier to accommodate in the backyard garden than watercress: It is able to grow in far drier garden conditions than moisture-loving watercress can abide. It can be cultivated in USDA Zone 3 and warmer.

Formerly classified as *B. praecox*, upland cress is also called land cress, winter cress, and Belle Isle cress. Because of its high vitamin C content, it is also known by the less poetic name scurvy grass. Its genus name, *Barbarea*, refers to the third-century martyr Barbara, the patron saint of miners, who is depicted in Raphael's "Sistine Madonna." According to tradition, she healed wounds by using upland cress, which is one of the few plants that is still green on her Saint's day, December 4.

Mature upland cress plants form a rosette that can reach more than 12 inches across. The dark green leaves are deeply cut in five to eight lobes and rounded at the tips, not unlike arugula or parsley.

When grown in combination with other early and late-season salad greens, 8 to 10 upland cress plants are probably sufficient for a family of four. To lengthen the harvest season, it is a good idea to sow successive crops of upland cress from early spring until late summer.

Moderately ornamental, upland cress can be incorporated in the flower garden or grown on a deck, patio, or rooftop in pots or boxes. Use a moderately large container with good drainage. Fill with a light, enriched potting mix, and keep plants well watered. Feed every 3 weeks with manure or compost tea.

HOW TO GROW

Upland cress thrives in spring and fall, when temperatures are cool. A late summer planting as far north as Zone 4 can produce a second harvest of salad greens until the snow flies. With some protection, such as a mulch of straw or other loose organic material, plants will overwinter and resume growth in the spring, providing greens for a few weeks until the plants begin to flower and go to seed. In warm regions, upland cress is normally grown in late summer or early fall for harvesting in winter and spring.

Stress-free conditions—moisture, good soil, and cool temperatures—produce the best-tasting upland cress. Grow it in humus-rich soil with a slightly acidic pH, between 5.8 and 6.5. For best flavor, be sure plants receive at least 1 inch of water a week. Upland cress will grow in full sun or partial shade. Afternoon shade helps protect late spring or early fall crops from warm summer temperatures. If the mercury in your garden soars in summer, consider planting this and other cool-weather greens on the east side of a trellis of peas or pole beans or in a north-facing bed.

Sow seeds—no cultivars are available—¼ inch deep, 1 inch apart, directly in the garden as soon as the soil can be worked, as early as 6 weeks before the date of the last expected frost, and/or sow in late summer for an autumn harvest. Germination takes about 6 days in 70°F soil, longer in colder ground. Keep the soil evenly moist until seedlings appear. Thin plants as they grow, ultimately spacing them from 4 to 6 inches apart. A weekly watering with dilute manure tea will provide a nutritional boost and keep plants growing vigorously. Plants mature in 50 days, although the leaves can reach harvestable size in less than 30 days.

Given adequate moisture and cool weather, upland cress is bothered by few insects or diseases. Aphids, which are troublesome if temperatures rise, can be controlled by using floating row covers. (See "Controlling Common Pests" on page 162 for more information and for control measures.)

HARVESTING

Begin picking individual leaves, which are rich in vitamin C, as soon as they are large enough to be used, harvesting from the outside of the plant. The outer leaves become unpleasantly hot-tasting as the season progresses. As plants grow larger, harvest new leaves from the plant's center rather than the outer leaves. Alternatively—for use as a cooked green like kale—cut entire plants when they reach maturity. Leaves can be stored in the refrigerator for up to 1 week.

Because upland cress is a biennial, saving seeds requires overwintering plants, which produce yellow flowers in midspring of their second year. Plants will not cross with others cresses, which are members of different species, but they may cross with *Barbarea vulgaris*, a closely related plant commonly known as winter cress and yellow rocket that has naturalized in North America. Seeds are viable for 4 years; store in airtight containers in a dark, cool location.

WATERCRESS

Nasturtium officinale. Mustard family, Brassicaceae. Perennial.

○ ◐ ☀ ❄ ▮

Peppery-tasting watercress is a popular salad green grown for its dark green compound leaves, but it isn't a plant for every garden. That's because it's an aquatic perennial and requires constantly wet soil, a nearly impossible condition to maintain in the average, well-drained backyard vegetable garden. Don't rule out growing watercress entirely, though, because there are realistic options for accommodating it that don't include buying property with a babbling brook.

Despite its genus name, *Nasturtium*, watercress is unrelated to the common garden nasturtium (*Tropaeolum majus*), a popular annual with peppery edible leaves and flowers. (In an odd turn of botanical nomenclature, nasturtiums are in the nasturtium family, Tropaeolaceae, while watercress's small summer clusters of white, four-petaled flowers mark it as a mustard-family plant.) The name *Nasturtium* is derived from the Greek *nasus*, for "nose," and *tortus*, "twist," the latter a term that the Roman Pliny applied to pungent plants.

A native of Europe, watercress has naturalized in many parts of North America since colonial times. Watercress's Johnny Appleseed may have been Ferdinand Hayden, the head of the U.S. Geological Survey of the Western Territories, whose trips in the mid-1800s led to Yellowstone becoming the first national park. Hayden reportedly planted watercress in every freshwater spring that his party passed, apparently as a hedge against scurvy.

Most seed catalogs list watercress under its generic name. When buying seeds, make sure you are purchasing *Nasturtium officinale*, not one of the other cresses, which belong to different genera. A few specialists may list cultivars with names like 'Springhead' or 'Waltham'. These are English towns where the strain has been grown, although they probably aren't significantly different from one another. 'Broad Leaf' is an improved cultivar with larger leaves than the species', which has small, round foliage and creeping stems that root easily, but it is not widely available. Plants are hardy in USDA Zone 3 and warmer.

Watercress

SITE & SOIL

Gardeners blessed with a stream or stream-fed pond on their property can accommodate watercress easily by planting it in the humus-rich soil at the water's edge, either in full sun or light shade. It is also possible to divert a spring or stream through a series of trenches dug in soil that has been amended with organic matter. In this case, dig the trenches so that water enters at the top of the bed and exits from the bottom, then plant watercress at the bottom of the trenches. Whatever the arrangement, however, grow watercress only on sites with clean, safe water, because the plants are sensitive to pollution; avoid locations contaminated by runoff from pastures or faulty sewage systems.

Container culture is also an option, although a high-maintenance one. Plant watercress in clay pots filled with a porous planting medium, such as a mix of compost, coarse sand, and vermiculite, and set the pots in pans of cool water, which must be changed daily to keep the water fresh. Another option is to set tubs of watercress in a water garden. Make sure the tubs have plenty of drainage holes, and prop them up on bricks so that they are even with the water surface.

HOW TO GROW

Once its demand for a constant source of cool, fresh, clean water is met, watercress is relatively easy to grow. Its pH preference is 6.0 to 7.0, and in the right site, plants will provide a bountiful harvest for years with few, if any, insect or disease problems. Plants not grown in running water may be attacked by aphids, but a stiff spray of water from the hose every few days will provide control.

To start watercress from seeds, begin indoors 6 to 8 weeks before the last-frost date or sow outdoors where the plants are to grow about 1 month before the last-frost date. The seeds are tiny—155,000 per ounce—and need light to sprout, so cover them only slightly and keep the soil moist. Germination should occur in about 1 week in soil with a temperature of 70°F. Watercress gets off to a slow start—about 90 days to mature plants. In long-season areas, plants may be large enough for a first harvest by fall, but in regions with more brief growing seasons, watercress won't be ready for cutting until the following year.

Far quicker and easier than starting from seeds is propagating from cuttings or divisions. Even watercress purchased from the supermarket usually will root—each piece should contain a node—and can be used to begin your patch of this pungent perennial. Set the pieces in a container of damp sand; roots will develop in about 1 week. Transplant outdoors as soon as new leaves appear.

HARVESTING

Watercress has two harvest seasons. The first is in spring, before plants flower; the second is in autumn, after the plants have died back and new growth appears. Harvest by shearing the top 3 or 4 inches of each plant or by pulling whole plants. Seeds, which appear on the plants in midsummer, can be harvested for sprouting. (See *Sprouts* on page 380 for directions.)

Watercress, which contains good amounts of vitamins A, C, B_1, B_2, and E, calcium, and iron, can be sealed in slotted plastic bags or can be set in a glass of water and stored for about 1 week in the refrigerator.

Watercress is best propagated from cuttings or divisions. Gardeners can save seeds for replanting, although the small, curved pods shatter easily, making the seeds difficult to collect. Watercress does not cross-pollinate with other cresses.

WATERMELON

Citrullus lanatus. Gourd family, Cucurbitaceae.
Annual.

○ ＊ ▮

Most gardeners are surprised to learn that although the watermelon is the sweetest member of the same family as muskmelons, cantaloupes, and honeydews, those crops are more closely related to cucumbers. Watermelon's closest cousin is the citron melon (*C. lanatus*, Citroides group), which has hard white flesh and is used for preserves and pickles, rather than eaten fresh. White-fleshed watermelons, although rare today, were popular in 19th-century America. `Ice Cream', which is still available today, started off with white flesh and white seeds. Over time, however, its flesh became pink, then red, and its seeds black, testimony to the ease with which watermelons cross-pollinate.

Mark Twain insisted that the watermelon, a vining native of tropical Africa, is "chief of this

Watermelon 'Birjuchekutskit'

world's luxuries . . . . When one has tasted it, he knows what angels eat. It was not a Southern watermelon that Eve took; we know it because she repented." The contemporary writer Charles Simic switched the religious reference to describe watermelon in his four-line poem:

Great Buddhas
On the fruit stand.
We eat the smile
And spit out the teeth.

Gardeners have been spitting out watermelon seeds for more than 4,000 years. At the same time, they've been saving seeds from the best melons and crossbreeding to produce both larger and smaller fruits, plants with compact vines, cultivars that mature faster and are disease-resistant and, beginning in the 1940s, seedless watermelons. The smile remains, but the teeth are gone.

Watermelons can be grown in USDA Zone 4 and warmer. To be successful, gardeners in colder areas may have to grow short-season cultivars and use heat-enhancing techniques.

DECIDING WHAT TO GROW

Days to maturity should be the home gardener's first thought when deciding which watermelon to plant. Most cultivars take more than 85 days from transplanting, which means more than 110 days in total. Space may be the second consideration. If your garden is small, choose a compact, or bush, cultivar, such as 'Garden Baby', which has 3-foot-long vines. These smaller cultivars also can be grown on a rooftop, deck, or patio. Use a large container, at least 24 inches deep, with good bottom drainage, and fill with enriched potting soil. Water frequently, and feed every 2 weeks with fish emulsion or manure tea.

Growing large (those weighing more than 25 pounds) and medium-size (18 to 24 pounds) watermelons should be left to gardeners with ideal conditions. Gardeners with short or cool seasons are better off trying the small "icebox" types—watermelons like 'Sugar Baby' that mature more quickly and weigh between 5 and 15 pounds.

Be warned, too, that seedless watermelons, hybrid triploid cultivars like 'Chiffon' or 'Seedless Sugar Baby', tend to be less vigorous and more difficult to grow than seeded cultivars. Begin seeds indoors, and make sure that your garden includes at least one "pollinating" plant, because seedless plants don't generate enough pollen to fertilize flowers and form fruits. The seed packet will contain pollinator seeds, which are usually marked by a pink dye.

Watermelon shape—round, oval, or oblong—has no effect on culture; however, flesh color may, with many gardeners claiming that nonred melons

---

WATERMELON CULTIVARS

Select watermelons cultivars that will ripen reliably in your climate. Beginners and gardeners with less-than-ideal conditions will have the best success with red-fleshed, icebox-size types. Keep in mind that days to maturity are from transplanting.

'Allsweet': 95 days; open-pollinated; red flesh; 25 to 30 pounds; disease-resistant.

'Chiffon': 80 days; hybrid; yellow flesh; 10 to 15 pounds; seedless; round fruits.

'Cole's Early': 80 days; open-pollinated; red flesh; 10 pounds; good short-season cultivar; heirloom.

'Cream of Saskatchewan': 85 days; open-pollinated; white flesh; 8 to 10 pounds; good short-season cultivar; heirloom.

'Crimson Sweet': 85 days; open-pollinated; red flesh; 20 to 30 pounds; vigorous plants; disease-resistant; widely adapted; AAS winner.

'Fordhook Hybrid': 75 days; hybrid; red flesh; 14 pounds; vigorous plants; early.

'Garden Baby': 75 days; hybrid; red flesh; 7 to 10 pounds; round fruits; compact plant; very early.

'Golden Crown': 85 days; hybrid; red flesh (gold skin); 8 pounds; few seeds; AAS winner.

'Jack of Hearts': 85 days; hybrid; red flesh; 10 to 13 pounds; seedless; superior disease resistance.

'Moon & Stars': 100 days; open-pollinated; flesh varies (pink, red, yellow); medium to large fruits (25 to 30 pounds.); needs long warm season; to mature; heirloom.

'New Orchid': 80 days; hybrid; orange flesh; 8 to 12 pounds; round fruits.

'Seedless Sugar Baby': 80 days; hybrid; red flesh; 8 pounds; seedless.

'Sugar Baby': 80 days; open-pollinated; red flesh; 8 to 10 pounds; round fruits; widely adapted; good home-garden cultivar.

'Sunshine': 75 days; hybrid; yellow flesh; 8 to 10 pounds; compact plants.

'Sweet Favorite': 80 days; hybrid; red flesh; 10 to 15 pounds; vigorous plants; disease-resistant; northern favorite; AAS winner.

'Tendersweet Orange Fleshed': 90 days; open-pollinated; orange flesh; 35 pounds; very sweet.

'Tiger Baby': 80 days; hybrid; pink to red flesh; 8 to 10 pounds.

'Tom Watson': 95 days; open-pollinated; red flesh; 25 to 40 pounds; productive; good short-season cultivar; heirloom.

'Yellow Baby': 75 days; hybrid; yellow flesh; 5 to 8 pounds; small seeds; AAS winner.

'Yellow Doll': 65 days; hybrid; yellow flesh; 5 to 7 pounds; round fruits; semi-compact plant.

(colors range from white to yellow, orange, and deep red) are more particular and difficult to grow. Interestingly, flesh color has little relationship to flavor or sweetness (on average, watermelons contain about 12 percent sugar). Watermelon rinds also vary—rinds can be everything from gold through dark green to near-black and may be a solid color to striped and mottled. The legendary heirloom 'Moon & Stars' gets its name from its unusual dark green rind, dotted with bright yellow spots.

One plant of a standard cultivar should yield three or four watermelons; bush cultivars average two to three fruits per plant. As with other melons, pollination is more important in determining overall yield than is the cultivar you are growing. Yields vary depending on how successfully bees and other insects pollinate the flowers. If conditions are poor—rainy and cold, for example—and bees few, yields will be down.

HOW TO GROW

The requirements and culture of watermelons are nearly identical to those of other melons: a long, hot growing season; full sun; and fertile, near-neutral soil. Since they are slightly more rambling than other melons are, give watermelons about 6 feet between hills; bush types can be set 3 to 4 feet apart. Trellising watermelons—with the possible exception of small icebox types—is not recommended.

Above all, don't rush into the garden when the soil and air are still cold. Watermelons won't tolerate even a hint of frost, and their seeds won't germinate in cold soil. Wait 2 to 3 weeks after the last frost—until the average air temperature is 65°F and the soil has also reached at least 65°F—before sowing seeds (1 inch deep) or transplanting seedlings. Fertilize plants with compost tea every 3 weeks, beginning when they flower and set fruits. (For detailed instructions, see *Melon* on page 296.)

Despite the name, watermelons are remarkably drought-resistant and less susceptible to diseases and insects than are other melons. By rotating crops and using plastic mulches and floating row covers, gardeners should be able to sidestep most potential problems. Watermelon mosaic virus, which results in yellow, mottled foliage, stunted vines, and deformed fruits, cannot be cured. Remove and destroy any affected plants. Next season, take special care to control aphids, which spread the disease. (For more

Watermelon 'Georgia Rattlesnake'

information about other watermelon foes—fusarium wilt, alternaria blight, anthracnose, and early blight—see "Controlling Common Diseases" on page 169.) Cucumber beetles and aphids can also attack watermelons. (See "Controlling Common Pests" on page 162 for control measures.)

Poor flavor and/or lack of sweetness can have several causes, beginning with growing a poorly adapted cultivar. Other causes are poor fertility, cool temperatures, overly wet weather, and inadequate foliage.

HARVESTING

It's not always easy to know when a watermelon, which contains vitamin C, is ready to pick. Experts recommend marking the time of full bloom—the first fruits should be ripe about 35 days later. Other signs of maturity? The tendrils, or curls, near the fruit stem yellow and die back; the "ground spot," the portion of the melon sitting on the soil, changes from white to cream or yellow; the melon rind takes on a dull cast and becomes slightly ridged or rough; and last, and least reliable, the melon gives off a hollow "thud" sound when thumped.

Cut, don't pull, watermelons from the vines, leaving a 1- to 2-inch stem. Whole fruits can be stored for about 1 week in a dark, cool location (50° to 60°F); watermelons that have been sliced into should be stored in the refrigerator.

Although they do not interbreed with other melons, all watermelon cultivars will cross-pollinate. To produce seeds that will come true, plant only one cultivar. Seeds are viable for 6 years; store in airtight containers in a dark, cool location.

WILD MARJORAM. See *Oregano*

WINGED BEAN

Psophocarpus tetragonolobus. Pea family, Fabaceae.
Perennial grown as an annual.

○ ✳ ❀

True winged beans are tropical plants, climbers that do well only in hot, humid climates. Although all the plant's parts are edible—seeds, leaves, flowers, pods, and tubers—it is the pods that most gardeners are after. Cultivated for centuries in Asia and India, winged beans thrive only where days are short, water is plentiful, and sunstroke is common—USDA Zone 7 and warmer. Variously referred to as gao beans, asparagus peas, asparagus beans, four-angled beans, Manila beans, and princess peas, the common names for winged beans overlap with other species, so check for the correct botanical name before you purchase seeds.

Winged beans have never been a popular crop in North America, although one 19th-century source called it "an agreeable dish, not unlike string-beans." In addition to sweltering temperatures, to foster winged beans, you'll need loose, organically rich soil that drains well and has an alkaline pH (7.0 to 8.0). If you can provide the right conditions, the reward is clusters of reddish brown flowers followed by long, waxy four-sided beans, each with fluted wings like those on the long necks of mythical sea monsters. Trellised plants can be used as a screen in the landscape or to form a background for an ornamental garden.

While there are named cultivars—'Bogor' and 'Chimbu' are the most common—most seed catalogs list this plant simply as winged or gao bean. Begin with six or eight plants for a family of four; if you want to preserve, increase the planting.

HOW TO GROW

If you don't have a long, hot growing season, cross winged beans off your list. Plants require a minimum of 125 days to produce mature pods and about 180 days to form tubers. Starting seeds indoors is no solution for a too-short season, because winged beans are light/dark-sensitive and won't bloom until late summer, when days grow shorter and nights longer.

But if you have at least 200 frost-free days, sow seeds direct, 1 inch deep, at the base of a sturdy 8-foot support, such as netting, a wire trellis, tepees, or heavy strings. Plants are largely untroubled by diseases and pests. Feed every 3 weeks with manure tea, and make sure plants receive 1 to 2 inches of water a week. To retain moisture and suppress weeds, mulch once the plants are established.

HARVESTING

Every part of winged beans, which are a first-rate protein source, can be eaten. Pick pods when they are immature and still tender, 6 to 8 inches long, and prepare them as you would common green beans. Harvest every day or two to keep up with the crop and to encourage plants to continue producing. Or allow the pods to mature, and shell them like soybeans. Harvest the small tubers, which are similar to Jerusalem artichokes, by digging them after the plants have been killed by frost.

Winged bean flowers are self-pollinating, so crossing is unlikely, even when cultivars are grown next to each other. Save seeds from the most vigorous and healthy plants. Seeds are viable for about 4 years; store in airtight containers in a dark, cool location.

WINTER CAULIFLOWER. See *Broccoli*
WINTER PURSLANE. See *Miner's Lettuce*
WINTER SAVORY. See *Savory*
WINTER SQUASH. See *Squash*
WITLOOF CHICORY. See *Chicory*
ZUCCHINI. See *Squash*

ASPARAGUS PEA

Asparagus pea, *Tetragonolobus purpureus*, is another member of the pea family. Its pods, which taste faintly of asparagus, look like miniature winged beans and should be harvested when they are tender and very small—at 1 to 2 inches in length. Plants are low and spreading, making them useful as groundcovers and in window boxes and hanging pots, where their pealike reddish flowers can be seen easily. Don't confuse this plant with asparagus bean, which is a large vining plant that prefers hot conditions; asparagus peas are half-hardy and do best in temperate regions, USDA Zone 4 and warmer.

APPENDIX

READING ABOUT GARDENING

Ashworth, Suzanne. *Seed to Seed: Seed Saving Techniques for the Vegetable Gardener* (Seed Savers Exchange, 1991)

Ball Blue Book: A Guide to Home Canning and Freezing (Alltrista Corporation, 1995; to obtain a copy, write to the Alltrista Corporation, Consumer Affairs Department, P.O. Box 2729, Muncie, IN 47307-0729)

Ball, Jeff. *Rodale's Garden Problem Solver* (Rodale Press, 1988)

Barash, Cathy Wilkinson. *Edible Flowers: From Garden to Palate* (Fulcrum Publishing, 1993)

Beard, Henry, and Roy McKie. *Gardening: A Gardener's Dictionary* (Workman Publishing, 1982)

Bennett, Jennifer. *The Harrowsmith Northern Gardener* (Camden House Publishing, 1982)

Bennett, Jennifer. *The Tomato Handbook* (Firefly Books Ltd., 1997)

Bowles, John Paul, ed. *Soils* (Brooklyn Botanic Garden, 1986)

Brown, Deni. *The Herb Society of America Encyclopedia of Herbs & Their Uses* (Dorling Kindersley, 1995)

Bubel, Mike, and Nancy Bubel. *Root Cellaring* (Rodale Press, 1979)

Bubel, Nancy. *The New Seed-Starters Handbook* (Rodale Press, 1988)

Buchanan, Rita, ed. *Taylor's Guide to Herbs* (Houghton Mifflin, 1995)

Burr, Fearing. *The Field and Garden Vegetables of America* (The American Botanist, 1988, first published 1863, 1865)

Campbell, Stu. *Let It Rot!* (Storey Communications, Inc., 1975)

Carr, Anna, *Good Neighbors: Companion Planting for Gardeners* (Rodale Press, 1985)

Christopher, Tom, and Marty Asher. *Compost This Book!* (Sierra Club Books, 1994)

Coleman, Eliot. *The New Organic Gardener* (Chelsea Green Publishing Company, rev. ed. 1995)

Coleman, Eliot. *The New Organic Grower's Four-Season Harvest* (Chelsea Green Publishing Company, 1993)

Creasy, Rosalind. *The Complete Book of Edible Landscaping* (Sierra Club Books, 1982)

Crockett, James. *Crockett's Victory Garden* (Little, Brown and Company, 1977)

Cutler, Karan Davis, ed. *Tantalizing Tomatoes* (Brooklyn Botanic Garden, 1996)

Cutler, Karan Davis, ed. *Salad Gardens* (Brooklyn Botanic Garden, 1995)

DeWitt, Dave, and Paul Bosland. *The Pepper Garden* (Ten Speed Press, 1993)

Doscher, Paul, Timothy Fisher & Kathleen Kolb. *Efficient Vegetable Gardening* (The Globe Pequot Press, 1993)

Dunphy, Paul, "Zap the Bunny: Install This Simple, Safe Electric Fence to Deter Garden Raiders," *Harrowsmith Country Life*, May/June 1993

Ellis, Barbara, and Fern Marshall Bradley, eds. *The Organic Gardener's Handbook of Natural Insect and Disease Control* (Rodale Press, 1992)

Forsyth, Turid, and Merilyn Simonds Mohr. *The Harrowsmith Salad Garden* (Camden House, 1992)

Foster, Steven. *Herbal Bounty: The Gentle Art of Herb Culture* (Gibbs Smith, 1984)

Foster, Steven. *Herbal Renaissance: Growing, Using & Understanding Herbs in the Modern World* (Gibbs Smith, 1993)

Fussell, Betty. *The Story of Corn* (Alfred A. Knopf, 1992)

Gershuny, Grace. *Start With the Soil* (Rodale Press, 1993)

Greene, Janet, Ruth Hertzberg, and Beatrice Vaughn. *Putting Food By* (The Stephen Greene Press, 4th ed., 1991)

Hansen, Michael. *Pest Control for Home and Garden* (Consumer Reports Books, 1993)

Henderson, Peter. *Garden for Profit: A Guide to the Successful Cultivation of the Market and Family Garden* (The American Botanist, 1991, first published 1867, 1884)

Hill, Lewis. *Cold-Climate Gardening* (Storey Communications, Inc., 1987)

Hill, Thomas. *The Gardener's Labyrinth* (Oxford University Press, 1987, first published 1577)

Kourik, Robert. *Designing and Maintaining Your Edible Landscape Naturally* (Metamorphic Press, 1986)

Kourik, Robert. *Drip Irrigation for Every Landscape and All Climates* (Metamorphic Press, 1992)

Larkcom, Joy. *Oriental Vegetables: The Complete Guide for Garden and Kitchen* (Kodansha International, 1991)

Lavery, Bernard. *How to Grow Giant Vegetables* (HarperCollins, 1995)

Leyel, Hilda (Mrs. C. F. Leyel). *Herbal Delights* (Faber and Faber, 1937)

McClure, Susan. *The Harvest Gardener* (Storey Communications, Inc., 1992)

Ogden, Shepherd, and Ellen Ogden. *The Cook's Garden* (Rodale Press, 1989)

Olkowski, William, and Shelia Daar, and Helga Olkowski. *Common-Sense Pest Control* (Taunton Press, 1991)

Parnes, Robert. *Fertile Soil: A Grower's Guide to Organic and Inorganic Fertilizers.* (agAccess, 1990; available from agAccess, P.O. Box 2008, Davis, CA 95671)

Patent, Dorothy Hinshaw, and Diane E. Bilderback. *The Harrowsmith Country Life Book of Garden Secrets* (Camden House Publishing, 1991)

Pleasant, Barbara. *Warm-Climate Gardening* (Storey Communications, Inc., 1993)

Raver, Anne, ed. *A New Look at Vegetables* (Brooklyn Botanic Garden, 1993)

Riotte, Louise. *Astrological Gardening: The Ancient Wisdom of Successful Planting & Harvesting by the Stars* (Storey Communications, Inc., 1989)

Riotte, Louise. *Sleeping With a Sunflower: A Treasury of Old-Time Gardening Lore* (Storey Communications, Inc., 1987)

Rupp, Rebecca. *Blue Corn & Square Tomatoes: Unusual Facts About Common Garden Vegetables* (Storey Communications, Inc., 1987)

Smith, Miranda, and Anna Carr. *Garden Insect, Disease & Weed Identification Guide* (Rodale Press, 1988)

Snyder, Leon. *Gardening in the Upper Midwest* (University of Minnesota Press, 1978)

Solomon, Steve. *Growing Vegetables West of the Cascades* (Sasquatch Books, 1989)

Solomon, Steve. *Water-Wise Vegetables* (Sasquatch Books, 1993)

Stout, Ruth, and Richard Clemence. *The Ruth Stout No-Work Garden Book* (Rodale Press, 1971)

The New Alchemy Institute, *Gardening for All Seasons* (Brick House Publishing Company, 1983)

Thompson, Bob. *The New Victory Garden* (Little, Brown and Company, 1987)

Vilmorin-Andrieux, MM. *The Vegetable Garden* (Ten Speed Press, 1993, first published 1885)

Watson, Benjamin. *Taylor's Guide to Heirloom Vegetables* (Houghton Mifflin, 1996)

SOIL-TESTING SOURCES

I.F.M
333 Ohme Garden Road
Wenatchee, WA 98801

LaRamie Soils Service
P.O. Box 255
Laramie, WY 82070

Peaceful Valley Farm Supply
P.O. Box 2209
Grass Valley, CA 95945

Symo-Life Inc.
RD 1, Box 102
Gap, PA 17527

FOR MORE INFORMATION

The following list contains a variety of sources—from non-profits to web sites—that may be useful to vegetable and herb gardeners.

NON-PROFIT ASSOCIATIONS

The Abundant Life Seed Foundation, P.O. Box 772, Port Townsend, WA 98368

American Horticultural Society, 7931 East Boulevard Drive, Alexandria, VA 22308

American Horticultural Therapy Association, Wightman Road, Suite 300, Gaithersburg, MD 20879

Bio-Dynamic Farming & Gardening Association, P.O. Box 550, Kimberton, PA 19442

Bio-Integral Resource Center, P.O. Box 7414, Berkeley, CA 94707

CORNS, R-1, Box 32, Turpin, OK 73950

Ecology Action, 18001 Shafer Ranch Road, Willits, CA 95490

Heirloom Seed Project/Landis Valley Museum, 2451 Kissel Hill Road, Lancaster, PA 17601

Herb Society of America, Inc., 9019 Kirtland Chardon Road, Mentor, OH 44060

National Gardening Association, 180 Flynn Avenue, Burlington, VT 05401

Native Seeds/SEARCH, 2509 N. Campbell #325, Tucson, AZ 85719

Old Sturbridge Village, 1 Old Sturbridge Village Road, Sturbridge, MA 01566

Seed Savers Exchange & Flower and Herb Exchange, 3076 North Winn Road, Decorah, IA 52101

Thomas Jefferson Center for Historic Plants, Monticello, P.O. Box 316, Charlottesville, VA 22902

GARDEN PUBLICATIONS

Kitchen Garden, 63 South Main Street, Newtown, CT 06470

National Gardening, 180 Flynn Avenue, Burlington, VT 05401

Organic Gardening, 33 E. Minor Street, Emmaus, PA 18098

GARDEN BOOKS BY MAIL

The American Botanist, P.O. Box 532, Chillicothe, IL 61523

Capability's Books, 2379 Highway 46, Deer Park, WI 54007

SEEDS BY MAIL

More than 1,000 mail-order seed companies and nurseries are listed in Barbara Barton's *Gardening by Mail* (Houghton Mifflin Company, 5th ed., 1997)

GARDENING ON-LINE

With the caveat that web sites appear and disappear at lightning speed, a few of the best—and most stable—are:

http://www.usda.gov (the United States Department of Agriculture, the door to an astonishing wealth of gardening information and resources)

http://www.reeusda.gov/new/statepartners/usa.htm (the State Partners of the Cooperative State Research, Education, and Extension Service, the door to all 50 state Extension Services)

http://www.hcs.ohiostate.edu/hcs/webgarden/FactsheetFind2.html (the WebGarden Factsheet Database maintained by Ohio State University, an index to more than 10,000 accessible Extension Service fact sheets and other publications)

http://www.nysaes.cornell.edu/ent/biocontrol (the Cornell University Biological Control: A Guide to Natural Enemies in North America site, which provides photographs, descriptions, and information about the major biological controls)

For more on-line gardening site and information, use a search engine, such as AltaVista or Yahoo. Be sure to narrow your request as much as possible: Entering "vegetables" or even "tomatoes" will generate several thousand listings. You may also want to participate in a Usnet newsgroup, such as rec.gardens, or sign up with one of several Listserv groups that specialize in gardening.

FROST DATES AND GROWING SEASON LENGTHS

This chart lists probable spring and fall freeze dates, as well as growing-season lengths (freeze-free periods). The dates given are based on temperature readings collected by National Climatic Data Center observation stations and indicate a 50 percent probability that freezing temperatures will occur after the date listed in spring, or *before* the date in fall. The cities and towns listed have observation stations and were selected to give as broad a picture of the frost dates in each state as possible. States (Hawaii) and portions of states (southern California, for example) that do not experience frost are not listed, for obvious reasons.

Use these dates to gauge planting times, determine when crops may need protection from cool weather, as well as figure out whether a particular crop will have time to mature in your area. Talk to other gardeners in your neighborhood or the local Cooperative Extension Service for even more local data. Since most of the observation stations take readings at 5 feet above ground, the dates here are for probability of temperatures below 36°F, a good indicator that frost has reached ground-level crops. Weather is fickle, though, so keep in mind that 50 percent probability means 5 years out of 10, freezing temperatures will occur after these dates in spring or before them in fall. Plan accordingly by using season-extension devices such as cloches or by delaying planting. In general, adding 3 weeks to the spring date improves your chances (to 1 year in 10) that tender transplants won't be damaged by frost.

| STATE | FREEZE DATES | | FREEZE-FREE PERIOD |
	SPRING	FALL	(DAYS)
ALABAMA			
Birmingham	April 10	Oct. 25	198
Mobile	March 14	Nov. 14	244
Selma	March 29	Nov. 4	219
Valley Head	May 5	Oct. 10	157
ALASKA			
Fairbanks	May 30	Aug. 27	88
Juneau	June 3	Sept. 8	96
Sitka	May 15	Oct. 14	151
ARIZONA			
Flagstaff	June 21	Sept. 5	76
Phoenix	March 1	Nov. 30	273
Prescott	May 31	Oct. 1	122
Tucson	March 23	Nov. 21	242
Yuma	Feb. 2	Dec. 18	312
ARKANSAS			
Fort Smith	April 13	Oct. 21	190
Hot Springs	April 7	Oct. 31	207
Jonesboro	April 10	Oct. 23	196
Texarkana	March 27	Nov. 3	221
CALIFORNIA			
Bakersfield	March 2	Nov. 23	265
El Centro	March 10	Nov. 26	260
Eureka	March 29	Nov. 28	244
Fresno	March 29	Nov. 12	227
Red Bluff	March 31	Nov. 16	230
Sacramento	March 25	Nov. 17	236
San Francisco	Feb. 7	Dec. 10	307
Santa Cruz	April 27	Nov. 9	196
Yreka	June 3	Sept. 29	117
COLORADO			
Boulder	May 18	Sept. 29	133
Canon City	May 15	Sept. 30	138
Durango	June 18	Sept. 9	82

STATE	FREEZE DATES SPRING	FALL	FREEZE-FREE PERIOD (DAYS)
CONNECTICUT			
Danbury	May 18	Sept. 24	129
Middletown	May 9	Oct. 3	146
DELAWARE			
Dover	April 23	Oct. 18	178
Wilmington	April 25	Oct. 16	173
FLORIDA			
Gainesville	March 16	Nov. 17	245
Tallahassee	March 26	Nov. 4	222
Tampa	Feb. 9	Dec. 8	301
GEORGIA			
Albany	March 26	Nov. 1	220
Athens	April 7	Oct. 29	204
Dalton	April 17	Oct. 20	186
Macon	April 1	Oct. 30	211
IDAHO			
Boise	May 21	Sept. 27	129
Coeur D'Alene	May 26	Sept. 20	116
Pocatello	June 6	Sept. 8	93
ILLINOIS			
Peoria	May 6	Oct. 6	152
Rockford	May 13	Sept. 30	140
Springfield	April 30	Oct. 10	162
Waukegan	May 15	Oct. 6	143
INDIANA			
Evansville	April 23	Oct. 17	176
Indianapolis	May 3	Oct. 9	158
South Bend	May 12	Oct. 6	146
Terre Haute	May 6	Oct. 6	152
IOWA			
Ames	May 9	Sept. 29	142
Decorah	May 18	Sept. 19	123
Ottumwa	May 1	Oct. 10	161

STATE	FREEZE DATES SPRING	FALL	FREEZE-FREE PERIOD (DAYS)
KANSAS			
Colby	May 14	Sept. 27	135
Dodge City	April 27	Oct. 12	167
Topeka	May 1	Oct. 6	157
KENTUCKY			
Hopkinsville	April 22	Oct. 15	175
Lexington	April 29	Oct. 14	167
Middlesboro	May 7	Oct. 8	153
LOUISIANA			
Alexandria	March 20	Nov. 5	229
Houma	March 6	Nov. 15	253
Monroe	March 28	Oct. 27	212
MAINE			
Agusta	May 11	Sept. 28	139
Portland	May 20	Sept. 19	122
Presque Isle	June 6	Sept. 3	89
Waterville	May 25	Sept. 18	115
MARYLAND			
Baltimore	April 9	Nov. 3	207
Cumberland	May 6	Oct. 2	148
Salisbury	April 25	Oct. 16	173
Westminster	May 2	Oct. 17	167
MASSACHUSETTS			
Framingham	May 8	Oct. 2	146
Nantucket	May 9	Oct. 19	163
New Bedford	April 18	Oct. 25	188
Springfield	May 7	Oct. 5	150
MICHIGAN			
Ann Arbor	May 10	Oct. 6	149
Lansing	May 26	Sept. 21	117
Midland	May 20	Sept. 24	126
Sault Ste. Marie	June 8	Sept. 13	96

STATE	FREEZE DATES SPRING	FALL	FREEZE-FREE PERIOD (DAYS)
MINNESOTA			
Albert Lea	May 11	Sept. 27	138
Alexandria	May 17	Sept. 22	126
Duluth	June 4	Sept. 11	98
Int. Falls	June 9	Sept. 4	86
MISSISSIPPI			
Biloxi City	March 7	Nov. 20	257
Meridian	April 4	Oct. 26	203
Picayune	March 24	Oct. 31	221
Tupelo	April 16	Oct. 19	185
MISSOURI			
Hannibal	April 28	Oct. 13	168
Joplin	April 21	Oct. 17	178
Poplar Bluff	April 21	Oct. 13	174
MONTANA			
Billings	May 26	Sept. 14	111
Helena	June 4	Sept. 8	95
Kalispell	June 12	Sept. 7	87
NEBRASKA			
Beatrice	May 5	Oct. 5	153
Chadron	May 24	Sept. 15	113
Grand Island	May 8	Sept. 28	143
NEVADA			
Carson City	June 18	Sept. 5	79
Elko	June 24	Aug. 28	64
Las Vegas	March 27	Nov. 14	232
NEW HAMPSHIRE			
Lebanon	June 2	Sept. 13	103
Nashua	May 30	Sept. 12	105
NEW JERSEY			
Cape May	April 14	Oct. 31	199
Plainfield	May 6	Oct. 7	153
Trenton	April 17	Oct. 25	190

STATE	FREEZE DATES SPRING	FALL	FREEZE-FREE PERIOD (DAYS)
NEW MEXICO			
Alamogordo	April 20	Oct. 22	184
Los Alamos	May 23	Oct. 2	131
Tucumcari	May 1	Oct. 15	166
NEW YORK			
New York	April 14	Oct. 30	199
Poughkeepsie	May 18	Sept. 24	128
Rochester	May 13	Oct. 2	140
Watertown	May 21	Sept. 25	126
NORTH CAROLINA			
Asheville	April 27	Oct. 14	170
Greensboro	April 23	Oct. 17	176
Morehead City	April 1	Nov. 6	218
NORTH DAKOTA			
Bismarck	May 30	Sept. 11	103
Minot	May 24	Sept. 13	112
OHIO			
Akron	May 14	Oct. 8	146
Cincinnati	April 27	Oct. 15	170
Columbus	May 7	Oct. 4	150
Sandusky	April 27	Oct. 17	172
OKLAHOMA			
Ardmore	March 31	Nov. 6	219
Bartlesville	April 21	Oct. 14	174
Tulsa	April 11	Oct. 24	195
OREGON			
Ashland	June 2	Sept. 29	119
Eugene	May 19	Oct. 6	139
La Grande	June 2	Sept. 13	102
Portland	April 29	Oct. 20	174
PENNSYLVANIA			
Allentown	May 4	Oct. 6	155
Meadville	May 27	Sept. 23	119

STATE	FREEZE DATES SPRING	FALL	FREEZE-FREE PERIOD (DAYS)
PENNSYLVANIA *continued*			
State College	May 8	Oct. 4	149
West Chester	May 1	Oct. 6	157
Block Island	April 24	Oct. 27	185
Kingston	May 22	Sept. 20	120
SOUTH CAROLINA			
Anderson	April 11	Oct. 22	193
Beaufort	March 24	Nov. 9	230
Columbia	April 16	Oct. 24	190
SOUTH DAKOTA			
Mobridge	May 16	Sept. 22	128
Sioux Falls	May 20	Sept. 21	123
TENNESSEE			
Clarksville	April 27	Oct. 14	169
Knoxville	April 9	Oct. 27	200
Memphis	April 3	Oct. 31	210
TEXAS			
Amarillo	April 26	Oct. 20	176
Austin	Mar 16	Nov. 16	244
Brownsville	Feb. 6	Dec. 24	322
Denton	April 1	Nov. 4	216
Galveston	Feb 13	Dec. 16	304
UTAH			
Cedar City	June 5	Sept. 21	108
Logan	May 20	Sept. 27	129
Moab	April 28	Oct. 9	164
VERMONT			
Burlington	May 24	Sept. 21	119
Montpelier	June 5	Sept. 11	98
VIRGINIA			
Blacksburg	May 14	Sept. 28	136
Norfolk	April 7	Nov. 4	210
Winchester	May 3	Oct. 7	157

STATE	FREEZE DATES SPRING	FALL	FREEZE-FREE PERIOD (DAYS)
WASHINGTON			
Aberdeen	May 8	Oct. 20	165
Seattle-Tacoma	April 22	Oct. 29	189
Spokane	May 23	Sept. 21	120
Yakima	June 6	Sept. 16	101
WEST VIRGINIA			
Beckley	May 29	Sept. 17	110
Martinsburg	May 5	Oct. 2	148
Parkersburg	May 4	Oct. 6	154
WISCONSIN			
Ashland	June 14	Sept. 5	82
Green Bay	May 24	Sept. 21	119
La Crosse	May 11	Sept. 30	142
WYOMING			
Laramie	June 22	Aug. 29	67
Sheridan	June 8	Sept. 10	93

Reprinted from Climatography of the United States No. 20, National Climatic Data Center, Asheville, NC.

USDA HARDINESS ZONE MAP

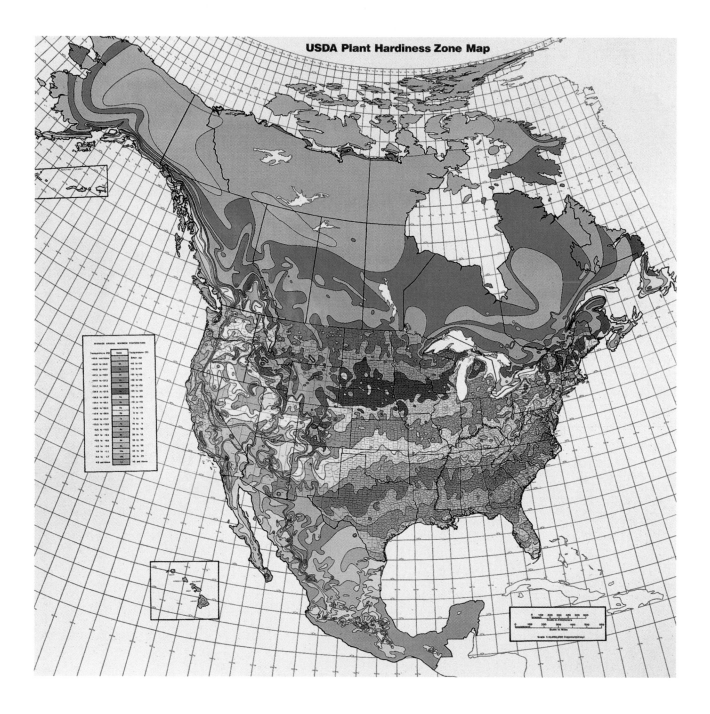

INDEX